Biggar And The House Of Fleming

William Hunter

BIGGAR.

AND

THE HOUSE OF FLEMING.

BIGGAR

AND

The House of Fleming.

BIGGAR,
DAVID LOCKHART,
MDCCCLXII.

BIGGAR

AND

THE HOUSE. OF FLEMING.

AN ACCOUNT OF THE

BIGGAR DISTRICT, ARCHÆOLOGICAL, HISTORICAL,
AND BIOGRAPHICAL.

BY WILLIAM HUNTER.

' Nescio, qua Natale Solum dulcidine cunctos
Ducit, et immemores non sinit esse sui.
Ov. Er., Lib. I.

BIGGAR:
DAVID LOCKHART, BOOKSELLER.

MDCCCLXII.

MURRAY AND GIBB, PRINTERS, EDINBURGH.

TO

ADAM SIM, ESQ.,

OF COULTER,

A GENTLEMAN DISTINGUISHED FOR HIS ZEALOUS AND UNWEARIED EXERTIONS

TO COLLECT THE ANTIQUITIES, DEVELOP THE HISTORY,

AND PROMOTE THE GENERAL IMPROVEMENT OF

THE UPPER WARD OF CLYDESDALE,

𝕿𝖍𝖎𝖘 𝖁𝖔𝖑𝖚𝖒𝖊,

WITH THE UTMOST GRATITUDE AND RESPECT,

IS DEDICATED,

BY HIS OBLIGED AND HUMBLE SERVANT,

THE AUTHOR.

PREFACE.

—◁◉▷—

'LONDON, says the Clydesdale peasant, is a big town, but there is one in Scotland that is Biggar. This is all, however, that can be said in aggrandisement of Biggar.' Such is the statement of Mr Robert Chambers, a very high authority at the present day in all matters relating to Scottish history and antiquities. In topographical works, Biggar is either ignored altogether, or, if alluded to, is discussed within the compass of a few lines. It may, therefore, appear presumptuous to write and publish a volume of considerable size in illustration of a locality, evidently regarded by the literary world as altogether uninteresting and obscure. In justification of the step that has been taken, it may be stated, that an idea was entertained by several persons, and among others, by the author of this work, that a few particulars regarding Biggar and Biggar men could be collected, which, although of no moment and consideration in the eyes of men of learning and research, might yet possess some degree of interest to the inhabitants of the district. It has accordingly been, for their instruction and gratification that the volume has been drawn up. If it fails to satisfy them, or to draw forth the history of Biggar from the obscurity in which it is involved, the fault must lie with the author, and not

in the want of materials for the purpose. These in the end
became so abundant, that it was found necessary to abridge some
portions of them, and to leave others out altogether, in order
that the work might be kept within a moderate space. The
attempt of the author to avoid one evil, has caused him to fall
into another, as he now finds that the rigorous curtailment, to
which he has subjected the contents of the volume, has given
serious offence to some parties, because information has been
excluded which, in their opinion, was of great importance, and
which they are confident would have enhanced the value of the
book, and the fame of Biggar.

The book, such as it is, owes its origin to a Lecture, which the
author was invited to deliver before the Athenæum of Biggar
in June 1859. He chose for the subject of discussion on that
occasion, ' Historical Incidents connected with Biggar and its
Neighbourhood.' Some time afterwards a suggestion was made
to the author by Mr William Ovens, merchant, Biggar,—a
leading member of the learned Institution referred to, and a
most able and intelligent correspondent,—that the information
contained in the Lecture might be extended and published,
either in a separate form, or in the columns of a periodical.
After much hesitation and delay, arising from the want of time
and facilities for executing such a work, it was at length resolved
to collect such additional particulars regarding Biggar as could
be readily got, and to publish the whole in a small volume.

In drawing up the work, the author has not thought it
necessary to quote his authorities, when the information was to
be found in the shelves of every public library; but in cases
where the facts were not so readily accessible, he has very frequently given not merely the name of the author, but also his

very words. He is well aware, from the predilections now prevalent, that these will be repulsive to some readers, and he anticipates that a considerable amount of censure will be bestowed upon him for their use. He can only say, that it would have been very easy to set them forth in a modern dress, and that his sole reason for retaining them in their original state is a very decided, though it may be an undue partiality, in favour of the peculiar orthography, the quaint expressions, and sage remarks of our old Scottish writers. The charm of these quotations would, at least to him, be lost, were they altered in the least degree from the way in which they were originally written.

The author has made a free use of various articles regarding Biggar, which at different periods he has written, and given forth in periodicals, etc. In a work drawn up principally from notes taken at various times, and from many different sources, and for the most part without any view to publication, it is far from unlikely, notwithstanding a careful revision, that some errors may have escaped notice. Since the work went through the press, the attention of the author has been directed to an Itinerary compiled by the Rev. Charles Henry Hartshorne, M.A., and published a few months ago in the First Part of the 'Collectanea Archæologica' of the British Archæological Association. This Itinerary clears up a point which the author, from want of proper information, has incorrectly stated at page 253, viz., the length of time that Edward II. remained at Biggar. According to this Itinerary, the King marched by Werk, Roxburgh, St Boswells, Selkirk, and Traquair to Biggar, at which town he arrived on the 29th of September, where he remained till the 3d of October, and then went back to Roxburgh. He returned to Biggar on the 5th, and remained there till the 10th, when he went to 'Carmil' (perhaps Carmichael), Lanark, Lin-

b

lithgow, and Renfrew, and came back to Biggar on the 18th. He finally left it on the 21st, and proceeded to ' Caremor' and Linlithgow, having been at Biggar altogether ten or eleven days.

The author would embrace this opportunity to tender his most grateful acknowledgments to those gentlemen who have given him assistance, either in supplying him with information or enabling him to obtain access to depositories of books and manuscripts not readily accessible to the general public. He would specially refer to Adam Sim, Esq. of Coulter. This gentleman not only allowed him ready access to his valuable library, but supplied him with important facts, pointed out sources of information, and afforded him the benefit of his extensive knowledge and critical acumen as the work went through the press. Above all, he handsomely offered, so soon as the work was projected, to furnish at his own expense the engravings by which it was to be embellished and illustrated. He has more than redeemed his original promise. A greater number of engravings has been given, and a higher style of art adopted, than was at first proposed. The consequence of this is, that the book is not only rendered much more attractive, but it is offered to subscribers at about one-half of its actual cost.

The author would merely mention the names of several other gentlemen, who have more or less lent a helping hand to the production of the book : viz., James W. Baillie, Esq., W.S., yr. of Coulterallers ; the late Captain John Dickson, yr. of Hartree ; David Laing, Esq. ; James Drummond, Esq., R.S.A. ; George Wilson, Esq. (of Messrs G. and G. Dunlop's, Edinburgh) ; Rev. John Christison, A.M., Biggar ; Rev. Dr David Smith, Biggar ; Rev. James Dunlop, A.M., Biggar ; Rev. Henry Scott Riddell, Teviothead ; Rev. Dr John B. Johnston,

Glasgow; Rev. David Crawford, Edinburgh; Dr Robert Pairman, Biggar; Mr Allan Whitfield, Biggar; Mr William Ovens, Biggar; Rev. William Whitfield, Biggar; Mr David Lockhart, Biggar; Mr James Watt, Biggar; Mr John Archibald, Biggar; Mr George Wilson, Edinburgh, etc., etc.

In conclusion, the author offers the volume as a small tribute of respect to his native district, and as an humble contribution to a work long projected and much desired—a complete History of the Upper Ward of Clydesdale.

PORTOBELLO, 12th May 1862.

CONTENTS.

P

CHAPTER VIII.

CHAPTER IX.

CHAPTER X.

CHAPTER XI.

CHAPTER XII.

CHAPTER XIII.

CHAPTER XIV.

CHAPTER XV.

CHAPTER XVI.

CHAPTER XVII.

CHAPTER XVIII.

LIST OF ILLUSTRATIONS.

BIGGAR AND THE HOUSE OF FLEMING.

CHAPTER I.

Prehistoric Remains in the Biggar District.

BIGGAR, a parish in the Upper Ward of Clydesdale, is bounded on the west by Libberton and the river Clyde, on the north by Dolphinton and Walston, on the east by Skirling, and on the south by Coulter and Kilbucho. The form of the parish is nearly triangular, and comprises 5852 Scots acres, or 11¼ square miles. It is chiefly of a hilly and undulating character, with exception of a level tract on the south, which is watered by Biggar Burn, and which forms part of what may be denominated the Strath of Biggar. This strath or valley is 628 feet above the level of the sea, and sends its waters, on the west, into the Clyde, and on the east, into the Tweed. The parish lies about 23 miles south-west from Edinburgh, and 32 miles south-east from Glasgow, and has ready communication by good roads, and now by railway, with all parts of the kingdom. The name of the parish in old documents is variously written, such as Bygare, Bygair, Bigre, Biger, Begar, and Bigar, and it is only of late years that its present orthography has been established. Its etymology, according to the learned George Chalmers, is to be traced to the Scoto-Irish words 'big,' soft, and 'thir,' land. It is far from unlikely that the title 'soft' was applicable to the lands of the parish at a remote period; for, even at the commencement of the present century, a large portion of the lowest parts of it consisted of marshes and peat-mosses. Others, again, think that 'big' may refer to a coarse kind of barley called bigg or bear, and, therefore, that the meaning of the word Biggar is the bigg or bear land. This is a sub-

A

ject, however, on which entire certainty will not be easily attained, and on which etymologists, in all probability, will continue to hold conflicting opinions.

The parish was, no doubt, peopled many ages previous to the existence of historical records, or the time at which the Roman invaders planted their eagles on our soil. The early inhabitants, like those of other parts of Scotland, would be very indifferently lodged, clothed, and fed. Their houses would be composed of turf, rough stones, and the branches of trees; their raiment would consist of the skins of wild or domesticated animals; and their food would be drawn from the spontaneous fruits of the soil, or the fish and venison which their skill and dexterity in fishing and hunting enabled them to procure. The parish, in these remote times, was evidently covered with forests of hazel, oak, alder, birch, etc., fragments of which have been dug up at considerable depths in its different peat-mosses. With the wild beasts with which these were tenanted, as well as with marauding neighbours, the inhabitants would wage a constant warfare. Traces of the early inhabitants are to be found in the stone weapons and utensils that are, from time to time, dug up in the neighbourhood. They belong to what is called the Stone Period; that is, a period when the metals were still unknown, and the implements used by man were composed of stone and wood. It has often been remarked, that where geology leaves the world's history, archæology takes it up. The one deals with the different processes that have taken place to form the earth's crust, and render it fit for the habitation of man; the other takes up the industrial developments of man from the rude and simple fabrications of aboriginal times, to the complicated and scientific productions of our own day. As the excavator and the miner have contributed much to geological science by laying open the wonders of the earth's crust, so the ploughman and the drainer have enriched archæology by the stores of relics which they have brought to light. Few districts have yielded a more plentiful crop of those remains of the past than the one around Biggar. A large portion of those dug up in recent times have fortunately found their way into the hands of Adam Sim, Esq. of Coulter. The collection of Lanarkshire antiquities in the possession of that gentleman is now exceeding rich, and, we may say, perfectly unique. With his kind permission, a few of those, more immediately connected with Biggar and its neighbourhood, have been selected for brief description and pictorial representation.

The stone hammer is a primitive implement that is very commonly to be met with. It is often found in the older cists, or burying-places; and hence by the vulgar it has been called a purgatory hammer, from the supposition that it was placed in graves in order to be used by the dead when they came to the gates of purgatory. It is on this account that in some districts it has been regarded as an object of religious veneration. The one here represented was found at Aikbrae on Crosscryne, about three miles from Biggar. It measures 8½ inches in length, and 2⅜ inches across the cutting edge.

The circular perforated stone here represented was found at Coulter, and is a specimen of what is very generally denominated a *flail-stone*. It has received this name from a supposition that it was a military weapon, which was made effective by suspending it by a cord or thong of leather from a short staff, and used in the same manner as the 'morning star' of the middle ages. As stones of this kind are often found in the graves of the aboriginal inhabitants, it has been conjectured by some person that they were personal ornaments, and worn as beads. The ornamentation on some of them would also favour this conjecture; but the fact is, that the real use of them cannot now be known.

Flail-stone.

Hammer.   Celt.

Another primitive stone weapon was an axe, or, as it is commonly called, a celt. It is a weapon that has been extensively dug up in almost every country in the world. It has been a matter of considerable speculation, to what use the celt was applied, and by what mode it was fixed to a handle. The likelihood is, that it was used both for warlike and domestic purposes, and that it was inserted in a wooden shaft or handle, and secured in such a way that it could be employed either in striking a foe, cutting down a tree, or constructing an article of domestic use. The one here represented was found at Biggar.

The practice of archery appears to be of a very remote antiquity in the Britannic Isles, and the number of flint arrow-heads, beautifully formed, that have been picked up on Bizzyberry, the Borrow Muir, and Biggar Shields, is a convincing proof that the Caledonian of Biggar 'put his reliance on his bow.' To shoot well with the bow, both in the battle-field and the more peaceful pursuit of the chase, would be regarded as a necessary accomplishment by the men of

Biggar; and at such places as Bowflat, now called Bamphflat, and Batts, or Butts, now called Springfield, it is more than probable that gatherings for practice were wont to take place.   The annexed wood-cut represents a fine specimen of a flint arrow-head found on the hill of Bizzyberry, that over-looks the town of Biggar.

The manner in which these arrow-heads were fabricated, and the places from which they were brought, are involved in obscurity.   They ap-pear to have been very extensively used, as they have been found in many different parts of the world, including the South Sea Islands and the immense continent of America.   As some of these regions are far remote from the spots where flint is a natural deposit, it is plain that, in the primitive times in which they were used, they must have formed an article of extensive traffic.   The rude material must have been dug up, and most likely fashioned, in places, such as the south of England, where flint for-mations abound, and then conveyed to distant parts of the country, to be bartered for other commodities which the natives could supply.

The flint arrow-heads, as is well known, were long associated with the superstitions of this and other countries.   They were termed elf or elfin bolts, and were supposed to be shot by the fairies, or other malignant spirits, and to produce the most fatal effects.   Hence, in some parts of the country, whenever they were found, they were carefully buried, in case some of these evil beings might find them, and use them in the accomplishment of their destructive designs. They seem also to have been worn in some districts as an amulet or charm.   They were in that case sewed in a part of the dress, and regarded as an effectual antidote against the spells of witches, and the injurious tricks of elfs and fairies.   In the Biggar district, till a very recent period, many of the diseases of cattle were attributed to the elf-shot.   One of the most remarkable statements regarding the fabrication of these elf-bolts, and the deadly effects which they produced, was made by Isobel Goudie, the famous witch of Auldern, on her trial before a commission in 1662.   In her second confession she said, 'As for elf arrow-heidis, the Divel shapis thame with his awin hand, and syne deliveris thame to elf-boyis, wha whyttis and dyghtis thame with a sharp thing lyke a paking neidle, bot quhan I was in Elfland, I saw thame whytting and dighting thame.   .   .   . Thes that dightis thaim ar litle ones, hollow and bossbaked.   They speak gowstie lyk.   Quhan the Divel giues thaim to ws he sayes,

> Shoot thes in my name,
> And they sall not goe heall hame.

And quhan we shoot thes arrowes we say,

> I shoot yon man in the Divel's name,
> He sall nott win heall hame ;
> And this sal be alswa tru,
> Thair sall not be an bit of him on lieiw.

We hau no bow to shoot with, but spang thaim from the naillis of our thowmbes. Som tymes we misse, bot, if they twitch, be he beast, or man, or woman, it will kill tho' they had a jack upon thaim. This, of course, is the declaration of a poor creature made mad by prolonged insults and torture, and deserves no consideration, further than it shows the strange hallucinations into which persons charged with witchcraft could be driven, and the gross absurdities which men, even of the highest rank and intelligence of the age, could be led to entertain and believe.

The annexed cut represents part of an ancient stone quern, or hand-mill for grinding corn, which was found at Coulter. The quern is an article of very great antiquity. The use of it would, no doubt, be almost coeval with the existence of the human race. Some rude contrivance of the kind was evidently requisite ere the grain furnished by the bountiful Creator could, to any extent, be converted into food. One of them would therefore be found  in every household. The people were attached to their use, and, after the introduction of water-mills, were decidedly averse to give them up. The Government, who wished to encourage the water-mills, therefore, in 1284, during the reign of Alexander III., passed the following enactment :—' That na man sall presume to grind quheit, maislhock, or rye, with hand mylnes, except he be compelled be storm, or be lack of mylnes, quhilk sould grind the samen. And in this case, gif a man grinds at hand mylnes, he sall gif the threttein measure as multer ; and gif anie man contraveins this our prohibition, he sall tine his hand mylnes perpetuallie.' This law failed to some extent to effect the end contemplated, and in some remote districts of Scotland the querns continued in use almost to our own times. At almost all the old farm towns in the Biggar district, these primitive and once useful utensils were lately to be found very generally built into the wall of some of the office-houses. Those of most recent date were hollowed out like a trough, and the corn, or rather the barley, was placed inside and bruised by a stone, or sometimes by a piece of wood called a knocker, and hence these utensils were usually denominated ' knocking stones.'

Another article that must be ascribed to a very remote antiquity

is the ornamented stone ball. It is found in various parts of Scotland.
Four or five very fine specimens are to be seen in the Museum of the
Antiquaries of Scotland at Edinburgh. They are nearly alike in size,
but they differ very much in their ornamentation. The one here represented (Fig. 1) was found at
Biggar Shields. It has six regularly arranged circles in relief, with
intervening spaces, which give it a
fine symmetrical appearance. The
use to which these balls were put
is not certainly known. It may

be that they were used for warlike purposes, as balls of a similar
kind have been so employed by some tribes of American Indians,
who enclosed them in leather, and attached to them a thong a yard
and a half in length. By some parties, on the contrary, it has been
conjectured that they were used in the process of grinding corn, and
hence they have been called 'corn-crushers.' They are frequently
dug up in cists; and this may be taken as a proof that, in remote
ages, they were held in respect. As might be expected, they have
been identified with the superstitions of subsequent ages, and have
been supposed to possess the same virtues, and to have the same claim
to awe and veneration, as elf-bolts, stone-hammers, adder-stones, etc.

In course of time several of the metals were discovered, particularly
copper and tin, as these, in some places, were found lying near the
surface. By smelting these two metals together, a substance was produced of much greater hardness than either of them possessed, taken
singly. This substance, which was called bronze, was, for a period,
most extensively used, and superseded stone as a material for the
construction of warlike and domestic implements. The introduction
of this metal marks an important stage in the history of human improvement; and it is interesting to note that articles, formerly composed of stone, were now produced in almost the same form in bronze.
The ancient Caledonians who inhabited Biggar, so soon as a knowledge
of the newly-discovered metals reached them, would no doubt throw
aside their stone implements as comparatively of little value, and adopt
those composed of the more durable and effective material. Several
remarkably fine examples of bronze axe-heads or celts, spear-heads,
and the weapons called paalstaves, have been found in the vicinity of
Biggar. Fig. 1 is a curious bronze implement, the real use of which
it is not very easy to divine. It may have been employed as a dagger, as in some specimens the blade contains two or three holes, for
the evident purpose of riveting it to a handle. It measures 7⅜ inches
in length, and, at the smaller end, 2 inches in breadth; but it is
evident that a portion of it has been broken off. It was found at
Coulter. In Fig. 2 we have a fine specimen of the bronze socket or
pot-celt. Its sides are ornamented with the groovings or tridental

marks common in this type, which have very frequently been met with in the north of England. It has a loop, intended either to fasten

it more firmly to the handle, or to suspend it from the girdle of the wearer. It is 4½ inches long, and was found at Hangingshaw in the parish of Coulter. The bronze axe-head here engraved (Fig. 3) was found in a cairn, within the camp on the summit of Wintermuir Hill. It is 6½ inches in length, and nearly three inches across the cutting edge.

The spear-head engraved (Fig. 4) was found in the neighbourhood, and has been selected as a good specimen of this early but beautiful weapon, and as in all likelihood the product of some of the ancient forges in the district. Another bronze implement here engraved (Fig. 5) is what is called a paalstave or paalstab. This weapon has, seemingly, been attached to a cleft handle, and might be used either as a spear or an axe. It was found at Aikbrae, on Crosscryne. Another very fine one in Mr Sim's possession was found at Kersewell, and several others have lately been discovered in this district. Paalstaves are met with in considerable variety, some of them being finely ornamented and engraved; but antiquaries are by no means agreed as to the purposes for which they were employed. It is very likely that they were used both as a warlike and a domestic implement, and perhaps, also, in the rites of some of the old religious systems that prevailed in the country.

The bronze ball (Fig. 2) represented in the woodcut, along with the one in stone, is the only specimen of the kind known to exist, being of the same type as those of stone formerly referred to. It is somewhat smaller, being only 1½ inches in diameter, and was found at Walston, three or four miles from Biggar. George Vere Irving, Esq. of Newton, in describing it in an Archæological Journal, says, 'It is beautifully incised with volutes, so as to produce six disc-shaped figures. It has been cast in two portions, each half being composed of a different metal, and of a different density. The workmanship of it would assign its production to a period subsequent to the occupation of this country by the Romans.'

The religion of the ancient inhabitants of the Biggar district is supposed to have been Druidism. It has, no doubt, been stoutly asserted by several authors that the practice of this system of religion in Great Britain was confined to the southern parts of the island, and they demand a proof to the contrary. Now, it must be admitted that no direct proof of the kind can be given. No ancient author has made any statement on the subject; and the Druids themselves left no writings, as it was one of their tenets that no record of their opinions and transactions should be kept. Cæsar, indeed, states that the Druidical system was in operation in South Britain, a region which he had himself visited; but this does not prove that it did not prevail in other parts of the country, which he never saw. However this may be, it becomes us to notice several remains of antiquity in the parish of Biggar and its neighbourhood, which have been generally set down as Druidical.

On the Shields Hill, in the parish of Biggar, several upright stones are still standing, which have been considered to be part of a Druidical temple. Here the Druids, with their flowing robes, their white surplices, their long beards, and their rods of office, may have expounded their religious opinions, and offered up human victims in sacrifice. At the west end of the town of Biggar is the Moat, or Moathill, which in Saxon signifies the meeting-hill. It is of a circular form, and measures 100 feet in height on the west side, 477 feet in circumference at the base, and 225 feet at the top. From the top of it, which is quite flat, three other moats of a similar form, though of less dimensions, are in sight,—one at Roberton, one at Wolf-Clyde, and another at Bamphflat. In the opinion of some, these were places on which the Druids held their courts of justice, as they are known to have acted in a judicial as well as in a religious capacity, and to have transacted their business and performed their rites in the open air. Here, then, the priests of the Druidical superstition may have tried many trembling culprits, pronounced on them the terrible sentence of excommunication, or sent them to expiate their crimes on the blazing pile. At a few miles distant, conspicuously in view, and forming a termination to the vista from the main street of the town of Biggar, is Tinto, the hill of fire, with its huge cairn, on which, on May eve, and on the 1st of November, yearly, the Druids are said to have lighted fires in honour of Beal or Belenus, the sun. Fires at the same time would blaze on the mountains of Lothian, Tweeddale, and others still more distant, till the whole island was lighted up with a ruddy glow. Then the fires on every hearth would be extinguished, and the people would hasten to the nearest mountain-top to obtain a portion of the consecrated fire to rekindle the fires in their huts or weems. No fire was, however, given unless the customary dues were paid to the Cairneach, or officiating priest; and no person dared to supply the defaulter, under the pain of excommunication, which is said to have been worse than death itself.

Two very fine specimens of an ornament, supposed to be Druidical, were found, in 1858, on a piece of newly broken up ground on the farm of Southside, in the parish of Kilbucho, about three miles from Biggar. They were at first thought to be merely pieces of tin, debris from the anvil of Moses Marshall, the tinker, and were taken to the farm-house, and thrown behind the kitchen fire. A relative of the farmer, Mr Core, who had visited America, happened to have his attention attracted by their singular appearance, and, on examination, found that they were composed of the  finest gold. They were taken to Biggar and weighed, and ultimately found their way into the hands of Adam Sim, Esq. That gentleman, on the 10th of June 1861, presented one of them to the Antiquarian Society of Scotland, and it is now to be seen in the Museum of that body at Edinburgh. The other still remains in his possession at Coultermains. Each of them weighs 1 oz. 8 dwt. 13 grs. They are in the form of a crescent or half-moon, measure at the broadest part 1⅜ inches, terminate at each extremity with a button or small disc, and have a slight ornamentation, consisting of faint lines and small depressions. They are both exactly alike; and it is remarkable that two of them were found at the same spot,—a spot at which other remains of a remote antiquity, in the shape of paalstabs and bronze celts, have been dug up. A representation of one of them is to be seen in the annexed woodcut.

The writers who consider that these ornaments were worn by the Druids, state that they were carried in the hand of the priest when he went to cut the sacred mistletoe on the sixth day of the moon, and that, as the Druids paid great attention to astronomy, this crescent-shaped ornament was intended to symbolize the moon at that stage of her course, and to indicate that the time of the festival had arrived. Such of them as had a button or disc at the extremities, are said also to have been worn on the head of the priest during sacrifices and other

B

ceremonies, and were then placed behind the ears, and fastened with a string looped to the buttons. In this position they very much resemble the nimbus or rays of glory which are usually made, in pictorial representations, to surround the head of Christ and His apostles. Another ornament of the same shape is said to have been worn on the breast of the Druidical priest. This was called the Iodhain Morain, or breastplate of judgment; and, according to the fables of Ireland, was believed to possess the power of squeezing the neck on the utterance of a false judgment. Representations of these ornaments, and the manner in which they are said to have been worn, are to be seen in the 'Collectanea de Rebus Hibernicis,' and in 'Meyricks and Smith's Costume of the Original Inhabitants of the British Islands.'

Though some authors have very strongly and positively asserted that these were the uses to which these ornaments were put, yet it must be admitted that their statements rest very much on conjecture. It is beyond question, however, that ornaments of the same kind were worn at a very remote era. They have been shown by Auberi, Montfaucon, and others, to have been represented on bas-reliefs and statues of great antiquity. Specimens of these ornaments have been occasionally dug up in the bogs of Ireland; but in Scotland they are more rarely to be met with, and hence the value of the two found at Southside.

CHAPTER II.

Invasion of the Upper Ward of Clydesdale by the Romans, and supposed Traces of the Invaders at Biggar.

THE Upper Ward of Clydesdale, during the first century of the Christian era, was inhabited by a tribe to which the Romans gave the name of the Damnii. They are described by Dion Cassius, Herodian, and others, as sunk in deep barbarism; and yet it is asserted that they fought in chariots, and made use of swords, lances, and bucklers, which, if correct, shows that they had by that time made very considerable progress in the useful arts. The whole history of the Roman invasion of the northern part of the island, abundantly shows that they were an athletic, warlike, and indomitable race. They never could be thoroughly subdued. It was, no doubt, in vain for them to contend, in a regular pitched battle, with the Roman invaders, who had attained the highest state of discipline, and had long been inured to war on the plains of Germany, Parthia, Gaul, and Palestine; but they lost no opportunity of surprising isolated detachments, cutting off stragglers, intercepting supplies, and attacking encampments. The consequence was, that the Romans were never able to keep a continuous hold of the Upper Ward. The first inroad made by them on this district was in the year 80, during the reign of Titus. At that time Caius Julius Agricola, at the head of a Roman army, overran the country, and built a chain of forts between the Forth and Clyde, to mark what he considered the bounds of his conquest. While Agricola was subduing the natives and strengthening his position, he was recalled by the Emperor Domitian, who had succeeded to the imperial throne on the death of his brother Titus. It is evident that on his departure the inhabitants of Clydesdale, with that invincible love of freedom which has ever distinguished them, gave abundant disquiet to the Roman legions left in the country, and rendered their position exceedingly disagreeable and hazardous. When the Emperor Hadrian, therefore, visited Britain in 117, he considered it impolitic to maintain the supremacy of Rome over the Lowlands of Scotland; and accordingly he erected a vallum or rampart between the Tyne and Solway, which he fixed as the boundary of the Roman Empire in Britain. His successor, Antoninus Pius, appointed Lollius Urbicus governor of Britain, and this commander again attempted the subjugation of Clydesdale. He marched an army into Scotland, and having cleared the way before him, he erected a rampart on the line of forts constructed by Agricola. After a few years tranquillity, the tract of country lying between the two ramparts became a scene of almost constant hostilities. The inhabitants, aided by the hardy and intrepid clans of the north, rose from time to time against their invaders, and, though often overcome, they strove with unflinching determination to expel them from their territories. In the reign of Commodus they defeated a Roman army, and slew the general. This obstinate resistance greatly incensed the Emperor Severus. No sooner did he find himself firmly seated on the throne, than he hastened to Britain, and in 208 entered Scotland at the head of a most formidable army, determined to spare neither sex nor age, and to lay the country in utter desolation. The natives were filled with terror, and proposed a peace; but he repelled all such overtures with disdain. Finding that the inaccessible state of the country gave shelter and protection to the inhabitants, he employed his legions in cutting down forests, in filling up marshes, in making roads, etc.; so the likelihood is, that it was his soldiers who hewed down the woods in the neighbourhood of Biggar, and left prostrate on the ground those numerous trees that from time to time have been dug up in the peat-mosses near the town. He penetrated a considerable distance to the north; but having lost 50,000 men, he was, in the end, glad to retire from Scotland, and take shelter behind the rampart of Hadrian. Mortified with the unsuccessful results of his expedition, he died shortly afterwards at York; and his son and successor, Caracalla, made peace on favourable terms with the northern tribes. For more than seventy years, almost nothing is related by the Roman historians regarding the proceedings of their countrymen in Scotland; but, in 367, Theodosius was sent into Britain, who, in several campaigns, contended successfully with the natives dwelling between the walls, maintained for a brief space the ascendancy of the Roman arms, and gave the territory the name of Valentia, after the Emperor Valentinian, then occupying the imperial throne. This success did not subdue the men of Clydesdale; they still continued their inroads and aggressions, till 422, when a Roman legion appeared against them for the last time. The barbarians of the north of Europe had now descended on the Roman Empire, and were threatening its existence. Its troops in the distant provinces had to be recalled to preserve it from impending destruction, and, in 446, the tribes of Britain were freed for ever from the thraldom and aggressions of the Romans.

No record is extant that enables us to fix on the parish of Biggar as the place at which any important movement was made by the Romans; but it is the concurrent opinion of all the writers, who have attempted to describe the operations of these invaders in Scotland, that the grounds in the neighbourhood of the town of Biggar were a Roman station, and lay on an angle of the great Iter, or road, commonly called Watling Street, that proceeded from Carlisle, by Annandale and the Vale of Clyde, to the Wall of Antoninus. It is evident that these grounds, from their local position, and the character of the country around, were well fitted to be a military post, especially at the time when the Romans attempted to hold sway over Scotland. They lie on the outskirts of what are called the Southern Highlands, and are situated about midway between two important Roman camps, the one at Corbiehall near Carstairs, and the other at Lyne near Peebles, both being distant about a moderate day's march. The gentle slopes of Bizzyberry and the Knock have space sufficient to accommodate sixty or even a hundred thousand men, while their summits present advantageous positions for exploratory posts. Here is a deep ravine well fitted to form one side of a strong rampart, or vallum, and along the bottom of it meanders a stream of excellent water, so necessary to a large encampment. The antiquaries, Gordon, Roy, Chalmers, Stewart, etc., all concur in thinking that the Moat Knowe was used as part of a Roman work. It may have been an outpost, while the camp itself extended along the grounds now composing the crofts of Westraw, or the minister's glebe and the burgh lands, on the north side of the town. Various Roman coins have been dug up here, the last of which was one of the Emperor Vespasian, and is now in the possession of a townsman, the Rev. Dr William Johnston, Limekilns. Bronze vessels, commonly called Roman camp-kettles, have been repeatedly found in the upper part of the Vale of Clyde, and in the district round Biggar, particularly at Carwood, Biggar Moss, Pyetknowe, Coulter, and Libberton. In the collection of antiquities at Coultermains, about a dozen of these kettles are to be seen, all of them found in the neighbourhood, and all, though of various sizes, of the same form and type. These vessels are generally broken or fractured, as if they had been thrown aside as useless. Moses Marshall, the celebrated Upper Ward tinker, was wont to say that, in the early part of his wandering life, he frequently bought them as old metal, at a mere trifle, and sold them at high prices, on account of the superior quality of the bronze of which they were composed. It has been asserted by some antiquaries that the quality of the metal is inferior to that used by the Romans, and that is one of the reasons why they consider that they are not of

Roman manufacture. However this may be, they are unquestionably articles of very great antiquity, and may have been used by the native inhabitants at a period even anterior to the possession of our country by the Romans. The woodcut represents one of the kettles found at Carwood Moss; and it is alleged that it was filled with gold and silver coins, but the finder, of course, would not allow this supposition to be entertained.

The Roman road that is supposed to have passed through the parish of Biggar has entirely disappeared. Gordon, in his 'Itinerarium Septentrionale,' published in 1727, states that traces of it were at that time distinctly to be seen in Westraw Moss, west of the town. This road or causeway is referred to so late as 1765, in the Records of the Baron Bailie's Court of Biggar, when a complaint of Robert Wilson, 'tacksman of ye grass of Westraw Moss, above ye cassaw leading through ye said moss,' was lodged against certain feuars in Westraw for cutting 'Roughheads,' and pasturing their cattle on parts of the moss, to which, it was alleged, they had no right. This 'cassaw' gave the name of 'Causeyend' to a small hamlet built at its western extremity, and some of the houses of which still exist. This causeway was, however, in all likelihood, of comparatively modern formation. The workmen, while engaged two years ago in making excavations in this moss for the line of the Symington, Biggar, and Broughton Railway, came upon a causeway of stones, about three feet below the surface, which had evidently been formed at an early period, and which, in all probability, was part of the Watling Street of the Romans. It was minutely examined by several gentlemen in the neighbourhood, and, from the systematic and skilful arrangement of the stones, no doubt was left on their minds that they had been placed there for the purpose of forming a road. By this Iter, then, most of the Roman troops would pass and repass on their marches to subdue, or, as Claudian says, 'to bridle the fierce Scots.' The probability, therefore, is, that Agricola, Hadrian, Urbicus, Calphurnius Agricola, Marcellus, Severus, Theodosius, and other commanders of the successive invading armies, halted at Biggar, and marshalled their legions on the adjoining plains.

Along the great Roman Iter, on each side of the valley of the river Clyde, circular earthen works are to be seen on the summits of the more isolated hills, and are supposed to be the strongholds of the early inhabitants. No less than eight or nine of these primitive fortifications are to be found in the parish of Coulter, and traces of them are to be seen on several of the Biggar hills, particularly one distinctly marked on Bizzyberry, immediately above the town. For a most learned and elaborate account of the ancient camps and Roman roads in the Upper Ward of Lanarkshire, we refer to the recently published papers in the 'British Archæological Journal,' by George Vere Irving, Esq. of Newton,—a gentleman who is gradually developing, by laborious researches, the ancient condition of his native district.

The Romans, as already stated, finally withdrew from Scotland during the fifth century. Their retirement led to the formation of what has been called the Regnum Cumbrense, or Kingdom of Strathcluyd. It existed till the close of the tenth century, and of course included the Biggar district; but we are unable to identify this district with any of the notable transactions that occurred during that lengthened period.

Drawn & Lithographed

B I G G A R.

1861.

by H. Wilson, Glasgow

CHAPTER III.

The Town of Biggar.

BIGGAR, in all likelihood, was an ancient British village. It may possibly be the Gadanica of the Romans, a town which was situated near the Clyde in this locality, but the exact site of which has much perplexed our modern antiquaries. However this may be, it can certainly boast of considerable antiquity, as it is mentioned in some of the earliest Scottish records extant. We have no means of knowing what sort of town it was in primitive times, but in all probability it was a mere accumulation of mud and turf cabins, possessing the miserable accommodation of the wigwams of the Indian or the huts of our own Highland population. During the early part of last century, the houses were still of small dimensions, and for the most part covered with thatch. The appearance of the town at that time was remarkable on account of the number of malt-kilns with which it was studded, several of the inhabitants being maltmen by profession, and the whole of them being evidently great drinkers of ale. Like most old towns, it was, down to a recent period, kept in a very dirty and unhealthy condition. Dunghills, peatstacks, noxious gutters, and fulzie of different sorts, were to be seen in all directions. This state of things has been now very much changed for the better. A number of good houses have been built, ornamental trees planted, gas-lamps to light the street put up, shops enlarged and embellished, old houses that incommoded the street pulled down, the common sewers covered, and all unseemly accumulations removed; so that the High Street, as may be observed from the engraving, has now a very spacious and respectable appearance.

The town of Biggar at present consists of a main street, two back streets, and a suburb called the Westraw. The houses in general are small, consisting of one and two stories. They are built of whinstone, from quarries in the neighbourhood, with corners, rybats, and lintels of freestone, brought from Deepsykehead, Libberton, and other places at a distance, as there is no sandstone in the immediate neighbourhood of the town. The covering of the houses are thatch and slates, roofing tiles being nearly unknown. In entering the town from the east, we have first a few isolated houses called the Townhead, and then the toll-bar,—'a merry place in days of yore,' when the toll-house was tenanted by Nicol Porteous. On the right or north side

of the street is Bow's Well, and a little below it the house occupied
for some time by John, eleventh Lord Elphinstone, in consequence
of Boghall Castle, the ancient seat of the family, having fallen into
disrepair. This same house was also long occupied by that burgh
worthy, Bailie Thomas Carmichael. He was appointed depute bailie
by Robert Leckie, head bailie and factor, in the year 1744, and
took a leading part in the management of the affairs of the town and
barony till his death, in 1795, when he had reached the patriarchal
age of eighty-two years. On the other side of the street is a large
house, once the residence of Dr Baillie, a distinguished Biggar physician of last century. The street here widens to a very considerable
extent, and is far more spacious than the streets usually found in old
towns. The reason of this, no doubt, was to afford space for the
large fairs annually held here. On the south side of the street is the
Langvout, so called from the houses, which once stood here, having
arched roofs. The Langvout of old was occupied by a family of
the name of Boe, most likely the progenitors of Drs Boe, father and
son, well-known physicians at one time in Biggar. The keystone of
the jambs of one of these vaulted houses was finely ornamented with
the Lockhart arms. When the house was demolished, this sculptured
stone came into the possession of Adam Sim, Esq. of Coulter, and
was presented by that gentleman to the late William Lockhart, Esq.
of Milton Lockhart. In the hall of Milton Lockhart House it is still
to be seen, placed on a bracket, and preserved with great care. Here
a wretched hovel was employed, for a number of years, as the town
prison; and here drunk beggars, the lunatic that fired Nannie Muir's
house, the tinker who felled his companion at the Ba' Green, and
other disturbers of the peace, were placed in durance vile. The
Langvout gate was, in olden times, the principal passage to Biggar
Moss.

A little farther down are Silver-knowes, long the property of a
family of the name of Brown. Andrew Brown, and his spouse Margaret Tod, flourished here during the first half of the last century.
They were succeeded by Richard Brown, weaver, whose spouse was
Isabella, or, as she was generally called, Tibbie Forrest. This worthy
couple had several children, of whom may be mentioned Andrew,
John, an officer of excise, and Janet, who long lived in the inheritance at Silver-knowes, and died there within the last thirty years.

Andrew, who was born in the year 1763, was the most distinguished. He early showed an aptitude for learning, and attended
different schools, but was chiefly indebted for instruction, in some of
the higher branches of education, to Mr Thorburn of Quothquan,
afterwards Dr Thorburn of Shields. One of his teachers, struck
with his aptitude and ability, said publicly, in the hearing of the other
scholars, 'You are a clever boy; you will one day be a minister of
Edinburgh;' a prediction which was afterwards verified. After going

through the usual curriculum of literary, philosophical, and theological study at the University, he was licensed to preach the Gospel by the Presbytery of Biggar. He was then employed for a short time as a tutor in a family, one of the female members of which became his first wife. In 1787 he was ordained to the pastoral charge of the Scottish Church, Halifax, Nova Scotia; and continued in this situation till 1795, when he was presented to the living of Lochmaben, in Dumfriesshire. On the passage home from Halifax, he had the good fortune to be on board the same vessel with Prince William Henry, afterwards William IV., who was delighted with his fine taste and literary acquirements, and took much pleasure in his conversation. In 1799 the Town Council of Edinburgh appointed him to the charge of the New Greyfriars Church, and during the year following translated him to the Old Church, as colleague to Dr Grieve. On the death of Dr Blair, in 1801, he was appointed by the Crown Professor of Rhetoric and Belles Lettres in the University of Edinburgh, being chiefly indebted, it is said, for this appointment to the efforts of his old acquaintance Prince William. In 1813 he had the honour of filling the dignified office of Moderator of the General Assembly of the Church of Scotland. He died at Primrose Bank, near Edinburgh, on the 19th of February 1834, in the seventy-first year of his age, and was interred in the Greyfriars churchyard.

Dr Brown's style was elegant and ornate, though somewhat diffuse, and his manner of delivery insinuating rather than commanding. He manifested much gravity and earnestness in his prelections from the pulpit, and indulged in an ample range of illustration, clothed in beautiful language that rendered them very effective. He excelled especially in prayer. His devotional sentiments were delivered with a fervour and an aptness of expression that led captive the thoughts and feelings of his fellow-worshippers. His lectures in the Rhetoric class were elegant and instructive, and from time to time were subjected to careful revision, in order to render them still more correct and complete. He spent a considerable portion of time in composing a history of America, and for the purpose of procuring information for this work, he paid several visits to London, and also to Paris. Persons to whom he read portions of it, spoke of it as highly elaborate and interesting, constructed on the model of the best historical specimens of the ancient classics, particularly in the curious conferences and harangues of the Indian chiefs. He delayed the publication of it in order to obtain fuller information, and thus to make it more complete; but he died before he had put it in such a state as he considered fit to lay before the public.

It is worthy of notice, that when the grave of Dr Brown's forefathers in Biggar churchyard was opened for the interment either of his brother or his sister, a box was found in it, three feet long, one foot broad, and upwards of one foot deep. On the outside of it was a

c

plate, ornamented with elegant figures, and bearing the following inscription :—' The remains of Jane, daughter of Sir T. A. S. of B., and wife of Sir T. A. S., Knt., who died abroad 14th of May 1799 ; together with those of her infant daughter and only child, who survived her but six weeks. Collected and brought home by the kind offices of a particular friend of her surviving husband, the Rev. A. B., and privately deposited at Biggar, N. B., 1805.' The box, on being opened, was found to contain the bones and skulls of the lady and her infant, embedded in a quantity of fine yellow and red sand. No person at Biggar was aware that this box had been deposited in the churchyard ; and many conjectures were hazarded, how it could have been placed there without being noticed, and who the parties were to whom the inscription referred. It was, no doubt, buried there by the directions of Dr Brown ; but everything else connected with it still remains an entire mystery.

· The part of the street in front of Silver-knowes was appointed by the Baron's Court as the place for the show and sale of stallions on fair and market days. Farther down was the Tron-knowe, where the public weighing beam stood, and where all weighable ware, such as butter, cheese, lint, etc., were exposed for sale. From this spot the engraved view of the town was taken. A little below was the Cross-knowe, a small eminence twenty or thirty feet in height, crowned with the Cross. The Cross had an octagonal basis of solid masonry, about four feet in height ; and from the centre of the platform above rose the shaft, which was without ornament of any kind. The Cross stone had a hole in its centre, and the date 1632 ; and the apex, which was square, had vertical dials on its four sides, and the initials 'J. E. W.,' John Earl of Wigton, with the date 1694. These two stones were, in the autumn of 1860, built into the south gable of the new Corn Exchange for preservation, with an inscription below them, intimating that they were 'part of the Old Cross of Biggar.' The oldest of these dates, viz., 1632, is not understood to be the period at which the Cross was erected. It can hardly be doubted that the Cross was at least as old as the time at which Biggar was created a burgh of barony, viz., in 1451. The dates, no doubt, referred to the time at which the stones on which they were inscribed were erected on the shaft, in place of others that had fallen into decay, or had been accidentally overturned and broken. At the Cross, state documents, acts of the Bailies' Court, and the different fairs, were proclaimed by tuck of drum ; and here the juveniles met for amusement, and the townsmen to discuss the topics of the day. Here, on market and fair days, assembled a motley crowd of people from the country round, to transact business ; while the sacred symbol above their heads reminded them of a leading point in their religious belief, and warned them to be candid and honest in their dealings, and to cultivate peace and good-will with their fellow-men. The shaft of the Cross, with the two

BIGGAR AULD CORSE KNOWE.

stones referred to, were taken down about fifty years ago; and the
pedestal, and the knowe on which it stood, were removed in 1823, to
make room for a hotel, which at that time was projected on the
Tontine system, but was never proceeded with. The removal of the
Cross-knowe, so prominent a feature in the Main Street of the town,
and so much identified with the recreations of the young and the
loungings of the old, furnished a theme of great lamentation to the
Biggar poets. James Affleck composed a dirge, in which he made
the knowe bewail its fate in very doleful terms, and preach a sermon
on the changeable character of all sublunary things. Remembering
with melancholy satisfaction the scenes which it had witnessed, it
exclaims :—

> ' I've been the haunt on market days,
>   The haunt o' monie a fair,—
> The lads and lasses, men and wives,
>   To me wad a' repair ;   ·

> ' And blythesome bairnies on my sides
>   Wi' pleasure they wad row,
> While worn-out age wad station keep
>   On Biggar auld Cross-knowe.'

It ended with this bit of serious moralizing :—

> ' I've served my time, and must away ;
>   Then why should earth repine ?
> Vain mortals ! view your coming fate,
>   It may be seen in mine.

> ' Before old age shall press you sore,
>   Still wiser may ye grow,
> Lay this to heart,—You must depart,
>   Like Biggar auld Cross-knowe.'

The most effective poem on the removal of the Cross-knowe was,
however, composed by Mr Robert Rae, a native of Biggar, and son of
Thomas Rae, a mason in that town. Mr Rae was born in 1805, and
at an early age removed, with his father and the other members of his
family, to the west of Scotland. While still a boy, he returned to
Biggar, and lived some time with his uncle, Robert Pairman, merchant.
In his fourteenth year he went to Glasgow, and filled various situations. While resident in that city, he published a volume of poems,
which met with a ready sale, particularly in Biggar, as some of his
pieces had a reference to that locality. Among others we may mention ' Hillrigs Jean,' and ' Wallace's Address to his Army after the
Battle of Biggar.' About ten years ago he went to London, and
obtained a situation in an extensive mercantile house. It was from
London that he addressed the verses on Biggar auld Cross-knowe to
his cousin, Dr Pairman, of Biggar. Mr Rae died at Glasgow in the

summer of 1861. As his poem on the auld Cross-knowe is the production of a Biggar man, as it contains many local allusions very happily expressed, and is pervaded by a fine genial spirit of affectionate attachment to scenes dear to every native of Biggar, we cannot forbear giving a considerable portion of it, more especially as it has never before been published. It is entitled—

'A YAMMERIN' AULD MAN'S LAMENT FOR BIGGAR AULD CORSE-KNOWE.

'O waes me for the auld Corse-knowe;
  Twice forty years hae come and gane
Sin' first I sprauchilt up its browe,
  A wee bit thochtless, happy wean.
Noo a' day lang I sit and grane,
  And scart wi' grief my lyart powe,
To think there's neither yird nor stane
  O what was ance the auld Corse-knowe.

'We grue to read hoo Vandals bar'd
  Their thirsty swurds owre auncient Rome;
And yet the heathen blackguards spar'd
  Aneugh to mark its dreadfu' doom.
But waur than Vandals hae been here
  (Deil rax their thrapples in a tow),
Wha left nae wee bit object near
  To tell whaur stood the auld Corse-knowe.

'Hoo strange that scenes we lo'ed when young
  Should sere auld age wi' pleasure fill!
The wud wi' hips and hazels hung,
  The wee burn dancin' down the hill,
The clatter o' the auld grey mill
  That peers owre Biggar's grassy howe,
Were dear to me; but dearer still,
  My heart's delicht,—the auld Corse-knowe.

'I've wander'd mony a far aff track,
  In mony a sweet wild spot I've been;
But aye my heart gaed yernin' back
  To bairntime's ever-hallow'd scene.
Whaur Hartree Hills, wi' simmer green,
  Dear Bizzyberry's rugged browe,
And Tintock, frae his azure screen,
  A' smiled upon the auld Corse-knowe.

'For O! a thousand memories kin'
  Roun' that dear hillock ever clung;
And aye its sounds o' auld langsyne
  (Sweet sounds!) owre a' my wandrin's hung.

The lowin' starns, that nichtly flung
　　Their glory owre the gloamin's browe,
Aye seem'd tae me as if they sung,
　　" There's nae spot like the auld Corse-knowe."

' In yon kirkyard, whaur, glimmerin' grey,
　　Heidstanes rise thick 'mang hillocks green,
Lies ae kin' chiel,* wha shar'd the wae
　　That brings the draps to my auld een.
His limner's han' and fancy keen
　　Did mak the ready canvas glowe
Wi' weel-kent groups, ilk face a frien',
　　A' clusterin' roun' the auld Corse-knowe.

' For mony a hundred years it stood,
　　And micht hae seen sax thousand fair,'
Defyin' time, and storm, and flood,
　　To lay its auld foundations bare.
Oure fathers lo'ed to linger there,
　　And see their wee anes roun' them rowe ;
But a' are gane, and never mair
　　Wi' joy shall ring the auld Corse-knowe.

' Hech ! Sirs ! the cronies o' my youth,—
　　Affleck, that kept us in a roar ;
The Fiddler, wi' his unco drouth,
　　Can't hae anither fortnicht's splore ;
The Elder cocks his thooms no more,
　　Nor Pinkles heckles at his tow !
Man ! Biggar's no like days o' yore,
　　It wants mair than the auld Corse-knowe.

' Yet aye I hear thro' memory's spell,
　　At dead o' nicht come doun the lum,
The tinkle o' Saunt Mary's bell,
　　Or tuck o' auld John Hilson's drum ;
Syne fancy leads me back to some
　　Tremendous hurlyhacket rowe,
Whan 'Roarin' Dillie,' lang since dumb,
　　Gaed thund'rin' doun the auld Corse-knowe.

' That rulin' power, auld Bailie Cree,
　　Aye cried the fairs wi' loud huzza ;
An', faith ! nae blateness show'd, whan he
　　To prick-the-garters gaed the law.
Nae mace had he, but baton braw,
　　The guid to fend, the bad to cowe ;
Nae chair o' state in gilded ha',
　　His rostrum was the auld Corse-knowe.

* John Pairman, artist, the poet's uncle, who painted the sketch of the Cross-knowe from which the engraving in this volume is taken.

'Oure farmers noo, ilk market day,
    Like donert nowte gang up and down,
And Biggar Fair and Whupman Play
    Are but a vain and empty soun'.
A bonfire still may licht the toun,
    But ah ! nae mair its sacred lowe
Can burn the auld year out, or croun'
    The young ane, on the auld Corse-knowe.

'Noo stoiterin' doun life's lanesome brae,
    Nae langer aught can pleasure gie;
For a' I lo'ed hae passed away,
    Like ripples oure the changefu' sea.
But sune I'll lay me doun tae dee,
    The yird will hap my weary powe,
And nane sall ever murn for me
    As I've dune for the auld Corse-knowe.

'But far abune yon murky lift,
    A warld o' sinless beauty lies,
Whaur frien'ships, scattered here like drift,
    Shall bloom beneath unclouded skies,
There 'mang the hills o' Paradise,
    Or where its gladsome rivers rowe,
Rejoicing in immortal ties,
    I'll weep nae mair the auld Corse-knowe.'

It is fortunate that a sketch of the Cross and the Cross-knowe, as they appeared when standing entire in 1807, was painted by Mr John Pairman, artist. His sketch, which was long in the possession of his brother Robert, merchant, Biggar, was presented by that gentleman to Mr Sim of Coulter. The engraving of it which adorns this volume will, no doubt, be duly appreciated by the inhabitants of Biggar, as to the old it will recall a spot associated with many youthful recollections, and to the young it will present a feature in the town which has for many years disappeared, but which must often, in their hearing, have been referred to and described. The figures with which the artist has peopled the Cross-knowe, were intended to represent various worthies, who were wont to frequent it on market days at the time the sketch was made. Among these may be mentioned, Colonel Dickson of Hartree; James Gladstone of Wester Toftcombs; John Paterson, farmer, East Toftcombs; William Lindsay, meal-dealer, Perryflats; John Minto, carrier, Biggar; David Loch, horse-dealer, Biggar; Mr Dickson of Baddinsgal, commonly called 'Old Barrinsgal;' Robert Tait, Spittal Muir, commonly known by the title of 'Sir Robert; James Stodart, Covington Hillhead.'

Immediately at the back of the Cross-knowe, as shown in the engraving, stood the Market House, or the 'Meal House,' as it was

generally called. What sort of building it was in former times, it is
not easy to say; but latterly it was a house of one storey, and had a
most melancholy look. It was opened every Thursday, the market
day, for the transaction of business, and occasionally on other days
for the sale of various commodities. Internally it was most uninvit-
ing, and was greatly infested with rats and mice, which rendered it
quite unsafe to deposit meal or grain within its walls. The rats and
mice were old colonists. Some fifty years ago, Affleck, the town poet,
penned a *jeu d'esprit*, which he termed an ' Address of the Rats and
Mice to two disputants (Nicol Porteous, toll-keeper, and William
Brechan, baker), who had disagreed about a bargain of oatmeal,
which was deposited by an order of the Sheriff in the Meal House,
Biggar, until the plea then pending should be settled.' This was
a glorious arrangement for the rats and mice, as they were thus
enabled to live for a time in the midst of abundance. This building
had long been felt to be nearly useless; and it was in so dismal and
dilapidated a condition as to be a discredit to the place. A number
of the leading men of the town and neighbourhood, therefore, resolved
to raise funds by shares, to erect a Corn Exchange of a more elegant
and commodious description. The site of the old Meal House, with
some adjoining ground, and also the right to levy the market customs,
were readily obtained, at a moderate price, from the late Colonel
John Fleming, the proprietor. Plans were procured from David
M'Gibbon, Esq., architect, Edinburgh; and the execution of the work
was intrusted to Messrs Jack and White, builders, Edinburgh. The
foundation-stone was laid with masonic honours on the 24th of
August 1860, by W. E. Hope Vere, Esq. of Craigie Hall and
Blackwood, Provincial Grand Master Mason of the Upper Ward of
Clydesdale, assisted by deputations of masonic brethren from twelve
different lodges. The completion of the building was celebrated by a
public dinner, which took place on Thursday, the 14th of November
1861, and which was presided over by Sir Edward Colebrooke, Bart.,
M.P., while A. Baillie Cochrane, Esq., M.P., acted as croupier. At
a meeting of the shareholders held a week afterwards—viz., on the
21st November—a code of regulations for conducting the business of
the market, along with a table of admission rates, and market and
storage dues, was agreed to, and the general business of the Exchange
was opened in a formal manner. The attendance of buyers and
sellers was numerous. The following is the statement of the day's
transactions as it appeared in the newspapers :—

'BIGGAR CORN MARKET, November 21.

' The supply of grain in this day's market amounted to 223 qrs.—viz., 200 oats ;
23 barley ; and 12 loads of oatmeal.

	Price per Qr.	Lbs. per Bush.	Av. Price.
Oats,..........19s. 0d. to 26s. 8d.	35 to 43½	£1 1 11
Barley,.......36s. 6d. to 30s. 0d.	52½ to 54½	1 7 8

Of the grain 173 qrs. were sold.'

The Exchange is a chaste and tasteful erection, in the Elizabethan style of architecture, and forms a great ornament to the street, as will be observed from the engraving of the High Street given in this work. A tower springing from the north-west corner, is intended to contain a clock, which will be a great benefit to the town. The basement storey is devoted to storage purposes; and above it are the large hall, sixty-two feet by thirty-five, for the disposal of grain and seeds; and in the higher part of the front of the building are a spacious reading-room and a consulting-room. The large hall, which is principally lighted from the roof, is so constructed that it will answer not only for commercial purposes, but also for public meetings, concerts, balls, etc. In the same quarter is John's Loan, the entrance to which is observable in the engraving of the Cross-knowe, the new Subscription School, and the Police Station, erected in 1860. A little farther down from the Corn Exchange are the spacious premises of the Royal Bank, conspicuous in the engraving of the High Street; and at some distance onwards are Malcolm's Well, the South United Presbyterian Meeting-house and Manse, and then the large building of the Commercial Bank, erected in 1833.

On the other side of the street, nearly opposite Silver-knowes, is the tenement once occupied by James Affleck, tailor and poet. James Affleck was born at Drummelzier on the 8th of September 1776. Owing to the poverty of his parents, he was kept but a short time at school, and went early to employment with the neighbouring farmers. He was then bound as an apprentice to Gilbert Tait, a tailor in his native village. He served with him three and a half years, and was chiefly employed, as was then the almost universal custom of country tailors, in sewing in the houses of his master's customers, having, as he said, 'not unfrequently to travel six or eight miles in a wintry morning, and work by candle-light for an hour or two before I received a morsel of breakfast, often wetted to the ankles in the morasses and rivulets which intersected our almost trackless way.' After the expiry of his apprenticeship, he resided a short time, first, at Netherton of Crawfordjohn, and then at the town of Ayr, and last of all set up his staff as a master tailor at Biggar, in the year 1793. In 1802 he published a volume of poetry, which sold readily, and brought him some pecuniary reward. He issued a second volume of poems in 1817, with a portrait from a painting by Mr John Pairman; and in 1818 he published a poem in two parts, entitled 'The Waes of Whisky.' A posthumous volume of his poems, with a biographical sketch, was published in 1836 by his son John, who, at the same time, inserted some poetical productions of his own.

Affleck's merits as a poet do not rank high. The divine afflatus was wholly awanting. His poems are very indifferent prose turned into rhyme. It would be difficult to select a single verse from his published works, and hold it up as a specimen of vigorous expression, original thought, or poetic inspiration. His poems, nevertheless, are interesting, as during a period of forty years his muse was ever busy with all sorts of local incidents, and, in fact, no event of any consequence transpired in the town or neighbourhood which did not evoke from him some poetic effusion. He was of an eminently social temperament. Shortly after his settlement at Biggar, he was initiated into the mysteries of freemasonry in the lodge of Biggar Free Operatives, and took a great interest and pleasure in the meetings and festivities of the brethren, always contributing not a little to their harmony and conviviality by the singing or recitation of his own productions, and, as chaplain, invoking a blessing on refreshments with such felicity of expression, and such manifestations of devotional feeling, as never failed to call forth the admiration of all present. He excelled in conversation, and was full of anecdotes and shrewd observations on life and manners. He was a great favourite in all the houses in which he was in the habit of being employed in the way of his profession. He made the winter evenings seem short, with his stories, his recitations, and remarks, and was commonly to be seen with a group of anxious listeners, to whom the words of Goldsmith were applicable :—

'And still they gazed, and still the wonder grew,
That one small head could carry all he knew.'

He was an excellent tradesman, and never allowed his conversational and poetical displays, nor the cultivation of the muse, to prevent him from producing a good day's work. It is to be lamented that in his latter days he became somewhat irregular in his habits. Intoxicating drink, which has mastered many a strong man, acquired, at times, too great ascendancy over him, and perhaps had some effect in laying him prematurely in the grave. He died on the 8th of September 1835, in the 59th year of his age, and was interred in the churchyard of Biggar.

A little farther down, and very near the spot at which the engraved view of the town begins, is an old house, once occupied by Richard Johnston and his spouse Nannie Muir, and subsequently by Mr Mathew Robertson, grocer. This house, or rather, perhaps, one which in former times stood on the same spot, was called the Tower or Fortalice. How it acquired this name, it is impossible now to say; but the probability is, that, as it stood in a commanding position, it was a fortified building for the defence of the town, or it may have been a stronghold of the Lords of the Manor at an earlier period than the castle of Boghall itself. The Tower House, and a half borrow land connected with it, belonged at one time to a Luke Tervat, in Toftcombs. On the 11th of July 1659, it was bequeathed by James Brown, merchant, Biggar, to the Rev. Alexander Livingston, minister of Biggar, and Alexander Hay, in Stane, and others, then

D

elders in the parish of Biggar, and their successors in office. The annual rent drawn from this property was, for a number of years, L.12 Scots, which was expended in aid of the funds for support of the poor. In 1774 it was sold by the kirk session, and ultimately fell into the hands of Richard Johnstone and his spouse Agnes Muir. After this period the Tower House witnessed more strange scenes than any other house in Biggar. It was for many years used as a lodging-house by its landlady Nannie Muir, and was, during that time, patronized by all the 'randy gangrel bodies' that frequented the Upper Ward. A score of teapots round Nannie's kitchen-fire on a morning was no uncommon spectacle. Drinking, dancing, and fighting at times, prevailed, though, in general, Nannie ruled her hostelry with a commanding hand. Had a Burns been admitted to its apartments during a winter's evening, he would have witnessed many a scene similar to those which he has so graphically described in his 'Jolly Beggars.'

On the same side of the street are the Elphinstone Arms Inn, where the omnibus is stationed in the engraving; the Freemasons' Hall and Commercial Inn; the Crown Inn, which, before the days of railways, was largely patronized by carriers; the North United Presbyterian Church; the old Burgher manse; the National Bank; the Established Church manse, rebuilt in 1805, and to which an addition was made in 1827; the parish school; the schoolmaster's house; the school green, and the kirkstyle, with its noble array of beech and ash trees skirting the road on the west. A little farther down the street is a large house, adjoining the one last seen in the engraving, but is not itself visible, which was once the property of a family of the name of Vallance, and now of the successors of the late James and William Paterson. This was one of the chief inns of Biggar during last century. It is remarkable as the house in which some of the officers of the Highland army, in December 1745, made their quarters during their stay in Biggar. The exact day of the arrival of the Highland army at Biggar has been preserved in the Session Records. The statement occurs in connection with the birth and baptism of James Carmichael, son of Bailie Thomas Carmichael, and his spouse Violet Craig. It is recorded that he was 'born 22d December 1745, and baptized 24th thereof, being the day Biggar was alarmed with the coming of the Highland army thereto, after their retreat from Prince William, second son to George II., King of Great Britain, etc., with whom they would not engage.' Unfortunately, no account has been preserved of the numbers of the Highland army that visited Biggar, the length of time which they remained, or the manner in which they conducted themselves. William Vallance, commonly called 'Laird Will,' with whom we ourselves, in our early years, have conversed, and whose father was proprietor and occupier of the inn to which we now refer, was in the habit of saying that he was some six or seven

years of age when the Highlanders came to Biggar. Intimation of
their approach having been obtained, he mounted his father's horses,
and fled to the solitudes of the Tweeddale mountains, to preserve them
from the fangs of the Hielandmen, who carried off or pressed into
their service all the horses on which they could lay their hands. A
little farther west are the Bridgend, the Wynd, and the Westraw.
In the landward part of the parish, in this direction, are Langlees, for
some time the property of the late Lord Murray; the Batts, now
called Springfield; the Lindsay Lands, Biggar Park (Alexander
Gillespie, Esq.), and Mosside.

Views of the town of Biggar have several times been sketched and
engraved. A view of the upper part of the town, and the Church, with
Bizzyberry in the background, was inserted in the 'Edinburgh Magazine' for May 1790. Another view of it, with an accompanying letterpress description, appeared in the 'Scots Magazine' for October 1815.
This is taken from Hartree, and embraces Hartree House, Boghall
Castle, the town of Biggar, and the adjacent heights to the north-west.
No artist, so far as we are aware, in more recent times, has considered
Biggar and its adjacent scenery picturesque and attractive enough to
induce him to expend time and labour in transferring a representation
of them to canvas. The people of Biggar, however, are thoroughly
convinced that their town presents some picturesque features, and
that the scenery around, if not striking, is pleasing and diversified.
At a meeting held at Biggar in 1848, under the auspices of the
Edinburgh Biggar Club, the Rev. John Christison, minister of the
parish, drew the following very playful contrast between Edinburgh
and Biggar:—'Any one standing between the old and new towns of
Edinburgh, and looking along the valley of the Nor' Loch, commanded
a very splendid view; but Biggar had an old and new town as well
as Edinburgh, and a beautiful valley lying between them, and as
pretty a stream winding through it as the eye could light on, on a
summer's day. (Cheers.) The whole, as many travellers had remarked,
formed no bad representation in miniature of the famous Links of
Forth. The view of the Edinburgh spectator would no doubt com-
prehend a greater variety of grand and picturesque objects; but would
it rival in sweetness the view of their own *burn braes*, on the one side,
beautiful in their pastoral simplicity,—"when unadorned, adorned
the most"—(cheers)—and on the other, crowned with lofty trees, the
growth of centuries, rising like towers, their leafy battlements scathed
with ages of elemental war? (Great applause.) The Edinburgh
view had many an architectural boast. Theirs had but one, but it
was a gem—the Church—(cheers)—old, venerable, grey, calling up
hosts of visions of the olden time, when it had its full establishment
of provost, prebends, singing boys, singing girls, tributary kirks, such
as Dunrod in far Galloway, etc., etc. Edinburgh had a splendid
viaduct stretching from town to town; but it must yield in historical

interest to their own *Cadger Brig*—(applause)—on which the foot of
the immortal Wallace was planted in one of the most heroic stands he
ever made. (Prolonged applause.) Edinburgh had its castle, itself
a magnificent object, and rich in associations of the past. He confessed it was difficult to find a parallel here, and, away from home, he
would scarcely have ventured on one. But in Biggar, which he knew
to be strong in local attachment, he thought he might refer to that
respectable eminence, *the Moat Knowe*—(laughter and applause)—from
which many a beacon had blazed in the days of yore, and which had
witnessed many a valiant fight—as, for instance, that memorable one,
the battle of Biggar, in which, if ancient chroniclers may be in aught
believed, not less than 60,000 men were routed in one day. Let the
people of Edinburgh, with all their scuffles about the castle, show
anything like that.' (Enthusiastic cheers.) The view from Biggar,
though embracing the now fertile vale that stretches from Tinto to
Broughton, is decidedly of an Alpine character. Hills appear on
every hand. The Common, 1260 feet above the level of the sea,
lies on the north-west, and was till recently covered with heather; but
has now been subdivided by belts of plantations, and subjected to the
inroads of the plough. Bizzyberry, 1150 feet above the level of the
sea, is on the north, commanding a fine view from its summit—
retaining not a few traces of ancient military operations, and having,
on the north side, a rock called Wallace's Seat, and Wallace's Well,
at which that hero is said to have quenched his thirst after the battle
of Biggar. On the east and south are the Broughton, Kilbucho, and
Hartree hills; the tops of some of them are encircled with deep
trenches, most likely dug in times of invasion in order to afford
security to the cattle of the district. Cardon and Coulter Fell are two
of the most conspicuous mountains in this direction, the latter of
which is said to be 2330 feet above the level of the sea, thus coming
within a few feet of the height of Tinto, and nearly verifying the old
rhyme—

> ' The height atween Tintock-tap and Coulter Fell
>   Is just three quarters of an ell.'

The most striking mountain near Biggar is certainly Tinto, which
rises majestically from the plain to the height of 2336 feet above the
level of the sea. It is crowned with a huge cairn of stones, on which
Druidical and beacon fires are said to have blazed in remote times,
and on which huge piles of combustibles have illumined the country
round in our own day, to mark seasons of rejoicing, such as the proclamation of peace in 1814, and the first visit of Queen Victoria to
the 'land of the mountain and the flood,' in 1842. Regarding Tintock-tap there is the following rhyme:—

> 'On Tintock-tap there is a mist,
>   And in the mist there is a kist,

And in the kist there is a caup,
And in the caup there is a drap;
Take up the caup, drink aff the drap,
And set the caup on Tintock-tap.'

In 1808 the late Sir Alexander Boswell published a ballad, entitled 'The Spirit of Tintoc, or Johnnie Bell and the Kelpie,' in which there is a special reference to the famed caup. Johnnie Bell, a droughty tailor, entertained as his guest auld Robin Scott, as great a lover of strong drink as himself. Robin was invited to 'pree' the contents of a graybeard, and, finding the liquor good, drank the whole at a single draught, much to the mortification of the tailor, who thus exclaimed:

'The graybeard's toom, I maun hae drink ;
I've no a plack to buy a drap.
My heart is up, and away I'll link,
There's drink for nought on Tintoc-tap.'

He instantly donned his blue bonnet, armed himself with a rowan-tree staff, and set out on his journey. During his progress he fell into a burn, and was seized by a water-kelpie, when a brownie whistled in his ear,—

'And muttered thrice the magic spell,
Thrice Cockatrice and Gallowlee,
When Kelpie shrieked, O Johnnie Bell !
My charm is broken, you are free !'

Gaining at length the summit of the hill, after much toilsome clambering, and having fortified himself with 'a quid o' the right Virginia,' Stilla, 'Queen of the Spirits of Fire,' appears to him, and bids him begone; but bold Johnnie Bell, not so easily to be daunted, defies the Queen and all the race of weird sisters, whom he overcomes by repeating the mystical words, 'Gallowlee and Cockatrice.' Thus compelled, and Stilla having

'—— stamped on the grassless yeard,
A fire and cauldron quick arose ;
The tailor rubb'd his head and beard,
And lick'd his lips, and cock'd his nose.

'The fire low'd, and the cauldron hiss'd,
And the hell-steam rose baith red and blue,
When the guardian-spirit of the kist
Swell'd to the wond'ring tailor's view.

'The lid o' the kist wi' a clap flew up—
And fou to the brim out flew the cap;
The thirsty tailor at ae sup
Drank it a', baith dreg and drap.

> ' The kist and cap, by cantrip spell,
>   Wi' whirring birr, in flinders flew ;
> But what became o' Johnnie Bell,
>   Gude kens ! I ken nae mair than you !'

The following reference is made to Tintock-tap in the well-known song of 'Tibbie Fowler':—

> ' Be a lassie e'er sae black,
>   Gin she hae the name o' siller,
> Set her up on Tintock-tap,
>   The wind wad blaw a man till her.'

With regard to the view from the summit of Tinto, Dr Mac-knight, in an excellent paper read before the '.Wernerian Natural History Society' on the 11th April 1812, says, 'The expanse of coun-try which it embraces appears unbounded on the west side, but towards the north it is terminated by the majestic Benlomond, and the lofty ranges of the Highlands, crowding irregularly into view in a manner extremely picturesque.   In the opposite direction of south-east, the prominent features of the view are the bold, undulating mountain lines, the finely grouped masses, and the ultimate swells and deep hollows of the Tweeddale hills.   Amongst the most remark-able is Coulter Fell, distinguished as the rival of Tinto itself, in size and height.   These magnificent objects, presenting themselves on the one hand, form an admirable and striking contrast to the delightful view, on the other hand, of the level country that stretches along the banks of the Clyde.   This noble stream, which shows in its course so many charms of natural scenery, and whose fine sweeps through the mountain valley and lower districts of Lanarkshire are so great an embellishment of the whole prospect, may, in truth, be said to carry along with it beauty and fertility from its very source.   It is equally pleasing and unexpected to find, at the height of 600 feet above the level of the sea, a tract of land so rich in soil, so well cultivated, and so extensively clothed with plantations, as the district spreading around the foot of the mountain, from Hyndford House to Syming-ton and Coulter, and up the river to a considerable distance.   The effect of the landscape is completed by the number of villas, and other marks of population and comfort, which everywhere appear in the vicinity of the Clyde.   There are few elevations in the United King-dom, where a finer assemblage of the grand and the beautiful in nature may be contemplated, than from Tinto.'

· The number of the inhabitants of the town and parish of Biggar in early times cannot now be ascertained.   The probability is, that in remote times the inhabitants of the landward part of the parish were much more numerous than what they are at present.   On most of the farms there were several cottars' houses, which have nearly all disappeared. Edmonstone or Candy had evidently a considerable population; and many dwelling-places, such as Batyhall, Hillhead, Johnsholm, Little Boghall, Foreknowes, Between the Hills, etc., mentioned in ancient records, do not now exist. The amount of the population in 1755 was 1098. In 1791 it had sunk down to 962; but after this period it continued for some time steadily, though slowly, to increase. In 1801 it was 1216; in 1811, 1376; in 1821, 1727; and in 1831, 1915. In 1841 it was 1865; in 1851, 2049; and in 1861, 2000.

The expense of erecting a house at Biggar, from the want of ready access to good and cheap building materials, has hitherto been considerable; and this has acted as a decided barrier to the increase of the town, as such a return in the shape of rent could not be obtained as to induce capitalists to expend their money in this direction. By the opening of a Branch Railway to Biggar, this disadvantage has, to some extent, been obviated; and therefore we may calculate that the town will, ere long, be largely increased.

CHAPTER IV.

Biggar Burn.

BIGGAR BURN rises in the north of the parish, and flows at first in a southerly and then in an easterly direction. After running a course of about nine miles, it falls into the Tweed nearly opposite Merlin's Grave, in the parish of Drummelzier. On its right bank, near its source, are the lands of Carwood, consisting of 947 Scots acres. At one period they formed a separate feu, and were for many years, as we learn from documents in the Wigton charter chest, held by a family of the name of Carwood. The male line becoming extinct, the heiress, Janet Carwood, was married to a younger son of one of the Lords Fleming, and the lands continued in this branch of the Flemings for a number of years. Richard Bannatyne says, that in 1572 they belonged to John Fleming, a brother of the then Lord Fleming. They were, at length, greatly encumbered with debt; and this being cleared off by Lord Fleming, they came back to the possession of the main branch of the Flemings. They consequently formed part of Admiral Fleming's Biggar estate, when the entail of it was set aside in 1830, and almost the whole of it was sold. Carwood, at that time, was purchased by Mr Robert Gray, son of the Rev. Thomas Gray, Broughton, and for many years a well-known grocer in Argyle Square, Edinburgh. That gentleman immediately set to the work of improvement with most laudable vigour. In a few years he reclaimed 400 acres of muirland, formed 50 enclosures of thorn, turf, and stone, and planted 200 acres with trees. In 1832 he erected an elegant mansion-house, and surrounded it with shrubberies and plantations. Carwood is now the property of W. G. Mitchell, Esq.

On the left side of Biggar Burn are the lands of Biggar Shields and 'Ballwaistie,' and a place called in former times 'Betwixt the Hills.' They comprise 1132 Scots acres. This extensive possession belonged at one period to the Fleming family. They appear to have sold it, or granted a wadset over it, previous to 1677; for, in November of that year, John Cheisley of Kerswell, near Carnwath, was retoured heir of his father John, 'in the lands and meadow of Scheills and Betwixt the Hills, a part of the lands called Balweistie, and lands of Heaviesyde, in the parish of Biggar.' In a rent-roll of the Earl of Wigton's Biggar property, in 1671, it is stated that the heritor of Biggar Shields and

Betwixt the Hills paid to his Lordship yearly 'fiftie punds of tiend duty, and eight bolls of tiend meal.' It was purchased in 1806 by Mr Joseph Stainton, manager of the Carron Company. At that time it was almost wholly a sheep-walk, and was let at a rent of L.150 per annum. In 1817 and the three following years, Mr Stainton carried on a series of very extensive improvements on this estate. 'He re-claimed 600 acres, drained extensively, erected 18 miles of stone dykes, and planted 15 miles of thorn hedges, and 265 acres with forest trees.' The yearly rental, we suppose, now exceeds L.1000.

Farther down the stream are the lands of Persilands, and of what were anciently called the Over and the Nether Wells, which most likely, by the time of Queen Mary, were disjoined from the Biggar estate, and held as a separate possession. Some years afterwards, viz., in 1614, the proprietor of these lands was William Fleming, no doubt a cadet of the family of the lord superior. In a document entitled 'The Rentall of the mealles, fermes, and other deuties payable to the Earl of Wigtoun furth of the Barrony of Biggar in 1671,' it is stated that John Muirhead was heritor of these lands, and paid five merks yearly as feu-duty. He was succeeded by his son James, who left the lands to George Muirhead, most likely his son, who died in 1751, and bequeathed them to his wife, Mary Dickson, a sister of the Rev. David Dickson, minister of Newlands. This lady afterwards married the Rev. John Noble of Libberton, and at her death left the estate of Persilands to her nephew, the Rev. David Dickson. This divine, after being licensed to preach the Gospel by the Presbytery of Biggar, was for some time assistant to his aunt's husband, Mr Noble. He was afterwards settled at Bothkennar, and ultimately translated to Edinburgh. He was a very popular preacher, and a strenuous partisan of the evangelical party in the Church. He died in 1820, and the estate of Persilands became the patrimony of his son, Dr David Dickson, a distinguished scholar, philanthropist, and divine, and for nearly forty years one of the ministers of the West Kirk, Edinburgh. He had thus an intimate connection with the parish of Biggar; but the pastoral duties and benevolent schemes with which he was always deeply engrossed, prevented him from visiting it often, or taking any great interest in its affairs. He died on the 28th July 1842, and the estate, after continuing a few years in his family, was sold to Mr Mitchell of Carwood. The farm-house and offices were recently re-built, and a carved stone, containing several initials, the date 1658, and two Latin inscriptions, one of them 'Nisi Dominus frustra,' and very likely belonging to one of the old mansion-houses of the Persilands, was placed for preservation in the end of a stable.

To the west of the Persilands is a spot where formerly stood a small farm-steading called Hillriggs. Towards the end of last century it was occupied by a shepherd of the name of Kemp. This was the father of George Mickle Kemp, who acquired so great celebrity as the

E

architect of the Scott Monument at Edinburgh. The architect was in
the habit of stating that he was born here; and we have not as yet
obtained any information to make us doubt that this statement is in-
correct. At all events, he lived here when a child under his father's
roof. In his tenth year, after his father had gone to reside in another
locality, he paid a visit to the famed chapel of Roslin; and being of an
impressible and poetical temperament, he contemplated the pillars,
arches, and emblematical devices of this edifice with wonder and
admiration. He was bred to the trade of a joiner; and on the expiry
of his apprenticeship, he set out on a tour for the purpose of improving
himself in his profession, and gratifying his taste for architectural
drawing. He wrought at his trade in many towns of Scotland, England, and France, and prolonged his stay especially in those which
contained remarkable specimens of Gothic architecture. He was in
the habit of studying all their details, and making a sketch of their
chief peculiarities. He spent also a portion of his time in acquiring
a knowledge of drawing and perspective, in which he made considerable progress.

Kemp at length returned home, entered into the marriage state, and
commenced business on his own account as a joiner. Not meeting
with the success which he expected, he threw aside the saw and
hammer, and devoted himself to the work of architectural drawing,
from which he derived a very small and precarious income. He still
practised his old habits of sketching the remains of ancient castles,
abbeys, etc.; and, in fact, at this time Burns' account of Captain
Grose was strictly applicable to him:—

> ' By some auld houlet-haunted biggin,
> Or kirk deserted by its riggin,
>   It's ten to ane ye'll fin' him snug in
>   Some eldrich part.'

He was engaged in taking sketches of the Abbey of Kilwinning,
when a professional friend, whom he chanced to meet, advised him
to try his hand at a design for the monument to Sir Walter Scott at
Edinburgh. Acting on this advice, he hastened home to his residence
in Edinburgh, and in five days produced the design of a splendid
Gothic cross, drawn in its principal details from Melrose Abbey. In
due time he lodged the drawing of his plan, to which he attached the
name of 'John Morvo.' The Committee appointed to forward the
monument had offered prizes for the three best designs; and when
they came to decide on the merits of those submitted for competition,
they fixed on John Morvo's cross as one of the three to which a prize
should be awarded. They were at a loss to know who John Morvo
was, not being aware that the name was assumed, and that, in fact, it
was the designation of a famous mason of former days, who, in an
inscription on Melrose Abbey, is said to have

‘ Had in kepyng al mason werk
Of Santandroys, ye Hie Kirk
Of Glasgow, Melros, and Paslay,
Of Niddisdaill, and of Galway.’

On the morning of the day on which the prizes were to be decided,
Mr Kemp had gone to Linlithgow to take drawings of some portions
of its ruined palace; and on returning in the evening, he was delighted
to find that some person had told his wife that a prize had been
awarded to the design of John Morvo. When it became known that
the beautiful and most appropriate Gothic cross was the production
of so humble and unassuming a man as George Kemp, a strong prejudice was manifested in some quarters against it, and the Committee
at first refused to adopt it. They advertised a second time for new
designs, and a few were obtained. Kemp stuck to his cross, and gave
in an improved drawing of his original plan. The Committee still
hesitated and objected. It was alleged to be a mere copy of some
Gothic building, and to be of so inaccurate and unsubstantial a construction, that it even could not be erected. Mr Kemp himself
satisfactorily showed that the first charge was entirely without foundation; and in regard to the second, Mr Burn, a professional architect
of high reputation, who was consulted by the Committee, declared
‘ his admiration of Mr Kemp’s design, its purity as a Gothic composition, and more particularly the constructive skill exhibited throughout,
in the combination of the graceful features of that style of architecture, in such a manner as to satisfy any professional man of the
correctness of its principle, and the perfect solidity which it would
possess when built.’ The Committee were, therefore, induced, in
March 1838, to recommend the adoption of Mr Kemp’s plan, as ‘ an
imposing structure, 135 feet in height, of beautiful proportions, in
strict conformity with the purity in taste and style of Melrose Abbey,
from which it is in all its details derived.’ It was afterwards resolved,
in order to give a still more impressive effect to the structure, to enlarge it to the height of 200 feet above the surface of the ground.

The building of the monument was entrusted to Mr David Lind,
and Mr Kemp himself was appointed superintendent of works. Mr
Kemp was now placed in circumstances of comparative comfort; he
had acquired a celebrity which he had hardly dared at one time to
contemplate, and he had the prospect of being largely employed, and
raised to a state of affluence. Unfortunately, one dark night when
on his way home, he fell into the Union Canal, and was drowned.
Mr Kemp was a remarkably modest and unassuming individual. He
was averse to anything like forwardness and obtrusion. His merits
were thus not readily observed, and often failed to secure him that
attention to which he was entitled. He was of a social disposition.
He loved to spend an hour with a friend to discuss the progress of
art, or the topics of the day. He had cultivated his mind with some

assiduity, and wrote tolerably good verses, some of which appeared
in newspapers and periodicals. His architectural genius was of a
high order. His Scott Monument was a noble conception, and will
perpetuate his name to distant ages. It holds, and is likely long to
hold, a chief place amid the splendid structures that adorn the capital
of our native land.

A little farther down is the farm of Foreknowes and Rawhead,
which some years ago belonged to the Hon. Mountstuart Elphinstone,
a brother of Admiral Fleming, and well known as a Governor of
Bombay, and afterwards of Madras, and as the author of an interesting work on the Kingdom of Cabul. He retired from the offices
which he held in India in 1827, and died at Hookwood Park, Surrey,
on the 20th November 1859. This property was purchased from Mr
Elphinstone by Mr Gillespie of Biggar Park, and sold by him to the
Free Church College, Edinburgh, having been purchased with funds
bequeathed for the benefit of that institution.

We next come to the mill which has ground the meal and malt of
the parishioners for a long period, as it is mentioned in some very old
documents connected with the parish. It is also referred to in one of
Dr Pennicuick's Poems, published upwards of one hundred and fifty
years ago, entitled 'The Tragedy of the Duke of Alva, alias Graybeard:
being the complaint of the brandy bottle lost by a poor carrier, having
fallen from the handle, and found again by a company of the Presbytery of Peebles, near Kinkaidylaw, as they returned from Glasgow
immediately after they had taken the test.' The graybeard, addressing their reverences, said,

'O sons of Levi! messengers of grace!
Have some regard to my old reverend face,
My broken shoulder and my wrinkled brow
Plead fast for pity, and supply from you.
Help, godly sirs; and, if it be your will,
Convey me safely home to Biggar Mill,
Where, wand'ring to the widow, I was lost.
Alas! I fear the Carrier pays the cost.'

In spite of these and other sympathetic appeals, the holy brethren
resolved that they would regale themselves with the inspiring contents of the graybeard, let the consequences be what they might.

'Right blythe they were, and drank to ane another,
And ay the word went round, Here's to you, brother.'

The poor widow of Biggar Mill was thus deprived of her jar of brandy,
and in all likelihood the carrier had to pay the expense of the carouse.

Biggar Burn, a little above the mill, enters a deep ravine called
the Burn Braes, and, after passing the mill, flows along in serpentine
meanders, like the Links of Forth in miniature. On the right bank
are the ruins of the wauk mill and dyeing establishment of Thomas

Cosh, and his son-in-law Angus Campbell, and the picturesque suburb of Westraw, with its finely sloping gardens. The indwellers in Westraw were wont to reckon themselves a sort of separate community from the inhabitants of the town of Biggar. They had distinct societies and coteries of their own. They had their own peat-moss, their own birlemen, and their own amusements. Between the boys of the two places there was a standing feud of old date. This was constantly manifesting itself in pugilistic encounters; but at a certain season of the year it broke out in a general bicker or *melée* on the Burn Braes. The weapons employed were slings, stones, and sticks. The tact and heroism at times displayed in attacking and defending these braes, would have done no discredit to a regular army. The wounds inflicted were often severe, and sometimes left scars and injuries that the sufferers carried with them to the grave. The baron bailie, Mathew Cree, and his henchmen the chief constables of the town, sometimes made a sally on the belligerents; and it was a rare sight to see these worthy powers put to flight by repeated volleys of stones, or at other times forcing the youthful warriors to shift their ground, and take refuge behind the mill-planting, or to scatter themselves over Cuttimuir or Kennedy's Oxgate. A lad having lost an eye in one of these encounters, the better disposed portion of the inhabitants at length rose against them, and happily succeeded in putting a stop to them, it is to be hoped, for ever.

The lands behind the Westraw swell into a gentle upland, now crowned with trees, called the Knock. These lands belonged at one time to the Knights Templars. So late as the 20th of March 1620, we find a precept of Sasine granted to John Smith, of two oxgates of Templelands, with the annuals or teinds thereof, in the Westraw of Biggar. In former times, it was a common thing to hold and compute land by oxgates. In the old writs of Biggar, of which there are a large number in the Wigton charter chest, we notice references to the following oxgates:—Chamberlain's, Fleming's, Goldie's, Hillhead, Mosside, Smith's, Spittle, Staine, Stainehead, and Telfer's. The lands of Westraw, or 'Wasterraw,' as it is often called in the old writs, consisted of eight oxgates. These oxgates were, in 1671, possessed by Archibald Watson, Thomas, James, William, and Alexander Robb, and William Valange, who 'payd for ilk oxgang twentie punds;' 'ane boll of meall, ane boll of beer, and ane boll and half of hill oats,' and for the whole twenty-four kain fowls.

On the left bank are the Kirkhill, the Kirk and the Kirkyard, the Moat-knowe, and the Preaching Brae. The Preaching Brae is the spot at which open-air discourses were delivered on sacramental and other extraordinary occasions. The tent was pitched near the edge of the Burn, and the crowd rose rank above rank on the rising ground in front. Many of the chief Dissenting divines of Scotland, especially those of former generations, preached here, and attracted

immense multitudes from the country round. The clergy, at these
assemblies, generally put forth their best abilities. Many persons
were wont to date from them their first serious concern for their
eternal interests. The spectacle was reverential and picturesque, re-
minding one of the conventicles of old, to see a large throng of people
worshipping their Creator under the blue canopy of heaven; and the
heart was touched to hear 'the sweet acclaim of praise' arise from
thousands of pious lips, and swell on the fitful breeze. The practice
of preaching here has been discontinued for well nigh forty years, so
that few of the present generation of Biggar inhabitants have seen a
Burn Brae conventicle at all approximating in magnitude and rapt
devotion to those of former times. .

On these braes the inhabitants have long carried on the practice of
washing and bleaching their clothes. Attempts have several times
been made to deprive them of this privilege. A keen war has hence
arisen between them and the tacksmen of the grounds; but the result
has hitherto been, that the wives and maidens have remained in
possession of the field.

A little farther down is a level spot called Angus's Green, on which
the Biggar gymnastic sports are annually held in the middle of June.
These sports have hitherto been popular, and have been largely
patronized; but, like similar amusements in other parts of the country, they are understood to be now on the wane, and, unless their
patrons make vigorous efforts to uphold them, the probability is that
ere long they will be abandoned. The curious excavations here, in
connection with the Moat-knowe, have, unfortunately, in the desire
for improvement, been filled up and defaced.

A little farther down, some thirty years ago, stood the hut of Janet
Watson, commonly known by the name of 'Daft Jenny.' She was
the daughter of John Watson and Isabella Vallance. In her early
days she was employed in hawking small wares about the country, in
a basket; but at length, manifesting decided symptoms of insanity, she
was placed in confinement, became dependent on the parochial funds,
and lived here in her solitary apartment for many years. Her
appearance was most singular. She had a wild and excited expression of countenance. She was commonly dressed in a blue cotton
gown, or in a blue flannel petticoat and jupe, or short-gown. She
wore on her head a plain mutch, or 'toy,' as it was here called, while
on one shoulder hung a plaid; and in her left hand she invariably
held an old tobacco pipe and a tattered Bible, which she frequently
kissed or held to her breast. She was fastened by the leg with a
strong iron chain, to prevent her from making her escape, and committing injury on the persons and property of the inhabitants. Her
language was rambling and incoherent, and largely interlarded with
snatches of songs, texts of Scripture, and the names of persons with
whom she had been acquainted. At times it was uttered in a low

and subdued tone, and all of a sudden it was poured forth with a vehemence and excitement that made all the neighbourhood re-echo. She was somewhat outrageous. She would heave the parritch cog, the frying pan, and other utensils in which she received her food, over the top of the adjacent houses, and assail persons who came near her with sticks and stones. When she broke her chain, or contrived to slip it off her leg, she commonly ran to the Relief Manse, erected on the site of her father's cottage; and there she broke the windows, or pulled up the bushes and plants in the garden. She was thus a great terror to the juvenile population; and when the cry arose, 'Jenny's loose,' every boy and girl made speedily to a place of protection.

Her father, surnamed the 'Whistling Laird,' was a singular sort of a man. In his early days he had spent some time in North America, and had there acquired a habit of making various articles of domestic use. In the side of a brae, near the place at which his daughter's hut stood, he erected a curious and primitive-looking building of stones, turf, and wood, and covered it with a roof composed partly of paper and pitch, and hence it was commonly known by the name of the 'Castle o' Clouts.' He made the whole of his own clothes, including his shoes and leathern cap; and he produced some rare pieces of joiner's work, in the shape of carts, wheelbarrows, etc. His first wife, Isabella Vallance, died early; and, during the war in Spain, he married a woman commonly called 'Jock's Jenny,' who had been previously married to a labourer in Biggar, at one time well known in that town by the soubriquet of 'Whistling Jock,' from a humming sort of whistle in which he indulged as he went from one place to another. During the exciting times of the Continental War, 'Whistling Jock' was fired with the ambition of being a soldier; so he deserted his wife, and went to fight the battles of his country in the Spanish Peninsula. He very likely carried on little epistolary correspondence with his wife, even when he first went abroad, but at length it ceased altogether; and as his regiment had frequently been engaged with the enemy, Jenny suspected that he had lost his life in some of the sanguinary contests then so common in Spain. She wrote a letter inquiring after him to the War Office, and, by some mistake or other, he was reported to have been killed. When the Whistling Laird, therefore, made proposals of marriage to her, she considered she was at liberty to accept them, as she said, in her stuttering manner, 'The War Office had told her that Dock was killed at Pain, far ayont Gasco.' They therefore were joined in wedlock, and lived contentedly till the conclusion of the war, when 'Dock' suddenly made his appearance in his tattered regimentals, and confronted the astounded pair. Jenny would rather have preferred to live with 'Don,' as she called her husband number two, as, in her estimation, 'he was a good religious man;' but Whistling Jock maintained, that, by priority of engagement, he had a preferable claim. With threats and pleadings, Jenny was prevailed on to go with Dock, and the Whistling Laird was left in solitary blessedness for the remainder of his life.

John Watson was a person of sagacity and information. He allowed himself, however, on one occasion, to be made the victim of a rather laughable, though to him a very mortifying hoax. One day he received by post a large letter with a huge seal, purporting to be from the Provost and Magistrates of Edinburgh, and inviting him to accept of the office of hangman, then vacant by the death of John High. He was not only thoroughly convinced that the letter was genuine, but he was vastly elated at the idea of receiving so great a mark of attention and honour from the municipal authorities of the Scottish metropolis. He said the post which they had conferred on him might not in general estimation be held to be very respectable, yet it was most necessary, and therefore laudable; because, if the laws were not duly carried out, society would soon be thrown into a state of anarchy. In spite of the remonstrances of his friends, he set out to Edinburgh, and presented himself at the Council Chambers. He boldly announced that he had come from Biggar to accept of the office of hangman. The clerks in the office informed him that it had already been filled up. This sad announcement at once laid all his bright hopes in the dust. He declared that he had been very unfairly treated, and produced the document putting the office in question at his acceptance. The communication was declared to be an arrant forgery, and John had no other alternative than to trudge back to Biggar, it may be a wiser, but certainly a most angry and disappointed man.

A little farther on are the Gas Works, erected in 1839 by a joint-stock company. Gas is supplied to the community at 7s. per 1000 cubic feet. The undertaking, while it has been a great advantage to the inhabitants, has also been a profitable speculation for the share-holders. We have next on the side of the Burn a range of premises used as a brewery by James Steel, and afterwards by Mr James Bell. No brewing has been carried on here for several years. Adjoining is the Wynd, dear to the recollection of Westraw callants, when it was tenanted by such worthies as John Davidson, tailor; David Loch, and Andrew Steel, carters, etc. Here is the Cadger's Brig, supposed to be a Roman work. It is far from unlikely that the Romans threw a bridge across this stream, which often in winter is considerably swollen, and is then not easily fordable; but the present erection is perhaps more modern. By whatever party it was built, it was, no doubt, largely taken advantage of by the numerous cadgers that at one time passed through Biggar to the great mart for their merchandise, the Scottish capital; and hence, in all likelihood, its name. The popular tradition, however, is, that it first received its name from the circumstance of its having been used by Sir William Wallace, when he visited the English camp at Biggar in the guise of a

John Jackson Del

Peter Priest Sculp

CADGER'S BRIG.

BIGGAR.

1862.

cadger. It is very narrow, and being without parapet-walls, it was crossed with great difficulty in dark nights. About forty years ago, a substitute for these walls was found in an iron railing, which was erected under the auspices of Mr James Bell, brewer. A little below is a bridge in connection with the turnpike road to Dumfries, built in 1823, and embanked at each end with the earth that formed the Cross-knowe.

Below these bridges is the Ba' Green, supposed at one time to have been the public park of the town, where, among other pastimes, football was played. Football was long a favourite amusement in this as well as in other districts of Scotland. It was cried down by the edicts of James I., and other sovereigns, who wished to substitute archery in its place; but it still prevailed. It was a rough and savage pastime. Severe wounds were often inflicted from falls and kicks, and fights were not uncommon from alleged instances of unfair play. The sport was also carried on in the Main or High Street of Biggar, particularly on public occasions, when a number of the country people were in town. It was then most irregular and tumultuous. Every one took what side he pleased. The fury and violence were terrible. A dozen or two of the combatants would be lying sprawling on the ground at one time, and an unhappy wight would be knocked through a window, or overturned in a filthy open sewer. This pastime has been discontinued. Draughts, quoits, curling, and bowling, are now the favourite amusements. The Bowling-green lies contiguous to the Moat-knowe. It is neatly constructed, is kept in excellent order, and conduces much to the recreation and health of a portion of the inhabitants.

On the side opposite to the Ba' Green is the small holding of the Blawhill; and here, by the side of the stream, is Jenny's Well, to which the inhabitants established a right about thirty-five years ago, when an attempt was made to shut up the road to it by the proprietor of the adjoining grounds. The meeting of Westraw wives, with Mr James Bell, brewer, at their head, to defend their ancient right, was a fine display of indignant and independent Biggar feeling. The proprietor entered the case before the Sheriff at Lanark; but in the end had sense enough to withdraw it, and pay all expenses. So this remarkably cool and copious spring will remain in all time coming to supply refreshing draughts to the Biggar people, and to remind them that in this free country might cannot always triumph over right.

On the right are the lands of Boghall Mains, now finely subdivided and improved. The farm-steading, built about thirty years ago, is one of the most elegant and substantial in the county. It cost the proprietor L.1500, and the tenant L.800 in cartages.

Biggar Burn, after receiving a small stream from Hartree, takes the name of Biggar Water. The first reference to Biggar Water in any of our public muniments, so far as we have observed, is in a document giving a detail of the perambulation of the Marches of Stobo,

F

which is supposed to have taken place between 1202 and 1207. This document, after referring to various boundaries of that parish, goes on to say, 'And so by the hill top between Glenubswirles to the Burn of Glenkeht (the Muirburn), and so downwards as that Burn falls into the Bigre.' The other tributaries of Biggar Water are Skirling Burn, Kilbucho Burn, Broughton Burn, and Holmes Water. In a ditch or small burn running from the Westraw Moss, the strange phenomenon is sometimes seen of a portion of the waters of the Clyde flowing into Biggar Water. This, of course, only takes place when the Clyde is greatly flooded; but it shows how small an effort would be requisite to turn the waters of Clyde into those of the Tweed. At the place where the level is most favourable for such a project, the Clyde has actually formed a channel of some length in this direction. The tradition regarding it is, that the wizard, Michael Scott, entered into a paction with the devil, by which he obtained liberty to take the Clyde across the Westraw Moss and the lands of Boghall as fast as a horse could trot, on condition, however, that he would not look behind him during the operation. He commenced the work; but the angry waters made such a terrific noise, that he could not resist the temptation to look back to see the cause of the uproar. The spell was thus broken, and the waters fled back to their old channel, but left a very decided trace of the devious course which they had been forced to take.

The Symington, Biggar, and Broughton Railway passes along the valley of Biggar Water. The first sod of this line was cut on the 30th of September 1858, by Mrs Baillie Cochrane of Lamington, amid the applauding demonstrations of a great concourse of spectators, who had marched to the spot from Biggar with banners and bands of music. It was opened on the 5th of November 1860. The length of it is little more than eight miles; and the tract over which it passes, being extremely level, presented little engineering difficulty. It crosses the Clyde, near the Moat of Wolf-Clyde, by a viaduct, the piers and abutments of which are of stone, and the arches, seven in number, of malleable iron. Three of the arches are each 62½ feet wide, and are what are called 'lattice' girders; and the other four are each 27 feet wide, and are called 'plate' girders. The whole weight of iron employed is 44 tons, and the cost was L.4150. At this point is the first station, the second is at Boghall, the third is at Braidford Bridge, and the present terminus is at Broughton, but steps are in the course of being taken to carry the line down the Tweed to Peebles. This railway can hardly fail to confer a great benefit on the district, in conveying agricultural products to the marts in the east and west, and in bringing coals, lime, and other articles which the district requires.

The tract through which Biggar water flows, especially on its north bank, was till recently a dreary, unprofitable, and deleterious waste, relieved only here and there with a stunted birch tree. It was composed of peat-moss, and vast quantities of peat for fuel had been dug here. The surface was consequently studded with deep excavations, filled with water, and almost impassable. When a stray stot or stirk ventured to intrude into this boggy and treacherous track, the probability was, that it plunged into a deep hole, or stuck fast in the mud; and then great was the labour of men and boys to drag it from its dangerous position, and preserve it from destruction. This waste appears to have been in early times called the Nether Moss, and latterly it was known by the name of Biggar Bogs. In 1832, a poem appeared in a periodical called the 'Edinburgh Spectator,' which contained a sort of ironical eulogium on the Bogs of Biggar. One of the stanzas ran thus :—

> ' O the Bogs of Biggar
> Both clean and trig are,
> With the frogs a chirping
>   Uncommon sweet ;
> And some bulrushes,
> And stunted bushes,
> To meet your wishes,
>   So small and neat.'

The growing crops in the neighbourhood of this dismal swamp, except in early years, were very liable to be damaged by frost, and were thus often rendered unfit for seed, and sometimes even for food. The feuars of Biggar, who rented nearly all the Bog parks, were occasionally subjected to heavy losses from this cause. The late Rev. William Watson, incumbent of the parish, had one of the Bog parks; but in consequence of the soil being drier, and lying at a greater distance from the swampy ground, his crops generally suffered less damage from the frosts than some of his neighbours, and thus excited their envy. One very frosty autumnal morning, Mr Watson met the late William Clerk, merchant, Biggar, and accosting him, said, ' William, this is a snell morning ; I am afraid the oats in the Bog parks must have sustained damage.' ' Aye, Mr Watson,' was the reply, ' there's nae respect o' persons this morning.'

Various efforts were, from time to time, made to bring some portions of this tract under cultivation. The great difficulty to contend with was the want of a sufficient descent, to carry off the superfluous moisture with which the lands were saturated. The whole valley was nearly a dead level, and the channel of Biggar Water was only a few inches below the surface. Drains, cut to any depth, were worse than useless. They only had the effect of bringing water in greater abundance on the adjoining grounds. To obviate these obstructions to drainage, the late Mr Murray of Heavyside cut a large ditch parallel to the stream, but at some distance from it, and at the termination of the ditch erected a water-wheel, with buckets, by which he lifted the water to a higher elevation, and thus was enabled to dry a considerable portion of his bog lands. This wheel, which wrought

very effectually, was the workmanship of the ingenious millwright of
Biggar, Mr James Watt. The adjoining proprietors at length resolved to deepen Biggar Water to such an extent as to ensure a proper declivity, and prevent it from being filled up with mud and
weeds, as had hitherto been the case. This important work was,
accordingly, carried out under the superintendence of Mr George
Ferguson, and completed in 1858. Some hundred acres of land along
the banks of the stream have, consequently, been drained and cultivated, and are now annually covered with most luxuriant crops, while
the atmosphere around has been rendered vastly more salubrious and
agreeable.

In this dreary flat stood a hamlet called John's Holm. John
Gairns and Archibald Brown were two of the tenants of this place, a
hundred and thirty years ago. The buildings have now entirely disappeared, so that it is difficult to ascertain the exact spot on which
they stood.

This level tract was, no doubt, at a very remote period, covered with
the sea. The stones, to a great depth, appear to have travelled from a
distance, and have the smooth rounded shape that is produced by the
action of water. Mr Robert Chambers, in his curious and interesting
work on 'Ancient Sea Margins,' states, that the central mountain range
of southern Scotland, from which the Tweed and Clyde take their
almost contiguous origin, bears marks of ancient sea levels at coinci-
dent heights on both sides. He enumerates various places at the
height of 628 feet on the Ettrick, Gala, and Tweed, which present
flat projections, supposed to be formed by the action of the sea, and
then says, 'It is remarkable, however, that the broad passage or col
between the Tweed and Clyde at Biggar, much of the basis of which
is occupied by a moss, is given at 628 feet above the sea. When the
sea stood at this height, the two estuaries of Clyde and Tweed joined
in a shallow sound at Biggar, and the southern province of Scotland
formed two islands, or rather group of islands.'

It is a matter of some regret that the Fleming family, so long connected with this parish, have, from time to time, disposed of nearly
all the extensive lands that they once possessed here and in the
neighbourhood. With Glenholm, Kilbucho, and Thankerton they
have long ceased to have any connection, and the whole of their inheritance in the parish of Biggar has now dwindled down to a few
acres. This regret is qualified by the circumstance, that they had
long allowed their lands in this parish to remain in a very neglected
state. They held out no inducement to improvement. Being non-
resident, and possessed of little superfluous wealth, they neither
showed any example of activity, nor expended the necessary capital
to promote the due cultivation of the soil; and thus it continued,
from year to year, in the same dismal and unprofitable state. When
the entail was broken, fully thirty years ago, and the portion of Big-

gar parish which they still held was sold, it fortunately fell into the hands of men who lost no time in commencing the work of improvement. New farm-steadings were built, drains were cut, dykes were erected, and trees and hedgerows were planted. Two thousand acres of land, by the enterprise and resources of the new proprietors, Lord Murray of Langlees, George Gillespie, Esq. of Biggar Park, Robert Gray, Esq. of Carwood, Thomas Murray, Esq. of Heavyside, and William Murray, Esq. of Spittal, very soon assumed a new appearance, and became vastly more valuable.

The whole lands in the parish of Biggar comprise, as we have said, 5852 Scots acres. The soil consists principally of clay, sand, gravel, loam, and peat-moss. It rears good crops of oats, barley, pease, turnips, and potatoes, but is not adapted for beans and wheat. The dairy is here an object of great attention. Most of the farmers keep a stock of milk cows; and the butter and cheese, both full milk and skim milk, which they produce, are held in high repute in the marts of the eastern and western metropolis, and very often receive premiums at the shows of the Highland and Agricultural Society of Scotland. In the north part of the parish, near the source of Biggar Burn, the soil is of a poor description, and appears to be too scantily supplied with the phosphates that are necessary for strengthening and fertilizing the soil. It is supposed that it is from this cause that the cattle are often attacked with a disease called the 'stiffness,' or 'cripple.' Those persons who wish to obtain information regarding this disease, which has hitherto been little investigated in this country, are referred to an article 'On Arthritic or Bone Disease,' by Mr William Thorburn, Henchilend, in the January number of the 'Veterinary Review' for 1861, and to various observations on the subject by Mr John Gamgee, both in that periodical and in his work on 'The Domestic Animals in Health and Disease.'

CHAPTER V.

Sunnyside and Candy.

A LITTLE to the north-east of the town is the elegant mansion of Walter S. Lorrain, Esq. It was formerly called Sunnyside, but its name has recently been changed to Loaningdale. Here James Scott, one of the Biggar poets, was born, about the year 1734. His father, who bore the same name, was by profession a mason. The name of Robert Scott, wright in Sunnyside, appears in the Session Records, under date 11th July 1734, in connection with negotiations for the construction of a new tent, 'for the benefit of the work of the Sacrament without doors;' but this, perhaps, was the poet's uncle. The parents of Scott contrived to give him a good education. On arriving at manhood, he devoted himself to the medical profession. He entered the army as an assistant-surgeon in 1755, and was stationed with his regiment at Fort George, Fort William, and several other places. In 1762, the Spaniards and the French having sustained a number of severe reverses from the English, thought fit, as a means of retaliation, to invade Portugal, which then was under the special protection of England. A large body of troops was therefore despatched from this country to the aid of the Portuguese, and, among others, the regiment in which young Scott served. Little or no fighting took place, as peace was shortly afterwards proclaimed, and the British troops were ordered home. Scott wrote a poetical epistle regarding this war and the subsequent peace, in which he says,

'Grim war, amid his horrid train,
Now leaves the desolated plain;
And now, by George's high command,
Again we seek our native strand,
Where, as I can no longer serve,
I have his gracious leave to starve.'

In a note on the last of these couplets he says: 'This is almost literally the case. After seven years spent in his country's service in a useful station for which no provision is made, the author was carried ashore at Portsmouth with a fever upon him, neither quite dead nor alive, where he had the pleasure of lying several hours on the beach, till, with much difficulty, somebody was found that had humanity enough to give him a lodging for three or four times its worth.

There his pay was struck off, and he was left to the care of Providence, who reserved him for—God knows what.' It is understood that Mr Scott settled ultimately as a medical practitioner in a town in England, but found leisure to pay an occasional visit to his relatives and his old scenes at Biggar.

Mr Scott, from his early years, had been a writer of verses. His object, he says, was the amusement of an idle hour, the diversion of a friend, or the gratification of an original propensity. In 1765 a collected edition of his poems was published at London by G. Burnet, in the Strand.* In the preface he states that some of his poetical productions had been previously printed in periodical papers and miscellaneous collections, and that he had had the misfortune to be complimented by his country neighbours with the praise of genius. This, he considers, had made a very erroneous and injurious impression on his mind, for he says that 'since he had cultivated a more intimate acquaintance with the writings of the poets, he has a thousand times heartily wished the labours of his muse at the devil.' He declares that, were all his productions in his power, he would without reluctance commit them to the flames; but as this was beyond his reach, he hopes he has sent them forth in their collected form in a state more worthy the acceptance of the intelligent reader. With a true portion of Upper Ward independence, but with a roughness of language scarcely pardonable in a sentimental poet, he adds, 'If, by ill luck, a critical reader should lay his hands on them, and find his delicacy shocked in the perusal, he is very welcome to throw the book in the fire, and damn the author for a blockhead.'

The author, to judge from his poetical effusions, was certainly not entitled to be characterized as a blockhead. Throughout his whole book he manifests much refined and correct sentiment, a warm appreciation of rural scenery, a high admiration of beauty and virtue, a devoted attachment to friendship and love, and a lively interest in the welfare and freedom of his fellow-men. At the time he wrote, the cultivation of poetry had sunk to a low ebb. The poetic race had become infected with a strained and sickly sentimentalism. They had forsaken the paths of nature, and took delight in nothing but weaving a succession of tawdry garlands for the brows of some feigned goddess, under the name of Melinda, Narcissa, Delia, etc. Our author did not escape the mannerism and defects of his times; but he frequently rises above them, and sings with a true, if not a very exalted note. His descriptive powers were considerable. Take as a specimen an extract from a poem 'On Solitude,' written in a beautiful wild glen near Fort Augustus :—

> 'See, the river winds along
> The wild and tufted hills among;

---

* A copy was presented by the author to his nephew, Robert Scott, saddler, Biggar, and is still preserved by one of the members of Mr Scott's family

> Placid now it flows, and deep,
> Now it thunders down the steep;
> With violence dashed, it foams and roars,
> And falling, shakes the lofty shores;
> And rocks and billows rave around,
> And woods and hills repeat the sound.'

His appreciation of the varied aspects of the year is manifested in many of his productions. For instance, he thus refers to spring, and the feelings which it excites, in an Elegy to Narcissa :—

> ' In pride of youth exults the jovial year,
> Again the groves put on their robes of green,
> Again the pleasant woodland song we hear,
> And Nature in her fairest form is seen.
>
> ' Along the banks of the wild warbling stream,
> With many an herb adorned, and fragrant flower,
> Cheer'd by the setting sun's inspiring beam,
> Oft wandering, I enjoy the peaceful hour.
>
> ' The solemn scenes dispose the tranquil breast
> To serious musing, and to thought refined ;
> And contemplation comes, a heavenly guest,
> And pours out all her blessings on the mind.'

His patriotism and loyalty found vent in a noble ode to the King on his birthday, 1756. We give one or two stanzas :—

> ' Industrious Commerce swells her train
> With all the treasures which the main
>   And distant lands can boast;
> While glittering gems, and golden ore,
> The wealth of every foreign shore,
>   She pours on Albion's coast.
>
> ' Here gentle love, with roses crowned,
> And peace, with olive garlands bound,
>   Their mingling charms unite;
> While art and science, hand in hand,
> Conspire to bless the happy land
>   With honour and delight.
>
> ' Fair Liberty, high o'er the rest,
> Exalted dwells in every breast,
>   By Britons still adored ;
> For her the angry god of war,
> Impatient, mounts his iron car,
>   And waves his flaming sword.
>
> ' See there her potent navy ride,
> Exulting o'er the foaming tide,
>   The tyrant's constant dread.

Soon may her awful thunder roar
O'er faithless Gallia's hostile shore,
   Ruin and terror spread.

' Favoured of Heaven, assert the cause
Of Britain, liberty, and laws ;
   And when with glory crowned,
Bid the fell rage of battle cease,
And, with the bands of love and peace,
   Embrace the nations round.'

The Scottish language, his native vernacular, was then considered rude and vulgar. It had not yet been raised to classic dignity by the genius of Burns and Scott. Hence he sedulously avoids the use of it in any of his productions. Neither his admiration of Scottish damsels, his musings by the ruins of Scotland's ancient royal halls, his wanderings among the Highland hills, nor his minute disquisitions on the equipments of a Scottish tea-table, could extort from him a word to indicate that he had spent his boyish days amid the hills and plains of Biggar, or was familiar with the streams of the Clyde and Tweed. His book was designed for English readers; and he would, no doubt, consider that Scotch phraseology would be unintelligible, and allusions to the obscure localities of Biggar little attractive to the Southrons. But notwithstanding any little drawback of this kind, Scott is certainly one of Biggar's chief literary men.

The grounds in this neighbourhood go under the names of Guildie, the Colliehill, the Cuttings, the Scabbed Rigs, and the Borrow Muir. They belonged, and still nearly all belong, to the feuars of Biggar. They are of excellent quality, and produce fine crops of oats, barley, turnips, and potatoes. A little to the east of Loaningdale is Cambus Wallace, formerly Whinbush, the pleasant residence of John Paul, Esq. We have then, in succession, Wester Toftcombs, Mid Toftcombs, Easter Toftcombs, Wintermuir, and Candy or Edmonstone.

The estate of Edmonstone was possessed for upwards of four centuries by the Douglases, Earls of Morton and Lords of Dalkeith. The Flemings of Biggar, however, held the superiority of it during that period, which may be taken to indicate that they were the possessors of it prior to the existence of any record in which it is mentioned.

In 1322, William, son and heir of the deceased Haldwine of Edmonstone, resigned the whole lands of Edmonstone, with their pertinents, in the barony of Biggar, to his superior, Gilbert Fleming of Biggar, in order that William, the son and heir of the deceased Sir James Douglas of Laudonia, might be infeft in the same. In 1382, Robert II. granted and confirmed to James Douglas, Lord of Dalkeith, and James, his son, the lands of Edmonstone in the barony of Biggar. On the 15th of July 1476, James Earl of Morton re-

G

signed the lands of Edmonstone and Wintermuir into the hands of
Robert Lord Fleming, the superior of these lands; and on the 18th of
the same month received a new charter of them from Lord Fleming,
to be holden for the service of ward and relief, and one suit in the
head court at Biggar.   A precept of Sasine of these lands was granted,
on the 4th of January 1496, by John Lord Fleming to James Douglas, son and apparent heir of John Earl of Morton.   In 1543, James
Earl of Morton and Lord of Dalkeith granted them to his daughter
Elizabeth, and to her husband, James Douglas, nephew of the Earl of
Angus.   The Earl of Morton dying without male issue, James Douglas, just mentioned, succeeded to his titles and estates.   He received
a new charter of these estates, and, of course, of 'the lands and barony
of Edmeston, with the maner, fortilace, mills, fishings, and orchards,
parts, pendicles, advowson and endowment of churches and chapels
and their pertinents lying within the barony of Biggar and sheriff-
dom of Lanark.'   This nobleman for some years played a very distinguished part in the public transactions of Scotland.   Being bold,
crafty, and avaricious, he attached himself to the side of the Reformers, and took part with the Earl of Murray in his opposition to
Queen Mary.   Attaining at length to be Regent of the Kingdom, with
a portion of the wealth which he then acquired, he commenced to
build the stately castle of Drochil on the Lyne, but did not live to
see it completed.   He was beheaded at the Cross of Edinburgh, on
the 2d of June 1581, for alleged complicity in the murder of Darnley,
by an instrument called 'The Maiden,' which he himself had been the
means of introducing into Scotland.   The estate of Edmonstone continued in the same family to the middle of the seventeenth century,
when it and the farm of Wintermuir were purchased by Christopher
Baillie of Walston.   These possessions then fell into the hands of a
family of the name of Brown, about the beginning of last century; and
in the hands of this family they still remain, the present proprietor
being Laurence Brown, Esq.   Some years ago, a very elegant mansion-house, in a castellated form of architecture, after a design by
James Gillespie Graham, was erected in a secluded valley on this
property.   It contained, and perhaps still contains, a collection of the
antiquities of the district; but no account of them, so far as we know,
has hitherto been published.

   On the estate of Edmonstone there was at one time evidently a
considerable village, which was generally called Candy.   It had its
own school, its own mill, its own alehouse, its own tailors, shoemakers, smiths, agricultural labourers, etc.   One of its inhabitants,
during last century, was Mr John Rob, tailor.   He was a good
specimen of the shrewd, intelligent, and pious men, who have long
abounded in this district.   He was a member of Mr Mair's congregation at Linton, and, afterwards, of Mr Low's at Biggar.   When the
controversy regarding the Burgess oath, which split the Seceders into

two separate divisions, was still raging, he entered the lists against the famous Antiburgher leader, the Rev. Adam Gib of Edinburgh; and, in 1755, published a pamphlet, in which, in the opinion of some judges, he completely demolished the positions of his doughty and energetic opponent. It was entitled, 'The Rod Retorted, or the Corrector Corrected; containing some remarks upon a pamphlet entitled, "A Rod of Correction, etc., by Mr Adam Gib." By John Rob, Tailor, Candy.' Copies of this brochure are now extremely rare. The only one that we have seen is in the library of Adam Sim, Esq., at Coultermains. We cannot forbear quoting one of the first paragraphs of this work, as a specimen of Mr Rob's style, and the manner in which the controversy was conducted. 'The first thing that I shall take notice of,' says Mr Rob, 'is, that he (Adam Gib) charges me with impertinence and unbecoming behaviour, like an *enraged kailwife*, as he calls it. I know that my speech is for ordinary high, but I challenge him, or any of the company, to condescend upon any one expression uttered by me unbecoming his character, although even from himself there was not wanting provocation; for I remember, when I met him at Biggar, how he prefaced his discourse. When the man told him I was coming for light in the present case, he proudly answered, "I have no manner of concern with such; let them take the length of the halter; perhaps they may worry in the band." Now, let any impartial reader judge how cross this spirit is to the very letter of the law, Exodus xxiii. 4, 5.'

John Rob had a son named Richard, who was a person of some humour, and a member of the same church. Being of a social turn of mind, he sometimes rather exceeded in his potations at fairs and on market days, and thus subjected himself to the animadversions of the 'unco guid.' The members of the Burgher session, who were very circumspect in regard to religious opinions, and sharp in their practice, summoned him before them to answer for his irregularities. When Richard appeared, he owned his fault; but he entreated his reverend judges, before pronouncing sentence, to answer the question, 'Is gluttony a sin?' This was at once admitted. 'Then,' said Richard, 'whan I was at the Little Wall the ither day, I saw John Young, a member of the session noo present, supping kail oot o' a calf's luggy. It was evident that on that occasion he was guilty of an act of gluttony; sae, if ye rebuke me, ye ought to rebuke him also.' The session were scarcely disposed to acquiesce in Mr Rob's analogy, or to comply with his demand; so they considered that it would be the best policy to dismiss him at that time with an admonition.

Mr Rob, on one occasion, accompanied Mr Low in his round of visitations to the houses of the members of his congregation in the neighbourhood of Candy. They entered thirteen different dwellings, and in each of them they were presented with spirituous liquors, of which the minister always partook. On parting in the evening, Mr

Rob very gravely accosted Mr Low, and said, 'I noo see wherein the sin o' drinking consists.' 'What is that, Richard?' said Mr Low. 'It maun consist, I think, in the paying,' replied Mr Rob; 'for I hae seen ye to-day tak a pairt o' thirteen drams, and a single word o' reproof or objection hasna faun frae your lips.'

Mr Rob one day played a sad trick on old Robert Forsyth, the bellman and grave-digger of Biggar. It has ever since been a standing story in the district, and used to be related with admirable drollery by the late James Sinclair, painter, Biggar. The minister of Biggar happening to have some very fine pigs, he promised to make a present of one to his friend the minister of Dolphinton. He therefore ordered Robert Forsyth to put one of them into a pock, and proceed with it to Dolphinton Manse. The obedient sexton did as he was ordered. While trudging on his way, and just as he approached Candy, where at that time a dram was sold, he met Mr Rob. 'Weel, Robert,' says the farmer, 'as the day is warm, and as you are doubtless fatigued wi' your load, ye had better step into Jenny's and I'll gie ye a dram.' To this proposal he readily assented. So the pock was thrown down by the side of the door, and in he went to quench his thirst and rest his limbs. While he was thus refreshing himself, the farmer went to the door, and succeeded, without being noticed, in making a young whelp occupy the place of the pig. At length our worthy resumed his journey to Dolphinton, and, on his arrival at the manse, announced his business with characteristic pomposity and importance. The minister and his domestics came out to view and examine the animal which had been so kindly sent by the reverend incumbent of Biggar; when, on being turned out of the sack, to the utter astonishment of all, it was not a sow, but a young dog. Old Robert 'declared, whatever it might be noo, he was sure it was a pig whan he pat it into the pock.' There was no help for it, but that the unfortunate sexton should again shoulder his load, and, much mortified and vexed, return as heavy as he went. Mr R., who was still purposely loitering about Candy, at length espied Robert coming down the brae very gloomy and disconsolate. What's the matter wi' ye noo?' said Mr R. 'Will the minister no tak the soo, that ye're trudging hame wi't on yer back, as melancholy like as ye had seen the deil?' 'Lord sauf us,' quoth Robert, 'it's nae langer a soo, it has turned into a doug; and as I'm a leeving man, I declare, whan I shook it out o' the pock afore the manse, my very heart played dunt, and I really thought that the deil had entered intill't as he ance did into the herd o' swine.' 'But Robie, my man,' said Mr R., 'this is a subject too kittle to be expounded here; we maun gae in again to Jenny's and hae anither gill.' While they were in the inn, the pig and the whelp, unknown to the unsuspicious sexton, again exchanged places. Having had a lengthened crack and a taste of the barley bree, they parted, and the sexton with his load made the best of his way to Biggar. He repaired at once to the manse, and told his reverence that by witchcraft or other diabolical means the sow had, during his journey to Dolphinton, become a whelp. 'A whelp!' exclaimed the minister, 'impossible; but let us see—turn him out;' and there now appeared before the dumfoundered beadle the veritable animal, in shape, size, and kind, which had been entrusted to his care when he started from Biggar. 'Why, Robert,' said the minister, 'that is surely the very animal which you put into your bag this morning.' 'Od,' says Robert, 'it may be ony thing it likes noo, but I'll minteen it was a whelp at Dolphinton.' 'Did you meet with anybody by the way?' inquired the minister, 'or were ye in any house?' 'To tell the truth,' said Robert, 'I gaed in a few minutes at Candyburn to hae a refreshment wi' Ritchie Rob.' 'Ah, Robert, Robert,' said the minister, 'I see through the whole affair; you have allowed that witty gentleman to play a sad trick upon you, as well as to offer an affront to me. You must never, when employed on important business, be allured into an alehouse again, lest a worse mischief befall you.'

A similar trick is ascribed, in the 'Laird of Logan,' to Laird Robertson of Earnock; but persons intimately acquainted with the Biggar worthies to whom I have referred, were in the habit of telling the story in a similar manner thirty or forty years previous to the appearance of that publication.

On the top of the hill above Candybank is a circular entrenchment, generally called a camp. No information regarding it exists, and the probability is, that it was constructed for the purpose of preserving the cattle and sheep during the times of invasion. It was in the course of removing a cairn of stones in this earthen work that the bronze implement, Fig. 3, page 7, was discovered.

CHAPTER VI.

The Castle of Boghall.

HE House or Castle of Boghall was one of the largest and most imposing edifices in the south of Scotland. It stood, as its name imports, in the midst of a bog, which in former times was impassable, even on foot, and which contributed greatly to its security. The habitable part of it was on the south; and, as the bog stretched behind it for several hundred yards, it had been deemed unnecessary to surround the back of it with a separate wall for the purposes of defence. An area in front, extending about two hundred yards both in length and breadth, and capable of holding all the grain and cattle in the barony, was enclosed by a square wall, three feet thick and thirty feet high, on the top of which ran a bartizan, and at each corner was flanked by a circular tower, with embrasures and loop-holes for small arms and cannon. The court was entered on the north by a spacious gateway, with two posterns, and above the gateway was a tower for the warder. The whole was surrounded by a broad and deep fosse filled with water, and spanned by a stone bridge opposite the gate. The ground, between the walls and the fosse, was planted with trees, and some very aged ones were standing within the last forty years.

The front of the habitable part of the Castle was two storeys in height, with attics, and presented a considerable degree of elegance, the lintels of the doors and the rybots of the windows being formed of carved freestone. In the centre of the staircase, which projected a little from the line of the building, the arms of the Flemings were carved in relief on a large square stone; and at the top of the wall was another stone, with the date 1670, which must have been placed there at the time some repairs were made on the Castle, during the time it was occupied as a residence by Anna Dowager Countess of Wigton. The lower part of the flanking tower on the south-east was used as a dungeon for the confinement of prisoners, and the upper part, it is understood, served the purposes of a girnel, in which the mails and duties of the vassals and tenants, payable in grain, malt, and me were stored. This building will be observed in the engraving to be a little detached from the habitable part of the Castle on the east side, or the left, facing the spectator. The girnel was

From an etching by John Clerk Esqr of Eldin

W & A K Johnston Lithog Edin

under the charge of a keeper, whose duty it was to receive the victual, to distribute it among the baron's retainers, and to sell or barter such portions of it as were required by the cottars and crafts-men located in the barony. References are often made to the 'gar-nar,' or 'girnel,' in the family documents and the Records of the Baron Bailie's Court. For instance, in the transactions of Anthony Murray, factor to John, Earl of Wigton, for the half year ending Martinmas 1667, we notice that he paid six bolls and three firlots of meal to William Thripland, my lord's 'garnar man' in Biggar, being half a boll for every chalder of thirteen chalders and nine bolls, which he did measure into the garnar, and measure out the same again, and did uphold the measure. James Carmichael, who was factor to William, Earl of Wigton, paid to the same William Thrip-land 'ye soume of twentie pund Scots for his service in his Lordship's girnal, fra Martinmas 1675 to Martinmas 1676.' The girnel at Bog-hall seems at that time to have undergone a repair, as there is an entry in the factor's books of L.51, 8s. 8d., paid 'for wrught work and seives to the girnall, and lyme to the house of Boghall, and leid to dress the windows.'

In the Records of the Baron's Court, we find that Bailie Alexander Wardlaw, on the 29th of July 1720, 'decerns the haill tennents, feu-ars, and others, lyable to the Earl of Wigtoun, to pay moulter and teind meall into the girnall, and any that hes gotten out meall upon trust, to pay to John Gledstanes, girnall man, one pund and fyve shillings Scots, for each boll, betwixt and teusday nixt, under the pain of poynding.' On the 28th of March 1747, Thomas Carmichael, keeper of the girnel of Biggar, made complaint before Bailie Robert Leckie, 'That sundrie of the Tennants, after grinding of their farm meall, doe allow the same to ly in ye miln, or in their own houses, a considerable time, without delivering the same into the garnell, by which means the meill is lyable of being spoiled and damnified. Therefore, the Bailliff enacts and ordains, that, for the future, the haill fewars and tennants of the barroneys of Boaghall and Biggar shall, immediately after their meall is grund att the miln, at least, within fourty-eight hours thereafter, deliver their farms into the gar-nell, and that under the penaltie of ten shillings Scots for each unde-livered boll, to be payed by the failziers to the said Thomas Carmi-chael, as garnell keeper, and his successors in office.'

An opinion has long prevailed at Biggar, and is referred to by Forsyth in his 'Beauties of Scotland,' that the habitable part of the Castle was originally of greater extent than it was in later times, and that it stood in the centre of the enclosed area. In trenching the ground, to a considerable depth, some years ago, no distinct trace of former buildings was, however, discovered; but this is certainly not decisive evidence on the point, as the buildings may have all been thoroughly removed. The deep morass on the south serving as a sufficient defence, was evidently the cause why the mansion-house, at least in the end, came to be placed in that quarter, and left unprotected.

The Castle of Boghall was, no doubt, built at a remote period. The exact time, however, cannot now be ascertained. David Fleming, second son of Sir David Fleming of Biggar, who was killed at Longhermonston in the spring of 1405, settled on some lands in Renfrewshire, which he called Boghall, a name which he most likely assumed out of respect to his paternal habitation. In an old book in the possession of Mr James Watt, Biggar, there is the following entry:—
'Note.—The Boghall Castle was built in the year of Christ 1492, by Malcolm Fleming of Cumbernauld.' Little dependence can be placed on this assertion, as it is unknown who made it, and is unsupported by any collateral evidence. It is very far from unlikely, however, that it was rebuilt at that period. It had certainly very much the appearance of having been built about the time of James IV. or James V. It had a degree of spaciousness and elegance that removed it considerably from the style of strongholds usually occupied by the Scottish barons, and led to the opinion that it had been constructed after the fashion of some of the large chateaux in France. Although not of extraordinary strength, it seemed able, if properly garrisoned, to withstand any attack, provided it was not made with heavy artillery. It must, for a long period, have been a principal residence of the Fleming family; but in the latter part of their history they seem to have given a preference to the House of Cumbernauld, which, at one time, was also a fortified stronghold.

After the death of the last Earl of Wigton, and the transference of the Biggar estates to the Elphinstone family, in 1747, the Castle of Boghall was more and more deserted. No repair was made on the buildings, and the consequence of course was, that they began gradually to fall into ruin. Between 1773 and 1779, when the sketch of the castle was taken, by John Clerk of Eldin, from which the accompanying view of it has been engraved, it was then almost entire. Captain Grose, whose name has been immortalized by Burns, visited Biggar in 1789, and also took a sketch of the Castle, which he afterwards published in his work on the 'Antiquities of Scotland.' By that time it had evidently undergone considerable dilapidation. The tower above the gateway had been partially demolished, and some of the stones had been removed from the top of the outer wall. In a view of it given in the 'Scots Magazine' for October 1815, it appears by that time to have been entirely dismantled, and many parts of the walls laid in ruins. The writer of a letterpress description of the town of Biggar and its neighbourhood, in the same number of the Magazine, says, in reference to the Castle, 'It is in a state of rapid decay, which, we are ashamed to understand, was accelerated some years ago by the appropriation of a part of its materials to the erec-

tion of a dog-kennel. It is still a ruin of considerable interest, and
we would entreat the proprietor to save it, and adorn the spot by surrounding it with planting.' No attention was paid to this remon-
strance; but, in 1821, Admiral Charles Elphinston Fleming, the proprietor, on some account or other, caused workmen to repair the walls
of the projecting staircase, in the centre of the habitable part of the
Castle, and to cover it with a roof of slate.

When the entail of the Biggar estate was broken in 1830, the farm
of Boghall Mains, and the other lands still belonging to the heir of
the Fleming family in the parish, were brought to the hammer. By
some misunderstanding or mismanagement, the remains of the Castle,
a short time afterwards, were nearly all carried away to fill drains and
build dykes. The only parts left were the recently repaired staircase,
and a portion of two of the flanking towers. These fragments, with
a few trees, now stand—sad relics of a glory that has passed for ever
away. How desolate and solitary is the scene around; how different
from the days of feudal splendour! Now the ample court, the fosse,
and the very site of the buildings, have been torn up by the plough,
and are covered with the successive crops of the husbandman.
Happily in our day a feeling of veneration for our ancient buildings
has sprung up; the writings of Sir Walter Scott, and others, and
the increased attention which has been paid to archæological studies,
have deepened and extended this feeling, and caused it to find practical manifestation in preserving our ancient and dilapidated castles,
abbeys, and cathedrals from further demolition, and sending thousands
and tens of thousands from all quarters to gaze on their time-worn
remains. The person who presumes to lay a violent hand upon them
is liable to receive very severe censure. We therefore cordially concur in the following remarks, in a recent address on Archæology, by
Professor Simpson of Edinburgh. 'I solemnly protest,' says he,
'against the needless destruction and removal of our Scotch antiquarian remains. The hearts of all leal Scotsmen, overflowing as
they do with a love of their native land, must ever deplore the unnecessary demolition of all such early relics and monuments, as can
in any degree contribute to the recovery and restoration of the past
history of our country and of our ancestors. These ancient relics and
monuments are truly, in one strong sense, national property; for
historically they belong to Scotland, and to Scotsmen in-general, more
than they belong to the individual proprietors upon whose ground
they accidentally happen to be placed.' 'Let us fondly hope and
trust,' he further adds, 'that a proper spirit of patriotism, that every
feeling of good, generous, and gentlemanly taste, will ensure and
hallow the future consecration of all such Scottish antiquities as still
remain—small fragments only though they be of the antiquarian
treasures that once existed in the land.' Many local poets have sung
in doleful strains the demolition of Boghall Castle. We have a

H

number of their productions lying beside us, and would gladly give
some of them a place, did our limited space permit. The engraved
view of it which we have been enabled to give, will, no doubt, make
many other persons than poets deplore that it has been so thoroughly
swept away.

The blame of the destruction of the Castle of Boghall is mainly to
be attributed to the Elphinstone family. It was they who left it to
entire neglect, who failed to expend a few pounds to
keep it in a state of repair, who carried off a portion
of its materials to build a dog-kennel, and who sold it,
without making the least reserve as to its preservation.
When these men, whose forefathers had built it, had
lived within its walls, and made it memorable by their
presence and transactions, not only felt no veneration
for it, but actually hastened its destruction, we could
scarcely expect that other parties, into whose hands it
might fall, would view it with feelings of warmer attachment, or would expend their efforts and their means to
preserve it from further demolition. Its removal, however, is to be regretted, as it was a noble feature in
the landscape, and as the district has little to show in
the shape of antiquities, and little to invest it with interest and attraction to strangers. We can only now
indulge the hope, that efforts will be made to preserve
such fragments of it as still remain.

A few relics of the Castle have been preserved. The
girnel-door is in the possession of Mr Allan Whitfield,
agent, Biggar. An antique clock, which formed part
of the furniture of the Castle, and which was presented by a member of the Boghall family, most likely
by Lady Clementina Fleming herself, to Dr Baillie,
who flourished as a physician in Biggar about the
middle of last century, is now in the museum of Mr
Sim at Coultermains. A huge key, which was found
near the ruins, and which is supposed to be the key of
the great outer gate, was, and perhaps still is, in the
possession of Laurence Brown, Esq. of Edmonstone.
Several cannon bullets, which appear to have been at
one time part of the munitions of the Castle, or to have
been shot against it during some of the assaults which
it sustained, are in Mr Sim's museum. A curious
sword-blade, with a waved edged, is shown in the
Museum of the Society of Scottish Antiquaries, as
having been found at the Castle of Boghall. It was
presented to the Society, by John Loch, Esq. of Rachan,
in 1829. In the letter which accompanied it, Mr Loch says that the

sword was presented to him by an old man, who assured him that it was found in the ruins of Boghall. How far this man's testimony may be relied on, it is impossible now to say; but it seems to have been credited by Mr Loch. Swords with waved edges were used in mediæval times for the purpose of making a greater impression on defensive armour than could be done by those which had their edges straight. They acted, in fact, as a kind of saw, being drawn with great force across a helmet or a coat of mail. The Boghall sword, a cut of which is here given, is 32¼ inches long, and has engraved on it the word Mini, repeated four times on each side of the blade, and some slight ornaments which very likely were trade marks.

Boghall Castle, in a historical point of view, is not so remarkable as some other strongholds that could be named. We really know nothing of its early history. We cannot say what scenes of joy and sorrow, of peaceful entertainment or tumultuous outrage, it may have witnessed in remote times. We only begin to get some notices of it after it had been comparatively deserted by the Fleming family for Cumbernauld House. Still it is not altogether destitute of interest. We have good reason for believing that it was often tenanted by the Scottish kings, in their frequent progresses through this part of the kingdom. It was, along with the town and burgh of Biggar, and the acres lying thereabout, erected into a barony, called the Barony of Boghall, by a charter from James V. in 1538. Malcolm Lord Fleming, in his testament executed in 1547, assigned it as the jointure house of his wife, Joan Stewart, in case of her surviving him; and she was to receive the whole 'insight,' or furniture, except the artillery, which was to be the property of his son and heir. It was besieged and taken by the Regent Murray, and many years afterwards by Oliver Cromwell. It was, during the persecuting times, the jointure house of Anna Ker, Countess of Wigton, and was made memorable by the conventicles held, under her auspices, within its walls. The last garrison that it ever contained was placed in it by the Government, to overawe the adherents of the Covenant in Tweeddale and the Upper Ward.

A large number of documents in the charter chest of the Wigton family refer to Boghall. We select one or two specimens of the accounts of the domestic expenses of William, Earl of Wigton, during his residence at the Castle, from a large mass of papers of a similar kind. The first is a statement entitled—

'Ane Accompt furnished to the hous of Boghall for his Lop's use, beginning the 15th March 1675, to the 23d thereof.

Imprimis, Six pound and a half of butter at 5/ the lb.			.	01	12	06
It.	Ane hundron veil	.	.	04	00	00
	Carry forward,	.	.	£05	12	06

	Brought forward, . . .	£05 12 06
It.	Ane sheep	06 14 00
It.	Six peices of salt beif & muttone . . .	01 10 00
It.	for eells	00 06 00
It.	for trouts	00 06 08
It.	for candle 3 pound	00 15 00
It.	ten dosen and a half of eegs at 1/8 the dozen .	00 14 02
It.	for seven loads of coalls	03 13 06
It.	for girding his Loᴿ's brewing loomes .	00 08 00
It.	for a choppine of brandie . . .	01 00 00
It.	for clowes measst & peper . . .	00 04 00
It.	for wild foulis	01 18 08
It.	for salt	00 01 04
It.	Given to my lord to give to the poor . .	00 06 00
It.	for a dosen of pypes . . .	00 02 00
It.	for corks peals & barme	00 06 06
It.	for two capounes	00 18 00
It.	for ane oyr chopen of brandie . . .	01 00 00
It.	mor fyve pynts of wyn out of Bigar . .	03 12 00
It.	mor ye 22ᵈ of March 1675 tuo pieces of salt mutton and half a pund of buter . . .	00 12 6
It.	mor tuo piece of muton to yr Lordship's super and tuo dosen of eges to yr brakfast . .	00 13 04
		£30 14 2'

From other documents we observe that, during the same brief period, two pecks and two forpits of bear, at the cost of 2s. 2d., were consumed at Boghall; and that two bolls of malt, which cost L.2 Scots, were 'browen' in the same place.

'Acompt of my Lord's expences at Bigair fra 8ᵗʰ of Octʳ to 12ᵗʰ yr of 1675.

Item givein to my Lord of Small mony ye 9ᵗʰ Octʳ .	00 06 00
Item payed at James Carmichell's on Saterday at night for four pynts of aill and 5 muchkines of seck . .	03 02 00
Item mor for 3 pynts of ail to ye servants . . .	00 09 00
Item for ane chopin of seck and a duble gill, and a pynt of aill in ye morning	01 08 00
Item half a dosen of pypes	00 01 00
Item mor at yr Lo's coming fra James Carmichell on Saterday at night ane duble gill . . .	00 05 00
Item your Lo lost or payed on Sunday a duble gill . .	00 05 00
Item for yr Loᴿ's footman qn you cam on Saterday morning at Js. Carmichell	00 05 00
Item On Monday morning yr wes a pynt of Seck, when yr Lo was wᵗ my lord Carmichell and ye rest of ye gentillmen, and two duble gills and 3 pynts of aill—Inde .	02 19 00
Carry forward, . . .	£09 00 00

Brought forward, . . .	£09	00	00
Item given to ye bellman at yr Lo's derection . .	00	12	00
Item to ye man yt went to Sunderland hall . . .	01	04	00
Item to ye man yt went for Whetsled and Glenkerk .	00	04	00
Item to ye woman yt brought ye gerse fra broughton .	01	04	00
Item to ye lase ye maid ye beds, and swyped ye house .	00	18	00
Item gven to Jon Chrictoune first 3 dolores qⁿ yr Loᴾ went to broughton and when yr Loᴾ came away thertie pund and to yr Loᴾ's self in small money fyve pund .	41	14	00

Acompt of qt cam to ye hous of boghall ye said tym.

Impʳ for tuo pund of salt buter and tuo pund of fresh buter	01	00	00
Item for ane sixpeny loaf and 5 small bread .	00	11	00
Item tuo dosen and a half of eges and a pynt of milk .	00	06	02
Item for a quarter of pund of raisines and a quarter of pund of plomdaimes	00	03	00
Item for half peck of ber and a for pairt of salt . .	00	07	04
Item for ane shep and a syd of mutton . . .	03	13	04
Item for tuo pynts of Seck and a pynt of Brandy . .	06	00	00
Item for six galants and a half of aill . . .	05	04	00
Item for a dosen of tubaco pypes . . .	00	02	00
Item for tuo pund of candell	00	10	00
Item Given to Hew Anderson for making ready my Lord's met	01	00	00
Suma totalis	£73	12	10'

A number of tacks, agreements, and deeds, still preserved, are dated 'att Boghall.' The following letter, preserved in the archives of the family, although containing no statement of any importance, may be interesting to some inhabitants of the Biggar district, from having been written by William Earl of Wigton within the walls of the Castle. It is addressed—'ffor Harie Drumond, Clarke to the Garisone off Dumbritoune Castell,'—his lordship being governor of that fortress, and head sheriff of Dumbartonshire:—

'BOGHALL, Sept. 20th, 1680.
' HARIE

I received yours with the Money, and the Counsell's Letter and proclamatione, I am not fully resolved as yett whither I keep the Meitting of the Shyre at Dumbartone, or the Counsell, they being both to hold, one the first twesday of October; but if I come not, I shall send tymous advertisment to the Shirff deput. Any letters you have to send to me from Dumbartone, send them with a sojer to John Carmichall, and he will send them to me. And send me a trwe account how the Major is. So this being all at present from

your assurred freind,
WIGTOUNE.

' Remember me to yr. wyfe. Be mindfull in getting my tarriers from M'farland. Remember me to Catiweillie and all aqwantances.'

On the death of William Earl of Wigton in 1681, the greater part of the old furniture of Boghall Castle was sold. An inventory of the sale has been preserved in the charter chest of the family; and as every scrap of information regarding this old fortress is interesting, we give a copy of this document. It is entitled an 'Acompt of the plenishing of the house of Boghall sold Julii 13, 1681.'

' Impri*. the mustfatt and yuilie fatt sold to the Lady of Cloburne	10	00	0
Item more to hir ane stand, ane say, ane kerne, and two four gallon trees	03	04	0
Item more to hir ane stooll and ane chamber pot . .	02	10	0
Item to John Carmichaell, in Carmichaell Myln, two stands, two punsiones, and two four gallon trees, and a washing tub	04	04	0
Item to Andrew Telfer two stands, three four gallon trees, two tubes	03	10	0
Item to him two old coverings	03	06	8
Item to Mr Anthony Murray, ane say, a handy, and a seck ruidle	00	18	0
Item to Mr Robert Scot ane fether bed, and three buffet stolles, and two barrelles	12	06	0
Item, ane fether bed and bolster, and two coads to the Ladie Cloburne	20	00	0
Item, two kapes to my lord Carmichael . . .	04	12	0
Item, for a wheel to Mr Anthonie Murray . . .	01	00	0
Item to him ane barrell	00	08	0
Item to William Tait two very old coverings .	01	10	0
Item to Mr Richard Broune ane fether bed and bolster £12 and ane suit of old strip hangings, £12, inde .	24	00	0
Item to bailzie Vallence for two suit of old reed Courtaings	08	00	0
Item to bailzie Kello ane fedder bed . . .	09	00	0
Item to the forsd John Carmichaell two calfe bolsters .	01	00	0
Item Jenet Threipland in the Mylne, ane old grein table cloath	00	14	0
Item to the Ladie Westshiell ane fether bed, ane bolster, and two coads	20	00	0
Cheiris resting that John Carmichaell is to Compt for with my ladie	100	17	4
Item two milk bowes to the Lady Cultermaines . .	00	13	0
Item to Hardingtoune's Woman halfe ane dozen of chaires, at 2/ sterling, the peice, two candlestikes, six shillings sterling, ane bolster and two coads £4. 6. 8 inde .	15	02	8
Item to hir ane chamber stooll and a chamber pot . .	02	15	0
Item to hir ane chimney	01	07	6
Item to bailzie Carmichaell's wife three pair of tonges, a pair-			
Carry forward, . . . £250	18	2	

Brought forward, . . .	£250	18	2
ing iron, ane pair of clipes 20/ ane cheese fork and a chamber pot £1 14/ ane calfe bed £1 16/ ane milk tub 14/. inde	03	14	0
Item for ane large fedder bed and bolster to the ladie hardingtoune	20	00	0
Item to Alexr. Bailzie, bailzie of Lammingtoune, ane fedder bed and bolster	16	00	0
Item halfe ane dozen of bassons to hir . . .	05	00	0
Item to bailzie Vallance halfe ane dozen of old reed chaires .	03	06	0
Item to bailzie Broune fyve chaires	06	00	0
Item to bailzie Kello ane pot	04	13	4
Item ane wheel to him	01	00	0
Item to the ladie Lamingtoune two chamber stoles .	02	00	0
Item to the ladie Cloburne ane stoll . . .	01	00	0
Item to Richard Broune 3 chaires	03	02	2
Item to the ladie Lamingtoune the chimney, in the drawing rowme	12	10	0
Item to Mr Richard Broune for a chimney . . .	01	07	6
Item to bailzie Vallence two beds	20	10	0
Item to James Aikman ane reed bed and a fether bed .	24	00	0
Item to Robert Fforsyth ane chair	01	04	0
Item to Culterallers ane Caldrone	66	13	4
The soume of the wholl charge is	£442	18	6'

CHAPTER VII.

Biggar Churchyard.

THE Churchyard of Biggar is of small extent. It is by no means in keeping with the populousness of the parish, and the spaciousness of the church erected in its centre. An addition was made to it, some years ago, by taking in a part of the glebe connected with the Established Church; but it is still narrow and confined, and affords no space for the walks, shrubs, and flowers with which the tombs, in more modern cemeteries, are now generally adorned. The graves are too much crowded, and the tomb-stones, especially on the south, stand too closely together. None of the tomb-stones are remarkable for their design, ornamentation, or antiquity. They almost entirely consist of the plain upright head-stone, or the horizontal slab, generally called a 'throughstane.' The oldest stones, so far as the inscriptions on them can be deciphered, do not go further back than the seventeenth century. The greater portion of them have been erected during the last fifty years, and few of them are without some lettering executed by the late James Watson, mason, Westraw, who might justly have been styled the 'Old Mortality' of the district, as he was often to be seen plying his mallet and chisel, not only in this churchyard, but in those of the country round.

Near the gateway is an obelisk, erected by the Lodge of Biggar Free Operatives, to the memory of Gavin Nicol, mason, an exceedingly bright and active member of the masonic fraternity, who died in 1819. Many persons yet alive will recollect the consequential strut and air which he assumed when taking part in the public masonic displays on St John's Day. In his latter years he was chiefly employed in conveying the mail-bags to and from Mountbog, mounted on an ass. During the Peninsular War, Gavin heralded to the inhabitants of Biggar the intelligence of all the famous victories achieved by the British arms. On these occasions his pocket-handkerchief was placed on the end of his staff in form of a flag, and his progress through the town was quite an ovation. No sooner did he appear at the town-head with his ass and his flag, and proclaim that some great battle had been fought and won, such as Salamanca, Vittoria, the Pyrenees, Waterloo, etc., than he was surrounded by an excited crowd; and the shop of Eben Young, tinsmith, was besieged, and his whole stock of tin-horns carried off. Then, amid the routing of horns and the cheering of the people, he was conducted to the dwelling of the postmaster, Mr Alexander Multrie, where the bag was opened, and the details of the battle were read to the crowd amid loud huzzas.

At no great distance from this monument is the burying-place of the Gladstones family. This family, it is understood, have had a long connection with Biggar. We know that in the early part of last century three of the chief men of the town bore that name, and had all families. These were William, a merchant, whose spouse was Janet How; James, who was by profession a maltman, and whose wife was Jean Telfer; and John, who was also a maltman, a burgess of the town, and proprietor of Mid Toftcombs. John was born in 1694, and took in marriage Janet Aitken, by whom he had a large family. His eldest son, Thomas, left his native place, and settled as a victual-dealer in the Coal Hill, Leith, where he prosecuted his business with success, and realized a considerable fortune. He married Helen, a daughter of Walter Neilson of Springfield, by whom he had a son, John, who commenced business in Leith; but being unsuccessful, he proceeded to Liverpool, where he embarked in the West India trade, and acquired so great wealth that he was able to purchase the estate of Fasque, and to give each of his sons, during his lifetime, L.100,000. He was created a baronet on the 27th of June 1846. By his second wife, Ann, daughter of Andrew Robertson, Provost of Dingwall, he had four sons—Thomas, Robertson, John Neilson, and William Ewart. The last named is well known as an eminent scholar, orator, and statesman. He is the author of various works, and at present, 1862, holds the high and very important offices of Chancellor of the Exchequer, and Rector of the University of Edinburgh.

Here we note the resting-place of the Kelloes, a very old Biggar family. In a list of the parishioners of Biggar, in 1640, in the archives of the Wigton family, John Kello is given as one of them. About the same period, George Kello and his son received a disposition of two oxengates of land in Biggar, and, in 1681, John Kello was one of the bailies of Biggar. On the family tomb-stone we notice the name of Agnes Kello, a lady who acquired some celebrity in her time, and therefore deserves to be specially mentioned. She was the daughter of Andrew Kello, tenant in Skirling Mill, and portioner in Biggar, who died in 1763, when she was a child. Her mother, whose name was Janet Watson, outlived her husband fifty-three years, and died in 1816, in the eighty-fifth year of her age.

Miss Kello was a lady of considerable personal attractions, great amiability of disposition, and of fortune somewhat beyond persons in her station of life. The charms of her person were set off to advantage by the neatness and elegance of her dress, particularly on Sundays, when she attended divine service in the Burgher meeting-house at Biggar. No young woman entered the old town on whom all per-

I

sons smiled so complacently, and none enjoyed a larger share of admiration and respect.   It is a proof of the impression which she made,
and the estimation in which she was held, that, though it is upwards
of sixty years since she was laid in her grave, her name is a household
word in Biggar to this day.

As might be expected, Miss Kello had many suitors for her hand.
They were, in fact, as numerous as those who came to woo 'Tibbie
Fowler of the Glen.'   Farmers, lairds, students, and tradesmen were
all ambitious to secure her favourable regard.   One of her most per-
severing suitors was William Sim, then schoolmaster at Quothquan, a
rare compound of bitter envy, spiritual pride, lofty aspirations, and
learned pretensions.   There is no proof that he ever received from her
the smallest encouragement; and so, wearied with sending her letters,
he took leave of her in an indignant epistle, which he addressed to her
on the 2d of June 1789, and a copy of which he has preserved in one
of the volumes of his manuscript memoirs.   A suitor of a far higher
stamp made advances to her at one time, and was accepted.   This
was the famed Professor Lawson of Selkirk.   The day for the nuptials
was fixed, and the intended bride and her relatives had made all the
necessary arrangements.   The Professor had a most extraordinary
memory for all kinds of sacred and human learning, but it appears
that he had a most unaccountable obliviousness regarding some of
the most important concerns of this world.   At all events, he forgot
the time that he had stipulated for the marriage.   The banns were
unproclaimed, and the lovely and amiable maid of Skirling Mill was
left to neglect.   She was, however, possessed of firmness and spirit ;
and when the oblivious Professor returned to consciousness, she rejected his advances, and resolutely refused to reinstate him in the
place which he had forfeited.

The admirer with whom she gained the greatest notoriety was
Patrick Taylor of Birkenshaw, in the parish of Torphichen, near Bathgate.   He first saw her at a Skirling Fair.   Her personal graces, and
the fact that she possessed a fortune of L.2000, made her very attractive in his eyes.   He subsequently paid his addresses to her, and being
a showy, specious fellow, succeeded in making some impression on her
heart.   By pursuing a course of reckless dissipation, he had reduced
himself to bankruptcy, and this rendered him altogether unacceptable
to Miss Kello's relations.   After an intimacy of eighteen months, he
gave her a document declaring her to be his just and lawful wife, and
received one from her of a similar import in return.   The following
is a transcript of the document presented by her to Taylor :—

'SKIRLING MILL, 16th Feb. 1779.

' I hereby solemnly declare you, Patrick Taylor, in Birkenshaw, my just
and lawful husband, and remain your affectionate wife,

' AGNES KELLO.'

These documents were kept secret by both parties; but the copy in

Miss Kello's hands having been discovered by her mother, she caused her to destroy it, and to write to Taylor, requesting him to give up his copy. This he refused to do, unless he received L.500. He continued, occasionally, after this period, to pay visits to Skirling Mill, and employed friends to intercede with Miss Kello's relatives in his behalf. He so far succeeded, that, in the spring of 1780, their banns were twice proclaimed; but some of the lady's friends, who were obstinately opposed to the union, prevented them from being proclaimed a third time. For two years afterwards their meetings were very unfrequent; and from 1782 to 1784 they ceased altogether.

Another candidate now appeared for the hand of Miss Kello. This was a gentleman of wealth and respectability from the neighbourhood of Whitburn. His suit was successful, and preparations were made for the marriage. Taylor, getting notice of this arrangement, immediately took steps to prevent its being carried into effect, by declaring that Miss Kello was already his wife. The case having been brought before the Commissary Court, was argued at great length; and the decision given was, that, according to the law of Scotland, they were married parties. Every effort was made, first by a bill of advocation, and afterwards by a reclaiming petition, to reduce this sentence in the Court of Session, but without effect; and therefore the case was carried, by appeal, to the House of Lords. Their lordships, on the 16th of February 1787, reversed the decisions of the Scottish Courts, declaring, 'that the two letters insisted upon in this process by the parties respectively, and mutually exchanged, were not intended by either, or understood by the other, as a final agreement; nor was it intended or understood that they had thereby contracted the state of matrimony, or the relation of husband and wife from the date thereof. On the contrary, it was expressly agreed, that the same should be delivered up, if the purpose they were intended to serve should prove unattainable, and if such delivery should be demanded; which last-mentioned agreement is further proved by the whole and uniform subsequent conduct of both parties.'

These harassing proceedings, although so far successful, had an injurious effect on Miss Kello's health and spirits. She never regained her former sprightliness and gaiety. She retired, in a great measure, from general society; and, along with her mother, took up her abode in the town of Biggar, where she died in 1796, in the thirty-second year of her age, and was interred in Biggar Churchyard.

Not far from the wall of the church is the resting-place of John Cree, Procurator-fiscal of Biggar, who died on the 17th December 1796, in the eighty-ninth year of his age; and also of his son Mathew, who held the office of Baron Bailie twenty-seven years, and died on the 7th of July 1832. He was one of the most mild and conciliatory magistrates that ever exercised authority in Biggar, or anywhere else. His common advice to disputants was, 'Tak a gill and 'gree;' and thus

seems to have been an implicit believer in Burns' opinion, that 'it's
aye the cheapest lawyer's fee to taste the barrel.' He long officiated
as an elder in the parish church. His only acting colleague in this
office, for many years, was John Pairman, who was generally denominated The Elder. These two worthies were great cronies, and had
many a pleasant confabulation over a single glass of whisky punch;
for they were remarkably circumspect in their conduct, and never
exceeded in their potations. The Elder was in the habit of pronouncing any untoward circumstance, 'A fair smook;' and this
phrase became quite proverbial in Biggar. On one occasion, a person called on the Elder in regard to a case of scandal, and invited
him to a public-house to talk over the steps he would require to
take, to be restored to his position in the Church. When the Elder
was thawed a little with the toddy, the offender ventured to hint that
there were two cases of scandal. 'Faith, then, Davie lad,' said the
Elder, 'we maun hae another half mutchkin.' On another occasion,
he complained bitterly to the parish minister of the annoyance received from the paupers of the parish, and the heavy demands made
for their support. The minister exhorted him to courage, and said,
'But, John, think of the reward promised in another world.' John's
answer was, 'Faith, a bird in the hand is worth twa in the buss.'

In the tomb of his forefathers also sleeps Gavin Cree, son of Mathew
Cree, just referred to. Gavin followed the same profession, viz.,
that of a nurseryman. In 1812 he was appointed paymaster to the
French prisoners who were located at Biggar, and ever afterwards
was extremely loquacious on the characters and proceedings of these
unfortunate sons of Mars. He long took a deep interest in the prosperity of his native town. He was an active manager of some of its
benefit societies. At the yearly display of the Whipmen's Society, in
the middle of June, he was always in high spirits, arranged the races
and sports that took place on the occasion, and catered largely for the
gratification of the juvenile portion of the population. He held the
rank of sergeant in the corps of the Lanarkshire Yeomanry Cavalry,
and regularly, for many years, attended the musters on Lanark Muir.
Mr Cree, however, gained his chief distinction by his laborious study
and exertions to improve the methods of pruning forest trees. His
attention was drawn at an early period to this subject, and one of
the first trees on which he experimented was the most notable in
Biggar. It was usually styled, the 'Deil's Tree;' and every youth
firmly believed that on very dark nights evil spirits were wont to hold
their rendezvous under its shade; and therefore a great amount of
courage was requisite to pass it after nightfall. Mr Cree procured a
ladder and a saw, and, greatly to the amazement of young and old,
cut off bough after bough, regardless either of fiend or fairy, and left
it one of the most stunted and uncouth objects that could well be
conceived. He continued his experiments wherever an opportunity

could be obtained, and he wrote several papers illustrative of his system, for the 'Quarterly Journal of Agriculture.' The Highland and Agricultural Society of Scotland having had their attention called to the subject, offered, in 1836, several prizes for essays on the best method of pruning forest trees. Mr Cree accordingly entered the arena as a competitor, and succeeded in carrying off one of the Society's silver medals. The distinguishing peculiarity of Mr Cree's system—the shortening the branches, instead of cutting them off by the trunk—attracted the attention of several distinguished botanists, among whom may be mentioned Mr Louden, and Professors Balfour and Low. Some of the systems propounded by others, particularly by Mr Bellington, one of the Keepers of the Royal Forest, were nearly similar to that of Mr Cree, but they failed to give so precisely the rule of practice; and therefore Professor Low, in his 'Elements of Agriculture,' states, that the country is highly indebted to Mr Cree for bringing his system to a point of improvement never before known. In May 1848, the London Society of Arts awarded Mr Cree a gold medal for the best essay, 'On the treatment of Forest Trees, where early pruning has been neglected; on the practice of Foreshortening, and how far advisable; and the physiological principles of its adoption.' This honour afforded Mr Cree the highest gratification. On all public occasions the medal appeared on his breast; and he spoke with rapture of the distinction of receiving an invitation to attend a meeting in London, to receive the medal from the hands of Prince Albert,—an invitation, however, with which he had been unable to comply. His system having thus been brought favourably under the notice of his countrymen, he was to be often seen in a solitary plantation, with his ladder and his saw, disencumbering the trees of their superfluous branches. On one or two occasions, he appeared in working order in the metropolis of Scotland, and, greatly to the horror of the uninitiated, committed sad havoc among the goodly boughs of the trees in the Meadows, and the Gardens of Princes Street, and the Royal Terrace; but these trees have long since borne ample testimony to the advantageous results of his operations. Some years ago, Mr Cree published his 'Essays on Pruning,' in a collected form, which, we understand, met with a ready sale. He died, after a short illness, on the 17th of June 1860.

Here is the resting-place of John Pairman, artist, who deserves to be noticed, not less on account of his merits as a painter, than on account of his amiable character, his cultivated understanding, and public usefulness. He was the second son of Robert Pairman, farmer, Staine, in the parish of Biggar, and was born in 1788. He received his education at the schools of his native place, and then went to Glasgow as an apprentice to a draper. At the expiry of his apprenticeship, he returned to Biggar; and there, in the shop now occupied by Mr George Johnstone, commenced business on his own account.

By this time he had begun to devote his thoughts and his leisure
hours to drawing sketches from the objects around him.   One of the
first portraits that he attempted, was that of his brother Robert, merchant, Biggar.   He wrought at this quite stealthily.   One day he
ventured to show it to his minister, the Rev. John Brown, who had
accidentally called at his shop.   He made no disclosure of the person
whom he intended to represent, but Mr Brown at once said, 'That is
your brother.'   This gratified him exceedingly, as it showed that he
could now sketch a countenance that could be recognised.   After
painting a number of portraits and local scenes, he abandoned his shop
at Biggar, and repaired to Glasgow, where he took lodgings, and,
though entirely self-taught, and without patronage of any sort, he
commenced business as a portrait painter.   After spending some years
in Glasgow, he left it, and proceeded to the Scottish capital, as likely
to afford a better field for his exertions, and there he fixed his head-
quarters till his death.   During the summer months, he was in the
habit of visiting some of the principal towns of Scotland, and there
painting portraits of clergymen and other noted personages.   The
first full-length portrait that he painted, was one of the Rev. John
Brown, Biggar; and though it is more than forty years ago, the
colours are still fresh, and the picture is considered a good likeness by
those who knew Mr Brown in his younger days.   At a later period,
he painted another portrait of Mr Brown, which was considered so
striking a resemblance that an engraving was taken from it.   Among
the portraits of other celebrities, painted by Mr Pairman, was one of
Professor Lawson of Selkirk, which was afterwards engraved.   Mr
Pairman, however, did not confine his attention to portraits; he also
painted landscapes, groups, and fancy pictures, somewhat in the style
of Wilkie.   These were sent to the different exhibitions in Edinburgh, obtained very favourable notices, and sold readily.   The last
landscape that he painted, was a bridge over the Almond, a small
stream not far from Edinburgh.   It is in the possession of his brother
Robert, along with a number of other memorials, particularly a view
of Tinto, taken from the High Street of Biggar.

    Mr Pairman was a member of the session of the congregation,
Broughton Place, Edinburgh, under the pastoral care of the Rev. Dr
Brown.   He took a deep interest in all matters connected with that
congregation, and was at the head of every scheme of usefulness.   He
paid great attention to the wants of the poor, and had an evident
delight in attending fellowship and district prayer-meetings.   He was
greatly esteemed for his mild, conciliatory manners, his ardent piety,
his unwearied diligence in doing good, and his enlightened and instructive conversation.   He died suddenly, at his house in Edinburgh,
on the 14th December 1843, in the fifty-fifth year of his age.

    We mark the tomb of Thomas Johnston, merchant, Biggar, and his
spouse, Janet Brown.   Beside them repose the remains of their eldest

son, Robert, who was born at Biggar on the 6th of December 1784, and was baptized on the 12th of the same month by the Rev. John Low. He received his education at Biggar parish school, and there made some progress in the ordinary branches of learning—reading, writing, and arithmetic, including the rudiments of Latin. After leaving school, he learned the art of weaving; and on the expiry of his apprenticeship, wrought some time as a journeyman weaver in the city of Glasgow. Returning to his native town, he settled down as a merchant, and carried on a fair business for a number of years. In 1808 he married Violet, daughter of the Rev. John Brown of Whitburn, and sister of the Rev. John Brown, then minister of the Secession congregation, Biggar.

Mr Johnston's vocation as a merchant not only brought him into contact with most of the worthies who, during his time, flourished in the Biggar district, but allowed him sufficient leisure to cultivate an acquaintance with literature, both ancient and modern. He was in daily converse with shrewd, practical farmers, learned and eccentric schoolmasters, grave and gifted divines, and intelligent and sagacious weavers, shoemakers, and other craftsmen. He would discuss a mathematical problem or an algebraical equation with Robert Whitlaw, the Symington weaver; canvass the merits of a favourite poet, or the contradictions of human nature, with James Brown, the Symington poet, or James Affleck, the Biggar tailor; dive into the perplexing intricacies of politics, or the abstruse subtleties of theology, with John M'Ghie, the Biggar shoemaker, or Daniel Lithgow, the Biggar weaver; enjoy the devotional gravities and amusing pedantries of Adam Thomson, schoolmaster, Quothquan, or William Sim, the peripatetic dominie and philosopher, Biggar; and then, as his nephew, Dr Brown of Edinburgh, has told us, he would every Friday evening repair to the Burgher manse, and with his gifted brother-in-law, the Rev. John Brown, range over all topics, from the elegancies and niceties of classic lore, to the humours and pleasantries of village gossip. Besides, he was very often chosen a referee in disputed cases, especially among the weavers; and thus his mental acumen was sharpened by coming into collision with such acute intellects as Andrew Brown, John Baillie, Allan Whitfield, etc. He thus acquired a very intimate knowledge of the inhabitants of the Biggar district, and to the last retained a very lively remembrance of their habits, peculiarities, and proceedings.

Mr Johnston cultivated a close and extensive acquaintance with the English classic authors. He never could be brought to devote any attention to the works of many modern writers, particularly of fiction, of whose productions the present age has been very much enamoured. He seemed to regard them as altogether unworthy of notice. But the works of Shakspeare, Milton, Pope, Swift, Hume, Addison, Burke, Johnson, he read over repeatedly, and knew all their sentiments and peculiarities of style intimately. He had a high appreciation of several of the Edinburgh Reviewers, particularly of Jeffrey, M'Intosh, Brougham, and Macaulay; and no literary productions ever afforded him greater delight than the poetry and novels of Sir Walter Scott. Down to the very close of his life, he every now and then perused one of Sir Walter's novels; and he seemed to enjoy its genial humour, its vivid portraitures of character, and its happy expositions of national feelings and peculiarities, with as much relish as ever. One of the most remarkable traits in Mr Johnston's character was the assiduous manner in which he devoted himself to acquire a knowledge of languages, both ancient and modern. He was, in his latter years, when we knew him best, well versant in Latin, Greek, Hebrew, French, Spanish, Italian, and German. He had read repeatedly the works of the best Greek and Roman authors, and particularly those of Virgil, Horace, Livy, Cæsar, Suetonius, Xenophon, Theocritus, and, above all, of Homer, as he made it a matter of conscience to read the Iliad and Odyssey from beginning to end every two or three years. He had perused the Greek New Testament so frequently, that he knew almost every passage in it by heart. He had read all the Hebrew of the Old Testament, but he did not cultivate so close an acquaintance with the Chaldee. With the works of Schiller, Tasso, and Cervantes, he was very familiar in the languages in which they were originally written; and he had a special pleasure in musing over the productions of Voltaire, Rousseau, Le Sage, Montesquieu, and other great French writers. He had, perhaps, a more minute acquaintance with the French language than any other, except his own; at least, it was the only foreign language in which he occasionally attempted to hold conversation.

Another department of learning to which Mr Johnston specially devoted himself, was geometry and algebra. Like most men of literary habits, he was rather of an indolent disposition, so far as manual labour was concerned; but in studying a classic author, or working out a mathematical demonstration, he would toil for days and weeks with the most unwearied application. He often gave himself a great deal of unnecessary labour. He disregarded all adventitious helps. He had no patience with glossaries and commentaries. An old text-book and a common dictionary were the only tools with which he would work. In algebra he had great enjoyment in evolving a general formula for himself, though it should cost him weeks of close study; and many of his processes were original deductions to himself. They had long been previously known to regularly educated men; and he might have been acquainted with them too, had he been disposed to take a little trouble to ascertain what discoveries had been made by other inquirers.

Mr Johnston's contributions to literature were not numerous, considering that he devoted a great part of a long life to the pursuit of knowledge. We know that he contributed to 'The Christian Repository,' edited at Biggar by his brother-in-law, the Rev. John Brown, a series of articles on the 'History of the Secession Church,' a paper on 'A Corn of Wheat Falling into the Ground,' and 'A Review of Sir Harry Moncreiff's Life of Dr John Erskine.' For a periodical called 'The Christian Gleaner,' he wrote 'A Memoir of Betty Gibson,' and, for the 'Eclectic Review,' a critique on Dr John Brown's 'Exposition of First Peter.' A sermon on the text, 'There remaineth much land to be possessed,' which was preached by the Rev. John Brown before the Secession Synod, and afterwards published, gave great offence to some of the friends of the Established Church, and called forth a number of very severe strictures. The Rev. Alexander Craik of Libberton, in particular, entered the lists, and published a censorious pamphlet against the assertions made in the sermon. Mr Johnston followed with a pamphlet, entitled, 'Letter by a Friend of the Church,' which his nephew, Dr Brown, characterizes as 'a capital bit of literary banter.' The following pamphlets were also from Mr Johnston's pen:—'On the Abolition of Slavery;' 'Calm Answers to certain Angry Questions proposed to Voluntary Churchmen;' and 'A Digest of the Evidence on the Connection of Bible Societies with the Circulation of the Apocrypha.' He furnished many articles to the 'Scottish Herald,' the 'Scottish Press,' and the 'Kirkcaldy Observer.' Two of the largest works with which he was connected were a translation of Calvin and Storr's work on Philippians, and a translation of the Messianic Psalms of Rosenmüller. To both of these works he furnished lengthened prefaces.

Mr Johnston was a person of very diffident and retiring habits. He had an extreme repugnance to put himself forward in any way before the public, or even before strangers with whom he accidentally came in contact. Every one who met him knew that he was a thoughtful, intelligent man; but it was only his intimate friends who were aware of the extent of his erudition, or the learned inquiries in which he was daily engaged. He had talents and acquirements fitting him to occupy a high position in life; but from an unconquerable aversion to push himself forward, and make his merits and his claims known, he passed through life in comparative obscurity. With one, or at most two intimate friends, he could descant whole evenings on themes of high import, delight them with anecdotes of Biggar men, or dissect the merits of a favourite author; but before a mixed company he was generally silent, or, if forced to speak, he generally made a very poor appearance. He, in fact, hated all public display, both on his own part and that of others. If left to his own judgment, he would not go a yard to see an exhibition, or attend a festive meeting.

Mr Johnston, in the latter part of his life, left Biggar with his family, resided for some years in Edinburgh, and then removed to Portobello. He died at this latter place, after a short illness, on Tuesday, the 17th April 1860, having reached the seventy-fifth year of his age. His wife, Violet Brown, was, in her way, a remarkable woman. Her intellectual powers were strong and discriminating, and her memory was wonderfully tenacious and accurate. It was always a pleasing treat to us to sit and hear her discant on the incidents of her early days, spent at Longridge and Biggar. She died at Portobello on the 22d of February 1861, and was interred also in the Churchyard of Biggar.

Mr and Mrs Johnston left behind them three sons and two daughters. The oldest son, Thomas, is settled in Glasgow as a medical practitioner. Like his father, he is fond of all sorts of books, and has a first-rate knowledge of his profession, and a great hatred of humbugs, especially of medical humbugs. He occasionally lectures on scientific subjects before some of the literary societies of Glasgow. Their second son, John, is minister of the United Presbyterian congregation, Duke Street, Glasgow. He was for some time editor of the 'Scottish Press,' and is the author of a work entitled, 'The Life and Remains of the Rev. Robert Shirra of Kirkcaldy.' He is a very popular preacher; and, a short time ago, one of the American colleges conferred on him the degree of Doctor in Divinity. The youngest son, Robert, is a United Presbyterian minister at Arbroath. He was educated at the High School of Edinburgh, and carried off the chief prizes at all the classes which he attended, including that of the Rector's. He also received the gold medal for being the best scholar of the senior Humanity class at the University of Edinburgh. He took the degree of LL.B. at the University of London, and at one time was employed in superintending some of the Latin educational works published by the Messrs Chambers of Edinburgh.

Mr Thomas Johnston, merchant, Biggar, had several sons besides Robert, to whom we have just referred. They all devoted themselves to the learned professions. James, a very amiable man, and a most respectable medical practitioner, is settled at Limekilns. Ebenezer, formerly connected with the Established Church, and now Free Church minister at Bannockburn, is a man of capital scholarship and great humour; and William, who is minister of the United Presbyterian congregation at Limekilns, is a person whose ability, learning, and great moral worth, have not only given him a high place in the United Presbyterian Church, but throughout a much wider section of the community.

In the north part of the Churchyard is a vault without grace or ornament, and, in fact, of so rude a construction as to be even an eyesore among the humble stones by which it is surrounded. Beneath it repose the ashes of Thomas Ord, the famous equestrian, and his first wife. Mr Ord's early history is obscure. It has been stated that he was the son of the Rev. Selby Ord, minister of Longformacus; that he was for some time a medical student; and that, being of a roving disposition, he threw aside the lancet and dissecting-knife, and enlisted into a cavalry regiment, in which he served till a friend of his father purchased his discharge. On the other hand, it has been asserted that he engaged himself, when a boy, to a distinguished equestrian of the name of M'Donald, with whom he served five years. In his sixteenth year, it is said, he started as an equestrian on his own account, and in this character made his *debut* at Kelso. However this may be, it is certain that, at an early part of his career as a master equestrian, he drew a company around him, and performed with *eclat* in many of the smaller towns of Scotland. Having great confidence in his own abilities, and encouraged by the success which had attended his previous efforts, he set up regular establishments in Edinburgh, Glasgow, Aberdeen, Dundee, Perth, Inverness, Dumfries, etc., and everywhere received substantial marks of public favour. He then made a descent into England, and performed in a number of the large towns in the sister kingdom; but here his good fortune forsook him. His heavy expenditure in attempting to cater for the amusement of the Southrons was not always covered by the receipts, and, in the end, he was forced to dispose of the greater part of his stud, to break up his troupe of artistes, and return to Scotland in comparative poverty. After this period he carried on his business in a more humble manner, keeping a small establishment, performing in the open air, and looking for remuneration to the disposal of lottery tickets. By prudence and economy, he amassed a sum of upwards of L.2000, which he invested in the Berwick Bank. This establishment, unfortunately, failed, and our equestrian again lost all his hard-won earnings. Nothing daunted, he still pursued his career, and ere long acquired such a sum as enabled him to purchase a small property at Biggar, which he afterwards regarded as his head-quarters. He had a higher appreciation of Biggar than any other town of Scotland, and here he erected his last circus, or amphitheatre, as it was called, in the spring of 1844. It was a substantial erection of wood, and had the singularity of standing on a part of his own grounds, and within a few yards of his own house. The interior contained the usual accommodation of boxes, pit, and gallery, and was fitted up with a considerable degree of elegance. The entertainments consisted both of equestrian and theatrical performances. On the 4th of April he presented a grand dramatic spectacle, written by a townsman, entitled 'The Battle of Biggar,' with appropriate scenery, such as the English Camp on the Burgh Muir, the Cadger's Brig, the Cave of Threpland, etc. This undertaking, notwithstanding his vigorous efforts to present attractive amusements, failed to command an adequate measure of support. In the bill announcing his benefit for the evening of the 11th of April, he consequently thought fit to publish the following card:

'Mr Ord respectfully takes leave to state to the gentry and public in general of Biggar and its populous vicinity, that, in consequence of the

very liberal encouragement he received on his former visits, he was determined to spare no expense in putting up an amphitheatre for their amusement, where equestrian exercises in the circle, and dramatic entertainments
on the stage, aided by appropriate scenery and wardrobe, might be alternately displayed, in the hope of a continuation of that patronage, which had
hitherto crowned his efforts to please. In the attempt he has entirely failed,
being a considerable *loser* from the opening of the establishment to the present time; and as the season is now at a close, he trusts he will not be
deemed impertinent in respectfully and earnestly soliciting the countenance
of his friends in particular, and the public at large, on this occasion, trusting
the numerous amusements selected will merit the approbation of the visitors
to his amphitheatre.

> ' 'Tis not in mortals to command success:
> I have done more, I've studied to deserve it.'

His last appearance on horseback was at Thornhill, on the 29th
September 1859. He proceeded with his company to Ayrshire, and
intended to take part in the performances at Galston and other towns;
but he became indisposed, and at his own request was conveyed to
his home at Biggar. Here he grew gradually worse, and at last
closed his earthly career on the 27th December following, aged upwards of eighty years, and his remains were interred in the vault to
which we have referred. A proposal was made, at the time of his
death, to raise a subscription to erect a monument to his memory; but
it appears never to have been actively prosecuted, and may now be
said to be abandoned. Mr Ord was temperate in his habits, charitable
in his disposition, and opposed to anything like fraud or gambling.
He was an equestrian of the first order. In the heyday of his strength
and success, he challenged the renowned Andrew Ducrow to a trial of
skill for L.500; but the latter refused to peril his reputation by entering the lists against so fearless and agile a competitor.

Several of the stones mark the resting-place of the baron bailies of
Biggar, some of whom presided over the destinies of the little community for many years. We specially notice that of Bailie Alexander
Wardlaw, to whose memory a marble slab was erected in the eastern
wall of the church, with an epitaph from the pen of the famous
Scottish poet, Allan Ramsay. The whole inscription on the tablet
is as follows:—

> ' Alexander Wardlaw, Chamberlain to the Right Honorable the Earl of
>   Wigtoun, dyed 15th March 1721, aged 67 years.
>> ' Here lyes a man whose upright heart
>>   With virtue was profusely stor'd,
>> Who acted well the honest part
>>   Between the tennants and their lord,
>>
>> ' Betwixt the sands and flinty rock,
>>   Thus steer'd he in the golden mein;

While his blythe countenance bespoke
A mind unsullied and serene.

' As to the *Bruce* the *Fleming* prov'd
Faithfule, so to the Fleming's heir
Wardlaw behav'd, and was belov'd,
For justice, candour, faith, and care.

' His merit shall preserve his name
To latest ages free from rust,
Till the Archangel raise his frame,
To joyn his soul amongst the just.
' Hoc monumentum ponit Joannes Wardlaw Alexandri filius.'

It is rather a noticeable feature in the tomb-stones of Biggar
Churchyard, that few of them contain poetical inscriptions. The only
other inscription of this kind which we have noticed or heard of, is
on a stone erected to the memory of Janet Jenkison. The whole
inscription on the stone is as follows:—

' Here lies the body of Janet Jenkison, daughter of James Jenkison,
burgess, Biggar, and spouse of Hugh Somerval, wright in Dolphinton,
who died the 20th day of February 1734, aged 33 years.
' At this cold pillow lies her head,
And hopes to rise with Jacob's seed ;
Prudent she was in virtue's walk,
And to do good in moderate talk.'

This is, no doubt, the composition of a local poet ; but it does not im-
press us with very exalted notions of the manner in which poetry and
grammar were cultivated in the district at the period to which it refers.

In this churchyard lie the ashes of many other men who, in their
day, enjoyed considerable local celebrity ; but it would swell this
work to an undue size to descant on their history and characteristics.

CHAPTER VIII.

Biggar Kirk.

DURING the 350 years occupied by the Romans in attempting to conquer Scotland, a revolution took place in the religious opinions of the people. The Druidical system, although embracing such truths as that there is only one God, that the soul is immortal, that men will be punished or rewarded in a future state according to the actions which they have performed on earth, etc., yet, consisting as it principally did of frivolous and debasing rites, particularly that of offering human sacrifices, it could not stand before the power and progress of divine knowledge. The individual or individuals who first introduced the light of Christianity into the British Isles, are not certainly known. The likelihood is, that during some of the rigorous persecutions carried on by the Roman emperors against the early Christians, which was the means of dispersing them over all parts of the known world, some of the converts found their way to Britain, and there promulgated the faith which they had embraced, and on account of which they had been called to suffer. The new faith, by whatever person it was introduced, appears to have made rapid progress in the minds of the people; and it is generally asserted that, in the year 203, Donald, King of the Scots, with his queen and many of his nobles, publicly embraced it, and were baptized. Then, from time to time, arose certain illustrious divines, whom our ecclesiastical historians have delighted to present in bright colours to the notice of their readers—such as St Ninian, St Columba, St Kentigern, etc. St Kentigern, or St Mungo, who flourished in the sixth century, after labouring with great zeal and success in Wales, settled at last in the Vale of Clyde, founded a stately church at Glasgow, and exercised a fatherly charge over the clergy in the adjacent districts. We may conclude that a fabric for the exercise of the Christian system had, by this time, been erected at Biggar, and that it was honoured with occasional visits from the Clydesdale saint. It is not, however, for fully 500 years after the time of St Mungo, that we have any authentic reference to the Church of Biggar. The earliest allusions to it, or rather to its clergymen, are to be found in the chartularies of the religious houses.

The Church was a rectory in the deanery of Lanark, and was dedicated to St Nicholas. Robert, the parson of Biggar, is mentioned as a witness of a grant by Walter Fitzallan to the monks of Paisley,

From a sketch by Mr Drummond R.S.A.

W & A K Johnston, Lithog Edin"

between 1164 and 1177. The name of Master Symon, the physician of Biggar, and also, as has been conjectured, the parson of the church, is given as a witness to a charter by Walter, Bishop of Glasgow, between the years 1208 and 1232. About the year 1290, Philip de Keith, son of William de Keith, Knight Marischall, was Rector of Biggar. In 1329 Sir Henry, Rector of Biggar, was one of the royal chaplains, and clerk of livery to the household of the king. Walter, Rector of Biggar, is mentioned in a charter of Malcolm Fleming, Earl of Wigton, during the reign of David II. After this, very little is known regarding Biggar Church and its incumbents for a period of two centuries.

In Baiamund's or Bagimont's Roll, which, in the state in which it now exists, may be held to represent the value of ecclesiastical livings in the reign of James V., the rectory of Biggar is valued at L.66, 13s. 4d., and in the Taxatio Ecclesiæ Scotianæ at L.58. By an indenture of assythment, and afterwards by a decreet arbitral in the reign of James V., it received an additional endowment of L.10 yearly from Tweedie of Drummelzier, ' to infeft ane chaplaine perpetualie to say mass in ye kirk of biggair, at ye hye altar of ye sayme,' for the soul of John Lord Fleming, whom Tweedie had murdered.

It is supposed that it was this endowment or mortification that first suggested to Malcolm Lord Fleming the propriety of founding a collegiate church at Biggar, and conferring on it a number of new endowments. He appears to have been a devoted Roman Catholic. He had identified himself with the party who, at the time, were striving, by every means in their power, to uphold the tottering fabric of the Romish Church, and he was, no doubt, anxious to give a notable manifestation of his zeal in the cause which they had so much at heart. The principles of the Reformation, first enunciated in Germany by Martin Luther in 1517, had now spread over all Europe, and were even making rapid progress in the comparatively obscure realm of Scotland, and alarming the fears of the devotees of the Romish superstition. Patrick Hamilton and George Wishart had proclaimed these principles with impressive effect, and had testified their sincerity by laying down their lives; and Sir David Lindsay of the Mount, and George Buchanan, had written and published most pungent satires on the pernicious doctrines and ungodly lives of the Romish priesthood. A corresponding desire was consequently manifested by the party, with whom Fleming was connected, to prop up the superstructure of Romanism, which had been so vigorously and successfully assailed.

The first intimation that we have of Lord Fleming's intention to build a collegiate church at Biggar, is contained in a writ still preserved in the archives of the Fleming family. It is from Gavin, Commendator of the Benedictine Monastery of Kelso, and bears date the 26th November 1540. It states that he had heard of Lord

Fleming's design to found and endow a college church at Biggar; that the right of patronage of the Church of Thankerton had been obtained by the Abbots of Kelso from his lordship's predecessors; that in these evil times, by the increase of Lutheranism, all true Catholics were bound to contribute to so good a work; and that he was most anxious that his lordship should not be diverted from his resolution, or suffer prejudice by the Abbots of Kelso continuing to hold the patronage of the Church of Thankerton. On these grounds, with consent of David Hamilton, then rector of the said church, he transferred to Lord Fleming, in name of the college to be founded and built, the right of patronage of that church, with its whole rents and emoluments, to be bestowed on one or more pre-bendaries of the foresaid college. The only reservation which he made, was that the Church of Thankerton should always be provided with a vicar pensioner, who should discharge the clerical duties of the charge, and have for his sustentation twenty merks Scots out of the first and readiest of the teinds of the parish, with a house, garden, and four acres of land. This writ was confirmed by the Archbishop of Glasgow, at Edinburgh, 1st May 1542.

The new church was founded in 1545, and erected on the site of the old building dedicated to St Nicholas. The parson of the old church at the time was Thomas Chappell, who, on the presentation of Malcolm Lord Fleming, was collated to his office by the Archbishop of Glasgow, on the 17th April 1542. It has been supposed by some persons, and among others by Grose, who took a sketch of the Church from a window of the manse in 1789, and published an engraving of it in his work on the 'Antiquities of Scotland,' that the present edifice is much older than the date above mentioned. This, to some extent at least, is certainly a mistake. From statements in the founder's testament, executed in 1547, and also in a charter of the Abbot and Chapter of Holyrood connected with this Church, and dated a few years afterwards, it is evident that the erection had been commenced and carried on, to some extent, by the founder, Malcolm Lord Fleming, but was evidently left unfinished at his death, in 1547. His son and successor, James Lord Fleming, belonged to the same religious and political party as his father, and was, no doubt, influenced by the same views and feelings in respect to the new collegiate Church. He is understood to have carried on the building, and to have left it in nearly the same state in which it exists at present.

The style of the architecture of the Church is Gothic, and the form of it is that of a cross. It was, no doubt, intended to be all composed of ashlar work. The choir, transepts, and tower have accordingly been built of dressed sandstone, brought evidently from a quarry in the parish of Libberton, near Carnwath; but the nave is constructed of rubble work, the stones employed being the rough whin which abounds in the neighbourhood. This may be a portion of the old

Parish Church made to harmonize with the original plan, or it may be a part of the building executed in this manner by James Lord Fleming, with the view of lessening the expense. It is said that the original plan embraced a spire, which would have been a great ornament to the town, and a fine feature in the landscape; but it was not built, and hence the unfinished state of the Church is very commonly cited in the locality as an illustration of the aphorism, 'Many a thing is begun that is never ended,' like Biggar Kirk. The walls of the tower from which the spire was to have sprung, have been formed into a parapet with embrasures and loopholes, as if it was intended to be a place of defence,—a use to which the towers and spires of churches in Scotland were, in former times, not unfrequently put. After all, however, it may be questioned if it was ever intended to carry the tower higher than it is at present. It is certainly the fact, that central towers in Gothic buildings very frequently terminate, not with a spire, but with a parapet containing loopholes and embrasures similar to those of Biggar Kirk.

The building on the outside is plain, presenting little more than the buttresses and mouldings peculiar to Gothic architecture. It had two principal entrances, one in the south transept, and the other in the western gable. The doorway in the west is extremely plain, and is now built up; and the one on the south is composed of an arch finely moulded. The corbels from which the mouldings spring, are much defaced; but enough of them remains to show that they have been ornamented with fine tracery work, and that the pattern of the one is different from the other. On the handle or latch of the strong wooden door, studded with nails, is the date 1697, referring most likely to the time at which the door was made, and placed in its present position. On the left side of this door are the remains of the ancient jougs, by which adult offenders were fastened to the wall, and forced to remain a space of time proportioned to their misdemeanors. On the right, at a lower elevation, are staples, batted into the wall with lead, which were evidently intended to suspend a pair of jougs for the confinement and punishment of juvenile offenders. An excellent representation of this door and the chain of the jougs is to be seen in the vignette to this volume. The buttresses on each side of the gable of the south transept have been surmounted by carved pinnacles; but these have long since disappeared, as well as the apex or finial of the gable, which most likely was an emblem of the cross. The remains of the cross on the apex of the north transept can still be very distinctly observed. On the lowest corbie, or, as they are here generally denominated, crowsteps, of the western gable, is a carved shield of the Fleming arms, with this peculiarity, that the cinquefoils, adopted from the arms of the Frasers, are in the first and fourth quarters, instead of the second and third, as they are usually found in the escutcheon of the Earls of Wigton.

L

A large portion of the hewn stones used in the building has the mark of the masons by whom they were prepared. The practice of marking stones is known to have been observed by masons for several thousand years. The design of it was to distinguish the stones wrought by each workman, so that the merit or demerit of the workmanship could at once be attributed to the proper individual. It is not uncommon to find two marks on one stone,—the one being the mark of the hewer, and the other of the overseer, who, after inspecting the stone, and finding it correctly wrought, put upon it the official stamp of his approval. The apprentices had generally what is called a blind mark, that is, one with an even number of points or corners; while the journeymen or fellow-crafts had one with an odd number, which might range from three points to eleven. In the ancient lodges of Freemasons, a ceremony was observed at the time of conferring a mark on a newly entered brother; and when this was over, his name and mark were inserted in a book. We accordingly find that this was one of the regulations adopted at a meeting of the masters of lodges, convened at Edinburgh, 28th December 1598, by William Schaw, 'Maister of Wark' to his Majesty James VI., and General Warden of the Mason Craft in Scotland. All the old operative lodges, therefore, practised mark-masonry, and some of them—and among others, the Lodge of Biggar Free Operatives—retain an interesting roll of the marks which their members adopted and used. The individuals who built Biggar Kirk were evidently mark-masons, and hence the frequent marks to be found on the stones of which a portion of it is constructed.

Two small buildings were at one time attached to the Church, the one on the north side of the choir or chancel, and the other on the south side of the nave. The one on the north side, the traces of which are still to be seen on the wall of the Church, as shown in the engraving of the Kirk, was the chapter-house, which in such buildings was rarely to be found west of the transept. It was used for the meetings of the provost and prebendaries, and most likely also as a mortuary chapel. The building on the south was originally, in all likelihood, the vestry, in which the sacred utensils and vestments were kept; and perhaps it also served the purposes of an eleemosynary, or almonry, in which alms were distributed to the needy poor. It was in the end—and, indeed, in the memory of some persons still living— used as a porch, and had seats all round the walls. These buildings were removed about sixty years ago; but for what reason, it is impossible, perhaps, now to say. Two buttresses on the north side of the nave, and an arched gateway that stood at the entrance to the churchyard, have also, in the course of time, been demolished.

The interior of the Church was fitted up with considerable elegance. It had four altars. The high altar and the altar of the crucifix stood in the choir or chancel, and the altars of the two aisles were placed one in the south transept and the other in the north transept, the two transepts being, in former times, very commonly called 'The Cross Aisles.' A screen divided the choir from the nave, and at the eastern extremity of the choir, which was finely lighted with three large windows, was the presbytery, into which no person was allowed to enter except the priests. A stone on the north side of the choir had a carved representation of a serpent,—an emblem which has a strange but emphatic significance in the rites both of Paganism and Christianity. In the nave were placed the pulpit, and the font for holding the holy water. The corbels from which the groinings and arches of the roof sprung, were highly ornamented with representations of doves, foliage, human heads, etc. These are now much mutilated; but the heads on each side of the eastern termination of the nave are nearly entire, and are most likely intended to represent the founder and his wife. In the north transept was the organ-loft, the door to which still exists in the staircase which admits to the tower. The ceiling, at least of the chancel, was originally of oak, richly carved and gilt; but was removed a number of years ago, and one of lath and plaster substituted in its place. In the tower is an apartment which appears never to have been completed. It is of square form, and has a small window on each side; but as these are filled with stone slabs, it is quite dark, and can only be examined by the aid of a candle. The walls are unplastered, and the floor and ceiling, if they ever existed, have disappeared. The oak joists, both above and below, are in a state of good preservation. A very singular-looking shaft rests on a joist below, turns on a pivot, and communicates with one of the joists above; while a second shaft, with a hole in it near its lower termination, is suspended from one of the upper joists. It would perhaps not be easy to discover the purpose to which this curious apparatus was applied. The apartment has a spacious fire-place, which seems to indicate that it was intended to be occasionally occupied; but no reliable account can now be got of the use which it was designed to serve. The tradition regarding it is, that it was the place to which the Fleming family retired, or intended to retire, before and after attending religious service in the Church, to assume and lay aside what was called their 'chapel graith.' It is certain that the family had articles of this kind, as is shown by the following bequests. The founder of the Church, in his testament, says, 'I leif to James, my eldest son and air,' 'the chapell graith of siluer; that is to say, ane cross with the crucifix, twa siluer spandellers, twa siluer croadds, ane haly water fatt, with the haly water stick, ane siluer bell, ane chalice with the patine of siluer, with all the haill stand of vestments pertaining to the samen.' James Lord Fleming, in the testament which he executed at Dieppe in 1558, bequeathed his 'chapel graith' to his brother John. It consisted of the following items:—'Ane silvere challice w^t ane pax, ane cryce of silvere, ane eucharest of silvere, ane haly watter fate, w^t ane styk of silvere,

and ij crouats of silvere.' From these extracts it is evident that the
Flemings had not only a set of sacred vessels, but a peculiar suit of
garments, which they used while attending or performing the rites of
the Romish Church.

The circular staircase already referred to was entered from the
inside by a door in the north-west angle of the chancel, and, besides
admitting to the organ-loft and the square apartment in the tower,
communicated also with the floor of the parapet or bartisan; and as this
is covered with lead, being open to the weather, it is usually called the
Lead Loft. The door in the inside of the Church was some years ago
built up, and one in place of it cut out of the staircase, as shown in
the engraving. On the north-west side of the interior of the staircase
are the initials W.M., and on the south-east side the initials I.H., and the
date 1542. With regard to the initials nothing can be said; and the
date is certainly puzzling, as it is three years prior to the time at which
the present Church was founded. The stone on which it is cut may
have belonged to the old Parish Church, or some person, at a period
subsequent to the erection of the present Church, may have cut it in a
mere spirit of wantonness, or with a design to mislead. We put no
confidence in it as calculated to establish the supposition of Grose and
others, that the whole of the Church is older than the year 1545, the
date of its foundation as a collegiate charge. The belfry was furnished
with a bell of a remarkably clear tone, which was heard for many
miles round, and was rung by a rope in the inside of the Church.
This fine bell, which was supposed to be as old as the Church itself,
was unfortunately cracked by a sexton, when tolling it at the funeral
of one of the proprietors of the parish, about forty years ago. The
present bell is one of much inferior quality, and is rung from the
outside of the Church.

In the inside of the Church a relic, now very rarely to be met with,
is still preserved. This is the cutty stool, on which the violators of

ecclesiastical discipline were wont, in the face of the congregation, to make expiation for their offences. The punishment of the cutty stool is referred to by Ferguson the poet as forming part of the gossip around the farmer's ingle :—

> ' And there how Marion for a bastart son
> Upo' the cutty stool was forced to ride,
> The waefu' scald o' our Mess John to bide.'

The cutty stool of Biggar Kirk has the date 1694, with the initials B. K., and is represented in the accompanying engraving.

Another relic preserved in the Kirk is a jug. It is apparently composed of pewter, and very much resembles a small claret-jug. It is usually denominated a holy water fatt or jug, as, according to tradition, it was used by the Roman Catholic priests in holding holy water. After the establishment of the rites of Presbyterianism, the jug was used in conveying to the Church the water used in baptism. As an old relic connected with the Kirk, we give the annexed engraving of it.

The Kirk, although it has undergone many barbarous mutilations from the violence of man, and suffered many injuries from the corroding hand of time, is still in a state of good preservation, and holds out the promise of serving as the Parish Church for ages to come.

A proposal has lately been made to renovate the interior of the building, and thus place it in a state similar, in some respects, to that in which it was in former ages, and more in keeping with the altered spirit of the times. This is to consist principally in filling the windows with stained glass; in taking down the present ceiling of lath and plaster, and substituting one of wood, with the groinings, pendants, and carvings, as near to the original as can now be ascertained; and in cutting away the oak joists in the centre tower, and forming the lead loft into a glass cupola, in order to shed a flood of light on the area of the Church. This proposal, with exception of the last alteration, appears to be highly worthy of commendation; and it is to be hoped that the present pastor of the parish, the Rev. J. Christison, who seldom fails in any undertaking in which he embarks, will take it up, and prosecute it to a successful termination.

Having given a description of the building, we may now refer to the Charter of Foundation. It is still preserved in the archives of the Fleming family, and, with its ancient style of penmanship, and its large seals, has a most venerable appearance. It is written in Latin, and is of great length. As a full translation of it would occupy too much space, we will give the substance of its most important points.

It is addressed by Malcolm Lord Fleming to Cardinal Beaton of St Andrews. After enumerating all that reverend father's high-sounding titles, it goes on to say that his Lordship, influenced by

examples of piety and devotion, and constantly desirous to increase
the means of religious worship, and to press forward more warmly
and earnestly in the practice of pious deeds, so far as justice and
reason might warrant him, had been induced to found, endow, and
effectually erect a College or Collegiate Church at Biggar, with the
collegiate honour, dignity, and pre-eminence. The funds for this purpose were to be drawn from the parish churches, benefices, chaplain-
ries, clerical revenues, and charities belonging to him by hereditary
right, and from other property bestowed on him by the favour of
Almighty God. He had erected and endowed this Church to the
praise, glory, and honour of the most high and undivided Trinity; of
the most blessed and immaculate Virgin Mary, under the title and
invocation of her assumption; of the blessed St Nicholas, patron of
the Parish Church of Biggar; of St Ninian the Confessor, and all the
saints of the heavenly choir. The object of the founder was the safety
of the soul of James V., late King of Scotland, of most worshipful
memory; the safety of his own soul; of the soul of his wife, Joan
Stewart, sister of the late renowned King; of the souls of his parents,
benefactors, friends, and relatives, predecessors and successors; and
of all the faithful dead, especially those from whom he had taken
goods unjustly, or to whom he had occasioned loss or injury, and had
not compensated by prayers or benefits. He had done all this with
consent of the most reverend father in Christ, Gavin, by the grace of
God Archbishop of Glasgow, and of the wise and venerable men, the
deacons and canons of the Metropolitan Church of Glasgow, in chapter
assembled. The foundation was to support a provost, eight canons or
prebendaries, four boys, and six poor men. The firm conviction of
the founder was, that in the solemnities of the mass the Son offered
himself to the Father Omnipotent, a rich sacrifice for a sweet-smelling
savour; and that to Him nothing more acceptable, gracious, and
worthy could be presented. His sincere belief in the Catholic faith
also convinced him that the mass had power to restore frail human
nature, often falling into sin, to the Father's favour, to rescue the souls
of the faithful from the pains of purgatory, and bring them to the
full enjoyment of happiness and glory. He wished to have an assurance that he would not be found among the number of those of whom
it was said in the beginning, 'They are a nation void of counsel,
neither is there any understanding in them. O that they were wise,
that they understood this, that they would consider their latter end!'
And he had pondered in his mind what is written in the Apocalypse,
'And I heard a voice from heaven saying, Write, Blessed are the
dead who die in the Lord from henceforth: Yea, saith the Spirit,
that they may rest from their labours; and their works do follow them.'

The founder's charity, piety, and desire for extending the means of
religious worship, having been thus evoked, he had, out of his hereditary patronages and acquired property, endowed the Collegiate

Church of Biggar, for the provost, canons, boys, and poor men, as already stated, and reserved only to himself, his wife, and his heirs, the disposition, presentation, and endowment of these officials, as often as the office of any one of them became vacant. The collation of the provost was to belong to the Archbishop of Glasgow, and the admission or installation of the prebendaries and boys was to be the duty of the provost, or, in his absence, the President of the College for the time being.

The provost was to be called the Provost of the Collegiate Church of the Most Blessed and Immaculate Virgin Mary, of Biggar. He was to celebrate the Assumption of the Virgin, in the Church of Biggar, as the principal festival; and he was to have for his sustentation, all and whole the produce, rents, revenues, tithes, and emoluments of the rectory and vicarage of the parish of Thankerton, in the diocese of Glasgow, along with its tributes and offerings, and its manse and glebe. He was, however, to pay L.10 Scots to a curate, who was to undertake the cure of souls in the parish of Thankerton, and to bestow on him two acres of land, near the Church, for a manse and garden. The said curate was constantly to reside in the parish, and discharge all the duties of his office in person. The provost was also to bear all burdens, and meet all liabilities, ordinary and extraordinary, that, in times past, attached to the Church of Thankerton.

The first prebendary was to be called Canon of the Hospital of St Leonards, and was to be master and teacher of the School of Song. He was to instruct the boys of the College, and others, who might attend, in plain song, invocation or pricksong, and discant. He was also to be well skilled in playing the organ for the performance of divine service. He was to receive for his support, throughout the year, the produce of the church lands of Spittal. The second prebendary, who was to be instructor of the Grammar School, was to be sufficiently acquainted with letters and grammar, and was to have, for his yearly sustentation, the lands of Auchynreoch. The third prebendary, who was to be sacristan of the College, was to have for his annual support the chapel founded on the lands of Garnegabir and Auchyndavy, and dedicated to the Virgin Mary, with its pertinents; and six merks of annual rent in Kirkintulloch, along with two acres of land, for a manse and garden, belonging to the chapel, and at that time in possession of Andrew Fleming of Kirkintulloch. The duty of this prebend was to ring the bells, to light the wax tapers and tallow candles on the high altar, the altars of the two aisles, and the altar of the crucifix. For the maintenance of the tapers and candles during winter, he was annually to receive L.5 Scots, drawn from the produce and emoluments of the priest's office in the Church of Biggar. This prebend was also to prepare the vestments and ornaments of the four altars; he was to wash, clean, and repair, as often as necessary, the cups, vestments, and ornaments; and when this was done, he was to cover them up in their respective places on the altars. For this service, he was to receive the annual sum of L.5 Scots, levied from the priest's office of the Church of Biggar. The same prebend was to provide bread and wine for the celebration of mass in the College; and for the expense of these elements, he was annually to receive L.4 Scots out of the produce, rents, and revenues of the rectory and vicarage of Biggar. The fourth prebendary was to have charge of the poor men, while they were engaged in their devotions in the College, and also the administration and distribution of the victuals and other emoluments belonging to them; and was to render an account of the discharge of his duties, in this respect, to the patron, or, in his absence, to the provost and prebends. This canon was to receive for his sustentation L.10 Scots, from the yearly rent of the lands of Drummelzier, and L.7, 6s. 8d. Scots, every year, drawn from the produce, rents, and revenues of the rectory and vicarage of the Church of Biggar. Each of the other prebendaries was to have for his support the yearly sum of L.17, 6s. 8d. Scots, levied from the revenues of the vicarage and rectory of Biggar, but the special duties which they were to perform are not detailed. One of them was to be vicar stipendiary of the Parish Church of Biggar, now erected into a college, and was constantly to take his place in the choir, to sing, and to exercise his divine office, unless when he was engaged with the special duties of his charge and the administration of the sacraments. The presentation of this vicar stipendiary was to belong to the founder and his heirs, but his collation was to devolve on the Archbishop of Glasgow for the time being.

The founder also ordained that there should be attached to the College, in all time to come, four boys with children's voices, who were to be sufficiently instructed and skilled in plain song, invocation, and discant, who were to have the crowns of their heads shaven, and to wear gowns of a crimson* colour, after the fashion of the singing boys in the Metropolitan Church of Glasgow. They were to have, divided amongst them, all and whole the produce of the priest's office of the Parish Church of Lenzie, in the diocese of Glasgow, except so much as might be necessary for the sustentation of a priest to discharge the duties of the cure of that parish. The presentation of these boys was to belong to the founder and his heirs, and their examination and admission to the provost and prebendaries. When they lost their boyish voices, by advancing age, or when they behaved in a disorderly and incorrigible manner, the provost and prebendaries were to have the power of dismissing them from their situations in the College. The produce and emoluments of the office from which they were to derive their living were, with the exception already stated, to be under the control of the boys, along with their

* The word 'blodie,' in the original, is rendered by Colvill and other English glossarists, 'crimson,' as derived from the Saxon 'blod,' blood; but Ducange considers that the proper meaning of it is blue.

parents and relatives, and were to be devoted exclusively to the payment of their aliment and other necessary expenses.

The founder ordained that the College should have six poor men,
commonly called 'beid men.' The qualifications for their admission
were to be poverty, frailty, and old age. They were to be natives of
the baronies of Biggar or Lenzie, if a sufficient number could be got
in these places, and they were to reside in the house of the Hospital,
with its garden grounds, which the founder had set aside for their
accommodation. They were to be presented, admitted, and installed
by the founder, so long as he lived, and after his death, by his heirs
and successors. They were to be annually furnished with a white
linen gown, having a white cloth hood; and every day, in all time to
come, they were to attend in the College at high mass and vespers;
and when the founder departed this life, they were to sit at his grave
and the grave of his parents, and pray devoutly to the Most High
God for the welfare of his soul, the soul of his wife, and the souls of
his progenitors and successors. For their aliment and support, they
were to have distributed amongst them, on the first day of each
month, two bolls of oatmeal, the whole amounting annually to twenty-
seven bolls; so that each bedesman, during the year, was to obtain
four bolls and two firlots of the said oatmeal. This sustenance was to
be levied from the first-fruits and tithes of the rectory and vicarage
of the Church of Biggar; and from the same source twenty shillings
annually was to be drawn for each bedesman, for purchasing his
gown and repairing his house. The bedesmen were also to have full
power, liberty, and access to cast, win, and lead peats and divots from
two dargs of the Nether Moss, in order to supply their hearths with
fuel.

The provost and prebends were to have suitable dwelling-houses
and gardens near the Church. The provost was to have one acre of
land for this purpose, and each canon half an acre; and they were,
besides, to have the privilege of casting, winning, and leading peats
in the barony of Biggar, and especially within the bounds of the lands
belonging to the Hospital of St Leonards. The patron, provost, and
prebendaries were, yearly, on the eve of the Feast of Pentecost, to
meet and select two of the prebendaries, whose duty should be to
collect all the produce, tithes, revenues, offerings, and emoluments of
the rectory, vicarage, and church lands of Biggar, and distribute them
in proper order and proportion. Whatever sum remained, after this
was done, was annually to be disposed of in such a way as the patron,
provost, and prebends might think expedient, for the use and advantage of the College. Each of these prebends, for their services in this
respect, was to receive annually the sum of 26s. 8d. Scots, derived
from the revenues of the rectory and vicarage of the Church of Biggar.

The founder ordained that the following masses should be celebrated in the Collegiate Church, and that a register of them should
M

be inscribed on a board, and suspended in the College. A mass in
honour of the blessed Virgin Mary was to be said in the morning,
between six and seven o'clock, before the commencement of matins,
in summer as well as in winter. The priest celebrating it was not to
be exempted from attending and singing at matins; and if he was not
present at the end of 'Gloria Patri,' or the conclusion of the first
psalm, he was to lose that hour, and be subjected to a fine. High
mass was to be celebrated immediately after ten o'clock with singing
the solemn Gregorian chant,* or discant, and playing such tunes on
the organ as the time might require. A mass was to be said daily to
any saint, according to the option of the celebrator, immediately after
the consecration and elevation of the body of Christ in high mass,
and not sooner; and no priest, present at chant and high mass, was
to absent himself, under the penalty of losing the hour during which
the mass was celebrated.

The following masses were to be celebrated on week-days, immediately after matins, viz. :—on the second day, or Monday, and on the
greater double feasts, a mass de requie, for the founder's soul, his
wife's soul, the souls of his parents, and all faithful dead; on the
third, Tuesday, a mass in honour of St Ann, the mother of the Virgin
Mary; on the fourth, Wednesday, a mass in honour of St Nicholas
and St Ninian,† bishops and confessors; on the fifth, Thursday, a
mass in honour of the body of Christ; and on the sixth, Saturday,
a mass for the five wounds of Christ; while on Sabbath a mass was
to be performed for the Feast of the Compassion of the Blessed Virgin
Mary.‡ The officiating priest, clothed in his white gown and surplice,
was, immediately after the celebration of high mass, to approach the
grave of the founder, and sing the psalm, 'de profundis,' with the
usual collects and prayers, and the sprinkling of holy water. Extraordinary mass, as well as the mass de requie, was also to be said daily
in the two aisles.

A chapter was to be held every week in the Collegiate Church. It
was to have the same constitution, and to be subject to the same rules,
as the Metropolitan Church of Glasgow. Whoever absented himself
from this meeting was to pay a fine of twopence. On the fourth day,
or Wednesday, immediately after the solemnities for all the saints, for
the purification of the blessed Virgin Mary, and for the Apostles
Philip and James, and St Paul ad vincula, a mass was to be sung for
the founder's soul, his wife's soul, and the souls of all those previously
mentioned,—the vespers and matins of the dead being performed on

* The 'Canto Fermo' was introduced into the service of the Romish Church by
Pope Gregory the Great, who flourished during the sixth century. It has continued
in use to the present day, and is generally known by the name of the Gregorian
Chant.

† A relative of the founder was Prior of the Monastery of St Ninian, at Whithorn
in Galloway.

‡ Compassion of the Virgin, or our Lady of Pity,—the Friday in Passion Week.

the evening preceding these solemnities, along with nine collects, and nine psalms, with their responses. Each prebend was, with the Gregorian chant, invocation, and discant, to celebrate matins, high mass, vespers, and complin, at the hours and seasons usually observed by prebendaries in other collegiate churches.

All the prebends and their successors were bound to make a personal residence at the College, and on all feast, Sabbath, and week days, and continued commemorations, were to celebrate and sing, without note, matins, high mass, vespers, and complin at the great altar in the choir of the Church; and, clothed in their clerical habits—viz., clean linen surplices and red hoods trimmed with fur,—were, every night after complin, except on the greater double feasts, to rehearse the responses in honour of the Virgin Mary, to sing the psalm, 'de profundis,' and to read the usual collects and prayers for the souls of the founder and all faithful dead.

The prebendaries, at the ringing of the bell, which was to commence every morning throughout the year at six o'clock, were to meet, clothed in their clerical vestments, and sing matins at seven. At ten o'clock they were to perform high mass; and at five, vespers and complin, except in Lent, when vespers was to be performed immediately after high mass, and complin at the usual hour. When met for these purposes, they were not to move up and down the Church, nor indulge in whispering and laughter, but to the close of the service were to remain in solemn silence, and to manifest all becoming gravity. They were exhorted, in the name of the Lord Jesus Christ, to perform their duties fully, honestly, and attentively; and, avoiding all light and frivolous proceedings, were to commence, continue, and pause in the singing all at once. Those who violated this rule were to be severely punished; for, by singing improperly and carelessly, the due honour of God was not manifested, the intention of the founder was frustrated, the well-ordered conscience was hurt, and the edification of others was not promoted.

The prebend who absented himself from the usual services of the Church on week-days or simple feasts, was, for each hour, to pay twopence; on Lord's days and the great feasts, threepence; and on the higher feasts, fourpence. The fines thus exacted were to be collected weekly by the provost or a substitute, and were to be expended in the purchase of books or ornaments for the Church. The provost, or his substitute, was also to have power of suspending offenders from the choir, and devoting the whole of their incomes to the uses already stated, or other objects of piety. On those who persisted in their disobedience, the general officer of the Church of Glasgow was to inflict still heavier penalties and higher ecclesiastical censures, from which they were not to be absolved till they had given the utmost satisfaction.

All the prebendaries were to be priests, or at least in deacon's

orders, and were to be well skilled in literature, plain song, invocation,
and discant; and, each day, were to take their places at the altars, and
in a private manner celebrate mass for the souls of those by whom
these altars were founded.   They were to possess all the advantages
common to the Romish Church, provided they made personal and
continued residence at the College; but, in the event of any one of
them absenting himself for five days without liberty, the provost, or,
in his absence, the president and members of the Chapter, were,
unless a necessary cause of absence was shown, to declare his office
de facto vacant.   At their admission, they were to take a solemn oath
of obedience to the provost and the founder, so long as he lived, to
observe the statutes and rules laid down in the constitution and ordinances of the College, and drawn up and ordained by the founder
and others to whom he gave authority.

In the event of any prebendary being prevented by infirmity or
indisposition from celebrating mass when it was his turn, another of
the brethren was to occupy his place; but should he refuse to perform this service when required by the provost or president, he was
to be fined twelve pence Scots.   Should any prebend be of a quarrel-
some disposition, and provoke his brethren to fight, or engage in
other improper contentions, he was, on his offence being proved, to
be removed without further process from his office.   A prebendship
becoming vacant in this or any other way, was not to be filled up till
after the lapse of thirty days, so that sufficient time might be afforded
for obtaining a suitable and well-qualified successor, who, previous to
his admission, was to undergo an examination by the provost and
prebendaries.

The charter ends by calling upon Cardinal Beaton, with concurrence
of the Lord Archbishop of Glasgow, to approve, ratify, and confirm,
to add, correct, or otherwise amend, the statutes, rules, and constitution laid down for the College, its endowments, and officials.   Malcolm Lord Fleming, in faith and testimony of all and every one of the
articles stated in connection with his religious foundation, subscribed
the charter with his own hand, and appended to it his armorial seal;
and the Archbishop of Glasgow, and the Chapter of the Church of
Glasgow, in token of their full concurrence and assent, attached to it
their respective seals, on the 10th of January 1545, in presence of
the following witnesses:—William, Bishop of Dunblane; Robert,
Bishop of Orkney; John, Abbot of Paisley; Thomas, Commendator
of Dryburgh; Malcolm, Prior of Whithorn; William, Earl of Montrose; John Lord Erskine; Alexander Lord Livingstone; John Lindsay
of Covington; William Fleming of Boghall; Thomas Kincaid of that
Ilk; Andrew Brown of Hartree, and many others.   This charter was
confirmed by the Pope's Legate on the 14th of March 1545.   The
charter of confirmation is a very lengthy document, written on parch-
ment, and is still preserved.

CHAPTER IX.

Biggar Kirk—*Continued.*

MALCOLM Lord Fleming, in his testament, executed in the spring of 1547, still further manifested his care for the erection of the Collegiate Church of Biggar. In that document he says, ' I leif my vestments that were indued to the Kirk of Biggar and Colledge of the samin, and all other profits, whilk belangs to themselves as the erection of the Colledge bears, to the utility and profite of the samen, ay and while the Kirk, Colledge, Alemosineress, and mansion-house be biggit; and putt ———— in their own places as the erection of the said Colledge bears, and ordines vᵒ merks of my own propir guddis to be tane to buy vestments, and bigging of the said Colledge, and manħions, chalices, or ony other necessar things that is needful for the said Colledge.' He further orders, ' All my clayths to be dealt betwixt my twa sonis gotten with my wife, and pairt of thaim to be given to the Colledge of Biggar, as my executors and oversman thinks expedient, and leif to the Gray-friers of Glasgow xx lib to pray for me, xx lib I leif to the ffour chaplains of the Lenzie and Biggar to pray for me, and to be divided as my executors find expedient.'

It is not unlikely that the old Parish Church of St Nicholas at Biggar was used as the burial-place of the Fleming family. In Catholic times a strong desire prevailed to deposit the remains of the dead in consecrated ground, particularly in a place so sacred and hallowed as the area of a church. Kings, nobles, priests, and indeed all ranks, were anxious that their ashes should lie in a spot where the exercises of religion were daily performed, where the constant presence of holy men shed a solemnizing influence, where no rude hand dared to commit violence, and where they would remain in calm and undisturbed repose till the time when the sound of the archangel's trumpet would animate them anew, and summon them into the presence of their Creator and Judge. It is certain, at least, that Malcolm Lord Fleming intended that his new church at Biggar should be the burying-place of his family. In his testament, after leaving his soul to Almighty God, the Virgin Mary, and all holy saints, he says, ' Gif it happynis me to decess in weiris or ony uther deid, as God pless, giffen my body be gottin quharever I decess, to be erdit in my Colledge Kirk of Biggar.' He also in the same document left orders that, immediately after the completion of the College, his father's 'cymmeter' was to be carried from the Castle of Boghall to that sacred edifice, 'whilk sall be born the xii day of October in the solemnest gate that can be devisit baith to the honour of God.' In the chancel of the new Church, at the spot where the high altar in former times stood, nearly all the members of the Fleming family have been interred from the days of the founder to the end of last century. The last person buried in it was Lady Clementina Fleming, who carried the Biggar estates into the family of Elphinstone, and who died in 1790. The banners and escutcheons of this noble family were wont to hang in ample fold over the graves of the deceased barons, but these have all disappeared for nearly a century. The only memorial of the dead interred below is a marble slab, inserted into the wall, to the memory of Jane Mercer, wife of the Honourable George Keith Elphinstone, who died in 1789. It is understood that a large number of other persons besides the Flemings were interred within the walls of the Church. It is certain that when excavations were made in the floor, some years ago, to introduce a heating apparatus, large quantities of the remains of mortality were dug up.

The practice of kirk burial was in popish times quite common throughout the whole country, and, therefore, the Presbyterian clergy, at the Reformation, set themselves with vigour to repress it, as it savoured, in their opinion, of Popery and superstition. In the General Assembly which met at Edinburgh in 1588, they passed an act against it; and in the General Assembly of 1643, they declared that all former acts and constitutions made against burial in kirks were again ratified, and that all persons, of whatsoever rank, were inhibited and discharged to bury within the body of the kirk, where the people meet for the hearing of the word and the administration of the sacraments, or to hang pensiles or boards, to offer honours or arms, or to make any such like monuments, to the honour or remembrance of any deceased person, upon walls or other places within the kirk. These acts set the landed proprietors and the Established clergy completely by the ears. The lairds, whose ancestors from time immemorial had interred their dead within the walls of the parish kirks, insisted on continuing the practice, maintaining that they had a right so to do, both by prescriptive usage and feudal superiority. The clergy took their stand on the acts of the General Assembly, and resisted with their usual warmth and obstinacy.

Some of the lairds in the neighbouring parishes had sad bickerings with the clergy in regard to this practice. They took forcible possession of the churches, and there interred their dead, in spite of all the acts and anathemas of their spiritual instructors, though, as might be expected, they had very generally in the end to submit to the fines and penances that were consequently imposed. We will give one or two instances from the records of the Presbyteries of Lanark and Biggar.

On the 22d of January 1624, John Chancellor of Shieldhill was summoned to appear before the Presbytery of Lanark at its next meeting, and answer the charge of burying within the Kirk of Quothquan. On the 17th of June following, it is reported that the Laird 'hes promised to gif satisfactioune to ye Session of Quodquan, and to find cawtione to abstain from kirk burial in all tyme coming.' The Laird, however, after all, was resolved to take his own way; and when his wife died, in 1639, he interred her forcibly in the Kirk of Quothquan. The clergy, led on no doubt by his own pastor, George Bennet, pounced upon him again, and summoned him to appear before them at Lanark, on the 28th of March of that year. The record says, 'Ye Laird of Shielhill compeiris and acknowledges his fault in burying his wife in ye Kirk of Quodquan, and is ordered to find cawtione to renounce his kirk buriell in tyme coming, under ye pain of xl lib, and is ordeined to be censured by ye Kirk Sessione of Quodquan, for breking up ye door of ye Kirk.' John Muir, the Laird of Anniston, was arraigned for committing a similar offence. The minutes of Presbytery record as follows: 'Qlk day, compeirit ye Laird of Anaston, and confessit his fault, both in taking ye key of ye kirk doore of Symingtoun from ye minister thairof, and also burying his faither within ye samen, for qlk faults he oblissis himself under ye pain of xl lib to satisfy the Injunctiones of Presbytery to abstain from kirk buriell in all tyme coming under the foresaid penaltie *toties quoties* be this act subscribed with his hand at Lanark 25th of Junii 1625.' Twenty years after this date, viz., on the 25th of February 1646, the next Laird of 'Anieston' was summoned before the Presbytery of Biggar, and accused of burying his father in the Kirk of Symington. He confessed the fault as charged, but pretended that he was not aware of the acts of the Church on the subject; that he was sorry for what had taken place, and promised forbearance in time to come. The Presbytery condemned him to make a public confession of his fault in the Kirk of Symington the next Lord's day, and to bind himself, under a penalty of a hundred pounds, not to offend in like manner again. We will only cite another instance. On the 10th December 1629, the Rev. James Baillie, minister of Lamington, was enjoined by the Presbytery to take security from Thomas Baillie, the Laird of Lamington, that he would be present at next meeting of Presbytery, to receive his injunctions for his offence in breaking up the door of Lamington Kirk, and burying his child within the walls thereof; and if he refused, his pastor was to proceed against him by public admonition. The Laird, however, appeared before the Presbytery on the 31st of the month referred to, and 'was ordeyned to mak his publick repentance in sack claith ane Sabbath day, and pay iiij lib in penalty.'

In May 1668, John, Earl of Wigton, was interred in Biggar Kirk with all due solemnity, just about the time that the kirk sessions were

battling with all their vigour against the practice of kirk burial.
Anthony Murray, factor at Biggar to his Lordship, enters in his
books that he had 'allowed to ye compter,' that is, himself, 'ye sowme
of ane hunder and two punds eighteen shillings and tuo pennies Scots
disbursed be him at Biggar at my Lord's funerall.' He also mentions
that he had given himself credit for the price of three bolls of meal,
at four pounds and half a merk per boll, which were consumed in
my Lord's house at the burial in May; and that six firlots of the
meal was at that time given to the poor.

The Flemings, most likely from being patrons of the parish, were
not disturbed in their kirk burial. No account has been left of the
ceremonials observed at the funeral of any member of the family.
These were, no doubt, very imposing, especially so long as the family
continued its adherence to the popish faith. A statement of the
funeral expenses of Lady Margaret Fleming, whose remains were
interred in Biggar Kirk in December 1675, is still preserved. It
details the expenses incurred before the body was brought to Biggar,
and after it arrived at that town. As this statement may be interesting
to some readers, we give a few of the items:—'To Georg Stark going
through ye Monkland w^t letters to ye buriall, L.1, 4s.;' 'for a dosen
of great prinies to prin ye mortcloath and horscloath, 2s.;' 'to ye
footman Anderson to go to Carluik to advertise ye peopell to have
provision for man and horse, 8s.;' 'for breid and drink at ye dryburn
qn ye corps halted, L.4, 6s.' The cortege remained during the night
at Carluke, and the bill of the inn in which the men and horses were
chiefly accommodated has also been preserved. It is dated at 'Carluik,
Dec. 22^d 1675,' and shows that the disbursements were for 8 gallons
of ale, L.6, 8s.; for bread, L.2; for beef and mutton, L.3; for brandy,
L.4, 10s.; for pipes and tobacco, 6s.; for coals and candles, 10s.; for
eight pecks and three capful, most likely of corn, L.5, 5s.; for straw
for seven horses, L.1, 8s.; for breakfast to the coachman and footmen,
L.1, 7s.; for additional breakfast, L.1, 4s. 6d. The amount of the
whole expenses in the inn was L.25, 18s. 6d. Some other disbursements took place at Carluke, such as L.4, 10s. 'for sex horse and sex
men that was not in yt house,' and 18s. 'given to ye bellman.' A
halt was next made at Carnwath, and the bill for refreshments at that
town was L.4, 12s. 8d.

Among the items of expense at 'Bigair' were '4 pund of candell,
L.1; 4 pund of buter, L.1; ane pund and a half of plumdames, 5s.;
ane quarter a pund of ginger, 3s. 4d.; half a peck of salt, 2s. 8d.;
4 hens, L.1, 10s.; two sheip, ane of ym L.5, and ane oyr L.6; 4 dosen
of pypes, 10s.; fyve loads of coall, L.1, 7s.; 2 cariag horse to bring
ye wyn and oyr necessaries out of Edinr., L.5; ane man for his hyr
and quarter yt was hyrd be Wm. bows to bring out ye links and
torches, L.3, 16s.; James Rob for coming to Carluik w^t ye torches,
L.1; ye man that brought ye mortcloath to Cumbernald, L.2; ye

cotchman and his man at bigair for horse stall and diat, L.4; a pynt of wyn and two gills of brandy and glase to James Carmichael's weif, L.2; Hew Anderson and his daughter besyd ane firlot of meal, L.1, 6s.'

At the death of the founder of the College Church, in 1547, the building, as we have already observed, was unfinished. His son and successor, James Lord Fleming, carried on the work; but, from some cause or other, he also failed to complete it, as well as the hospital for the bedesmen, and the manses for the priests. On the 5th of May 1555, he obtained a charter from the abbot and convent of Holyrood, conferring on the College of Biggar the patronage and emoluments of the Church of Dunrod, in the diocese of Whithorn, avowedly on the ground of the scanty provision made for the provost and prebendaries of the College. This charter has been preserved in the chartulary of the Monastery of Holyrood, and is of considerable length. As everything of this kind possesses not merely a local, but a general interest, we will give an abridged translation of its principal points. It is addressed by Robert Stewart, commendator of the Monastery of the Holycross, to the reverend father in Christ, Andrew, by the grace of God Bishop of Candida Casa, and Dean of the Chapel Royal at Stirling. It sets out by saying that all sincere endeavours to promote the worship and honour of Almighty God, made by the faithful, ought to be extolled, approved of, and assisted by every person to the utmost extent of his power. The abbot and monks of Holyrood had, therefore, fully appreciated the singular affection, piety, and beneficence displayed towards God and the holy Catholic Church by the late noble and potent Malcolm Lord Fleming, who in these miserable and heretical (Lutheranis) times, and at his own expense, had erected a magnificent church at the town of Biggar, in honour of Almighty God and the Virgin Mary, and commonly called the College of 'The Blessed Mary of Biggar,' in which a provost and a certain number of other religious men had been appointed, established, and set apart to the service of God and the blessed Virgin. James Lord Fleming, son and heir of the late Malcolm Lord Fleming, had lately presented to the said abbot and monks a petition, which showed that his Lordship, moved by pious zeal and devotion, was striving to follow in the footsteps of his excellent father, and was endeavouring not merely to uphold the College, but to improve it with most watchful care. The petition also reminded them that they had in their hands the right of patronage of the Church of Dunrod;* and they felt that in these evil times it was incumbent on them, so far as their ability extended, to increase the means of religious worship, and render assistance to Lord Fleming, so that he might not be deterred from pursuing his excellent

* Dunrod formed the south part of the parish of Kirkcudbright. It was granted, with its church, to the Monastery of Holyrood so early as 1160. The remains of its church are yet to be seen, and its cemetery is still in use.

N

purpose and design, and feel too great inconvenience from the slender
endowment and scanty revenue of the numerous religious men officiating in the College at Biggar. They had therefore resolved, in chapter
assembled, after mature consideration, and with the consent of the
venerable John Stevenson, prothonotary apostolic and precentor of the
Metropolitan Church of Glasgow, first provost of the College of Biggar,
and present vicar of the Parish Church of Dunrod, to give up all and
whole the produce, rents, rights, and emoluments belonging to the
vicarage of Dunrod, so far as their power extended, in order that they
might be united, annexed, and incorporated with the provostship of
the said College. They provided, however, that a vicar stipendiary
should be appointed to discharge the duties of the Parish Church of
Dunrod, and should receive for stipend twenty merks Scots annually,
together with a house and garden, and an acre of arable land. They
conclude by calling on the bishop of the diocese to approve and confirm the nomination of the paid vicar, and the annexation and incor-
poration of the produce and rents of the vicarage and other things, as
already stated; to supply any omissions that they had made; and to
accept the signatures of their agents, acting in their name. To the
charter is appended the seal of the monastery, and the subscription of
the abbot and monks, and of John Stevenson, provost of the College
of Biggar.

John Stevenson, or Steinstoune, as he spelled his name, was the
last Roman Catholic precentor of the Metropolitan Church of Glasgow.
He was the first provost of the Collegiate Church of St Mary's of
Biggar, and held, besides, the office of a Lord of Session. An interesting relic of this ecclesiastic, long preserved by the late Principal
Lee, is now in the possession of Adam Sim, Esq. This is a copy of
the historical fragments of the Babylonian priest Berosus, which belonged to him, and which has his autograph both on the title-page and
on the last leaf. The following is the inscription on the last leaf:—

' Spe expecto,
Sum ex libris magistri Johannis Steinstoune, Metropolitane Glasguensis
præcentoris, de Collegiat. Eccles. Be Marie de Bigger præpositi—et Ami-
corum, 1548.'

The glory of Biggar Kirk, as a collegiate establishment, was short-
lived. The provost, canons, singing boys, and poor men, scarcely felt
themselves warm and at ease in their new possessions, when they were
roused and perturbed by the thunders of Knox and other leaders of
the Scottish Reformation. The crusade against popish idolatry burst
forth with destructive fury in 1559. The monasteries and other
religious houses were attacked and demolished by the ' rascal multitude,' and their revenues reverted to the Crown, or were seized by
the rapacious and turbulent nobles. How far the principles of the
Reformation had at that time made progress among the burgesses of

Biggar, it is perhaps impossible now to say. The powerful influence exerted over them by Lord Fleming, in virtue of his feudal rights and prerogatives, would no doubt prevent them from laying violent hands on the new ecclesiastical edifice of Biggar Kirk, had they been so disposed. The monuments of idolatry connected with its walls were, at any rate, few. The heads of two or three saints, the emblems of a dove, or even of a serpent, were not calculated greatly to rouse the destructive propensities of the Reformers, who may have sprung up within the bounds of the burgh and barony. Some of the most offensive may have been defaced in the manner in which they are now to be seen. The altars would be overturned, the sacred furniture and utensils would be carried off, the priests would cease to perform their masses, the organ and the singing boys would become silent, and the poor bedesmen would no longer sit at the graves of the founder and his relatives, and pray for the safety of their souls.

A great difficulty was felt in supplying the places of the Romish priests. A sufficient number of regularly ordained Protestant clergymen was not to be found. It was, therefore, laid down in the 'First Book of Discipline,' that 'To the churches where no ministers can be had presentlie, must be appointed the most apt men, that distinctlie can read the common prayers and the Scriptures, to exercise both themselves and the Church till they grow to greater perfection, and in process of time he that is but a reader may attain to a further degree, and by the consent of the Church and discreet ministers, may be permitted to minister the sacraments,' etc. The names of bishop and archbishop were distasteful to the Presbyterian Reformers, and therefore they appointed persons whom they called superintendents, who were employed in visiting the churches in a district assigned them, and preaching the word from parish to parish. Under this arrangement, William Millar was reader at Biggar in 1567, and William Hamilton in 1571, with a salary each of L.20. It is not unlikely that these two officials had been prebendaries in the collegiate establishment of Biggar, as it is known that this class was largely employed at the period as readers and exhorters. In 1574 a new ecclesiastical arrangement, carried into effect by the Earl of Morton, then Regent of the kingdom, provided that several parishes should be placed under the pastoral superintendence of one minister, while the readers were still to continue to discharge their duties in each parish.

During the existence of this plan, Ninian Hall was appointed minister of Biggar, Lamington, Hartside, Coulter, Kilbucho, and Symington, with a salary of L.114, 13s. 4d. The readers in these parishes, and their salaries, were as follows, viz.: at Biggar, David Makkie, L.20; at Lamington and Hartside, John Lindsay, L.22, 4s. 5½d.; at Coulter, William Millar, L.16; at Kilbucho, Andrew Jardine, L.16; and at Symington, John Lindsay, L.16. In 1576 Walter Haldane was minister of Biggar, with a stipend of L.112, and the kirk land of Biggar;

and the reader was John Pettilloch, with the former salary of L.20. Walter Haldane had also the oversight of the parishes of Coulter, Lamington, and Symington. He appears in the end to have committed some misdemeanor; for in May 1588 he was deposed, as unworthy to fill his sacred office. The readers and exhorters were debarred from celebrating marriages or administering the sacraments, but it appears that in many instances they overstepped the bounds prescribed to them. We find, for instance, in the records of the Presbytery of Glasgow, that James Waugh, reader at Quothquan, was accused of celebrating irregular marriages; and was, besides, a drunkard, a fighter, a wanton, and inconstant. It was therefore declared by the General Assembly, in 1580, that 'thair office is no ordinar office within ye Kirk of God;' and in the year following it was enacted that this office should be finally abolished, that the churches should be arranged into a number of presbyteries, and that none but a regularly ordained clergyman should be permitted to discharge the duties connected with public worship.

Although the ecclesiastical system of Scotland was changed at the Reformation, it yet seems that, for a considerable period afterwards, some of the clerical staff of Biggar College was kept up, at least in name. William Fleming, a son of John Fleming of Carwood, was presented to the office of provost, and the parsonage and vicarage of the Collegiate Church of Biggar, by John Lord Fleming, on the 1st of January 1573. This person, or perhaps another of the same name as he, is styled a servant of Lord Maitland of Thirlestane, obtained a tack of the teinds of the parsonage and vicarage, in 1590, from commissioners appointed by John Lord Fleming to sell or wadset such of his teinds and benefices as they should see fit, during his absence from this country. William Fleming, who obtained this tack, procured a decreet from the Lords of Session, on the 26th November 1593, against the feuars, farmers, parishioners, tenants, tacksmen, rentallers, and others indebted in payment of the teinds, fruits, rents, and emoluments of the provostrie of the College of Biggar, and the parsonage and vicarage of Thankerton, united and annexed to the said provostrie, commanding them to make payment, under the penalty of having diligence executed against them, and being committed to ward in Dumbarton Castle. A gift of the provostship, with its fruits, rents, emoluments, and casualties, was conferred by John, Earl of Wigton, on Patrick Fleming of Ballach, on the 31st of March 1661. John, Earl of Wigton, patron of the College Kirk and prebendaries thereof, with consent of William Fleming, the provost, on the 14th of May 1616, granted a disposition in favour of James Duncan of the prebendship that was endowed with the teinds of Auchynreoch, and the two acres of land lying in the town and territory of Kirkintulloch. Whether these persons officiated as the parish ministers of Biggar, we have not been able to ascertain.

As we formerly stated, the parish of Thankerton was joined to the Collegiate Kirk of Biggar previous to the Reformation. It was this circumstance that led the Commissioners for the Plantation of Churches, on the 5th of December 1617, to unite and annex the Church and Parish of Thankerton to the Church and Parish of Biggar, and to decern that the Earl of Wigton, patron of these churches, and tacksman of their teinds, should provide and maintain a passage-boat on the Clyde, for the accommodation of the parishioners of Thankerton, when they attended divine service at the Kirk of Biggar. The people of Thankerton by and by became averse to repair to the Kirk of Biggar, and they rebelled in the same way as the people of Libberton afterwards rebelled in regard to the Kirk of Quothquan. On the 13th of May 1630, the minister of Biggar lodged a complaint with the Presbytery of Lanark, that the parishioners of Thankerton refused to attend the Kirk of Biggar, on the ground that it was inconvenient to travel so far to the examinations, by which they were prepared for participation in the sacrament of the Supper. The parishioners were therefore summoned before the Presbytery, to show the grounds of their refusal. On the 27th of the same month they appeared by commissioners before the Presbytery, and positively asserted that they would not attend divine service at Biggar; 'quhairfore ye breether ordaine ye censures of ye kirk to proceed against thame for contumacie.' On the 10th of June following, they again appeared, and informed the Presbytery that they had held an interview with the Earl of Wigton, and that he had promised with all possible diligence to meet with the Presbytery in order to concert some method, 'how ye Kirk of Thankerton may be served.' The Presbytery therefore thought it advisable to proceed no further with the infliction of spiritual censures on the people of Thankerton. The dispute, however, was not so soon settled. We find that in the spring of 1635, the Archbishop of Glasgow wrote a letter to the Presbytery of Lanark, ordering George Ogstoun, minister of Covington, to signify to the parishioners of Thankerton that they should repair to the Kirk of Biggar, in accordance with the decision of the Commissioners for the Plantation of Churches. The Presbytery, however, brought the subject before the Synod; and the result in the end was, that Thankerton was joined to the parish of Covington.

Thomas Campbell was minister, or what was called parson and vicar of Biggar, about the beginning of the seventeenth century. On the 13th February 1607, he granted a tack of the teinds of Biggar, during his lifetime, to John, Earl of Wigton, for the payment of four chalders of oatmeal, between 'Youl and Candlemas,' and relieving his Lordship of the communion elements and all stents and taxation. In 1644, when the Presbytery of Biggar was formed, a Thomas Campbell was still minister of Biggar; but whether this was the same individual who granted the tack to the Earl, it is very difficult to say. At

that time Mr Campbell was an old man, incapable of discharging the
duties of his office. The pulpit of Biggar was therefore, for several
years, supplied by members of the Presbytery. Many applications
were made to the Earl of Wigton to issue a presentation in favour of
some acceptable minister, but nothing was done till October 1646,
when a letter was laid before the Presbytery of Biggar from his
Lordship, 'whairin he did nominat Mr Alexander Livingston, now
minister at Carmichael, for ye Kirk of Biggar;' and a 'supplicatione'
from the parishioners was at the same time presented, calling on the
Presbytery to take all necessary steps to forward so desirable a settlement. The Presbytery therefore lost no time in prosecuting the
matter before the Presbytery of Lanark; and this Presbytery having
obtained a decision favourable to the translation from the Commission
of the General Assembly, and being satisfied that Mr Livingstone was
inclined to accept the presentation, they agreed to transport the said
Alexander Livingstone to the Kirk and Parish of Biggar. Mr Livingstone was most acceptable both to the Presbytery and the people of
Biggar. He was an eloquent and effective preacher. On the 27th of
January 1647, he preached a popular sermon, from Eph. iv. 11, 12,
before the Presbytery, preparatory to his settlement, which gave the
members so great satisfaction, that they put on record that they praised
God for the gifts and graces which He had bestowed on their intended
colleague. The following extract from the report of his induction, on
the 3d of February 1647, can hardly fail to be read at the present day
with interest by the parishioners of Biggar:—'And haveing seriouslie
exhorted ye whole people of that congregatione, especiallie ye present
elderis of ye same, that in regaird they had been so long destitute of a
pastor, and now that they had received one soe hopefull to doe good
among theme, and one whome they had so earnestlie socht for, that
they wold testifie yr thankfullnes to God for him, and that they wold
reverence and obeye him as yr pastor in all things in the Lord.
Thairafter the said ministeris, elderis, deacones, and parochiners respective, in signe of yr consent, did tak the said Mr Alexander Livingstone be ye hand, and gave to him most heartilie ye richt hand of
fellowschip.' Mr Livingstone, as is well known, demitted his charge
in 1662, rather than comply with the new ecclesiastical arrangements
then established by law. His future history is shrouded in obscurity.

No record exists, so far as we know, that describes the ecclesiastical
condition of the parish of Biggar during the persecution, from 1662
to 1688. It appears to have been favoured with the ministrations of
one or two successive curates; and there is evidence to show that
some hot contentions took place in consequence of the withdrawal of
the parishioners from the Parish Kirk, and their attendance on conventicles.

The first curate at Biggar, of whom we know anything, is Richard
Brown. His name appears repeatedly in the books of the Earl of

Wigton, as having received his stipend, which appears to have been paid partly in money and partly in victual. For instance, it is recorded that there was allowed 'Richard Brown, minister at Bigyar, the soume of fourscore pund qlk completes his silver stippand cropt 1674.' The following order regarding the payment of his victual stipend, from William, Earl of Wigton, to Bailie James Law of Biggar, is still preserved:—'James Law, at sight heirof, pay to Mr Richard Broune, our minister at Bigger, twelve bolls victuall, tow pairt meal and third pairt beir, faill not heirin, as ye will be answerable to us; and this, with his receipt, shall be your sufficient warrand. Given under our hand at Bigger Januar sixten, jaj vi seventie-fyve (1675) years.

'WIGTOUNE.'

Mr Brown's receipt is written on the same sheet; and whatever may have been his merits in other respects, we can say at least that he was a good penman. At what time Mr Brown was settled we have not discovered, but we have found references to a kirk session at Biggar in 1666. He was most likely settled by that time, and, though an Episcopalian, appears to have had a kirk session. At that time, and for many years subsequently, the Earls of Wigton paid L.60 Scots, as interest, or, as it is called, annual rent, on a sum of L.1000 to the kirk session of Biggar. The next Biggar curate whose name has been preserved is John Reid, who was translated from Walston to Biggar in the end of the year 1685.

After the Revolution, William Jacque appears to have been for some time minister of Biggar. He was succeeded in 1697 by Robert Livingstone, who was translated from Libberton. Mr Livingstone died in 1733. A Mr Jack was appointed his assistant and successor in 1732; and he continued to officiate here till the 27th April 1749, when he was translated to Carnwath.

The curators of the heirs of John, Earl of Wigton, viz., William, Earl of Panmure, and William Fleming of Barrochan, in 1751, issued a presentation to the Kirk of Biggar in favour of Mr William Haig. The call to this gentleman was supported by Lady Clementina Fleming, and her husband, Mr Elphinston, by Mr Chancellor of Shieldhill, Sussana Lockhart, widow of Mr Dickson of Hartree, by Robert Forsyth, Robert Hamilton, and his sister Margaret Cooper. But, on the other hand, it was opposed by Lady Persilands, Mr Brown of Edmonstone,—James Telfer, Laurence Boe, James Bertram, John Gladstanes, James Smith, and James Melrose, all resident heritors except James Melrose; by four of the elders, twenty-five feuars of the town of Biggar, and one hundred and twenty-five householders. The Presbytery, in these circumstances, decided that they could not proceed to the settlement of the presentee, and resolved to apply to the patrons to be relieved from any further trouble in the matter; but Gideon Lockhart, writer, Lanark, as agent for the presentee, protested and appealed to the Synod of Lothian and Tweeddale. The case,

accordingly, came before the Synod, and afterwards before the General Assembly. The deliverance of the Assembly was, that 'in present
circumstances it is not expedient to appoint the settlement of the presentee, and do remit to the Presbytery of Biggar, to deal with all
concerned, in order to bring about a comfortable settlement of the
parish.'

As the parishioners, almost unanimously, still persevered in their
opposition to the settlement, the Presbytery found that they could
proceed no further in the case; and therefore another appeal was
made to the higher ecclesiastical courts. The Commission of the
General Assembly appointed a committee to deal with objections.
The following objections were laid by the elders before the committee:—'1st. He began on a high enough key, but he was not able
to hold out the whole length of the service. 2d. That he was so un-
wieldy and infirm, that they had no prospect of his being able to
perform the duties of his office by visiting his parishioners, particularly the sick.' The whole people intimated that they adhered to
these objections. The committee thereupon exhorted them to be
cautious what they said, as every statement made would go to proof;
and reminded them that further opposition on their part would have
the effect of keeping the Church longer vacant. The answer of the
parishioners was, that they were determined to persevere in the course
on which they had entered, as in their opinion the settlement of Mr
Haig would be no better than a vacancy. The consequence of this
decided opposition was, that Mr Haig was induced to write a letter
to the Presbytery from Edinburgh, on the 8th of June 1754, resigning any right which he might have acquired to the incumbency of
Biggar.

On the 27th of June, Bailie Carmichael appeared before the
Presbytery, and laid on the table a presentation to the Kirk of Biggar
in favour of Mr John Johnston, minister of the Gospel in the Castle of
Edinburgh. John Gladstanes, one of the elders, at the same time
presented a petition, signed by all the elders, the resident heritors,
and a large number of the heads of families, craving that the Presbytery would proceed to the settlement of Mr Johnston with all convenient speed. Mr Johnston was consequently inducted to the charge
of Biggar on the 26th September 1754. Mr Johnston died on the
15th of October 1778. The next incumbent of the parish of Biggar
was Mr Robert Pearson, who, as elsewhere related, was violently
obtruded in 1780. Mr Pearson dying in 1787, Mr William Watson
was admitted to the charge on the 23d October 1787. This divine
died in 1822, and was succeeded in 1823 by the present incumbent,
the Rev. John Christison, A.M.

The Flemings, from an early period, were patrons of the Parish
Church, and also of an hospital dedicated to St Leonard. No account
of this latter institution can now be obtained, and the very spot on

which it stood is not known. It is supposed that the lands belonging to it were those of Spittal on Candy Burn, and that it was from this circumstance that they acquired their name; Spittal being a corruption of the Latin word hospitium—a house of entertainment. We know that Malcolm Lord Fleming, who founded the College Kirk of Biggar, bestowed the church lands of Spittal on this establishment for the endowment of one of the prebendaries, who was to be called Canon of the Hospital of St Leonards. The charter chest of the Wigton family contains many documents which refer to the patronage both of the Church and the Hospital. There is, for instance, a precept of Sasine, granted by James II., for infefting Robert Lord Fleming in the lands of Biggar, and the patronage of the Church and Hospital, which bears date 31st May 1446. This was relative to a charter proceeding upon the personal resignation of David Lord Hay of Yester. A claim, it would seem, was made by Lord Hay to these patronages, and a lawsuit was the consequence. Commissioners appointed to settle the dispute held a meeting at Glasgow on the 31st of July 1469, and gave forth a decreet, by which they declared that the patronage belonged to Robert Lord Fleming, as the true, loyal, and only lawful and undoubted patron of the Church of Biggar. Reference is also made to Lord Fleming's right of patronage to the Church and Hospital of Biggar in documents dated 1470 and 1472. The patronage of Biggar Kirk has remained with the Fleming family and their descendants ever since, and at present (1862) is the property of Lady Hawarden, the daughter of the late Admiral Fleming.

The stipend of the Parish Church of Biggar, which, in 1821, was fixed at seventeen chalders, half oatmeal and half barley, was two years ago augmented to nineteen. The sum derivable from this source is stated to be L.307, 3s. 0¾d. per annum. An allowance of L.8, 6s. 8d. is also given for communion elements; and the glebe, extending to ten acres, is said to let at L.4, 4s. per acre. The free teind in the parish is still upwards of L.200.

CHAPTER X.

The Presbytery of Biggar.

THE Presbytery of Lanark was originally composed of twenty-one parishes. About the year 1640 an agitation was set on foot to constitute a new Presbytery, the seat of which should be at Biggar, and which should consist of eight parishes in the Upper Ward connected with the Presbytery of Lanark, and four in Tweeddale connected with the Presbytery of Peebles. At the General Assembly in 1641, John Lord Fleming, who was the representative elder for Biggar parish, presented a petition in favour of this scheme, which was referred to the visitation of the bounds. The agitation was still kept up; and at the General Assembly which met at Edinburgh in August 1643 the subject was amply discussed; and after due trial, and the hearing of all parties, it was resolved to erect the new Presbytery, and to grant to it full power of jurisdiction, the exercise of discipline, and all the liberties and privileges belonging to any other Presbytery. At the same time, it was agreed that the formal establishment, or, as it was called, the entry and possession, of the new Presbytery, should be suspended during the pleasure of the General Assembly. Principal Baillie says that this was done 'because of my Lord Fleming's small affection to the common cause.' The meaning of this most likely is, that by this time his Lordship had deserted the cause of Presbytery, and gone over to the side of the King and Episcopacy. The ministers and elders of the parishes embraced in the new Presbytery presented a petition to the General Assembly which met at Edinburgh in June 1644, craving that the reverend court should without further delay constitute the Presbytery. This 'supplicatioun being read in audience of the General Assembly, and thereafter the Commissioners from the Presbyteries of Lanark and Peebles personally present being at length heard, in what they could say or allege therein; And the said supplicatioun and desire thereof with the alledgiances and objections made against the samine being taken into consideration by the Assembly, and they therewith being fully and ripely advised, the Assembly, after removing of the parties, and after consideration of the premises and voycing of the foresaid desire, Ordaines the entrie and possessione of the foresaid Presbyterie of Biggar, consisting of the particular kirks above mentioned, to begin now presently; And appoints and ordaines all the ministers and ruling elders of the forsaid kirks above specified, whereof the said Presbytery consists, to meet and convene with all conveniencie at the said Kirk of Biggar, which is the place and seat of the samine Presbyterie ; And the Assembly refers to the Commissioners, to be appointed by them for the public affairs of the Kirk, to determine to what Synod this the said new erected Presbyterie shall be subordinate, as also to prescribe the order and solemnities that shall be necessar for entering and possessing the ministers and elders in the said Presbyterie.'

The following are the names of the clergymen who, along with a ruling elder from each parish, formed the Presbytery of Biggar at its institution in 1644 :—Thomas Campbell, Biggar ; Robert Brown, Broughton ; Alexander Somervail, Dolphinton ; Kenneth Logie, Skirling ; George Bennet, Quothquan ; Andro Gudlatt, Symington ; John Currie, Coulter ; Robert Elliot, Kilbucho ; William Dickson, Glenholm ; Thomas Lindsay, Walston ; and George Ogstoun, Covington. The Kirk of Wandel and Lamington was at the time vacant, and one of the earliest cases that came before the new Presbytery was a dispute regarding the settlement of this parish. The previous incumbent, Mr James Baillie, died in 1642 ; and a violent controversy arose between Douglas, Earl of Angus, proprietor of Wandel, and Sir William Baillie, proprietor of Lamington, as to which of them had the right to appoint a successor. As they could come to no agreement, both of them exercised the right of patronage. Baillie presented John Currie, and Douglas, Andrew M'Ghie. The case came before the Presbytery of Lanark, and afterwards before the higher ecclesiastical courts. A decision was given in favour of Douglas, and consequently of M'Ghie. The Presbytery of Lanark having, accordingly, appointed M'Ghie to preach before the people of Lamington in March 1644, the Lady of Lamington, aided by several other women, took possession of the pulpit in a tumultuous manner, and prevented the presentee from obtaining an entrance, and, of course, a hearing,—her Ladyship stoutly declaring, ' that no dog of the house of Douglas should ever bark there.'

This was too heinous an offence to be lightly passed over by the divines of the Lanark Presbytery. They lodged a complaint against the lady and her abettors with the Privy Council; and the consequence was, that a decree was issued, commanding the accused to enter their persons in ward in the Tolbooth of Edinburgh. This was accordingly done ; and they remained in confinement till a fine imposed on them of 1000 merks was paid to the Lanark Presbytery. The members of this court were not yet satisfied. They wished her Ladyship to appear before them, and make a public expression of her deep contrition for an offence ' so scandalous for the present, and so dangerous for the time to come.' Before this part of the case could be finally disposed of, the Presbytery of Biggar was formed, and the Lady of Lamington was now within its jurisdiction. The Presbytery of Lanark desired that her Ladyship and the other delinquents should be sent by the

Presbytery of Biggar to Lanark to make atonement before the court, the authority of which she had violated. After much altercation, the answer of the Biggar Presbytery was, 'That they would do nothing of that kind till they should receive a pairt of the soume lately determined by the Council to the Presbytery of Lanark.' The ground on which this claim was made, was that several members of the Biggar Presbytery had, while members of the Lanark Presbytery, expended money in prosecuting the case.

The Presbytery of Biggar itself resolved to deal with the Lamington ladies; and, accordingly, they were cited to appear before it on the 25th December 1644. The minute of that date states, 'This day compeired the Ladie Lammingtoune; and being accused of ane scandell committed be her in ye Kirk of Lammingtoun by her resisting and stopping of Andro M'Ghie (expectant sent yr be ye Presbyterie of Lanark), who came yr upon ye Lord's day to preach, schoe did confesse the samyn resistance, bot withal did solemnlie protest that she had no ill intention, neither any thocht either to profane God's Sabbath or house, or to hinder preaching, bot onlie schoe satt and stayed Mr Andro to enter ye pulpitt, and went into the samyn, onlie for fear of losing her husband's richt (he being absent for the tyme in England in the publick service), or for fear of some ill or greater inconvenience which might have fallen furth. And nothwithstanding whairof, yett was content to refer herself to ye Presbyterie to mak satisfactione as they pleased. Whairupon the Presbyterie, after dewe advyse, did ordaine her, the next Lord's day, in her awin kirk, and in her ordinary saitt, to confess her fault, and in most humble manner to crave pardon, when schoe suld be called upon be the preacher efter his sermon. And being also desyred to delaite these who were her helpers and attendants in the said resistance, schoe did declare ingenuously upon her conscience that none of all her folkes did stirre, or move out of yr places, except two, who went to the pulpitt doore with her, to witt, Catherine and Jennet Bailyie. Whairenent the Presbytery having called in ye wholl summoned persones, did absolve them except these two, whom they enjoined to mak yr public repentance, the same day and place, and in manner foresaid. And to that effect did ordaine Mr Thomas Lyndsay to preach yr ye said day, and receive the confessiones and testificationes of the repentance of ye said offenders, and to report ye next day.' The report given in at next meeting of Presbytery was, that the Lamington ladies had in every respect complied with the sentence of the Presbytery.

Andro M'Ghie, after all, was not settled at Lamington. He seems to have withdrawn; and John Crawford, another nominee of the Earl of Angus, was settled in that parish on the 11th of August 1645. On that day, it is recorded that possession and collation were given to this gentleman, by the Presbytery handing him the key of the kirk-door, going to the manse and putting out the fire of the former occupants, and ' bigging on a fyre for the said Mr John,' and by delivering ' eard and stane' in the manse, yard, and glebe land, lying within the barony of Wandel.

One of the most notable proceedings of the Presbytery was the visitation of the churches within its bounds. This was conducted in a most searching and inquisitorial manner. After the minister of the parish to which the visit was paid had preached a sermon, he was removed, and the elders were called in one by one, and strictly interrogated if their pastor preached sound doctrine; if he was painful in preaching twice on Sabbath and once on a week-day; if he regularly visited his parishioners, and particularly the sick; if he kept up family worship in his own household, and enjoined it on others, etc. The elders were then removed, and the pastor himself was called in, and questioned if he had any complaint to make regarding his elders, or the state of the kirk and parish. The answers elicited on these occasions involved not merely the Presbytery, but the inhabitants of a parish, in a great amount of vexation and trouble. When the members of Presbytery once entered on a case, they were most indefatigable in searching out every particular regarding it, and most inexorable in exacting due homage to their authority and laws. During these visitations, we find that John Currie of Coulter had complaints to make regarding the ruinous condition of his kirk and kirkyard dykes. George Bennet of Quothquan was annoyed at the enmity that prevailed between his parishioners in Libberton and Quothquan, the Libbertonians refusing point blank to attend religious ordinances in the Kirk of Quothquan. Robert Brown of Broughton had accusations brought against him for having advised Sir David Murray of Stanhope to join Montrose. William Dickson of Glenholm 'regraitted' that his kirk was in bad condition, and that the kirkyard was likely to be carried away with the water. George Ogstoun of Covington was offended because Sir Francis Douglas had buried a child in his kirk. Andro Gudlatt of Symington was blamed that he preached doctrine noways edifying; that he delivered only one discourse on Sabbath; that he did not introduce the 'Directorie' in proper time; that he had baptized a child at Biggar without knowing whether it was dead or alive; that he had failed to repair his manse, which is described as being 'as base as a cottar's house;' and that he was puffed up with self-pride. And Kenneth Logie of Skirling complained that he did not receive the amount of stipend to which he was entitled.

Another point on which the members of Presbytery were most exacting, was the visitation and catechizing of families. They drew up a set of regulations and questions, which were first to be expounded from the pulpit, and then used when the pastor went from house to house. The principal points into which he was to make inquiry were, if the family made prayers morning and evening; if the Lord's day was properly observed, by prayer, reading the Scriptures,

attending religious ordinances, and abstaining from frequenting common inns, from lascivious, worldly, and idle conversation, from feeing
- servants, or making any kind of merchandise; if every household had
a Bible and a psalm-book, and every member of it could read; if any
scandalous persons were in the family, and, if there were, to report
them to the kirk session; and, lastly, if all the social duties of husband
and wife, parent and child, master and servant, were duly observed.

Another subject which engaged the attention of the Presbytery, in
1645, was the introduction of the 'Directory for Public Worship.'
This was readily adopted by the Presbytery, and all the members
began to introduce it in the month of August of that year, having
first read and expounded it to the people of the several parishes
from the pulpit. The only exception was Andro Gudlatt of Symington, who thus justified himself when called on by his brethren to
explain his conduct: 'He thocht it best,' he said, 'to delay and not to
be over sudden, until he did see a farther settling, for he feared
changes; and if the King should prevail and bring in Bishops, they
wold call us false knaves, and say we wold turn to any thing, and not
spair to embrace ye masse.' This reply gave the brethren great offence,
and led, with other delinquencies, to the suspension of the 'holy brother.'

The whole of Britain, at the time at which the Presbytery of Biggar was formed, was in a very disturbed state, in consequence of the
war between Charles I. and a portion of his subjects, and in Scotland
particularly by the campaigns of Montrose. The members of Presbytery were alternately swayed by hopes and fears. They held
solemn days of thanksgiving for the victory of Fairfax in Northamptonshire, the capture of the town of Newcastle by the Scots army,
and the defeat of Montrose at Philiphaugh by General Leslie. On
the other hand, they had to fast and mourn for the triumphs of Montrose, and the invasion and victories of Cromwell. After the battle
of Kilsyth, five of them fled from their manses and their flocks altogether, and the meetings of Presbytery were suspended for two months,
which is termed a 'long vacancie occasioned be the insolencie of ye
barbarious enemie approaching to this parte of ye countrie.' No
sooner was Montrose defeated at Philiphaugh, and all apprehensions
of immediate danger were removed, than the fugitives came out of
their hiding-places, and returned to their charges. They now assumed
a vast amount of courage; and in order to cover the disgrace of their
retreat, they had the audacity to take to task those who kept their
posts and boldly faced the danger. The minute on this subject is so
interesting and amusing, that it must be quoted entire. The day on
which this trial took place was the 15th October 1645. 'This day ye
Presbyterie took tryell of the breether's carriage, who had stayed at
home, and not fled ye tyme of the enemie's abode in thir quarteris,
after this manner,—first, ye said breether (being saxe in number, to
witt, Robert Brown, William Dickson, Andro Gudlatt, George Og-

stoun, George Bennet, and Thomas Lindsay) being desyred to answer certain queries, did give satisfactorie answers yrunto, as I. if they did sie James Graham in his Leaguer—the answer negative, II. if they had socht or received protection from the enemie—the answer negative; III. if they did preach and pray against the enemies of God's Kirk and these wicked men—the answer was affirmative, every one of them remembering his text of Scripture and sundry of the doctrines, whilk the Presbyterie did consider was to the purpose and a clear evidence of yr honestie and good affectione; IIII. if they had bocht any plundered gear—yr answer was negative; V. if they did blame thair breether for flieing—yr answer negative; VI. if both in privat and publick they had dissuaded yr people from compliance with ye enemy—yr answer wes that they did so; VII. if they had read or caused read James Grahame's orders—the answer was negative: Next, because they willingly did offer themselves to any tryell: And lastly, in respect the voyce of the countrie was, that they carried themselves both honestly and courageously, therefore the Presbyterie were satisfied with them, and every one giving praise to God, did rejoice one with another.'

From repeated expressions in the records of the Presbytery, we might infer that the army of Montrose visited the Biggar district. The members talk of 'ye approach of ye barbarous enemie to this part of ye countrie,' and inquire what the carriage of each other was during 'ye tyme of ye enemies' abode in ye countrie,'—if 'they bocht any plundered geir' from the soldiers, and if they saw Montrose, or James Graham, as they invariably call him, in his leaguer. These statements, though not entirely explicit, would yet seem to indicate that Montrose's army had come nearer the Upper Ward than the camp or leaguer established at Bothwell, which was about thirty miles distant. We can, however, find no account in any history that Montrose's army, or even a detachment of it, visited the Biggar district, either during the time the chief leaguer was maintained at Bothwell, or during the march to the south of Scotland previous to the battle of Philiphaugh.

It was one of the lamentable results of the unhappy contentions which at that time prevailed, that the Presbyterian clergy resolved to regard certain political opinions and actions as ecclesiastical offences. Malignancy, or an adherence to the cause of Royalty, was held by them to be one of the most grievous delinquencies, and they set themselves with uncommon zeal to ferret out every person in their respective parishes that, by word or deed, could in the least degree be regarded as leaning to the side of their Sovereign. The Presbytery was divided into sections, each consisting of two or three parishes, and in these a most thorough search was made for malignants. This brought the members of Presbytery into collision with the local gentry, most of whom were attached to Montrose and the cause of Royalty. The most notable offenders on whom they pounced were—

Sir David Murray, Gideon Murray, John Weir, and John Lauder, of
Broughton; Sir Francis Douglas of Covington; Christopher Baillie of
Walston; John Baillie of St John's Kirk; Thomas Sommerville and
Alexander Rodger of Quothquan; John Brown of Coultermains; and
William Lindsay of Birthwood, and his son Andrew. All of these
persons were in the end forced to appear before the Presbytery, to
acknowledge their offence, and to crave pardon.

It is interesting to note that the members of Presbytery, on the
morning of the 5th of September 1650, hastened to Biggar, without
any previous concert, but every one of his own accord. They found
the town in a sad state of uproar. This was occasioned by the arrival
of news of the defeat of the Scots army at Dunbar. After calling on
the name of the Lord, the Presbytery appointed next day to be observed as a day of solemn fasting and humiliation for the sins of the
land, and the manifestations of divine displeasure which had afflicted
the people. Nearly a hundred years afterwards, the Presbytery
appointed Tuesday, the 10th of September 1745, as a day of fasting,
prayer, and humiliation for the abuse of the long-continued peace,
and the gross immorality and wickedness of all ranks; 'recommending
it withall to the several ministers to warn their people of their present
danger from a Jacobite party at home and a popish power abroad,
to maintain their loyalty to our present Sovereign King George and
his royal family, and to adhere to our present happy constitution,
both in Church and State.' The whole members of Presbytery, as
elsewhere stated, left their livings in 1662, rather than comply with
'a tyrant's and a bigot's bloody laws.'

For some time after the Revolution, the Presbyteries of Biggar
and Peebles held their meetings conjointly. The members were few,
and they had no fixed place of meeting. We find that they assembled
at Biggar, Peebles, Kilbucho, Kirkurd, Linton, but most frequently
at the Hills of Dunsyre, a place previously occupied by the famous
preacher, Mr William Veitch, who, after the Revolution, was settled
for some time at Peebles. James Donaldson of Dolphinton, and
Anthony Murray of Coulter, are the only members of the Biggar Presbytery that appear to have survived the storms of twenty-eight years'
persecution, and to have been restored to their pulpits after they had
been vacated by the hated curates. In a few years these aged divines
were also removed, so that shortly after the close of the seventeenth
century we find the Presbytery composed of entirely new incumbents.

The records of the Presbytery are contained in fourteen volumes.
In the early part they are very imperfect, whole years' transactions
being altogether awanting. The period from 1650 to 1660 is a blank,
and so is also the period between 1662 and 1688. For a number of
years after the Revolution, they are of a very abbreviated character;
but from the commencement of last century they are of ample extent,
and complete.

CHAPTER XI.

The Covenanters of the Biggar District.

JAMES VI. was at first, by profession at least, a zealous Presbyterian. After he was assailed by a mob while attending a meeting in the Tolbooth of Edinburgh, and especially after he had a certain prospect of ascending the throne of England, he began to look coldly on Presbyterianism, as being, in his opinion, incompatible with the prerogatives of monarchy. He therefore laboured till he succeeded in introducing the office of bishop into the Church, and also several religious ceremonies, such as the confirmation of youths, the observance of holidays, private baptism, private communion, and kneeling at the Eucharist, which were commonly called the Five Articles of Perth, from having been adopted at a General Assembly held at that town. He was contemplating still further innovations, when he died, in 1625, leaving it as an injunction on his son and successor Charles, to prosecute with all vigour the scheme on which he had himself so foolishly entered. In this way he laid the foundation of an unhappy contest, that raged in Scotland for more than half a century, that caused an incalculable amount of disorder, cruelty, and bloodshed, and in the end was the means of driving the Stewart dynasty from the throne of these realms.

Charles I., true to the doctrines in which he had been educated, and madly bent on executing the scheme projected by his father, at length ordered that a liturgy and book of canons should be introduced into the service of the Scottish Kirk. The great body of the Presbyterian clergy met this order with the most strenuous opposition, as they regarded it as an unwarrantable innovation on the proper mode of conducting public worship, and as wholly invalid, inasmuch as it had not received the sanction of the General Assembly. The bishops, finding the order disregarded, caused the Privy Council to pass an Act to enforce its observance, under the pain of horning. The minister of Biggar, and most of the other ministers of the Presbytery of Lanark, refused to introduce the service-book and book of canons into their ministrations. The Bishop of Glasgow, in whose diocese they were, therefore, sent a messenger of arms to the Presbytery with a letter, commanding every member to buy the obnoxious books, and on his refusal to put him to the horn. The Presbytery were nothing daunted. They met, and resolved to petition the Privy Council against the introduction of the two books; and as their moderator, Mr

John Lindsay of Carstairs, who was a subservient tool of the Bishop
of Glasgow, would not join in the petition, they requested him to resign his office. Lindsay, therefore, closed the diet, and, with two or
three others, left the meeting. Those who remained, constituted
themselves into a new meeting of Presbytery, and chose Alexander
Somervail of Dolphinton as moderator *pro tempore*, when the petition
was unanimously adopted. The Privy Council, instead of lending an
ear to this petition, and others of a similar kind, passed an Act making
it treason for any body of men to meet for the purpose of adopting
such memorials.

This arbitrary step, and the commotions which took place in Edinburgh on the first introduction of the service-book in the Church of
St Giles, on Sabbath, the 23d of July 1637, led to an organization of
all ranks, and ultimately to the adoption of a Solemn League and
Covenant. This document was signed on the 28th February 1638,
in the Greyfriars Church, Edinburgh; and copies of it were immediately transmitted to every parish, to receive the names of those who
stood well affected to the Presbyterian cause. Before the end of
March it had been read in nearly all the churches of the Upper Ward,
and signed, amid demonstrations of weeping and enthusiasm, by nearly
the whole people. The only notable exceptions to this unanimity
were the parishes of Douglas, Carmichael, and Carstairs, in which
clerical or baronial influence prevailed in favour of the innovations.

The General Assembly that met at Glasgow in 1638, set the authority of the King's Commissioner at defiance. It declared the proceedings carried on and sanctioned by the six previous Assemblies to
be null and void, and denounced and abolished the canons, the liturgy,
the High Commission Court, the Articles of Perth, the forms of consecration, and the whole Episcopal system, root and branch. The
gauntlet was thus thrown down to the King. He took it up, and
both sides prepared for war. The Earl of Wigton, and his son John
Lord Fleming, had signed the Covenant, and publicly declared that
they would always maintain the doctrine and discipline now established by the General Assembly and the voice of the nation. Lord
Fleming immediately took the field at the head of his father's retainers.
His Lordship, and Lords Montgomery, Loudon, Boyd, Lindsay, and
others, seized the Castle of Strathaven, and compelled all the gentlemen in Clydesdale suspected of favouring the royal cause to give
security that they would not rise in arms. They then marched to
Douglas, where they expected a hot reception from the Marquis of
Douglas. They had no cannon, and entertained little hope of being
able to make a successful assault on the strong Castle of Douglas;
but the Marquis did not remain to offer any resistance; so they readily
obtained possession of the Castle, and left it garrisoned with a detachment of their troops.

Lord Fleming, in all likelihood, came to Biggar from Douglas, and

completed his levies. He soon marched down the Tweed and joined
the other Covenanters, who had now assembled in considerable numbers under the command of General Leslie, an old veteran, trained to
war under the renowned Gustavus Adolphus, King of Sweden. The
King had also raised a considerable army, and the blazing balefires
soon gave token that he had crossed the border, and was penetrating
into the country. He published a proclamation at Dunse, requiring
the rebels to submit within ten days, fixing a price on the heads of
the leaders, and confiscating their estates. He intended also to make
this proclamation at Kelso, and a strong detachment was despatched
thither under the command of the Earl of Holland. The Scots getting
information of this intended movement, Lords Fleming, Munro, and
Erskine, with their followers, to the number of a thousand horse and
foot, met them before they could accomplish their purpose, and
offered them battle. The English, however, did not relish the encounter, and fled, losing two hundred men in the pursuit. Principal
Baillie says that it was thought that Holland's commission was to cut
off all opposition; but his soldiers that day were a great deal more
nimble in their legs than their arms, except the cavaliers, whose right
arms were no less weary in whipping than their heels in jading their
horses.

The Scottish army afterwards encamped on Dunse Law, and presented a strange spectacle of military and religious enthusiasm,—the
din of warlike evolutions intermingling with the voice of psalms, and
the prayers and sermons of the preachers. 'Every company,' says
Baillie, 'had fleeing at the captain's tent-door a brave new colour
stamped with the Scottish arms, and the motto, "For Christ's Crown
and Covenant," in golden letters. Our soldiers were all lusty and
full of courage, the most of them stout young ploughmen; great
cheerfulness in the face of all. They were clothed in olive or grey
plaiden, with bonnets having knots of blue ribands. The captains,
who were barons or country gentlemen, were distinguished by blue
ribands worn scarf-wise across the body. None of our gentlemen
were anything the worse of lying some weeks together in their cloaks
and boots on the ground. Every one encouraged another. The
sight of the nobles and their beloved pastors daily raised their hearts.
The good sermons and prayers morning and evening, under the roof
of heaven, to which the drums did call them instead of bells, also
Leslie's skill, prudence, and fortune, made them as resolute for battle
as could be wished.' The King, seeing the resolution and warlike
spirit of the Scots, considered it hazardous to risk an engagement,
and therefore an agreement was entered into, to settle the differences
by negotiation. A conference was accordingly held at Berwick by
commissioners on each side; but their proceedings were in the end
rendered abortive by the obstinacy and duplicity of Charles, who
would not recede from his design to establish Episcopacy in the

northern part of his dominions.   No alternative was left but a fresh
appeal to arms.

The Scots had disbanded their army, but the tocsin of alarm was
again sounded.   The barons summoned forth their retainers, and the
clergy beat the 'drum ecclesiastic' with fury and effect.   Lord John
Fleming once more set up his standard at Biggar, and called on the
retainers of his house, and others in the district well affected to the
cause, to assemble around it.   At a meeting of the Presbytery of
Lanark, on the 25th June 1640, a communication was read from his
Lordship, desiring every minister in the Presbytery to intimate from
his pulpit, that the muster of men, according to the stipulated number, would take place at Biggar on Thursday first.   The Presbytery
at the same time chose Alexander Livingstone, minister of Carmichael,
and afterwards of Biggar, to be chaplain to his Lordship's Upper
Ward Regiment.   He was to continue a month at this post, and at
the end of that time was to be relieved by George Bennet, minister
of Quothquan, who was assured that, in the event of his not receiving
payment from the general fund for support of the army, he would
be paid by the Presbytery at the rate of 30s. per day.

The Scottish army, amounting in all to 23,000 infantry and 3000
cavalry, struck their tents in the month of August 1640, and marched
into England.   On arriving at the Tyne, they found that General
Conway, the commander of the English army, had erected batteries
on its banks near Newburn, to oppose their passage.   The Scots were
nothing discouraged.   They opened so severe a fire from their artillery
that the English were forced to abandon their guns; and a detachment of the Scots having crossed the river, encountered the English
cavalry, and put them to flight.   Conway's army was thus thrown
into a state of rout and confusion, and the cavalry retreated to Durham, and the infantry to Newcastle.   The Scottish troops were induced, by the solicitations and subsidies of the Puritan party in
England, to prolong their stay till their grievances were redressed.
After some negotiation with the Royalists, it was ultimately agreed
that all oppressive courts should be abolished, that no money should
be levied without consent of Parliament, and that Parliaments should
be summoned every three years.   The Scottish army, on the completion of these transactions, received L.300,000, in name of brotherly
assistance, and returned to their native country.

At the very time at which Lord Fleming and his retainers from
Biggar were in England upholding the cause of the National Covenant,
and contending against the arbitrary designs of the King, a meeting of
nineteen Scottish noblemen was held at Cumbernauld House to support
the royal cause.   They subscribed a bond, in which they declared
that, from a sense of the duty which they owed to their religion, their
king, and country, they were forced to join themselves in a covenant
for the maintenance and protection of each other.   Their country,

they said, had suffered by the special and indirect practising of a few individuals, and therefore their object was to study all public ends which might lead to the safety of the religion, laws, and liberties of the poor kingdom of Scotland. This meeting was convened principally by the efforts of James, Marquis of Montrose, who, at first, took part with the Covenanters, and was at Dunse Law and Newburn; but, conceiving that his merits had been overlooked, and feeling special offence that Argyle was made his superior in the Senate, and Leslie in the field, he had obtained a secret interview with Charles when in England, and pledged himself to support his cause. The document, signed by the Earl of Wigton and the other noblemen,—' Montrose's damnable Band,' as Baillie terms it,—was ordered by the Committee of Estates to be burnt by the hands of the common hangman, and Montrose was seized and thrown into prison.

The Earl of Wigton, having thus embraced the side of the Royalists, was honoured by receiving several letters from the King's own hand. They are still preserved, and present a very creditable specimen of caligraphy. In one of them, dated Oxford, 21st April 1643, the King, after expressing his desire to preserve the affections of the people of his native kingdom, and to do everything to contribute to their happiness, goes on to say: ' but knowing what industry is used (by scattering seditious pamphletts, and employing privat agents and instruments to give badd impressions of us and our proceedings, under a pretence of a danger to religion and government) to corrupt their fidelities and affections, and to engadge them in ane unjust quarrell against us their King, wee cannot, therefore, but remove those jealousies, and secure their feares from all possibilitie of any hazard to either of these from us. Wee have, therefore, thought fitt to require you to call together your freinds, vassalls, tenents, and such others as have any dependencie upon you, and, in our name, to show them our willingnes to give all the assurance they can desire, or wee possibly graunt (if more can be given than already is), of preserving inviolably all those graces and favours, which we have of late graunted to that our kingdome, and that wee doe faithfullie promise never to goe to the contrarie of any thing there established, either in the ecclesiasticall or civil government, but that wee will inviolably keip the same according to the lawes of that our kingdome.'

The Earl himself does not seem, after all, to have taken a very active part in the support and advancement of the cause of Charles. It was otherwise with his son John, who had been suspected of leaning towards the King when he was with the Scottish army in England, and who now fairly turned his back on his old friends the Covenanters. After his relative Montrose had gained the brilliant victories of Tibbermuir, Inverlochy, Aulderne, Alford, and Kilsyth, he threw off all disguise, and at the head of a body of his vassals, joined the army that had fought so gallantly and successfully in behalf of the King.

He marched with Montrose to Philiphaugh, near Selkirk; the object
of that general being, now that all opposition was beat down in Scotland, to make a diversion in favour of the Royalists on the soil of
England. Montrose posted his infantry on an elevated piece of ground
on the left bank of the Ettrick, while he himself and his cavalry occupied
the adjacent town of Selkirk, and thus allowed the river to divide his
forces into two portions. General Leslie, who had been despatched
from England with a detachment of 5000 or 6000 men to oppose
Montrose, taking advantage of a thick mist, on the morning of the
13th September 1645, fell on both flanks of his opponent's infantry
at one time. The left flank was immediately thrown into confusion,
and driven from the field; but the right occupying a more advantageous
position, with a wood in the rear, fought for some time with great
obstinacy, but in the end had to yield to the furious onsets of the
Covenanters. Montrose, with Lords Fleming, Napier, and Erskine,
Sir John Dalziel, and other officers, so soon as the din of the battle
was heard, rallied the cavalry, and hastened to the scene of action.
They did everything that skill and bravery could suggest to retrieve
the disasters of the day; but all their efforts were unavailing. They
were forced to retire, and seek safety by speedy flight. They hastened
up the Yarrow, struck along the bridle-road over Minchmuir, and
came to Traquair House. Receiving little countenance here, although
the Earl of Traquair was also a partisan of the King, they proceeded
up the Tweed to Peebles, where they halted a short time during the
night, and early next morning pursued their journey. They came to
the Upper Ward and crossed the Clyde, and here they met with the
Earls of Crawford and Airley, who had escaped by a different route.
Montrose and a number of his friends fled to the Highlands, while
Lord Fleming and others concealed themselves in the Lowlands.

The Convention of Estates were not disposed to pass over the
delinquencies of those who had taken up arms against them, and
subjected them to so much terror, inconvenience, and expense. They
appointed a section of their number, called the Committee of Processes
and Money, to institute actions against those persons who had taken
part in what they termed the Rebellion of Montrose.

Lord Fleming remained concealed for some time, but the Committee
of Processes permitted him, on the 9th of February 1646, 'to repair
home to his owne dwelling house on his giving James, Earl of Callender, as a cautioner, that he would appear before the Committee on
the 8th of March following, at Linlithgow, or where they should
happen to be sitting at the time, and that he would conduct himself
with all due propriety, under a penalty of fiftie thousand punds.'
The Committee, on taking his case into consideration, decided that he
should pay a fine of L.6400; but agreed to remit a portion of it,
should the allegation of his Lordship, that he had expended large
sums in the support of troop horses, foot soldiers, dragoons, and others

in the public service, be satisfactorily established. In a document which his Lordship laid before the Committee, he stated that he had possession of no lands or teinds belonging to his father's estate, 'except onely twentie chalders victuall payed to him of the estate and lands lyand about Biggar, within the shyre of Cliddisdaill, quhilk is allowed upon him be his father for keiping his purse and buying his cloathes.' He declared that he had no casual rent, no money owing him by 'band' or otherwise, and no moveable goods or geir that could be escheated. He had borrowed, he said, L.20,000, which he had expended in the public service, viz., 'be out reicking himself ane colonel at the first two expeditions, be buying of armes and uther necessre furnitour for his regiment, and by paying his officers and men,' and supporting himself, as he had never received any of the public money at all. Besides, there were the charges, expenses, and pay of a garrison of forty soldiers, with a captain and lieutenant, who had occupied the Castle of Boghall of Biggar since the 14th of September last, and had been maintained solely out of his own portion, and the revenues of his father's estates; large sums were also due for the soldiers that had been quartered, and the depredations that had been committed on his father's lands in and about Biggar and Cumbernauld; and further, all public orders had been obeyed, the monthly contribution paid, and 'twenty horsemen of trouperis and dragounners with forty-aucht foot sojouris had been out reicked and put furth be my Lord's rent and estaite sufficientlie armed and mounted since the said fourteine day of September last bypast.' The whole expense incurred in the equipment and maintenance of twenty dragoons and ninety-eight foot soldiers, including those lying in the Castle of Boghall, amounted to 8090 merks. The Committee, having duly weighed all the pleas advanced, decided that the account rendered by John Lord Fleming was sufficient to 'exhaust the wholl fine abovewritten imposed upon him for his delinquency, doe therfor discharge the said John Lord Fleming of the said fyne.' His Lordship thus appears to have got rid of the heavy exaction imposed on him for the crime of taking part in what was then called the Rebellion of Montrose.

Charles II. had scarcely been restored to the throne, when he utterly repudiated the engagements into which he had entered in the days of his adversity, to uphold and maintain the Presbyterian form of church government, and the covenanted work of Reformation. He resolved to overturn the whole fabric of Presbyterianism, and to set up Prelacy in its stead, which the great majority of the Scottish people hated nearly as much as Popery itself. The Covenants were repealed; the opposition to Episcopal church government was denounced as sedition; the clergy who had been admitted to livings subsequent to the abolition of patronage were declared to have no title to them, and were required within four months to obtain presentation from the patrons and collation from the bishops, with assurance, if they did not

comply, that they would be ejected by military force. The consequence of this edict was, that about the end of 1662, no fewer than
three hundred and fifty clergymen threw up their livings rather than
do violence to their conscientious convictions. The valedictory sermons which they delivered, the high esteem in which they were held,
and the destitute circumstances to which they were reduced, made
their flocks rally round them, and listen to their instructions with a
keener relish than ever. Hence arose the practice of holding meetings for public worship in the fields, which became so obnoxious to
Government, that an Act was passed prohibiting the ejected ministers
from approaching within twenty miles of their former parishes, and
declaring it sedition for any person to contribute to their support.
The people disregarded the edicts of the drunken and infuriated man
who at that time swayed the destinies of Scotland, and doggedly
refused to abandon their old pastors and wait on the ministrations of
the ignorant and subservient curates who now occupied their pulpits.
Hence fines, imprisonments, tortures, and death, were resorted to; and
the people on several occasions were goaded on to repel aggression,
and assert their liberties and their rights, with arms in their hands.

From a list published by Wodrow, it would seem that in 1662
the whole of the ministers of the Presbyteries of Lanark and Biggar
left their pulpits. This is rather surprising, as some of them are
understood to have had a strong leaning towards Episcopacy, and, in
fact, to have been the creatures of the bishops. It may be that even
these parties were indignant at the violent and tyrannical conduct of
Middleton and his drunken associates, and were thus induced to throw
in their lot with their brethren. Wodrow's list of the members of
the Biggar Presbytery is as follows:—Alexander Livingstone, Biggar;
Anthony Murray, Coulter; James Donaldson, Dolphinton; Patrick
Anderson, Walston; James Bruce, Archibald Porteous, Alexander
Barton, John Rae, Symington; John Crawford, Lamington; William
Dickson, Glenholm; John Greg, Skirling; and Robert Brown,
Broughton. These men chose rather to throw themselves on the wide
world, and to subject themselves to all the hardships of an unsettled
life, and all the contumely and persecution of an infuriated Government, than do violence to their convictions of duty, and succumb to
the dictates of tyranny. It must ever be a matter of regret, that
almost nothing of their subsequent history is known. John Rae,
minister of Symington, as mentioned by Wodrow, was apprehended
in 1670 for preaching and baptizing in his own house, and sent to
Edinburgh, where he was confined in the Canongate Tolbooth. After
an examination he was sent to Stirling, but his fate is not stated.
Anthony Murray of Coulter was held in high esteem by the Nonconformists, though we are not aware that he got into further trouble on
account of his adherence to the covenanted work of Reformation, than
being forced to abandon his manse and stipend. Wodrow states that

he was a relative of the Duchess of Lauderdale, and that in consequence of this connection, he was selected by a number of influential ministers to present an address to the Duke in favour of the Covenanters. It is a tradition, we are told, that after leaving his clerical charge, he continued to reside in the parish of Coulter, and employed himself in practising the healing art, facetiously remarking, that he would now make the doctor keep the minister. At this period, an Anthony Murray acted as factor for the Biggar estate of the Earl of Wigton. We have examined several of the books of his accounts, which are still preserved in the Fleming archives; and as he appears to have resided in Biggar or its neighbourhood, and to have enjoyed much of the confidence and respect of his employer, we have been rather disposed to think that this is the same person as the outed minister of Coulter. It will be observed, that his name appears twice in the inventory of old effects sold at Boghall Castle in 1681.

The work of imposing fines for nonconformity was early commenced in the Upper Ward. Middleton's Parliament, which met at Glasgow in 1662, fined the parish of Biggar L.1071, 5s., Quothquan L.181, 2s. 6d., Walston L.308, 8s., Dunsyre L.177, 12s., Carnwath L.6739, 19s. 8d., Lanark L.5000, etc. Heavy fines were imposed on many individual gentlemen in the same district. Among others may be mentioned, Christopher Baillie of Walston, L.9600; William Brown of Dolphinton, L.1200; Andrew Brown of the same parish, L.600; William Bertram of Nisbet, L.480; James Baillie, St John's Kirk, L.240; Thomas Gibson, Quothquan, L.360; John Kello, there, L.260; and John Braid, Hillhead, Covington, L.600.

The Covenanters who rose in arms, in 1666, in the south-west of Scotland, after capturing Sir James Turner at Dumfries, proceeded to the Upper Ward. They halted a short time at Douglas, and then marched to Lanark, where they listened to sermons preached by some of the clergymen who accompanied them, and with great solemnity and uplifted hands renewed the Covenants.

From the strong leaning of the people of Biggar and its neighbourhood in favour of the principles of the Covenant, and the intense indignation which they felt at the tyrannical measures of the Government, it is likely that some of them took part in this insurrectionary, or, as it may rather be called, defensive movement. We know that Major Learmont, proprietor of Newholm, in the parish of Dolphinton, and the Rev. Wm. Veitch, tenant in the Westhills of Dunsyre, and son of the Rev. John Veitch, for forty-five years minister of Roberton, joined the Covenanters at a hill above Galston, and took a leading part in their proceedings. Major Learmont was appointed to the command of one of the divisions of cavalry, and escorted Sir James Turner out of the town of Lanark, to protect him from the assaults of the inhabitants. The Covenanting army marched from Lanark to Bathgate in the midst of extremely stormy weather, and ascertaining

Q

that they were to receive no assistance from the inhabitants of the
Lothians and the city of Edinburgh, they resolved to make a detour
by the end of the Pentland Hills and march to Biggar. Mr Veitch
was sent in disguise to Edinburgh, to hold an interview with their
friends in the city; but he was apprehended and detained as a prisoner. On his expressing his readiness to march against the Whigs,
he was less strictly guarded, and effected his escape, and thus witnessed the conflict at Rullion Green, and arrived that same night at
the herd's house in Dunsyre Common. Major Learmont fought
bravely on the field of Rullion Green. He commanded the party
that defeated the second charge of the enemy. General Dalziel, seeing his men give way, hasted forward a detachment to their rescue,
when Major Learmont was attacked by four horsemen, and his horse
was shot under him. He started to the back of a fold dyke, shot the
first trooper that approached, mounted his horse, and escaped.

It was near the close of day when Dalziel advanced his whole
army to the last charge ; and as his numbers were 3000 against 900,
the poor Covenanters had no alternative but to scatter themselves
among the deep defiles of the Pentland Hills, where they were safe
from the pursuit of the cavalry, and where they were soon hid by the
darkness of the night. Large numbers on the day following hasted
to their homes by Carnwath and Biggar.

James Kirton, who from 1655 to 1657 was one of the ministers of
Lanark, in his 'History of the Church of Scotland,' has brought a
severe charge against the inhabitants of these towns, for their cruelty
to the poor distressed fugitives. His information, he says, was obtained at the spot, and therefore was entitled, as he insinuates, to the
most implicit credit. His statements, which are deeply tinctured with
the superstitious notions that prevailed at the period, can, however,
at the most, only apply to a few individuals, and not to the mass of
the inhabitants. He refers to the subject more than once, but we will
quote only one of his passages. He enumerates various reasons why
the people listened more readily to the ministrations of the outed
clergymen than of the curates, and among others gives the following,
viz.: 'Another reason was the strange judgments seen upon those who
were or had been persecutors. It is well known and observed what
happened those who injured the poor Whigs who fled from Pentland.
In the Upper Ward of Clydesdale, when some of them fled through
Carnwath, one of the townsmen carried some of them into the moss
and murdered them. It was told by the people of the village to myself within a little time thereafter, that frequently a fire was seen to
arise from that place in the moss where the murder was committed,
and thereafter creeping overland, it covered the murderer's house.
Himself, as I was told, perished, and his children are beggars to this
day. What curses befell the people of Biggar who were equally
guilty of this fact, and how poor Laurence Boe died in high despair,

accusing himself of the secret murder of two, was well known, and as well remembered by the neighbours.' It would be most interesting to us at the present day to know what the curses were to which Kirton refers. They were, he says, well known at the time he wrote his history; but whatever they were, they are now utterly forgotten.

The curates who were thrust into the pulpits of the Upper Ward were, from all accounts, weak and despicable individuals; and some of them, particularly the curate of Carnwath, were known to lead profligate and licentious lives. The description given by Bishop Burnet of the curates generally, was, no doubt, applicable to those of the Upper Ward. 'They were,' he says, 'the worst preachers ever I heard; they were ignorant to a reproach, and many of them openly vicious. They were a disgrace to their order and to the sacred function, and were indeed the dregs and refuse of the northern parts.' Such preachers were not likely to recommend the cause of Prelacy, and induce the people to wait upon their ministrations. Some of the Upper Ward churches appear to have been entirely deserted. We may refer in this respect to the Church of Symington. The manse and church, in consequence of standing some time unoccupied, fell into a state almost of ruin. On the 21st of June 1676, Gavin Steven and Hugh Telfer, masons and wrights, Biggar, at the instance of the curate, Robert Lawson, who, at that time, had most likely been newly appointed, underwent a lengthened examination, on oath, before some clerical brethren, regarding the state of the manse and church. They declared that it would take 400 merks Scots to put the manse in habitable order, making it, as they said, 'water tight and wind tight, with new theiking, glass windows, boards and cases, locks, sneckes, and slots, and casting the house without and within.' In regard to the kirk, they reported that the west gable had slidden, and had a rift in it, and that if it were not helped it was likely to fall, and that very shortly; and that, as there were no glass in the windows, no pulpit, and no reader's desk, it would be necessary to supply them. The whole expenses for the repair of the kirk, it was estimated, would be L.48 Scots. On the 5th of July following, Robert Lawson, the curate, reported, at a meeting of his clerical colleagues, that after a search he had succeeded in finding the kirk box, the session book, the iron stauncher, and the iron holder, in which the sand-glass stood; and that the only thing now awanting was the key of the kirk box.

The practice of attending field-meetings, or conventicles as they were called, was still obstinately maintained in the Upper Ward, as well as in many other districts in Scotland. The Parliament, in 1670, passed a severe enactment against these meetings. Every unauthorized person, who should preach, expound Scripture, or pray in any place, except in his own house and with his own family, was to be imprisoned till he found caution, to the amount of 5000 merks, not to be guilty of a similar offence again, or otherwise agree to remove out

of the kingdom altogether; but if he so officiated at a meeting in the
fields, he was to suffer death and the confiscation of his goods. It
was also enacted, that all persons who should attend such ministrations should be fined *toties quoties* in certain specified sums, according
to their stations in life; and that these sums should be doubled if the
ministrations were conducted in the open air. The fine of a landed
proprietor was the fourth part of his annual rent; of a farmer or master tradesman, L.25 Scots; of a cottar, L.12 Scots; and of a servant,
the fourth part of his yearly fee. Notwithstanding the severity of
the Government, a number of conventicles were held in the neighbourhood of Biggar. The Rev. John Kid, who was taken prisoner at the
battle of Bothwell Bridge, and executed at the Cross of Edinburgh on
the 14th of August 1679, preached one day on the hill of Tinto, to a
large assemblage of the inhabitants of this district. Patrick Walker,
the packman of Bristo Port, Edinburgh, who wrote the lives of several Covenanting worthies, and who most likely was present on this
occasion, tells us that Mr Kid, in the course of the service, gave out a
part of the second psalm to be sung, and accompanied the reading of
it with a commentary. When he came to the sixth verse, viz.,

> 'Yet, notwithstanding, I have Him
>   To be my King appointed;
> And over Sion, my holy hill,
>   I have Him King anointed,'—

he exclaimed, with many tears, 'Treason, treason, treason, against
King Christ in Scotland. They would have him a King without a
kingdom, and a King without subjects. There is not a clean pulpit in
all Scotland this day, curate nor indulged. Wherefore, come out
from among them, and be separate, saith the Lord, and touch not
these unclean things; and I will be a Father unto you, and ye shall be
My sons and daughters, saith the Almighty.'

The hill of Tinto, situated in the midst of a populous district, and
affording concealment and security in its deep declivities, was a favourite preaching place with several of the other heroes of the Covenant. Donald Cargill, who was in the habit of saying that he felt more
liberty and delight in preaching and praying in the glens and wilds of
the Upper Ward of Clydesdale than in any other place of Scotland,
came to this district in the beginning of June 1681, after a tour
through Ayrshire and Galloway, and intended on the Sabbath following to preach on Tinto. Mrs Baillie, the Lady of St John's Kirk,
who professed a warm attachment to the Covenant and its champions,
but who was looked on with suspicion by some of its more zealous
and rigid partisans, as a person whose fidelity was likely to give way
in the hour of trial, had begun to feel uneasiness at the frequent conventicles held in her neighbourhood. When she learned Cargill's
design to preach on Tinto, she held a correspondence with some of

the leading Covenanters in the country round; and it appears that they entered so far into her views as to permit her to issue an announcement, that the meeting on Sabbath would take place on a common in the parish of Glenholm, at the back of Coulter Heights. Mr Cargill had taken up his abode in the house of John Liddell, at Heidmire, in the neighbourhood of St John's Kirk; but though communication could thus have been very readily held with him, he received no notice that the place of meeting had been changed. He rose early on the Sabbath morning, and going out to meditate in the fields, he observed numbers of people travelling to the south. On learning from some of them to what place they were going, he said, 'This is the Lady's policy to get us at some distance from her house, but she will be discovered.' He did not return to Mr Liddell's house to get breakfast; but being anxious that the great multitudes from Biggar and the surrounding country, whom he understood were flocking to the place of rendezvous, should not be disappointed, he immediately set out on his journey. The day was very warm, and the road was long and difficult; the consequence was, that by the time he reached the sequestered spot where his friends were assembled, he was very much exhausted. Before he commenced his labours, a man went to a rivulet and brought him a drink of water in his steel bonnet, and supplied him with another draught in the same way between sermons; and these were all the refreshments which he tasted during the day. He discoursed on the 6th chapter of Isaiah in the forenoon, and in the afternoon delivered a sermon on the words in the 11th chapter of Romans, 'Be not high-minded, but fear.' We can easily conceive the thrilling effects that would be produced by religious discourses preached in a region so solitary and mountainous, and by the lips of a man so full of ardour and faith as Donald Cargill. Holmes' Common can never be surveyed without identifying it with that great meeting.

A short time afterwards, Cargill preached his last sermon on Dunsyre Common, on the text, in the 20th verse of the 26th chapter of Isaiah, 'Come, my people, enter thou into thy chambers,' etc. Walker the packman, who was present, says, 'He insisted what kind of chambers these were of protection and safety, and exhorted us all earnestly to dwell in the clefts of the rock, to hide ourselves in the wounds of Christ, and to wrap ourselves in the believing application of the promises flowing therefrom, and to take our refuge under the shadow of His wings, until these sad calamities pass over, and the dove come back with the olive leaf in her mouth.'

After sermon, he did not leave the muir till it was dark, as he was afraid of falling into the hands of his enemies, who, he knew, were eager to apprehend him, and obtain the reward of 5000 merks offered by the Government for his person. The Lady of St John's Kirk was present, and desired him to accept accommodation at her house; but he felt a great reluctance to comply, as he could not bring himself to

regard her with entire confidence, and was in the habit of saying,
' Whatever end she might make, there would be foul wide steps in her
life.' Mr Walter Smith and Mr Boig, two lay gentlemen who had devoted
themselves to the work of upholding the persecuted faith in Scotland,
insisted that he would accept the invitation, and he so far yielded
that he accompanied the lady to Covington; but refusing to go
farther, he and Messrs Smith and Boig found accommodation in the
house of Andrew Fisher, Covington Mill.

James Irvine of Bonshaw, a brutal individual, and a dealer in
horses, having got a commission from the Privy Council to hunt down
and apprehend all persons who attended field conventicles and were
obnoxious to Government, and hearing that a great Covenanting meeting was to be held in the Upper Ward, left Kilbride on Sabbath
evening with a party of dragoons, and arrived about sunrise at
St John's Kirk. He searched the house very closely; but finding
none of the individuals of whom he was specially in quest, he proceeded to the Murrays, or Muirhouse of Thankerton, the residence of
a well-known Covenanter, Mr James Thomson. A fine opportunity
was thus presented to the Lady of St John's Kirk to apprise her friends
at Covington Mill of their danger; but the good lady was too much
paralysed with her own fears to cause anything of this kind to be done.
Bonshaw, disappointed in not finding any of the leading Covenanters
at the Murrays, set off with his troop to the house of Andrew Fisher,
and his spouse, Elizabeth Lindsay, at Covington Mill, and there he
apprehended Messrs Cargill, Smith, and Boig. He was vastly elated
with his success, and blessed the day that he had been born to find
so rich a prize. He carried the prisoners to Lanark, and lodged them
in the Tolbooth till he obtained refreshments; and then mounting
them on the bare backs of horses, he tied Mr Cargill's feet below the
horse's belly, with circumstances of great cruelty. In this posture he
conveyed them hastily to Glasgow; and after halting a short time
in that city, transferred them to the prison of Edinburgh. They
were arraigned before the Court of Justiciary on the 26th of July
1681, found guilty of high treason on their own confessions, and
condemned to be hanged next day at the Cross of Edinburgh, and
their heads to be placed on the Nether Bow. This was accordingly
done; and thus their names were added to the roll of martyrs who
have laid down their lives for opposition to tyranny and in defence of
religious liberty. Irvine of Bonshaw, as is well known, a short time
afterwards, was killed in a squabble with one of his drunken associates
at the town of Lanark; and it has ever since been considered by some
persons as a special mark of divine vengeance, that he suffered
punishment in the place where he had exercised his cruelties on
Donald Cargill.

After this period Mrs Baillie, or, as she was usually termed, the
Lady of St John's Kirk, fell into considerable odium with the more

rigid of the Covenanters. It was rumoured that she had been accessory to the capture of her late friends at Covington Mill. The rumour, it appears, had even reached those men in their confinement in the Tolbooth of Edinburgh, short as the time was which they were allowed to live. One of them, Walter Smith, in his dying testimony, as inserted in the 'Cloud of Witnesses,' however, exonerates her from that charge. In reference to this he says, 'As to my apprehending, we were singularly delivered by Providence into the adversaries' hands, and, for what I could know, betrayed by no one, nor were any accessory to our taking more than we were ourselves. And particularly, let none blame the Lady of St John's Kirk.' This lady, in the killing years that followed, actually, it is said, became a persecutor, and allowed no person to dwell on her lands unless they took the oath of abjuration, and attended the ministrations of the curates. When Mr John Johnston in Grangehill of Pettinain, and Francis Leverance of Covington, two of her old Covenanting friends, waited on her to remind her of her solemn declarations in favour of the covenanted work of Reformation, and to remonstrate with her on her inconsistent and injurious conduct, she refused to hold conversation with them, and ordered the door to be shut in their faces. The dread of imprisonment and the forfeiture of the family estate, had, no doubt, produced this change in her professions and deportment; and this incident furnishes another illustration of the unhappy effects produced by persecution for religion's sake.

But two of the most remarkable religious meetings that took place in the Biggar district were held in the Castle of Boghall, under the personal auspices of the Dowager Countess of Wigton, a daughter of Henry Lord Ker, and widow of John Fleming, Earl of Wigton. These meetings were addressed by various outed ministers, and were largely attended by the inhabitants of Biggar and the country round. So daring a contravention of the Act to which we have referred, of course attracted the attention of the tyrants who conducted public affairs in Scotland, and, therefore, the following persons were, at the instance of John Nisbet of Dirleton, his Majesty's advocate, summoned to appear before the Lords Commissioners and Lords of the Privy Council at Edinburgh, on the 25th of July 1672, viz., Anna, Countess of Wigton, James Crichton, John Kello, James Brown, John Dalziel, John Henderson, John and Laurence Tait, James Brown, wright, John Tod, mason, Alexander Gardiner, tailor, John Nisbet, and Alexander Smith, all residing in Biggar;—James Paterson, Carwood; James Crichton, Westraw; William Cleghorn, Edmonston; Alexander Story, there; William Thomson, Boghall; Malcolm Brown, Edmonston; James Cuthbertson, there; Peter Gillies, Skirling Waukmill; John Robertson, procurator, Lanark; John Watson, notar, Carnwath; Thomas Crichton, Wolfclyde; James Glasgow, Whitcastle; John Tweedie, Edmonston; Robert Lohean, Skirling; William Forrest, there; John Newbigging, Carstairs; John Hutchison, Harelaw; John Lochie, Ranstruther; Malcolm Gibson, Wester Pettinain; Ronald Spence, Thankerton; James Thomson, Muirhouse of Thankerton; and James Adam in Netherwarnhill. All of these persons obeyed the summons, and appeared in Edinburgh on the day appointed. The first person brought before the Privy Council was John Robertson of Lanark. He admitted that he had been at the conventicles kept at Boghall; and being commanded to declare upon oath all that he knew regarding the persons who were present at these meetings, and the business that was transacted, he refused to do so, and therefore was ordered to be carried to prison, and there to remain until he should receive further sentence. The Privy Council very likely saw that it would be a difficult and tedious matter to deal with so many offenders, and it was on this account, perhaps, that they appointed the Earls of Linlithgow, Murray, and Dumfries, a sub-commission, to examine the others, and to imprison such of them as would not become informers and give satisfactory answers, and to impose fines on those who were less resolute, and promised to attend no more conventicles in future. Fourteen of them, whose names deserve to be held in remembrance,— viz., James Crichton and John Dalziel, Biggar; James Paterson, Carwood; William Cleghorn, Malcolm Brown, and James Forrest, Edmonston; Peter Gillies, Skirling Waukmill; Thomas Crichton, Wolfclyde; James Glasgow, Whitcastle; James Lindsay, Netherwarnhill; James Thomson, Muirhouse; John Newbigging, Carstairs; John Hutchison, Harelaw; and Malcolm Gibson,—were then examined before the Committee, and as they resolutely refused to give the satisfaction required, they were condemned to suffer imprisonment. What the ultimate fate of these individuals was, and of the others who were arraigned on the same indictment, we have not been able to ascertain. Some of them were, no doubt, subjected to as heavy fines as they could bear, and others may have endured a long captivity on the Bass, or in the dungeons of Dunottar, or even may have been banished to the plantations of America. The Countess of Wigton was fined in the sum of 4000 merks, which she was ordered to pay to Sir William Sharp, his Majesty's Treasurer.

One of those who attended the conventicles at Boghall was Peter Gillies, of the waukmill of Skirling. His subsequent fate is well known to those who are conversant with the history of the Covenanting struggles. He had given refuge to some of the hard-hunted and oppressed preachers of the Covenant, sheltered them for a night under his roof, and supplied them with such victuals as his humble cottage afforded. This act of humanity had been reported to James Buchan, the curate of Skirling, and this professed servant of Christ was never at rest till he got Sir James Murray, the proprietor of Gillies's little tenement, to throw him and his family adrift on the world. After wandering about for some time, he settled at length in the parish of Muiravonside, in the county of Stirling. Gillies was none of those faithless and faint-hearted individuals that could be daunted by persecution, and led to change their opinions and their practices to please the minions of power. He was still a staunch Presbyterian, and readily attended a conventicle, or befriended an outed minister, as often as an opportunity occurred. He thus incurred the resentment of Andrew Ure, the curate of the parish in which he had settled; and in 1682 this worthy obtained a troop of dragoons to apprehend him, but at this time he happily escaped their fangs. He at length returned to his family, and continued to pursue his humble vocation till April 1685, when the curate caused another party of soldiers to apprehend him, and John Bryce, a weaver from West Calder. The soldiers treated him most brutally, and threatened to kill him before his wife, who a day or two previously had been delivered of a child. They searched his house, carried off everything that they could readily transport, and then hurried him away with them to the west of Scotland. On the 5th of May he was served with an indictment at Mauchline, charging him with having cast off the fear of God, and his allegiance and duty to the King; with having approved of the principles of rebellious traitors and blasphemers against God, and of the practice of taking up arms against the King and those commissioned by him; with adhering to the Covenant, and refusing to pray for his most gracious majesty the King. He was tried on these charges before Lieutenant-General Drummond and a jury of fifteen soldiers, found guilty, and condemned to be hanged next day at the Town-end of Mauchline. This sentence was accordingly carried into execution. No coffin was prepared for his remains; some of the soldiers and two countrymen dug a hole in the earth, and there deposited his body in the same state as it had been cut down from the gibbet. Thus died the once humble tenant of Skirling Waukmill, the friend of suffering humanity, the victim of relentless persecution, and the unflinching adherent of the covenanted work of Reformation.

Biggar and its neighbourhood furnished a contingent to the muster of Covenanters that took place, in June 1679, at Bothwell Bridge. The number of countrymen who assembled on this occasion was considerable, and they might have produced very important effects on the Government of Scotland, had they been commanded by proper officers, and not allowed themselves to be torn asunder by contentions regarding topics which, however important they might be in themselves, were completely out of place at such a juncture. On the 22d of June they were attacked by the royal troops under the command of the Duke of Monmouth, and completely routed. Many of the men of the Biggar district escaped. In the fugitive rolls of the period, we find the names of the following, among other persons, who either had been at the Battle of Bothwell Bridge, or had sheltered some of those who fled from that unhappy conflict, viz.: James Crichton; Gideon Crawford, merchant; John Gilkers, heritor; Robert Aitken, merchant; and

R

Alexander Smith, weaver, all belonging to Biggar;—John Fisher, Covington Mill; Robert Brown, smith, Covington Hillhead; James Thomson, Muirhouse, Thankerton; James Weir, Lamington; Andrew Gilroy, Walston; and Hugh Sommerville, Quothquan.

The names of all the persons connected with the Biggar district, who were taken prisoners at Bothwell, cannot now be ascertained. The following have been preserved on account of the fate that ultimately befell them, viz.: John Rankin, Biggar; and James Penman, James Thomson, and Thomas Wilson, Quothquan. The prisoners owed their lives to the clemency of the Duke of Monmouth. Some of the Royalists, and particularly Claverhouse, who was smarting from the defeat which he had, a short time before, sustained at Drumclog, urged that they should all be shot on the field; but Monmouth, who had a leaning towards the Covenanters, would not listen to such a barbarous proposal. Numbering in all about 1400 men, they were marched in a most deplorable state to Edinburgh, and confined like so many cattle in an enclosure called the Inner Greyfriars Churchyard. They were pent up in this place without any covering from the blasts and dews of heaven, and were forced to lie all night on the cold ground; and any one that stirred or made a noise was liable to be fired at by the sentinels. Their allowance of food was four ounces of bread and a small quantity of water daily. Many persons in Edinburgh pitied their condition, and were willing to contribute to their comfort; but the food, clothing, and money which they sent, were, in many instances, not admitted, or appropriated by the sentinels to their own use.

After they had continued in this wretched state for some time, a proposal was made that they should sign a bond not again to take up arms against the King or his authority. Nearly a thousand signed this bond, and were set at liberty; but the remaining four hundred obstinately refused to sign it, and no entreaty, nor even the report that they would all be put to death, could induce them to comply. Day after day they submitted to the most severe privations, and endured the most acute sufferings. As the rigours of winter drew on, the hearts of the authorities began a little to relent, and they were treated with more indulgence and humanity. A few huts were erected to shelter them from the inclemency of the weather, and a more ready access was given to their friends. The consequence was, that about a hundred of them effected their escape, either by climbing over the walls, or being disguised in women's clothes; and a few more, at the earnest solicitation of some Presbyterian ministers, were induced to sign the bond. Their numbers were now reduced to 257 individuals. From the want of sufficient nutriment and exposure to the weather by day and night, their bodies were fearfully emaciated, and many of them were afflicted with acute diseases. It was understood that some of them were now rather disposed to submit to the requirements of Government; but the Privy Council, irritated perhaps by their obstinacy, passed, on the whole of them, a sentence of banishment to Barbadoes. Early on the morning of the 15th November, after they had been confined in the churchyard nearly five months, they were marched to Leith, and put on board a vessel belonging to William Paterson, merchant, Edinburgh, where their sufferings, from want of water, food, and fresh air, and from being jammed together in a narrow hold, were worse than ever. They sailed from Leith Roads on the 27th November, and on the 10th of the following month, when passing the Orkney Islands, were overtaken by a storm, and the ship was ultimately dashed on the rocks. The captain had ordered the hatches to be locked and chained down; and when the vessel struck he refused to open them, but provided for the safety of himself and his men. The consequence was, that some time elapsed before the prisoners could get on deck. About forty of them, by means of boards, reached a place of safety, and the remainder found a watery grave amid the tempestuous surges of the Pentland Firth. Among those saved was James Penman, Quothquan; and among the drowned were James Rankin, Biggar, and Thomas Wilson and James Thomson, Quothquan. Biggar thus furnished at least one unflinching martyr in the cause of the Covenant, whose name is entitled to be held in remembrance in the annals of the town.

The Rev. Dr Robert Simpson of Sanquhar, in his work entitled 'Gleanings among the Mountains,' relates an incident of the Covenanting times, which, he says, occurred at Biggar. It is to the effect that two brothers, of the names of Thomas and James Harkness, were apprehended in the wilds of Nithsdale by a party of dragoons, and conveyed to Edinburgh, where they were placed in confinement. By some means or other they contrived to escape, and, in returning to their native place, had occasion to pass Biggar. The good town, it seems, still possessed some of the persecutors spoken of by Kirton, and, among others, the leader of the very party who had captured the two brothers. Resolving to give him a taste of the terrors which he was in the habit of occasioning to others, they obtained firearms, went to his house, and demanded to see him. His wife denied that he was at home, but a little boy betrayed the place of his concealment. He was instantly seized, dragged to the fields, and ordered to prepare for death. The brothers having blindfolded him with a napkin, caused him to kneel and offer up a prayer; and this being done, they presented their muskets and fired. Their intention, however, was not to kill him; so after the volley they plucked off the napkin from his eyes, and raised him in a state of almost entire insensibility to his feet. This event made a powerful impression on his mind. He began to reflect on his previous course of life, and was struck with its injustice, cruelty, and sinfulness. He ceased to be a persecutor, and entering on a new course of conduct, became an entirely altered man. How far this story may be founded on fact, we have no means of deciding.

Graham of Claverhouse, in course of his murderous raids through the western shires of Scotland, paid occasional visits to the Upper Ward, and there exercised the cruelties for which, in all succeeding times, he has been so infamously distinguished. He was ranging up and down this district in 1685, when he met with James Brown of Coulter, fishing in the Clyde. He caused him to be searched; and a powder-horn having been found on his person, he denounced him as a knave and ordered him to be shot. He commanded six of his troopers to dismount and carry his sentence into execution; but the Laird of Culterallers, who happened to be present, interceded in his behalf, and so his life was spared till next day. He was bound with cords and carried off to the south by the soldiers. He was ultimately confined in the Tolbooth of Selkirk, from which he contrived to escape, and thus eluded the fangs of that stern persecutor, who seldom felt much scruple in imbruing his hands in the blood of his fellow-men.

In order more thoroughly to overawe the people of Biggar and the country adjacent, a detachment of soldiers was stationed in the Castle of Boghall. These soldiers no doubt embraced every opportunity of exercising their cruel and tyrannical propensities on the poor and oppressed inhabitants, and carrying out the behests of a blind and infuriated Government. We find that the Committee on Public Affairs, on the 16th July 1684, wrote a letter to Sir William Murray of Stanhope, Sir Archibald Murray of Blackbarony, and John Veitch of Dawick, stating that they had been informed that conventicles had been held at Carnhill and Colston's Loup, in the county of Peebles, and complaining that these gentlemen had furnished no information regarding the persons who had been present, in violation of the terms of the proclamation of Council, in 1682. They were therefore ordered to make diligent search for, and to apprehend, both the preachers and hearers on these occasions; and to avail themselves in this work of the assistance of the garrison of Boghall.

The Covenanters in the Upper Ward, in spite of all the efforts of Government, kept up their meetings. By means of the Societies which were first formed in December 1681, they maintained a complete organization, and were, no doubt, regularly trained to the art of war, in order to be ready to take advantage of any favourable juncture that might arise, to assert their claims. They carried on a continued correspondence with the Prince of Orange, mainly through Sir Robert Hamilton; and when that Prince arrived in England, they lost no time in holding a great meeting, in the Church of Douglas, on the 29th April 1687, at which it was resolved in fourteen days to raise two battalions, each to consist of ten companies of sixty men each. The result of this step was the formation of a regiment, which still exists, under the name of the 26th, or Cameronian Regiment, and which, on various occasions, has greatly distinguished itself by achievements on the battle-field.

CHAPTER XII.

The North and South United Presbyterian Churches.

IT was the remark of a shrewd Biggar worthy, that Biggar has long been famed for the support which it gives to 'divinity and diversion.' It is certainly the case, that from the time of the Covenant downwards, the people of the Biggar district have been noted for the extent of their theological acquirements, their critical acumen in discussing abstruse points of faith, and the strictness of their religious opinions and practice, and their strong dislike to the undue interference of the State with the Established Church. It was naturally to be expected, then, that the immediate descendants of the men who had contended and suffered in this district for the covenanted work of Reformation, would look with approving countenance on the stand made by the founders of the Secession Church against the defections of the times. They could not submit to what seemed to them such serious errors as patronage restored, the Covenants despised, heretical opinions openly promulgated, vice and profligacy passing unrebuked, and a slavish subserviency to the ruling powers pervading the leaders of the Church, without feeling extreme sorrow and indignation, and applauding the men who stood boldly forward to oppose and rebuke them. This feeling was greatly deepened by the conduct of their own pastors, in reading from the pulpit a document regarding the apprehension of the persons concerned in the execution of Captain Porteous, on the 7th September 1736, in the Grassmarket of Edinburgh, and hence commonly called the Porteous Paper. This document was ordered by the Government to be read publicly by the Established clergy before their congregations, on the first Sabbath of each month, for a whole year, under the penalty, in case of refusal, of being declared incapable, for the first offence, of sitting and voting in any Church Court, and for the second, of 'taking, holding, or enjoying any ecclesiastical benefice in Scotland.' This enactment was held by many of the clergy, and a large majority of the people, to be a manifest and daring usurpation, by the civil magistrate, of powers which belonged exclusively to the Church itself,—in short, to be downright Erastianism. Many of the inhabitants of the Biggar district, at this period, therefore left the Established Church, and attached themselves to the Associate Presbytery, formed in 1733,

and consisting at first of four ministers, viz., Ebenezer Erskine, Stirling; James Fisher, Perth; Alexander Moncrieff, Abernethy; and
William Wilson, Kinclaven. It was augmented, in 1737, by the
accession of the Rev. Thomas Mair of Orwell, and the Rev. Ralph
Erskine of Dunfermline.

The Dissenters of Biggar and its neighbourhood, being far distant
from the towns in which the fathers of the Secession were settled, could
only listen to their ministrations by making long journeys and at rare
intervals; and therefore they petitioned that some of their number
would favour them with occasional visits, till such time as they were
sufficiently organized, and could obtain the services of a settled pastor.
In compliance with this petition, these worthy divines, in the midst of
numerous engagements, found time to come at intervals to this district, and dispense the ordinances of religion to a congregation collected from many surrounding parishes. It was at length decided
that an eligible place for the erection of a church was West Linton,—
a village eleven miles east from Biggar. Accordingly, Ralph Erskine
and Thomas Mair, by order of the Presbytery, proceeded to West
Linton, on Friday, the 24th of March 1738; and there, after sermon
by Ralph Erskine, an election of elders took place, 'by the lifting up
of the hand.' The elders thus chosen were then subjected to an
examination; and on the Sabbath following were formally installed
in their office. On that occasion both of the reverend gentlemen
preached discourses to 'a great and grave auditory,' and they were
afterwards gratified by learning that many persons present were much
refreshed. In August 1738, Ralph Erskine, and James Fisher, then
removed to Glasgow, were sent on a missionary tour to the south of
Scotland, and on the 30th of that month preached at West Linton, and
baptized several children. In the autumn of 1739, Ralph Erskine,
and the Rev. James Thomson of Burntisland, who had also joined
the Secession, were engaged in another of these tours. On Wednesday, the 12th of September, Mr Thomson preached at West Linton,
and dispensed the ordinance of baptism; and in the afternoon they
rode to Symington, three miles to the west of Biggar, where the families who had left the Established Church had fixed the day following
as a season of fasting and humiliation. Both the reverend gentlemen
here preached impressive discourses to an audience whose descendants,
in most cases, continue Dissenters to the present day. At length Mr
James Mair was ordained the permanent pastor of the West Linton congregation, on the 29th of May 1740; and on this occasion the sermon
was preached by the Rev. James Fisher, and was afterwards published.

For twelve or fifteen years the Seceders of Biggar and its neighbourhood waited on the ministrations of the Rev. James Mair, and
Sabbath after Sabbath travelled to West Linton, though many of
them resided twelve and fifteen miles distant. One of the most
zealous Dissenters and constant attenders at West Linton, was Robert

Forsyth, afterwards bellman and gravedigger, Biggar, and father of Robert Forsyth, the distinguished author and advocate. Robert went to Linton in all kinds of weather. Neither 'summer's heat nor winter's snow' stopped his journey. One tempestuous Sabbath morning he rose early, as usual, and, in spite of the remonstrances of his mother, took the road. In passing up the town, he saw James Brown, joiner, another zealous Dissenter, and grandfather of the late Robert John-' ston, merchant, Biggar, standing at his door and gazing on the sky, to discover any symptom of the speedy clearing up of the weather. 'Weel, Jeemes,' said Robert, 'are ye no gaun east the day?' 'As there's nae appearance of the wather rackin' up, I was thinkin' about stayin' at hame,' said James. 'Hoot, man,' replied Robert, 'Mr Mair wull think mair o' us if we gang on sic a day as this, than if we gaed on twa or even three gude days.' So saying, he took his way in the midst of the storm, by Candy, Sandyhill Nick, Slipperfield Muir, and West Water, to Linton.

A movement was at length set on foot to form a Secession congregation at Biggar. The members of Mr Mair's congregation at Biggar, Skirling, Walston, Libberton, and Glenholm, were joined in this movement by the persons in Symington, Covington, and Carnwath, who attended the ministrations of the Rev. David Horn at Davies-dykes, in the parish of Cambusnethan. The exact year in which the congregation was formed is not now known. It seems to have been a short time previous to the year 1754, because during that year a petition, craving a supply of sermon, was presented to the Edinburgh Secession Presbytery from the congregation of Biggar. The main cause which led to the formation of the Biggar congregation was, no doubt, the inconvenience of travelling so far to attend religious ordinances as West Linton and Cambusnethan; but minor causes seem also to have been at work, such as the erection of the Antiburgher meeting-house at Elsrickle, and the attempted violent settlement of Mr Haig in the Parish Church of Biggar. A meeting-house having been built on a piece of ground immediately behind the north side of the High Street, the congregation proceeded, on the 16th of October 1760, to give a call to Mr Samuel Kinloch to be their pastor. This call Mr Kinloch thought fit to decline; and, therefore, the congregation, on the 7th of May 1761, gave a call to Mr John Low, who had studied divinity under Professor Fisher at Glasgow, and who had a short time previously been licensed to preach the Gospel. Mr Low accepted this call, and was ordained on the 30th of September, O.S. The members of the Edinburgh Presbytery present on that occasion were—the Rev. William Hutton of Dalkeith, the Rev. Archibald Hall of Torphichen, the Rev. James Mair of West Linton, the Rev. Mr Pattison of Edinburgh, and the Rev. Mr Kidston of Stow. The leading men in the congregation, and all of them holding the office of elder at the settlement of Mr Low, were—James Telfer, Whinbush;

William Watson, Kirklawhill; James Brown, joiner, Biggar; James
Steel, Elsrickle; James Sommerville, 'Carnwath; John Bertram, and
Robert Wilson. Very little regarding these worthy men is now
known: so quickly does the memory of even good and once prominent
men fade away without the assistance of written records.

Mr Low was a faithful, laborious, and much-respected minister.
In the pulpit his appearance was commanding, his voice rich and
powerful, and his delivery impressive. His discourses were pervaded
by a strain of ardent piety. His theology was that of the severest Cal-
vinism ; and, of course, he was well versed in all the subtleties of that
abstruse creed. It is worthy of notice, that at the time of his settlement he had a valuable collection of theological works. They consisted of 56 folio volumes, 44 quarto volumes, and 70 volumes of
inferior sizes, all of a solid and standard character. The only relic
of his library that we have seen, is the well-known controversial
work on the origin and authority of episcopal church government,
entitled 'Altare Damascenum,' etc., by the historian, David Calder-
wood. It has Mr Low's autograph on the margin, and is now in
the library of Mr Sim, at Coultermains.

Mr Low had a somewhat irritable temper, that brought him into
occasional troubles, both with the members of his own flock, and the
adherents of other churches. The most minute record of some of the
squabbles in which he was embroiled, is to be found in the manuscript
memoirs of William Sim, schoolmaster, who had his headquarters at
Biggar, and was a member of Mr Low's congregation. Mr Low,
shortly after his settlement at Biggar, entered into the marriage
relation with a lady whose name was Janet Henderson. By this
lady he had the following children :—Margaret, Helen, Robert, John,
Janet, James, and Ebenezer. Mr Low continued to discharge his
ministerial duties at Biggar for a period of forty-three years, and
died on the 1st of November 1804.

The successor of Mr Low was the Rev. John Brown. He was the
son of the Rev. John Brown, Whitburn, and Isabella Cranston, a native
of Kelso, and was born on the 12th of July 1784. He studied
general literature and philosophy at the University of Edinburgh, and
theology at the Divinity Hall, Selkirk, under the direction of Dr
Lawson. He was licensed to preach the Gospel, by the Presbytery of
Stirling and Falkirk, on the 12th Feb. 1805, and, after a short proba-
tion, received calls from Biggar and Stirling. The Synod, which at
that time held the power of deciding in the case of competing calls,
assigned him the charge of Biggar. He was ordained on the 6th
Feb. 1806. The weather at the time was remarkably stormy; and the
consequence was, that only three members of the Presbytery of Lanark
attended on the occasion. Dr Harper of Leith, a son of the Rev.
Alexander Harper of Lanark, at the jubilee services of Dr Brown, in
Broughton Place Church, Edinburgh, on the 8th April 1856, said, 'I

have a boyish recollection of the event which you are met to com-
memorate, and of being almost, I cannot say altogether, a spectator
of Dr Brown's ordination. On the morning of that day I sat at the
fireside wrapped up, and ready to be placed by my father in a nook
of the conveyance in which he and a friend were going to the ordination at Biggar. There had been a heavy fall of snow through the
night; and the friend I speak of used to remind me that there was a
little face in the corner that had its own share of gloominess as well
as the weather, when a messenger, who had been sent out to ascertain the state of the roads, reported that it was doubtful whether a
horse and gig could pass. There was no help but to leave me behind.'
Mr Brown's own father preached the ordination sermon; and on the
Sabbath following he was introduced by the Rev. James Ellis of Saltcoats. The congregation at Biggar, to which Mr Brown ministered,
was characterized by great spiritual devotion and general intelligence.
Some of the members were his equals, if not his superiors, in classical
knowledge and literary attainments; while many of them were as deeply
versant as himself in the abstruse tenets of Calvinistic theology, and
in the history and principles of the religious body to which they
belonged. He was thus stimulated, in the highest degree, to diligence
in his preparations for the pulpit, and the diets of examination which
he held in the houses of his members. He studied carefully everything that he delivered in public. He wrote out at full length, and
mandated his discourses, prayers, and casual addresses. Besides the
ministrations in his own pulpit, he was in the habit of preaching in
barns and school-rooms in the adjoining villages, and not unfrequently
in the open air. His son John, in his supplementary chapter to
Dr Cairns' life of his father, gives an anecdote illustrative of his
achievements on his good grey mare in fulfilling an engagement of
outdoor preaching. 'He had,' he says, 'an engagement to preach
somewhere beyond the Clyde on a Sabbath evening, and his excellent
and attached friend and elder, Mr Kello, Lindsaylands, accompanied
him on his big plough horse. It was to be in the open air on the
river side. When they got to the Clyde, they found it in full flood,
heavy and sudden rains at the head of the water having brought it
down in a wild *spate*. On the opposite side were the gathered people
and the tent. Before Mr Kello knew where he was, there was his
minister on the mare swimming across, and carried down in a long
diagonal, the people looking on in terror. He landed, shook himself,
and preached with his usual fervour.'

He delivered a monthly lecture in his own church, the collection at
which was expended in the education of poor children; and he was
among the first who established a minister's library of costly and not
readily accessible theological works—an institution of great importance
to clergymen of limited means in country districts. In the United
Presbyterian body there are now not fewer than 160 libraries of this

s

kind; and the number is from year to year increasing. His little church was, every Sabbath, filled with an auditory that listened with profound attention and admiration to the clear, forcible, and impressive exposition of Scripture truth that proceeded from his lips. The old church was pulled down and a new one built; and a new manse was also erected in a more retired situation, on the south side of the town, finely overlooking the strath of Biggar and the Hartree Hills.

In August 1807, he married Miss Jane Nimmo, a daughter of Mr William Nimmo, surgeon, Glasgow. As her son, Dr John Brown, has justly said, she was modest, calm, thrifty, reasonable, tender, happy-hearted. She was his student-love, and is even now remembered in that pastoral region for 'her sweet gentleness, and wife-like government.' Their union was blessed with four children—two sons and two daughters. They enjoyed the greatest earthly felicity in each other's society; but cruel and envious fate snatched her from him in 1816. He mustered up courage to preach her funeral sermon, and descanted on her virtues and his own loss, amid the sobs and tears of an attached and sorrowing congregation. She was interred in Symington Churchyard, according to her own wishes; and her husband there erected a tablet to her memory.

Down to the year 1815, Mr Brown confined himself, in a great measure, to the discharge of his pastoral duties at Biggar. It was the careful preparation of his discourses for the devout and intelligent people of the Biggar district that laid the foundation of that skill, that eminence in the exegetical and critical examination of Scripture, to which he afterwards attained. It was in Biggar, too, that he commenced that wonderful career of authorship, which is so marked a feature of his life. He was in the habit, at an early period of his ministry, of contributing occasional papers to the 'Christian Instructor,' then under the editorial care of the Rev. Andrew Thomson. In 1816, he started a periodical styled 'The Christian Repository and Religious Register,' which, besides his own articles, received contributions from Dr Lawson, Dr Peddie, Dr Marshall of Kirkintilloch, Dr Balmer, Berwick, Robert Johnston, Biggar, etc. Five volumes of this magazine had been published at the union of the Burghers and Antiburghers in 1820, when it was merged into a conjoint periodical, called 'The Christian Monitor.' The 'Repository' was ably conducted. Its papers were of a highly intellectual rather than a popular cast. To men of education and reflection they were most acceptable; and they can still be read with pleasure and profit. It is interesting to con them over, and think that every one of them was carefully revised in the calm solitude of that retired manse, with its trim garden, standing behind the Silver-knowes of Biggar, and looking forth on the green mountains of Tweeddale.

Mr Brown's first separate publication at Biggar was 'Strictures on Mr Yates's Vindication of Unitarianism.' This was followed in succession by a volume of 'Sacramental Discourses;' by a sermon preached before the Edinburgh Missionary Society, entitled 'The Danger of Opposing Christianity, and the Certainty of its final Triumph;' by 'Remarks on the Plans and Publications of Robert Owen, Esq., New Lanark;' by 'Three Discourses on the Character, Duty, and Danger of those who Forget God;' by a volume 'On Religion, and the Means of its Attainment;' by 'Notes of an Excursion into the Highlands of Scotland;' and 'A Sermon on the State of Scotland in reference to the Means of Religious Instruction.' The statements contained in this last-mentioned discourse, which was preached before the Associate Synod on the retirement of Mr Brown from the office of Moderator in April 1819, were strictly accurate, and all parties have long since admitted their truth; but at the time of its delivery and publication, a considerable party in the Established Church were unwilling to acknowledge that their ecclesiastical institution was chargeable with any defects, and were indignant at any one that attempted to point them out. Hence the Rev. Alexander Craik of Libberton, near Carnwath, and others, opened a heavy battery on Mr Brown for his strictures; but he bore the assault with wonderful equanimity, and lived to see very extraordinary efforts made within the pale of the Establishment itself, to remedy the very evils of which he had complained.

Mr Brown, in the latter part of his ministry at Biggar, was very much occupied with labours of a more public and extensive kind than the sphere of that town afforded. He preached the anniversary sermons of several public institutions, and he was sent out on various missionary tours. On one occasion he visited England, along with the Rev. A. O. Beattie, then Burgher minister at Kincardine, and the Rev. David Dickson and the Rev. Henry Grey, both of the Established Church, Edinburgh. They returned with a subsidy of L.3000. In 1820, on the death of Professor Lawson, Mr Brown was nominated as one of the candidates for the vacant Divinity Chair; but the choice ultimately fell on Dr Dick, Glasgow. In 1817, he refused a call to the congregation of North Leith; but in 1822, receiving a call from the congregation of Rose Street, Edinburgh, the Synod decided that he should accept it; and he took farewell of his Biggar flock in a sermon which he preached from 1 Cor. xv. 1–4. On the occasion of his jubilee, in 1856, he thus referred to the congregation of Biggar:—'A more cordial pastoral relation, I believe, never existed. I respected them for their Christian intelligence and worth, and loved them for their unaffected kindness. They made abundant allowance for my youth, and showed that peculiar kind of affection which is cherished by the mature Christian for the young disciple; for a large proportion of the congregation, when I went to them, were beyond the midst of life, experienced in religion as well as stricken in years. I had great advantages for study; and, I hope, did not entirely neglect them. The acquisitions made in my first charge lay at the foundation of any measure of usefulness to which I may have attained in other situations. Biggar was much endeared to me as the scene of very sweet enjoyments and very deep sorrows. "The dews of youth" lay heavy on these scenes, and their recollection refreshes the heart. It certainly was in my heart to live and die with my people there; but the Head of the Church ordained it otherwise. My connection with that congregation was not dissolved with my own hand. We parted in sorrow, but in peace. Long before I became their minister, their former pastor, the Rev. John Low, a man of a warm temper but kind heart, said to his friend, my father, speaking of his own ministerial life, "We have had our brangles; but they are a sonsy, kindly folk." This is a true saying. I found them "a sonsy, kindly folk;" but we never had any brangles.'

Mr Brown, after leaving Biggar, pursued a successful career of public usefulness. In 1829 he was translated to the congregation of Broughton Place; in 1830 received the degree of D.D. from Jefferson College, United States; and in 1834 was appointed Professor of Exegetical Theology to the religious body with which he was connected. In 1835 he entered into the relation of marriage with Miss Margaret Fisher Crum, only surviving daughter of Alexander Crum, Esq. of Thornliebank, near Glasgow; and by this lady he had one son and two daughters. During the latter part of his life he published, in rapid succession, a number of those valuable expositions of Scripture which he had sketched at Biggar, and which he had perfected during his succeeding pastorates and his professorship in Edinburgh. His separate publications are numerous, amounting to upwards of fifty. They will long be held in esteem by those who value correct sentiment, clear and vigorous expression, and extraordinary critical acumen. He died at his house, Arthur Lodge, Newington, Edinburgh, on Wednesday, 17th October 1858, and was interred in the New Calton Buryingground, beside his second wife, who had predeceased him several years.

Dr Brown's successor in the Associate Congregation, Biggar, was the Rev. David Smith, who was born in the year 1792, in the village of Rattray, near Blairgowrie, Perthshire. In 1807 he went to London, and remained there till 1815. He had now resolved to devote himself to the work of the holy ministry, and with this view he returned to Scotland, and attended two sessions at the University of Glasgow, and one—that of 1817-18—at the University of Edinburgh. In August 1817 he entered the Divinity Hall of the Associate Synod, then under the charge of Professor Lawson of Selkirk. The Professor died before Mr Smith had finished his theological course, and he completed it in September 1821, under Dr Dick, Glasgow. He was licensed to preach the Gospel in December of that year, and received a call from the congregation of Biggar in ·the spring of 1823. This he thought fit to accept, and was ordained on the 19th of August following. He married Janet Brown, a daughter of the Rev. John

Brown of Whitburn; and by her he has 'had six children—three sons and three daughters.

In the discharge of his duties as a pastor, Dr Smith has been most faithful and laborious. He has taught the word of life from the pulpit with earnestness and power; he has been no stranger in the domiciles of his flock, praying in the family circle, or by the bedside of the sick and dying, and raising their thoughts to Him who has the issues of life and death in His hand, and who makes every event contribute to His glory; and he has taken no lukewarm interest in the condition and instruction of the young, but has laboured assiduously to furnish them with the knowledge that is profitable for the life that now is, and that which is to come. In the quiet seclusion and retirement of the Secession manse he has found time to compose and give to the world the following works :—'Devotional Psalter;' 'Sacramental Manual;' 'Chamber of Affliction;' 'Token of Remembrance for Children;' 'Golden Sayings;' 'Memoirs of the Rev. John Brown, Whitburn;' 'Memoirs of the Rev. William Fleming, West Calder;' 'Memoirs of the Rev. Charles C. Leitch, India;' Tracts on Baptism and the Lord's Supper; and Sermons on 'How Old art Thou?' and on 'Prosperity and Peace, or the Church and the World of the Last Days.' These various works not only testify to the diligence of Dr Smith, but to his zeal and ability in promoting the cause of his Divine Master, and in contributing to the gratification and improvement of his friends and the world at large. In 1850 the College of Dartmouth, United States, conferred on him the degree of Doctor of Divinity. He has received calls to other congregations, but his resolution appears to be to live and die with his attached flock at Biggar. At the meeting of the Synod of the United Presbyterian Church in May 1861, Dr Smith was proposed as Moderator by Dr William Johnston of Limekilns, himself also a Biggar man. Dr Johnston assigned four reasons in favour of Dr Smith's election. He said he proposed him, 'first, because Dr Smith was a senior minister; secondly, because he had always taken a deep interest in the affairs of the Church, and had been a close attender of the Synod's meetings; and thirdly, because the Church was under obligation to him for his writings. Last year he preached a sermon which he (Dr Johnston) considered to be one of the best he had ever heard, and which he would not be afraid to put in competition with any sermon preached in Scotland within the last twelve months. The sermon was published, and each might judge for himself. Fourthly, he proposed Dr Smith because he had in a remarkable degree aided the missionary operations of the United Presbyterian Church.' These, as Dr Johnston said, were good reasons why Dr Smith should be honoured with the Moderator's Chair. Dr Robson of Glasgow had, however, been brought forward as a candidate for this honour; and on the vote being taken, ninety-one voted for him, and eighty-seven for Dr Smith.

Though Dr Smith was thus unsuccessful, yet the large number of votes tendered in his favour show the high estimation in which he is held by the religious body to which he belongs.

On the 15th October 1861, a very interesting and gratifying meeting took place in Dr Smith's church. This was the celebration of the centenary of the settlement of its first pastor, the Rev. Mr Low. On this occasion, the Rev. Dr Cairns of Berwick preached a sermon in the forenoon; and in the afternoon a soiree was held, at which Dr Smith presided, and gave a sketch of the rise, progress, and present state of the congregation under his charge. He was then presented by Mr John Archibald, president of the congregation, with a purse containing 135 sovereigns, as a testimony of respect for his long and faithful services. Addresses were afterwards delivered by a number of gentlemen, among whom were the following natives of Biggar:— John Brown, M.D., Edinburgh; Dr William Johnston, Limekilns; Dr John Brown Johnston, Glasgow; the Rev. William Scott, Balerno; and the Rev. Robert Johnston, Arbroath.

Shortly after the union of the two kingdoms, the State began to impose fetters on the Church of Scotland, with the view of checking its free republican spirit and constitution. These, in course of time, introduced a state of laxity, subserviency, and degradation, that made a departure from the doctrinal standards of the Church appear an offence less heinous than the violation of an ecclesiastical or legislative act, however unjust and unwarrantable it might be. This State interference, and the corruption it engendered, have lain at the foundation of all the secessions which have taken place in Scotland for more than a century past.

The body of Christians that at one time existed, called the 'Relief,' had their origin in the exercise of the law of patronage, which had been thrust on the Church in the reign of Queen Anne. Captain Philip Anstruther, in 1749, issued a presentation to the parish of Inverkeithing, in favour of the Rev. Andrew Richardson, minister of Broughton, in the Presbytery of Biggar. The parishioners of Inverkeithing, almost unanimously, opposed the settlement of Mr Richardson, and on this account the Presbytery of Dunfermline refused to take the usual steps to instal him in that charge. This led to a course of rigorous and summary proceedings in the superior Church Courts, which ended in the deposition of the Rev. Thomas Gillespie, minister of Carnock, in 1752. Mr Gillespie, the Rev. Thomas Boston, Jedburgh, and the Rev. Thomas Colier, Colinsburgh, Fife, on the 22d October 1761, constituted themselves into a Presbytery of Relief.

The Relief congregation, Biggar, had its origin in the violent settlement of a minister in the Parish Church. The Rev. John Johnston having died on the 15th of October 1778, a presentation to the vacant charge was issued in favour of Mr Robert Pearson, probationer. At a meeting of the Biggar Presbytery, on the 25th of March 1779, the presentation was laid before the members by Bailie Carmichael, and sustained; and the presentee was instructed to preach once before the Presbytery, and twice before the people. Mr Pearson obeyed; but his discourses gave so little satisfaction, that, without any formal meeting or concerted resolution, the people came to a unanimous determination to abstain from any concurrence in his call. The Presbytery delayed taking any further steps till the 6th of July, to see if any one would move for the moderation of a call; but, as no person came forward, the Court fixed the 30th of July for that purpose. On this occasion the Moderator asked several times, if any parishioner present was disposed to subscribe the call. But no one would either put pen to paper, or give an oral assent; and, therefore, it was decided that the call should lie in the clerk's hands for some time, to obtain subscriptions, even in a private way. On the 19th of October, not a single name had been appended; and, therefore, the Presbytery finding themselves in a dilemma, resolved to apply for advice to the Synod of Lothian and Tweeddale. The Synod did not advise the Presbytery to proceed to a settlement in the circumstances, but requested the Presbytery to deal with the people, in order to induce them to accept of the presentee. The people of Biggar were indignant at this recommendation, as they held that the Presbytery should have received instructions to deal with the presentee as well as with themselves, so that he might not persist in thrusting himself on a flock who, to a man, were opposed to his settlement. Six months elapsed before any further steps were taken, publicly; but, in the interim, great efforts were made to obtain concurrents to the call, either by fear or favour. At a meeting of the Presbytery, on the 9th of May 1780, Mr James Saunders, writer, Edinburgh, appeared as agent for the patroness and the presentee, and laid on the table the result of these efforts, in the shape of letters of adherence to Mr Pearson from four non-resident heritors—viz., the Hon. John Elphinstone, General James Lockhart of Lee, Geo. Brown of Heiston, and Charles Brown of Coulston,—one non-resident feuar, and four or five individuals, dependants on the patroness. The despicable amount of support thus obtained, and the resolute opposition of the people, staggered the members of Presbytery, and made them refuse to proceed further with the settlement. The agent of the presentee therefore protested, and intimated his intention to carry the case by appeal to the ensuing General Assembly. It accordingly came before the Supreme Court on Monday, the 29th May. It was felt to possess a somewhat singular character, as, properly speaking, there was only one party— the presentee—with his four or five resident supporters; while almost the entire body of parishioners made no appearance, but stood doggedly aloof, and did not offer even any tangible objections. It, nevertheless, gave rise to a long and keen discussion, and at length the following motion was submitted, viz.: 'To remit the case to the Pres-

bytery, and enjoin them to moderate in a call to the presentee, *de novo*,
betwixt that time and the 1st of October next, and to proceed towards
the settlement according to the rules of the Church.' A counter motion
was then proposed: 'That the Assembly do sustain the concurrence to
the presentee; appoint the Presbytery to proceed towards a settlement
of the presentee, with all convenient speed, according to the rules of
the Church; and empower the Commission, in November, to judge in
any question that may be regularly brought before them concerning
the settlement of the parish, by complaint, reference, or appeal.'
These motions were put to the vote, when 77 members supported the
first, and 85 the second, and judgment was given accordingly.
Against this decision twenty-eight members entered a protest; and
the chief reasons which they assigned for taking this step were as follows, viz.:—'Though it hath been often a matter of dispute what
number of subscriptions were necessary to constitute that call upon
which the Church can proceed to the settlement of a minister, yet
there is not any one instance in which this Court ordered a settlement to proceed without something which had at least the form
and the name, however little it might have of the nature, of a call;
but in the present case, the Assembly hath ordered a settlement
to proceed *according to the rules of the Church*, although to this
moment the call is a sheet of blank paper, without a single name.
The concurrence came eleven months after the moderation of a call;
and was, therefore, strictly inadmissible in any form. If the unau-
thenticated extrajudicial subscriptions of, or a promise to subscribe, a
call, were to be regarded, why not turn them into a legal shape, and
remit for that purpose to the Presbytery to moderate a call *de novo?*
The regular course was plain; nor was there the smallest reason for
deviating from it by an extraordinary stretch of power. By ordination a mutual relation is constituted; and for this purpose the consent
of both parties is equally essential. In what manner the consent of
the people is to be expressed, hath been clearly laid down in the law
and practice of the Church; and when it is not thus expressed in what
is generally named a call, or something equivalent to a call, an ordination is an absurdity, if not worse. "That no person shall be intruded into any office of the Church, contrary to the will of the congregation to which he is appointed," nay, "that it is not lawful for
any person to meddle with an ecclesiastical function without the consent of the congregation," are express and repeated enactments of our
ecclesiastical law; they are ratified and approved by numberless Acts
of Parliament; the strict observance of them is solemnly sworn to by
every office-bearer in the Church of Scotland; and every member of
Assembly, in particular, holds his commission with an express injunction as he shall be answerable, to decide accordingly. All this notwithstanding, the Assembly hath, in the present case, appointed a settlement, not only without the consent of the congregation, but directly

in the face of express opposition by every heritor, elder, and head of family in the parish. For, with respect to the seven persons who, out of 1200 parishioners, have been prevailed on to promise a concurrence, they are of such singular characters, and in such singular circumstances, that the Hon. Counsel (Mr Henry Erskine) who supported the presentation candidly gave them up; and with respect to the letters from the non-residing heritors (who, by the by, are most of them not of our communion, and all together do not much exceed a third part of the heritors that pay the stipend), they cannot in the present view be of any consideration whatsoever, they can have no weight in a call which is the foundation of a pastoral connection between a minister and his people. However much some people may think proper to despise, and even wantonly to provoke and insult the people, yet this is certain, that all the laws respecting our ecclesiastical constitution are expressly founded on the inclinations, and enacted with a view to promote the happiness and tranquility of *the whole Christian people*. We cannot, without the utmost regret, imagine the idea of a church without a people, ministers without congregations; we cannot, in duty to God and our constituents, but protest in the strongest terms against measures which have such a tendency; and though we must hang our harps upon the willows, yet we shall always pray, that He who stills the raging of the sea, and the tumults of the people, may preserve peace within our Jerusalem's walls, and pour down prosperity upon the Church of Scotland.'

On the 30th of June the Presbytery of Biggar met, when Bailie Carmichael appeared, and presented a mandate, craving that the Presbytery should proceed with the settlement of the presentee. Mr Pearson, accordingly, was subjected to trials for ordination; and these having been sustained at a meeting of the Presbytery in September, his ordination was fixed to take place on the 28th of November.

The Rev. Thomas Gray of Broughton was appointed to serve the edict on the people, and the Rev. David Dickson of Libberton, to preach and preside on the occasion of the ordination. Against this step John Gladstone, one of the elders, tabled a protest, signed by himself, John Black, and John Wilson, elders; and by Richard Lithgow and William Aitken, parishioners. The protesters stated, that as the right of society, both civil and sacred, to choose their rulers and representatives had always been held sacred and inviolable, they could not sit entirely silent, and see themselves deprived of all choice, voice, or hearing, by having a minister intruded upon them, in the most arbitrary manner, by the lordly exertion of Church power, and in opposition to all the Acts of the Church of Scotland since the Reformation. They then referred to the Acts of the Church against the intrusion of ministers, and declared that the proceedings in this case left the parishioners nothing but implicit obedience and subjection, and thus made them mere nullities; that they subverted the

T

constitutional principles of the Church and good order; that they were the fruitful cause of debates, schisms, and divisions, and plainly tended to mar the success of the Gospel. On these grounds, they, in their own name, and in the name of all who should adhere to them, entered their protest against the steps proposed to be taken to settle Mr Pearson.

The people were now greatly incensed. Threats were freely used that the proceedings at the ordination would be prevented by violence. Several females had declared their intention of providing themselves with 'lapfuls' of stones, and pelting the Presbytery so soon as they made their appearance in the Kirkstyle. On the other hand, a rumour prevailed that a troop of dragoons would be brought from Edinburgh, to protect the members of Presbytery in the discharge of their duties. Everything betokened that the 28th of November would be a day of great commotion in the little town. The excitement was still further increased by the conduct of the Rev. Mr Dickson of Libberton. He caused a *pro re nata* meeting of the Presbytery to be held on the 25th of September; and there positively and solemnly declared that he would not preach and preside at Mr Pearson's ordination. He ended his statement by saying, that in the event of the Presbytery still insisting on his performance of the duty which they had assigned him, 'I will be reduced to the painful necessity of immediately giving in a resignation of my charge and office as minister of Libberton, which appears to me the most respectful manner of preventing any further trouble to the Presbytery.' The members of Presbytery were placed in a complete dilemma. None of them were prepared to incur the odium and brave the fury of the Biggar people, by taking an active part in the obnoxious settlement. It was in the end agreed, that a hint should be given to the presentee, that it would be necessary for him to bring some of his clerical friends from a distance to perform the chief part in his ordination. He accordingly arrived at Biggar on the evening of the 27th of November, along with the Rev. Mr Steel of Cockpen, and the Rev. Mr Whyte of Liberton, near Edinburgh.

Next day a meeting of Presbytery was constituted in a small apartment of one of the inns of the town. The place was immediately crowded to suffocation, and numbers were unable to gain admittance. The moderator called on the parishioners, if they had any objections to the presentee, to state them at once. John Gladstone, in name of the parishioners, stepped forward and presented a number of objections; but the Presbytery decided that they could not be sustained, as none of them inferred immorality of life, or heterodoxy of doctrine. A protest and appeal to the Synod of Lothian and Tweeddale was next tabled; but the Presbytery, considering that these were now irrelevant, resolved to proceed to the settlement. The parishioners, in a body, therefore, left the apartment, and at the same time the Church of their forefathers. They formed themselves into a congregation, and obtained a supply of sermon from the Synod of Relief.

The proceedings in this case led to the publication of a poem of considerable length, but of little literary merit. Copies of it are now extremely rare. It details the proceedings under the similitude of a marriage;—the bride being the flock, the bridegroom the presentee, and the attendants or witnesses the Presbytery. The presentee or bridegroom, and the two strange priests that were to officiate at the nuptial ceremony, are described as starting on their journey from the east, and halting by the way at the alehouse of Harestanes, to fortify themselves with potations of strong drink to enable them to brave the dangers to which it was apprehended they would be exposed at Biggar; and to spend time, so that they might enter the town after nightfall, and thus elude the assaults of the old women, who had threatened to salute them on their entrance with a shower of missiles. Addressing the landlord,

'Make haste, they cry, bring us a gill,
Till Phœbus get behind the hill ;
For we'll stay here till night is gone,
Because we love to walk unknown.'

The marriage then takes place, amid the protests, appeals, and lamentations of the bride. Her language is strong and furious. Addressing the officiating priests, she says,

' Your works proclaim, and loudly tell,
That you're but sons of Belial,
To wreath so hard upon my neck
A yoke from hell made by Old Nick.'

In looking round and seeing the desolation which they had made in her tabernacle,

' Where once so many lov'd to dwell,'

And

' Which once did shine with Gospel grace,'

Her bosom was filled with convulsive pangs, and she despairingly exclaimed,

' O when shall wicked rulers cease
To hurt the Church and mar her peace!'

Her outraged spirit, in form of a ghost, then visits all the members of Presbytery in succession, commencing with 'Cauldrife John of Symington;' and not neglecting Mr Pearson and his two friends, Whyte and Steel. She exposes with unsparing hand all their foibles, heresies, and shortcomings, and upbraids them for the part they had acted in robbing her of her rights and reducing her to a state of slavery. The ghost then returns to Biggar, bemoaning her sad fate, and praying that the reign of the 'wild wolf' that had intruded into the Gospel-fold would be short.

One of Mr Pearson's clerical friends, who had assisted at the ordination, by and by comes back to Biggar, to see what sort of congregation he had collected. He finds it composed of the 'mongrel
gentry,' of 'rustic John that mettle knave,' of the 'scandalous tribe,'
of 'the poor and needy,' and 'the thoughtless and the ignorant;' in
short, of those who had no fear of God, or who expected to reap some
worldly advantage by their attendance. The devil himself at last
appears on the stage, and expresses his entire satisfaction with the
conduct of Mr Pearson. Addressing Pearson, he says,

'O Pearson! thou'rt a champion bold,
Thy use to me here can't be told,
My kingdom here you do defend
Against all such as heav'nward bend.
You have now banished from the Kirk
All such as did me hurt and wreck ;
My flock all gather unto thee,
Because their ills ye will not see ;
And while ye keep this easy way,
No rake from you I'm sure will stray.'

The devil then gives him many advices. He was to hold no diets of
examination, nor put troublesome questions about Bible truths, as
these things disturbed the minds of those who loved to dwell at ease.
In his sermons he was to say nothing of Christ or righteousness, and
he was not to fright his hearers with statements of coming wrath. He
was to choose as his intimate associates the licentious and untruthful,
the careless and indifferent. If he did all these things, he would continue to be very dear to his Satanic Majesty, and would receive from
him no harm or molestation.

The most active individuals in opposing the settlement of Mr Pearson, and in forming the Relief Congregation at Biggar, were John
Gladstone, Richard Tweedie, and Andrew Ritchie. These persons
and their associates lost no time in purchasing half a burgh land,
lying on the south side of the town, and belonging by inheritance to
Isabella Vallance, wife of John Watson, the 'Whistling Laird,' to
whom we have already referred. The Burgh land, of which this
formed a part, consisted, as usual, of ground fronting the High Street,
Croft land running to the south, and part of the Moss, the Borrow
Muir, and Colliehill of Biggar ; and prior to 1712 was the property
of Sir William Menzies of Gladstane. It was purchased from that
gentleman by William Baillie, merchant, Biggar, who sold it to that
distinguished burgh worthy, Bailie Luke Vallance. On the death of
Luke, it went by inheritance to his brother Alexander, who left it to
his two daughters,—Isabella, married to John Watson as already
stated, and Janet, married to Thomas Bryden, baker, Biggar. On the
portion of this Burgh land which the founders of the Relief congre-

gation thus acquired, they erected a meeting-house, and subsequently a manse and office-houses. The congregation having been regularly constituted by the Synod of Relief, the following are the members who attended the first meeting of session, viz.: John Gladstone, John Wilson, John Small, John Thomson, John Waugh, John Reid, Richard Tweedie, Andrew Ritchie, William Gilbert, and James Johnstone.

The first minister of this new congregation was the Rev. James Cross. He was ordained towards the close of the year 1780. His connexion with the congregation was of short duration, as he accepted a call to Newcastle in 1782. Their next minister was the Rev. John Reston. He was ordained in 1783. He received a call to the Relief Church, Kilsyth, in November 1792; and the case having been brought before the Relief Presbytery of Edinburgh, he said that he saw no sufficient reason for leaving his present charge, but submitted the matter for decision to the Presbytery. The Presbytery, by a unanimous vote, decided that the call should not be sustained. Mr Reston, in the year following, demitted his charge, and went to Charleston, South Carolina. He was afterwards the pastor of a Relief congregation that met in Carrubber's Close, Edinburgh, and was ultimately translated to Bridgeton, Glasgow. Their third minister was the Rev. Robert Paterson, who had been for a number of years pastor of the Relief congregation at Largo, in Fife. He came to Biggar in December 1794; but in consequence of a great storm of snow, the Presbytery were unable to come up to induct him for eight weeks afterwards. Mr Paterson died on the 10th of August 1802, in the sixty-first year of his age and the thirty-second of his ministry, and was interred in Biggar Churchyard, where the congregation erected a monumental stone to his memory. The fourth pastor was the Rev. Hugh Macfarlane. On the 23d of March 1803, the Relief Presbytery of Edinburgh met at Biggar. The edict having been served, and no objections to the settlement of Mr Macfarlane offered, the Rev. Mr Ralston preached a sermon from 2 Cor. ii. 16; the eloquent Mr Struthers of College Street, Edinburgh, put the usual questions, and offered up the ordination prayer; after which Mr Macfarlane was solemnly set apart, by the imposition of hands, to the office of the holy ministry and the pastoral charge of the congregation of Biggar. The Rev. Mr Thomson of James Place, Edinburgh, then gave the charge to the congregation; and Mr Macfarlane's name was added to the roll of the Presbytery. On the 4th of March 1806, commissioners from the congregation of Biggar laid a libel against their pastor on the table of the Presbytery of Edinburgh. In consequence of some irregularity, it was not entertained till the 2d of July. The names attached to the libel were—John Paterson, farmer, Toftcombs; John Waugh, tenant in Thankerton; Andrew Ritchie, currier, Biggar; and John Small, miller, Skirling Mill. A number of witnesses were examined in support of the libel, and Mr Macfarlane himself appeared in his own defence.

The Presbytery found three counts in the libel proven: 1st, that the rev. gentleman had been guilty of disrespectful behaviour to the congregation of Biggar; 2d, of the mean habit of drunkenness; and 3d, of taking the name of God in vain.   The decision of the Court was, that the Rev. Hugh Macfarlane should be solemnly rebuked, and his connection with the congregation of Biggar dissolved.   The congregation afterwards paid L.200 for behoof of Mr Macfarlane, which was entrusted to the Presbytery, to be advanced as they saw proper.   On the 3d of March following, the Presbytery agreed to restore Mr Macfarlane to the office of the sacred ministry; but it soon became more plainly apparent that his reason was impaired, and that he was incapable to discharge the duties of this office.   He then became unsettled in his habits, and travelled over the country from place to place. In the course of his wanderings, he came occasionally to Biggar, visited some of his old hearers, particularly the late George Cuthbertson, Westraw, and received such small gratuities of food, money, and clothes as he would accept.

The fifth pastor of this congregation was the Rev. Andrew Fife. He was ordained on the 23d of July 1807, and translated to Dumfries in May 1808, in opposition to a protest and appeal to the Synod on the part of the congregation of Biggar.   The rev. gentleman, after ministering for nearly thirty years in Dumfries, attempted to carry his congregation and the place of worship over to the Established Church, but he met with only partial success; and the consequence was, that the congregation was rent asunder and nearly annihilated. The sixth pastor was the Rev. Daniel M'Naught, who had been previously settled at Riccarton, near Kilmarnock.   He was inducted to the charge at Biggar on the 4th December 1808, and after labouring with considerable acceptance for upwards of ten years, he died on the 5th of May 1819, and was interred in the area of the Church, in front of the pulpit.

The seventh pastor of this congregation was the Rev. Hugh Gibson, who was ordained on the 16th of May 1820.   He was a man of quiet and unobtrusive habits; but his manner and style of preaching were dry and unattractive, especially to strangers.   On the 29th of December 1835, Mr Gibson petitioned the Presbytery to dissolve the pastoral relation between him and the Biggar congregation, in consequence of his belief that he could no longer be useful.   A congregational meeting was held a few days afterwards, which was presided over by the Rev. Francis Muir of Leith, when it was unanimously resolved to agree to a dissolution of the pastoral relation between them and Mr Gibson.   The Presbytery gave effect to the petition and resolution on the 5th of January following; and Mr Gibson shortly afterwards left this country and proceeded to America.   The eighth minister of this congregation was the Rev. James Caldwell.   His ordination took place on the 27th January 1837.   Mr Caldwell was a popular preacher, and was much esteemed by his flock; but, having received a call from the Relief congregation, Greenock, in 1846, he resolved to accept of it, and leave his charge at Biggar. He had not been long settled at Greenock, when the congregation charged him with some improprieties of conduct, and he found it necessary to give up his connexion with them. He was afterwards pastor of a church in England, and ultimately departed to the United States of America.

The ninth and present pastor is the Rev. James Dunlop, A.M. He was ordained on the 14th of April 1847. He is an earnest and faithful expounder of divine truth. He has distinguished himself by his untiring efforts to awaken a spirit of vital godliness in the district. His labours to erect a Subscription School for the burgh, and thus to supply a want which was long felt, and which did much injury, cannot fail to evoke the grateful feelings of many generations of Biggar inhabitants.

The Relief congregation, called, since the union of the Associate and Relief Synods, the South United Presbyterian Church, has been subjected to considerable disadvantages, in consequence of the frequent change of pastors. The subsequent establishment of the neighbouring congregations of Newlands, Roberton, Lanark, and Peebles, has also had the effect of withdrawing many of its adherents and narrowing the sphere of its operations. Death and change of residence have further had the effect of removing not a few of its most zealous and substantial members. In spite, however, of all these adverse circumstances, it is still a numerous and influential body, the communicants on the roll being at present upwards of five hundred.

CHAPTER XIII.

Biggar Schools and Libraries.

THE instruction of the people of Biggar in the secular branches of education, in the times preceding the Reformation, when some even of the dignified clergy were scarcely able to read, was, no doubt, very limited and imperfect. It would perhaps be too much to assert that the means of education were then altogether awanting in Biggar. We know that Malcolm Lord Fleming, who founded the Collegiate Church of Biggar, ordained that one of its prebendaries should be teacher of the Grammar School. This School, in all probability, existed previous to that period, and was, no doubt, continued at the Reformation, as it was an enactment both of Parliament and the Church that a school should be planted in every parish. The readers who were appointed to many of the parishes of Scotland on account of the paucity of properly qualified and regularly ordained pastors, in many instances acted also as schoolmasters for some years after the introduction of the new ecclesiastical system. It is, no doubt, on this account that the parish schoolmasters in many parishes, continued to act as readers down to a very recent period.

It is worthy of notice, that at one time a law existed in Biggar, that no seminary of learning should exist in the town and parish, except the Public or Parish School. In 1722 the various Acts on the subject were renewed by the Baron's Court, in the following terms, viz.: 'The whilk day, the Bailie renews the former Acts of Court in favour of the Public School in Biggar, and discharges all private schools within the same to be kept, under the pain of five punds Scots, *toties quoties.*' These enactments evidently did not carry with them the sympathy of the whole inhabitants, as parties appeared, from time to time, who violated them, and received a portion of public support. We, therefore, find that on the 28th of March 1747, Mr James Philips, the parochial schoolmaster, laid a complaint before Mr Robert Leckie, the Bailie, that 'diverse and sundrie private schools were kept in the town and neighbourhood, to the great hurt and prejudice of the said Mr Philips, the legal schoolmaster.'' The Bailie, therefore, 'inhibited and discharged all and sundry the private schoolmasters, within the said town and paroch, from holding and keeping schools, for the future, excepting in as far as in such parts of learning the said Mr James Philips was not capable to teach, and that under the penalty of L.12 Scots, for each transgression, *toties quoties.*'

These enactments appear to us at the present day to be somewhat arbitrary and injurious. They infringed the liberty of the subject; they prevented well qualified men from communicating useful knowledge, and thereby earning an honest subsistence, and benefiting society; while they deterred the inhabitants from countenancing and supporting useful and meritorious instructors, put a ·check on the diligence and attention which are generally evoked by wholesome opposition, and restricted the education of youth to a person who might be objectionable from the want of talent, activity, impartiality, or good temper.

These local enactments were most likely based on an Act passed by the Scottish Parliament in 1567. The object of this Act was to provide 'that the youth be brocht up and instructit in the feir of God and gude maneris;' and, therefore, it was statuted and ordained, 'that all sculis to burgh and land, and all universities and collegis, be reformit, and that nane be permittit nor admittit to have charge and cure thereof, in tyme cuming, nor to instruct the youth privately or openlie, but sic as salbe tryit be the superintendents, or visitouris.' The patrons and clergy having thus got a control over the instructors of youth, exercised it rigorously in many places down to the middle of last century. The parish schoolmasters of Biggar being invested with an almost entire monopoly in the article of education, were evidently disposed not to allow the laws in their favour to remain a dead letter. They caused edict after edict to be sent forth, backed with all the terrors of the Baron's Court, to dislodge or scare away any poor wight that might be disposed to communicate his store of information to the youths of the town. This state of things has passed away, and any person is now at liberty to open a school in the parish for imparting instruction in such branches of learning as he may be proficient, or the inhabitants may require. The consequence of this has been, that Biggar, for well nigh a century, has always had one or two adventure schools, taught by men who, if they did not possess great learning, were, at least, distinguished for industry, fidelity, and success.

Notwithstanding the desire of the parish schoolmasters of Biggar to enjoy a monopoly in the supply of instruction to the young, an additional school was for many years maintained, even under the auspices of the Kirk Session, at Edmonston. The schoolmaster there appears to have had a small salary, for in the Session records, under date 3d July 1730, we find the following entry:—'The Laird of Edminstone (James Brown) produced a discharge for the sum of L.5 Scots, being one half year salarie, from Martinmas 1729 to Whitsunday 1730, for a schoolmaster in Edmistone, due by contract between the Session of Biggar and the Laird of Edmistone.'

Few of the early Biggar schoolmasters are remembered by the inhabitants. Schoolmasters are a quiet unambitious race, who pass through life doing a vast amount of good, but, in general, leave few

U

tangible memorials behind them. We will, therefore, very briefly
notice a few of those men who, in their day and generation, contributed not a little, during the last two centuries, to form the minds of
the Biggar youths, and to uphold the character of the town and parish
for intelligence and sagacity.

After the Reformation, the readers of Biggar—to whom we have
referred in a former part of this work—most likely acted also as
schoolmasters. It is not, however, till after the formation of the
Presbytery of Biggar, in 1644, that we obtain any direct references
to the schoolmasters of Biggar.

In 1646, Mr Andrew Threpland was schoolmaster of this parish.
He was, perhaps, an aspirant to the work of the ministry; for on the
14th of January of that year, he appeared before the Presbytery and
delivered a discourse in Latin, and underwent an examination in
Chronology, in the Hebrew and Greek languages, and in the interpre-
tation of difficult passages of Scripture. He acquitted himself so
much to the satisfaction of the Presbytery, that a very favourable
certificate was ordered to be given to him by the clerk. The next
schoolmaster with whose name we are acquainted, was James Reid.
We know that he held the offices both of schoolmaster and reader;
and that he had resigned his situation, and retired on a small allowance, previous to the year 1675. He was succeeded by Thomas Carmichael. The Earl of Wigton's proportion of his salary was 'ye soume
of thretie-three pund six shillings and eight pennies.' The next
schoolmaster appears to have been John Watson. He is mentioned
as presenting himself at a conjoined meeting of the Presbyteries of
Biggar and Peebles, held at the Hills of Dunsyre, on the 27th of June
1689, and stating that he wanted a door to the kirk; but the Presbytery decided that they could not interfere in the matter. It is more
than likely that he kept his school in a part of the Parish Kirk, and it
was, no doubt, on this account that he was so anxious to procure a
proper door for that edifice. The circumstance of the kirk standing
without a door may be taken as a proof of the disrepair into which
it had fallen during the times of persecution, and the incumbency
of the curates. From the date 1697, on the latch of the present
strong door, studded with large-headed nails, as shown in the
vignette to the present volume, it would seem to have been put up a
few years after the period referred to. Shortly after this period,
Alexander Forsaith, or Forsyth, is mentioned in the records of Presbytery as the parish schoolmaster. In 1695, the Earl of Wigton presented Mr Thomas Fleming to the office. The Presbytery was rather
surprised at this step, as Forsyth was still in the discharge of his
duties, and consequently the office was not vacant. The members of
Court, therefore, refused to take Mr Fleming on trials; but a short
time afterwards Mr Forsyth was induced to resign, and Mr Fleming
was immediately installed. The next schoolmaster appears to have

been Mr George Grant. After his settlement, in 1720, Mr Alexander Wardlaw, one of the Bailies of Biggar, at a meeting of the Head Court of the Barony, held on the 4th of February of that year, gave the following deliverance regarding the emoluments of the School, viz. :— 'And considering that the dues of the said scoall is too small incuradgement for fitt and quallified persons in the said office; and it being agreed to by the heritors present att this Head Court, that the dues of the said scoall should be augmented to the said Mr George Grant and his snocessors in office; therefore, it is statut and ordained that the dues of the said scoall shall be quarterly in tyme coming, viz., for the teaching of each boy in the Latine tongue, twenty shillings Scots, per quarter; and for the teaching of each lad or lass in Inglish, ten shillings Scots, per quarter; and for the teaching of each lad or lass in arithmatick, fyfteen shillings Scots, per quarter; and it is declared, that the yearly sellarie due to the scoallmaster is ane hundred punds Scots, by and attour the dues of said scoall.—And this Act is ordained to stand in all tyme coming.' The next schoolmaster of the Parish School of Biggar was Mr John Girdwood, a son of Mr Daniel Girdwood, schoolmaster, Carnwath. He was presented to the office by the Earl of Wigton in 1780. It was the practice of these times that the schoolmaster should be precentor in the Parish Church. Mr Girdwood, considering himself unqualified to lead the psalmody, refused to accept the appointment, unless he was allowed to find a substitute in his office as precentor. This liberty appears to have been granted.

Mr James Philips, to whom we have already referred as complaining, in 1747, against the existence of private schools, was most likely the next parish schoolmaster. One of the parties who appears to have roused his discontent, was Mr John Scott. This person was an exciseman, and greatly excelled as an arithmetician. He published a work on this subject, but copies of it are now extremely rare. He opened a school in Biggar, and his fame as a man of figures attracted a large attendance. Many of the Biggar worthies that flourished during the close of last century were wont to ascribe their skill in arithmetic to the zeal and abilities of their instructor Mr Scott. He was the instructor of Mr James Smith, who was originally a weaver, but who afterwards was factor for Smollet's estate at Symington, and a distinguished land-measurer at Biggar for half a century.

For many years during the latter half of last century, Biggar rejoiced in the instructions of a parish dominie called Mr John Porteous. He was a man of eccentric habits and some talent. He had a turn for poetical composition, and published a poem, entitled 'The Christian Life,' but we cannot speak of its merits, as, after repeated inquiries, we have been unable to find a copy. He took an active part in the general agitation against Popery in the year 1779. At that time the whole of Scotland was put into a flame by a proposal made to repeal the penal statutes against the Roman Catholics.

Societies, or Committees of Correspondence, for defence of the Protestant interest, were formed in Edinburgh and other towns, and under
their auspices resolutions and petitions were got up and published
by many towns, parishes, public bodies, etc. The town and parish of
Biggar, of course, sent forth a short declaration on the subject. It is
dated Biggar, February 8th, 1779, and is signed by John Porteous,
preses, and John Telfer, clerk. It may be noticed that John Dickson,
Esq., advocate, Coulter, took a leading part in this movement. He drew
up a pamphlet, entitled 'A Short View of the Statutes at present in
Force in Scotland against Popery; the Nature of the Bill proposed to
be brought into Parliament for Repealing these Statutes; and some
Remarks showing the Propriety and Necessity of Opposing such
Repeal, with a few Hints on the Constitutional and Prudent Mode of
Opposition.' This pamphlet went through two editions, and was
widely circulated.

Since the days of Porteous, the ferula of the Parish School has been
successively wielded by Messrs Johnstone, Scott, Gray, Wilkie, and
Morrison; while the adventure schools have been conducted by
Messrs Spence, Robertson, Slimon, Alton, Campbell, Ingram, Bogle,
Brown, Scott, Blair, Ramage, and Crichton. It is worthy of notice, that
on a vacancy taking place in the Parish School in the early part of the
present century, Dr A. R. Carson, who afterwards held the office of
Rector of the High School of Edinburgh, and became distinguished
for his eminent scholarship, and his success as a public instructor,
appeared as a candidate; but the Presbytery of Biggar considered
that at that time he did not possess sufficient qualifications to fit him
to hold such a situation.

Biggar, besides male teachers, has long had a succession of laborious
and painstaking female instructors, who have taught sewing and other
branches of a female education. One of these, some forty years ago,
was a Mrs Logan, a retired, prudent, gentle matron, with two children.
She had a passage of romance in her history, in the desertion, restoration, and death of her husband. This passage being related to a fair
authoress, was woven by her into an interesting story, which was
inserted in two successive numbers of 'Chambers's Journal' for November 1858, under the title of 'The Second Widowhood.' The
writer has brought in a few fictitious incidents for the sake of effect;
but many of her statements are in the main correct. Mrs Logan's
settlement at Biggar—'a moorland village,' the writer is pleased to
call it—her opening a school, and the branches of education she taught,
the return of her husband on a Sabbath forenoon, her hasty summons
from the church, and the illness and death of her husband, are all stated
very nearly as they occurred. The following reference in these articles
to the progress of education in Biggar since the time at which Mrs Logan
opened her school, though a little exaggerated, is understood to be
based on fact:—'At that time there were only two pianos in the

district; now they are as common as tables. Then, neither in Mrs
Armour's school, nor in that of her masculine competitor, did the
pupils quote Milton, or read memoirs of Shelley,—they do both now;
and it is not uncommon to find Macaulay's ballads done into crochet-
work covers, reposing on tables under the shadow of bead-baskets.'

Education, of late years, has unquestionably made progress at
Biggar. The branches of learning taught are more numerous, and
the mode of tuition is more efficient. It is a rare thing for the child
of any of the settled inhabitants to grow up without receiving, at least,
the rudiments of education. From time to time, Biggar schools have
sent forth not a few pupils who have, in after years, become clergymen, surgeons, lawyers, authors, editors, etc.; while many others who
have betaken themselves to industrial and commercial pursuits, have
risen in their professions, and realized considerable fortunes. We
will very briefly sketch the career of one or two of the scholars of
Biggar School.

The late Robert Forsyth, advocate, and author of works on various
subjects, was a native of Biggar, and a scholar at the Parish School.
His father was Robert Forsyth, bellman and gravedigger, to whom we
have already referred; and his mother's name was Marion Pairman.
This worthy couple were united in marriage in 1764, and their only
child, Robert, was born on the 18th January 1766. Their condition
in life was very humble, and they had to struggle with all the disadvantages and sorrows of extreme poverty; but they resolved to give
their son, who early showed an aptitude for learning, a good education, in order to qualify him for the work of the ministry. He was
sent early to the Parish School; but being the son of a poor man, he
was treated with marked neglect, and made small progress. He soon,
however, became extremely fond of reading. He borrowed such books
as his neighbours could supply, and read them in the winter nights to
his parents, to Robert Rennie, shoemaker, and others, who commended
him highly for his industry and ability, and thus encouraged him to
renewed exertions. In this way he became acquainted with such
works as 'The History of the Devil,' 'Satan's Invisible World Discovered,' the histories of Knox, Cruikshanks, and Josephus, Ross's
'View of all Religions,' the poems of Butler, Young, Milton, Ramsay,
Pennicuik, and Sir David Lindsay. It is remembered at Biggar, that
one evening he was busily engaged in reading aloud the poems of
Sir David Lindsay, by the blaze of a piece of Auchenheath coal, after
his mother had gone to bed, when that worthy matron said, 'O Robie,
man, steek the boords o' Davie Lindsay, and gies a blad o' the chapter
buik (the Bible), or I'll no fa' asleep the nicht.'

As he made slow progress in his classical studies at the Parish
School of Biggar, he was sent in his twelfth or thirteenth year to the
Burgh School of Lanark, then taught by Mr Robert Thomson, a
brother-in-law of the author of the 'Seasons.' Here he made more

advancement in a few months than he had done for years previously. When attending this seminary, he returned to Biggar every Saturday, and remained till Monday. His aged grandmother was wont to 'hirple' out the Lindsaylands road to meet him on his way home; but young Forsyth sometimes spent a few hours in climbing trees at Carmichael, or looking for birds' nests at Thankerton; and this sorely tried the patience of the old dame, as she sat by the wayside chafing at his delay, and longing for his return.

Forsyth then studied four years at the University of Glasgow, and manfully struggled with all the obstructions arising from the 'res angusta domi.' During one of these years, a severe and protracted storm of frost and snow occurred, and prevented all communication from place to place by means of carts. The Biggar carrier was consequently unable to pay his usual visits to Glasgow for several weeks. Old Forsyth was thrown into great distress regarding the state in which he knew his son would be placed from want of his ordinary supply of provisions. He therefore procured a quantity of oatmeal, and carried it on his back, along the rough tracks on the top of the snow, all the way to Glasgow, a distance of thirty-five miles, and just arrived when young Forsyth had been reduced to his last meal.

After the usual attendance at the Divinity Hall, Edinburgh, Forsyth was licensed to preach the Gospel when he had attained his twentieth year. He was an eloquent, energetic, and popular preacher. He officiated several times in the church of his native parish, and he did so on one occasion when a severe disease had made sad ravages among the population, and had carried off some of his friends and acquaintance. He therefore commenced the morning prayer with the words, 'Our fathers, where are they? We stand where our fathers have stood, and we worship where our fathers have worshipped. We look around us, and behold but the green mounds that cover them.' 'He had scarcely uttered these expressions,' we are told, 'when all around were overwhelmed by a burst of grief.'

He preached in a number of the pulpits of the Established Church in Edinburgh, and thus had an opportunity of bringing himself under the notice of men of power and influence; but year after year passed by, and no patron had discrimination and generosity enough to present him to a living. After long and anxious cogitation, he resolved to change his profession, and to seek for admission into the Faculty of Advocates. At that time the men of the Parliament House were more exclusive than they are at present. They cared little for a new adherent to their ranks, unless he came recommended by his connection with some aristocratic family. The idea of a *sticket* minister, and the son of a gravedigger, obtaining admission into their dignified order, was intolerable to the Dundases, the Forbeses, the Wedderburns, the Erskines, and others, who in those days ruled the roast in the Parliament House. One of their number, connected with the

Biggar district, but never distinguished for obtaining any great amount of practice, was specially opposed to Forsyth, and one day had the audacity to say, 'Who are you, sir, that would thrust yourself into the Faculty? Are ye not the poor bellman's son of Biggar?' 'I am so,' said Forsyth, coolly but sarcastically; 'and I have a strong suspicion that had you been a bellman's son, you would have been your father's successor.' Forsyth was not discouraged by the rebuffs and opposition which he had to encounter. He still persisted in his application. He renounced his profession of a preacher, and thus removed one of the objections which had been urged against him; and Lord President Islay Campbell interfered in his behalf, so that his opponents were forced to give way, and he was admitted to trials, and passed in 1792.

For a long time he had little practice. He attached himself to the party called the Friends of the People, who sympathized with the principles of the French Revolutionists; and this subjected him to a larger amount of obloquy and persecution, and operated still more in preventing him from obtaining employment at the bar. He was not idle. He studied mechanics, botany, chemistry, etc., and engaged largely in literary composition. At an early period he had composed and published a poem, entitled 'Nature,' and had made some progress with an epic poem in celebration of the achievements of Sir William Wallace; but he destroyed this production before it was completed. For the 'Encyclopædia Britannica' he now wrote the articles 'Asia,' 'Botany,' 'Britain,' and 'Agriculture,' the last of which was afterwards enlarged, and published in two volumes. In 1805, he published a volume of considerable size, entitled 'Principles of Moral Science.' This volume is written in a clear, trenchant style, and contains many ingenious speculations and useful disquisitions; but it abounds with most untenable paradoxes and reckless assertions. Such doctrines as that there is no moral evil and no guilt in the eye of God, and that those persons only who have made a certain intellectual and moral progress will continue to exist in a future life, would, we suspect, have subjected him to the charge of heresy, had he remained a preacher in the Established Church. He wrote a Life of Dr Samuel Johnson, which was published in connection with an edition of the Doctor's works in 1806; and that same year appeared his 'Beauties of Scotland,' in five volumes, illustrated with engravings. This work contains a large amount of interesting information regarding Scotland; but it has been superseded by several publications of the same kind, which have appeared since the period of its publication, particularly the 'New Statistical Account of Scotland.' In 1830 he published 'Political Fragments;' in 1834, a pamphlet, entitled 'Remarks on the Church of Scotland;' and in 1838 he wrote 'Observations on the Book of Genesis,' which, along with some sermons and a lecture, were published in 1846, shortly after his death.

In person Mr Forsyth was tall and commanding, his complexion
was dark, his features strongly marked, and his constitution hardy
and vigorous. He had an extensive knowledge of law, and was a
powerful and successful pleader. In the latter part of his life, he, in
a great measure, abandoned the more public part of his profession,
and was principally known as a Chamber Counsel, great weight being
attached to his opinions, whether oral or written. He became a rigid
Conservative; and the bellman's son, and one of the Friends of the
People, was in the end considered a fit associate and coadjutor of the
greatest aristocrats in the land.

The Rev. Henry Scott Riddell, who has risen to distinction by his
poetical productions, was also at one time a scholar at Biggar Parish
School. He was born in 1798 at Sorbie, in the Vale of Ewes, Dumfriesshire. His father, who followed the occupation of a shepherd,
shortly afterwards removed to Langshawburn, a sequestered spot in
the wilds of Eskdalemuir; and here the poet heard the songs in the
Ettrick Shepherd's first publication so often read and sung, that he
could repeat nearly all of them before he was able to read. His father
had occasion to make several other changes in his herdings; and as
they were all situated in solitary spots among the mountains of the
south of Scotland, the education of the young poet was very desultory
and imperfect. His first regular occupation of life was the tending of
his father's cows at the farm of Cupplefoot, on the Water of Milk.
By and by he rose to the higher trust, and more congenial rural
employment, of herding sheep. He acted one year, while yet a boy, as
assistant-shepherd at Glencotho, on Holmswater; and thus, for the first
time, became acquainted with the Biggar district. It was while resident at this place that he first made an attempt to write regular rhyme,
by linking the names of the different localities of the farm together.

Mr Riddell's occupation as a shepherd was favourable to the deve-
lopment of his latent poetic powers. The scenes amid which he daily
moved, if not rugged and sublime, were, with their green mountains,
their sequestered valleys, and brawling rills, full of wild pastoral
beauty, and well fitted to invigorate the frame, and inspire the soul
with lofty imaginings. As he grew up to manhood, the care of his
flocks, the perusal of books, and the recording of his poetic concep-
tions, occupied his attention by turns, as he wandered among the
mountains, or loitered in the sunny nooks and green bracken dells of
Ettrick Forest, whither he had now been removed.

Regarding this period of his life he says,

> ' My early years were passed far on
> The hills of Ettrick, wild and lone;
> Through summer's sheen, and winter's shade,
> Tending the flocks that o'er them stray'd;
> In bold enthusiastic glee,
> I sung rude strains of minstrelsy.'

· Mr Riddell having, from the proceeds of his employment, saved a little money, and having at the death of his father received his portion of his effects, he resolved to put in execution a scheme which he had for some time contemplated, viz., acquiring a more accurate and extended education, and devoting himself to the profession of the ministry. On throwing aside 'the crook and plaid,' his early imbibed predilections induced him to come to Biggar, where he continued to reside for some years. He placed himself under the tuition of the late Mr Richard Scott, parochial schoolmaster, who was a good classical scholar, and a man of genial disposition and varied information, but of somewhat indolent habits. He had, especially, a rooted aversion to the drudgery of teaching little children such elementary knowledge as is contained in spelling-books. Mr Riddell, although arrived at the years of manhood, resolved to attend day by day in the school, amid all its din and distraction. He found the task which he had imposed on himself somewhat irksome; and in the bright days of summer, he says that he felt the solitary paths, woods, and wilds, not far distant from the town, eternally wooing his steps to retirement, and his mind to solitary contemplation. The following verses, expressive of his feelings, were written in Biggar school, and which, therefore, we venture to quote:—

> ' Discontented and uncheery,
>   Of this noise and learning weary,
>   Half my mind to madness driven,
>   Woos the lore by nature given.
>   'Mong fair fields and flowing fountains,
>   Lonely glens, and lofty mountains,
>   Charmed with nature's wildest grandeur,
>   Lately wont was I to wander;
>   Wheresoever fancy led me,
>   Came no barrier to impede me;
>   Still from early morn till even,
>   In the light of earth and heaven,
>   Musing on whatever graces,
>   Livelier scenes or lonelier places,
>   Till a nameless pleasure found me,
>   Living like a dream around me;
>   How, then, may I be contented,
>   Thus confined and thus tormented?

> ' Still, oh! still, 'twere lovelier rather
>   To be roaming through the heather;
>   And where flowed the stream so glassy,
>   'Mong its flowers and margins mossy,
>   Where the flocks at noon, their path on,
>   Came to feed by birk and hawthorn;

x

Or upon the mountain lofty
' Seated, where the wind blew softly,
With my faithful friend beside me,
And my plaid from sun to hide me,
And the volume ope'd before me,
I would trace the minstrel's story,
Or mine own wild harp awaken
'Mid the deep green glens of bracken,
Free and fearlessly revealing
All the soul of native feeling.

' 'Stead of that eternal humming,
To the ear for ever coming—
Humming of those thoughtless beings,
In their restless pranks and pleaings,
And the sore-provoked Preceptor
Roaring "Silence!" o'er each quarter.
Silence comes, as o'er the valley,
Where all rioted so gaily,
When the sudden bursting thunder
Overpowers with awe and wonder,
Till again begins the fuss,
"Maister, Jock's aye nippin' us!"
I could hear the fountain flowing
Where the light hill-breeze was blowing,
And the wild winged plover wailing
Round the brow of heaven sailing,
Bleating flocks and sky-larks singing—
Echo still to echo ringing—
Sounds still, still so wont to waken,
That no note of them is taken,
Yet which seem to lend assistance
To the blessing of existence.
Who shall trow thee wise and witty,
Lore of the Eternal City,
Or derive delight and pleasure
From the blood-stained deeds of Cæsar?
Thus bewildering his senses
'Mong these cases, moods, and tenses;
Still the wrong-placed word arranging,
Ever in their finals changing;
Out and in, with hic and hockings,
Like a loom for weaving stockings;
Latin lords and Grecian heroes—
Oh, ye gods, in mercy spare us!
How may mortals be contented,
Thus confined, and thus tormented!'

A number of the young men of Biggar, inspired with a rage for theatricals, formed themselves at that time into a dramatic company, and acted ' the Douglas Tragedy,' and the farce of ' Barnaby Brettle. Some of them were good singers, and between the pieces gave several songs, one of which was Burns's song, ' O let me in this ae Night,' the two parts of which were sung by different performers, with the accession of proper stage scenery. Mr Riddell, being known as a song-writer, was solicited by these amateur actors to compose for them an appropriate lyric, which they might sing on their humble stage in one of the malt lofts of the Brewery. He accordingly, to an air of their own selecting, produced a piece in the form of dramatic plot, which, as he himself says, being sung by alternate voices, was well received, and enhanced his fame as a composer of lyric poetry.

At this time also, a Mr Watson, one of those gentlemen who are usefully employed in going from town to town teaching vocal music, came to Biggar, and opened an evening class for singing in the Parish School. He was rather a good singer,—at least he was an enthusiast in his profession. Besides psalmody, he taught song-singing; but several of his songs were far from select, the music only rendering them passable. One of his songs was entitled the ' Plough Boy,'— a very poor production, but with rather a good air. Mr Riddell, who used to attend Watson's class, composed as a substitute the song of ' The Crook and Plaid ' to the same air; and it immediately became popular with the Biggar singers, and ere long found its way over all Scotland.

Mr Riddell, while residing at Biggar, composed a Border Romance, which he submitted to the examination of the Ettrick Shepherd, and whose remark on returning it was, that there were more rawness and more genius in it than any work he had seen. He also contributed several papers to the ' Clydesdale Magazine,' a periodical published at Lanark by William Murray Borthwick, a son of the late John Borthwick, farmer, Langlees, Biggar. One of his acquaintances while at Biggar, was the Rev. James Proudfoot, then parochial schoolmaster, Skirling, and now minister of the Free Church, Coulter. Mr Proudfoot had distinguished himself at College by carrying off a prize for the best poem on the subject of Waterloo; and a congeniality of taste and sentiment naturally led to a bond of intimacy between him and Mr Riddell, and in company they made a tour to Yarrow, and held converse with that gifted son of song the Ettrick Shepherd. Another of his Biggar associates was James Brown, weaver, Symington, a good poet, and an amiable man, of whom notice will be taken in another part of this volume. Mr Riddell was also on terms of intimacy with the family of a farmer in the neighbourhood; and for one of its members, who had the charge of one of the hirsels of his father's flocks, he composed the well-known song, ' The Wild Glen so Green.' One of Mr Riddell's school associates was Mr W. B. Clark, a native of Biggar, afterwards parochial incumbent of Half Morton,

and, after the Disruption, for some time pastor of the Free Church,
Maxweltown, Dumfries.* Through this intimacy he became acquainted with Mr Clark's sister, Eliza, who, after a courtship of a
goodly number of years, became his wife. A Mr Harrower, who was
a son of Mary Black, Biggar, and who had realized a considerable
fortune in Demerara, came home at this time, and took up his residence at Biggar. He soon formed an intimacy with Mr Riddell, invited him frequently to his table, and put his horse at his disposal.
After the poet left Biggar to attend the University of Edinburgh,
Harrower several times paid him a visit, and on one occasion brought
with him two English friends. The whole party made a pilgrimage
to the scene of the battle of Pinkie, and the Englishmen bantered
Harrower and Riddell a good deal concerning the defeat which the
Scots there sustained. Riddell, since he could not make a better of
it, resolved at least to have the last word in the strife ; and before he
slept, composed, in support of his country's cause, the popular song,
'Ours is the Land of Gallant Hearts.'

Mr Riddell, after attending the Universities of Edinburgh and St
Andrews, was licensed to preach the Gospel. He was ultimately
settled at Teviothead, as minister of a chapel erected by the Duke of
Buccleuch ; but, after labouring for a number of years in this situation, he was visited with severe affliction, which for a considerable
period laid him aside from the discharge of his duties. On his recovery he did not resume his pastoral charge, to which another in the
interim had been appointed. The dwelling-house which was built for
him by the Duke of Buccleuch, he still continues to occupy, and re-
ceives from his Grace an annuity, with other perquisites. Mr Riddell's
publications are—'The Songs of the Ark;' 'A Monody on the Death of
Lord Byron ;' 'The Christian Politician, or the Right Way of Thinking ;' and a volume of poems and songs. In 1855 he made a translation of the Gospel of St Matthew into the Scotch language, executed
for Prince Lucien Bonaparte. More recently, he also for his Highness translated into the same language the Psalms of David and the
Song of Solomon. As these translations were for linguistic purposes
of the Prince, only a limited number of copies of each was printed.

All the emanations of Mr Riddell's muse manifest much poetical
power; they everywhere breathe an ardent attachment to liberty, to
country, to rural scenes and domestic enjoyments. His larger pieces
contain many choice sentiments and felicitous expressions, which we
love to con over and over again; but, on the whole, and for our own
part, we feel disposed to give the preference to his songs. It is in
his lyrics that the divine inspiration of genius shines most conspicuously forth. In these, the ardour of patriotism, the affections of the
heart, the beauties of nature, and the endearments of home, are de-
veloped in such glowing and apt illustrations, that they will charm

* He is now minister of Chalmers' Free Church, Quebec.

and delight so long as lyric poetry holds a place in the literature of
our country. As might be expected from the genial sympathies of the
bard, he has always cherished a warm attachment to the Biggar district and its inhabitants. A short time ago, in a communication to
ourselves, he said, 'My recollections concerning Biggar and its surrounding localities are vivid, manifold, and, I may add, pleasurable,—
unless in so far as they are mingled with my regret in leaving them,
and for the departure of those friends from them with whom I was
wont to associate in the days of other years. Still, these things are
like what Ossian says of departed joys, "They are sweet and mournful
to the soul."' In several poetical productions he has given expression
to his regard to the scenes and the people of this district. We regret
that our space only admits of our giving from these effusions a few extracts. In a poem entitled 'The Folk o' the Clyde,' he says :—

　'O there is not a vale in the wide world in which
　　The hearts are so kind, and the scenery so rich,
　　Wi' its woodlands so green, and its homes and its domes,
　　Where the wind wanders free, and the waterfall foams,
　　Where the wild wood is grand, if the moorland be grey,
　　And its bosom lies veiled in the beauty of day.
　　As bold as a bridegroom, and blythe as a bride,
　　And there is not a vale like the vale of the Clyde.

　'The world frae Tintock gang ye and survey,
　　It's no fault of his, if sight fails by the way, .
　　But of all the scenes that may beam on the eye,
　　Ye'll see these the loveliest close round him that lie ;
　　For where is the beauty will ever excel
　　Its bowers in the bosom of wild Coulter Fell,
　　Where David sings sweetest of a' at eve-tide,
　　O' the wild glen sae green, to the lads o' the Clyde ?

　'And there are the maidens sae modest, yet free,
　　And sweet as the breath o' the new-blown haw tree,
　　As fair as the wild flower, and blythe as the day,
　　And untainted as dew in the morning of May ;
　　Wi' blinks in the e'e that will ne'er let alane,
　　Till they warm a' the heart, tho' the heart were like stane ;
　　And if there ere now I had won not a bride,
　　I wad woo night and day at the lasses o' Clyde.

　'Ye lads o' the hill, and the holm, and the shaw,
　　I'll long for your welfare while breath I shall draw ;
　　And when sleeps the bard that ye wont so to hail,
　　O bring ae sweet daisy frae Clyde's lovely vale,
　　And plant the fair flower on the turf o' his tomb,
　　For methinks it will sweeten the sleep of its gloom ;
　　And may health, peace, and plenty, for ever betide
　　The warm generous hearts on the banks o' the Clyde.'

In a song written for the Edinburgh Biggar Club, and sung at its anniversary meeting, 7th January 1848, he thus gave utterance to similar sentiments :—

'On Yarrow Braes and Ettrick Shaws beat leal, leal hearts and warm,
    In men and dames, and lovely maids that cheer alike and charm ;
But lealer hearts and fairer forms are no in Scotland wide,
    Than those that trace and sweetly grace the bonnie banks o' Clyde.

'The Tweed rows down his waters far alang yon mountain glen,
    Where lonely rills and lofty hills are roun' the hames o' men ;
But Tintock rears a prouder crest, and guards a fairer tide,
    In casting his broad shadow o'er the valley o' the Clyde.

'There glow the hearths as erst they glowed ere them we left behind,
    Where love and worth combined to bless the kindest o' the kind,
And bright intelligence lits up the fare the free provide,
    When cantily they crack within the happy hames o' Clyde.

'May peace and plenty dwell wi' them who still are dwellers there,
    May love the sunny ringlets wreathe, and wit the hoary hair,
And sympathies that aye are young inmingle life's ain tide,
    While harps are strung and sangs are sung upon the banks o' Clyde.'

        .   .   .   .

The only other extract which we will give is from a lengthened and very excellent poem, which he wrote for the same Club also in 1848 :—

'Climb to green Bizzyberry's top,
    And say, as round you cast your eye,
If lovelier scene on Nature's lap
    E'er spread its breast to Nature's sky.
Lo! Coulter Fell and wild Cardon,
    Themselves with heaven's own hues invest,
And Tintock lifts his summit lone
    Far 'mid the stillness of the west.

'Around lie stream, and glen, and grove,
    And mansions fair, and woodland wide,
Reflecting smiles of light and love,
    To hail the mountain of the Clyde.
Even Tweed's lone hills, dark and sublime,
    As if awakening from a dream,
Look longingly across the clime
    To greet the guardian of our stream.

'But can the distant hill or dale
    Forth in the soul sensations draw,
Such as awake when thought must hail
    Our own blythe Biggar and Westraw ?

O'er these, the haunts of early days,
   Emotion into rapture swells,
While fondest feeling warmly says,
   There worth with love and beauty dwells.

'From out these village homes and trees,
   Afar the children's mingled hum,
Comes floating on the light hill-breeze,
   As erst our own was wont to come.
And, lo! that venerable pile,
   Grey with the garniture of years,
Gives forth its echo, hark! the while,
   Awakening other hopes and fears.
There sleep the loved of soul and heart,
   The death-departed of our line,
Who scorned to play a servile part
   In aught, if secular or divine.

'Their power could foreign pride o'erawe,
   And smile amid the triumphs won,
When Scotia's Lion raised his paw,
   And shook his grey beard in the sun.
Their voice of freedom bore away,
   And energy, they say, that shook,
When passing from the lip away,
   The dial on yon Castle nook.'

It is only doing justice to the author of these poetic productions, here to state, that our limits only allowing us to adopt verses here and there out of each of them, they, as thus given, fail to develop the regular train of sentiment, and consequently to produce the same impression which they are calculated to do in their original condition.

The parochial school-house of Biggar was erected about the commencement of the present century. It is a building of two storeys, which formerly contained a large apartment for a school-room and accommodation for the teacher, rather beyond what the statute then prescribed. The school-room was by and by found to be rather small, and an addition was made to it some thirty-five years ago, but it did not altogether prove satisfactory. The Rev. John Christison, therefore, set vigorously to work to get a new and separate building erected; and in this he entirely succeeded. The school-house put up under his auspices, and mainly by his efforts, is one of the most elegant and commodious that can be found in the whole country. As the erection of this building is a notable event in the history of the town, and is most creditable to all parties concerned, we will quote a letter from Mr Christison to James Sommerville, Esq., S.S.C., Edinburgh, showing the steps which were taken to raise the necessary funds:—

'BIGGAR, 10th February 1849.

'MY DEAR SIR,—I received your letter the other day, wishing some information about the building of our Parish School, and I must apologize for
not replying sooner. The heritors of this parish agreed to build a new
school-house, at an expense of L.340, on the site of the old one; but as this
site had no playground attached to it, and was otherwise bad, I urged them
to purchase a new one. They declined doing this, but agreed to allow the
parishioners, at their own expense, to furnish a new site, and to improve
the style and accommodation of the building, if they chose. A subscription
was immediately set on foot for these purposes, and went on with great
spirit. In a short time we realized subscriptions in money to the amount
of L.125. Besides this, everybody who had a horse assisted in driving
materials; the value of the labour thus contributed was L.28. We had
then a public sermon, at which a collection was made. We had a concert;
and we were presented with the gratuitous services of the architects, Messrs
Clark and Bell of Glasgow. We got by these means L.24. We had now
raised L.177, and I had become liable to the contractors for L.50 more,
trusting to the generous spirit which had already given so much, and which
did not appear to me to be yet exhausted. I was not deceived. Our next
device was a sale of ladies' work. Every needle in the parish, and not a
few elsewhere, went cheerfully in the cause. A tempting show was set
before the public, and at the close of the sale we found that it had yielded
us L.59. We were still short, however, of what we required, for we had
again gone ahead; and when we were considering what we should do next,
the young people of the parish took the matter out of our hands, by getting
up a ball, and sending us the proceeds, which amounted to L.21. We had
now raised in all L.257, which, added to the L.340 expended by the heritors,
amounted to nearly L.600. With this we have built one of the best
parochial schools in Scotland. We were fortunate in getting a beautiful
site, and a very elegant design from Messrs Clark and Bell; and we adopted
all the recent improvements as to ventilation, and the proportion of area to
each child. The main school-room is 53 feet long, by an average breadth
of 26 feet. We also built an additional class-room of 16 feet by 14, and
a lobby, which may be occasionally used as a class-room, 16 feet by 11.
The class-room and a tower outside the building are, in the mean time, unfinished, but we do not despair of completing them by and by.* When
these are finished, the whole will have cost about L.650.

'You may easily conceive that all this was not done without a struggle,
but the result has richly repaid us. Not only has the direct benefit been
great, but a very gratifying proof has been given of the readiness of the
people to support and honour the cause of education.—I am, my dear Sir,
yours truly,   'JOHN CHRISTISON.

'Js. SOMMERVILLE, Esq.'

The want of a suitable apartment in which to hold a subsidiary,

* These parts of the building were finished in a short time afterwards, and the
tower was furnished with a clock, a proprietor in a neighbouring parish subscribing
L.20 for this very useful object.

or, as it is now called, an adventure school, was long felt at Biggar. Those persons who attended the schools taught by Messrs Robertson, Slimon, Stephens, and Alton, will recollect the miserable apartments, dark, dirty, and confined, in which they were held. About thirty-five years ago, a somewhat better apartment was obtained in one of the office-houses connected with the Relief manse; but the ceiling of it was low, and it had no playground except the public road. The erection of a larger and more appropriate building had, therefore, become absolutely necessary, to keep pace with the educational wants of the parish and the progress of the times. The new Parish School contains accommodation for 180 children; but the number of children in the town and neighbourhood who ought to be at school was found to be 330, thus leaving 150 to be otherwise provided for. A scheme was, therefore, set on foot for the erection of a building, to be used as a school for the burgh. Liberal subscriptions were obtained from many of the most wealthy inhabitants of the town and neighbourhood, and a suitable site, of half an acre in extent, was obtained at the head of John's Loan, on one of the small fragments of ground that the descendant of the Flemings still possessed in the parish. A suitable plan having been obtained, the foundation-stone was laid with masonic honours, by Br. Alexander Baillie Cochrane, Esq. of Lamington, assisted by the Lodge of Biggar Free Operatives, on the 27th of October 1859. The part of the building devoted to the purposes of tuition, including an industrial department, was finished in the autumn of 1860, and was opened in October of that year. It is capable of containing 120 scholars, and has cost L.500. A house for the accommodation of the teacher has since been erected, adjacent to the school. The chief and indefatigable promoter of this undertaking has been the Rev. James Dunlop, M.A., of the South United Presbyterian Church; and it will stand, we hope, for many generations, a monument to his honour and a benefit to the district. Biggar has been fortunate in having two such clergymen as Messrs Christison and Dunlop, who felt and understood the educational wants of the district, who set to work with heart and hand to remove them,—who could not be driven from their design by any amount of lukewarmness or opposition, and who have now daily the satisfaction of seeing the beneficial effects of their labours, in the increased comfort and improvement of the youths of the town and parish with which they are connected.

The cause of education in Biggar has been promoted to some extent, among the poorer classes, by the benefactions of two individuals, whose example is worthy of imitation. One of these was William Law, skinner, Biggar, who built and occupied a house near the Cadger's Brig, the lintel of the outer door still showing his initials and the date 1751. This individual, in 1767, mortified L.41 sterling for the education of poor children in the parish. The other person was William Nesbit, who had his dwelling in the School Green, and used

Y

to make a livelihood by hawking salt. At his death, in 1817, he
mortified L.40 for the same laudable purpose.

Another benefactor of the poor of Biggar, in respect to education,
was the late Alexander Mitchell, Esq., tanner and currier, Glasgow.
Mr Mitchell, it has been stated, was a native of the neighbouring
parish of Kilbucho, and when young removed to Biggar with his
father, who lived for some years in the Kirkstyle, and was employed
as a kilnman at Biggar Mill. When Mr Mitchell acquired sufficient
strength to toil for his daily bread, he was engaged as a labourer in
the nurseries of Bailie Cree. He left Biggar, and proceeding to Glasgow, got employment in a tanner and currier's establishment in that
city. Here, by his steadiness, his shrewdness, and attention to business, he rose, by degrees, to be the head of the establishment which
he had entered as a workman, as well as to be one of the directors of
the City of Glasgow Bank. At his death, which took place in 1860,
he left L.90,000, and among other legacies he bequeathed L.1000 to
the Kirk Session of the Established Church of Biggar, to be invested
for the support of education in that town. He further bequeathed
'to the Kirk Session of the United Presbyterian Church at Biggar,
in behoof of the school connected with that congregation, the sum of
L.1000.' These sums are not payable till after the decease of the testator's widow. As two United Presbyterian Churches exist in Biggar, a difference of opinion has arisen as to the one indicated by the
testator in his trust settlement. Both of them, we believe, have laid
claim to it, and it may be necessary to make an appeal to the gentlemen of the long robe before the controversy regarding it is settled.

A society, called the Edinburgh Biggar Club, which was instituted
in 1847, has for one of its objects, the promotion of education in the
parish of Biggar. On several occasions, it has given a number of
books to the schools as prizes for the reward of merit,—a proceeding
worthy of commendation, as it not only stimulated the scholars to industry, but distributed a number of useful works in various depart-
ments of literature among the families of the town, and thus conduced
to the knowledge and mental improvement of both young and old.
The Edinburgh Upper Ward Club for some years prosecuted the same
object, by giving prizes to the schools; but, singularly enough, finding
these not appreciated in some quarters, it discontinued them, and for
several years it has given a sum of money to the most proficient
scholar in the Upper Ward, for the purpose of enabling him still further to prosecute his studies. Mr John Jamieson, a native of Abing-
ton, and for a number of years one of the partners of the firm of
Gillespie, Moffat, and Co., Montreal, having realized a competent fortune, returned to his native district, and resided some time in the
parish of Coulter. At his death, in 1848, he left the sum of L.600,
to be invested for the purpose of founding a bursary in the University
of Edinburgh. Candidates for this bursary must be the sons of

schoolmasters, farmers, mechanics, etc., whose yearly income does not exceed L.100; and they must have been born and educated in the parishes of Biggar, Coulter, Lamington, Crawford, Crawfordjohn, Wiston, and Roberton. They require to undergo an examination in Greek, Latin, and arithmetic, and the successful competitor holds the bursary for four years; the amount at present being L.21 per annum. The patrons are the Principal of the University and ten professors.

A number of years ago a society was established at Biggar, called 'The Scientific Association.' Its object was to diffuse information on scientific subjects, by means of lectures, discussions, and books. After flourishing for some time, it fell into abeyance, and in 1854 was superseded by a similar institution, called the 'Athenæum,' which still exists, and has a library, a reading room, and a course of lectures on miscellaneous subjects, during the winter months. It is supported by an annual subscription of 5s. from each member. Institutions of this kind are with difficulty upheld in our largest cities; and it will certainly reflect credit on Biggar, if, with a population scarcely so large as is to be found in many a single street of these cities, it should be able to maintain its 'Athenæum' in the same efficient state which it has hitherto done, and thus hand down to succeeding generations an institution productive of much rational entertainment, useful instruction, and mental improvement.

Biggar has a number of other public libraries in addition to the one connected with the Athenæum, but none of them are of a very old date. The Biggar Library, founded in 1797, principally by the exertions of the Rev. Patrick Mollison of Walston, contains about 1000 volumes, and has been supported almost exclusively by the higher classes of the town and neighbourhood. The number of members is now few, and it is understood to have been in a languishing condition for some years. The present librarian is Mrs Tait. Biggar Parish Library, was founded in 1800 by the working classes of the town and neighbourhood. This library, thirty-five years ago, had fallen very much into a state of dormancy. The members had dwindled down to eleven in number, the income had become a trifle, and the addition of new books had, in a great measure, ceased. The merit of restoring it to more than its primitive vigour is due to Mr Allan Whitfield, who, at the time referred to, was elected president. That gentleman got a new catalogue and a new set of regulations drawn up and printed, and commenced an active canvass for entrants. The consequence was, that in the course of a year or two, the members were increased to fifty; and the library has continued down to the present time in a flourishing and satisfactory state. The number of members at present is upwards of ninety, and the volumes amount to fully 1200. The entry money is 6s., and the annual payment 2s. At one time this library was under the charge of John M'Ghie, shoemaker, one of the most shrewd and intelligent men of his time in

Biggar. He had read all the books in the library, and many of them several times over. As he was endowed with a most tenacious memory, he could give a summary of the contents of any one of them to which his attention might be directed, as well as a very correct estimate of its merits. His conversational powers were of a high order. It was a treat of no ordinary kind to sit beside him while engaged with his *elshin* and his *lingle*, and hear him discourse with fluency and critical acumen on poetry, philosophy, politics, religion, and general literature. He was a notable specimen of not a few men living in obscure corners of our country, and pursuing an humble vocation, who have, nevertheless, entered into the very depths of the great masters of literature, and have had a powerful influence in stimulating and moulding the minds of the generation around them. The present librarian is Mr James Small, shoemaker.

The Evangelical Library was founded in 1807, and, as its title imports, it is composed of books of a religious cast. It contains 900 volumes. The entry money and annual payment are 2s. each. This library is scarcely in so flourishing a state as could be desired. Biggar Kirk Library contains upwards of 1100 volumes, and is supported by collections at evening sermons, delivered under the auspices of the Established Church. The Biggar Relief Juvenile Library has a very useful collection of books, amounting to nearly 700 volumes; and is conducted by a committee of the congregation. The entry money is 6d., and the annual payment 1s. 1d.

The existence of these libraries bears abundant testimony to the reading habits of the inhabitants, and the desire generally felt to spend their leisure hours in rational and profitable exercises. It is very desirable, however, that a movement should be set on foot to unite the most of these libraries into one institution. Were this done, and a suitable apartment built for their accommodation, and a fair remuneration given to a person to take charge of them, not only would the books be preserved from the risk of being dispersed, but an additional impetus would be given to that mental cultivation and rational amusement which are to be derived from the perusal of good books.

One of the branches of education long sedulously cultivated at Biggar is that of music, both vocal and instrumental. An excellence in this department is one of the things in which the inhabitants have taken great pride. No town of so small a size has sent forth so many really good singers; and none has had a succession of better instrumental performers. So far back as 1513, mention is made of the piper and fiddler of Biggar, who played to James IV. on one of his visits to the town. When the Collegiate Kirk of Biggar was erected, one of its prebendaries was appointed to play the organ and to teach music, both to the singing-boys of the Kirk, and to the parishioners at large. After the Reformation, the parish schoolmaster was generally the precentor in the church, and, no doubt, the teacher of psalmody. When

John Girdwood was presented to the office of schoolmaster in 1730, as formerly stated, he refused to accept the appointment, unless he was allowed to find a substitute to precent for him in the church. About the beginning of last century, John Scott was the chief 'violer,' or fiddler, of the parish. From the parish records we find that, in 1740, John Murray was one of the professional fiddlers of Biggar. At the commencement of the present century, John Simpson, a blind man, flourished as the chief musician. He fiddled at all the merry meetings in the country round, and could travel everywhere without a guide. Nay, what was very remarkable, though he was stone blind, he took great delight in the chase, and was often seen following the pack of hounds, which, for some time, was kept in the parish by Lord Elphinstone; and seemed to enjoy the sport with as much relish as any one present.

Some thirty or forty years ago, one of the town fiddlers was Mr Thomas Davidson. He was not only a musician, but a tailor, weaver, optician, musical instrument maker, and philosopher. Two of his favourite tunes were the 'Button Hole' and the 'Hen's March,' which he played with comical grimaces and rare effect. In his old age, he tried to learn to perform on the flute, but he complained that he constantly lost the blast; and therefore he invented a curious apparatus for applying wind to the instrument with greater ease than by the usual mode of sounding it by blowing into the embrochure. He could thus sound the instrument, but the notes wanted the delicacy and precision produced by the ordinary mode of playing; so in the end he abandoned the task, as beyond the powers which he then possessed. Had he lived in the days of James IV., he could, with his uncommon tunes, his curious instruments, and his ingenious speculations, have afforded that mirthful monarch rare entertainment during his repeated visits to Biggar.

Another musician that flourished at the same period, was John Brown, usually denominated 'The Fiddler.' He was a good performer, especially of reel, strathspey, and contra-dance tunes; and his services were in almost constant requisition at fairs, penny weddings, and dancing schools. Like most Biggar men of his time, he was shrewd, intelligent, and occasionally witty. Many of his good things are still remembered in Biggar. Let us merely give a specimen or two. On one occasion he was at a Broughton Fair, furnishing music, as usual, for penny reels in a barn. He got considerable supplies of usquebae during the day; and at night, after his labours were over, he had a carouse with some boon companions in the Green Inn. He at length set out towards Biggar when the morning was somewhat advanced, and by the way feeling squeamish and sick, he sat down by the roadside, and was seized with an apprehension that his final end was near. After ruminating for some time, he suddenly started up and exclaimed, 'If I maun dee, I may as weel dee gaun as sittin'.'

On another occasion, after indulging in a round of rather hard
drinking, he fell into the horrors.   He viewed his conduct with anything but complacency.   He considered that a feeling of sorrow and
regret was not a sufficient atonement for his delinquencies, but that
he was fairly entitled to receive some personal chastisement.   Labouring under this impression, he went forthwith to the late Mr James
Paterson, commonly called 'Oggie,' from having lived with his father
on the farm of Oggscastle, near Carnwath.   Having found him, he
said, 'Jeames, I maun hae the len' o' a gun frae ye this mornin'; I'm
gaun to tak a bit daunder doon the length o' Bogha' Castle.'   'The
len' o' a gun, John,' said James; 'that's a very unusual request.
What on earth are ye gaun to dae wi' a gun?   Ye dinna mean to shute
yersel'?'   'No exactly that, Jeames,' said John; 'but of coorse I mean
to gie mysel' a deevil o' a fleg.'

Biggar has had several instrumental bands, who, for a time, have
cultivated music with great spirit and success.   These bands, in so
small a town, are not easily kept up, as the young men are being
constantly draughted off to fill situations in other districts, and their
places in the band cannot be readily supplied.   The consequence has
been, that after flourishing a few years, they have, one after another,
been broken up.

CHAPTER XIV.

Physicians connected with Biggar.

BIGGAR, from a remote period, has had a staff of medical men. So early as the fourteenth century, mention is made, in a charter, of Simon the Physician of Biggar. We know very little regarding the Biggar doctors, however, prior to the beginning of last century. At that time Andrew Aikman flourished as a surgeon in Biggar. The earliest notice that we have of him is on the 28th of June 1720, when he and James Thrypland were brought before the Bailie's Court, and fined 'in the soume of fyve punds Scots to the fiscall,' for having, in the course of casting peats in Biggar Moss, encroached on their neighbour's room. In 1723, he and his family appear to have been greatly annoyed by William Liddell, a horse-couper, one of those restless and outrageous individuals who give their neighbours and the powers that be a great amount of trouble. He therefore arraigned him before the Bailie's Court; and Luke Vallange, the presiding magistrate, condemned him, under a penalty of 'fyve hundred merks Scots,' to keep the doctor, 'and his wife, bairns, family, and others, harmless and skeathless, in their bodyes, lives, goods, and geir, and not to molest him nor his in any sort, directly or indirectly, in tyme coming.' Mr Aikman was an active member of the Biggar Lodge of Freemasons, and, in 1726, held the office of boxmaster. He died on the 8th of April 1730, in the forty-fourth year of his age.

Drs William Baillie and William Boe were distinguished physicians at Biggar during a considerable part of last century. Biggar, during the time they flourished, acquired some celebrity as a medical school. It was a common practice at that time, for young men who wished to acquire a knowledge of the medical art to serve an apprenticeship to some eminent practitioner. The fame of these two Biggar worthies drew round them many young men, some of whom distinguished themselves in their profession in after years. We may specially refer to Dr Robert Jackson. Mr Jackson was born at Stonebyres, near Lanark, in 1750, and was a near relative of the late William Jackson of Coulter Mill, and his brother James Jackson, who for nearly half a century was well known in the streets of our towns and villages as a blind minstrel. Old James had a fine musical ear, and sung a number of popular Scottish songs, accompanying himself on the fiddle. We

ourselves conversed with him a short time previous to his death; and
it was gratifying to find that, amid all his vicissitudes and wanderings,
and even when he had 'grown weary and old,' he still retained a
lively recollection of the men and incidents of a former generation
connected with the Biggar district.

Robert Jackson received his elementary education at a small school
at Wandel, and afterwards at the Parish School of Crawford, then
taught by a Mr Wilson, a teacher of some local celebrity.   In 1766,
he came to Biggar to study the medical art under the care of Dr
Baillie.   After remaining some time at Biggar, he proceeded, for the
further prosecution of his medical studies, to the University of Edinburgh, then enjoying a high reputation, on account of the genius and
learning of several of its professors, such as Munro, Cullen, and Black.
After the completion of his college curriculum, he went abroad in
pursuit of employment, and encountered such a variety of difficulties,
disasters, and adventures, as to invest this period of his life with a
most engrossing interest.   He, however, surmounted them all, and
gradually rose to eminence.   He wrote some valuable treatises on
contagious fevers in jails, ships, hospitals, etc.; and a number of
medical reports on climate, sanitary arrangements, and hospital diseases.
By his writings and personal exertions, he effected great reforms in
the treatment of soldiers, and therefore was generally spoken of as
'the army physician.'   He died at Thursby, near Carlisle, on the 6th
of April 1827, in the seventy-seventh year of his age.

Another surgeon, who was a good deal about Biggar last century,
and who for upwards of thirty years worshipped every Sabbath in
the Burgher chapel of that town, deserves to be here noticed.   This
was the well-known James Meikle.   Mr Meikle was born at Carnwath on the 19th of May 1730.   From his earliest years, he was
of a serious and devout turn of mind, and spent much of his time in
secret prayer and reading the Scriptures.   In his fifteenth year he
heard a sermon delivered by one of the Secession fathers, and this
made so strong an impression on his mind, that he was led to make
inquiries regarding the opinions and proceedings of the new sect.   The
result was, that he joined Mr Horn's church at Daviesdykes, and
continued a staunch adherent of the Secession Church ever afterwards.
The leading aim of his early years was to be a preacher of the Gospel;
but the poverty of his family, and the death of his father in 1748, formed
an insuperable barrier to the attainment of his wishes.   Through the
efforts of a gentleman who took an interest in his advancement, he was,
at one time, elated with the hope of enjoying a bursary at one of our
universities; but he was doomed to disappointment so soon as it was
known that he was a Seceder. He therefore devoted himself to the study
of medicine; and soon afterward commenced practising in Carnwath
as a surgeon and apothecary, with the view of earning a subsistence,
and procuring means for the prosecution of his theological studies.

His income from the profession on which he had now entered was small and precarious, and therefore he formed the resolution of going to sea, and serving as a surgeon's mate on board of a man-of-war. After various disappointments, he left Carnwath on the 10th of March 1758, and having passed an examination at Surgeons' Hall, London, was appointed second surgeon's mate to the 'Portland,' a 50-gun ship, lying at Portsmouth. Mr Meikle was now introduced to scenes which his soul utterly abhorred. The officers and crew, being men of immoral habits, were constantly guilty of profane swearing, excessive intoxication, gross debauchery, and Sabbath profanation. Amid all the wickedness by which he was surrounded, he nobly maintained his integrity, and found time to compose a great part of 'The Traveller,' 'Solitude Sweetened,' 'The Secret Survey,' etc., which were afterwards published, and which will long preserve his name among our Scottish worthies. He continued in the 'Portland' four years. During that time he visited various parts of the world, and was present at two engagements, in which victories were gained over the French.

Mr Meikle returned to Carnwath on the 24th March 1762, and immediately joined the newly-formed congregation at Biggar. He attended regularly every Sabbath, and had thus to travel a distance of fourteen miles. He seems to have enjoyed great pleasure in meditating on divine things on his journeys to and from the church. In reference to this exercise, he on one occasion says, 'It was a sweet day, and no disturbance but from a wandering heart;' and on another, 'I had pleasure in meditation: the sermon was divine and edifying.' On the 18th of August 1779, he married Agnes Smith, daughter of a farmer in the neighbourhood of Carnwath. She belonged to a small body of Antiburghers, who, previous to 1760, had erected a chapel at Elsrickle, a village about midway between Biggar and Carnwath, but lying a little to the east of the direct road. Previous to entering into this marriage relation, he and his future partner signed a series of articles regarding their conduct to each other. One of them was as follows, viz.: 'As there is a difference of our views in some things, instead of suffering this to breed discord and contention between us, let it beget in us a proper concern for the divisions of Reuben, and continued supplication for the peace and prosperity of Zion; that, as there is one Lord, so His name may be one in all the earth.' It was in this truly Christian spirit that he conducted his wife on Sabbath mornings to the little Antiburgher chapel at Elsrickle, and, after worshipping at Biggar, returned by that village in the evening, and accompanied her home. It was in the same spirit of toleration and liberality that, on several occasions, he exerted himself to procure pecuniary contributions for the support of the Rev. J. Anderson, the pastor of the little flock of which his wife was a member. Mr Meikle was ordained an elder of the Biggar congregation in July 1789, after he had been twenty-

z

seven years a member, and held this office till his death, which took place on the 7th December 1799.

Dr James Boe, Dr Bertram, Dr Renton, and Dr Wilson are Biggar surgeons still remembered by the older portion of the inhabitants. Biggar at present has a number of meritorious medical practitioners; but the only one of them who has distinguished himself as an author, is Mr Robert Pairman. Mr Pairman was born at Biggar on the 23d November 1818. His father is Mr Robert Pairman, merchant, who, during a long life, has been characterized for his integrity, and his calm and Christian deportment.

The Doctor received the rudiments of his education at Biggar Parish School, then taught by the late Mr Richard Scott. At the age of twelve, he was sent to a classical seminary in Edinburgh, at which he studied for four years. He matriculated as a medical student in the University of Edinburgh in November 1834, and finished his curriculum, and obtained his diploma, in 1838. At the close of that session, he carried off several very distinguished prizes: first, one of two medals awarded by Professor Lizars to the two most distinguished students of his class for proficiency in surgery; second, the highest prize in the class of Dr George A. Borthwick, Lecturer on Clinical Medicine at the Royal Infirmary; and third, the first prize in the Materia Medica Class, of nearly two hundred students, conducted conjointly by Dr J. Argyle Robertson, and Dr W. Sellar, F.R.C.P., Lecturers at the Argyle Square School of Medicine.

On leaving the medical schools with these distinguished honours, he immediately settled in his native town, and commenced practice. Amid the toils and disquietudes of the life of a country surgeon, he has found leisure to compose several valuable little works. The first, published in 1848, is entitled 'Sceptical Doubts Examined.' This work is in the form of a dialogue, and states, with great plainness and perspicuity, and with many happy illustrations, the deistical doubts which are apt to arise in the mind of a young and ardent inquirer; and the telling and conclusive solution which can be given to these doubts by a person of learning, experience, and religious convictions. His next work was a popular 'Exposi' on of Asiatic Cholera,' which he delivered before the Biggar Athenæum, on the 20th March 1856. This treatise contains a clear elucidation of the manifestations and effects of this mysterious disease, the proofs which can be adduced in support of the theory that it has its origin in a damp and foul condition of the atmosphere, and the methods which ought to be adopted for its prevention. This work called forth very hearty commendations, both from medical men and the public press. A third work of Dr Pairman's is a series of four tracts on 'Fever Poisons in our Streets and Homes,' which were composed at the request of the Glasgow City Mission. They have been extensively distributed, not merely by the Society for which they were originally written, but by other kindred institutions.. For instance, the Ladies' Sanitary Association of Aberdeen, in the year 1859, circulated 2000 copies. Several passages from these tracts, that appeared in a work by Miss Brewster, having attracted the notice of the Committee of Council on Education, J. S. Lawrie, Esq., one of the officials connected with that Committee, addressed a communication to the author in 1858, requesting permission to make extracts for educational purposes. To this request the Doctor readily acceded, his great object in composing them having been to lend his aid to the movement for the instruction and temporal elevation of the poorer classes of society. This application must have been a source of gratification to the worthy Doctor as well as to his friends, as it showed that his labours were recognised and appreciated in the very highest quarters. The tracts are written in the Doctor's usual clear, shrewd, earnest manner. They are divested of all perplexing technicalities, so that all classes can read and understand them with ease. They treat of themes of the highest importance to the health, happiness, and social amelioration of the community, and therefore deserve to be scattered broadcast among all ranks, the rich as well as the poor.

It gives us pleasure to notice a medical gentleman, a native of Biggar, who has risen to distinction. This is Dr John Brown, son of the late Rev. Dr John Brown of Broughton Place, Edinburgh. Dr Brown was born in the Secession Church manse, Biggar, on the 22d of September 1810. He lived at Biggar till his twelfth year. Being educated privately, he did not mix much with the adventurous, and perhaps somewhat mischievous, youths, who at that time flourished in the little town; but, nevertheless, we know that he retains a very lively recollection of the scenes and the men with whom he was familiar in his early years. In 1822, he removed, along with his father, to Edinburgh, attended the High School and the University of that city, took his degree as an M.D., and for some years was connected with a medical institution in Minto House, Argyle Square. He entered at length into the marriage relation, and set up his staff as a physician in the same city; and there he still lives, and enjoys a very respectable amount of practice.

Dr Brown, however, has achieved higher fame as a *littérateur* than as a physician. He had long been known as a person of mark and likelihood,—as a contributor to some of our most popular periodicals,—and as possessed of that warm devotion to letters and study that has characterized his family for three previous generations; but it was not till he published the first series of his 'Horæ Subsecivæ,' in 1859, that his reputation as a literary man was established. This work consists of a collection of literary, scientific, metaphysical, and professional papers, composed, as their general title imports, at spare hours,—hours snatched from the toils and fatigues of a laborious profession. These papers are written in a free, hearty, dashing style, with a disregard, we are sometimes apt to think, of the usual rules and conventionalities of literary composition; but still with a preci-

sion and correctness which, on examination, we cannot but admire.
They stamp the author as a bold, independent thinker, as possessing a
clear insight into the intricate workings of the human heart, and
capable of ranging from a vein of singular quaintness and humour to
a flow of most gentle but touching pathos. His tale of 'Rab and his
Friends,' which has been widely circulated in a separate form, which
has been translated into German by Mrs Montague, and sent forth
with attractive pictorial embellishments, from the pencil of George
Harvey, Noel Paton, and other distinguished artists, has fascinated
many a heart, and drawn a tear from many an eye. It is to his connexion with Biggar that we owe this charming tale. He was solicited,
through the medium of his uncle, the Rev. Dr David Smith of the
North United Presbyterian Church, Biggar, to deliver a lecture before the members of the Athenæum of that town. He consented, but,
like many persons in a similar predicament, he felt a difficulty in
selecting a suitable topic for discussion. He at length fixed on the
story of Ailie, a story that had made a profound impression on his
own heart, and over which he had often thoughtfully pondered. He
sat down to his desk one midsummer evening at midnight, and by
four o'clock next morning he had committed it to paper. 'I read it
to the Biggar folk,' he says, 'in the school-house, very frightened, and
felt I was reading it ill, and their honest faces intimated as much in
their affectionate and puzzled looks.' A second series of 'Horæ Subsecivæ' was published about two years ago, and was also well received.
A new and large edition of these papers, in one volume, somewhat
abridged, has just (March 1862) been issued, and has at once been
taken up by the trade, which is a proof of the high estimation in
which the Doctor's writings are now held by the public.

Dr Brown, after the reformation effected a few years ago in the
management of the University of Edinburgh, had the honour of being
elected one of the Assessors of the University Court, which consists of
eight members. He received this honour from W. E. Gladstone, Esq.,
the Rector. The following is a copy of Mr Gladstone's letter to Dr
Brown, appointing him to this office :—

'November 25, 1859.

'SIR,—I take the liberty of requesting that you will permit me, as Rector
of the University of Edinburgh, to nominate you as an Assessor and member
of the University Court.

'Not having upon you the claim of even the slightest personal acquaintance, I may with the more freedom assure you, that I prefer this request
upon public grounds alone, under the influence of an anxious wish that, in
the exercise of every power with which I may be intrusted, I may be enabled to direct it steadily and solely towards the good of the University.

'I have the honour to be, Sir, your faithful servant,

'W. E. GLADSTONE.

'John Brown, Esq., M.D., etc., etc.'

Mr Gladstone's grandfather, as formerly stated, was a Biggar man. His ancestors, for generations, held a prominent place in that town, not merely as men of substance, but as active useful members of the community, and leaders especially in all ecclesiastical movements. It was, therefore, a singular coincidence—a coincidence of which the Rector himself was probably unaware—that a native of Biggar should have been nominated to the office of Assessor by a gentleman descended from an ancient stock of Biggar men.

CHAPTER XV.

Biggar a Burgh of Barony.

ONE of the favours which James II. conferred on Robert, Lord Fleming, was the erection of Biggar into a free burgh of barony. The original charter is still preserved in the archives of the Fleming family. Like other early charters, it is of no great length. It states expressly, that, for the love and favour which the King had for Robert, Lord Fleming of Biggar, he erected Biggar into a free burgh of barony, with all the usual privileges, and particularly a weekly market on Thursday. This charter was given under the great seal, at Edinburgh, on the 31st of March 1451, It was renewed by the Scottish Parliament on the 25th November 1526, in the reign of James V., in the following terms:—'Our sourane Lord, with avis and consent of his thre estatis, ratifyis and apprevis ye charter of new infeftment maid be our sourane Lord to Malcolme, Lord Flemyng, making ye toun of Beggar and Kirktulloch burghis in baronyis, with ye mercat dais, in all punctis and artiklis, efter ye forme and tenor of ye said charter of infiftment maid yareupon.' New ratifications of this charter were made by James VI., on the 6th of January 1588; by Charles I., on the 1st of February 1634; and by Charles II., on the 10th of May 1662.

The privileges of a burgh of barony were, in general, the, holding of a weekly market and certain annual fairs; the exaction of a custom on all merchandise brought into the burgh for public sale; the trial of all disputes and offences which took place within the bounds of the barony, with the punishment of offenders by fine, imprisonment, and even in some instances by death; and, lastly, the recovery of the baron's mails, duties, profits, multures, and mill service.

It is a popular tradition, that the burgh of Biggar, at one time, possessed the power of self-government; and that it was thus, in point of jurisdiction, similar to a royal burgh, or a burgh of regality. Thi power, it is said, was taken away by the influence or active interference of a lawyer in Edinburgh, who in his youth had been a vagrant, and who, on account of some depredation committed at Biggar, had been rather roughly handled by the authorities and the inhabitants. The following rhyme is understood to have a reference to this transaction, from which it would seem that the individual in question had been drummed out of the town:—

'The laddie had tricks that cost him fu' dear,
    For he was a runnagait loon;
But their ain licks and their ain drumsticks
    Hae fared as ill for the toun.'

No written proof exists, so far as we know, to lend anything like
confirmation to this tradition, though it is by no means unlikely that
the Flemings, for services performed, conferred extra privileges on
the burgh, and that some incident occurred which caused these privileges to be taken away. It is evident, however, that the Flemings
treated the inhabitants of Biggar with considerable liberality. The
whole land in the immediate neighbourhood of the town was conferred on the burgh, and was divided into twenty-four portions, called
Burgh or Borrow lands; and besides these, there were also two Cotlands. A burgh land was of sufficient extent to allow one or two
houses to be erected on it, fronting the street, and to afford ample
space for a garden and a croft. The possessors of these burgh lands,
who, both in common parlance and in legal documents, were styled
burgesses, had each of them a right to a piece of land, on the east of
the town, called the Borrow Muir, on which they raised crops and
pastured their cattle, and had, besides, a 'darg' or 'room' in one of
the mosses in the neighbourhood of the town, from which they drew
large supplies of peats and divots, or, as they are generally called,
roughheads. The burgh lands were not all of the same extent. They
ranged from five to eight acres, and each of them was valued at L.12,
13s. 1d. Scots, so that the extent appears to have been regulated by
the quality. Taking them at an average of six acres each, this shows
that upwards of 140 acres of the best land of the parish were in the
hands of the burgesses. Few of the burgh lands remain entire.
They have been much subdivided, and some portions of them have
been sold to the conterminous proprietors, and persons not connected
with the burgh. The feuars, however, still hold about forty acres of
arable land, and also thirty-five acres of moss, to which they have a
conjoined right, and which are lying in a very dismal and unprofitable
state. They are quite unfit for pasture, and are of little use as a
source to supply fuel, as coals, by means of the railway, can now be
got at a moderate rate. It is therefore very desirable, that efforts
should be made to bring them into a state of cultivation.

When a burgh land was sold or bequeathed to a successor, a certain sum was paid for Lord Fleming's confirmation. On the 23d of
January 1668, John Brown, senior, burgess, Biggar, paid 'ane hunder and six punds threteen shillings and four pennies Scots' for the
confirmation of his rights to that burgh land sometime possessed by
Mr John Kello. James Brown, who succeeded his father John, in
1678, paid L.40 for my Lord's confirmation of his right to the burgh
land, he being a singular successor. The sums paid for this warrant
appear to have differed very much, and to have depended on the

value of the land, and the person into whose hands the land was transferred.

The burgesses appear, like the other vassals of the Flemings in the parish, to have also had a certain right to the Common of Biggar, an extensive hilly tract lying to the north-west of the town. The different claims to this Common led to a series of litigations between the vassals or feuars and their superior, the Earl of Wigton, before the Court of Session, in the beginning of 1739, a short time before the Biggar estate was last entailed. Notices of these cases are to be found both in Kilkerran and Morrison's Decisions. We will give one or two of these notices, and refer those curious in such matters to the works just mentioned for a detail of the others.

'*Jan.* 23d, 1739.

'THE EARL OF WIGTON *contra* HIS VASSALS.

'In the process of division in the Common Muir of Biggar, at the Earl of Wigton's instance, against his vassals, some of whom were proprietors, others had only servitudes, wherein the Earl claimed not only a proportion of the Muir, according to the valuation of his adjacent property lands, but also a præcipuum of a fourth, agreeably to the decision of the Muir of Foggo in 1724. The division was not opposed, and though it had, it is believed that it would have been sustained, in respect there were common proprietors. But the objection being made to the præcipuum by those having only servitudes, that there was no foundation for any such præcipuum in the Act of Parliament, and that they were entitled to a proportion of the whole commonty sufficient for their servitudes, the Lords " found the superior not entitled to a præcipuum, and that those having servitudes were entitled to a proportion of the Common sufficient for their servitudes."'

'*Feb.* 1st, 1739.

'THE EARL OF WIGTON AND LOCKHART OF CARNWATH *contra* THE FEUARS OF BIGGAR AND QUOTHQUAN.

'In the division of the Common Muir of Biggar, it being controverted, whether certain of the charters of property produced by the vassals imported a right of property, or servitude in the Muir,—the Lords found, that where lands were disponed with parts, pertinents, and pendicles, or where they were disponed with mosses, muirs, commonties, and parts and pertinents in general, whereon possession in a common muir had followed for forty years, it did import a right of property ; but where lands were disponed with parts, pendicles, and pertinents, with common pasturage used and wont, though the possession in the muir had, for forty years, to all intents been the same as in the former case, it was found to import only a right of servitude in the common muir.'

The likelihood is, that the Earl of Wigton, previous to effecting a new entail of his lands, purchased the rights of the feuars of Biggar to the Common, and thus all knowledge of these rights has, in a great

measure, faded from the remembrance of the present generation of
feuars.

The burgesses of Biggar, for their possessions, were bound to render the superior the usual service; that is, to attend his court, to follow
him to the battle-field, to cast and win his peats, and to lead both his
peats and corn, so far as they had horses, and received command to
do so. Besides this, the feuars and burgesses of Biggar were bound
by their original charters to pay to the lord superior six chalders of
malt, with exception of two pecks and a half. This, at least, is stated
to be the case in 1675, by an entry in one of the Earl of Wigton's
books of that period. After the rebellion in 1745, an Act was passed
for abolishing heritable jurisdictions; and thus the holding of land
for military service was changed into what is called feu or blench
tenures, that is, the payment of an annual sum of money, or some
honorary acknowledgment of vassalage; and by this means the burgesses of Biggar were, like all other vassals, released from their obligation to follow their lords superior through the gory ranks of war.

In a burgh of barony the chief magistrate was the baron himself;
but as that dignitary often found it inconvenient to attend to all the
duties of his office, he generally deputed his powers to a substitute,
called his Bailie. The Chief Bailie of the Flemings, at least in later
times, was most commonly a lawyer, who had charge of all their
estates; and being often non-resident at Biggar, he had power to
appoint one or two deputes. Biggar had thus almost always two
bailies, and sometimes three. It had three in 1729. The Chief Bailie
at that time was John Wardlaw. Luke Vallange, tailor and burgess,
and a man of very considerable wealth, had, for a long time, held the
office of Depute-bailie; but his advanced age and increasing infirmities
rendered him unable to discharge efficiently the whole duties. Bailie
Wardlaw, therefore, gave him a colleague in the person of Alexander
Baird; and these two worthy deputes sat on the judicial bench in the
Tolbooth together. The next official in the burgh was a Procurator-
fiscal, who seems to have been joint prosecutor with the Bailie, and
to have received the fines imposed in the Baron's Court. Besides
these, there were a Clerk, to draw up indictments, record the transactions of court, etc.; a Dean of Guild, to take the oversight of the
buildings; Inspectors of Markets, to examine the goods exposed for
public sale, and ascertain if they were of good material and workmanship; Quartermasters, to secure lodgings for travelling soldiers, and
horses for the conveyance of their baggage; Referees or Birliemen,
as they were called, to settle disputes, inspect the fences, and decide
upon boundaries; and lastly, an Officer or Constable, to apprehend
offenders, issue summonses, and warn the vassals to pay their feu-duties,
rents, kains, customs, and casualties. A Head Court was held once
or twice a year, and an ordinary Court once a month, and, at times,
once a week.

2 A

The Court of the Lands and Barony of Biggar was long held in the Tolbooth of the burgh. This was a strong vaulted building, which stood on a spot behind the present Corn Exchange. One part of it was used as a court-house, and another as a prison. It was the scene of many a curious trial, and a place of resort to the burgesses to hear the sentences and the laws given forth by the Baron Bailie. It was, in a great measure, discontinued as a court-house about the year 1737; but the cause is not now known. The court, after this period, was generally held in an apartment of the Bailie's own house.

Had the records of the Court of the Lands and Barony of Biggar, during the three hundred years that it existed, been preserved, they would, to us at the present day, have been extremely interesting, and would have been worthy of being published by some of the literary clubs, which have done so much to extend a knowledge of rare books and ancient manuscripts connected with Scottish history. The only memorial of this court known to exist, is a mutilated fragment of the last volume of its transactions, extending from 1719 to 1781; but the entries after the abolition of heritable jurisdictions, and the death of the last Earl of Wigton in 1747, are few and of little importance. The perusal of it, however, brings very vividly before the mind of the reader a considerable portion of the inhabitants of Biggar, and their doings in the earlier part of last century. We will give a few extracts from it, illustrative of the rights, liberties, and proceedings of the inhabitants at that period.

One of the first entries shows the great care that the Bailie manifested in preserving the horses of the parish from infectious diseases :— ' Court of Lands and Barrony of Biggar, holden in the Tolbooth thereof upon the 12th day of November 1719, by Alexander Wardlaw, factor to the Earl of Wigton, and the suits called and the court fenced and affirmed; the whilk day the Bailie statutes and ordains, that no person nor persons keep colded nor scabbed horses, or otherwise insufficient, within the parroch, under the pain of ten punds Scots, by and attour of repairing their neighbours' skaith and damage. And where such horse or mare is found in the fields, that they be taken up and sighted, and if found insufficient, that the magistrate of the town caus dispatch them, and the owners thereof punished as said is.'

The appointment of the birliemen was vested in the Head Bailie; and it appears, as we have already said, that the suburb of Westraw had a set of these functionaries of its own. At the Head Court held on the 19th May 1720, the Bailie, Alexander Wardlaw, appointed ' David Tweedie and Thomas Aitken, Westraw, to be birliemen there for ane year, and for that effect has taken their oaths *de fidele administratione*.' The sort of cases in which the birliemen gave their decision, is shown by the proceedings which took place at the Court held by Luke Vallange on the 28th of June following, viz.: 'The same day the Bailie fynes Andrew Aikman and James Thrypland, ilk ane of them, in the soume of fyve punds Scots, for cutting peats in their neighbour's peatt moss roumes, and that conform to ye birliemen's declaratione.'

The dealers in horses, or horse-coupers, as they were usually called, are now characterized in the Biggar district for their orderly habits, and the honesty of their transactions. Within the memory of persons still living, the state of matters was different. Then, cheating in horse-dealing was proverbial; and the evenings of the fairs at Biggar and Skirling often presented scenes of swearing, fighting, and tumult among the generation of horse-coupers, truly appalling. Similar exhibitions, it appears, were common one hundred and forty years ago. The old record states, that Bailie Alexander Wardlaw, taking into consideration 'the many complents made to him anent drinking, fighting, cursing, swearing, and cheating, by reason of selling and exchanging of horses under night, when mercat tyme is over, for remeid whereof, the Baron Ballie statuts and ordains, that no person whatsoever buy, sell, or exchange any sort of horses after daylight is gone, under the pain and penalty of five pund Scots, *toties quoties*, for each transgression, and all bargains, after daylight is gone, are hereby declared null and of no effect. He renews all former Acts of Court anent forstallers of mercatts, and keeping up horses, and not presenting them to the mercat, in tyme of day, and ordains this Act to be proclaimed at the Mercat Cross, on Thursday, in tyme of mercat.'

Notwithstanding this enactment, the horse merchants could not be altogether deterred from pursuing their evil courses. We have evidence of this from the following sentence pronounced by the Bailie a short time afterwards :—'The same day, the Baillie fines and amerciates Richard Steill, horse merchant, in Biggar, in ye sum of ten pound Scots, for contumacy in not compearing, being personally summoned, at ye fiscall's instance, and likewise fines him in ye sum of five pounds Scots, for his cursing, swearing, and breaking ye peace of ye fair.' Richard appears to have been rather an outrageous knave, for on his appearing next court-day, the Bailie fined him in the additional sum of five pounds Scots, for cursing and swearing in the face of Court, and using other opprobrious language.

The horse merchants of Biggar, it appears, were guilty of the practice of forestalling the market; that is, the sale of their horses before exposing them in the public market place. This practice was constituted a crime by an Act of the Scottish Parliament in 1592, and was punishable by the escheat of moyeables. The horse merchants, however, were not the only dealers at Biggar who were chargeable with this crime. On the 12th April 1729, the Bailie, Luke Vallange, fined Gilbert Bannatyne, Thomas Forrest, James Watson, and William Bertram, and on the 2d of May following, Andrew M'Watt and Gilbert Reid, all meal-mongers in Biggar, 'ilke ane of them in L.5 Scots,' for not presenting their meal to the market, in market time of day.'

It is a proof of the traffic then carried on at Biggar, that it had at least six dealers in the article of meal.

The following is a specimen of the punishment inflicted by the bailies for the crime of theft. At the Court held on the 20th October 1720, by Bailie Luke Vallange, Margaret Stevenson, a native of the parish of St Ninian's, was arraigned, at the instance of the Fiscal, for the crime of breaking into the house of John Wilson, shoemaker, Biggar, on the fast-day before the Sacrament, and theftuously carrying off all his clothes. The culprit confessed that 'she took from him ane coat, ane gown, ane weast coat, ane pair of stockings, and twa shifftis. The Bailie having considered the complaint, and the defender's judicial confession, ordains her to stand in ye jugs for the space of ane hour, and to be banished out of ye toun by touok of Drum.'

The customs of Biggar were farmed by one of the burgesses, and were generally exposed every year to public competition. The Bailie, at a Court held in the end of October, intimated that a meeting of the burgesses would take place in the afternoon, when the customs would be rouped; and that none were to bid who could not produce a suffi-cient cautioner, under the penalty of L.50 Scots. This meeting, though primarily intended for business, appears to have also partaken of a festive character, as the customer, or person into whose hands the customs fell, was, at least on some occasions, bound to pay for 'a chopin of brandy' to regale the company. At the hour appointed for the meeting, the officer set up the half-hour sandglass, and cried 'three several Oyesses,' and the highest bidder, when the last particle of sand had run down the glass, was declared the 'customer' for the ensuing year. The customs of the two fairs of the town of Biggar were 'set' in 1671 to Andrew Telfoord, my Lord's officer, for twenty-eight pounds Scots yearly. The sum yearly obtained from the customs of Biggar during the early part of last century, ranged from L.60 to L.70 Scots. In 1730, Bailie John Wardlaw drew up a revised tariff of customs for Biggar, and ordered it to be engrossed in the Court books, and observed in all time to come. It is interesting, as showing the rate of custom at the time, and the kind of commodities that were exposed for sale at the fairs and markets of Biggar. It is divided into two parts, the dead and the quick customs; and fixes a higher rate of custom for fairs than for the ordinary market days. On market days, it appears, there were exposed for sale, shoes, smith work, pewter dishes, spinning wheels, chests, ploughs, harrows, caups, sieves, riddles, candle, coal, butter, cheese, salt, tallow, lint, horse, nolt, sheep and dog skins, webs of cloth, and such merchandise as were hawked about in horse and foot packs. At fairs, a stand for a horse pack was 1s. 4d., and for a foot pack 8d.; a stone of lint was 2s.; and a stone of tallow, tobacco, cheese, butter, and other weighable ware, was 1s. 4d. Each shoemaker, smith, cooper, wheelwright, and joiner, paid 8d.; while a horse-load of caups, sieves, and riddles was

8d., of pewter utensils, 1s., and of any other ware, 1s. 4d. A web of cloth was 8d.; and each load of meal was the full of the town-ladle, neither heaped nor stropped. On ordinary market days, the rate of custom was, in general, about one-half less than what it was on fair days. The quick customs, which were levied only at fairs, and upon both buyer and seller, were 2s. Scots for a horse, 1s. for a cow, 3s. 4d. for each score of old sheep, and 2s. for each score of lambs. The custom on cattle still belongs to the superior, and the custom on grain has been let on a long lease to the shareholders of the New Corn Exchange at Biggar.

Some of the young women of Biggar, it would seem, in former times occasionally amused themselves with a reprehensible pastime, which in our own day is termed larking. An instance of this occurred in May 1728, as appears from the following entry:—'The same day the Bailie fines Marion Rob, in Easter Toftcombs, and Janet Rob, servant to William Liddell, Biggar, ilk ane of them in the sum of two punds Scots to the fiscal, for their masquerading, and breaking and overturning of muck carts in Biggar, under cloud of night, when all the inhabitants were at rest.'

In the days when the Flemings and their bailies reigned in Biggar, it is evident, from the records which they have left, that the inhabitants had to submit to a considerable amount of interference with their liberties. Let us give one or two instances:—The Bailie not only ordered a number of the burgesses, in 1723, to dispose of their horses, cows, and other bestial, within eight days, under a penalty of L.10 Scots, on the ground of their not having a sufficient quantity of provender for their support, but on the 14th of February of the year following, statuted and ordained, 'that none within the toun of Biggar, nor Barronie thereof, belonging to my Lord Wigtoun, sell any fodder until the toun and tennantrie belonging to his Lordship be served therewith—they always paying such reasonable prices as others pay for the same, under the pain and penalty of twenty pounds Scots, toties quoties.

Another prohibitory act of the Bailies of Biggar, which seems to have been supported by a regulation of the Justices of the Peace of the county, but which has been unknown in practice for a long time past, was the prevention of servants from hiring themselves out of the parish, so long as there was within its bounds any demand for their services. The following is an enactment of Bailie Alexander Wardlaw on this subject, on the 17th February 1721:—'The whilk day the Ballie having considered the grivancess of the parroch of Biggar anent there servants, not only fieing without the said parroch, but in going to the neighbouring shyre for the love of extravegant fies, contrair to the act of the Justices of the Peace within this shyre, so that servants cannot be had in the parroch for laboring and manuring the ground, ffor remeid whereof the Ballie statutes and ordains, that no man nor woman servant lass nor lad flit nor remove from there master

or mistress out of the said parroch in tyme coming, until the people
of the said parroch be served, under the pain of ten punds Scots to
each transgression, *toties quoties*, and that by and attour the loss of
what fies and bountiths shall be resting them by their masters or
mistresses at the time of there going out of their service; and every
such servant suspect to contravene this Act, shall be obliged to find
caution to obtemper the same under the pain of imprisonment, and
ordains this Act to be intimat at the cross of Biggar the next
mercat day.'

The powers and prerogatives of Biggar as a burgh, if they are not
now extinct, are at least in abeyance. It may be questioned if it now
possesses a fully accredited Baron Bailie. It has no Procurator-fiscal,
no legally appointed Birliemen, no Dean of Guild, no Inspector of
Markets, no Burgh Clerk, and, perhaps, not even a Burgh Officer.
A Baron Bailie's Court has not been held for years. A proclamation
at the Market Cross, in all its state and ceremony, has not been seen
by the present generation. The preservation of the public peace is
now in the hands of one or two officials of the county police, who
have recently got a location in the neighbourhood of the place on
which, in former days, stood the Tolbooth of the burgh. However
active and efficient these men may be, they appear to us to be a
miserable substitute for the Baron Bailie with his staff of assistants.
Biggar may now be compared to a state ruled by foreigners instead of
its native princes. Disputes and offences, instead of being brought
before its own magistrates, and disposed of by their decision, are now
dragged away to Lanark, and subjected to the fiat of a Sheriff-substi-
tute of the county. We anticipate, however, a time when Biggar,
increased in size and importance, will once more possess the power of
self-government, and take its place among the burghs of the kingdom.

CHAPTER XVI.

The Commerce and Trade of Biggar.

THE Biggar district, in former times, had a number of markets and fairs. Some of these, for many years, have been abandoned. The Scottish Parliament, on the 15th of June 1693, passed an Act in favour of Andrew Brown of Dolphinton, 'for two free faires to be holden at the town of Dolphinton,' the one upon the last Wednesday of May yearly, to be called New Whitsunday Fair, and the other upon the 8th of October, to be afterwards named; and also a weekly market upon Tuesday, with the usual privileges, immunities, customs, casualties, and duties. The Dolphinton annual fairs and weekly market, if they were ever established, have long been discontinued.

'The Edinburgh True Almanack for the year of our Lord 1692,' states that 'there are two notable fairs at Lamington, within the shire of Lanark, where are to be had good schap horse, neat, sheep, and corns, meal, etc. The first on the 15th of June, with a horse-race for a saddle at 40s. value, set out by the laird of Lamington; the second, on the 22d of October yearly, with a weekly market every Thursday.' The fairs and the market of Lamington have also, for a long period, been abandoned.

Broughton, five miles from Biggar, has from time immemorial had an annual fair. It is, or was, a hiring fair, and was famed for the numerous assemblages of the rural population, male and female, that frequented it from the mountainous region around, and the desperate combats in which the Tweeddale ploughmen and shepherds engaged when under the maddening influence of love and drink. This fair, of late years, has much declined,—in fact, it is now almost extinct. Skirling, two miles distant, has three annual fairs;—the first in May, the second in June, and the third in September.

The June fair of Skirling was long one of the largest markets in Scotland for horses and cattle. It has now much fallen off. A large painting, showing its appearance in the days of its prosperity, by the celebrated artist, James How, a native of Skirling, is now in the possession of Adam Sim, Esq. of Coulter, along with another picture of a similar size, by the same artist, representing a show of stallions on Skirling Green. These pictures, while they give abundant proof of Mr How's great skill as an animal painter, at the same time show

that he had a strong appreciation of the ludicrous and grotesque.
They exhibit scenes of great fun and comicality,—scenes which he
himself, no doubt, witnessed and enjoyed in his early days, while
living under his father's roof. The Biggar district has produced no
painter of greater genius than How. No artist of his day could give
a more lifelike representation of the horse, the cow, the sheep, the
dog, and other portions of the animal creation. His professional
merits raised him to distinction; and they might have made him
wealthy, respected, and happy, had they not been counterbalanced by
great defects. His Panorama of Waterloo alone, by prudence and
proper management, might have placed him in a state of affluence;
but he allowed that and other golden opportunities to pass by without
yielding him any solid advantage. What money he gained by indefatigable industry and the exercise of his rare talents in one day, he
squandered away the next in reckless profusion and the debasement
of his noble faculties; and in the end he died in poverty and neglect,—
affording another example of the calamitous fate that too frequently
befalls the sons of genius.

When Skirling was erected into a free burgh of barony, in 1592,
by James VI., ' in consideratione of ye gude and thankfull service to
hir Majesty, and umquhile our dearest mother, by the late Sir James
Cockburne of Skraling,' it was provided that it should have a weekly
market on Friday, and an annual fair on the 4th of September. The
reason assigned for this was the distance of Skirling from the principal
burgh of the shire, 'quhairby they (the inhabitants) cannot goodly
repair at the fairs and mercat days of the said burgh for doing of
their lawful affairs, and traffic of goods, corns, and other merchandise.'
It would appear from this, that, at the time, it was thought desirable
that the traffic of a county should as much as possible be confined
within itself,—an opinion very different from that which now prevails.
To what extent the weekly market of Skirling was patronized by the
farmers and traffickers of the district, we cannot now say; but it
appears, for a long time, to have fallen into disuse.

The fairs or large markets at Biggar are numerous; and some of
them have been long established. The first of the year is held on the
last Thursday of January, old style, and is usually called Candlemas
Fair. The business principally transacted at it is the sale of horses
and cattle, and the hiring of servants. The second takes place on the
first Thursday of March, and used to be called Seed Thursday, because
its principal transactions consisted in the disposal of corn, potatoes,
etc., for seed. The third fair is held on the last Thursday of April.
It was only instituted a few years ago, but has been attended with
success. At this market servants are hired, stallions are shown, and
horses, cattle, pigs, etc., are disposed of. The next fair takes place
on the third Thursday of July, O. S. This fair, in the charter re-
erecting Biggar into a burgh of barony, granted by James VI., in

1588, in favour of John, Lord Fleming, is called St Peter's, and is appointed to take place on the festival of that saint, on the 29th of June,—fairs in ancient times being very commonly held on the festival of some saint. It was wont to be called Midsummer Fair, and was a great market for the sale of lambs, but it began at length to decline; and, about forty years ago, it was agreed to hold it two weeks later in the year, in the expectation that this would operate as an inducement to the farmers in the adjacent pastoral districts to patronize it again with their flocks. When a place of business begins to fall off, it is no easy matter to restore it to its former state of prosperity. This was fully exemplified in the case of this fair. It is now wholly deserted as a sheep and lamb market; but some business is still done in wool, and reapers for the harvest are engaged. It was, down to a recent period, a practice for a foot-race to be run on the evening preceding the fair, immediately after it had been proclaimed by the Baron Bailie at the Cross by tuck of drum. The reward given to the successful competitor was a pair of white gloves. As the expense of the gloves was paid by the lord superior, it is likely that the race was instituted by some of the Flemings to encourage the practice of athletic sports.

The cattle show of Biggar, held on the last Thursday of August, is another great agricultural display. In the year 1808, a Farmers' Society was established at Biggar, the principal objects of which were the discussion of agricultural subjects, the establishment of an agricultural library, and the punishment of depredations on the property of the members. The library was, however, never formed. In 1820, it was resolved to change the name of the Society to that of 'The Biggar Farmers' Club,' and to extend its design, by having an annual show of live stock and seeds. This show, with the exception of seeds, has accordingly taken place every year since, and has been largely patronized. The Club comprises the names of all the principal proprietors and farmers in the district; and it cannot be questioned that it has, in a great degree, contributed to evoke and keep alive a spirit of wholesome emulation in rearing stock, in cultivating the soil, and improving the products of the dairy. It has caused increased attention to be paid, among other matters, to the breed of horses, for which this district has long been famed. The powerful Clydesdale horse is now held in repute not only in Scotland, but in various other parts of the world. Several fine young stallions reared in the Biggar district, have of late years been exported to New Zealand and Australia. The prices realized for these animals are very considerable. We may specially refer to a very fine specimen, that was recently sold by Mr William Muir of Hardington Mains to Mr D. Innes, Parriora, Canterbury, New Zealand, for the large sum of L.325. The farmers in the Biggar district, as might be expected, very often succeed, at the great shows held under the auspices of the Highland Society, in carrying

2 B

off some of the chief prizes for the breed, not merely of horses, but of sheep and cows, as well as for the produce of the dairy.

The last fair of the year is held on the last Thursday of October. It is called the 'Old Fair,' and is a large market for the sale of horses, cattle, and the hiring of servants.

It is evident from the entries in the old record of the Bailie's Court, that sad scenes occasionally took place at the fairs of Biggar. On the 1st November 1723, the Bailie fined James Young, servant to James Anderson, Bridgend of Dolphinton, in the sum of five pounds Scots, and to remain in prison until it was paid, for committing 'a blood and battery on Steven Gilles in Biggar Fair.' On the 9th February 1721, the Bailie fined James Aitken and William Fleming in the sum of L.10 Scots, for refusing to assist in quelling a tumult in the market of Biggar on the last Thursday of January. On the 2d July 1724, the Fiscal arraigned before the Bailie, James Millar, in Biggar, and his spouse, John Rob, servant to Alexander Forsyth, and David Murdoch, son to William Murdoch, officer of Excise, for a riot committed by them on the 1st of July, being Biggar Fair, upon Robert Reid of Broughton Mains. The Bailie continued this case till next court-day, but the decision is not recorded. On the 2d July 1728, John Rob, son of Thomas Rob in Westraw, was fined in the sum of five pounds Scots, and to remain in prison until it was paid, for fighting and making a disturbance in the fair on the day previous. It was in consequence of such disturbances as these that the Baron's officer, and one or two assistants, armed with halberts, perambulated the ground during the continuance of the fair. Their duty was to prevent all tumults and riots, and to apprehend individuals disposed to be outrageous and unruly, lodge them in the Tolbooth, and arraign them before the Baron Bailie. The halberts used on these occasions are still preserved, and a representation of the head of one of them is given in the annexed engraving. We are far from thinking, however, that the fairs of Biggar are more distinguished for dis-

turbances and immoralities than the fairs in other districts. The rustics of Biggar, like those everywhere else, have a high flow of animal spirits, and when they get free from the thraldom in which

they are held all the year round, they are apt to be a little hilarious
and uproarious; but this is nothing more than might be expected from
persons rejoicing in the vigour of youth, and placed in similar circumstances. At the same time, no right thinking man will condemn the
efforts recently made to withdraw them, on these occasions, from the
consumption of intoxicating drinks. The unseemly exhibitions of
swearing, rioting, and fighting, that at times take place, are, in almost
every instance, the direct result of the use of these beverages.

The hiring of servants in a public market is also a degrading spectacle. It savours very much of the marts of slavery. Men and
women there expose, if not their persons, at least their physical capa-
bilities, to public sale, and are subjected to a scrutiny in some respects
similar to that which the slave-merchant gives to the human chattels
placed on the auction block. Moral character here goes but a short
way, while physical strength is reckoned of higher value, and is in
far greater request. It may appear difficult to find a substitute for
these human exhibitions,—the rustics themselves may cling to them
with the greatest tenacity, like the slave hugging his chains; but the
employers of labour, by subjecting themselves to a little temporary
inconvenience, and by adopting a proper mode of registration in the
towns and chief villages, might, in a short time, change the whole
system of hiring, and obviate the great evils and defects with which
the present method is chargeable. At the same time, let servants,
like other classes, have their holidays. Incessant bondage and toil
are by no means conducive to the physical and moral well-being of
mankind. It is good to have seasons of cheerful reunion, when
change of scene and innocent recreation give a zest to human existence, and scatter the clouds that are too apt to settle down on the
brows of the sons and daughters of toil. Biggar has recently commenced a great movement for the amelioration of the condition of
farm servants. The public meetings, and the addresses of Dr Guthrie
and others, at two Biggar Fairs, have drawn upon it the eyes of all
men. We hope it will not be found wanting, but will persevere in
its efforts till the objects which it contemplates have been crowned
with success.

At the fairs and markets of Biggar, in the olden time, one of the
most notable and gratifying spectacles was the ample array of the
products of female industry that was then displayed. Every house-
wife in the rural districts was a spinner and a manufacturer. Her
primary object was to clothe and adorn her own household; but not
unfrequently, by diligence and economy, she was able to supply
domestic wants, and also to have a considerable surplus to dispose of
to others. Hence, the gudewife appeared at the marts of commerce
with her lint and her wool, her hanks of yarn and her webs of cloth;
and, by the sales then made, she increased the family finances, and received encouragement to enter on new schemes of domestic industry.

Some remains of the ancient implements of female industry and thrift, once so common in the Biggar district, are still to be found. In preparing wool to make a very fine worsted thread, a comb of the following construction was used. This implement has long been discontinued, and a specimen of it is very rarely to be met with.

The implements of spinning, till within the last hundred years, were the distaff, the spindle, and whorle. These implements, which were remarkably simple, had been in use from the earliest periods of which we have any record. They are mentioned by Homer; and Solomon declares that a virtuous woman 'seeketh wool and flax, and worketh willingly with her hands; she layeth her hands to the spindle, and her hands hold the distaff.' St Catherine, in more recent times, was the patroness of the art of spinning; and its votaries, and the implements which they used, had the 7th of January set apart to their honour, and hence called 'St Distaff's Day,' or 'Rock Day.' An assemblage of young people for industrial purposes was, on this account, called a 'Rockin.' The readers of the poems of Robert Burns will recollect a reference to a meeting of this kind in the opening stanza of his first epistle to Lapraik. We quote from the original manuscript of this epistle, now in the possession of Adam Sim, Esq.:—

> 'On Fasten e'en we had a rockin,
> To caw the crack, and weave our stoken,
> An' there was meikle fun and jockin,
>   Ye need nae doubt ;
> At length we had a hearty yokin'
>   At sang about.'

In some districts of the country, the instruments of spinstry were borne in procession before a newly married bride. In an old work we find the following reference to this custom :—'In olde tyme there was usually carried before the mayde, when she should be married, and come to dwell in hir husbandes house,—a distaffe, charged with flaxe and a spyndle hanging at it, to the intent that she might be myndefull to lyve by hir labour.'

The whorles, which are commonly made of black stone, are found in abundance in the Biggar district. Like many of the early stone implements, they have had a certain superstitious veneration attached to them, and were ranked among the charms that had power over evil influences. Distaffs are now articles of great rarity. They were not merely composed of perishable material, but, when they were no longer applied to their original purpose, they were specially liable to injury and destruction, from their shape, which readily suggested their conversion into another useful domestic utensil, viz., a parritch-stick. Distaffs and whorles were wont, in ancient times, to be highly ornamented, and many curious and valuable specimens are carefully preserved. In a respectable family in the neighbourhood of Biggar, a finely carved distaff is still kept, and regarded as a family relic. The distaff, spindle, and whorle here engraved, were the property of one of the oldest families in the village of Coulter, and the initials of one of the members of the family are cut on the top of the distaff.

The yarn, after being spun, was formed into hanks by means of a hand-reel, which is represented below with a portion of the yarn upon it. When the winding of the thread was in progress, something like the following words were used :—

'Thou's no ane, but thou's ane a' out ;
Thou's no twae, but thou's twae a' out.'

The thread was not full till it had passed in a certain manner round the reel, and so many rounds formed the hesp or hank.

Thursday, 'dies Jovis,' is the day expressly mentioned in the original charter constituting Biggar a burgh of barony on which the weekly market of that town was to be held. We are, therefore, surprised to find, that when the General Assembly of the Scottish Kirk fixed on Saturday, the 26th of July 1645, to be observed as a solemn national fast, for the purpose of craving a blessing on the Parliament about to assemble at St Johnstone, and of giving thanks

for the victory gained by Fairfax in Northamptonshire, the Presbytery of Biggar, in making arrangements for the fast, decided that, 'because Satterday is ye ordinar day of Biggar mercatt, it was recommended to

ye baillies of Biggar to discharge ye mercatt for that day.' Nay, in
the charter of 1661, reconstituting Biggar and Kirkintulloch burghs
of barony, it is stated that their market days were changed from
Sunday to Saturday. However this may be, it is a fact, that the
weekly market of Biggar, as well as its annual fairs, have, for a period
beyond the memory of any man now living, been always held on
Thursday. On market days the farmers, and other portions of the
rural community, visit Biggar. Grain, meal, potatoes, and other
agricultural produce are disposed of, the news of the district are discussed, the progress of rural labour on the different farms is reported,
bank business is transacted, farming implements and household commodities are purchased, and the wants of the inner man are supplied
by a due modicum of refreshments in the 'Crown,' the 'Commercial,'
or the 'Elphinstone Arms.'

The amount of business done at the fairs and markets of Biggar is
considerable. It is, indeed, far beyond what any person who takes a
cursory look at the town would suppose. No better proof of this can
be given than the fact, that Biggar supports the branches of three
different banks, the 'Commercial,' the 'Royal,' and the 'National,'
besides a Savings' Bank. Some forty years ago the directors of an
Edinburgh Bank applied to the late Mr Robert Johnston, Biggar, to
obtain an opinion from him, if Biggar could support a branch of their
bank. Mr Johnston supposed that he knew the trade of the district
well; but, after all, he was so little aware of its wealth, and the traffic
it carried on, that he gave his decision against the establishment of
any such institution. The Savings Bank was established in 1832, and
was attended with so much success, that the Directors of the Commercial Bank were satisfied that a branch of their establishment
might also be opened with advantage. They immediately erected
suitable premises, and the branch was opened in the end of 1832,
under the management of the late Mr James Purdie. The present
manager is Mr Thomas Paul, jun. A branch of the Western Bank
of Scotland was opened on the 25th April 1840, and was conducted
by Mr John Wyld till September 1848, by Messrs Wyld and Jackson
till 1853, and by Mr David Thomson till the suspension of the Bank
on the 9th November 1857. A branch of the Royal Bank was established in place of the Western, on the 28th November of that year,
and has, to the present time, been conducted by Mr Thomson. A
branch of the City of Glasgow Bank was opened in January 1857;
and on the partial suspension of that Bank in November of that
same year, the business was taken up by the National Bank of Scotland on the 1st of December following. The branch of the National
is under the management of Mr Adam Pairman.

The Rev. John Christison, in his Statistical Account of the parish,
makes the following statement regarding the retail trade of the town.
'Some idea,' says he, 'may be formed of the retail trade of Biggar by

the following quantities of excisable articles sold during the year ending 5th July 1835: 2608 gallons British spirits, 80 gallons brandy,
136 gallons ginger wine and other shrubs, 88 dozen of foreign wine,
2528 lbs. tea, 1876 lbs. tobacco and snuff.' The quantity of these
articles sold in the shops of Biggar, particularly tea, the annual sale
of which exceeds 7000 lbs., is now, 1862, very considerably increased.
This has been caused by the prosperous state of agriculture, and an increase in the number of wealthy families resident in the neighbourhood.

The inhabitants of Biggar devote themselves to all the industrial
pursuits common in little towns. Its weavers, masons, joiners, shoemakers, and tailors very much predominate, in point of numbers,
over the other tradesmen. About thirty years ago, according to the
Statistical Account of Scotland, there were no fewer than 210 weavers
in the town and parish. The webs, which consisted of stripes, checks,
ginghams, druggets, etc., were supplied by manufacturing houses in
Glasgow, through the medium of agents. One of the weavers' agents
at Biggar at that time, was Mr James Brown, who deserves to be
specially noticed on account of his amiable manners, his Christian
deportment, and poetic talents. He was born at Libberton, near Carnwath, on the 1st of July 1796. His father, who was miller of Libberton
Mill, was considerably advanced in years at the time of his birth, and
died when he was only six years of age. His mother was Grizzel
Anderson, a person held in esteem for her kind and amiable disposition. As soon as Mr Brown had acquired sufficient strength, he was
apprenticed to a weaver, and after serving the usual period, he removed
to Symington, and there wrought for a number of years as a journeyman. He devoted his leisure hours to the cultivation of his mind, or
the enjoyment of solitary rambles on the adjacent uplands of the
Castlehill and Tinto. He established a club for mutual improvement,
which met periodically at his house. He wrote a number of poems
and songs of considerable merit, which enjoyed some portion of local
celebrity; but he obstinately refused to commit any of them to
print. In 1823, he obtained a situation in the wareroom of a manufacturer in Glasgow; but this employment not suiting his constitution, he was appointed agent of the firm in Biggar. Here he
lived several years; but his health, never robust, gradually gave
way. When he saw that the time of his departure was at hand, he
desired to be taken to Symington, the scene of his early manhood,
and there he died on the 12th September 1836. His manners were
rather grave and austere, and his disposition retiring and reserved;
but he possessed a kind and benevolent heart, and his belief in the
truths of divine revelation was firm and sincere. Several of his productions were published for the first time, two or three years ago, in
Rodger's 'Scottish Minstrelsy.'

The agents at Biggar also supplied webs to weavers at Symington,
Thankerton, Covington, Quothquan, Newbigging, Elsrickle, etc.,—these

places containing, perhaps, not less than 150 weavers. The number of webs received from Glasgow weekly, at least from 1824 to 1835, would average about eighty, and the amount of weekly payments would be about L.200. The rate of remuneration was highest in 1812, and a few years subsequently. The weaving of an ell of stripe, 1000 reed, was then paid as high as 8½d.; but the rate at length began gradually to decline, so that the same fabric in 1840 was paid as low as 1¾d. per ell,—a rate at which it was scarcely possible to earn the scantiest subsistence. The supply of work, even at so low a rate, was very limited; and this induced some of the agents, and especially Mr Allan Whitfield, to exert themselves to introduce new fabrics. Their efforts met with partial success, and for some years a considerable amount of heavy work, consisting of cotton warp and woollen weft, was obtained. The application of steam-power to weaving, and the erection of large weaving establishments in the west of Scotland, appear, however, to have had a permanently injurious effect on hand-loom weaving in such places as Biggar and its adjacent villages. While we write, 1862, the weaving trade in Biggar is in a most depressed state. The number of weavers in that town at present does not exceed 50, and these are by no means fully employed,—the number of webs from Glasgow being reduced to an average of ten weekly, and the aggregate amount of wages to L.15.

The other branches of industry in Biggar continue in a prosperous state. It is no small proof of the progressive character of the town, that it is now able to support a printing press. From this press issue trade circulars, announcements of sales, public meetings, etc., all conducive to the enterprise and prosperity of the district. The spirited proprietor of this press, Mr David Lockhart, in 1860, laid before the public the first volume ever printed in Biggar. It is entitled, 'Tales and Legends of the Upper Ward of Lanarkshire.' This volume contains no inconsiderable portion of Upper Ward history, interlarded, no doubt, with a large amount of fable. The style in which these 'Tales' are couched, and the industry of the author in ferreting out old traditions and incidents connected with the locality, are worthy of commendation; but, upon the whole, the stories rather disappoint the hopes which they are calculated at first to raise. We hail them, nevertheless, with great cordiality, as the first intellectual fruits of the Biggar Press, to be followed, we trust, by many worthy and successful publications.

On the authority of an intelligent statistician, we give a list of the different occupations at Biggar, and the number of persons connected with each:—Weavers' Agents, 4; Architects, 3; Auctioneer, 1; Bakers, 13; Bankers, 5; Beadles, 3; Besom-maker, 1; Bill-poster, 1; Bird-stuffer, 1; Boot and Shoemakers, 20; Builders, 3; Cabinetmaker and Upholsterer, 1; Carriers, 4; Chimney-sweepers, 2; China, Glass, and Earthen Ware Dealers, 7; Clergymen, 4; Cloggers, 2; Coach and Post Horse Hirers, 3; Coal Agents and Merchants, 2;

Coffeehouse Keepers, 2; Contractors, 4; Coopers, 2; Dress and Straw Hat Makers, etc., 26; Druggists, 2; Fleshers, 4; Gardeners, 2; Gasfitters, 2; Glaziers, 3; Grocers, Tea and Spirit Merchants, and Ironmongers, 24; Gravediggers, 2; Horse Dealer, 1; Hawkers, 7; Inn and Hotel Keepers, 7; Jewellers, 2; Joiners, 12; Land-surveyors, 2; Last and Boot-tree Maker, 1; Letter Carrier, 1; Librarians, 5; Machine Makers and Millwrights, 4; Manufacturers, 2; Masons, 21; Midwife, 1; Millers, 2; Nailmakers, 9; Newspaper Agent, Stationer, and Printer, 1; Notary Public, 1; Nursery and Seedsman, 1; Painters, 2; Paper-hangers, 2; Pavement Merchants, 2; Perfumer, Barber, and Hair-dresser, 1; Physicians and Surgeons, 5; Plasterers, 2; Plumbers, 2; Porter and Ale Brewers, 3; Quarriers, 2; Saddlers and Harness-makers, 11; Sawyer, 1; Skinners, 3; Slaters, 4; Smiths, 11; Stationers, 2; Tailors, 24; Teachers, 3; Thatchers, 4; Turner, 1; Umbrella and Parasol Manufacturer, 1; Valuator, 1; Veterinary Surgeon, 1; Victuallers, 2; Watch and Clock Makers, 6; Weaver Utensil-makers, 2; Woollen and Linen Drapers, 16.

Biggar was long a depôt for lead from the mines at Leadhills. These mines were wrought for some time by James IV. and James V. The latter monarch, at length, granted permission to a company of Germans to work the whole mines of Scotland for forty-three years. In January 1562, John Achisone, Master of the Mint, and John Aslowne, burgess in Edinburgh, obtained a license from Queen Mary 'to wirk and wyn in the Leid Mynis of Glengoner and Wenlek, sa mekill leid ure as they may gudlie, and to transport and carie furt of this realme to Flanderis, or ony utheris pairtis beyond sey, 20,000 stane wecht of the said ure comptand sexskoir to ye hundreth trone wecht.' These parties were to deliver to the Queen's Mint at Edinburgh, forty-five ounces of pure silver for every 1000 stones of lead ore which they carried away. The lead which these persons dug, was conveyed on horses' backs to Biggar, and thence to Leith, where it was shipped for Flanders. There the silver incorporated with the lead was extracted, by a process with which the Scots were at that time unacquainted. About thirty years afterwards, Thomas Fowlis, goldsmith, Edinburgh, obtained a lease of these lead mines, and assumed as partner a skilful and enterprising English miner named Bewis Bulmer. In the records of the Privy Council, it is stated that the broken men of the Border were in the habit of assailing the servants of this mining company while employed in transporting the ore on the backs of horses, and depriving them of 'their horses, armour, clothing, and hail carriage.'

After the use of carts became common, and the process of smelting the lead ore was carried on at Leadhills and Wanlockhead, the practice was to cart the lead in bars from these places, and deposit it at Biggar, where each mining company had an agent, and then convey it in the same way from Biggar to Leith, principally by

2 C

carters from Edinburgh and Leith, who took what they called a 'rake o' leed,' when business was slack at home, or when they had occasion to be at Biggar or its neighbourhood with other loading.   About the beginning of the present century, the number of bars that were annually deposited at Biggar, on their way to Leith, ranged from 10,000 to 18,000.   Each bar weighed about 120 lbs.   Taking the medium number of bars to be 14,000, and each cart to carry 15 bars, upwards of 900 cart-loads of lead would thus each year, on an average, be conveyed to and from the depôt at Biggar.

The number of carts constantly coming and going in connection with this traffic, caused no small stir at Biggar, and brought a considerable amount of patronage to the houses of the stablers.   The construction of the Caledonian Railway deprived Biggar of the advantages which it derived from this source, and removed the piles of lead bars which for a long period formed a marked feature in the High Street of the little town.

Besides the transmission of lead, a considerable number of carriers from the south of Scotland passed every week through Biggar on their way to and from the metropolis.   Biggar was one of their stages; and on certain nights of the week, ranges of well-laden carts, with a due portion of canine attendants, were to be seen on the street.   Biggar, standing on the great highway from the south to Edinburgh, was visited by a constant succession of travellers on foot or horseback, in gig or chariot.   Being the capital of a considerable district, extending from Tweedsmuir to Covington, and from Dolphinton to Crawford, its markets and marts of commerce were frequented by a considerable population, and thus its monotony was relieved, and its wealth increased.   Biggar, neither in remote ages, with the exciting presence of its feudal barons, nor in more recent times, with its spirit, industry, and traffic, could therefore, with any fairness, be called a dull and lifeless community, or was so 'entirely cut off from the great world, and thrown upon its own solitary reading and reflection,' as some persons have ventured to suppose.

CHAPTER XVII.

The Benefit Societies of Biggar.

THE people of Biggar and its neighbourhood have not been inattentive to the advantages of associating themselves for the purpose of social intercourse, and mutual relief in case of accident or sickness. Efforts of this kind are meritorious, as they encourage prudent and economical conduct, promote good fellowship, and provide a security against destitution, when, by some stroke of calamity, the usual sources of income are dried up. Thirty years ago, Biggar could boast of possessing four benefit societies, with a conjoined membership of 733 persons. These were the Masons', the Friendly, the Whipmen's, and the Weavers' Societies.

The oldest Society in Biggar is the Masons. Like many Masons' Societies in Scotland, it has lost its oldest records, and therefore its early history is shrouded in an obscurity never likely to be dispelled. When we first become acquainted with it, we find it in active working order; but we obtain no information regarding the way in which the members acquired their masonic knowledge, or the time at which they first associated themselves together. It is perhaps not going too far to say, that a masons' lodge of one kind or another has existed in Biggar from the commencement of the building of Biggar Kirk, in 1545. The men who erected that edifice were evidently, from the marks left on their work, Freemasons; and little doubt can exist that they practised their rites during the time that they carried it on. The Lodge then formed would be frequented by the operative masons in the district; and these men would continue the organization long after the builders of the Kirk had taken their departure. This is so far confirmed by the fact, that the Freemasons of Biggar continued, to a recent period, to practise mark-masonry, and to use marks similar to those found on the stones of Biggar Kirk. A record of the Lodge marks for a number of years is still preserved, and possesses no small interest to the student of the principles of masonic science. The law of the Lodge in regard to marks, as expressed in a minute dated 27th December 1797, was, 'that every brother, in all time coming, using any mark, for any purpose whatever in masonry, shall have the same registered by the Mark Masters, for which he shall pay the sum of one mark Scots, which shall go to the funds of the Lodge, and that any mark that is not so registered, cannot serve him for any purpose in masonry;

and further, that no brother can, on any pretext whatever, use a mark employed by another brother after it is registered.'

The first entry in the records of the Lodge of Biggar Free Operatives that has been preserved, is dated 12th January 1726, and states that William Ireland and George Young were then entered apprentices, and Alexander Crichton was passed fellow-craft. A reference is made in one of the minutes to an Act, passed in 1725, against absentees from the meetings of the Lodge; and this is the earliest date that we can find regarding its operations. The Biggar Society of Freemasons was, strictly speaking, what is called an Operative Lodge; that is, a large portion of its members were operative masons. It apparently practised at first only two degrees of St John's masonry—the entered apprentice and fellow-craft. It is not till the year 1765, that special notice is taken of the raising of entrants to the sublime degree of Master Mason. The Lodge, at first, was presided over by a deacon, who was assisted by a warden, a box-master, a treasurer, a clerk, and several managers; but after the formation of the Grand Lodge of Scotland, in 1736, the present order of officials,—viz., a master, two wardens, two deacons, two stewards, a treasurer, secretary, etc.,—was adopted. On St John's day 1726, the principal office-bearers chosen were—Robert Scott, deacon; Alexander Baillie, warden; and Andrew Aikman, box-master; and the most active members, at that time, were Thomas Cosh, John Tod, Daniel Aitken, James Vallange, John Gladstones, George Bertram, and William Baillie.

At a meeting of the members of the Lodge, on the 27th May 1727, it was resolved to petition the Lodge of Linlithgow to be incorporated with that Lodge—'to be made,' as was stated, 'a part and pendicle of it, and to obtain the rights, powers, and privileges thereof.' Accordingly, the Lodge of Linlithgow, at a meeting held at Queensferry on the 11th of July following, was pleased to grant the prayer of the petition, and to present a charter on stamped paper to a deputation from the Biggar Lodge, that were in attendance. The expenses incurred in carrying through this transaction, amounted to L.58, 17s. Scots, and the Biggar Lodge became bound to pay to the Linlithgow Lodge one pound Scots yearly. On the 27th of May 1734, the Biggar Lodge received a visit from the deacon and warden of the Linlithgow Lodge, and spent L.12 Scots in giving them a treat.

It was the practice of the Lodge at that time, as it still is, to have an annual procession on the anniversary of St John the Evangelist, viz., the 27th of December. On the 24th December 1736, the members resolved to have a new flag for their annual display. Accordingly, they bought a piece of silk cloth from William Johnston, and 'yellow wattens from Janet Wilson to munt the said flag,'—the price of the whole being L.4, 2s. Scots. On St John's day following, they chose Alexander Crichton ensign, and Daniel Aitken adjutant, and marched through the town five men deep, all with blue bonnets, white aprons, white gloves, yellow cockades, and hand-rules. On these occasions, it was the custom of the brethren to ascend the Cross-knowe, and while encircling the ancient Cross, to drink the usual loyal toasts in whisky, brandy, or ale. This was done with great acclaim on the 27th December 1745, during the time of the rebellion; but whether the toasts on that occasion referred to Prince Charlie or George II., the record saith not. We are told, however, that the brethren got a present of a pint of whisky from John Laidlaw, merchant, and that, in the exuberance of their generous feelings, they invited to dinner the following townsmen, viz.:—Andrew Vallange, John Gibson, Bailie Carmichael, William Forrest, Robert Craig, John Laidlaw, George Bertram, and 'ye Drummer,' and defrayed the whole expense out of the funds of the box. It is certain that the Biggar Masons were intensely loyal to the House of Hanover during the early part of the reign of George III. On the King's birthday—the 4th of June—the brethren were wont to assemble, and, clothed in the paraphernalia of their order, to proceed to the Cross, and there drink his Majesty's health amid loud huzzas and volleys of musketry.

The order of procession on St John's day was fixed, in 1796, as follows:—

Music, preceded by three Halbertmen.
Tyler in uniform.
Stewards with white rods.
Brethren out of office, two and two.
Treasurer and Secretary, with the badges of their offices.
The Bible, with Square and Compass, borne on a crimson cushion, and supported by the two Deacons, with black rods.
The Chaplain.
The Wardens.
The Past Master.
The R. W. Master, supported by the Depute and Substitute Masters.

It was the practice, for a number of years, to have a sermon preached on St John's day in the Parish Church. In 1794, the sermon was preached by the Rev. William Strachan of Coulter; in 1795, by the Rev. James Gardner of Tweedsmuir; in 1796, by the Rev. Robert Anderson, preacher of the Gospel at Symington; in 1797, by the Rev. John Ritchie of Dunsyre; in 1798, by the Rev. Bryce Little of Covington; and in 1799, by the Rev. Patrick Mollison of Walston.

In 1736, Biggar Lodge sent a representative to Edinburgh, when William St Clair of Roslin resigned his office as hereditary Grand Master, and the Grand Lodge of Scotland was constituted in its present form. The name of the representative is unfortunately obliterated in the old record, from exposure to damp, but it is supposed to have been Sir William Baillie of Lamington. A misunderstanding, it appears, arose between Sir William and the Lodge, which he was in-

disposed to take any steps to clear up. When the Grand Lodge sent
a communication to the Biggar Masons, in March 1737, requesting a
delegation at the Quarterly Communication on the 13th of April, the
brethren set Sir William aside, and elected, in his place, Brother
Thomas Simson. They furnished this brother with a copy of their
charter from the Lodge of Linlithgow, and the names of the entrants
since the formation of the Grand Lodge; and they instructed him to
ascertain if they were recognised as a regularly constituted Lodge,
and, if this was the case, to pay the stipulated fee of half-a-crown for
the enrolment of each of their entrants since November last. It may
be conjectured that there was either some hesitation on the part of
the Grand Lodge to admit the Biggar brethren, or that these brethren
themselves were slow in complying with some of the Grand Lodge
regulations. At all events, the Lodge of Biggar was not placed on the
roll, and the brethren very soon began to cool towards the governing
body. In 1738, they therefore came to the decision, that, as they had
many widows and orphans to support, it would be better to keep
their half-crowns at home than to send them to the Grand Lodge.
The Lodge continued its connection with the Lodge of Linlithgow,
although that Lodge had set the example of resigning its independent
powers, and giving its adherence to the supreme ruling body established in Edinburgh; and it was not till the year 1785 that the
Biggar brethren resolved to obtain a charter from the Grand Lodge.
This accordingly was granted them on the 6th of November 1786,
and cost the sum of L.7, 19s. 2d. The Biggar Lodge was placed on
the roll as number 222, which was afterwards changed to its present
number, 167; but had it persevered in its original design of joining
the Grand Lodge at its formation, it would have taken its place among
the oldest lodges in the country. The charter, which it thus obtained,
is preserved with great care; it is always read at the annual meetings
on St John's day, and during processions is carried in an ornamental
box by the Tyler.

The meetings of the Lodge were at first held in the inns and private
houses of the town. Those most frequently mentioned are the houses
of Thomas Cosh, dyer; John Cree, gardener; John Gladstones, maltman; Andrew Brown, Silver-knowes; and John Jardine and Thomas
Wilson, vintners. A lodge was occasionally opened in the country
for making masons. Among other places in the neighbourhood, may
be mentioned Elsrickle, Bogsbank, and Cormiston; and on one occasion a dispensation was granted to make masons for the Biggar Lodge
in England. In 1793, the members purchased a house in the centre
of the town from Mathew Cree and Andrew Nicol, and converted one
of its apartments into a lodge-room; but it was far from being suitable
or commodious. The brethren at different times held deliberations
regarding the propriety of erecting a proper hall. In 1796, Lord
Elphinstone, superior of the barony, proposed to erect a new Meal-

house and a Tolbooth; and, therefore, the brethren put themselves in communication with his Lordship to get liberty to put an additional storey on the top of this projected building, to be used for the purpose of a hall; but his Lordship's design does not appear to have been carried into execution. In 1808, a committee, composed of three delegates from each of the Benefit Societies of Biggar, held several meetings to decide on the erection of a common hall. To this committee a report was given in, that a hall, 55 feet long and 28½ feet wide, could be erected for L.450. This project also failed, and the consequence was, that the Masons erected a new hall for themselves, in 1814, adjoining their own tenement. It is plain but commodious, and on great festive days is ornamented by the Master's chair, made in 1794, and by a portrait of Robert Burns, painted for the Lodge by a townsman and brother mason, the late John Pairman. This portrait was presented to the Lodge in December 1821, along with the following letter addressed to the Right Worshipful Master :—

'R. W. MASTER,—As an humble but sincere mark of respect to you and the brethren of Biggar Free Operatives, St John's Lodge, I beg to present for your acceptance a portrait of the late Robert Burns, the Ayrshire poet. In fixing on him for your hall, I do not wish to hold him up as a faultless character, but I may be allowed to say that, with all his faults, Burns will merit a place in the affections of every brother. When living, he was ardently devoted to masonry; and since his death, his songs have, in an eminent degree, contributed to the innocent pleasures of masonry. With best wishes to you and the brethren whom you have the honour to represent, —I am, etc.,

'JOHN PAIRMAN.'

As a small return for Mr Pairman's kindness, the Lodge elected him an honorary member, and presented him with a diploma.

At the meeting on St John's day 1796, some Knight-Templars who were present, insisted on taking precedence of the other brethren, who were only Blue Masons. This led to a keen discussion. The Lodge itself was not disposed to give any deliverance on the subject, but Brother George Inglis protested against the conduct and pretensions of the Templars, and appealed to the Grand Lodge. That body, on the 1st of May 1797, gave the following decision :—'A petition and complaint was read from sundry brethren of the Lodge Biggar Free Operatives, respecting certain brethren of the Order of Knight-Templars, insisting that, in consequence of their possessing that degree in masonry, they are entitled to precedency above Master Masons of said Lodge. The Grand Lodge declare in the negative, and that the present office-bearers of every regular Lodge shall, according to their respective offices, as expressed in their charter, take precedency of every other member of said Lodge; and that no other distinction shall be known in a Lodge of the brethren thereof, but that which rises from superior knowledge in masonry and exemplary behaviour.'

A number of the French prisoners stationed at Biggar on their parole of honour, towards the close of the war with France, were freemasons. In the beginning of 1813, they applied to the members of the Biggar Lodge for the use of their hall, the master's chair, the warden's tools, etc., in order that they might constitute a lodge of their own. This application was acceded to, and Brothers Elias Berger and Francis Renaudy became security for any damage that might be done. The French masons were here wont to practise their rites, which were somewhat different from those of the Scottish brethren. One of their number, resident in the Westraw, having died, was interred with masonic honours, and a funeral lodge was held out of respect to his memory. The Biggar Lodge had the honour of enrolling in its ranks one of these prisoners, a distinguished Polish nobleman and a freemason named Francois Mayskie, and received from him a fee of one guinea.

The Lodge of Biggar has taken part in various public ceremonials of the craft. It was well represented at laying the foundation-stones of the Lodge Hall of Lockhart St John, Carnwath; the National Monument at Edinburgh; the Bridge over the Mouse at Cartlane; the County Buildings, Lanark; the Freemasons' Hall, Edinburgh, etc.; and it turned out in great force at the demonstration at laying the foundation-stone of the Corn Exchange, Biggar.

Members are admitted into the Lodge between the ages of sixteen and thirty-two years. On being entered apprentices they pay L.1, 6s. 6d., and 10s. 6d. additional on being raised to the sublime degree of Master Mason. The quarterly payment is 1s. 3d. Members, when sick, are entitled to 6s. weekly for the space of seventeen weeks; and if they continue longer in a bad state of health, they receive 4s. weekly till the expiration of a year. After this period, they are allowed such a sum as the managers think proper. On the death of a member, the Lodge pays L.2 in name of funeral expenses. The annual income of the Society has been somewhat fluctuating. In 1837, it was as low as L.93, 1s. 4d., while in 1849 it was as high as L.172, 5s. 6d; and in 1860, it was L.132, 3s. 2d. The expenditure has varied in the same way. In 1836, it was L.70, 12s. 6d.; and in 1855, it was L.159. The Society is at present in a flourishing condition, and the number of members on the roll is 245. The amount of good which this Society has done is, no doubt, very great. It has not only aided hundreds of poor men when in distress, and after their death caused their funeral obsequies to be observed with decent solemnities, but it has relieved the wants of many a poor wanderer. The entries in the books are numerous of small sums disbursed to travelling brethren, to assist them on their journey.

A benefit society, established in 1787, was called the 'Friendly Society.' In 1835, it had one hundred and fourteen members, with a capital of L.250. It continued after this period gradually to decline.

Few new members joined it, and the demand on its funds increased from year to year. It was therefore dissolved.

Another benefit society was established at Biggar in 1806, and is called the 'Biggar Whipmen's Society.' During the first year of its existence, it enrolled 190 members. At its first annual procession, which took place on the 17th of July 1807, no fewer than 164 members appeared on horses, gaily caparisoned with ribbons, flowers, etc. The privilege of carrying the colours or flag was rouped, and brought the sum of four guineas. The members then proceeded to Coultermains, the seat of John Brown, Esq., and afterwards to Hartree House, the residence of Colonel Alexander Dickson. The annual processions at first were fixed to take place on the day after Biggar Midsummer Fair, but they have been changed to the day after Skirling Fair, in June; and on this day the Biggar gymnastic sports are also held. The Whipmen's Society allows its sick members 5s. per week for twelve weeks, 3s. a-week for twenty-four weeks, and then one guinea quarterly so long as sickness continues.

The fourth benefit society was instituted on the 3d of December 1806, and was called the Weavers' Society. Its annual meeting and procession took place on the first Friday of July. On this occasion the members paraded the town clothed with white aprons, sashes, and other insignia. The Weavers' parade was a gala day at Biggar. The music for many years consisted of a drum and a fife, supplemented with one or two fiddles. The allowance to sick members was somewhat similar to that of the Masons' Society, and the funeral money was the same. The Weavers' Society, from being founded on erroneous calculations, from having too many very poor and infirm members, or receiving no adequate accessions of young men to its roll, began to give symptoms of decay. It lingered on for some years; and though it was a law that any member who should propose that the Society should be dissolved, or its funds divided, should instantly and for ever be expelled, yet this idea was not only propounded, but entertained, and this once flourishing institution was brought to a close in 1841. The colours or flag of the Society, which waved in the breeze on every annual procession, are preserved by Mr George Johnston, merchant, Biggar. They are adorned with the Weavers' arms, and the motto—

'Imperial thrones
Our art adorns,
But to the poor
Here is our alms.'

2 D

CHAPTER XVIII.

The Witches of the Biggar District.

A BELIEF in witchcraft and sorcery, it is well known, prevailed at one period throughout the whole of Europe. The minds of all men were, for a season, given up to gross delusion on this subject; a delusion, unfortunately, that did not remain visionary and passive, but manifested itself in acts of the most unrelenting cruelty. It is impossible at this day to read the details of the tortures and deaths that were inflicted on old helpless men and women, accused of these imaginary crimes, without experiencing a thrill of intense horror, and breathing a prayer of grateful acknowledgment that we live in times more rational and enlightened. The Romish Church, when it held undisputed sway over the nations, waged, with its papal bulls and inquisitorial proceedings, a terrible and unremitting warfare with the supposed possessors of these black arts. The Reformation, which had a great effect in eradicating errors, enlightening the mind, and banishing intellectual torpor, instead of dispelling the belief in witchcraft, rendered it more inveterate and intense, and fanned the rage against it to a state of fiercer activity than ever. The Scriptures were more diligently searched, and in many respects better understood; but all classes of men were still unable fully to discriminate between what was peculiar and temporary in a dispensation that had passed away, and what remained obligatory in the religious system that had taken its place. The Old Testament declared that witches, wizards, enchanters, familiar spirits, etc., not merely existed, but that the law of God was, that they should not be suffered to live. Those rulers among the ancient Jews who had signalized themselves in attempting to effect the utter extermination of these unfortunate beings, had received very special commendation, and therefore, it was argued, that men in authority, in all ages, should act a similar part. Fortified with such notions, the whole mass of the people became blind to the utter improbability that the Almighty, either directly or indirectly, would permit old, ignorant, crazed individuals to possess powers so extraordinary as to be able to raise storms, blast the produce of the field, inflict diseases and disasters on man and beast, metamorphose themselves into various animals, fly through the air from place to place, hold personal intercourse with the enemy of mankind, pry into the dark future, and foretell the designs of Providence and the fate of human beings.

The Scottish Parliament, in the reign of Queen Mary, enacted that 'witchcraft, sorcerie, necromancie, the vsurers thereof, and all persons seikand any helpe, responsé, or consultatione fra any sic vsurers, or abusers, are punished to the death with all regour.' The consequence of this was, that vast numbers of aged persons, especially women, were seized and arraigned for crimes, which we now know were purely imaginary; and, in order to extort a confession of guilt, were subjected to the most excruciating tortures. The boots and the thumbkins * were often called into requisition in such cases; men called prickers were employed to thrust large pins into the flesh of the accused; a terrible instrument, called the branks, or witches' bridle, * was placed on their heads, which fastened them to the wall of their cells, and prevented them from speaking; relays of men were appointed to guard them in prison and keep them from falling asleep; and a special and stand- ing commission of the Privy Council was empowered to try the wretches accused of the supposed crime. Many of the persons seized, made mad by oppression, emitted before this tribunal the most extra- vagant, absurd, and incredible confessions; and, in most cases, were sent without delay to the gibbet or the stake. The effect of these severities was, that the numbers of the accused, instead of being diminished, were increased to an immense extent. Witches, war- locks, and charmers abounded in every parish, prisons sufficiently large could not be got to contain them, and terror and frenzy reigned in every quarter. The most active instruments in the discovery, pro- secution, and destruction of witches, were the Reformed clergy. These men pursued this object with an unrelenting determination, that while it bears ample testimony to their energy and zeal, at the same time reflects no great credit on them as men and Christians. They seem to have divested themselves of all feelings of humanity, and to have gloried in evincing an amount of error, delusion, and barbarity utterly alien to the enlightened and benevolent principles which they had undertaken to enunciate to their fellow-sinners.

Warlocks and witches, during the sixteenth and seventeenth cen- turies, of course, abounded in the Upper Ward of Clydesdale, as well as in the other districts of Scotland. Every parish had its quota, but it appears, from the records of the Presbytery of Lanark, that they were especially numerous in the parishes of Douglas, Crawford, and Crawfordjohn. The Presbytery of Lanark, for a number of years, had their hands so full of business connected with these persons, that it engrossed a large portion of their time.

In former times, great attention was paid to certain wells. They were held to possess a sovereign efficacy in curing diseases, and were dedicated to some saint or angel, who was supposed to preside over them, and to confer upon them their curative virtues. Bands of people walked in procession to them on the festivals of the holy beings

* Good specimens of these instruments are to be seen in Mr Sim's museum.

to whom they were dedicated; and on these occasions they were
decorated with flowers and boughs of trees, and libations of their
water were poured out with great ceremony and solemnity. Pilgrims
from distant parts of the kingdom were often to be seen seated by
their side, imbibing their water, or washing the sores with which
their persons were afflicted. The leaders of the Reformation resolved
to suppress these superstitious practices; and, accordingly, a statute
was enacted, in 1579, prohibiting all pilgrimages to wells. This law,
however, had not the desired effect. It was to little purpose that the
civil authorities threatened and prosecuted, or that the Reformed
clergy thundered against the practice, and inflicted their spiritual
censures. The people could not be deterred from the observance of
their old custom, or led to believe that the wells, once so sacred and
efficacious, had lost their virtues. The Privy Council, in 1629, issued
an edict, in which they lamented that pilgrimages to chapels and wells
were still common in the kingdom, to the great offence of God, the
scandal of the Kirk, and disgrace to his Majesty's Government, and
enacted that Commissioners should cause diligent search to be made
'at all suche pairts and places where this idolatrous superstition is used,
and to take and apprehend all suche persons, of whatsoever rank or
qualitie, whom they sall deprehend, going in pilgrimage to chappellis
and wellis, or whome they sall know themselffes to be guiltie of that
cryme, and commit thame to waird,' until measures should be adopted
for their trial and punishment. Notwithstanding the severity of this
enactment, it is evident from the records of the Presbytery of Lanark,
and from other sources of information, that the practice was still, more
or less, continued. For instance, in September 1641, Mali Lithgow
was reported to the Presbytery of Lanark, by John Hume, to be
guilty of charming in the parish of Skirling; and William Somervail,
minister of Dunsyre, was appointed to make diligent search for her,
and send her to the Session of Skirling to be tried. On the 5th
November following, Mali was brought before the Presbytery, and
confessed that she went to the Well of Skirling,* and was ordered to
appear before the Kirk Session of Skirling, and answer for her incan-
tations. And the Session records of that parish, if they have been
preserved, no doubt contain a detail of her trial and sentence. The
principal wells in Biggar and its neighbourhood were, and still are,
Bow's, Malcolm's, Duncan's, Jenny's, Gum's, and the Greystane. Some
of these were, no doubt, locally famous, in former days, for their
healing virtues. The practice was common, till a recent period, of
young persons going to them early in New Year's day morning, and,
after thrusting into them a bunch of straw, drawing forth what was
considered of sovereign excellence, the flower of the well.

It can hardly be questioned that Biggar, during the sixteenth and

* The Well of Skirling was held in considerable repute in ancient times, and was
dedicated to the Virgin Mary.

seventeenth centuries, would have its quota of witches and sorcerers, as well as the adjacent parishes. It is not yet fifty years since persons were pointed out in the town, who were supposed to possess supernatural powers, and whom their neighbours did not like to displease. Tradition has preserved the names of several women in the town and parish of Biggar, who were reputed witches at an earlier period, and who underwent the operation of 'scoring abune the breath,' that is, having several incisions made with a knife, or other sharp instrument, across the forehead. This operation, like that of cutting off the locks of Samson, was understood to deprive them of their supernatural powers. One of the most noted of these witches was Bessie Carmichael, who lived in the neighbourhood of Biggar, and was regarded with awe on account of her 'grewsum' looks, her intercourse with the weird folk, and her extraordinary powers in curing diseases, etc. One day a man in her neighbourhood was going to the mill of Biggar, with one or two loads of grain on a horse's back—then the usual mode of conveyance—and Bessie requested him to take, either her 'pock,' which hung in the mill, to receive the gratuitous offerings of the farmers when they had a 'melder' at the mill, or a quantity of grain with him, which she had gleaned or received as a gift from some of the farmers. The man refused to do this; and Bessie told him, in the hearing of some persons, that he would soon rue it. In course of disloading the horse, at the mill, the animal became restive, and gave the man so violent a kick, that he was laid lifeless on the spot. The whole country round soon rang with this terrible instance of the witch's revenge, and the universal desire was, that she should be burnt. By the time this incident happened, the days of judicial burning for witchcraft had passed away; but it is said that some persons, in disguise, broke into her cot, and maltreated her in such a way, that they hoped she would no longer 'keep the country-side in fear.'

In 1640, a case of alleged witchcraft engaged a great portion of the attention of the Presbytery of Lanark. As it shows the untiring energy of the Presbyterian clergy in the prosecution of such cases, we will give an outline of the proceedings. The person accused of this crime was an aged woman called Marion, or, as she was commonly termed, Mali M'Watt, who lived at Nisbet, in the parish of Coulter. Previous to her coming under the cognizance of the Presbytery of Lanark, she had been arraigned by the Presbytery of Peebles, and had undergone a lengthened examination in the Kirk of Glenholm, in presence of David Murray of Stenhope, the Laird of Hadden, and other members of that reverend court. These parties appear not to have followed up the examination with any further prosecution of the case, as the accused most likely removed herself out of the bounds of the Presbytery, and took refuge among the Coulter Hills, in the county of Lanark. Here, however, she was found out by John

Currie, minister of Coulter, and summoned to appear before the
Presbytery of Lanark on the 14th of May 1640. She appeared, but as
a copy of her confession in the Kirk of Glenholm was not forthcoming,
she was dismissed till next meeting, after giving John M'Watt,
in Cagill, and William M'Watt, in Baitlaws, as cautioners for her
attendance, under the pain of L.100 Scots. She, accordingly, presented herself before the Presbytery on the twenty-eighth day of the
same month, and showed a disposition to deny what it was understood she had confessed at Glenholm; but she admitted that she had
charmed a stream of water with an axe, by crossing it in the name of
the Father, Son, and Holy Ghost, and then giving three knocks on the
threshold of the door; that having been sent for to John Black's cow,
she had caused it to take the calf, and then prayed to God that it
might give milk, which it did; and, lastly, having been sent for to see
Alexander Ram's mare, she had also prayed to God for its recovery.
We are now apt to think, if no further charge could be brought
against her than is contained in her confession, that it would have
been amply sufficient, in so frivolous a case, to have dismissed her
with an admonition to abstain from any absurd symbolism in future,
when she attempted to purify the water, or cure the bestial in her
neighbourhood; but the Presbytery thought otherwise, and therefore
set themselves with the most restless activity to take the life of this
poor woman. In the times to which we refer, it was a practice observed by the Presbyteries of the Scottish Kirk, to hold diets of visitation in each parish within their bounds. The Lanark Presbytery,
therefore, at their meeting on the 11th June, instructed the visitors
of the Kirk of Coulter to be careful and diligent to find out everything they possibly could against Mali M'Watt, and report the result
of their investigations at next meeting. On the 16th of July, the
Rev. John Currie of Coulter, and the Rev. George Bennet of Quothquan, gave in a 'process,' which they had drawn up, and which, after
deliberation, it was agreed should be delivered to the Commissary of
Lanark for his revision. At this diet of the Presbytery, James Bryden, a son of the accused, was present, and became bound, under a
penalty of L.100 Scots, that his mother, till Whitsunday next, would
at any time appear before the Presbytery when summoned. The Commissary of Lanark, it appears, had requested to be furnished with a
copy of the proceedings instituted against Mali by the Presbytery of
Peebles, and therefore John Currie was instructed to proceed to
Peebles to procure one; but he either did not go, or was unsuccessful,
for, on the 21st of January 1641, a committee, consisting of the Rev.
Richard Inglis of Wiston, the Rev. James Douglas of Douglas, and
the Rev. George Bennet of Quothquan, was appointed to hold a meeting at Coulter with some members of the Presbytery of Peebles, but
the result is not stated.

In the meantime, it was resolved to apply to the Committee of

Estates for a commission to try Mali for the crime of witchcraft.
The Commissary of Lanark, however, told the Presbytery that, in his
opinion, Mali had been guilty, at the most, of charming, and that such
an offence did not infer the penalty of death.   The Presbytery were
evidently chagrined and annoyed by this decision; but it did not
deter them from the prosecution of their bloodthirsty design.   They
instructed the moderator, and the committee previously named, to
revise the whole process against Mali, and, if possible, to get it signed
by the members of the Presbytery of Peebles; and ordained the Rev.
James Baillie of Lamington to summon Mali and her cautioner, James
Bryden, to appear before them on the 1st of July.   In these unhappy
times, it often happened that old women accused of witchcraft were
deserted by their relatives, and left to the tender mercies of their
persecutors, without a friend to console and defend them.   This happened on the present occasion.   The old woman trudged away from
Nisbet to Lanark, and presented herself, on the day appointed, before
the Presbytery; but as no person, not even her son, was present, who
would vouch for her future appearance, she was committed to the
prison of Lanark.   Her own minister, John Currie, was one of her
most inveterate persecutors; but on this occasion he insisted that
she should either be declared guilty of witchcraft, or that the charge
against her should be abandoned.   The Presbytery were not yet
prepared to decide either the one way or the other; they still deside-
rated further proofs of her guilt; and therefore they appointed John
Currie and George Bennet to attend the Presbytery of Peebles, 'to
labour,' as they called it, for additional information, and to request
that a committee of the Presbytery of Peebles should meet at Biggar
on the 21st of the same month of July, to hold a conference with the
following committee of their own body, viz.,—the Rev. Alexander
Somervail of Dolphinton, the Rev. George Bennet of Quothquan, the
Rev. John Currie of Coulter, the Rev. Andrew Gudlatt of Symington,
and the Rev. John Veitch of Roberton; and to summon all parties
interested to attend the said meeting.   This meeting accordingly took
place, and the result of its deliberations, as embodied in a report, was,
that many of the charges against Mali M'Watt were found proven, and
that there were just grounds for arraigning her before the civil tribunals
of the country.   The Presbytery thereupon once more took courage,
and acting, as they said, on the Scripture warrant, 'Thou shalt not
suffer a witch to live,' they ordained John Currie to repair to Edinburgh to wait upon the Earl of Angus, Sir William Baillie of Lamington, Sir William Carmichael, and Sir John Dalziel, to induce them to
lend their assistance to procure a commission to apprehend Mali, who
had been set at liberty, and subject her to such punishment as the
laws of God and the country authorized.   John Currie, as instructed,
went to Edinburgh; but he was met with the objection, that his application for a commission was informal, so long as Mali continued at

large, and practised her charms and cures. The Presbytery, when they heard this, with one consent, requested the elder for Lamington, Sir William Baillie, or, in his absence, his bailie, Alexander Menzies of Culterallers, to apprehend poor Mali with all expedition, and to keep her in confinement at Coulter, or to send her to the county jail, to be under the vigilant eye of the bailies of Lanark.

The Privy Council had begun, by this time, to be wearied with the endless prosecutions raised by the clergy against old women; and, in the case of Mali M'Watt, they could not, at any rate, see that the charge of witchcraft could be sustained. The clergy were determined, however, not to be baffled; and on the 24th of March 1642, the day on which Mali was lodged in Lanark Jail, they met and resolved to appoint a committee to revise her process, and to make a fresh effort to obtain a commission for her trial. The committee, consisting of the Rev. William Somervail of Dunsyre, the Rev. Alexander Somervail of Dolphinton, the Rev. George Bennet, and the Rev. John Currie, met at Dolphinton, and, after revising the process, drew up a petition to the Lords of the Privy Council, which was signed by the clerk in name of the Presbytery, and conveyed to Edinburgh by the indefatigable John Currie. When John arrived in Edinburgh, he found that the Privy Council would hold no meeting sooner than the 1st of June; and thus he and the Presbytery were once more baulked in their design. The Presbytery, nevertheless, ordered John to repair to Edinburgh so soon as the Council met, and agreed to allow him two dollars to pay his expenses; but when the day arrived, John had become unwell, and could not leave his manse. The Presbytery, still unwearied in their efforts, resolved to take the advice of the Synod on their procedure in Mali's case, and also to consult the Commission of the General Assembly and the legal agent of the Church; but what advice they got, or what further steps they took, their records, so far as we have seen them, give no information. The likelihood is, that Mali M'Watt, after undergoing a most harassing and protracted persecution from the Presbyteries of Peebles and Lanark, lived and died in her own quiet home in the Vale of Coulter.

For several years after the formation of the Presbytery of Biggar, the members of that reverend court appear to have taken no part in the prosecution of witches. Their persecuting zeal, however, broke out, all of a sudden, in 1649. At a meeting on the 28th of November of that year, it was reported that one Janet Bowis, a confessing witch, was imprisoned at Peebles; and therefore Robert Brown of Broughton, and John Crawford of Lamington, were instructed to wait on the Commissioners appointed to try cases of witchcraft, to ascertain if, in her depositions, she had accused any one connected with their congregations of being guilty of that crime, and to request liberty to bring Janet to Biggar, to be detained in confinement there, and to be confronted with such old women as she might declare to be witches.

These two reverend gentlemen, accordingly, repaired to Peebles, and obtaining an interview with Janet, the confessing witch, they received from her the names of a number of persons in the parishes of Broughton, Lamington, and Walston, whom, she alleged, had been guilty of the crime of witchcraft. The authorities at Peebles, however, refused to allow Janet to be taken out of their hands, and transferred to the Tolbooth of Biggar. The two delegates, therefore, repaired to the moderator of the Presbytery, and laid before him the result of their proceedings; and that dignitary lost no time in sending a communication on the subject to Sir John Christie. Through the influence of this gentleman, a commission was granted by the Committee of Estates to sit at Biggar on the 19th of December, with power to try all witches within the bounds of the Presbytery; and an order was at the same time issued for transporting Janet Bowis, the confessing witch, to Biggar. The Commission met at Biggar on the day appointed. The whole members of Presbytery attended. It is a matter of regret that no report of what took place at that meeting can now be obtained. We only know that the divines of the Presbytery were greatly disappointed and dissatisfied with the result; and particularly with the conduct of the confessing witch, of whom they expected to make so much. She appears to have broken completely down under the searching examination to which she was subjected. The divines resolved not to give her up. They appointed a meeting to take place on the 29th, and summoned her before them. The minute referring to what then took place is curious, and therefore we give it entire:—
'The brethrine in yr attendance upone ye Commissioneres appoynted for tryall of suspected witches, within ye boundis of ye Presbyterie, haveing perceived that Jennett Bowis, ye confesseing witche (brocht to Biggar for yat end), that schoe micht be confronted with suche persones as schoe had delated and affirmed to be guyltie with her of ye said cryme of witchcraft, had clearlie contradicted herself in these declarationes in verie many points, and that the most part of her dispositiones wer full of variationes, bothe in regaird of persones, names, tymes, places, matter, and everie other circumstance; all whiche haveing maid them suspicious of her, that schoe had lyed upone some innocent persones, and concealed ye guyltiness of others, tending to the prejudice of ye work of tryall, and discoverie of that fearfull sinne, and to ye advantage of Satan, did therefore aggrie togeder to sett aparte this day for humiliatione and prayer. And being (at least ye most parte of yr number) convenit this day in ye Kirk of Biggar, and ye said Jennett Bowis being brocht before theme, efter manie exhortationes from ye word of the Lord, and pouring furth of prayers and supplicationes to God (by turns), entreating his Majestie to open her mouthe to confess her guyltiness in this point, and with manie wurds exhorteing her to yat effecte. At last ye said Jennett burst furthe in clamours and teares, and said that schoe had condemned her awin

2 E

sillie saule in sweareing falselie, and, in signe yrof, schoe presentlie
cleared about fortie eight persones, whoes guyltiness before schoe had
affirmed. Whairupone the breethrine of ye Presbyterie thocht fitting
to referre, as be ther presents they doe referre, ye matter to ye consideratione of ye Commissioners for tryall, that they may bothe advyse
what to doe, and also (if need be), to represent the samyn to ye
Committee of Estaitts for directione, what sall be done anent ye said
Jennet Bowis.' No further statements regarding her appear in the
records of Presbytery, and therefore her ultimate fate cannot now be
ascertained.

At that period, so many persons were apprehended for the crime of
witchcraft, that the ordinary prisons could not contain them. An
order was therefore issued, that each parish, in its turn, should furnish a
quota of men to guard them and prevent their escape. The members
of the Biggar Presbytery, in their great zeal against witchcraft, resolved
that they would, along with their parishioners, take their turn in
watching. On the 7th of May 1650, they even went the length of
resolving to call in the services of a person called Cathie, 'a searcher
for ye Devill's mark on witches,' who dwelt at Tranent, and who had
recently been pursuing his vocation within the bounds of the Presbytery of Peebles. They therefore requested the Presbytery of Haddington, in conjunction with a magistrate, to bind him down to answer
before the Judge Ordinary when he should be called.

At this period, the members of the Presbytery of Lanark were
equally active in the prosecution of witches. In 1650, they caused a
very considerable number of old women to be apprehended in the
parishes to the west of Biggar, and lodged in the Tolbooth of Lanark.
We may briefly refer to one or two of these cases:—On the 10th of
January of that year, Marion Hunter, one of the suspected persons
incarcerated for witchcraft, compeared before the Presbytery, and
declared,—1st, That the devil appeared like a little whelp between
Haircleuch and Littleclyd, and evanished in a bush; 2d, Like a brown
whelp at Haircleuch, and, a good while afterwards, like a man, between
Haircleuch and Glispen, and nipped her in her shoulder, and requested
her to be his servant; 3d, That she was in Gallowberriehill, and rode
upon a 'bunwede,' and that of those who are at present in prison,
the following were with her on this occasion, viz.—Lillias Moffat,
Marion Watson, Helen Aitchison, Marion Moffat, and Mali Laidlaw;—
the last, she said, was of special service to her, for she 'drew her
when she was hindmost, and could not winne up.'

In a month or two afterwards, Janet Birnie, from Crawford, was
tried by a committee of the Presbytery, and the following points were
found proved:—First, That she followed William Brown, slater, to
Robert Williamson's house in Watermeetings, and there craved him
for something that he was due her. A quarrel thereupon ensued
between them; and in twenty-four hours thereafter he fell from a

house and broke his neck. Second, 'Ane outcast' having taken place between her family and the family of Bessie Aitchison, the said Janet prayed that the Aitchisons might soon have bloody beds and a light house; and after that, Bessie Aitchison's daughter took sickness, and cried, 'There is a fire in the bed,' and died; and Bessie Aitchison's 'gudeman dwyned.' And, Third, She was blamed for causing discord between Newton and his wife, and procuring the death of William Geddes. The Presbytery, notwithstanding these grievous charges, agreed to set her at liberty, provided the bailies of Lanark would enter into recognisances, to the amount of 1000 merks, that she would appear before them when called on.

On the 21st March of the same year, 1650, the Presbytery received papers from Richard Inglis, which contained the confession of 'ane warlock called Archibald Watt, alias Sole the Paitlet, freelie given by him in the Tolbooth of Douglas.' The brethren read over the papers, and considered that it was clearly set forth that this warlock had made a paction with the devil, that he had held frequent meetings with his satanic majesty and several witches in different places, and that he had been guilty of many horrid abominations. They were unanimously of opinion that it was their duty to obtain a commission of the Lords of Council to try him; and therefore they appointed Mr Robert Lockhart to proceed to Edinburgh for this purpose, with all convenient speed. Mr Inglis requested that, as the warlock had once before escaped out of the prison of Douglas, he should be brought to the Tolbooth of Lanark; and further, that a committee of the Presbytery should be appointed to confer with him on his arrival. All this was agreed to; but the records of the Presbytery fail to show what was the fate of this unfortunate and infatuated individual.

CHAPTER XIX.

The Vagrants of the Biggar District.

THE Biggar district was, from a remote period, overrun by swarms of tinkers, gipsies, chapmen, beggars, etc. Some of these wanderers were well known, and kindly treated. They went regular rounds, obtained quarters at certain farm-houses, and claimed and received an 'awmous,' or small benefaction, in the shape of a coin, a bannock, or a handful of meal, at the doors of the charitable, and bestowed a benediction in return. The sturdy beggars, sorners, and bluegowns of a bygone age, carried in their capacious wallets what was called an awmous dish, which was round in shape and composed of wood, and, in fact, bore a close resemblance to a large quaich or drinking cup. On calling at a house, the gaber-lunzie held out this dish to receive the alms of the gudewife, which, in that case, generally consisted of a handful or two of barley or oat-meal. By this method he was able to ascertain the exact amount of the dole bestowed, and to measure out in return a corresponding amount of benison to the giver. The meal was then deposited in the appropiate meal-pock, and the awmous dish had its place of honour in one of the pocks in front. We can thus see the appropriatenees of the comparison used by Burns, when he says, that one of the heroines of his 'Jolly Beggars'

> 'held up her greedy gab,
> Just like an aumos dish.'

The accompanying engraving represents an awmous dish, carried, we believe, by one of the sturdy beggars that at one time frequented the Upper Ward of Clydesdale. These vagrants in the long winter nights, when seated at the back of the ample hearth, enter-tained the family circle with the news of the district, or with stories of their  experience and adventures in their early years. The pedlars, male and female, carried a tempting collection of wares from house to house, and conveniently supplied persons far remote from shops with articles of ornament or utility. The tinkers mended pots and kettles, sold trenchers, horn spoons, heather besoms, rush mats, pottery ware etc. The men were expert hunters and fishers, and some of them excelled as musicians, while the females practised the art of fortune-telling. Their encampments, by the side of plantations, or in secluded corners of the country, with their blazing fires, and their array of asses, horses, and dogs, had a romantic effect, and impressed the mind with a primitive state of existence, 'ere the base laws of servitude began.' They paid scrupulous respect to the property of those who treated them kindly and afforded them shelter; but plundered, without mercy, all those who drove them from their doors, or refused them the corner of a field on which to pitch their encampment. Besides these wanderers, there were a number of idiots, who roamed the country at large, afforded amusement by their antics, witticisms, or mimicry, or were regarded with terror for their sudden resentment and their savage malignity.

The laws against the sturdy vagabonds that prowled idly about the country were numerous and very stringent. They were consolidated into one comprehensive statute, in 1579, during the reign of Queen Mary, and provided that vagrants, on being apprehended, 'sall be put into the King's waird or irons, so lang as they have ony gudes of thair awin to live on. And fra they have not quhairupon to live of thair awin, that thair eares be nayled to the trone or to an uther tree, and thair eares cutted off, and banished the countrie; and gif, therafter, they be found againe, that they be hangit.' These laws, and others of a similar kind, afterwards enacted, appear to have become, in a great measure, a dead letter; and if we can fully credit the statements of Fletcher of Salton and others, the country about the close of the seventeenth century was overrun by thousands of vagrants, of whom the settled inhabitants knew little, except being kept in terror by their brawls, depredations, and exactions.

The authorities of Biggar made various attempts to keep the town free from the riots and annoyances of the unsettled and lawless hordes that frequented the Upper Ward. The enactments against them were renewed on the 22d April 1727, in the following terms :—'The same day, the Bailie renews all former Acts of Court made anent resetting of sturdy beggars, by giving and selling to them meat and drink, whereby they abuse the hail inhabitants of the town; and therefore prejudice to all former Acts, statutes and ordains, that no person or persons within the town of Biggar resett such sturdy beggars, sorners, gypsies, or give unto them drink for yr money, under the pain of ten punds Scots, *toties quoties*.' On the 15th October 1728, Bailie Luke Vallange fined John Rob, indweller in Biggar, in the sum of ten pounds Scots, for entertaining thieves and beggars, the 'fangs' (plunder) being found in his house.

The Baron Bailie, on the 28th March 1747, gave the following decision:—'The same day, complaint having been made upon Samuel Bell, innkeeper in Biggar, and Agnes Noble, his spouse, that for some

time past they have been in use of hounting and allowing vagrants,
tinklers, sorners, and sturdy beggars to lodge in their house. The
Bailiff passes them for all bygone transgressions of that nature, but
appoints them to find caution, that from this time to the term of Whitsunday next, at which time they are to leave this place and reside at
Linton, that they shall not harbour any such vagrants or sturdy beggars, under the penalty of twelve punds Scots for each transgression,
toties quoties, by and attour repairing what damage neighbours shall
sustain by and through their harbouring them, as said is.'

The gipsy hordes that roamed about the Upper Ward in former
times, consisted of distinct families or clans. The principal of these
were—the Jardines, Browns, Baillies, Faas, Shaws, Ruthvens, Keiths,
and Wilsons. They were the source of great annoyance and disquiet
wherever they went, both on account of the brawls which took place
among themselves, and the depredations which they committed. Two
of these parties, the Faas and Shaws, had a terrible fight at Romano,
in Tweeddale, about ten or twelve miles from Biggar, on the 1st of
October 1677. They had been at a Haddington fair, and were on
their way to Harestanes, to meet two other gangs, the Baillies and
the Browns; but they quarrelled about a division of the spoil taken at
the fair, and a fight ensued. The Faas consisted of four brothers
and a brother's son; and the Shaws, of the father and three sons, with
several women on both sides. The combat was keen and bloody, and
victory at last inclined to the side of the Shaws. Sandie Faa and his
wife were killed dead upon the spot, and Geordie Faa was dangerously
wounded. Old Robin Shaw and his three sons were, some time afterwards, apprehended; and having been convicted of the murder at
Romano, they were hanged in the Grassmarket in February 1678.
Dr Pennecuik, to whom the estate of Romano belonged, erected, in
1683, a dovecot on the spot on which this fight, or 'polymachy,' as
he calls it, took place, with the inscription,

> 'The field of Gipsie blood, which here you see,
> A shelter for the harmless dove shall be.'

The late Robert Johnston, merchant, Biggar, was wont to relate a
story concerning the gipsies and his paternal great-grandfather,
James Brown, who was tenant in Skirling Mill nearly a century and a
half ago. We give it in nearly his own words. On one occasion, a
strong band of tinklers quarrelled with the country people assembled
at a Skirling fair. The business of the market was stopped, and many
persons left it in consequence of the violent behaviour of these ruffians, when James Brown and his brother-in-law, Richard Burns,
armed themselves with trusty Andrea Ferraras, and at the head of a
courageous body of countrymen attacked the tinklers, and drove
them quite out of the village. One of them, however, determined on
revenge, and, running off in the direction of Skirling Mill, was over-

heard threatening, with the bitterest imprecations, that the whole of
the buildings would be immediately in flames. Several persons, on
hearing this threat, followed him with all speed, to prevent him from
executing his design; but what was their surprise, on reaching the
court in front of the house, to find the fellow stretched on his back,
and a man above him holding his throat with a grasp which, in a
short time, must have put an end to his existence. This man's name
was John M'Ivor. He was a native of the 'north countrie,' and had
been out in 'the fyfteen.' Leaving his native mountains, he came to
the low country, and employed himself as a hawker, and that morning had come to the mill after the male portion of the family had
gone to the fair. Being fatigued with a long morning's journey, he
had sat down to rest himself in the barn before proceeding to the fair,
and had fallen asleep, when he was awoke by the screams of the terrified females, and, rushing out, knocked the intended incendiary down,
and held him fastened to the ground till competent assistance arrived.
Many years afterwards, the gudeman of the mill had occasion to make
a journey some distance from home. In a solitary part of the road he
saw an encampment of tinkers, which he could not avoid passing.
Revenge was a peculiar characteristic of these vagabonds. The gudeman, at the sight of them, in a place far remote from any assistance,
felt a sudden tremor creep over him; but he resolved to show no signs
of fear, and therefore faced them boldly. While engaged in conversation with them, one of them brought forth a sword and said, 'Gudeman, what think ye o' that swurd? Is it as lang and sharp as the ane
ye used at Skirling Fair?' To these questions the gudeman made a
jocular reply. No violence, however, was offered him, and he was
allowed to wend his way home in safety. The sword used by Mr
Brown, on the occasion of clearing the fair, is still preserved by Mr
Johnston's family.

The family of gipsies that had the most intimate connection with
the Biggar district, were the Baillies. The chief of this clan, towards
the close of the seventeenth century, was William Baillie, who professed to be a descendant of the family of Lamington, and assumed an
air of importance accordingly. He travelled constantly about the
Upper Ward, and was sure to be present at all the fairs in this extensive district. He was a bold and successful marauder, and derived
his living almost wholly from plunder. The dairy, the hen-roost, the
meal-ark, the mountain, and the river, were all laid under contribution,
to supply the wants of himself and his dependants. Many anecdotes
were wont to be told of his exploits, as a thief and pickpocket, round
the hearths of the Upper Ward, but these are now nearly all forgotten. We give the following one:—At an old fair of Biggar, which is
held in November, the clan of the Baillies had been singularly unsuccessful; and the sun had sunk behind the lofty mountain of Tintock, and the gloamin' was throwing its dusky shades over the noisy

assemblage which was still congregated around the Cross-knowe, and
yet scarcely an article of any value had been captured. It was the
practice of these marauders to fix upon some house or place, at which
one of their number was stationed, to receive the booty from the
hands of those by whom it had been purloined. On this occasion, a
room for this purpose had been taken in an old house which was
burnt a number of years ago; and here several of the gang assembled,
and lamented their want of success, cursed the vigilance of the town
officer and his assistants, and projected schemes for future attempts.
Will, during these discussions, happening to observe a rustic pass with
a large plaiden web on his shoulder, exclaimed, 'I'll wad ony o' ye a
pint o' Lucky Vallance's best usquebae, that ere ten minutes that web
will be in my possession.' The bet was taken; and Will, having provided himself with a darning-needle and thread, followed hastily after
the man, who was proceeding up the town. The darkness and noise
which prevailed, enabled Will, unperceived, to stitch a corner of the
web, that hung at some distance from the man's back, to the lappel
of his own coat. He then tripped the man, and seizing the web,
placed it on his own shoulder. The man, on regaining his feet,
grasped at the web, and demanded it as his. 'Na, na,' quoth Will,
'this is no your web. Some o' the tinklers maun hae run aff wi' the
ane that ye had; and really, gudeman, ye ought to mak your gear
mair sicker when there are sae mony o' thae thievish fellows in the
fair. See, man, how I hae secured mine (showing him the web
stitched to his coat; and had ye followed the same plan, ye might hae
defied Will Bailie and a' his gang to tak yours awa without your
kennin.' On saying this, Will walked coolly off, leaving the poor
man overwhelmed with grief and amazement at the loss of his web.

William Baillie's wife, Mary Youston, was also a very remarkable
character. In height she was nearly six feet, her eyes were dark and
penetrating, her face was much marked with the small-pox, and her
appearance was fierce and commanding. She was even more dreaded
than her husband, as she was more audacious and unscrupulous. Few
persons cared to give her offence, because, if they did, they were sure
in the end to suffer some loss or injury. It was a common saying, in
reference to anything that was done to prevent further injury, 'It is
like Mary Youston's awmous, gien mair for her ill than for her guid.'
She was, like her husband, a dexterous thief and pickpocket, so that
it was a common observation regarding her, 'Whip her up Biggar
Street, on a market day, wi' a man at ilka oxter, and she wad steal a
purse ere they got her to the head o't.' Many stories of her sayings
and exploits were, at one time, prevalent among the peasantry of the
Biggar district. We give a specimen or two. One day Mary arrived
at the village of Thankerton, with several juveniles, who were usually
transported from place to place in the panniers of the cuddies. She
commenced hawking her commodities amongst the inhabitants, when

some of the children of the village came into the house where she was, and cried, 'Mary, your weans are stealing the eggs out of the hen's nest.' Mary quite exultingly exclaimed, 'The Lord be praised! I am glad to hear that the bairns are beginning to show some signs o' thrift.'

One harvest morning during her peregrinations, she called, with a number of followers in her train, at a farm-house a few miles from Biggar. The family were all employed, at some distance from the house, in cutting down the grain, except the gudewife, who had just dished the parritch for the morning's meal. Mary declared, that as she and her attendants were excessively hungry, they must have a portion of the parritch. It was in vain that the gudewife remonstrated, and declared that the quantity prepared was just sufficient for the shearers. A pock on one of the cuddies was opened, a number of ram-horn spoons were procured, and the contents of the bickers disappeared in a twinkling. Mary, in her rounds afterwards, never failed to call at the farm-house, to solicit an awmous, or the sale of some of her wares. The gudewife invariably told her to go about her business, as she wished to have nothing further to do with her. Mary's constant rejoinder was, 'Lord sauf us! gudewife, wull ye never forget the drap parritch?'

Mary, it is understood, did not originally belong to a gipsy tribe, but was the daughter of honest and respectable parents. William Baillie, in his wanderings, having accidentally met her, 'cust his glamour ower her,' and she immediately forsook her home, and followed the commanding and fascinating gipsy. In her subsequent career, she showed herself so apt a scholar in the arts of gipsy life, that she greatly surpassed all her compeers, and commanded obedience wherever she went. Though her husband stood greatly in awe of her, he does not seem to have preserved strict fidelity to his marriage obligations. In the records of the Presbytery of Biggar, it is stated, that at a meeting of that reverend court, on the 9th of June 1695, Margaret Shanklaw being summoned, and called, compeared, and judicially acknowledged the crime of adultery with William Baillie the gipsy; and being seriously exhorted by the moderator (the Rev. John Buchanan of Covington) to mourn over her sins, she was referred back to the Session of Lamington, to satisfy, according to the Acts of the General Assembly of the Church. William Baillie, we are told, was killed at Biggarshiels, in a fray regarding the distribution of some plunder that had been obtained at a neighbouring fair; and Mary died at an advanced age, in an old kiln at Harelaw, and was interred in the Churchyard of Carstairs. They had at least two children, Mathew and Nannie. Nannie married one of the Keiths, and continued to pursue the same wandering life as her forefathers.

Mathew, who succeeded to the authority and dignity of the chief of the clan, travelled over the country and practised the same arts as his predecessors. He contrived, somehow, to amass a little wealth,

2 F

and affected to occupy a higher standing than his forefathers. At
fairs, and other public occasions, he made a considerable display with
his broad-tailed coat, his wrist-frills, and silver shoe-buckles. He
fixed his headquarters at Biggar. He erected a house in Westraw,
which is still standing; and which, above one of the doors, has his
initials, M. B., and the date 1752, along with the letters M. E. C. I.,
and a mason's mark. His name appears several times in the records
of the Baron Bailie's Court during the year 1765, in connection with
the right which, in virtue of his feu, he acquired to the Westraw
Moss. He was twice married, and had a family by both wives. By
his first wife he had Jock, Jamie, Mary, and another daughter, who
was married to one of the Morrisons. By his second wife, whom he
brought from the north, and whose name was Margaret Campbell, he
had Mathew, Leezy, and Rachel. Mathew appears, from the Session
records of the parish of Biggar, to have been born in the house at
Westraw, on the 4th of September 1754.

Mathew's children, for the most part, connected themselves in
marriage with the gangrel tribes who, at the time, frequented the
Upper Ward. They sold the house in Westraw to Mr George Cuthbertson, and it is now the property of Adam Wyld, Esq. The most
noted of their immediate descendants was Peter, or, as he was most
commonly called, Pate Baillie, who for many years settled about
Loanhead and Bonnyrigg in Mid Lothian, and who excelled as a
player on the fiddle. He certainly was gifted with musical abilities
of a very high order. Had these received due cultivation, and had
he not possessed the wayward and obstinate disposition and the unsettled habits of the gipsy, he might have taken a high place as a
musical performer. He devoted his attention almost exclusively to
Scotch music; and certainly the variations which he improvised, when
playing some of our best tunes, were highly original and striking.
His rude and offensive manners prevented him from receiving that
patronage from the higher classes of society which he would, no doubt,
have otherwise obtained; but he was often employed by the country
people at penny weddings, kirns, and other merry "splores," when he
was largely plied with intoxicating drink, and it was alleged that he
played as well when he was drunk as when he was sober. He died
some twenty years ago, and was interred, we believe, in the Churchyard of Lasswade.

One or two of the other most noted wanderers that frequented the
Biggar district during the present century, may be very briefly noticed.
John Thomson, commonly called 'Langleathers,' was a person of
great strength, and carried a budget of old iron implements and other
articles on his back that few persons could lift. He was decidedly
fatuous; and the report was, that he had received such a shock on
witnessing the destruction of the city of Lisbon by an earthquake in
1755, that he never again entirely recovered his reason. He used, in

his contemplative moods, often to mutter to himself, 'I saw a city sunk.' He was inoffensive, except when roused by the annoyances and tricks of mischievous boys. He then became exceedingly noisy and outrageous; and being a dexterous 'hencher' of stones, it required great nimbleness on the part of his youthful tormentors to avoid his aim. When he happened to be at Biggar on Sabbath, the boys and he were sure to come into collision, and then a great deal of noise and disturbance was the consequence. He had rather a fondness for these encounters, and was not easily prevailed on to give them up. When any person remonstrated with him, and said that he ought to pay more respect to the Sabbath, 'Weel, weel, then,' said Jock, 'I'll aff to Crawfordjohn; there's nae Sabbath there.'

Daft Francie was another well-known wanderer. He was remarkably quiet and inoffensive. His thoughts ran almost constantly on the subject of religion, and he considered that he had a special vocation in the exercise of prayer. When he entered a house, with the inmates of which he was on familiar terms, he generally proposed, let the season or the hour be what it might, to engage in devotional exercises. At certain times, that was by no means convenient; and the consequence was, that the poor fool was often left praying alone. He attended religious worship in the nearest church every Sabbath day; and at every tent-preaching for twenty miles round he was sure to be present, especially on sacramental occasions. His grimaces, mutterings, and ludicrously devout appearance, often provoked laughter in the church, and disturbed the equanimity of the preacher. A clergyman, on proceeding to his church one Sabbath morning, observed Francie stationed by the wall of the church, waiting till the ringing in of the last bell. He had been often annoyed by the fool's extravagant conduct in the church; so he went up to him and said, 'Now, Francie, you must promise to sit quietly on your seat; you must make no faces, and speak not a single word.' 'I'll doo your biddin',' said Francie. The minister then directed his steps to the church door, when Francie hastened after him, and cried out, among the assembled loungers outside the church, 'Minister, I want to speak wi' ye.' 'What is it?' said his reverence. 'Wull a body no be allooed to host?' inquired Francie, with a tone of such solemn gravity and earnest simplicity that the bystanders could not refrain from a shout of laughter. One Sabbath afternoon, the inhabitants of a parish adjacent to Biggar, in returning from church, met Francie, who had been hearing one of his favourite preachers elsewhere. 'Francie,' said one of them, 'ye war ill away frae ower kirk the day. The minister, I'm shure, wad hae pleased ye, for the Gospel cam spewin' oot o' his mouth just like a flood.' 'It must hae been an unco effort,' said Francie, 'for it's nae easy wark spewin' wi' a toom stomach.' Francie very often engaged in the work of public exhortation himself. When he worshipped in a parish church, his practice was to slip out immediately on the conclusion of the service, and, mounting a through-stone in the churchyard, to hold forth with great vehemence and volubility to all who would stop and hear him. On one occasion, being very much dissatisfied with the services of the Rev. Thomas Gray of Broughton, he commenced to preach in the churchyard with such vehement shouts and vociferation, that two horses, who were grazing in a neighbouring field, were alarmed, and, pulling up their tethers, ran off at full speed, and did not halt till they had reached the top of an adjoining eminence, called Jockie's Brae. This poor wanderer came to an untimely end. He was travelling one very dark night in the parish of Eddleston, and, having lost his way, he stumbled into a sheet of water called the West Loch, and was drowned.

One of the most remarkable mendicants that ever travelled the Upper Ward, or drank a glass of usquebae at a Biggar alehouse, was James Abernethy. Of his history very little is now known. He was born in Edinburgh March 1722, and was bred a corkcutter. In his eighteenth year he was inspired with a warlike spirit, and, being not less than six feet four inches in height, he enlisted into the King's Life Guards. The two incidents of his military career to which he most frequently referred, was his presence at the disastrous battle of Fontenoy, fought in 1743, and his being one of the detachment of picked men who, in the year 1761, formed the escort to the Princess Charlotte of Mecklenburg Strelitz, when she arrived from the Continent to marry George III. He received his discharge about the year 1764, and returned to his native place, where he obtained employment at Craigleith Quarry. He here met with an accident which rendered him lame for life; and after this he betook himself to the profession of begging, which he continued to prosecute for the long period of fifty years. His appearance was striking. His stature, as already stated, was considerably above the usual size; his aspect was fierce and commanding, and manifested no symptom of the usual humility and condescension of a mendicant; and a curious old hat, with the brim cocked up, which he invariably wore, gave him a semi-military air. Several wallets, including his meal-pocks, hung round him, and were partially concealed by a plaid; and the staff, or 'kent,' by which he supported himself in the course of his peregrinations, was fully two yards in length, and of corresponding strength. No person in the Biggar district carried so formidable a kent, with exception, perhaps, of James Forrest, who dwelt at Langlees, and was famed for his love of 'parritch,' and his strong antipathy to potatoes, which he constantly denounced as 'vile roots, unfit to be men's meat.' The accompanying engraving, which is taken from a print published during the mendicant's life by a bookseller in Paisley, gives a tolerably fair representation of his usual appearance when he was greatly advanced in years, and shortly before he abandoned for ever the scene of his wanderings. The print was taken from a sketch made by a young man, son of Mr Robert Hamilton, factor to the Earl of Hynd-ford, at Mauldslie Castle. James entertained a strong aversion to the idea of having his likeness taken, and resisted all efforts to induce him to sit for this purpose. This object, in the end, was gained by stratagem. In the course of his rounds, he came to the locality where Mr Hamilton resided, and, on calling at one of his favourite houses, he was invited into the kitchen, and some bread and cheese and a stoup of whisky set before him. Young Hamilton was concealed in a closet, which commanded a view of the place where the mendicant sat, and thus was enabled to take a correct sketch of his countenance and general appearance.

Abernethy was a contemporary of Andrew Gemmells, and in many respects was a counterpart of that remarkable mendicant, who has been immortalized by Sir Walter Scott under the name of Edie Ochiltree. He went regular rounds, and called only at certain houses for an alms. He considered that he had a prescriptive right to be served at these houses, and would seldom take a refusal. On one occasion, he called at one of his farm-houses near Biggar, and de-manded his usual dole. The gudewife, being busily engaged in churn-ing, told him that she had not time to attend to his wants just now, but promised to give him a double gratuity the next time he came round. Abernethy was by no means disposed to give credit, and therefore setting out, and, making a complete circuit of the farm premises, returned and demanded his promised supply. The gudewife was hardly disposed to admit that he had gone his usual round; but amused at the artifice resorted to, and seeing there was no use in attempting to stave off the claims of the mendicant a second time, she, with the best grace she could, gave him a double 'gowpen' of oatmeal. After he commenced his wanderings, he would seldom engage in any manual labour, but regarded begging as his sole vocation. One day he arrived at a farm-house in Peeblesshire, where the cattle were scant of fodder, and a young lad was the only person left to thrash in the barn. The farmer thought he would tempt Abernethy to give him assistance by offering him a shilling for a day's thrashing. The mendicant rejected the offer with disdain. 'Why, man,' said he to the farmer, 'if ye'll serve me for a day, and carry my meal-pocks, I'll gie ye half-a-crown for your pains; and I'm shure ye'll no find it half sae sair wark as your thrashin'.' Abernethy had great fondness for a glass of good spirits, and sometimes partook of considerable quantities without any apparent injury. One day he entered a grocer's shop in Biggar, and said to the shopkeeper, 'Tammas, draw me a gill of whisky oot o' yer best barrel; there's a good king's coin to pay for't; and let me hae a bit parliament cake to taste it wi'.' The grocer filled the stoup and set it down on the counter; and then turning round to obtain a parliament, Abernethy with singular dexterity lifted the measure, drank off its contents, and placed it on the counter, wholly unobserved. Abernethy appearing in no hurry to taste the liquor, the grocer inquired the cause. 'I'm waitin' till ye fill the stoup.' 'Fill the stoup! the stoup is filled already. If it is no fou, I'll gie ye a gill for naething.' 'Done,' said Abernethy, and turning the stoup upside down, showed that it was entirely empty. The bewildered grocer drew another gill, and set it down. Abernethy, though a beggar, was a man of honour. He explained how the first gill had disappeared, drank the second, and paid for both. On another occasion, he called at a spirit-dealer's shop at Carnwath, and asked for a gill. The shopman drew the liquor, and asked where was his bottle. 'I'll shune let ye see that,' said James; and lifting the stoup, emptied its contents at a single 'waucht,' and demanded another fill. The astonished publican hesitated to comply. 'I maun hae't,' said the sturdy vagrant; 'I've got ane for the tae side, I maun hae anither to balance it.' It was drawn, and immediately swallowed as before. 'Noo,' said the drouthy gaberlunzie, 'if I had a third for the centre, I wad be a' richt.'

Abernethy, like his contemporary Andrew Gemmells, often used great familiarity with persons in the higher stations of life, and sometimes even retorted on them with bitter effect. One day, on his way to Hyndford House, he took a near-hand cut through the grounds, and accidentally met with the Earl of Hyndford himself. The Earl, displeased at the trespass, accosted James somewhat angrily, and said, 'Get off, ye coward; what are you wanting here?' The mendicant, not at all abashed, replied, 'I'm nae greater a cooard than your Lordship.' The Earl, amused at this reply, asked for an explanation. 'That can shune be gien,' said James. 'Your Lordship fled frae Dunkirk, and I fled frae Fontenoy. Ye rade, and I ran; wha is the greatest cooard?' The Earl, pleased with the repartee, gave James a sixpence, and sent him to the house for refreshments; and ever after James received sixpence and plenty of food, as often as he visited Hyndford House. Like most members of the wandering train, he had to maintain a constant warfare with the canine race. On approaching a farm-house, he was usually assailed by all the collies and mastiffs about the place. The mendicant never flinched, but, shouldering his kent, boldly advanced to the attack. If any unwary cur ventured within range, he received such a 'lounder' as sent him at once howling to his den. On one occasion, he was passing along the Main Street of Carnwath, and there met a mastiff that was dissatisfied with his appearance, and seemed disposed to offer him battle. James accepted the challenge, and, ascending the steps of the Cross, provoked the dog to come to close quarters. The bruilziement soon attracted a number of spectators, and, among others, the owner of the dog, the Rev. Mr Mark, who dwelt near, and who was well acquainted with the vagrant. 'James,' cried he, 'you will surely not hurt my dog.' 'Your doug!' said James, 'I'm sorry that he's yours; for if he had been ony ither body's, I wad shune hae laid his yaffing for ever.'

Abernethy travelled the country till he had reached his one hundred and third year. By the increasing infirmities of age, he was now unable to walk to any distance, and was generally conveyed from place to place in a cart. He relished this mode of travelling very ill, as he could not get time to sun himself about the dykes, and particularly to visit his favourite ale-houses. Notwithstanding his tippling propensities, he contrived somehow to save a little money; and, in 1825, he relinquished his peripatetic habits, and took up his abode in an institution in Edinburgh, where he stipulated that he should, at least, receive two glasses of whisky daily, and a due modicum of tobacco. It is understood that he did not long survive the close of his wanderings. His favourite toast is said to have been the following:—

> 'Here's health to the sick,
> Honour to the brave,
> Success to the lover,
> And freedom to the slave.'

John Robertson was one of the most expert and clever knaves that ever prowled about the Upper Ward. He had received a good education, was well acquainted with Scripture, and excelled as an expert penman. His knowledge of men and manners was extensive and accurate; his conversational powers were of a superior order, and his apprehension was remarkably quick and acute. He usually feigned himself to be deaf and dumb, and then professed to tell fortunes. With his chalk-writing, he made astounding disclosures to the rustics ranged round the fire on a winter evening. To persons with whom he was intimate, he was wont to give the following explanation of his mode of fortune-telling :—' Such is the propensity of human nature to pry into futurity, that I am very successful as a spaeman; and as I take no money, I am less apt to be committed as a vagrant. I can hide my tongue in such a manner that it cannot be observed; and though I am dumb, I am not deaf: I hear in one house what is going on in another, and can easily make a tolerable history. I first kneel down on the floor, then draw a magic circle with my chalk; next, I write the initials, J. S., which will serve for John Smith, James Sommerville, Joseph Sym, Jacob Simpson, and a thousand more. On seeing the initials, a girl perhaps whispers, " I'll wager that's our Johnnie that's at the sea." Having found a clue, I draw a ship, and write Mediterranean, or whatever can be elicited from the tattle of the maidens. If, on inspecting the initials, they look grave, or give a hint about death, I draw a coffin; but if the initials do not suit any absent friend of the parties, I make them a sentence, " I say," and follow it up with a new set of letters till I can fabricate a story.'

It was understood that Robertson had studied at the University of Glasgow, at the time at which it was attended by Campbell the poet, and the late Rev. Hamilton Paul of Broughton. He had afterwards fallen into dissipated and irregular habits, and had served both as a soldier and a sailor. In the end he betook himself to a wandering life, principally in the counties of Lanark, Ayr, Dumfries, and Renfrew; and he calculated that it took him nearly two years to complete his rounds. He contrived to pick up a sufficient amount of food in the houses which he visited to supply his daily wants; and he usually spent the money which was bestowed on him for his fortune-telling, and out of compassion for his pretended deficiencies of hearing and speech, on strong drink, to which, of course, he was much addicted. He had, naturally, a strong constitution; so he was never at a loss for a bed. When he could not obtain the corner of a barn or a byre, he thought nothing of ensconsing himself at the back of a dyke, where he slept as soundly, and with as little apparent harm, as if he had been accommodated in the most elegant and comfortable quarters.

One of the last of the noted Upper Ward tinkers, was Moses Marshall. He did not belong to the gipsy race, but was born at New-ton-of-Ayr, where his forefathers had resided for several centuries. He was bred a currier, and, when a young man, 'listed into the Royal Artillery. After serving with this corps for eighteen years, he deserted in the West Indies. He was afterwards pressed on board a man-of-war; but embraced the earliest opportunity of deserting from this service, which he hated even worse than the Artillery. He then commenced a wandering sort of life, which he continued till within a week or two of his death. He wrought as a tinsmith, and dealt in hardware goods; but as he was addicted to occasional rounds of hard drinking, he often exhausted his whole stock in trade; and it was a matter of some mystery how he contrived to get it replaced. In person, he was tall and powerful; and at one period was excessively pugnacious, when under the influence of strong drink. He was engaged in constant broils, and thus became a terror wherever he went; while punishments of various kinds, inflicted on him for his outrages, seemed to be employed in vain. He was often met in personal combat, and would have been more frequently defeated than he was, had his principle on these occasions not been that 'a's fair in time o' war.' One day he encountered a strong fellow at Bathgate, and would have received a sound pommelling, had he not, as a last resort, caught the man's nose with his teeth, and by a terrible wrench deprived him of this facial appendage, and made him roar out for mercy. On another occasion, he 'took up' the toll-house at Tarbrax, when a shepherd in the neighbourhood, hearing the noise, came in and attempted to subdue the infuriated Moses. A determined encounter took place; but ere long the herd was glad to relinquish the fray with the loss of a finger. During his latter years, Moses became more pacific in his disposition, or at least in his practice. His declining strength, no doubt, made him less able to use those weapons with which he had achieved victory on many a hard-fought field.

Moses had a great dislike to live in the lodging-houses that are usually to be found in the towns and villages of the district. He earnestly petitioned the proprietors of land within the bounds of his wanderings to allow him a small corner to pitch his encampment; and this request was generally granted. He could, in fact, use a considerable degree of familiarity with the local gentry. A proprietor in the parish of Coulter one day came upon Moses' encampment, and found him busily engaged in preparing dinner. Among other viands round the fire was an excellent leg of mutton, which he appeared to watch with great care. 'Moses,' said the laird, 'you seem to keep a very vigilant eye on the mutton.' 'Muckle need,' said Moses; 'were I no to do that, it wad very soon disappear.' He seemed to be apprehensive that some of his followers would lay hands on it before the feast began. 'Mr ———,' said Moses, addressing the laird, 'as I hae often dined at your expense, I shall be very happy if ye'll tak a bit chack wi' me the day, as you're here at ony rate.' The laird thanked Moses, but declined the invitation, on the ground that he was previously engaged. After a short illness, Moses died at Coulter, on the 15th of May 1860, in the eighty-sixth year of his age.

CHAPTER XX.

Crime in the Biggar District.

THE Biggar district has long been inhabited by an industrious, intelligent, and moral population. It has acquired no celebrity for the perpetration of the higher class of criminal acts. Quarrels, fights, petty thefts, etc., have occasionally taken place; but instances of forgery, housebreaking, arson, and murder, committed by the native inhabitants, have been remarkably rare. We may refer, however, to one or two instances of crime connected with the district, which caused some sensation at the time at which they happened, and which are still more or less remembered.

We may, in the first place, notice the case of Janet Brown, daughter of John Brown, Biggar, who, on the 25th of June 1614, was tried before the Justiciary Court of Edinburgh, for the crime of child-murder. The child was illegitimate, and the alleged father was John Stevenson. The indictment charged her with concealment of pregnancy, as none of her neighbours were aware that she was with child, and as she had left her father's house and gone to the fields in the neighbourhood of the town, where she was delivered of a female child without the help of a midwife. She was further charged with having immediately strangled the child, and having taken its body to a dykeside, and there covered it with a number of turfs, and thus was guilty of murdering 'the said bairn.' In her confession, she denied the murder, and asserted that the child died shortly after it was born, and 'sae she earthed it in the grund of a turf stack.' The assize, by the mouth of William Fleming of Persilands, Chancellor, 'fand and pronouncit the said Janet to be fylt, culpable, and convict of the murder of the said infant;' and her sentence was, that she 'be tane to the Castlehill, and be hangit quhill she be deid, and her moveable goods to be escheat.' This is the only native of Biggar, so far as we are aware, that ever suffered the ignominious doom of capital punishment.

A case of a somewhat similar kind, but, so far as we can ascertain, without such sanguinary results, occurred in 1646. On the 15th of July, of that year, the bailies of Biggar reported to the Biggar Presbytery 'that some folkes of yr toun had fund a young bairne in Biggar Mosse, covered over, and being alyve, had broucht it furth; and also, that they had apprehended the mother, who had confessed the haynous and unnaturall facte done be her to her chyld.' The advice of the Presbytery was, that the bailies should detain the woman in prison till their next meeting. The members offered to contribute along with the town to her maintenance, and they instructed the moderator to write to the King's advocate to obtain his opinion regarding the nature of her crime, and his advice as to her disposal. The answer of the King's advocate was, that she should be sent to the Justice-General at Edinburgh; and, therefore, the Presbytery called on the bailies of Biggar to put her confession on record, and send her forward to Edinburgh. The fate of this person, as we have already indicated, is not now known.

An instance of murder occurred at Biggar, on a fair afternoon, in the latter part of last century, under very peculiar circumstances. Two individuals who happened to meet in John Craig's public on that occasion, were J. M'Ghie, farmer, Mossside; and George Paterson, an old soldier, and at the time a labourer. Mr M'Ghie had been in the habit of employing Paterson on his farm, and it appears that, in the course of their transactions, some misunderstanding had arisen. The quarrel was resumed over their potations, and was carried to such a height that a scuffle ensued, and M'Ghie was laid prostrate on the floor. At this juncture M'Ghie's son James came in, and seeing his father maltreated by Paterson, seized a pair of tongs, and struck Paterson so severe a blow on the head, that he was instantly deprived of life. Young M'Ghie was shortly afterwards apprehended, and committed to prison. Lord Elphinstone and other persons exerted themselves in his behalf, and the consequence was, that, on being brought to trial, he was sentenced to receive what, even at the present day, would be regarded as a lenient punishment, viz., banishment for a few years furth of Scotland.

We will now refer to a murder committed near the village of Newbigging, which made a great sensation in the Biggar district, and was closely associated with a man well known in Biggar at the commencement of the present century. An old man, named Adam Thomson, with his wife and a daughter, occupied a solitary hut at the place referred to, and employed himself in the manufacture of heather besoms, straw mats, and similar articles. About 11 o'clock on the night of Monday, the 17th of June 1771, when the inmates had retired to rest, a loud knocking was heard at the door and windows by several persons, who peremptorily demanded that Thomson should rise and show them the way across the muir to Peebles. He accordingly got up, and, on reaching the door, was struck a heavy blow on the head, and knocked down. The ruffians then tied his hands behind his back, and maltreated him in a brutal manner. Mrs Thomson, alarmed by the noise of the scuffle, sprung out of bed, and went to the door, when she was instantly struck also, and laid prostrate on the ground. The daughter, hearing the violence that had

been inflicted on her parents, made her escape by a back window,
and proceeding, with all speed, to the nearest house, gave the alarm.
In a short time, several persons, who had been hastily collected,
hurried to the cottage, and found that Thomson and his wife had
been seriously wounded; that the house had been rifled, the chests
broken open, and a quantity of linen, a silver watch, several bank-
notes, and a red plaid carried off. A surgeon with all haste was
brought from Carnwath. The old man was found to have received
some deadly strokes on the head, and at six o'clock next morning
breathed his last. Mrs Thomson was less dangerously injured, and
in course of time recovered.

Great efforts, by offering rewards and otherwise, were made to
discover the perpetrators of this foul outrage. Several persons were
apprehended on suspicion, and all manner of reports was put in circulation; but no satisfactory discovery was made, and most persons
began to consider that further search was hopeless.

Adam Thomson, a son of the deceased, a man of strange notions
and eccentric habits, and then schoolmaster of the Parish of Walston,
after pondering for a long time over the mysterious death of his
father, resolved to make personal efforts to discover the murderers.
From time to time, so often as his vocation would permit, he left his
native locality, and travelled over the greater part of Scotland and
England, making minute inquiries after suspicious characters, visiting
jails, and mixing with thieves, tinkers, and vagabonds of all sorts.
Again and again he returned home, baffled and disappointed. One
evening, as he lay in bed ruminating on the painful subject which
had taken so firm a hold of his mind, he felt a strong and irresistible
impulse once more to renew his search. He rose early next morning
and wended his way to Jedburgh, where, as was his wont, he repaired
to the Tolbooth. Here he made the usual inquiries at the prisoners,
if any of them knew the perpetrators of his father's murder; and it is
understood that he obtained such information as enabled him to take
effectual steps to apprehend them and bring them to justice. It
was thus ascertained that the murder was committed by two men,
John Brown and James Wilson, and two women, Martha Wilson
and Janet Greig. At what place James Wilson was apprehended,
we have not ascertained; but John Brown was captured in a house
near the Fort of Inversnaid, by a party of soldiers from the garrison,
on Sabbath, the 3d of January 1773, and conducted first to Stirling,
and then to Edinburgh. As no person had seen them commit the
act, it would have been difficult to obtain a conviction against them;
but the two women basely agreed to turn king's evidence. The trial
of the two men was fixed to take place on the 28th of June; but it
was postponed till the 12th of August, on the plea that at least one
of the panels could bring evidence to prove an *alibi*. The individual
who at length came forward and made this attempt, was a person of

their own kidney, called William Robertson; but his statements were so inconsistent and contradictory, that the Court committed him to prison. The jury unanimously found the prisoners guilty; and the sentence pronounced upon them was, that they should be executed in the Grassmarket, Edinburgh, on Wednesday, the 15th September, and their bodies given to Dr Munro for dissection.

Previous to their execution, they emitted their 'last speech, confession, and dying words,' all of which were attested by Richard Loch, inner-turnkey of the Tolbooth, and printed and published by H. Galbreith, Edinburgh. James Wilson declared that he would make no public confession of particular crimes, and that he would confess to God alone. His last speech, therefore, throws no light on the murder, or the manner in which he and his associates in crime were detected. John Brown, in his declaration, was more explicit. He said, 'I do acknowledge that I was at the house of Adam Thomson, in Carnwath Muir, on Monday, the 17th of June 1771, along with Martha Wilson and Janet Greig; but as they did not tell the truth, the whole truth, I will give a simple declaration of it to the world. I declare that I never knew that house before; neither had I any intention to call at it that night, until I was led to it by Martha Wilson and Janet Greig; neither did I knock at the door, as they declared; it was the man that was with me that went to the door. I acknowledge that when Adam Thomson came out, I was standing by; but I did not give him the first stroke, neither did I give him the last; but the women, Martha Wilson and Janet Greig, struck both the woman and the man most desperately with sticks. As to the story they told as to my beating him with a potato-dibble, it is entirely false; yet I do acknowledge that I gave him several strokes. I acknowledge also that I gave the woman the first stroke, although it was declared before the judges that it was the other man, for which I sorely repent, as I acknowledge myself art and part in the murder. As to robbing the house, I touched nothing in it; but when I went in to desire the women to come out, I saw one of them at a chest, and another at the amry.' He made a number of other statements, but none of them bearing particularly on the murder and robbery.

The execution of Brown and Wilson took place on the day appointed; and Adam Thomson, it is said, appeared with them on the scaffold, and offered up a solemn prayer, an exercise of which he was very fond, and in which, it is allowed, he greatly excelled. On his return home, he erected a stone at the grave of his father in Carnwath Churchyard, with an inscription in Latin. It was long an object of attraction, and was visited by many persons at a distance, who had heard the story of the murder, the extraordinary efforts made by young Thomson to discover the perpetrators of it, and the singular epitaph which he had composed. A relative of Thomson, some years ago, removed the stone to the neighbouring churchyard of Libberton;

and there barbarously caused the inscription to be defaced or erased, and another one, regarding his own immediate relations, to be put in its place. So far as can be remembered, the inscription ran as follows :—

'Hic jacet Adamus Thomson, qui xv. ante Cal. Julii 1771, cruentis manibus, Joannis Brown, Jacobi Wilson, et duarum feminarum, apud Nigram Legem prope Novam Ædificationem, crudelissime trucidatus erat. Illi, Adamo Thomson, defuncti filio et ludimagistro de Walston, detecti erant. Ob quod crimen nefandum, Brown et Wilson, capitis damnati, et xvii. Cal. Oct. 1773, suspensi erant.

'Hoc monumentum extructum fuit Adamo Thomson, rectore Academiæ de Walston.'

The late Rev. William Meek of Dunsyre was wont to quote the above inscription, as a curious sample of the latinity of the dominies of the Upper Ward, putting special emphasis on the rendering of Blacklaw near Newbigging, by 'Nigram legem prope Novam Ædificationem,' and the fine conceit of Thomson in styling himself 'ludimagister' and 'Rector' of the Academy of Walston. Mr Thomson some time afterwards left the 'Academy' of Walston, and became teacher of the School of Quothquan. He was a frequent visitor to Biggar, and his appearance and oddities were familiar to all the inhabitants. Many anecdotes regarding him were at one time current in the district, all of which tended to show that he was a man of simple manners, devout feelings, and eccentric habits.

We will only give another incident of a criminal kind, which made a considerable noise in the Biggar district, and indeed over all Scotland; and which is the only instance, so far as we are aware, of individuals suffering the last sentence of the law for injury inflicted on a Biggar man.

Nearly fifty years have elapsed since the incident happened. At that time, in the Wynd of Westraw, Biggar, dwelt a man named David Loch, and his spouse, Jeanie Dodds. In his early days, David pursued the vocation of a pedlar, and realized a little money; but tiring of this wandering profession, he settled down at Biggar, and became a carrier and a dealer in old horses. He frequented the principal fairs in Scotland, and few men in the Upper Ward put so many old hacks through their hands. When not attending markets, he employed his 'auld yades,' as he called them, in driving coals to Biggar from Ponfeigh, and visited regularly, once a week, in the capacity of a carrier, the old burgh of Lanark.

A gentleman having occasion to proceed to the south, from Edinburgh, hired a horse to convey him the length of Biggar. David Loch, who was going to Edinburgh next day on some business, engaged to take the horse back to its owner. He accordingly left Biggar, mounted on the hired horse, between one and two o'clock in the afternoon of Wednesday, the 23d of November 1814, and was soon jogging along at a slow trot, by Toftcombs and Candy Burn. In his pockets were four bank-notes and twenty shillings of silver, a tobacco spleuchan, made of a piece of calf's skin, and a twopenny loaf, put there by the affectionate attention of his spouse, Jeanie Dodds, that he might have the wherewithal to appease any gnawing of hunger that might arise, and have no pretext to misspend his time and his means, by indulging in refreshments in the many tempting ale-houses by the way. At that time the country had been put into a state of great alarm by the perpetration of a number of most daring highway robberies. In almost every quarter, men and women had been knocked down and maltreated, and their money, and in many cases their clothes, carried off. Participating in the general apprehension, David felt anxious to reach the metropolis at an early hour in the evening, and therefore steadily pursued his journey, and, although the day was piercingly cold, manfully resisted all the allurements of Bridgehouse, Ninemile Burn, Howgate, and Lothian Burn, favourite resting-places in those days for the wayfaring man. The days at that season of the year being short, the shades of night began to descend ere he had reached House of Muir, but, as the sky was unclouded, and the ground covered with snow, the night was by no means dark.

He had now passed the Buckstane and the Brigs o' Braid, and was descending the road towards Morningside, congratulating himself that he had escaped all danger, when, near a solitary thorn-bush, which long bore his name, he met two men, one of whom inquired at him if he knew what the clock was. David slackened the pace of his steed a little, and replied that 'he didna ken, but he believed it wad be about sax.' 'Sure enough,' said the one who had not spoken, 'it is as near eleven.' David took them to be two drunk rustics, who had been in Edinburgh at the market, and was about to proceed, when one of them rushed forward and seized the bridle, while the other dragged him off the horse, and tossed him into a ditch by the wayside. Instantly the two ruffians were above him with their knees, and in the struggle several of his ribs were broken. Age, and an attack of paralysis, had greatly weakened his bodily powers, and, consequently, he was able to offer very little resistance, but he roared out 'Murder, murder,' as loud as he was able. One of the villains then struck him several severe blows on the head with the butt end of a pistol, and threatened, if he would not be silent, to knock his brains out. He still, however, kept crying 'Oh dear;' and the noise which he made reached the ears of Mr Andrew Black, blacksmith, Braidsburn, who had been convoying one Samuel Payne towards Edinburgh, who had passed the robbers a few minutes before, on the road, nearer the city, and had remarked to his companion that they were gallows-looking scoundrels, whom he would not like to meet in a solitary place with a hundred pounds in his pocket. Andrew hastened with all speed to the spot, and the villains seeing him ap-

proach, ran off across the fields, carrying with them all the articles
contained in David's pockets, formerly mentioned. Andrew pursued
them for some distance, when one of the robbers wheeled round and
discharged a pistol at him, which caused him to halt and turn back.
He found David still lying in the ditch, all covered with blood, and
the horse standing about thirty yards distant. Andrew, having procured some assistance, got David conveyed to Mr Scott's of Myreside,
and afterwards to the Police Office, Edinburgh, where his wounds
were dressed, and where he made a statement of the assault and
robbery to the authorities.

Suspicions had for some time been entertained that two Irishmen,
named Thomas Kelly and Henry O'Neil, were concerned with some
of the numerous robberies which had been recently committed.
Their houses in the West Port were searched, and several articles
found, which had been taken from persons who had been robbed,
and among the rest was David Loch's spleuchan. It was shown to
David, who recognised it at once. Some of the legal gentlemen inquired how he was able to identify it as the article which he had lost.
Davie replied, 'I ken the spleuchan weel eneugh frae the look o't,
as I hae putten mony an ounce o' tobacco in till't, and also frae having
shu'd a slit in't the morning afore I cam' awa' frae Biggar.' The
spleuchan being unrolled, David's rude needlework was discovered,
and its identity thus established beyond a doubt. The Irishmen were
accordingly forthwith lodged in the old Tolbooth, and, in a few days,
served with an indictment to stand their trial before the High Court
of Justiciary, on the 16th of December, little more than three weeks
after their robbery of David Loch.

The trial took place on the day appointed, and excited a very
lively interest. The culprits having been placed at the bar, the indictment was read, which contained three separate charges,—1st, for
having, on the 22d of November, attacked and robbed William
Welch, parish schoolmaster of Stenton, East Lothian, near the farm-
house of Howmuir; 2d, for having, on the same day, attacked and
robbed James Leigo and Thomas Wilson, farm servants in the parish
of Haddington, on the high road between Haddington and Dunbar;
and 3d, for having attacked and robbed David Loch, carter in Biggar,
as already stated. Although the panels had, in their declarations,
confessed their perpetration of the crimes laid to their charge, they
now chose to plead not guilty, and so the case went to an assize. A
number of witnesses bore testimony against the prisoners, and among
others, Andrew Black, the smith at Braidsburn, who, on that occasion, was highly complimented by the Court for his humanity and
attention. The evidence being closed, the Solicitor-General addressed
the jury on the part of the Crown, and Messrs Gilles and Brodie on
behalf of the prisoners. The charges against them having been clearly
proved, the jury, without leaving the box, unanimously returned a

verdict of guilty. The sentence of the Court was, that they be carried, on Wednesday, the 25th of January, between the hours of one and four in the afternoon, from the Tolbooth, to the spot at which they had committed the robbery on David Loch, and that they be there hanged till dead.

The sentence was carried into effect on the day appointed, in presence of a large concourse of spectators, many of whom came from a great distance. Two large square stones, in which the beams of the scaffold were placed, still remain in the public road, to mark the spot at which the execution took place; and, as they consist of sandstone, they have a dark damp appearance, even in summer, and are thus conspicuous to the eye of the traveller. The thorn-tree, so long a terror after nightfall, was, a few years ago, cut down; but the incident of the robbery and execution is still fresh in the memory of many of the citizens of the Scottish Capital.

CHAPTER XXI

The Battle of Biggar.

THE Battle of Biggar is a theme well known to all readers of Blind Harry's renowned poem, 'Ye Actis and Deidis of ye illuster and vailzeand Campioun, Shyr Wilham Wallace, Knycht off Elrisle,' and of the metrical abridgment of it by Hamilton of Gilbertfield. Much discussion has taken place regarding the actual occurrence of this battle; but whatever opinion may be entertained regarding the veracity of the Minstrel, it nevertheless becomes us, in a work of this kind, to give a detail of the incidents of the conflict as he has recorded them.

In 1297, Sir William Wallace, to revenge the murder of his wife, attacked the garrison of Lanark under cloud of night, and by fire and sword put almost every one of the English who composed it to death. This notable exploit soon resounded over the country, and brought together a large number of men who were desirous of striking a blow for the freedom of their country. Wallace was unanimously chosen their leader. The English garrisons who had been left to keep the country in subjection, were of course much alarmed by these warlike demonstrations, and Aymer de Vallance, then dwelling at Bothwell, despatched a courier with intelligence of them to Edward. The king having set his heart on the entire subjugation of Scotland, and having been at infinite pains to effect this object by artful schemes of diplomacy, as well as by several military inroads, was excessively grieved and enraged at this intelligence, and instantly resolved to march again into Scotland, to chastise the insolence and audacity of the Scots, and put them under more rigorous bondage than ever. The queen vainly endeavoured to persuade him against this expedition, representing the outrage and injustice he was attempting to perpetrate on Scotland, by depriving it of its ancient sovereign power, and reducing its people to slavery. Deaf to all remonstrances, the king despatched his heralds over the country to summon his vassals to meet him in warlike array, and to follow him to Scotland. One of Edward's pursuivants, by birth a Scotsman, and well known in Scotland afterwards by the name of Jop, on learning the intentions of the English king, left the court and hastened to Scotland to give information of them to Wallace, whom he found in Ayrshire. Wallace lost no time in setting up his standard at Lanark, and sending notice to his friends, especially in

Ayrshire and Clydesdale, to join him without delay. Adam Wallace, the young laird of Richardtown, Sir Robert Boyd, the ancestor of the Earls of Kilmarnock and Errol, Sir John Graham, Sir John Tinto of Crympcramp, Sir Thomas Sommerville of Linton and Carnwath, Sir Walter Newbigging of Newbigging, near Biggar, Nichol Auchinleck, and other men of note, hastened with their followers to obey the summons. On mustering their united forces, they were found to amount to 3000 horsemen, well equipped, and a considerable number of foot; but these were in a great measure destitute of arms. The Scots, learning that Edward was approaching with a powerful and well-appointed army, and being aware that they could not cope with him in the open field, betook themselves to a strong position on the hill of Tinto, about four miles from the town of Biggar.

The English army marched up the Tweed from Berwick, and after winding among the hills of Peeblesshire, descended on the plains of the Upper Ward of Lanarkshire, by the ancient pass of Crosscryne. The Scots, from their elevated encampment, no doubt beheld this 'awful ost,' as the Minstrel calls it, defile over the mountain's brow. It amounted to 60,000 warriors, clad in complete armour, led on by the most warlike and politic monarch of the age, and supplied with everything that could contribute to their comfort, or inspire them with confidence and courage. Still the little patriotic band on the side of Tinto manifested no symptoms of fear, nor thought for a moment of dispersing themselves and providing for their safety. The English pitched their camp near Biggar, on a piece of ground rising gently from the valley traversed by Biggar Water, and having a deep and inaccessible morass on the south and east. Here

> ' Yai planytyt yar feild with tents and pailzonis,
> Quhar claryouns blew full mony mychty sonis:
> Plenyst yat place with gud wittaill and wyne,
> In carts brocht yair purwiance dewine.'

From this place Edward despatched two heralds to Wallace, commanding him to submit to his authority, and promising if he should do so to take him into his service and favour, and to confer upon him the most ample rewards; but in case of disobedience, he threatened to hang him the first time he should fall into his hands. Wallace, after consulting his friends, wrote back to the king that he rejected his offers with disdain; and that, so far from being intimidated by his threats, he was determined to contend against him until he was driven from the kingdom; that the Scots would sacrifice him without mercy should he ever become their prisoner; and that they would be prepared to offer him battle at no distant period.

A young knight, the king's nephew, either out of curiosity, or for the purpose of ascertaining the numbers and reconnoitering the position of the Scots, had accompanied the heralds in disguise; but Jop

recognising this youth, having often seen him before while living at
the English court, gave intimation of his rank and condition to
Wallace.   In these chivalrous times, it was considered highly dishonourable for a true knight to act as a spy, or for any one to assume
the character of a herald who did not belong to that order; and the
person who did so was held to have forfeited all claim to be treated
with mercy.   The Scots, smarting under the wrongs inflicted on them
by the English, indignant at the haughty and imperious message sent
by the king, and especially enraged at the duplicity of the young
warrior and his companions, instantly resolved to punish them in a
most severe and summary manner.   The knight was conducted to an
eminence above the camp, and had his head struck from his body;
the tongue of one of the heralds was cut out, and the eyes of the
other extracted with a pair of pincers.   The two heralds, in this
dreadful plight, were ordered to return to the English camp with the
head of the knight, and to inform the king that he might regard what
the Scots had done as a proof that his threats and his powerful army
had not been able to strike them with terror, or bring them to sub-
mission.   When Edward learned what had taken place, he was for
some time struck dumb with sorrow and indignation; and at length,
when his feelings were somewhat tranquillized, he vowed not to leave
Scotland till he had taken the most ample vengeance on Wallace and
the Scots for the outrage they had perpetrated.

Wallace had now resolved to take a very daring step.   He was
quite well aware that his small army was no match for Edward's in a
fair field, and that his only chance of success lay in some well-con-
certed and vigorously-executed stratagem.   To carry out such an
object, he was convinced that it would be of great advantage were he
to visit the English camp in disguise, and thus ascertain its means of
defence, and the positions occupied by the king and his generals.
He communicated his design only to Sir John Tinto, and enjoined him
to observe the strictest secrecy.   He accordingly disguised himself, and
left the camp unnoticed.   On his way between Coulter and Biggar, he
met a poor man driving a horse laden with pitchers of earthenware.
Wallace entered into conversation with him, and finding him to be an
itinerant merchant, instantly entertained the idea that he might gain
admission into the interior of the English camp by pretending to be
a hawker of earthenware.   He accordingly purchased the man's horse
and his stock in trade; and still thinking his disguise not sufficiently
complete, proposed an exchange of garments—a proposal which greatly
increased the man's astonishment, but to which he readily assented.
Equipped in the hawker's habiliments, consisting of a threadbare hood,
a grey doublet, and hose daubed, or, as Harry says, 'claggit' with
clay, closing one of his eyes as if it had been deprived of vision, and
driving the mare, he set forward, to the great amusement of the old
hawker, towards the town of Biggar.   In this guise, tradition says

that he passed along the old narrow bridge which crosses Biggar Burn; and that from this circumstance, as we have already stated, it first got the name of the 'Cadger's Brig,' which it still retains.

About twilight he entered the English camp, and while seemingly intent on the sale of his commodities, he was, at the same time, carefully observing the arrangement of the encampment,

'Quhar lords lay and had yair lugyng maid,
Ze kings palzone quharon ye libards baid,
Spyand full fast quhar awaill suld be,
And couth weyll luk and wynk with ye ta e.'

The soldiers, no doubt struck with his singular appearance, soon began to treat him with considerable freedom. Some of them broke his pots, while others indulged in jokes upon his blind eye. It is a tradition, that one man declared that if the hawker had not been blind of an eye and lame of a leg, he was certain that he was Wallace himself. This declaration was afterwards put into rhyme, and is still well known at Biggar. It is as follows:—

'Had ye not been cripple o' a leg, and blind o' an ee,
Ye are as like William Wallace as ever I did see.'

Wallace finding his situation becoming perilous, made haste to retire without exciting further suspicion.

He returned to his own camp just in time to save the life of his friend, Sir John Tinto. A great discontent had arisen among the Scots when it was known that Wallace had secretly left the camp, as it was conjectured that he had, after all, deserted his friends, and might betray them to the enemy. As he had been last seen in communication with Sir John Tinto, that knight was called on to disclose what he knew regarding the movements of their leader; but as he positively refused to do this, he was put under restraint, and a cry was raised that he should forfeit his life for his obstinacy. When the excitement was at the very height, and Tinto was expecting nothing else than that he would fall a victim to the general indignation, Wallace made his appearance, ordered him to be set at liberty, and commended him highly for his unflinching fidelity to his obligation. The chiefs gathered round Wallace to hear an account of his adventures, the recital of which afforded them much amusement; but it called forth a strong expression of dissatisfaction from Sir John Graham, who maintained that such conduct was unchieftainlike, and altogether unbecoming the commander of an army. Wallace, in reply, said that before Scotland was free, it would be necessary for them all to subject themselves to far greater hazards, and to perform still more daring exploits.

The Scottish army retired to rest, but with instructions that every man should be on foot before daybreak, and ready for the march.

When the trumpet, at the appointed time, blew a rallying blast, they all sprang up, ready armed, and eager for the fray. They were immediately drawn up in three divisions. The first was led by Wallace himself, and under him were Sir Robert Boyd and Nicol Auchinleck; the second by Sir John Graham, and under him were Adam Wallace, younger of Riccarton, and Sir Thomas Sommerville of Carnwath; and the third by Sir Walter of Newbigging, and under him were Sir John Tinto, and David, son of Sir Walter. The foot, being badly armed, were drawn up in the rear, and received orders not to engage rashly, but reserve themselves till a fitting opportunity, or till they were properly supplied with arms. Wallace then summoned the chieftains around him, and strictly enjoined them to prevent their followers from being allured from the combat by the pillage which the English camp might present. He reminded them, that those who betook themselves to plunder before the victory was gained, generally lost both their life and their booty. He expressed the utmost confidence that they would, on this occasion, strike a blow worthy of freemen, and exert themselves with all their might to inflict punishment on a false tyrant who had come to wreathe fresh chains on the necks of their countrymen. All of them readily consented to attend to his orders.

They had scarcely commenced their march, when, through the faint gloom of the summer's morning, they beheld a body of armed men approaching from the south, which naturally filled them with alarm. These, however, turned out to be a party of three hundred hardy and stalwart borderers, under the command of Thomas Halliday and his two sons, Wallace and Rutherford; and with them also came Jardine of Applegirth, and Rodger Kirkpatrick, Lord of Torthorald; the whole being on their way to join the Scottish patriots who had taken up arms in defence of their country. This welcome accession of strength was hailed with great satisfaction, and still further raised the spirits of the Scots.

The combined force now proceeded with the greatest celerity towards Biggar. The English, to prevent surprise during the night, had posted pickets at some distance from their camp; but as dawn began to appear, these had been withdrawn. The English, being aware of the comparatively small number of the Scots, entertained no suspicion that an attack would be made upon them by day. When the first division of the Scottish horsemen, led on by Wallace himself, therefore, rushed upon them, they were taken somewhat by surprise. The knowledge which Wallace had acquired by his visit to the English camp, was of the greatest use, as he knew the ground, the disposition of the tents, and the best mode of conducting the assault. He therefore rushed with his division into the very heart of the camp, with the view of reaching the tent of the king; but he found this was impossible, as the English soldiers in great numbers rallied round it, particularly the Earl of Kent, with a detachment of 5000 men. The Scots, finding themselves encumbered with their horses, dismounted, and carried on the affray on foot. As they were all stalwart men, expert in war, and animated with a deadly resentment to the English, they fought with the most desperate valour, and made a prodigious havoc among their terrified, disordered, and half-armed antagonists.

Graham and Newbigging, with their divisions, followed by the foot, who had now obtained an abundant supply of weapons, also pressed hastily forward, overturning the tents in their way, and slaughtering every opponent they could reach. The battle still raged round the king's person with great obstinacy; and the Scots, having joined their forces, began to drive the English back towards the valley, covered with deep marshes on the south, and in the confusion the royal tent was overturned. The Earl of Kent, proud of displaying his martial skill and prowess in the presence of his sovereign, rallied his troops once and again; and, with a ponderous battle-axe, committed great havoc among the Scots. Wallace, finding the course of victory arrested by the powerful arm of this intrepid and indomitable warrior, sought him out amid the throng, and engaged him in single combat. When these two distinguished champions had fairly encountered, the surrounding warriors, on both sides, almost suspended the work of death, to watch the issue of a conflict so tremendous and heart-stirring. Both fought with great fury, but with admirable courage and dexterity, till, at length, Wallace, with an irresistible stroke, smote him lifeless to the ground. At this sight the English were discouraged, and mounting the king on horseback, forced him, much against his inclination, to quit the field. In this encounter 4000 of the English were cut down, and the remainder, in terror and confusion, fled from Biggar, taking the direction of Coulter by the Causeway, which crossed the moss on the west. The Scots pursued them to Coulter Hope, about four miles distant. Here the English rallied in great force, and Wallace, knowing that he was no match for them in the open field, withdrew his followers to Biggar, after they had slain 7000 men in the pursuit, as no quarter was given. Here, finding provisions and valuable commodities in abundance, and being exceedingly hungry and fatigued, they sat down to a sumptuous repast; and after regaling themselves with bumpers of wine, proceeded to take some repose. Their rest, however, was of short duration, as Wallace was afraid that the English, apprized of the smallness of their numbers, would return, for the purpose of recovering their camp, and therefore deemed it prudent to draw off his forces to a place of strength and security, called Davis Shaw, and to convey the booty obtained in the camp to Rops's Bog.

The English were now drawn up in Coulter Hope, on a place called John's Green, and were lamenting the disaster that had befallen them, and the loss of their comrades and commanders, among the latter of

whom were the king's son, his two uncles, and the Earl of Kent, when
two cooks, who had concealed themselves in the camp, and skulked
off after they saw the Scots indulging in repose, came and informed
them that the Scots were lying in the camp, overcome with sleep and
intoxication, and might easily be overpowered. The king was unwilling to credit this story, as he considered it unlikely that Wallace
would be so remiss and unguarded in such circumstances. He therefore declared it to be his determination to retreat, as there was little
hope of recovering their provisions at Biggar, and no adequate supplies could be obtained amid the mountains by which they were surrounded. The Duke of Lancaster urged, that the circumstances in
which they were placed rendered it imperative that an effort should
be made to regain the camp; and though the king himself would not
return, he requested to be furnished with a strong detachment, with
which he hoped to recover the supplies, of which they would soon
stand so much in need. The king was prevailed on to allow him to
take 10,000 men, and promised to wait on him till next day, expecting to be able to supply the wants of his troops with such bestial as
he might find among the hills. The Governor of Calais and the
Lord of Westmoreland resolved to accompany the Duke, and each of
them obtained the command of 1000 men; Sir Aymer de Vallance
also joined them with a considerable reinforcement. These united
parties marched back to Biggar, but found the camp plundered and
deserted, and strewed with dead bodies that had been stripped bare.
For some time they were at a loss to conceive what place the Scots
had retired to, but some scouts soon brought intelligence that they
were posted at Davis Shaw, which is supposed to have been situated
on the sloping sides of the hill of Bizzyberry, little more than a mile
from Biggar. They accordingly marched in that direction, but were
descried by the Scottish videttes, who gave the alarm. Leaving their
horses in the Shaw, the Scots passed on foot into Rop's Bog, as a place
of greater security from the attacks of the English division, which
consisted principally of cavalry. The English seeing them pass into
the bog, and being deceived by its fair and solid appearance, rode
towards them with great impetuosity. The consequence was, that the
front line of horse was soon embogued in the morass, and overborne
by those that pressed on behind. In this state of confusion the
soldiers were assailed by the Scots, and, being unable to extricate
themselves, were slaughtered almost to a man. The Scots, embold-
ened by this success, crossed the bog and fell upon the English, who
were bewildered and intimidated by the fate of their comrades, and
the boldness and success of their opponents. The conflict, however,
was sharp and long-continued, and great valour was displayed on
both sides. The mode of fighting at that time generally rendered a
battle a series of single combats. Some notable encounters of this
kind took place during the engagement. The Governor of Calais,

clad in complete armour, and expert in all warlike exercises, assailed Sir John Graham, who, with his trusty blade, warded off his attacks, and, at length, struck him such a blow as pierced his harness, and laid him lifeless on the spot. Wallace, espying Aymer de Vallance, one of Edward's most active and resolute captains, and noted for his cruel oppression of the Scots, was anxious to engage with him; but the Earl of Westmoreland, coming between them, received a stroke from Wallace on his steel basinet, which instantly deprived him of life. Robert Boyd encountered the Governor of Berwick, and, after an obstinate combat, also succeeded in slaying him by a 'straik awkwart ye crag,' which cutting

> 'Throuch all hys weid in sondyr straik ye bane.'

The English, now panic-struck, left the field to the victorious Scots, and fled back to John's Green.

Such was the Battle of Biggar; and if Harry is at all to be credited, it was productive of most important consequences. Edward considered it prudent to return to England, without gaining the object of his expedition. Many persons of distinction came and ranked themselves under the banner of Wallace, and, in a short time after, that undaunted and inflexible patriot was chosen Warden of Scotland, at an assembly of his countrymen held at Carluke Church, then called Forest Kirk.

The spot on which the English are supposed to have had their encampment, and on which the Battle of Biggar was fought, lies to the east of the town, and comprehends what are now called the Back Well Park, the Stanehead, Guildie's Oxgait, and the Borrow Muir. A little farther to the east is the extensive morass, then called 'Rop's Bog,' and now Biggar Moss, a right to it having, at a later period, been conferred on the town. A small stream, which runs out of this bog, is said to have been dyed with blood on the day of the battle, and, therefore, got the name of the 'Red Syke,' by which it is still known. A little to the north is the hill of Bizzyberry, on which the wood called Davis Shaw is said to have been situated, on which evident traces of military works are still to be seen, and which has some parts of it associated with the name of Wallace to this day.

The story of the Battle of Biggar, as is well known, has been regarded by historians as a mere fable, and has brought down on the head of the poor Minstrel a perfect torrent of contempt and abuse. The main cause of this is, that no historian or state document of the period mentions the expedition of Edward I. which ended in the Battle of Biggar. It is stated, too, by some historians, and among others by Holinshed, that Edward was in France in 1297, the year in which Harry says the Battle of Biggar was fought. Now, all these circumstances do not put the Battle beyond the bounds of probability. Documents of that period, whether written by statesmen or historians,

2 I

were neither very detailed nor accurate, and were often, in the course
of a few years, destroyed or lost.   Supposing Blind Harry's narrative
to be correct, it is far from unlikely that the king was at pains, so far
as he possibly could, to obliterate every trace of an expedition so dis-
appointing to his hopes, and so damaging to his military reputation.
It is not a decisive statement to say that Edward was that same year
in France, because he may have gone to that country shortly after the
battle was fought; and even supposing that he was the whole of the
year there, the details given by Harry may be perfectly correct,
although he may have made a mistake as to the exact date.   Several
reasons might be assigned in favour of attaching credit to the Minstrel's story.   The causes which are said to have led to the battle, viz.,
the sanguinary proceedings at Lanark, do not rest on the testimony of
Harry alone.   They are recorded by Fordun in his 'Scotichronicon,'
and by Wyntoun in his 'Ckronykill of Scotland;' and are generally
regarded as facts beyond all cavil or dispute.   The slaughter of Hesi-
rig, Thorn, and the English garrison at Lanark, and the gathering
together of the Scots, under Wallace and other competent leaders,
were certainly events sufficient to rouse Edward to make a fresh inroad into Scotland.   The complete subjugation of this country was
regarded by that monarch as a matter of the last importance.   For
the attainment of this object he had plotted and contended for years;
he had held important national assemblies; he had overrun the greater
part of Scotland; he had vanquished its armies; he had destroyed or
carried off the memorials of its national independence; he had filled
its strongholds with his troops; and he had forced its king and its
barons to submit to the most bitter mortifications, and to bend before
him as their lord superior.   Though detachments of English troops
were stationed in different parts of Scotland, it does not appear that
there was at that time any concentrated force that could effectually
cope with the patriots who had banded themselves together.   In these
circumstances, nothing was more likely than that Edward should again
march into Scotland at the head of a large army.

It serves somewhat to confirm the statement that Edward was at
Biggar, and fought a battle there, that fragments of ancient armour,
according to report, have been repeatedly dug up in the neighbourhood of the town; and coins of his reign have been found in the
adjoining fields.   One of these, found on Gum's Meadow, by Adam
Wyld, Esq., Biggar, is still in the possession of that gentleman; and
another, found some forty years ago by Mr Peter Williamson on the
Borrow Muir, is now in the possession of William Ballantyne, Esq.,
manufacturer, Glasgow, a native of Biggar.   A few years ago, an
immense number of these coins were dug up at a spot on the south
side of Crosscryne, about three miles from Biggar, which tradition
points out as lying on the exact line of the march of the English
army.   That zealous antiquary, Mr Sim of Coulter, visited the spot,

and he found the coins scattered about in such abundance, that he was led to entertain the opinion that a portion of Edward's military chest had been there deposited, either from the circumstance of a waggon breaking down, or for the purpose of concealment. As might be expected, Mr Sim has in his repositories a number of these coins, which he delights to show to his friends, as forming, it may be, a slight corroboration of the old Minstrel's narrative of the Battle of Biggar.

The details given by Blind Harry are by no means improbable. The visit of Wallace to the English camp cannot be a matter of great surprise, when we know that the Duke of Wellington, one of the most cautious of generals, was in the habit, both in Spain and France, of going alone, and in disguise, almost close to the pickets of the enemy, to ascertain, with his own eyes, the nature of the ground, and the best modes of carrying out his movements. The disparity of numbers is, no doubt, very great; but the battle is not described as a regular engagement in the fields, but as, in the first place, an unexpected assault on the enemy's camp, and in the second, a stand against an attack of cavalry in a bog, in both of which a small body of powerful and intrepid men might successfully oppose and overcome five or six times their own number. The removal of the booty by the Scots to a place of security, the return of the English to Biggar, and the position taken up by the Scots on a piece of ground defended by a morass, are all circumstances most likely to occur; while the nature of the ground, and the relative position of the places mentioned, are accurately described, and lend additional confirmation to the Minstrel's tale.

It is not to be denied that there is much confusion of dates, and even of statement, in Blind Harry's book. In the end he dispenses with dates altogether. His narrative, however, agrees in many points with that given by old historians, particularly by Fordun and Wyntown; and recent researches have tended rather to establish than invalidate the events which he describes. If he tells the truth in very many respects, it is rather surprising that he should be guilty of an entire fabrication in regard to the Battle of Biggar. Harry lived at a time when, no doubt, much authentic information, both written and oral, existed regarding the career of Wallace. He refers to various works as his authorities, which unfortunately do not now exist, such as 'The First Line of the First Stewarts,' 'Con's Cronykle,' and, above all, a Life of Wallace, written in Latin by his chaplain, Robert Blair, and Thomas Gray, parson of Libberton, in the neighbourhood of Biggar, and confirmed for truth by Sinclair, Bishop of Dunkeld, who had himself been a witness of many of the exploits of Wallace. These works may have borne out the Minstrel's narrative in very many particulars. As it is evident that he was an enthusiast in the cause of his hero, he would spare no pains in collecting the stories then current regarding his achievements. He mentions several parties who had supplied him with facts, particularly Wallace of Craigie, and the Laird of Liddle. His own declaration regarding his book bears such an appearance of simplicity and candour, that it would almost satisfy an inveterate sceptic of his entire sincerity in the narrative which he has given.

> ' All worthy men yat redys yis rurall dyt,
> Blaym nocht ye buk set I be unperfyt.
> I suld haive thank, sen I nocht trawaill spard,
> For my labour na man hecht me reward.
> Na charge I had off king or oyir lord,
> Gret harm I thocht hys gud deid suld be smored.
> I haiff said her ner as ye process gais,
> And fenzied nocht for freindschip nor for fais.'

We have no intention to stand up and implicitly maintain that a battle, with all the incidents detailed by Blind Harry, actually took place at Biggar; but, at the same time, we have little doubt that in these unsettled times some engagement or another was fought at this place, on which the narrative of the Minstrel was, in a great measure, founded.

CHAPTER XXII.

Military Movements and Royal Progresses at Biggar.

THE encampment of Edward II. of England at Biggar, in 1310, is an important event in the history of the town. By this time Wallace had been betrayed into the hands of the English, and had been most unjustly and ignominiously put to death as a traitor; and his savage executioner, Edward I., who had caused so much injury to Scotland, had also paid the debt of nature, without obtaining the great object of his ambition, the entire subjugation of the Scots. His son, Edward II., now reigned in his stead; and though possessed of far less energy and discrimination than his father, he still pursued the same unjust and aggressive policy in respect to the northern kingdom. He had, however, to contend with Robert Bruce, a most politic, indefatigable, and valiant champion of his country's rights and liberties. Bruce, at first, had met with reverses and discouragements sufficient to crush any ordinary man; but, at the period to which we refer, he had rallied his scattered friends, and was overpowering in detail the generals whom Edward had sent to overawe and subjugate the country. The English king, on learning the reverses of his troops, and the successful career of Bruce, resolved to levy a formidable army, and once more make an inroad into Scotland, hoping that his imposing array of military force would put an end to all further efforts on the part of Bruce to oppose his designs. He summoned his vassals from all parts of his dominions, and, in a short time, arrived at Berwick with a mighty body of armed men, his principal generals being the Earls of Gloucester and Warrene, Lord Henry Percy, and Lord James Clifford. Leaving Berwick, they ascended, by leisurely marches, the vale of Tweed, and arrived at Biggar on the 12th or 14th day of October. The English monarch was, most likely, desirous of an engagement; but Bruce was now well aware of the advantages of stratagem and caution. He saw that he was more likely to defeat a large army by allowing it to march up and down a barren and desolated country, than by encountering it in the open field. He therefore kept hovering on the flanks of the English, intercepting their supplies, and cutting off such stragglers and foraging parties as fell in his way. On one occasion he pounced on a detachment of 300 men, and before a reinforcement could be sent to their aid, cut them to pieces.

From the long-continued wars in which Scotland had been engaged, tillage had been greatly neglected, and the country, at the time, was suffering from the direful effects of famine. Any corn and forage that existed had been carefully removed to places not easily accessible to the English. This was a leading feature in the policy of Bruce; to which he gave prominent expression in what is called his Testament, originally written in Latin verse, and afterwards translated into Scotch by Hearne. In speaking of the manner of dealing with invaders, he says,

> ' In strait placis gar keip all stoire,
> And birnen the planen land thaim befoire,
> Thanan sall thai pass away in haist,
> Quhen that thai find nathing bot waist. '

Had the sound advice given in this testament been attended to by the Scots in after times, it would have saved them from many a sad disaster; and, at this day, we would not have had to lament such woeful defeats as those of Flodden, Pinkey, and Dunbar.

While Edward lay at Biggar, his troops began to suffer very much from the want of provisions, and, therefore, he issued an edict to the sheriffs of the different counties of England to levy and forward supplies of corn, etc. As this is the only state document, so far as we know, that ever was issued from Biggar, we will venture to give a translation of it from the Norman French in which it was written, and which was so long the language of the English court, although the statements contained in it are not, historically speaking, of any great importance :—

' *The King to the Sheriff of Warwick, greeting.*

' Whereas we lately commanded you, by our letters bearing the stamp of our great seal and the special seal of our Exchequer, to make diverse purveyances of corn and other things for the sustentation of us and our army in Scotland ; and we have since learned by intelligence from some people, that you have begun to make these purveyances in an undue manner. We again command and charge you, on the faith which you owe to us, that you cause these purveyances to be made in a manner so expedient, as not to incur the ill-will of our people, whom God protect. Our will in this respect is, that you do no wrong on account of this levy of provisions, and that you do not, under a pretence of purchase, carry off the goods of any one, without their consent; but that, by the best methods that you can adopt, you will cause the said victuals to be provided with all despatch, under warrants of your bailiffs, by way of purchase, voluntary presentation, and the favourable disposition of well affected people. And should it happen that the whole of our own revenues are not sufficient to procure these purveyances without having recourse to the property of others, we command you that with all despatch and

care you levy the whole of our dues which you have, or may have in
charge, from our resources, and the sums in our Exchequer, and by
other express orders from us in your possession. You must exempt
no one from the sums due to us unless he can show a discharged
account or other acquittance, or you have instructions from us that he
is to be specially exempted from the taxes which you have levied, or
may levy, as well as from all other warrants issued by your bailiffs.
Make, then, fully and without delay, the purveyance already referred
to, and in the manner specified; and see that you fail not, as you regard the honour of us and our realm, and wish to avoid the heavy
penalty which you will incur for any loss that we may thereby sustain.

' Given at Biggar, the 18th day of October.

' The same instructions are given to the sheriffs underwritten; that
is to say, Kent, Norfolk, Suffolk, Essex, Hertford, etc., etc.'

For six days, the English king and his army remained at Biggar;
but Robert Bruce, true to the cautious policy which he had adopted,
kept at a distance, and afforded no prospect of surrendering to his
opponents, or coming to an engagement in the field. They struck
their tents, therefore, and marched down the Clyde to Renfrew; but
finding in the west the same uniform scenes of poverty and desolation,
they soon reversed their march and came to Linlithgow, where they
remained twelve days, and then returned to Berwick, at which town
they arrived on the 10th of November. The whole expedition was a
complete failure, being nothing better than a piece of empty ostentation and bravado. It awed and subdued nobody. Edward, in writing an account of it to the Pope, however, claims the credit of completely overawing the Scots. He says,—' When we lately marched
into Scotland to suppress the rebellion of Robert Bruce and his
accomplices, traitors alike against us and your Holiness, they lurked
in hiding-places like foxes, not daring to oppose us in the field.' He
had a very different tale to tell a few years afterwards, when he met
Bruce on the famous field of Bannockburn.

Biggar was the place appointed as the rendezvous of the Scottish
warriors, who, in February 1802–3, were summoned to repel an invasion of the English. Here assembled an army of 8000 or 10,000
men from Dumfriesshire, Ayrshire, and Clydesdale,—districts famed
throughout the whole of our history for containing the boldest and
most unflinching champions of freedom, civil and religious. The
principal commanders were Sir John Comyn, Lord of Lenzie and
Badnoch, and one of the guardians of the kingdom, and the brave
Sir Simon Fraser of Oliver Castle, in Peeblesshire. Walsingham and
some other English historians state that Wallace held the chief command; but as this circumstance is not confirmed by Fordun or any
Scottish writer, it is probable that the great hero of national inde-

pendence was not present, but, at the time, was living in retirement,
or had gone to France, disgusted with the selfishness and treachery of
the greater part of the Scottish nobility. We can readily imagine the
lively interest with which the inhabitants of Biggar would regard the
array of brave and patriotic men, who had assembled on their plains,
not for the purpose of a mere holiday review, but of using their good
broadswords, and imperilling their lives to repel the swarm of invaders that Edward of England had again sent to ravage their country.
The English, amounting to 20,000 men, under the command of Sir
John Segrave, marched about Lent from Berwick to Edinburgh, and
then commenced to move in three divisions to the south. The Scots
at Biggar appear to have got notice of their movements, and being
nearly all horsemen, they hastened by a night march to meet them,
and stop their progress. While it was yet dark, they fell on the first
division near Roslin, commanded by Segrave, and ere it had time to
draw up in battle order, routed it with great slaughter, and took a
large number of prisoners, among whom were Segrave himself, sixteen
knights, and thirty squires. The Scots, thinking they had gained a
complete victory, began to collect the booty, when the second division,
under the command of Ralph Manton, the cofferer or treasurer,
appeared in sight, and no alternative was left but to slay the prisoners,
and engage in a second combat. The Scots made the attack with
such irresistible fury that they bore all before them, and captured the
cofferer and many other persons of distinction. Scarcely had this
combat been decided, when the Scots saw the third division, under
the command of Sir Robert Neville, hastening to the scene of action.
Worn out by their night march from Biggar, and their exertions in
the two previous engagements, their first thoughts were turned to a
retreat from the field; but the enemy was too close upon them to permit this to be done with safety, and they were compelled to fight a
third time, and a third time they were victorious. Neville was laid
lifeless on the field, and the whole of the English army were either
killed or scattered in hopeless confusion over the plains of Lothian,
while the Scots were rewarded by the rich booty left in their hands.

At a convention held at Stirling, on the 15th May 1565, Queen
Mary expressed her intention to enter into the marriage relation with
her cousin, Lord Darnley. Lord John Fleming and the barons present gave their sanction to this union, and it was accordingly solemnized on the 20th of July following. Unfortunately, the step gave
great dissatisfaction to some of her principal nobility. Professing a
warm attachment to Protestantism, they viewed Darnley with special
dislike on account of his adherence to the Romish faith. The Duke
of Chatelherault, the Earls of Murray, Glencairn, Rothes, and Argyle,
Lords Boyd and Ochiltree, and others, usually styled the Lords of
the Congregation, drew together their followers, and broke out
against her in open rebellion. Whatever may have been the faults

and failings of Mary Stewart, she was certainly not destitute of courage and activity. She lost no time in summoning her faithful subjects around her, and, at the head of 5000 men, marched against the rebel lords, then assembled in the west of Scotland. The Queen expected to encounter them at Hamilton; but they eluded her, and proceeded to Edinburgh. Finding that they were to receive little support in the capital, they left it in a few days, and retreated, first to Lanark, and then to Hamilton. Considering their position insecure in the west, they proceeded to Dumfries, so that, in case of necessity, they might readily retire across the border, and take refuge in the dominions of Queen Elizabeth, who secretly favoured their rebellious designs. Queen Mary and her friends, on the rebel lords first leaving Hamilton, went to Stirling, and then to St Andrews, from which she issued a proclamation calling on the rebels to lay down their arms, and appear before her in six days, to answer such charges as might be brought against them; but, as none of them appeared, they were denounced as rebels, and put to the horn. Her authority being thus set at defiance, she sent forth a summons to her faithful subjects to assemble at Biggar on the 8th of October, 'all boden in feir of weir,' with twenty days' provision, 'under pane of tinsell of lyff, landis, and guddis.' The author of the 'Diurnal of Remarkable Occurents,' in referring to the 8th of October 1565, says :—'Upon the samen day our souranis with thair army depairtit of Edinburgh towart Biggar.' The equipment of the Queen was decidedly warlike. She rode a stately charger, and had a pair of pistols stuck in holsters at her saddle-bows ; and it is said that her scarlet and embroidered riding dress covered a suit of defensive armour, and that under her hood and veil she wore a steel casque. Darnley was also gaily mounted, and wore a splendid suit of gilt armour. These royal and illustrious personages were received at Biggar by an enthusiastic host of 18,000 men, all ready to march against the foes of their sovereign, and to fight to the death in defence of her rights and authority. Mary, no doubt, honoured her cousin, Lord Fleming, by taking up her abode in the Castle of Boghall during her brief stay at Biggar. Its old walls would then resound with the enthusiastic shouts that welcomed Scotland's fair Queen and her husband to repose within its towers and battlements.

Biggar never saw a more gallant array of Scottish chivalry than was, on this occasion, displayed on its adjacent acclivities. Here had assembled a large portion of the nobles, barons, and knights of Scotland, with their retainers, from almost every part of the kingdom. The names of the chief leaders of this army, and the posts which they were to occupy in the different battalions, as given by some of our old historians, are as follows :—The vanguard was led by the right noble and mighty Lord Mathew, Earl of Lennox, Lieutenant in the western parts of the realm, who was supported by the Earls of Cassillis and Eglinton, Lords Semple, Ross, Cathcart, and Sanquhar, the Sheriff

of Ayr, the Laird of Garlies, Sir James Hamilton, and other lieges
of the Queen, within the Earl of Lennox's jurisdiction. The rear-
guard was led by George, Earl of Huntly, John, Earl of Athole, and
David, Earl of Crawford; and these noblemen were accompanied
by Lords Ruthven, Glamis, Forbes, Drummond, and Innermeth, and
the Commendator of Deer, who took the place of his father, the Earl
Marischall. The main body was under the command of Lord Darnley,
the husband of the Queen, who was supported by the Earls of Morton,
Bothwell, and Mar; Lords Fleming, Ogilvie, Livingston, Sommerville,
Borthwick, Yester, Lindsay, and Hume, and 'the haill remnant of
ye realme.'*

The Queen was the life and soul of this warlike assemblage. She
directed its movements and inflamed its martial ardour. Her youth
and beauty won every heart; and her courage in taking the field in
person, to imperil her liberty or her life in defence of her rights, no
doubt lent strength to every warrior's arm, and made him resolve to
conquer or die in her behalf. The review of her troops on the gently
rising grounds of Biggar, therefore, far surpassed in thrilling interest
any martial demonstration that has taken place in our country in recent times. It was not a mere holiday display, or a muster for a
sham fight. It was not a spectacle got up for amusement, and
theatrical effect; but an array of men who had seized their weapons
of war, left their homes and usual employments, and taken their place
in battle order, ready to be led against their foes, and to engage in
deadly combat.

The Queen led forth her loyal and devoted warriors from Biggar
on the 10th of October, and proceeded by Coulter, Lamington, and
Crawford towards Dumfries. The rebel lords fled at her approach,
and, crossing the border, took refuge in England. Mary, two days
after she left Biggar, entered Dumfries; but finding none in arms to
oppose her, she disbanded her army, and with all the *eclat* of a blood-
less victory, returned to her capital by way of Moffat, Tweedsmuir,
and Peebles.

After the battle of Langside, so disastrous to the claims and power
of Mary Stewart, the Regent Murray proceeded to inflict vengeance
on the adherents of the unfortunate Queen. His policy was rather to
plunder their estates and overturn their strongholds, than to shed
their blood on the scaffold. He is consequently described in a history
of the time as running in a rage 'throwe the cuntrie like a wilde
boare, depopulatinge the landis of the Queenis faithful subiects, robbing them of ther goodis, and pullinge down ther holds and houses,

* The Council of war, at which the above arrangement was agreed to, made the
reservation 'that the present ordouring and disposing of the Battellis foersaidis, be
nawayis prejudiciall to the Erle of Angus, his titile and interes qnhatsumever.' The
Earl of Angus had a hereditary right to lead the van of the royal army, but it appears
that he was not present at Biggar on this occasion.

persuinge them with fire and sworde whithersoever he came, and confiscatinge all ther mowables for his owen particular uise.'

One of his first expeditions of this sort was up the Vale of Clyde, and to the southern parts of Scotland. He 'put out proclamations commanding all men to ryse with fifteen days provisions,' and appointed the rendezvous to be at Biggar. He set out from Glasgow in the beginning of June with 2000 men in his train, and three pieces of artillery; one of the noblemen who accompanied him being James Douglas, Earl of Morton, and Laird of Edmonston. On his way he took and destroyed the Castles of Hamilton and Draffen, belonging to those zealous partizans of the Queen, the Hamiltons. Herries, in his 'Historical Memoirs of the Reign of Mary Queen of Scots,' states, that the Regent, on his arrival at Biggar, 'found four thousand hors and one thousand foote with fyrlocks.' With this force he plundered and devastated the domains of the supporters of the Queen in the Biggar district, with absolute freedom and impunity.

Lord Fleming was particularly obnoxious to the Regent, both because he was a zealous and indefatigable partisan of the Queen, and especially because he obstinately continued to hold the strong and important fortress of Dumbarton in her interests. He was, of course, absent from Biggar at this time; so the full weight of the Regent's vengeance fell on his tenants and vassals. We know from a journal of the Regent's proceedings in Clydesdale, preserved in her Majesty's State Paper Office, that he laid siege to the Castle of Boghall, and took it, after overcoming some resistance, and most likely demolishing a portion of the buildings. He then led a detachment of his men to Skirling, the domain of Sir J. Cockburn, who, at the time, was a fugitive in England. The Regent, meeting with no opposition, found little difficulty in obtaining possession of the castle of that barony. This stronghold was situated in a morass, which now forms part of the glebe of the parish minister, and was of considerable size and strength. It was principally defended by the morass; but this being somewhat accessible on the south-west, the building in that quarter was protected by strong turrets. The ordinary access was by a causeway and stone bridge. The Regent, being determined to leave behind him a sensible token of his displeasure, caused a large quantity of gunpowder to be deposited in one of the lower apartments, and this being fired, the edifice was immediately reduced to a heap of smoking ruins. It was never rebuilt. The remains of it continued standing till the present century, when they were unfortunately removed by the Rev. Mr M'Alpine, a late incumbent of the parish, during some improvements which he made on the glebe. The ground has now been so much changed by drainage and cultivation, that it is very difficult to discover the spot on which the Castle stood.

Detachments of the Regent's troops were also sent out to ravage the lands of the other adherents of the Queen in the neighbourhood of Biggar. The tenants of Baillie of Lamington, Baillie of St John's Kirk, and Chancellor of Shieldhill, were assailed and plundered without mercy. The fortalice of the Chancellors, which at this period stood at the village of Quothquan, was of course attacked and laid in ruins. It was not rebuilt; and when times became more settled under the rule of James VI., the laird erected a habitation on the spot on which the House of Shieldhill still stands. The Regent thus left the Biggar district a scene of suffering and desolation; and the expedition, on this account, received the name of the Raid of Biggar. In the records of Justiciary, we find that on the 4th January 1570–1, James Spens, in Glenduke, William Russell, in Glaslie, and John Dick, elder, in Easter Cartmoir, were 'delatit for remaning fra the Raids of Langsyde, Biger,' etc. The Court deserted the charge against them at that time; but the Judge ordered them to find caution to appear and underlie the law on the 15th of February next. No record has been left to show whether they were ultimately punished or acquitted.

After the execution of Charles I., the Scots proclaimed his son Charles successor to the throne. They despatched Sir William Fleming and other Commissioners to hold an interview with the young King at Breda, to invite him to Scotland, and proffer him support, on condition of his accepting and signing the Solemn League and Covenant. Charles by no means relished such terms; but, at the time, seeing no other way of arriving at the throne of England, he came to Scotland and accepted them, but with a secret determination to violate them so soon as circumstances would permit. The Scots, by the support thus tendered to the King, were brought into collision with the Republicans of England. Oliver Cromwell was recalled from Ireland, and despatched to Scotland with a force of 16,000 men, in order to compel the Scots to renounce their adherence to the King, and to submit implicitly to the Commonwealth. The Scots mustered a considerable army to oppose the English general, and would have forced him to leave the country, had not the improper interference of the Presbyterian clergy caused them, in spite of the remonstrances of their commander, General Leslie, to hazard an engagement at Dunbar, on the 3d of September 1650. As might be expected, they were thoroughly defeated. This disaster caused great consternation in the Upper Ward. The brethren of the Biggar Presbytery, as we have elsewhere stated, on the morning of the 5th, two days after the battle, hastened spontaneously to Biggar, and found the whole town in an uproar, 'be reason of the sad newes of ye defeat of our army.' They called the people together, and offered up supplications to the Almighty, that they might be preserved from the outrages and devastations of war, and that their enemies might be rebuked and scattered. Before dismissing the people, they resolved to meet again next morning, and spend the day in fasting and humiliation, on account of their own sins and the sins of the land, which had so signally evoked the judgments of divine Providence. The Presbytery of Lanark also met on the 5th, and spent the day in devotional exercises, and, at the same time, resolved to set apart the 22d, as a day of fasting and humiliation, in the parishes within their bounds. Accordingly, on that day suitable discourses were delivered, collections were made for defraying the expenses incurred by attendance on the sick and wounded, and ex hortations addressed to all able-bodied men to lose no time in repairing to the camp at Stirling, where the scattered remains of the Scottish army had been gathered together under the banner of the King.

Cromwell lost no time in improving the advantages which he had gained by the victory at Dunbar. He bombarded and took the Castles of Roslin, Tantallon, Hume, Borthwick, Neidpath, and others; and their shattered remains still bear witness to the effects of his destructive assaults. In the end of November he despatched a force of 4000 men, chiefly horsemen, to the Upper Ward, who took possession of the town of Lanark, and committed a series of ravages on the country round. It is supposed that it was this force, or a part of it, that laid siege to the Castle of Boghall. The camp which the soldiers of the Commonwealth are said to have occupied, is situated a few hundred yards to the south-west of the Castle, and though much obliterated by the progress of agricultural improvement, can still be very distinctly traced. It completely commanded the habitable part of the Castle; and as it was no doubt furnished with a battering train, a few shots would serve to show that the walls could not long withstand the effects of a cannonade by heavy ordnance, and that the garrison had no alternative but to surrender. At all events, it seems to be certain that the Royalist troops were expelled, and that the Castle was held for some time by the soldiers of the Commonwealth. These men committed great devastation on the country round. The only retaliation inflicted on them, that we have heard of, is recorded by Captain Armstrong in his 'Companion to the Map of Tweeddale,' published during the latter part of last century; but we suspect that his statement rests on no higher authority than tradition. He tells us that a party of sixteen horsemen from Oliver Cromwell's camp at Biggar, penetrated the hills of Tweeddale. They had reached a place in the parish of Tweedsmuir called Talla or Fala Moss, where they were surprised and made prisoners by Porteous of Hawkshaw, and a party of country people. After some deliberation, it was resolved that the whole of them should be put to death; and the captors at once rushed upon the defenceless soldiers, and plunged their swords in their breasts. One of the soldiers having received only a slight wound, ran several miles; but being overtaken, was cut down with a number of blows. The others were interred at the part of the moss where they had been massacred.

The Scots, although encountering many disasters, still prosecuted the war against Cromwell. They rallied round the standard of Charles at Stirling, and manifested a most resolute determination not to yield to the invader. Cromwell at length set out to prosecute hostilities in Perthshire; and the way to England being thus left open, Charles formed the desperate resolution of marching into England, where he hoped he would be joined by a large number of adherents. He therefore set out on his march, and in a day or two arrived at Biggar. David Leslie, his major-general, summoned the Castle of Boghall to surrender; but the governor, according to Whitlocke,* returned a resolute refusal, declaring that he held the Castle for the Commonwealth of England. As the Royalists were anxious to cross the border with all possible haste, they did not halt sufficient time at Biggar to attempt a reduction of the Castle by force. Cromwell followed hard in the track of the royal army, and therefore the likelihood is that he also visited Biggar in person, and took up his quarters for a night in the Castle of Boghall.

No sooner did it become generally known in 1715 that the Earl of Mar had set up the standard of rebellion in the north, than a meeting of Jacobites was held at Edinburgh. At this meeting it was resolved that troops should be raised to join the squadrons expected to be levied in the south of Scotland, and that the rendezvous should be at Biggar. This muster accordingly took place; but the number of troops that assembled at Biggar on this occasion cannot now be ascertained. We know that a troop of horse came from Carnwath, commanded by Philip Lockhart, a brother of the distinguished Sir George Lockhart. This gentleman, who was a captain in the royal army, and, at the time, was on half pay, possessed good natural abilities, which had been cultivated by a liberal education, and was now influenced, by the persuasions of his brother and the movements of the Earl of Mar, to draw his sword in behalf of the Chevalier St George. His brother, in speaking of the Carnwath troop that joined the Jacobite muster at Biggar, says, ' In respect of the goodness of the men, horses, and arms, and being commanded by three brave experienced officers, besides several private men that had served in the army, and whom I prevailed with and engadged at no small charge to enter the service, was reckoned the best troop in the little army.'

The men assembled at Biggar were all cavalry; and, after a short halt, marched to the south to join the Earls of Kenmure, Nithsdale, Winton, and Derwentwater, Lord Widrington, Thomas Forster, and others, who had levied a number of horsemen in the south of Scotland and the north of England for the service of the Pretender. As they felt unable to make any decided movement from the want of infantry, the Earl of Mar despatched a body of 1400 Highlanders, under the command of M'Intosh of Borlum, commonly called Brigadier M'Intosh, to their assistance. These several forces formed a junction at the

* Whitlocke wrote a Journal, or Memoirs, as he calls them, of the transactions which took place from day to day, from the beginning of the reign of Charles I., to the restoration of Charles II.

town of Kelso, and, after some debate, resolved to march into England.

In this resolution the Highlanders obstinately refused to acquiesce. They had an extreme aversion to enter the sister kingdom. They drew up in battle order on the Muir of Hawick, and, cocking their muskets, declared that they would not go into England to be kidnapped and sold as slaves; and that, if they were doomed to destruction, they would prefer to die in their own country. The greater part of them were ultimately prevailed on to cross the border; but 400 of them broke off from their companions, and attempted to regain their native mountains. The people of the country through which they passed hovered about them, captured the stragglers, and prevented them from plundering. Ten of them were taken prisoners by Robert Jardine, at a place called Briery Hill, and marched to Dumfries. The rest proceeded in a body by Moffat to Erickstane; and here they divided themselves into two parties, one of them taking the route by Crawford and Douglas, and the other striking through the hills towards Lamington. Two countrymen, who had been watching their movements, knowing the passes of the hills, hastened on before them, and arrived at Lamington about midnight. Baillie of Lamington, who was favourable to the House of Hanover, lost no time in despatching messengers in every direction to summon the well-affected to hasten with all speed to Clydesbridge, above Lamington, to assist in capturing the poor Highlanders. Accordingly, next morning, the 2d of November, a large multitude from the country round assembled at the place of rendezvous, headed by the Lairds of Lamington, Nisbet, Glespen, and Mosscastle, Mr Mitchell, factor to the Laird of Hartree, Mr Campbell of Moat, and, what is not a little surprising, considering that the Earl of Wigton was, at the time, in prison for his Jacobite attachments, Luke Vallange, one of the bailies of Biggar. They were all well armed and accoutred, and having been divided into several companies, they penetrated the hills, and, after a little search, found the poor wanderers, in number about 200, quite worn out with hunger and fatigue. Meeting with little or no resistance, they took them all prisoners, and marched them off to Lamington Kirk, where they were detained all night, and next day were conducted to Lanark, and afterwards to Glasgow. Rae, who recounts this incident, has failed to tell us what was the ultimate fate of these wretched men.

The main body of the insurgents pursued their march into England. At length they reached the town of Preston, and here they were attacked by Generals Willis and Carpenter, and, after a series of desperate encounters, were forced to surrender to superior numbers. Captain Lockhart, and five other officers who held commissions in the regular army, were tried by a court martial, and condemned to be shot. This sentence was carried into execution on all of them, with the exception of Ensign Dalziel, a brother of the Earl of Carnwath,

who was found to have resigned his commission previous to his
engaging in the rebellion.

During the sixteenth and seventeenth centuries, Biggar received
many visits from royalty. One of the reasons which conduced very
much to this, was the celebrity of the shrine of St Ninian at Whithorn. St Ninian, who was the son of a British prince, about the
year 370, paid a visit to Rome; and the Pope, finding him well instructed in the mysteries of the Christian faith, and zealous for their
promulgation, ordained him as a missionary to the heathen tribes of
Britain. On his return, he built a church at Whithorn, which he
dedicated to his uncle, St Martin of Tours, and which, being built of
stone, was generally known by the title of 'Candida Casa,' that is, the
White House. St Ninian was interred within its walls, and it continued to be the Cathedral Church of the district for several centuries.
Fergus, Lord of Galloway, in the reign of David I., erected near this
church, which by that time had fallen into ruins, a priory for monks
of the Premonstratensian Order; and gathering together such relics
of St Ninian as had been preserved, deposited them in this sacred
edifice. From that time down to the Reformation, the memory of St
Ninian, and the sanctity and efficacy of his supposed relics, were held
in the highest estimation. All ranks, from the King to the beggar,
made pilgrimages to Whithorn, and paid their devotions at its shrine.

In the summer of 1473, Margaret, the Queen of James III., made
a pilgrimage to the shrine of St Ninian, attended by six ladies of her
bedchamber, who were attired in new dresses for the journey. They
no doubt passed through Biggar, and lodged in the Castle of Boghall,
as Biggar lay on the direct road to Whithorn from the Royal Palaces
of Edinburgh, Linlithgow, Stirling, and Falkland. The monarch who
made the most frequent pilgrimages to this shrine was James IV.
Although James was one of the most gallant and courageous men that
ever lived, he was deeply tinctured with the superstitious notions of
the times. He had strong compunctions regarding the part which he
had taken in the movement that led to his father's death; and, in
token of his penitence, wore an iron belt, to which he added a link
yearly; and the priests of the Chapel Royal, both at matins and vespers, made daily lamentation in his presence for his having been
'counsalled to cum againes his father in battell.' Once, and sometimes twice, every year, the King repaired to St Ninian's shrine to
pour out his sorrows, and pray for strength and consolation. On
these occasions he was attended by a considerable retinue, and particularly, as he was fond of music, by a number of minstrels. It was,
besides, always the practice of the local musicians to turn out and
entertain the King with their minstrelsy, on passing through their
villages and towns. In the accounts of the Treasurer of the Royal
Household, we find, that James, during these pilgrimages, disbursed
considerable sums to pipers, fiddlers, and luters, and also to tale-

tellers, priests, and poor men. For instance, in 1502, on passing through Wigton, he gave 14s. to the pipers of that town for playing during his progress. On the 24th of February 1503, there is the following entry in the Treasurer's books, viz. :—'Item, That samyn nycht, in Bigar, to ane piper and ane fithelar, be the King's command, xiijs.' On the 10th of February 1505-6, Margaret Tudor, his Queen, bore a son and heir to the Scottish throne, and her life having been placed in extreme peril, her royal spouse set off as usual on a pilgrimage to the shrine of St Ninian, to pray for her recovery. He walked the whole way on foot, and was accompanied by four Italian minstrels, who, being unable to bear the same amount of fatigue as the robust and spirited monarch, completely broke down, and had to be borne forward on horseback. It would be a rare sight for the people of Biggar to see the King, with his staff in his hand, marching on foot, while his foreign minstrels were mounted on horses, like so many noblemen. When James arrived at the shrine, he prayed most powerfully; and it was noted that the Queen began to recover at the exact time at which he was engaged in this pious work. So soon as the Queen was able to go abroad, a pilgrimage on a grand scale to the shrine of a saint so propitious and influential was resolved on. This took place in July 1507. The Queen, being still weak, was borne on a litter, the wardrobe and baggage of the King were carried by three horses, and the paraphernalia of the Queen required no fewer than seventeen. Another horse was laden with 'the King's chapel geir,' and the 'chapel graith' of the Queen was borne along in two coffers. They were attended by a large retinue, and occupied nearly a month in the journey to and from the shrine.

James V. also made several pilgrimages to Whithorn, particularly in the years 1532 and 1533. According to the statements of the author of the 'Memoire of the Sommervilles,' James also paid frequent visits to the Upper Ward, with the view of visiting Catherine Carmichael, a daughter of the Captain of Crawford, of whom he became enamoured by seeing her in Cowthally Castle, at the marriage of the eldest daughter of Hugh, Lord Sommerville, to the Laird of Cookpool in Annandale. As his sister Joan, or Janet, was married to Malcolm, Lord Fleming, it is natural to suppose that he was no unfrequent guest at the Castle of Boghall. The Bannatyne Club, in 1836, published a work, entitled 'Excerpta e libris Domicilli Domini Jacobi Quinti, regis Scotorum,' from 1528 to 1533, consisting of a statement of his household expenses at various places which he visited, written in a sort of Frenchified Latin. It is extremely curious and interesting, as it not only shows the various kinds of viands with which the royal table was supplied, and the prices at which they were purchased, but also the different journeys which he undertook, and the places at which he occasionally resided. Although Biggar is not mentioned in this book, yet it is easy to infer that, in passing from

2 L

Peebles to the Upper Ward, he would take the Castle of Boghall in
his way, and receive entertainment from Lord and Lady Fleming. At
Peebles and Lanark he had everything to buy, and hence we have in
the book referred to, long lists of articles furnished at these towns for
breakfast, dinner, and supper, consisting of bread, ale, mutton, sal-
mon, soles, turbot, skate, pike, trouts, chickens, capons, rabbits,
woodcocks, redshanks, plovers, butter, cheese, onions, pears, apples,
mustard, not forgetting occasionally the favourite Scotch dish of
capita arietum et pedes ovium, that is, sheep's heads and trotters; but
at the Castle of Boghall, as well as at the Castle of Cowthally, he would
get the best of these viands without any expense, and hence the
Master of the Household would be under no necessity of making any
entry in his books of the dishes with which he was there entertained.

Biggar appears to have been honoured by several visits from James
VI. From a despatch, preserved in her Majesty's State Paper Office,
from George Nicholson to Mr Bowes, we know that this monarch, in
the month of January 1595, was living at Biggar, and no doubt in the
Castle of Boghall. His object, we are told, was to enjoy the sport of
hawking. The Biggar district was, no doubt, at that period plentifully
stocked with various kinds of wild fowl. We know that the marshy
grounds, and the banks of the Clyde and the Tweed, abounded with
herons, which afforded excellent sport to the falconer, and, in all
likelihood, greatly attracted the attention of the royal huntsman.
The most famous heronry in the neighbourhood in olden times, was
in an old orchard at Dawick, where the herons, by carrying trouts and
eels to their nests, furnished the strange spectacle of fish, flesh, and
fruit, on the same tree. The sojourn of James and his court in the
Castle would create some stir and excitement in the little town.
Messengers of State would be constantly coming and going; the
servants of the household would be frequenting the shops, and pur-
veying for the royal table; and the inhabitants would be on the alert
to witness the movements of the King, and to give him a joyous welcome as often as he appeared. We can fancy the sapient monarch,
mounted on a stately charger, surrounded by some of his nobility,
and followed by a goodly train of falconers and other retainers, issuing
from the spacious gate of the Castle, proceeding along the broad
avenue that led to the highway, and then, amid the defiles of the
Tweeddale mountains, or on the gentle ridges of the Common, the
Lindsaylands, or the Shields, participating in the exhilarating pastime
of the chase as then pursued. It will be long, we fear, before another
monarch courses a maukin or brings down a muircock in the same
district.

CHAPTER XXIII.

Historical Sketches of the Fleming Family.

IN the twelfth century, the Flemings were perhaps the most active and enterprising people in Europe. Finding their own territories in Flanders too limited for their ambitious aspirations, they emigrated in considerable numbers to England, during the reigns of William Rufus and Henry I.; and, some years afterwards, took an active part in the civil war waged by Stephen to obtain the English throne. Henry II. having, in the end, vanquished his opponent Stephen, the Flemings were consequently banished the kingdom; and numbers of them taking refuge in Scotland, entered into the service of David I., then on the Scottish throne. Many other Flemings are understood to have come, about the same time, directly from their native regions to Scotland. These strangers, settling in towns and rural situations, contributed greatly, by their skill in agriculture and other industrial arts, to the improvement of the country.

One of these Flemish leaders, it is said, obtained a grant of the lands of Biggar from David I., and settled there with his followers; and thus became the founder of a family that for several centuries reigned as lords superior in that parish. We propose to give a brief account of the most notable incidents in the history of this family, and particularly of the battles and warlike expeditions in which the successive members of it took part. These are entitled to special notice in a work on Biggar. The Flemings of Biggar, in addition to their anxiety to support and advance any cause to which they might be attached, were bound by the feudal law, not merely to appear in the field themselves, at the call of their sovereign, but to bring with them a certain number of their retainers. These retainers, or vassals, were in their turn bound, in consideration of occupying their farms and feus, to give their superior suit and service, both in his court and in the field, as often as these should be required. It is, then, a matter almost of certainty, that in all the battles in which the Flemings fought, they were attended by a portion of the inhabitants of Biggar. In fact, some of the charters by which the Scottish kings conferred honours or rewards on the Flemings, make express reference to the services of their retainers on the battle-field. For instance, in the commission of Chancellorship to James, Lord Fleming, granted under the Great Seal on the 12th of November 1553, during the minority of Queen Mary, it is stated that this honourable office was conferred

on Lord Fleming, specially in consideration of 'the good, faithful, and
gratuitous service to our late most noble father, of happy memory,
whose soul may God benefit, and to us, by our late well-beloved
cousin, Malcolm, Lord Fleming, our Great Chancellor, who, under our
banner, with diverse of his relatives, servants, and friends, was slain
in the camp of Pinkey Cleugh.' In the warlike proceedings in which
the Flemings took part, the men of Biggar, no doubt, then, fought by
their side, and sometimes lost their liberties or their lives in contending with them to revenge a wrong, to repel invasion, or maintain
the independence of their country.

The first proprietor of Biggar, of whom we know anything, was
Baldwin, who at first was styled Baldwin Flamingus, but who afterwards, as was the usual custom of the period, took also from his lands
the title of Biggar. He was appointed by Malcolm IV., the grandson
and successor of David I., to the office of Sheriff of Lanarkshire—the
shire of Lanark, at that period, including also the territory now forming the county of Renfrew. He, along with his stepson John, who settled at Duneaton, and gave his name to Crawfordjohn, between 1147
and 1160 witnessed a charter of Arnald, Abbot of Kelso, granting
the lands of Douglas Water to Theobald, also a Fleming, and said by
some writers, though perhaps without sufficient authority, to be the
founder of the distinguished House of Douglas. He was also a witness of a charter of Walter, son of Allan, the Steward of Scotland, to
the monks of Paisley, between 1165 and 1174; and he himself
granted to Hugh de Padenan the lands of Kilpeter in Stragrife. In
the Register of the Monastery of Paisley a charter still exists, setting
forth that Baldwin, Sheriff of Lanark, gave and granted to God, and
the Church of St Mirin of Paisley, and the monks serving God there,
the Church of Innerkyp, with all the lands lying near the river where
the church is founded, with the entire parish and its pertinents, to be
held in free and perpetual gift.

Baldwin was succeeded by his son Valdeve, who, most likely, was
also appointed to the office of Sheriff of Lanarkshire, as this office
seems to have continued in the Biggar family for several generations.
The most remarkable incident in his life, that has been preserved, is
his capture by the English, along with William I., surnamed the Lion,
at the siege of Alnwick Castle, in 1174. It may be stated, that the
kings of Scotland, sometime previous to this period, held considerable
possessions in the north of England, and had been deprived of them
by the superior power of the English. William the Lion made a
demand for the restoration of these provinces, but Henry, the English
king, refused to comply. William, therefore, proclaimed war against
Henry; and, during the year 1173, inroads were made, on both sides,
into the territories of each other; and though much property was
destroyed, and many lives lost, yet no decisive advantage was gained.
Next year, William levied a numerous but undisciplined host, con-

sisting of Scots, Flemings, and Gallowaymen, and invaded England. He laid siege to Alnwick Castle; but on the 13th of July 1174, with a lamentable want of prudence and caution, he separated himself from the main body of his army, and, attended by Valdeve of Biggar and about sixty horsemen, rode to some distance. The day was dark and misty, and, before they were aware, a body of horsemen had approached within a few hundred yards of them. The King at first took them to be a detachment of his own army; but they soon turned out to be a party of four hundred Englishmen, headed by several gallant Yorkshire barons, who had mustered this force, and were hasting to the assistance of their countrymen. When the King perceived his mistake, he disdained to flee, but cried out, 'Let it now appear who among you are good knights,' and instantly charged against the foe. The King and his followers fought desperately, but, in the end, were overpowered by superiority of numbers; and the king, Valdeve of Biggar, and others, were taken prisoners. They were conducted to Newcastle, and then to the town of Northampton, where William, and most likely his fellow-captives of note, were presented before King Henry, with their legs tied under their horses' bellies, as if they had been the most ignominious felons. The Scottish King was kept a prisoner for some time in the Castle of Richmond, and then sent to Falaise in Normandy, that continental sovereigns might behold an instance of the successful achievements of the English. Whether any of the other captives accompanied the King to the Continent, history has not declared; but he was not himself released till the 8th December, when the Scottish nation had to submit to the deep mortification and disgrace of giving up to England the Castles of Edinburgh, Berwick, Roxburgh, Jedburgh, and Stirling, and seeing the King do homage, not merely for his lands in England, but for the whole kingdom of Scotland.

For several generations, nothing very remarkable regarding the family of Biggar is known. Their names, however, appear very frequently as witnesses of important charters granted by the Scottish kings and barons, and the abbots of religious houses. For instance, William Flandrensis, most likely a son of Valdeve of Biggar, along with Hugo Cancellarius, who died in 1199, witnessed a deed of William I. to the monks of Kelso, and also a charter of the same monarch confirming the teinds of Linlithgow to the nuns of Manuel. He was also a witness of a donation of Richard le Bard to the monastery of Kelso, which was confirmed by Alexander II. in 1228. Hugh of Biggar, a grandson of Valdeve by his son Robert, as patron of the Church of Strathaven, granted, on the 14th February 1228, to St Machute's of Lesmahagow, and the monks there, in pure and perpetual gift, all the tithe land of Richard le Bard lying on the south part of the river Avon, the great Kyp, the lesser Kyp, Glengenel, Polnebo, and Louchere. The names of the witnesses to this charter are in-

teresting, as showing some of the principal men then holding possessions in the neighbourhood of Biggar. They were, William Fleamang,
probably the uncle of the donor, Malcolm Loccard, most likely of
Symington, Robert of Robertstun, Radulph of Cormaceston, and
Richard, parson of Coulter. Peter of Biggar is mentioned in a
charter of Anneis de Brus, granting the Church of Wodekyirch, or
Thankerton, to the monks of Kelso; but, as is commonly the case in
very old charters, the precise date is not given. In 1232, Symon of
Biggar is a witness of a charter of the Archbishop of Glasgow, transferring the Churches of Roberton, Wiston, Symington, Dunsyre, etc.,
to the monks of Kelso. Sir Malcolm Fleming, most likely a son of
William formerly mentioned, witnessed the donation of the Church of
Largs to the monastery of Paisley, by Walter, the High Steward, who
died in 1246. In a charter of Malcolm, Earl of Lennox, of which
he was a witness, he is styled, 'Vice Comes de Dunbarton,' which
shows that during the reign of Alexander III. he had been appointed
to the office of Sheriff of that county. Nicholas of Biggar, Knight, is
mentioned in a deed dated at Lesmahagow in the year 1269, and he
appears to have been Sheriff of Lanarkshire in 1273. He died previous to 1292, when the marriage of his wife Mary, and the ward and
marriage of his daughters Marjory and Ada, were granted by Edward
I. of England to Robert, Bishop of Glasgow. It has been asserted
by some writers, that the Lairds of Biggar to whom we have already
referred, were a different family from the Flemings who afterwards
were proprietors and superiors of this barony. A Fleming, they say,
married one of the daughters of Sir Malcolm de Biggar just referred
to, and receiving with her the lands of Biggar, became the progenitor
of the family who possessed the Biggar estate for some centuries. So
far, however, as we can ascertain, this assertion is based entirely on
conjecture.

Robert Fleming, who probably was the son of Malcolm, attended
the assembly of bishops, earls, abbots, priors, and barons, which took
place at Brigham, 12th March 1289-90, to consider the proposal
made by Edward I. of England, to marry his son Edward to the Maid
of Norway, heiress to the Scottish throne, and thus to unite both
kingdoms under one sovereign. Robert Fleming, along with the
others present, agreed to this proposal, and appended his name to a
letter addressed to the English monarch, in which it is stated that
they were overjoyed to hear the good news that the 'Apostle' had
granted a dispensation for the marriage of Margaret, their dear lady
and Queen, to Prince Edward; and requested to be furnished with
early intelligence regarding the steps taken to forward this important
measure, with assurance of their full and ready concurrence, provided
certain reasonable conditions were agreed to, which would be specified
by commissioners, who were to attend in London at the meeting of
the Parliament in Easter. This scheme, after all, was defeated by

the early death of the Maid of Norway, in September 1290. Robert Fleming, previous to the year 1305, appears to have thrown off his allegiance to Edward of England, and to have joined the patriots who fought for their country's freedom. According to Holinshed, he was in the Castle of Lochmaben when Robert Bruce, escaping from the murderous fangs of the English king, arrived, in the February of that year, at the stronghold of his forefathers. At that time, the Justiciars, Roger de Kirkpatrick and Walter Burgheton, held their courts at Dumfries; and Bruce, as a freeholder in Annandale, was, no doubt, summoned to give suit and service for his lands, by appearing in the retinue of these dignitaries. He, at all events, set out to that town, attended by his brother Edward, and Robert Fleming; and during their journey, it is said, they met a servant of the distinguished Sir John Comyn, who had been Governor of Scotland, and who, as a sister's son of Baliol, was also one of the claimants of the Scottish throne. This servant was bearing despatches from his master to the English king; and as Bruce had begun to suspect that Comyn was a traitor to his country, and faithless to certain engagements into which he had entered with himself, he felt no scruple in attacking the servant, and depriving him of the documents with which he had been entrusted. In these he found that Comyn strongly urged Edward to lose no time in putting Bruce to death, alleging as his principal reason for giving this advice, that so long as he continued to live, it would be difficult to suppress the efforts of the Scots to throw off the yoke of England. At Dumfries, Bruce met with a number of the barons and freeholders of the southern districts of Scotland, and among others with Comyn, Roger Kirkpatrick, and James Lindsay. It is said that Bruce embraced this opportunity to convene a meeting of his countrymen, at which he urged them to make a stand once more in defence of their liberty and independence, and ended by advancing his own claims to the Scottish throne, and expressing his determination to assert and maintain them at all hazards. Many of the gentlemen present signified their intention of giving him support; but Comyn, as was to be expected, opposed his pretensions and designs, and attempted to show that he had a preferable claim to the Scottish throne, as the heir of Baliol, and for the services which he had already rendered to his country.

The meeting appears to have broken up without coming to any decided resolution; and Bruce shortly afterwards met Comyn in the Church of the Greyfriars, and taxed him with his duplicity. A warm altercation ensued, and in the heat of the moment Bruce so far forgot himself, and the sacred place in which he stood, that he drew his poniard, and smote Comyn to the ground. Struck with horror at committing so atrocious a deed, he instantly rushed to the door, and there met Fleming, Kirkpatrick, and other friends. Seeing him pale and trembling, they asked the cause. 'I doubt,' said Bruce, 'I have slain Comyn.' 'Doubt!' said Kirkpatrick; 'then I'll mak sicker;' and along with the others hurried into the Church. They were resolutely opposed by Robert Comyn, who defended the body of his brother; but they very soon despatched him, and then plunged their weapons into the breast of the dying baron. On their return, Bruce inquired if Comyn was dead. Fleming, holding up his bloody sword, exclaimed, 'Let the deed shaw;' and it is said that henceforth this expression was adopted as the motto on the crest of the Flemings of Biggar. Robert Fleming continued to be a strenuous supporter of Robert Bruce, and, no doubt, so long as he lived, fought in his battles and shared in his varied fortunes.

Robert Fleming died previous to 1314, and thus was not destined to take a part in the glorious and decisive battle of Bannockburn. He left two sons, Malcolm and Patrick. Patrick is usually styled Lord of Biggar, and he may have received the barony of Biggar for his patrimony. He married one of the daughters and heiresses of Sir Simon Fraser of Oliver Castle; and thus the Flemings obtained considerable possessions in Tweeddale, and also a right to add the arms of the Frasers—viz., second and third azure, and three cinquefoils argent —to their escutcheon. It was, no doubt, in consequence of obtaining these possessions that he was appointed to the office of Sheriff of Peeblesshire. We see no reason to credit the statement given by Crawford, and repeated by many subsequent writers, that Patrick Fleming received the barony of Biggar as part of his wife's heritage. We can, in fact, find no proof whatever that her father, Sir Simon Fraser, was ever proprietor of the lands of Biggar. The documents in the charter chest of the Fleming family throw no decided light on this subject. The oldest family document in which the Flemings of Biggar are mentioned, is dated 1357. This is a charter granted by Malcolm, Earl of Wigton, to his kinsman, Malcolm Fleming, Laird of Biggar, of all his lands of Auchmoir, etc., with their pertinents, wadset to him by Sir Thomas Morham, Knight, for 200 merks. There is, indeed, an old paper in the chest referred to, entitled, 'Catalogue of the knights, lords, and earls of the house of flemyng, as they ar recorded in their Charters,' and evidently written during the seventeenth century, in which it is stated that a Sir Malcolm Fleming of Biggar lived in the reign of David I. This statement was made, perhaps, on the authority of a charter, though it cannot now be found; but, if it rested on nothing better than tradition, it at least shows that the family, two or three centuries ago, entertained the opinion that the Flemings of Biggar were as old as the days of that monarch.

Malcolm, the elder son, appears to have given a warm support to the cause of Robert Bruce. He was, no doubt, present with his retainers at the battle of Bannockburn. Robert Bruce, in consideration of his eminent services, conferred upon him the charters of several lands. We give a translation of one of them as a specimen. 'Robert, King of Scotland. Be it known that we have given, and by this our present charter confirmed, to Malcolm Fleming, our well-beloved and faithful soldier, for his homage and service, the whole barony of Kirkintilloch, with its pertinents, which formerly belonged to John Comyn, Knight, holding and to be held by the said Malcolm and his heirs from us and our heirs, by all its proper boundaries and divisions, and with all its liberties, commodities, easements, and just pertinents, as freely, quietly, fully, and honourably as the said John held or possessed, for some time, the said barony and its pertinents; the said Malcolm and his heirs rendering to us and our heirs the service of a knight in our army, and suit in the court of the Sheriff-dom of Dumbarton.' He also received from Bruce charters of the lands of Achyndonan and their pertinents in the Lennox, which had been resigned by Malcolm de Drummond, and of the lands of Poltown in the county of Wigton. Bruce also appointed him to the offices of Sheriff of Dumbarton, and Governor of the castle of that name; and Walter, the High Steward, on the Feast of St Dunstan, 19th May 1321, rewarded him with an annuity out of the revenues of the Abbey and Convent of Holyrood, drawn from the barony of Cars.

Sir Walter Scott, as is well known, makes Malcolm Fleming a leading character in his last published novel, 'Castle Dangerous.' He is described in that work as fighting at the capture of Douglas Castle, the Castle Dangerous of the novel, and there vanquishing in single combat Sir Aymer de Vallence, on Palm Sunday, 19th March 1306-7. He has, of course, a sweetheart, whose name was Margaret de Hautlieu. Her father was a Norman baron, who, in quest of adventures, came to the Scottish court, and in the war for independence took the side of Baliol. His daughter Margaret, in course of the story, says, 'Among those soldiers of the soil, Malcolm Fleming of Biggar was one of the most distinguished by his noble birth, his high acquirements, and his fame in chivalry. I saw him, and fell in love with the handsomest youth in Scotland.' Her father had designed to wed her to a youth, bred at the English court, and, therefore, was utterly opposed to her union with Malcolm Fleming, a keen partisan of the opposite faction of Bruce. Fleming, who was inspired by a similar passion, resolved not to be thwarted by any ordinary obstacle, and therefore, along with Sir William Wallace, concerted a plan to carry her off by force. They assailed the house in which she lived, and a combat ensuing, Wallace attempted in the midst of the confusion to carry her down a ladder; but this being overturned, they were both precipitated to the ground, and the form of the fair Margaret was seriously injured and disfigured. On recovering from her wounds and bruises, she became a nun at Douglas, and during the contentions of the period, was carried off by a band of marauders to the borders. She was, however, rescued; and the last sentence that

2 M

Scott published as a novelist, is as follows:—'In a short time it was made generally known throughout Scotland, that Sir Malcolm Fleming and the lady Margaret de Hautlieu were to be united at the court of the good King Robert, and the husband invested with the honours of Biggar and Cumbernauld, an earldom so long known in the family of Fleming.'

Previous to completing the novel of 'Castle Dangerous,' Sir Walter paid a visit to the scene in which it is laid. Having been subjected to several attacks of apoplexy, his health was at the time in a precarious condition; and a few weeks previously, he had been assailed with a strong burst of popular indignation at Jedburgh, in making an attempt to oppose the movement for Parliamentary Reform. Accompanied by Mr John Gibson Lockhart, his son-in-law, he left Abbotsford on the morning of the 18th July 1831, and, travelling through many scenes hallowed by his magic pen, he arrived at Biggar in the afternoon, where he was detained for some time, in consequence of the horses belonging to the chief inn being engaged elsewhere. A report spread rapidly through the town that the great minstrel of Scotland had arrived; and instantly the weavers left their looms, the smiths their forges, the shoemakers their stalls, and the merchants their shops, and hastened forth to obtain a sight of a man who had afforded them so much delight, and who had conferred so great fame and honour on his country. In general, Scott was annoyed when he was made the object of vulgar gaze and attention; but, on this occasion, Lockhart says that he appeared gratified by the respectful notice of the people of Biggar, and he accounts for it by saying, 'Jedburgh, no doubt, hung on his mind, and he might be pleased to find that political differences did not interfere everywhere with his reception among his countrymen.'

It is to be regretted that the temper of our great novelist, in the enfeebled state in which he was at the time, was ruffled by an incident which occurred a few minutes after he left the town of Biggar. It is thus related by Lockhart:—'About a mile from Biggar we overtook a parcel of carters, one of whom was maltreating his horse; and Sir Walter called to him from the carriage-window with great indignation. The man looked and spoke insolently; and, as we drove on, he used some strong expressions about what he would have done had this happened within the bounds of his sheriffship. As he continued moved in an uncommon degree, I said, jokingly, that I wondered his porridge diet had left his blood so warm, and quoted Prior's

> " Was ever Tartar fierce or cruel
> Upon a mess of water-gruel ? "

He smiled graciously, and extemporized this variation on the next couplet,

> " Yet who shall stand the Sheriff's force
> If Selkirk carter beats his horse ? " '

Malcolm Fleming was succeeded by his son Malcolm, who remained stedfast in his attachment to David, the youthful son of Bruce, whom that monarch left to inherit his perilous and unstable throne. Fleming, therefore, threw in his lot with the Earl of Mar, the Douglases, Sir Andrew Murray, and others, who, after the Battle of Dupplin in 1332, refused to concur in the usurpation of the Scottish throne by Edward Baliol. Having succeeded his father as Governor of Dumbarton Castle, he was able to afford a refuge in that fortress to David during the disastrous state of his affairs that ensued from the loss of that battle. The party with whom Fleming acted, having attacked Baliol and his adherents at Annan, drove them across the border. Edward III. of England, who favoured Baliol in consequence of having received from him an acknowledgment as his lord superior, proclaimed war against the friends of Bruce, and having levied a large army, laid siege to Berwick. This town was gallantly defended by the Earl of March and Sir Alexander Seton. A stipulation was entered into with Edward, that the Scots would deliver Berwick into his hands unless they were able, before the 19th day of July 1333, to throw 200 men into the town, or defeat the English in a pitched battle. The adherents of David Bruce immediately raised an army, and marched to the relief of the beleaguered town. The Governor representing that the inhabitants were reduced to the last extremity, the Scots resolved to hazard a battle, and, crossing the Tweed, took up their position at a place called Dunse Park. On this movement, Edward withdrew his army to an eminence on the west of Berwick, called Halidonhill, and both sides prepared for the combat. The English were drawn up in four battalions, flanked by those terrible archers who often contributed so much to gain the battles of the English. The Scots were also arrayed in four battalions; and their principal leaders were, Lord Archibald Douglas of Galloway, Regent of the kingdom; the Steward of Scotland, a youth of seventeen years of age; the Earls of Ross and Moray; and James and Simon Fraser. Fleming and his retainers were placed in the first division of the second battalion. A morass intervened between the two armies, and the Scots, with their national impetuosity, resolved to cross it and attack the English. The morass, as might naturally be expected, retarded their advance, and threw them into confusion. 'And then,' as an old author states, 'the Englische mynstrelles beten ther tabers, and blowen ther trompes, and pipers pipden loude, and mad a grete schoute uppon the Skottes, and then hadde the Englische bachelers eche of them 11 wingis of archers, whiche, at that meeting, michtly drewen ther bowes, and made arrowes flee as thik as motes in the sonne beme, and so thai smote the Skottes that thai fell to the grounde by many thousands.' A considerable body of the Scots, led on by the more intrepid of the nobility, succeeded in clearing the marsh, and pressing up the hill on which the English army stood. They fought, however, under great disadvantages. Their ranks were disordered; they had to ascend a rising ground, and to encounter a body of men greatly superior in numbers, drawn up in close array, and occupying a commanding position. They renewed the charge several times, but they were ultimately driven back, and the whole Scottish army was completely broken and scattered in irretrievable confusion. Fourteen thousand warriors, including a number of the nobility, were laid lifeless on the field. Fleming was fortunate enough to escape, and fled to his strong Castle of Dumbarton. Edward overran the country, appointed sheriffs, garrisoned castles, and managed all matters as if Scotland had been thoroughly and irretrievably subdued, and had become an integral part of England. Fleming, therefore, began to suspect that Dumbarton might not be strong enough to protect the King and Queen; and on this account he privately conveyed them to France, where they remained for eight years. They returned to Scotland on the 4th of May 1341, when their interests in Scotland had begun to be again in the ascendant.

David, whatever may have been his defects in other respects, was fully alive to the great and notable services which had been rendered to him by Malcolm Fleming. At the town of Ayr, on the 9th of November, about six months after his return from France, he conferred on him a charter, by which he was raised to the dignity of Earl of Wigton, and obtained very important rights and privileges. The following may be given as the substance of this charter, from the original Latin:—David, by the grace of God, King of Scotland. Be it known to all good men on the face of the earth, lay or clerical, that we have given, granted, and, by this our charter, confirmed to Malcolm Fleming, our well-beloved and faithful Knight, for his homages and laudable service paid and to be paid to us, all our lands of Faryes and the Rynnes, and the whole of our burgh of Wigton, with all their pertinents, and all my lands of the whole Sheriffship of Wigton, by their proper boundaries and divisions, viz., along the Water of Cree to the sea, and along the sea-coast to Molereunysuage, and from that point to the bounds of Carrick, and from these bounds to the head of the Water of Cree. All these lands are to be held by Malcolm and the heirs-male, lawfully begotten, or to be begotten, of his body, from us and our heirs, in feu and heritage, by the bounds and divisions described, in free Earldom, with homages and services of the said lands, with feus and forfeitures, with courts and escheats, with pit and gallows, with sok and sak, thol and theam, with infang-thief, with multures, mills, and their sequels, with fowlings, fishings, and huntings, with all other liberties, commodities, easements, and just pertinents, that may belong to the free Earldom at present, or at any future time, named as well as not named; together with the advowson of churches, and the right of patronage of the monasteries and abbacies existing in the Earldom, reserving only to us and our heirs the patronage of the episcopal seat of Whithorn, and continuing to the burgesses of Wigton the same liberties which they justly possessed in the times of our predecessors. And because the place of Wigton is held to be the principal manor of the whole Sheriffdom, we ordain and perpetually confirm that Malcolm and his heirs take hence the title of Earl and Earls of Wigton ; and because the said Malcolm has always conducted himself faithfully and laudably towards us, in times both of prosperity and adversity, we add, as a perpetual memorial of such service, to the grant of the said Earldom, that he and his heirs hold it in free regality, and have power to judge, in its courts, in the four pleas of the Crown,*—the said Malcolm and his heirs rendering to us and our heirs the service of five knights in our army.

The alliance which for centuries existed between France and Scotland, was often the cause of great disasters to the Scots. It repeatedly involved them in war with England, during which their country was invaded and their armies defeated. David II. had been hospitably entertained in France during the eight years that he resided in it; and Philip, the French king, had aided his adherents in Scotland with contributions of arms and money. When war broke out between France and England in 1346, the French naturally desired that David would make a diversion in their favour by invading England. The Scottish king, therefore, summoned his subjects to repair to his standard at Perth ; and thither accordingly went Malcolm Fleming, now Earl of Wigton, his cousin, Sir Malcolm Fleming of Biggar, and their relatives and retainers, to devote their energies and their lives to the service of their sovereign. The Scots, under the command of the King himself, marched to the borders ; and rashly supposing that, as Edward III. was in person carrying on the war in France, the English would be incapable of making any defence, they crossed the border, and ravaged the country as far as Durham. Had David possessed any forethought, or been amenable to advice, he would have lost no time in retreating, and securing his booty in the less accessible places of his own country ; but he allowed time for the English to assemble an army of 30,000 men, under the command of Ralph Nevil, Lords Henry Percy, Musgrove, Scrope, Hastings, etc. The English very soon advanced to meet the Scots, who were encamped at Bear Park, near the town of Durham. Their position was ill chosen. It consisted of an undulating common, intersected with hedges and ditches, which prevented the different divisions from readily supporting each other. David drew up his army in three divisions. He led the centre himself, while the right wing was commanded by the Earl of Moray and the Knight of Liddesdale, and the left by the High Steward and the Earl of March. When the English bowmen advanced, they began, as usual, to discharge a shower of arrows, which did considerable execution ; and this caused Sir John Graham to hasten to the King,

* These pleas were robbery, rape, murder, and arson.

and request a detachment of cavalry to disperse them; but though this was the movement that decided the Battle of Bannockburn, the King infatuatedly turned a deaf ear to the request, and Graham, stung with disappointment, rallied such followers as he could command, and rushed on the foe. His heroism was unavailing. The deadly shower of arrows laid numbers prostrate in the dust; and when his own horse was shot down, it was with difficulty that he made his way back to the main body.

The whole forces of the English were now in sight, and the number of gorgeous banners and crucifixes carried by the warriors of the Church made an imposing display. Moray's division having been galled by the archers, and attacked by the men at arms, was put into disorder; and the English cavalry improving the advantage, rushed on the broken ranks with irresistible fury and impetuosity. Moray himself was slain, and his division nearly cut to pieces. The force of the English attack was now directed to the centre of the Scots, under the command of the young King. It was assailed on the flank by 10,000 bowmen, but it bravely stood its ground, and, for three hours, carried on the fray with great vigour. The King would not flinch a foot. His nobles fell thick around him. Hay, the Great Constable, Keith, the Great Marshall, Charters, the Chancellor, and Peebles, the Lord Chamberlain, were all cut down; and two arrows penetrated the King's person, but he would neither surrender nor flee from the field. Copland, an English knight, at last broke in upon him, and engaged him in a hand-to-hand encounter, in the course of which the King drove out two of Copland's teeth with his dagger; but in the end he was overpowered, and taken prisoner. The High Steward and the Earl of March, thinking that opposition was now hopeless, withdrew their division, and sustained little loss. It is estimated that 15,000 of the Scots were slain in this battle; and among the prisoners taken, besides the King, were the Earls of Wigton, Fife, Monteith, and Sutherland, Douglas, Knight of Liddesdale, and about fifty other barons and knights, including Sir Malcolm Fleming of Biggar. They were conducted under a strong escort to London, paraded along the streets with great ostentation, and then lodged in the Tower. The Earl of Wigton, and his cousin, Sir Malcolm Fleming of Biggar, were captured by a person named Robert Bertram, and it appears that they were afterwards committed to his charge. This individual either set them at liberty, or allowed them to escape; and for this conduct, was denounced an enemy to his king, and punished with imprisonment in the Tower, and the confiscation of his lands and goods.

The English, taking advantage of the defenceless and disordered state of Scotland after the Battle of Durham, overran the Merse, Ettrick, Annandale, and Galloway. Considering that these districts had all been thoroughly and irretrievably subdued, they fixed on a

new boundary between the two kingdoms, which was to extend from
Cockburnspath to Soultra, and from Carlops to Crosscryne. As
Wyntoun in his ' Cronykill' says,

'At Karlinlippis and at Corscryne,
Thare thai made the marches syne.'

The Earl of Wigton was present at the Parliament held at Edinburgh, 26th September 1357, and gave his consent to the appointment of a commission to conclude a treaty for the ransom of David
II. This negotiation was completed at Berwick in October following,
and the Scots agreed to pay 100,000 merks, and to give a number of
persons connected with the chief families, as hostages for the faithful
performance of their part of the treaty. The Earl of Wigton appended
his seal to the documents in this case, and gave his grandson Thomas
as one of the hostages, his son John having died about the year 1351.
The Earl, who seems to have had very extensive possessions, conveyed
the lands of Kilmaronock in Dumbartonshire, and the island of Inch-
cailloch in Lochlomond, to his son-in-law, John Danielson; the lands
of Kyllynsith in Dumbartonshire, to Robert de la Vall; the lands of
Hallys and Letbernald, to Robert Dunbarton, Clerk of Register; and
he gave a donation to the Monastery of Newbattle, in the beginning
of 1346, to say prayers for the safety of his soul. He himself obtained
a charter of the five merk land of Carmnole and Knockiebirvan. He
died about the year 1862, and was succeeded by his grandson Thomas.

Thomas, the second Earl of Wigton, was a hostage for David II.,
when he was permitted to visit his dominions, 4th September 1851;
and, as we have already stated, he was one of the hostages for the
fulfilment of the treaty that set David at liberty, 3d July 1354.
David conferred on him a new charter of the Earldom of Wigton,
dated at Perth, 25th January 1865; but he withheld the right of
regality, out of deference, it is supposed, to the wishes of Archibald
Douglas, Lord of Galloway, who was grievously dissatisfied that
another person should exercise such a jurisdiction in a territory with
which he was connected. The right of regality was of great importance. By it the possessor was made absolute in his own domains.
He held his own courts; was supreme judge in all cases, civil or
criminal; had the power of death or imprisonment in his own dungeon;
and could reclaim any of his vassals from the court even of the High
Justiciar himself. A quarrel at length arose between the Earl and
the native population of Wigtonshire, most likely originated and
fomented by the same Archibald Douglas; and this rendered his position so disagreeable, that he was induced to dispose of his lands,
privileges, and title in Wigtonshire to that nobleman. A copy of the
deed conveying these still exists; and as the transaction is one of very
rare occurrence in Scottish history, we give the following translation :—' Know ye that I, Thomas Fleming, not by force or fear in-

duced, nor by error misled, but of my pure free will, firmly resolved, in my great, urgent, and inexorable necessity, and especially because of great and grievous discords and deadly animosities lately arisen between me and the natives of the Earldom of Wigton, have sold, and by title of sale for ever granted, to the noble and potent Sir Archibald of Douglas, Knight, Lord of Galloway, on the east side of the Water of Cree, my whole foresaid Earldom; and have purely, simply, absolutely, and for ever transferred to the said Archibald all right and claim competent in future to me, my heirs and assignees, in the said Earldom, with its pertinents, for a certain considerable sum of money paid to me in my foresaid great and urgent necessity, to be holden by the foresaid Archibald, his heirs and assignees, in fee and heritage, by all its bounds and marches, in meadows, grazings, moors, marshes, roads, paths, waters, pools, mills, multures, with servants, thralls, and their progeny, with fowlings, huntings, and fishings, with pit and gallows, sok and sak, toll and teme, infangthief and outfang-thief, with fees, forfeitures, and escheats, wards, reliefs, and marriages, tenandries and services of free tenants; as also, all and whole the other liberties, commodities, easements, just pertinents, and free customs, belonging, or that can by any right or title whatsoever be-long, to the said Earldom, as freely, quietly, fully, and honourably, and entirely in all and through all, as I, the foresaid Thomas, or any of my predecessors, held and possessed the same Earldom. In testi-mony whereof, I have appended my seal to these presents. Given at Edinburgh, the 8th day of February, in the year of our Lord 1371.'

This sale was confirmed by Robert II. on the 7th of October 1372. The sum which Thomas Fleming obtained for the Earldom, with all its important rights and possessions, was L.500. One of the most notice-able things connected with this transaction, is that a sale was made, not merely of the lands and their privileges, but also of the title. In a royal charter granted by Robert II. in 1375, Fleming is styled Thomas Fleming of Fulwood,* formerly Earl of Wigton. The family of Douglas, however, did not assume the title till a considerable time after the sale took place.

Thomas Fleming, having no children, appears to have alienated most of his estates during his life. In 1371 he granted an annuity of twelve merks to William Boyd; on the 20th June 1372, he gave in pledge the barony of Lenzie for the sum of L.80; and he gifted the town of Kirkintilloch to Sir Gilbert Kennedy, which was confirmed 13th May 1373.

The successor of Thomas Fleming was Sir Malcolm Fleming of Biggar, a son of Sir Patrick, who married the daughter of Sir Simon Fraser. As formerly stated, he was taken prisoner at the Battle of Durham; and afterwards received from David II. charters of the barony of Dalliel, and of the lands of Rinns of Wigton, and Sthboger

* The lands of Fulwood lie on the banks of the Greif in Renfrewshire.

in the barony of Lenzie. His cousin, Malcolm, Earl of Wigton, gave him a grant of the lands of Achmoir and Seymoir in 1357, as already stated; and his predecessor Thomas, previous to his death, conferred on him the barony of Lenzie, and this gift was confirmed by Robert II. on the 20th September 1382. He was appointed Sheriff of Dumbarton in 1364, and had an assignment of the pledge made of the barony of Lenzie by Thomas Fleming to William Boyd for L.80. He had a charter from Robert II. of a tenement in Cramond, resigned by Marjory Fleming, 16th January 1380.

Sir Malcolm left two sons, David and Patrick. Patrick, in April 1369, exchanged his lands of Dalnoter and Gartscandane, in the Earldom of Lennox, for the lands of Bord, Tweoures, Croy, etc., in the barony of 'Leygneh,' belonging to Sir Robert Erskine, and became the progenitor of the Flemings of Bord.

David Fleming of Biggar played a distinguished part in the public transactions of his time. In 1362 he received from David II. a charter of certain annual rents; on the 20th of May 1365 he obtained a safe conduct to visit England; and in 1388 accompanied Douglas in the expedition to England which terminated in the Battle of Otterburn, so much celebrated in our annals, as one of the most chivalrous encounters that ever took place between the inhabitants of the two kingdoms. The Scots, on this occasion, numbering about 5000 men, penetrated into the mountainous district of England on the eastern frontier, and then emerged into the flat and richly cultivated country, burning, plundering, and slaying wherever they went. The Percies of Northumberland lost no time in levying an army, and throwing themselves into Newcastle. In the course of a sally which they made from the town, Douglas captured the spear of Henry Percy, commonly called Hotspur, and bragged that he would carry it as a trophy into Scotland. Hotspur, indignant at the thought of this disgrace, resolved to make every effort to prevent the design from being carried into effect. In the meantime, the Scots, having accomplished the object of their expedition, retreated up the vale of the little river Reid, and on the 19th of August pitched their tents at Otterburn, about twenty miles from the Scottish border. They were closely but stealthily followed by the English, who were much superior in point of numbers, and who, during the night, approached within a short distance of their camp, with the design of making an attack on its flank.

As soon as the alarm was given, Douglas drew up his men on a piece of ground still more advantageously situated for an engagement than that occupied by the encampment. The English supposed that the Scots by this movement had beat a retreat, and, therefore, were surprised when, by the light of the moon, they discovered them drawn up in battle array, and awaiting the encounter. The combat instantly commenced, and raged with great fury, both sides being inflamed

2 N

with national animosity, and putting implicit confidence in the skill
and bravery of their leaders. The Scots, oppressed with numbers,
were on the point of giving way, when Douglas ordered his banner to
be advanced, and, attended by his best knights, rushed forward,
shouting his usual war-cry, 'A Douglas! a Douglas!' and smote all
down before him with his battle-axe. He at length fell, pierced by
three mortal wounds; but he urged those around him to conceal his
disaster, and to carry on the combat with redoubled fury. This was
done; and in a short time the English were entirely routed, and all
the chief men of Durham and Northumberland were either killed or
taken prisoners, and among the latter were the Percies themselves.
Froissart, who obtained his information from persons on both sides
who had taken part in the battle, says in his Chronicles:—'Of all the
battles which I have made mention of heretofore in this history, this
of Otterburn was the bravest and the best contested; for there was
neither knight nor squire but acquitted himself nobly, doing well his
duty, and fighting hand to hand without either stay or faint-hearted-
ness.'

Sir David Fleming, or, as the monks of Holyrood used to call him,
'Davie Fleming of Biggar,' came out of the encounter at Otterburn
with no small reputation for bravery and martial prowess. It was
most likely as a reward for his gallant services that he obtained from
Robert II. grants of various lands and sums of money. On the 14th
March 1390, he received from that monarch a charter of annual rents
of the value of L.50 sterling, due to the Crown by the abbot and
monks of Holyrood from the lands of Cars in Stirlingshire; and
charters of the lands of Auchlan, in the barony of Kinnedward,—of
Barbethe, Caslis, Galnethe, and Glentall, in the parish of Straiton in
Ayrshire,—of Cambusbarron and Blaregis, in Stirlingshire,—of the
chapels of Kirkintilloch, the lands of Drumtablay, in Dumbartonshire,
—the lands of Wodland and Meiklgall, in the barony of Monycabow,
and the lands of Cavers and the Sheriffship of Roxburgh.

With the consent of his son and heir Malcolm, he, in his turn,
gave the lands of Mureton to the Monastery of Cambuskenneth, in
order that the monks of that establishment might constantly pray for
the welfare of the souls of Malcolm, his father, of Christian, his
mother, of himself, and his wife Isabella. At that period, he seems
to have been in a very generous and pious turn of mind; for in a few
days after, viz., on the 25th of the same month, he granted a charter
to the abbot and monks of Holyrood, which was drawn up at Stirling,
and confirmed by Robert III. A copy of it still exists in the chartulary of the Monastery of Holyrood, and, strange enough, is written in
the contracted vernacular Scotch of the period, and not, as was usual,
in Latin. 'It contenis and bearis witness that ye said Davi Lord of
Bigare and Lenzie has giffen in pure and perpetuale almous to ye
said religious men, twenty marks of annuale rent to pay a channon

singand perpetually at ye altare of St Nicholas, in ye said Abbay, quare ye said Davi has ordanit his sepulture. Item the said Davi has giffen five marks of annuale rent in pure and perpetual almous for the repair of St Nicholas' altare, both within and without, with glass windows, and his arms on them. Finally, he has giffen ten pound of annuale rent for the offering up of continual prayer for his own soul and the souls of his relatives.' It further provides, that David Fleming or his heirs might redeem these annual offerings by paying down to the abbot and monks, on the high altar of Holyrood, the sum of one hundred pounds. He also mortified his whole lands of Drumtablay, with a portion of the miln thereof, to the Chapel of the Blessed Virgin in Kirkintilloch, to say masses for the salvation of his own soul, the soul of his wife, his parents, and others. This mortification was confirmed by Robert III. in 1379.

Robert III., though possessed of a mild and generous disposition, was a weak and indolent monarch. He had been injured in boyhood by a kick from a horse, and was thus prevented from engaging in those martial and violent exercises in which the nobles took delight, and which they thought indispensable in a king. The Duke of Albany, the King's brother, was a far more spirited and energetic individual, and took the chief management of public affairs. The Duke of Rothesay, the King's eldest son, gave great uneasiness to his father by his riotous and irregular behaviour; and, with the view of reclaiming him to more settled habits, it was proposed to unite him in marriage with a daughter of one of the nobles. Albany, in carrying out this arrangement, made it a condition, that the daughter of that nobleman would be preferred who would pay down the largest sum of money. The Earl of March at first proposed to give the largest sum, and his daughter and the Prince were betrothed. The Earl of Douglas afterwards offered a still larger sum; and Albany, with great injustice, broke faith with the Earl of March, and united the Prince to Margery Douglas. This marriage was exceedingly unhappy. The Prince continued his irregularities; and two ruffians, at the instigation, it is said, of Albany and Douglas, seized the unhappy young man, and immured him in the dungeon of Falkland Castle, where he was starved to death.

The Earl of March, filled with indignation at the dishonourable treatment which he had received in this matrimonial transaction, fled to England, and at the head of an English force committed great havoc on the Scottish border. The Earl of Douglas, to revenge this inroad, levied an army, and marched into England; but he was routed at Homildon by an English force under the command of the Percies, and taken prisoner. A short time afterwards, the Percies, in conjunction with other discontented nobles, broke out in rebellion, and in the war which they waged against their sovereign Henry IV., received the assistance of Douglas, whom they had set at liberty. At the Battle

of Shrewsbury, Douglas fought with great bravery, but his horse
stumbling, he was wounded and taken prisoner; while the Earl of
Northumberland and Lord Bardolph, escaping from the field, took
refuge in Scotland. Henry IV., addressing himself to the Duke of
Albany, proposed to set at liberty Murdoch, the Duke's son, the Earl
of Douglas, and other Scottish prisoners in England, on condition that
the English refugees were immediately put to death. Albany entered
into this base project; but Sir David Fleming of Biggar having discovered it before it was ripe for execution, apprised his friend, the
Earl of Northumberland, of the fate intended for him, and advised
him to seek safety in flight. By this means the English exiles escaped
the bloody fangs of the Duke of Albany, greatly to the mortification
of the Douglases, who resolved to embrace the earliest opportunity of
taking vengeance on Fleming.

Robert III., being well aware of the ambitious and unscrupulous
character of his brother, the Duke of Albany, was careful to have his
second son, James, Earl of Carrick, brought up in a place of security.
He was, therefore, educated in the Castle of St Andrews, under the
superintendence of Henry Wardlaw, then Bishop of that See. The
death of his brother in the Castle of Falkland, and the unsettled state
of the country, made the King apprehensive that there was no place
in Scotland beyond the reach of violence, and therefore he resolved
to send his son to France to complete his education. A vessel was
prepared for the voyage, and stationed at the Bass; and a strong body
of armed men, under the command of Sir David Fleming and the
Earl of Orkney, were ordered to escort the Prince from St Andrews
to Edinburgh, and then to North Berwick. These barons performed
the duty assigned them with great promptness and fidelity, and the
Prince, with the Earl of Orkney and a small suit, were safely put
aboard the vessel. They were, however, not destined to reach the
shores of France; for, on passing Flamborough Head, they were captured by an armed English vessel, carried to London, and thrown into
the Tower, in direct violation of a truce, which, at the time, existed
between the two kingdoms.

The Duke of Albany and the Douglases being full of indignation
against David Fleming, both on account of the escape of the English
refugees and the departure of the young Prince, collected a number
of their retainers, and placed them under the command of Sir James
Douglas of Balveny and Alexander Seton. These individuals fell
upon Fleming and his party at Longherdmanston, on their way from
North Berwick; and, after an obstinate encounter, Fleming and a number of his followers were slain. The body of Fleming was conveyed
to the Abbey of Holyrood, and there, according to his own arrangement, was interred under the altar of St Nicholas, the patron saint of
the old Parish Kirk of Biggar. Wyntoun thus speaks of his prowess
as a warrior, and the esteem in which he was held by the King:—

'Schire Davy Flemyng of Cumbirnald
Lord,—a knycht stout and bald,
Trowit and luvit wal wyth ye King,
Our Prynce resavit in his keiping.'

Of his death and burial the same poet says :—

'Fra this, Schire Davy thare wes slayne,
Der Lords all passit hame agane,
And ye cors wes on ye morne
Through Edinbruch wyth honoure borne
Til Halyrudhouse, yare he lyes,
His spirite intil Paradys.'

Sir David Fleming was twice married. His first wife was Jean, daughter of Sir David Barclay of Brechin; and by her he had a daughter, Marion, who became the wife of Sir William Maule of Panmure. By his second wife, Isabel, heiress of the Baron of Monycabow, he had two sons, Malcolm and David. David was the founder of a respectable branch of the Fleming family, who settled at a place in Renfrewshire which was called Boghall.* The elder son, Malcolm, succeeded to the family estates of Biggar and Cumbernauld. He married Elizabeth, daughter of the Duke of Albany, niece of Robert III., and thus was closely connected with the royal family of Scotland. He was knighted by that monarch, and received from his father-in-law a charter of the lands of Torwood, most likely as the dowry of his wife. He, of course, inherited the lands in the parish of Drummelzier, acquired by the Flemings from their marriage with the family of Sir Simon Fraser. The father of Sir Simon, who died in 1291, had bestowed a portion of the lands of Kingledoors on the monks of Melrose. These lands, in ancient times, were divided into Craw Kingledoors and Chapel Kingledoors; Chapel Kingledoors being so called from a chapel which stood on it, dedicated to St Cuthbert. A dispute arose between the monks of Melrose and the Lairds of Biggar, regarding the party on whom devolved the burden of repairing and upholding the chapel, and had the right of appointing a priest to officiate at its altar. Malcolm Fleming, of whom we are now treating, put an end to this long and keenly controverted point, by renouncing, in 1417, 'all right and claim in the chapel and its priest had, or to be had, from the beginning of the world to the end of time.'

The Earl of Carrick, whom we mentioned as having been conveyed by Sir David Fleming to the Bass, and as having been captured and imprisoned by the English, became, on the death of his father, in 1406, James I.; but for eighteen years was detained a prisoner in

* The lands of Boghall, on the death of their proprietor, John Fleming, in 1581, came into the hands of John, Lord Fleming, who disponed them to his second son, James, in 1593. In course of time they went out of the hands of the Flemings, and became the property of the Earls of Dundonald.

England. He was allowed to visit his dominions in May 1421, and Malcolm Fleming was one of the hostages for his return to captivity. A war breaking out between France and England, in 1419, many of the most bold and adventurous Scots embarked for France, and took part in the contest against the English in that country. The English carried the Scottish king to France, in order that he might exert his authority to prevent his subjects from taking any further part in the war; but they refused to obey his orders so long as he was not a free agent; and this circumstance made the English more readily disposed to listen to proposals to set him at liberty. A treaty was at length concluded at London on the 4th December 1423, by which it was stipulated that the Scots should pay L.40,000, as a compensation for the expense which the English had incurred in the maintenance and education of James, and also give a number of the principal barons as hostages for the due fulfilment of the terms of this treaty. The names of the hostages, and the yearly income of each, are given in 'Rymer's Fœdera.' 'Malcolmus, Dominus de Bygare,' was one of the hostages; and his yearly income is set down at 600 merks, which, if the value of a merk at that time was equal to L.10 of our present currency, would amount to L.6000.

James I. was no sooner established on his throne than he began to administer justice with a severity that, in a short time, cost him his life. Among other persons whom he brought to trial, was Murdoch, Duke of Albany, his cousin, who had succeeded his father as Regent of the kingdom during the confinement of the King in England; and both he and his two sons were condemned for abusing the King's authority, and beheaded at Stirling, in May 1425. Sir Malcolm Fleming of Biggar, being the brother-in-law of Murdoch, was apprehended at the same time; but, as most likely no satisfactory plea could be advanced against him, he was soon set at liberty.

In those days of feud and faction, very strange and unexpected alliances were often formed. It would naturally be supposed that Malcolm Fleming, having lost his father by the craft and malignity of the Duke of Albany and the family of Douglas, would hold them in deadly enmity; but, instead of this, he married the daughter of the one, and became the intimate friend and counsellor of the other. At that time no noblemen were more powerful, or comported themselves with a more haughty and imperious bearing, than the Earls of Douglas, of whom it was nothing uncommon to hear, that they were marching through the country with a band of several thousand armed men in their train. In fact, their power and authority became dangerous to the Stewart dynasty, more especially as, by marriage with the royal family, they had acquired some hopes of succeeding to the throne. Archibald, the fifth Earl of Douglas, died on the 26th of June 1439, and left two sons, William and David. William, who at his father's death was only seventeen years of age, was a youth of good abilities,

gallant demeanour, and generous disposition ; and, had his lot been
cast in more peaceful and settled times, he might have been one of the
most distinguished members of his illustrious House. Malcolm Fleming of Biggar was his near neighbour, and his age and experience
might point him out as a most proper friend and adviser. At all
events, the recent feud between the two Houses was forgotten, and a
great intimacy springing up between them, Douglas sent him and
Allan Lauder of the Bass to France, to carry his oath of allegiance to
the French king, and to receive investiture in the Dukedom of Tou-
raine, which had been bestowed on the grandfather of Douglas, for
his gallant services to the French nation. Charles VII., then King of
France, gave Fleming and Lauder a very kind reception, and, as we
are told by Lindsay of Pitscottie, 'grantit gladlie to thair requeisit
and message, and gave to him (Douglas) and his procuratouris the
haill landis and rentis in France, quhilkis his guidschir had a befoir.'

At the period of which we are now speaking, Scotland was in a
very miserable condition. James I. had been cruelly murdered at
Perth, and his son and successor was only a few years old. No single
person possessed sufficient power and authority to exercise, with
effect, the administration of public affairs, to cause the laws to be
respected and obeyed, to overawe the factious, turbulent, and bloodthirsty barons, and promote the peaceful arts of industry and commerce. The two noblemen who claimed and exercised the largest
share of power were Alexander Livingston of Callender, who held the
office of Governor ; and William Crichton of Crichton, who was Chancellor of the kingdom. These barons carried on a constant rivalry
with one another, each of them being resolutely bent on obtaining the
superiority, and equally industrious in issuing edicts, calling on the
people to give him exclusive obedience. The minds of the population
were thus distracted; the adherents of one party perpetrated every
species of enormity on the other; the lands remained uncultivated;
and famine, with all its dire concomitants, was the result. The young
Earl of Douglas, amid these unhappy dissensions and calamities, is
alleged to have conducted himself in a very imperious and lawless
manner, riding up and down at the head of several hundred armed
troopers, and burning, slaughtering, and pillaging wherever he went.
The Governor and Chancellor having, at length, effected a reconciliation, came to a resolution to crush, by dissimulation and violence, the
exorbitant power of Douglas. A letter was written to him, representing that the affairs of State could not be conducted without his
aid, and requesting him to repair without delay to Edinburgh. It
is stated that other inducements were given to draw him into the
snare, such as holding out a prospect of advancing him, or his uncle,
Malise, Earl of Strathern, to the supreme power, in preference to the
son of James I. ; but the fact is, that the reasons which they adduced
are not certainly known. Whatever they were, they were sufficient

to puff up the vain young man with very confident and exalted notions, and made him deaf to all the entreaties and remonstrances of his
friends to keep aloof from the society of Crichton and Livingston,
whose hasty reconciliation made them apprehensive of impending
danger. Accompanied by his brother David, his friend Malcolm
Fleming, and a small escort, he set out towards Edinburgh, and by
the way was met by Crichton, the Chancellor, who conducted him
and his attendants to the Castle of Crichton, and- there splendidly
entertained them for several days. They at length left Crichton's
festive halls, and proceeded to the Castle of Edinburgh, where they
were seemingly welcomed with the greatest cordiality. Lesley, Pitscottie, and perhaps some other of our older historians, state that they
were here entertained at a sumptuous dinner, and that, in the course
of it, a bull's head was placed on the table, which was a sign of condemnation to death. This, it is said, gave rise to the popular
rhyme,—

' Edinburgh Castle, town, and tower,
    God grant ye sink for sin ;
  And that even for the black dinnour
    Earl Douglas gat therein.'

Tytler, in opposition to the statements of the old historians, rejects
the story of the bull's head as a mere fiction; but his opinion rests on
nothing better than supposition. It is certain, at least, that Douglas
and his principal attendants were immediately accused of treason and
placed under restraint. The Earl and his brother were subjected to
the forms of a mock trial, and condemned to be taken to the Castlehill and beheaded. This sentence was accordingly carried into execution, in presence of the young monarch, on the eve of the Festival
of St Katherine, viz., the 24th November 1440.

It has been generally asserted, that the trial and execution of Sir
Malcolm Fleming took place at the same time with the Douglases.
This is a mistake. It has been ascertained that he was not tried and
executed till the fourth day after his friends had been deprived of life.
After a form of trial, as illegal as it was insulting, he was brought to
the Castlehill, the usual place of execution at the time, and there his
head was struck from his body by the axe of the headsman; thus
ignominiously losing his life for no other crime that history has left
on record than that he was a friend to the youthful Douglas, and
obnoxious to men inflamed with mad ambition, and ready to make a
cruel and unwarrantable use of the power that had fallen into their
hands.

Malcolm, by his wife Elizabeth Stewart, who in old writs is termed
Lady Biggar, had two sons, Malcolm and Robert. Malcolm was one
of the hostages for James I., and appears to have been released from
this duty on the 20th January 1432. He predeceased his father, and
therefore his brother Robert succeeded to the estates. One of Robert's

first acts was to make several public protests against the sentence of death and forfeiture which had been pronounced against his father. Copies of several of these instruments are still preserved. We may refer to one of them, written partly in Latin and partly in the vernacular Scotch of the time, which was made at the Cross of Linlithgow. It commences by invoking the name of the Deity, and wishes all men to know by this public instrument, that on the 7th day of January, in the year of our Lord 1440, and the 14th year of the Pontificate of the most holy Father in Christ, Lord Eugenius, by Divine Providence Pope, and in presence of the witnesses whose names are subscribed—Walter Buchanan and Thomas Muirhead, Esquires, and procurators of Robert Fleming, son and heir of the late Malcolm Fleming, Lord of Biggar, having power and sufficient instructions, as is shown by legal documents, went to the Market Cross of the burgh of Linlithgow, and there, before William Houston, Sheriff-depute, and in name of the said Robert, falsified a certain sentence pronounced, or violently carried out, upon Malcolm Fleming, father of the said Robert, on the Castle Hill of Edinburgh ; all this being done according to due mode and form, and for the reasons written below, the tenor of which follows in the vulgar :—

'We, Waltyr of Buchquwane, and Thomas of Murhede, special procuratoris and actourneis, conjunctly and severally, to Robert Flemyng, son and ayr to Malcolm Flemyng, sumtyme Lord of Bigar, sayis to thee John of Blayr, Dempstar, that the Doyme gyffin out of thy mouth on Malcolm Flemyng in a said court haldyn befor our soverane Lord ye King, on the Castle-hill of Edynburch on Mononday the acht and twenty day of the moneth of November, the yere of our Lord M^{mo}c,c,c,c^{mo} and fourty zeris sayande, "that he had forfat land, lyff, and gud aschete to the King, and that yow gave for doyme," that doyme forsaid giffen out of thy mouth is evyl, fals, and rotten in itself ; and here, We the fors^d Walter and Thomas, procuratoris to the said Robert, for hym, and in his name, fals it, adnul it, and again cancel it, in thy hand William of Howston, deput to the Sherray of Lithgow, and tharto a borch in thy hand ; and for this cause the courte was unlachful, the doyme unlachful, unorderly giffen, and agane our statut ; for had he been a common thef takyn redhand, and haldyn twa sonys, he sulde haff had his law dayis, he aakande them, as he did befoir our soverane Lord the King, and be this resoune the doyme is evyll giffyn, and weil agane said ; and here we, the forsaid Walter and Thomas, procuratoris to the forsaid Robert, protests for ma resounys to be giffyn up be the said Robert, or be his procuratoris, quhan he acht in lawful tyme.'

The said sentence, as thus set forth, being false and void, the procurators of Robert Fleming took a pledge to pursue the adnulification and falsification of the said sentence, in the hands of Robert Nicholson, serjeant of our Lord the King, who received the same pledge.

The procurators afterwards offered a falsification and adnulification
of the sentence, under the seal of Robert Fleming, to William Houston,
Sheriff-depute, who refused to receive it, alleging that the reception
of such a document pertained to the Justiciar and not to the Sheriff;
and thereupon the agents publicly protested against this refusal being
the cause of any prejudice to the said Robert in time to come.
Upon each and all of these points the procurators took public instruments in the hands of a notary public, at the Cross of Linlithgow, at
ten o'clock of the day already stated, and before a number of competent witnesses.

On the 16th of August 1443, Sir Alexander Livingstone, as is
shown by a document still preserved, in presence of Robert Fleming
and four bishops, solemnly purged himself, upon oath, of having
given any counsel, assistance, or consent to the slaughter of Sir
Malcolm Fleming. It would thus seem that the death of Sir Malcolm
is to be ascribed solely to the vindictive feelings or ambitious aspirations of Crichton the Chancellor.

When James II. arrived at the age of maturity, he became convinced that great injustice had been done in putting Malcolm Fleming
to death, and forfeiting his estates. He therefore caused precepts to
be addressed to the sheriffs of the different counties in which Fleming's
estates were situated, ordering them to infeft Robert Fleming of
Biggar as the heir and successor of his father, who had been proved,
by the testimony of several persons, to have died at the faith and
peace of his sovereign. He also, on the 6th of June 1451, bestowed
on him a charter of the twenty-four merk lands of Petkenny, Cule-
venny, and Balrody, and their pertinents, lying in the barony of
Kinghorn, to be held of the King by rendering the usual services.
On the following day, viz., the 7th of June, he conferred on him a
charter of all and whole the lands of Auchtermony and their pertinents,
lying in the Earldom of Lennox, to be held of the King by rendering
a silver penny Scots if sought. It was, no doubt, James also who
raised Fleming to the peerage, though the date at which this took
place is not exactly known. But the favour received by him from
the King, which possesses the greatest interest to the people of Biggar,
is the erection of Biggar into a free burgh of barony, as we have
elsewhere stated.

CHAPTER XXIV.

Historical Sketches of the Fleming Family—*Continued.*

IT was a very common thing for the nobility in former days, to enter into a bond or league with each other for mutual defence, or the attainment of some object. The main plea in justification of this step was the defective administration of the laws. The executive department of government was often powerless; and the consequence was, that the strong oppressed the weak, and rapine, slaughter, and confusion prevailed. On the 10th of February 1465, Robert Lord Fleming entered into a remarkable bond, or 'Indenture,' as it was called, with Gilbert Lord Kennedy, and Sir Alexander Boyd of Duchal. The object of it is thus stated: ' Ye said lordis ar bundyn and oblisit yaimselfis, yair kyn, friendis and men, to stand in afold kendness, supple, and defencs, ilk an til odir in all yair causis and querrell, leiful and honest, movit and to be movit, for all ye dais of yair liffis, in contrery and aganis al maner of persones yat leiff or dee may.' Reservation was made with respect to the 'bands' which these barons had previously made with other parties; and from this it appears that Lord Fleming had bands with Lord Livingstone and Lord Hamilton. The document goes on to bind Lord Fleming not to give his consent or assent to any proposal to take the King from Lord Kennedy and Sir Alexander Boyd, or the persons whom they might appoint his keepers in their absence; and to use all his power of good counsel to prevail on the King to be kind to them, 'yair bairnis, and friendis yaiat belong to yaim for ye tym.' If he did this, he was to have such reward as follows: ' Gif yair happynis a large thyng to fall, sic as vard, releiff, marriage, or offes, yat is meit for hym, the said Lord Flemyng sal haff it for a resonable compocion befoir udir.' It appears that two individuals, 'Thom of Sumerwel' and 'Wat of Twedy,' were special friends of Lord Fleming; and therefore Lord Kennedy and Sir Alexander were bound to have them in special maintenance, supply, and defence in all their actions, causes, and quarrels, lawful and honest, for Lord Fleming's sake, and for services done, or to be done. The document ends with this solemn sanction: ' All to be lelily kepit bot fraud and gil, after they have given to each other yair bodily aithis, the hali euangelist tuychit, and set to thair sealis.'

In the records of 'The Acts and Proceedings of the Lord Auditors

of Causes and Complaints, from 1466 to 1494,' Robert Lord Fleming
frequently appears as a party in the lawsuits then carried on.   We
will briefly refer to one or two of the cases with which he was more
especially connected.   On the 30th July 1473, an action was raised
by Henry Livingstone of Middlebinning against Robert Lord Fleming
and John and Thomas Anderson, for their spoliation and withholding
of ten oxen and cows and two bulls from the lands of Weltown and
Castlecary, belonging to the said Henry, and the improper holding of
his lands.   The Lords decreed that Lord Fleming had done wrong in
taking the said animals, and ordained him to restore them, and, in all
time coming, to desist from annoying the said Henry ' in the browkin
and joysing' of his lands, as well as to pay him 20s. for his costs and
expenses, his three witnesses 15s. for their costs, and, if necessary, to
distrain his effects for payment.   On the 16th May 1474, Lord Crichton
raised an action against Lord Fleming for the payment of L.150, which
had been awarded by a decreet of arbitration.   The Lords decided
against Lord Fleming, and ordered his lands and goods to be dis-
trained.   On the 14th October 1479, Lord Fleming appeared in an
action against Lord Crichton, for wrongously withholding from him a
basin and ewer of silver gilt, valued at L.80, which he had laid in
' wad' to the said Lord Crichton for L.20.   The Lords continued the
case to the 17th of January following, to afford Lord Fleming time to
bring forward proof of the value of the basin and ewer, and to Lord
Crichton to return them, or give the balance of their value ; but the
final result is not recorded.   On the 12th June 1478, the Lords
decreed and delivered that Robert Lord Fleming should content and
pay to Patrick Baron, burgess of Edinburgh, the sum of 26 merks,
owed by him and his son Robert Fleming, for certain merchandise
which he had received, as was proved by Baron's account books, and
that letters should be written to distrain his lands and goods for payment.   Lord Fleming alleged that his son owed 20 merks of this
account; and therefore the Lords continued the case till the 3d of July,
to give him time to summon witnesses to prove what he had stated.
It appears that his Lordship either had been afflicted with that great
evil, a scarcity of money, that he had an avaricious desire to obtain
the property of others, or had a natural aversion to discharge his pecuniary liabilities ; for his name occupies rather a discreditable place in
the record, not less for his violent possession of the effects of others,
than for his unwillingness to pay the debts which he had incurred.

Robert Fleming died in 1494.   He was twice married, first to Janet,
daughter of Lord Douglas, and second to Margaret, daughter of John
Lindsay of Covington.   By his first wife he had two sons, Malcolm
and Robert, and two daughters, Elizabeth and Beatrix ; but by his
second wife he had no children.

Malcolm, the elder son, was one of the Commissioners appointed to
negotiate a marriage between James, Prince of Scotland, to Cecilia,

daughter of Edward IV., on the 18th of October 1474. He died before his father, and by his wife Euphemia, daughter of Lord Crichton, had two sons, David and John. David, as the heir-apparent of his grandfather, had a charter of the family estates of Biggar, Thankerton, Cumbernauld, etc., about the year 1480. He died early. His brother John, in 1482, some years previous to his accession to the estates, appeared with the retainers of the family at the Boroughmuir of Edinburgh, on the summons of James III. to assist in opposing Edward IV. of England, who had raised a force for the purpose of invading Scotland. The Scottish army marched to Lauder; but the barons, dissatisfied with the King, on account of his partiality to tradesmen and persons of low degree, seized one Cochrane, his master-mason, whom he had raised to the peerage by the title of the Earl of Mar, and who had conducted himself in a very supercilious and offensive manner, and hanged him over the bridge of Lauder, disbanded the army, and conveyed the King prisoner to Edinburgh Castle. When the King was restored to liberty by his brother, the Duke of Albany, and the Duke of Glo'ster, he attempted to take revenge on his rebellious nobles, and, among others, committed John Fleming to prison; but he was soon after released.

Fleming again joined the discontented party—Angus, Hume, Both-well, and others—who seized the young Prince, afterwards James IV., and proclaimed him King, declaring that his father, on several grounds, had forfeited his right to the crown. Both parties mustered their vassals, and an engagement took place on the 18th June 1488 at Sauchieburn, in which the King's forces were routed. The King fled from the field, and on descending a declivity at Beaton's Mill, near Stirling, he was thrown from his horse, and, being encased in armour, was much hurt. He was conveyed to a bed in the miller's house, and was there murdered, and his body carried off by a person whose name remains unknown to this day. The rebel lords were unable to obtain any intelligence of the King, and therefore it was supposed that he had gone on board one of the ships of war that had been sailing up and down the Firth of Forth, under the command of Sir Andrew Wood. They therefore requested a conference with Sir Andrew; but he refused to meet with them, unless two noblemen were placed on board as security for his own safety. The noblemen selected for this purpose were Lords Fleming and Seton; and, so soon as they were on board, Sir Andrew landed, and had a lengthened conversation with the Lords, during which he spoke very freely of their rebellious con-duct, but, of course, could give no information regarding the King. Pitscottie says, 'The lordis sieing nothing in Captane Wood bot disphyghtfull answeiris and proud speakingis, they war not content thairwith; yitt they durst not put hand in him to doe him any skaith, becaus of the lordis that war pledges for him: ffor if the had done him any skaith, they wold incontinent have hanged the lordis that war pledges for him, quhilk as it was, escaped narrowlie, becaus of the long stay of the said captane. The Lords haisted away the captane to his schipes, and inquyred no moe tydings of him. This being done, the lordis pledges war delyvered and tane on land againe, who war richt flied, and schew the Prince and the lordis, if they had holdin Captane Wood any longer, they had been both hanged.'

A war having been proclaimed between France and England, James IV. of Scotland, about the year 1511, was urged by the King of France to invade England. He refused to do so, on the ground that a bond of alliance existed between the English King and himself; but he promised to send a reinforcement to the assistance of the French. He accordingly fitted out a fleet of considerable size, appointed Lord Hamilton Admiral, and Lord Fleming Vice-Admiral, and placed under their command a body of 10,000 men. The ship in which Fleming sailed was called the 'Margaret,' and the Admiral's ship was the 'Micheall,' which was built by James, and was the largest vessel in Scotland, being 240 feet long, and 46 feet over all. She carried 1400 men, and cost upwards of L.40,000. This armament set sail; but instead of directing its course to France, it approached the coast of Ireland, burnt the town of Carrickfergus and some of the neighbouring villages, and then returned to Scotland. The Admiral and his men landed at the town of Ayr, where they 'played thamselves, and reposed be the space of fourtie dayes.' The King, when he heard of their conduct, was in a terrible rage, and sent Sir Andrew Wood and several heralds to order Lord Hamilton to give up his command; but his Lordship disregarded the King's authority, and having put his men on board, he again set sail. The expedition was a complete failure, and apparently was one of the causes which induced James to muster a land army and march into England, where he lost his life on the disastrous field of Flodden.

At the death of James IV., in 1513, his son James was only two years of age, and therefore his Queen, Margaret, was appointed Regent of the kingdom. During the year following, Lord Fleming, and James Ogilvie, Rector of Kinkell, and afterwards Abbot of Dryburgh, were sent on an embassy to France, and acquitted themselves with so much fidelity and success, that Fleming, on his return, was chosen a member of the Queen's Privy Council. He was shortly afterwards entrusted with another embassy to France, and brought back a considerable quantity of arms and ammunition, and 10,000 francs, to assist the Scots in defending themselves against the English. The Queen, in consequence of entering into a marriage with the Earl of Angus, was called on to resign her office of Regent; and was so incensed at the idea of being deprived of power, that she requested assistance from her brother, Henry VIII. of England, to enable her to retain possession of her office. It appears that Lord Fleming had by this time deserted her party, and incurred her resentment; for in the letter in which she requested this assistance, she says, 'It is told me that the Lord adversaries are prepared to siege me in the Castle of Stirling. I would, therefore, that Lord Chamberlain Fleming be held waking in the meantime with the Borderers. I trow I shall defend me well enough from the others till the coming of the English army.' The passion of the Queen having been thoroughly roused, she appears to have stickled at nothing by which she might blacken the character of Lord Fleming, and fire the indignation of her brother against him. In one of her letters, she accuses him of having been guilty of a most atrocious crime. 'For evil will,' says she, 'that he had to his wife Euphemia Drummond, caused poison three sisters, one of them his wife; and that is known as truth throughout all Scotland. And if he be good to put about the King, my son, God knoweth.' The sudden death of Lord Drummond's three daughters, Margaret, Euphemia, and Sybilla, by poison, is a historical fact; but, so far as we know, not a shadow of proof remains to implicate Lord Fleming in a tragedy so foul and unnatural. During his subsequent career, no one ever publicly charged him with being either an accessory or a principal party in the perpetration of this crime, which would not very likely have been the case had it been supposed that he was guilty. James Stewart, then Duke of Rothesay, and afterwards James IV., was passionately attached to Margaret, one of the daughters who was poisoned. Many historians assert that he had actually married her privately, and that, as the union was within the prohibited degrees, he was only waiting for a dispensation from the Pope to have it legally solemnized. Three parties in the state were violently opposed to this marriage—first, the clergy, because it was within the degrees prohibited by the Church; second, a portion of the nobles, because they wished the Prince to ally himself in marriage with the royal family of England; and third, the Kennedys, because the Prince had carried on a love intrigue with Lord Kennedy's daughter Jane, whom it was expected he would marry. It was, no doubt, by some of these parties that the deed was committed, and not by Fleming, who apparently had no motive in murdering not only his own wife, but the wife or mistress of the young Prince, and her sister. Had James IV. really believed him to be the murderer, he would, considering his passionate attachment to Margaret Drummond, and his grief at her untimely death, very quickly have brought him to the ignominious doom that he would, in that case, have so justly deserved.

The Queen was succeeded in the regency by the Duke of Albany, grandson of James II., who had previously lived in France. Lord Fleming, by his zeal and abilities, very soon secured the favour and countenance of the new Regent, who appointed him to the office of Lord Chamberlain in 1516, on the execution of Lord Chamberlain Home, for the cowardly and unpatriotic part which he had played at the Battle of Flodden. The office of Lord Chamberlain, or Treasurer,

which remained in the family of Fleming for several generations, was
one of great trust and dignity.   It required the person who held it to
be constantly resident at court, to have charge of the household of
the sovereign, and to disburse all sums that were necessary for the
maintenance of the royal establishment.   The accounts of the Trea-
surers of Scotland have been preserved from a remote period, and
are extremely interesting, as well as useful in illustrating the movements of the court, and the manners and customs of the times.   Lord
Fleming, so far as we know, first signed himself ' Camerarius Scotiæ,'
in a letter of date 7th October 1517, which was sent by the Regent
and Parliament to Henry VIII. of England, regarding a suspension
of hostilities between the two kingdoms.

The Duke of Albany soon found his position as Regent beset with
so many difficulties and troubles, that he longed to return to the calm
privacy which he had formerly enjoyed in France.   He therefore
departed to that country, holding out as the cause, that he wished to
enter into a personal negotiation with the French King regarding the
assistance which he would render in the event of the English invading
Scotland ; but he remained so long absent, that Lord Chamberlain
Fleming was despatched to France to urge his return.   A copy of the
instructions which he received on this occasion is preserved in the
charter chest of the family ; and from this document it is made to
appear that the Regent was detained in France by the influence of the
French King, and that the Council of Scotland threatened, if he was not
very soon sent back, they would enter into an alliance with England,
break off all connection with France, and declare the office of Regent
vacant.   As a specimen of this document, we quote the 'Item' in which
the threat is held out of an alliance with England:—' That the Conseil
of Scotland is aduisit that gyf thai have na sickyr tydingis of my lord
gouernour be Monsyeur de Flemyng, or the said Vitsonday, thai wil tak
pece witht Ingland as is offerit thame, straytar than the auld and
alluterly agains France ; quharfor thai have ellis send for ane sauf
conduct to Ingland for thair ambassadouris to tret the sammyn.'   Lord
Fleming was, however, successful in gaining the object of this mission ;
and he returned to Scotland in the retinue of the Regent in November 1521.

Albany, after his return, wished to get possession of the person of
James V., then resident with his mother and his brother, the Earl of
Ross, in the Castle of Stirling, and for this purpose levied an army of
7000 men, and invested the Castle.   The garrison, ere long, was
induced to surrender ; and Queen Margaret, seeking an interview with
the Regent, caused the young King to place the keys of the Castle in
his hands.   The Regent then committed the King to the guardianship
of the Earl Marischall and Lords Fleming and Borthwick, in whose
fidelity he placed entire confidence ; and this proceeding was ratified
by public instrument in November 1523.

The Regent Albany, at the instigation of the King of France, involved Scotland in a war with England; but he conducted it in a way that reflected little credit on his energy and skill, and entailed many calamities on the country over which he ruled. Born and brought up in France, he never had any warm attachment to Scotland, and seemed always well pleased to escape from its plots, its turmoil, and miseries. He left it in May 1524, and never again set foot on its soil. After his departure, the country was placed, if possible, in a still more disordered state than ever. The young King, who was only thirteen years of age, was incompetent to take on his shoulders the cares of government; and he had no person around him of sufficient power and energy to grasp the reins of administration, and keep the country in proper awe and subjection. His mother had obtained a legal separation from her second husband, the Earl of Angus, and had entered into a new matrimonial connexion with Henry Stewart, a younger son of Lord Evandale, and had thus lost all political influence. Her late husband, the Earl of Angus, now rose into power; but was opposed by a faction, who wished to place the King, young as he was, at the helm of public affairs. In the unsettled state of the country many disorders arose, and many barbarities were perpetrated. One of the most remarkable of these was the murder of Lord Fleming, on the 1st of November 1524, by the Tweedies of Drummelzier and a band of accomplices.

The Tweedies, who long occupied a considerable portion of the wild and mountainous region in the upper part of Tweeddale, were a numerous clan, distinguished for their arrogance, turbulence, and ferocity. Outrages committed by them are found repeatedly recorded in the annals of the criminal courts of Scotland. For instance, at a Justice Aire held at Peebles by Lord Drummond, on the 15th Nov. 1498, John Tweedie of Drummelzier, and five others, came in the King's will, and were each fined five merks, for art and part in an act of oppression committed on Oswald Porteous, and his wife Janet Fleming, in ejecting them from their holding in Upper Kingledoors. In the reign of James IV., Gilbert Tweedie, John Beres, and Andrew Chancellor, were arraigned for the slaughter of Edward Hunter of Polmood; and on the 4th Feb. 1502, John Tweedie of Drummelzier, Walter Tweedie of Hawmyre, and William Tweedie, became sureties for the appearance of the said Gilbert Tweedie at the next Justice Aire at Peebles, under the penalty of 100 merks. On the 26th January 1565-6, 'Adam Twedy of Drawey was dilatit of (the crime of) cutting Robert Raimagis luggis, and demembring him.' A feud broke out in the upper part of Tweeddale in 1590; and as it affords a good illustration of the turbulent character of the Tweedies, we quote the account, somewhat abridged, which has been given of it by Mr Robert Chambers in his 'Domestic Annals.' 'The fact from which it took its rise,' he says, 'was the slaughter of Patrick Veitch,

2 P

son of William Veitch of Dawick (now New Posso), by or through James Tweedie of Drumelzier, Adam Tweedie of Dreva, William Tweedie of the Wrae, John Crichton of Quarter, Andrew Crichton in Cardon, and Thomas Porteous of Glenkirk. These persons were in prison in Edinburgh for the fact in July of this year; but the case was deferred to the *aire* of Peebles. Meanwhile, on the 20th of the month just mentioned, two relatives of the slain youth—James Veitch, younger, of North Synton, and Andrew Veitch, brother of the Laird of Tourhope—set upon John Tweedie, tutor of Drumelzier and burgess of Edinburgh, as he walked the streets of the capital, and killed him. Thus were the alleged murderers punished through a near relative, probably uncle, of the principal party. Six days after, the two Veitches were "dilated" for the fact; and we find Veitch of Dawick taking their part in true Scottish style, by joining in surety for their appearance at trial to the extent of ten thousand merks. After some further procedure, the King was pleased to interfere with an order for the liberation of the Veitches. It would appear that, within a short space of time, the Tweedies of Drumelzier took revenge to a considerable extent on the Veitches: in particular, they effected the slaughter of James Geddes of Glenhegden, who seems to have been brother-in-law to a principal gentleman of that family. The recital of James Geddes's death in the Privy Council Record, affords by its minuteness a curious insight into the manner of a daylight street-murder of that time. 'James,' it is stated, 'being in Edinburgh the space of aught days together, haunting and repairing to and fra openly and publicly, met almaist daily with the Laird [of Drumelzier] upon the Hie Street. The said laird, fearing to set upon him, albeit James was ever single and alane, had espies and moyeners [retainers] lying await for him about his lodging and other parts where he repairit. Upon the 29th day of December [1592], James being in the Cowgate, at David Lindsay's buith, shoeing his horse, being altogether careless of his awn surety, seeing there was naething intendit again him by the said laird divers times before when they met upon the Hie Gait; the said laird, being advertised by his espies and moyeners, divided his haill friends and servants in twa companies, and directit John and Robert Tweedie, his brothers-german, Patrick Porteous of Hawkshaw, John Crichton of Quarter, Charles Tweedie, household servant to the said James, and Hob Jardine, to Cow's Close, being directly opposite to David Lindsay's buith, and he himself, being accompanied with John and Adam Tweedie, sons to the Guidman of Dreva, passed to the Kirk Wynd, a little bewest the said buith, to await that the said James sould not have escaped; and baith the companies, being convenit at the foot of the said close, finding the said James standing at the buith door with his back to them, they rushit out of the said close, and with shots of pistolets slew him behind his back." The guilty parties were summoned, and, not appear-

ing, were denounced as rebels. In June 1593, we find James Tweedie
of Drumelzier released from Edinburgh Castle, under surety that he
should presently enter himself in ward in the Sheriffdom of Fife. We
next hear of the two belligerent parties in January 1600, when they
were commanded to come and subscribe letters of assurance " for the
feid and inimitie standing betwixt them."'

The principal residence of the chief of the clan Tweedie, was
situated on the banks of the Tweed at Drummelzier. It was a building of great size and strength, but its situation was ill chosen either
for assault or defence. To compensate for this disadvantage, they
erected a fort on a neighbouring eminence, which was called the
Thane's Castle, but more commonly, by the country people, Tennis
Castle. It is a tradition that it was a custom of the Tweedies to
demand an act of homage from every person that passed these strongholds, and to inflict severe punishment in case of refusal. This imperious conduct brought them at times into collision with the Scottish
kings, who made them feel the full weight of the royal displeasure.
An instance of this is still related by the peasantry of Tweeddale and
Clydesdale, and is more or less detailed in several publications. It is
to the following effect:—One of the Jameses having heard of the
overbearing and tyrannical conduct of the Tweedies, resolved to visit
Drummelzier *incognito*, and witness, in person, the treatment which
they bestowed on strangers. He went, as was a very common practise with our Scottish monarchs, to hunt the fallow deer in the wilds
of Tweedsmuir and the Forest of Ettrick, attended by a considerable
retinue. Having made some of his courtiers privy to his design, and
enjoined them to keep themselves concealed among the hills, but to
remain within hail, he disguised himself, and as a solitary traveller
descended the Vale of Tweed. At a place not far distant from the
Castle of Kittlehall, the ancient seat of the Geddeses of Rachan, he
came up to an old man, a cobbler to trade, tending a cow, and entertaining himself with a spring on the bagpipes. This man, whose
name was Bertram, and who occupied a small hut in the neighbourhood, readily entered into conversation with the traveller, and at last
invited him to his humble dwelling to partake of refreshments. The
King at once complied, and having been regaled by the homely fare
set before him, resumed the conversation, and made minute inquiries
regarding the conduct of the neighbouring barons. Time flew rapidly
by, and evening coming on, the King being greatly delighted with
the kindness and intelligence of the cobbler and his wife, readily
consented to take the shelter of their cot during the night. Next
morning, to the great astonishment and even consternation of his
host, he disclosed his rank and condition, and his design of passing
the Castle of Drummelzier, and requested Bertram to act as his guide.
The King and Bertram immediately set out, and on coming to the
Castle of Sir James Tweedie, not only offered no act of homage, but

took pains to manifest their contempt, and then pursued their journey.
The indignation of the Tweedies was roused. Sixteen of them mounted
their steeds, and following the refractory couple with all speed, had
almost overtaken them at a spot called Glenwhappen, when the King
blew a loud blast on his bugle, and immediately a party of horsemen appeared in sight. So great was the insolence and audacity of
the Tweedies, that they nevertheless threatened to inflict corporal
chastisement on the fugitives for the affront which they had offered
them. The King instantly stript off his disguise, and ordered the
Tweedies to be seized and disarmed. Sir James, finding himself
caught in a snare from which he could not escape, fell on his knees
and begged the King's pardon. The King with some reluctance
granted his request, on condition that in future he and his retainers
would refrain from all aggressions on travellers. Bertram was highly
honoured, and rewarded with a grant of sixteen acres of land adjoining his dwelling, with the right to pasture a mare, and a foal, and a
sow, and nine pigs, on a piece of ground at the foot of Holmes Water.
The descendants of Bertram long held this possession, which was
called Dukepool, and acknowledged no superior, and paid no tax or
assessment. In course of time it was much curtailed by the disposal
of portions of it to the neighbouring proprietors, and such of it as
remained, fell some time ago into the female line, and is now the
property of James Tweedie Esq. of Quarter.

Between the Tweedies and Lord Fleming a feud had arisen. The
cause is not very accurately known, but it seems to have been regarding the disposal or marriage of Catherine Frizzel, heiress of Fruid in
Tweedsmuir. Catherine was a descendant of the old family of Frizzel
or Fraser, who held large possessions in the upper part of Tweeddale
in the twelfth and thirteenth centuries. By the marriage of Patrick
Fleming of Biggar with one of the heiresses of Sir Simon Frizzel, the
Flemings, along with the Hays of Yester, whose ancestor married
another of the heiresses, acquired some control or superiority over
the lands of Fruid. We have a proof of this in 1445, when Lord
Fleming's bailie and Hay of Yester granted a sasine of the lands of
Fruid to William Fraser. John Lord Fleming, it appears, was
anxious that Catherine of Fruid would marry one of his sons, whose
name was Malcolm,—not his legitimate son and heir of that name, but
another, most likely illegitimate. On the other hand, the Tweedies
were determined that she should wed no other than James Tweedie,
eldest son and heir of John Tweedie of Drummelzier. From casual
expressions in some of the old documents on the subject, it would
seem that she had actually been married to Malcolm Fleming, as she
styles him her husband. This, no doubt, fired the indignation of the
Tweedies. Having got notice that Lord Fleming was to enjoy the
sport of hawking over his lands in Kilbucho, Glenholm, and Drummelzier, they assembled to the number evidently of not fewer than

forty or fifty men, and waylaid his Lordship and his small retinue
among the hills. When the parties met, a hot altercation ensued, and
in the course of it young Tweedie of Drummelzier drew his sword
and slew Lord Fleming on the spot. Miss Agnes Strickland, in her
'Lives of the Queens of Scotland,' says that it was Douglas, 'Lord of
Drommellar,' who attacked and murdered Lord Fleming, and that
this was done on the threshold of St Giles's Church, Edinburgh. She
does not cite her authority for these statements; but they are not
borne out by the records of Justiciary, the documents in the Wigton
charter chest, or the assertions of our old historians. Not a word is
said in any of these authorities, so far as we have seen, that in any
way implicates the Douglases in this transaction; and Lindsay of
Pitscottie expressly says, that Lord Fleming was slain when enjoying
the sport of hawking.

The party in attendance on Lord Fleming was small, consisting
merely of his son and a few domestics. After the slaughter of his
Lordship, the Tweedies plundered his servants and carried off young
Fleming, and kept him in confinement in the Place of Drummelzier.
While this young nobleman was in their custody, they extorted a
promise from him that he would confer on them the ward and
marriage of Fruid—that is, a sum equivalent to two or three years'
rent that the heir of a vassal was bound to pay to the superior on his
marriage and accession to the estates; and it is likely, also, that he
consented that Catherine Frizzel should give up her engagement to
his brother, and should marry young Tweedie. In order to obtain
his liberty, and as a pledge that he would fulfil the agreement which
he had made, he put into the custody of the Tweedies Malcolm Fleming
his brother, Robert Stewart of Minto, and William Fleming of Boghall; and these persons were for some time kept in confinement in
the Place of Drummelzier.

Malcolm Lord Fleming, on regaining his liberty, wished to resile
from this engagement; but being afraid of the vindictive character of
the Tweedies, he signed an instrument to show that he sent Catherine
Frizzel, with the writs and evidents of her lands, to the Place of Drummelzier, solely for the purpose of obtaining the liberation of his friends,
and from a dread of the disastrous consequences that might otherwise
ensue. Several other legal instruments, still preserved, also show that
Catherine had been compelled to go to Drummelzier Place against her
inclination, and that her object was to set her husband, Malcolm
Fleming, and the other gentlemen held in custody, at liberty, and
further, to testify that whatever she might say or do on that occasion,
could not legally be used to the prejudice of her, her estates, or
marriage. These documents are dated the 17th and 25th of November 1524.

The civil authorities lost no great time in making efforts to bring
the Tweedies and their accomplices to justice. In the course of

fourteen days after the murder was committed, it appears that a
number of them had been seized or bound down 'to thole an assize;'
for at that time a respite for one year was granted to James Tweedie,
son and apparent heir to John Tweedie of Drummelzier, and other
persons, for the cruel slaughter of 'ye vmquile John Lord Fleming,
and treasonable taking and presonyng of Malcolme, Maister of Fleming,
his sone and are, ye king's fre man, in priuate presone; and for reif
of certain gudis fra yame and yare seruandis ye samyn tyme.'

From an indenture made at Edinburgh 23d November 1524, and
still preserved, it appears that by some influence or other, it was
'appoyntit, aggriet, and finalie concordit,' between Malcolm Lord
Fleming and James, son and apparent heir of John Tweedie of Drummelzier, that a reconciliation should take place and all previous wrongs
forgiven. This document intimates that James Tweedie and his accomplices went 'to ye mercat croce of Peblis in their lynning claithes, viz.,
sark alane, and yair thai haif offerit yr naykit suords to ye said Malcolm, his kyn and friendis,' that they bound themselves to be his
servants 'all ye dayis of· yr livis,' and gave him a band of manrent
thereupon. Lord Fleming, on the part of himself and his friends,
received James Tweedie and his accomplices 'in faithful troth and
afald kindness,' and forgave them the rancour which they had shown,
and the injury which they had inflicted; and in token of his sincerity,
extended to them the right hand of fellowship at the Market Cross of
Peebles, at the time the foresaid sword was delivered, and agreed to
support and defend them in all their actions honest and lawful, 'bot
fraud or gyle.' Tweedie and his accomplices engaged 'to gang, or
gar gang,' the three head pilgrimages of Scotland, viz., St Ninian's in
Galloway, St Duthus in Ross, and St Andrews in Fife, and at all of
these places to make offerings and cause masses to be said for the
welfare of Lord Fleming's soul; and they were to infeft a chaplain to
say mass at the high altar of Biggar Kirk for the same purpose. It
was finally agreed that the son and heir of Tweedie should be married
to one of Lord Fleming's sisters, that an honest and competent livelihood should, at the sight of friends, be bestowed on the young couple
by Tweedie, and that Tweedie was to receive the ward and marriage
of the heir of Fruid. It appears from several documents still extant,
that the terms of this agreement were not strictly adhered to, and
that the vengeance of the law still pursued the Tweedies and their
accomplices.

On the 6th of June of the following year, a respite was granted for
nineteen years to James Tweedy, Drummelzier, John Veitch of Kingside, James Tweedy of Kirkhall, David Newton of Mitchelhill, William
Porteous of Glenkirk, and twelve others, for the crime of murdering
Lord Fleming. On the 18th of August 1525, a petition, in connexion
with this foul transaction, was presented to the Lords of Council by
George Geddes of Kittlehall, near Rachan. As it is curious, we will

give it in the original words:—'My Lordis of Counsal and Auditoris of Chekker, vnto zour l huimlie menis and shewis I, zour seruitor, George Geddes of Cuthilhall: That quhare Williame Tuedy, ane scolar, wes delatit of airt and pairt of ye slauchter of vmquhile John Lord Fleming, and is innocent yairof, considering ye tyme of ye committing of ye samin, he wes at ye scule in Edinburghe: And becaus I duell amang his frendis, yai sollist and listit (enticed) me to be souerte for him, for his entre to ye law: And becaus he durst nocht compier, he being innocent, for feir of his parti, I am vnlawit for his nonentre befor ye Justice; howbeit as I traist, I suld nocht have bene ressauit souerte, nor suld have bene vnlawit, considering I wes and is of lessage within xv yeiris, and may nocht nor suld nocht be souerte, of ye law. Heirfor I besek your l, to have consideratioune herof, and gif command to ye Justise Clerk to draw me out of Adiornal, sua yat I be nocht poinded for ye said vnlaw. According to justice and zour ansuer I beseik.' The Lords ordained that, as the complainant at the time of his signing the document was in his minority, he should be relieved from his engagement, and his name erased from the books of adjournal.

On the 22d October 1528, the Tweedies were declared to be fugitives from the law, and were put to the horn, and their goods forfeited and conferred as a gift, under the Privy Seal, on Malcolm Lord Fleming. In the spring of 1529, the case was still unsettled; but it appears that at that time some impetus was given to the tardy wheels of justice, for we find that John Tweedie of Drummelzier, John Tweedie dwelling with him, Thomas Tweedie of Oliver Castle, James Tweedie of Kilbucho, and James Tweedie of Wrae, were compelled to find security to appear at the Justice Aire of Peebles, and underly the law for art and part in the cruel slaughter of John Lord Fleming; and as these parties had been previously put to the horn, John Hay of Yester was taken as security for their appearance, by warrant of the Privy Council, and with consent of Malcolm Lord Fleming. James Tweedie, younger of Drummelzier, John Veitch of Kingside, David Newton of Mitchellhill, and eight others, were also summoned to appear at the same time, and offered Sir Walter Scott of Branxholm as their cautioner, to answer at the same time and place for the above crime. On the 18th September of the year mentioned, Champnay, messenger-at-arms, was despatched with the King's writings, to summon a 'condign' assize, to convene at Peebles the 13th day of October, betwixt the Laird of Drummelzier and Lord Fleming of Biggar.

This assize did not give a deliverance on the merits of the slaughter and disputes, but referred the whole case for arbitration to the Lords of Council. Their Lordships, on the 4th of March 1530, pronounced a decreet-arbitral, by which it was decerned that John Tweedie of Drummelzier should found a chaplainarie in the Church of Biggar

and endow it with a yearly stipend of L.40 out of his lands and heritages, to pray for the soul of the umquhile John Lord Fleming, and
the Lords Fleming to have the patronage. It was further ordained
that James Tweedie, heir-apparent of Drummelzier, and the other
persons guilty of the slaughter of Lord Fleming, should go out of the
kingdoms of Scotland and England within three months, and should
remain for three years, or during his Majesty's pleasure; and that the
parties in the dispute should, in presence of the King and Council,
take each other by the hand, and bind themselves for the orderly
behaviour of their respective kin and followers. In regard to the
marriage of Catherine Frizzel to James Tweedie, a thing which was
claimed by Malcolm, Lord Fleming's brother, it was decided that the
Tweedies should cause Lady Fruid infeft heritably and irredeemably
the said Malcolm and his assignees in the L.4, 10s. land of old extent
of Mossfennan, in the 40s. land of old extent of Smallhopes and the
mill thereof, and in the 40s. land called Urisland, etc. All this was
to be done without prejudice to the concord made between Lord
Fleming and the Lairds of Glenkirk and Polmood; and the penalty
of failure was to be 10,000 merks. This decreet was confirmed by
James V. on the 22d of March 1531.

Malcolm, the eldest son of John Lord Fleming, who was murdered
by the Tweedies, was born in 1494. He was educated, as became his
rank, in all the learning of the time; and on arriving at manhood,
was distinguished for his abilities, acquirements, and upright character.
His merits were highly appreciated by James V., who conferred on
him many favours. On the death of his father in 1524, he was
appointed to the vacant office of Lord Chamberlain, and received
charters of the lands of Drummelzier, Hopcastle, Halmyre, Cardrona,
Rachan, Glencotho, Covington, Kilbucho, Over Kingledoors, Over
Menzion, Oliver Castle, Auchtermony, Kerse, Lenzie, Cumbernauld,
Boghall, Thankerton, Biggar, and many others. On the 26th Feb.
1524-5, he obtained a dispensation from Pope Clement VII. to marry
Joahanna or Janet Stewart, a natural daughter of James IV., as she
was related to him in the third degree.

On the 24th July 1526, Lord Fleming accompanied James V. in an
expedition to the border to settle disturbances and punish thieves.
After this had been effected, the royal party set out on their march
homewards, and had reached the bridge of Melrose on the 29th, when
the Laird of Buccleuch presented himself at the head of a thousand
horsemen. The King, it appears, had come to be of opinion that he
was kept too much in bondage by the persons by whom he was daily
surrounded, and had sent a secret message to Buccleuch to raise his
clan and come to his rescue. The Earl of Angus, who commanded
the King's troops, demanded to know what Buccleuch's design was in
coming with so great a force. Buccleuch replied that he had come
to do the King honour and service, and to show him his retainers and

friends. Angus at once ordered him to depart on the pain of treason, and on his refusal, a combat ensued; but Buccleuch in the end was routed, and eighty of his men slain.

The Scots, about this period, warmly resented the interference of Henry VIII. in their national affairs; and the consequence was, that a war ensued between the two kingdoms. The inhabitants of the Biggar district have ever been distinguished for their loyalty to their sovereign, and for their contendings in behalf of their native country; and therefore one is surprised to find that about seventy of them were arraigned for treasonable intercourse, during the war, 'with Alexander Forrester, Jonkin Storie, and others their accomplices, Inglishmen and traitors, dwelling upon levine and reset of them within the realm.' The names of the principal parties arraigned were, Malcolm Lord Fleming, James Murray of Fawlohill, Gilbert Brown of Threpland, Andrew Brown of Hartree, Richard Brown of Coultermains, Patrick Porteous of Hawkshaw, Walter Hunter of Polmood, James Kincaid, the Laird of Crympcramp, John Murray of Lewinshope, William Murray of Sundhope, William Boyd of Bathenheugh, William Carwood of that Ilk, and William Murray of Rommano. On the 16th of August 1526, a respite was granted them for nineteen years; and it does not appear that they were ever subjected to any further legal proceedings, which is apt to make us believe that the accusations brought against them were false and unfounded.

Lord Fleming, in 1535, accompanied James V. on his matrimonial expedition to France. Ambassadors had, a short time before, concluded a marriage treaty between James and Marie de Bourbon, daughter of the Duke of Vendosme. Henry VIII. of England had by this time quarrelled with the Pope regarding the divorce of his wife, Catherine of Arragon, and had embraced the doctrines of the Reformation. He was consequently anxious to withdraw his nephew James from the matrimonial connection already stated, believing that it would tend to confirm the young King more devotedly in his attachment to the Romish Church. James finding himself opposed by his uncle, resolved to repair secretly to France to see the object of his choice, and complete the marriage. He set sail with a considerable retinue; but the nobles who accompanied him being disposed in favour of the English alliance, embraced an opportunity, when the King was asleep, to reverse the course of the ship, and ere James was aware, he was brought back to the coast of Scotland. James, in a fit of passion, ordered the captain to be hanged; and this would have been done, had not the nobles taken the whole blame on themselves. The King, determined not to be driven from his design, again set sail, attended by many of the nobles, among whom was Lord Fleming, and, in ten days, arrived at Dieppe. Notwithstanding his previous engagement to Mary of Vendosme, he fell in love with Magdalene, daughter of the French king, a lady of great beauty, but of weakly constitution,

2 Q

and was married to her in the Church of Notre Dame, Paris, on New Year's day 1537. In the spring the King returned with his Queen and attendants to Scotland; but the fair and youthful Magdalene sickened and died, forty days after she set foot on the shore of her adopted country.

The misunderstanding between James V. and his uncle Henry VIII. still continued. James refused to wed Henry's daughter, Mary, and formed a matrimonial union with Mary of Guise, a lady whom Henry himself had shown a disposition to add to the list of his wives. Henry was anxious that a conference should take place between James and himself at York, to discuss various matters of importance to both kingdoms. James was disposed to meet his uncle, and made a promise that he would do so; but, influenced by the remonstrances of the Romish priests, who were apprehensive that James would be drawn from his allegiance to the Church of Rome by the entreaties and reasonings of his uncle, who had become a zealous champion in support of the principles of the Reformation, he failed to keep his appointment. Henry was greatly enraged at the conduct of his nephew, and, in retaliation, caused several rich merchant-vessels belonging to Scotland to be seized and detained. James demanded satisfaction, which was refused; and the result of the whole was, that a war broke out between the two kingdoms. The success, at first, was decidedly on the side of Scotland; and this caused Henry to raise an army of 40,000 men, which he placed under the command of the Duke of Norfolk, and sent to invade Scotland. James, on his side, summoned his subjects to assemble on the Boroughmuir, near Edinburgh, and, in a short time, at the head of a large army, marched to Fala. The Duke of Norfolk, harassed by detachments of the Scots, suffering from the want of provisions, and opposed by a formidable army, in a short time beat a retreat across the border. Now was the time, as James thought, to retaliate with effect on the English; but, to his extreme surprise and mortification, his principal barons refused to advance a step farther. Many of them had become dissatisfied with his conduct in annexing estates to the Crown, limiting the power of the nobles, refusing to meet with his uncle Henry, and manifesting a stubborn determination to uphold the principles and the patrimony of the Church of Rome. It was in vain that James upbraided them, and declared that they no longer possessed the spirit of men and patriots. His words were disregarded; and he had no alternative but to disband an army with which he expected to deal a decisive blow upon England. The alienation of these barons threw the King still more thoroughly into the arms of the Romish priests and their bigoted adherents, who, elated with the confidence reposed in them, strove to gratify the wishes of the King by contributions of men and money. In a short time James saw himself at the head of an army of 10,000 men, whom he despatched, in November 1542, with all haste to the border. He accompanied them himself in person, but being overtaken with indisposition, he halted at Caerlaverock Castle. The army, nevertheless, hastened on their march, and had scarcely disentangled themselves from the dangerous sands and bogs of the Solway, when they were filled with surprise and indignation by a proclamation, that Oliver Sinclair, the King's gentleman-in-waiting, had been appointed to the chief command. A shout was instantly raised by the army that they would not follow such a leader; and a scene of complete insubordination and disorder immediately ensued. The English wardens, Dacre and Musgrove, with 400 horsemen, happened at this juncture to advance for the purpose of reconnoitring, and, observing the confusion of the Scots, instantly assailed them with levelled lances, and drove them in irretrievable rout from the field. A number of them were slain, and many of them taken prisoners, among the latter of whom were the Earls of Cassillis and Glencairn, and Lords Fleming, Sommerville, Maxwell, Gray, and Oliphant. These barons were marched to London, and, on the 19th of December, lodged in the Tower. On the second day after their arrival, they were clothed in gowns of black damask, furred with black rabbit-skins, and coats of black velvet, decorated with the red cross of St Andrew; and in this guise were publicly paraded through the streets of London to Westminster Hall, where Audeley, the Lord Chancellor, reprimanded them for invading the territory of England, and waging war with its sovereign and people. He, however, stated, 'that his Majesty meant to return good for evil, and to give a signal instance of the benignity of his most princely nature by releasing them from personal restraint; and that, taking only their word of honour for remaining in England prisoners at large, he would allot them their lodgings with the Archbishop of Canterbury, the Duke of Norfolk, and other persons of high consideration.'

James V., fourteen days after the rout of Solway, died of a broken heart in his palace of Falkland, in the thirty-first year of his age. When his uncle, Henry VIII., heard of his death in circumstances so melancholy and deplorable, he treated the Scottish prisoners with more kindness and forbearance, hoping to make them instrumental in promoting the political designs which this sad event now led him to entertain in regard to Scotland. He invited them to a grand entertainment on the 26th December, and after bestowing on them the most flattering marks of respect, he propounded to them his new scheme of uniting the two kingdoms by a marriage between his only son Edward and the infant Queen of Scots, who was born a few days before her father's death. This design, had its accomplishment been sought by fair and honourable means, had much to commend it, as it held out the prospect of conducing to the peace and prosperity of both nations; but Henry clogged it with conditions that were highly reprehensible. He insisted on receiving the custody of the young Queen, in order that she might be brought up and educated in Eng-

land, on being declared lord superior of Scotland, and on placing
English troops in the principal fortresses of that country. Seven of
the prisoners, viz., the Earls of Cassillis and Glencairn, and Lords
Fleming, Sommerville, Gray, Maxwell, and Oliphant, signed a bond
to use their exertions to carry this design into effect, and were released,
on giving hostages that they would return to captivity by a prescribed
time, or, failing in this point, to pay the sum of money at which they
were valued. Lord Fleming gave as his hostage his eldest son James,
and his ransom was fixed at 1000 merks. The Scottish barons began
their journey homewards on the 1st of January 1543, and by the way
visited Enfield, where the young heir-apparent of the English throne
resided, and were greatly pleased with his intelligence, his fine features,
and graceful deportment.

Lord Fleming, for some time after his return to Scotland, continued
faithful to his engagement to the English monarch. In the Parliament
which met at Edinburgh on the 12th March 1543, he defended the
proposal of a marriage between Mary of Scotland and Prince Edward
of England, as likely to put an end to the feuds and wars that so often
prevailed between the two kingdoms. He was consequently, in opposition to the wishes of Cardinal Beaton and his party, appointed, along
with Lords Erskine, Livingstone, and Ruthven, a guardian of the
young Queen, who, at that time, was kept in Stirling Castle. Sir
Ralph Sadler, the English ambassador, in his state papers, bears testimony to the strict manner in which these barons discharged their
duties. They would neither allow the Cardinal to lodge in the Castle,
nor above one or two of his accomplices to enter the gates at the same
time. In a conversation which Sir Ralph had with Lord Fleming in
April of this year, his Lordship attributed the opposition to the matrimonial project of Henry VIII. principally to the Regent, the Earl of
Arran, and the Douglases; his Lordship stating that the Regent had told
him that he would rather take the young Queen and carry her with him
into the isles, and dwell there, than consent to marry her into England.
His Lordship, as a proof of his own zeal for the English interest,
declared that his reply was, that if the Regent should take this step,
the English King, for L.10, might get one of the 'Irish cettericks'
(banditti) there to bring him the Regent's head. Sir Ralph says that
Lord Fleming and the Douglases were at that time at variance regarding a sheriffship; and he assigns this as the main cause why he
spoke so strongly against them, and especially against Arran the
Regent. At the same interview, Lord Fleming declared that he would
proceed to England before the day appointed for his return, and would
lay his opinion regarding public matters before Henry in person, as
'he was fully determined to serve his Majesty to the uttermost of his
power, according to his promise.'

By the month of August following, a complete change had been
produced in Lord Fleming's mind regarding the English alliance; and

hence Sadler, writing on the 10th of that month, says that, by the assistance of one of the spies in his employment, he had discovered that Fleming and other noblemen had secretly signed a bond against the matrimonial connection with England, which had been drawn up by Cardinal Beaton at Linlithgow. He further says, that it had come to his ears that Lord Fleming had declared that he would never go back to England, whatever became of his son; and that he had resolved to pay the sum fixed for his ransom, and thus shake himself free from all obligation to the English king. This, in reality, was the course pursued by his Lordship. He broke off all connection with the English party, paid the 1000 merks for his ransom, and became one of the most zealous and devoted partisans of the Queen Dowager, Cardinal Beaton, and their confederates, all bigoted adherents to the Romish faith and the interests of France. The step which he thus took was so far justified by the decision of the Scottish Parliament, which, on the 11th December 1543, by a solemn act, declared that all negotiations regarding the proposed matrimonial union were at an end. The consequence of this decision was, that war broke out between the two kingdoms with renewed vigour. Henry, greatly incensed at the conduct of the Scots, resolved to chastise them with the greatest severity, and therefore sent invading armies into Scotland that committed every species of havoc, burning towns, villages, and religious houses, and slaughtering and plundering the people. In some of the battles which were at that time fought, Lord Fleming took part. He obeyed, for instance, the proclamation which was issued for the lieges of the Queen to assemble at Dunbar on the 29th November 1544, and march to the border. Seven thousand men having mustered, they received several pieces of artillery and other weapons, taken out of the Castle of Dunbar, and then proceeded to Coldingham, which at the time was in possession of the English. They opened their batteries on the town; but their operations were feebly and unsuccessfully conducted. The English made a sortie, broke their ranks, and chased them for miles back into the country.

Malcolm Lord Fleming, to manifest his zeal in the cause of Popery, resolved to erect and endow a Collegiate Church at Biggar. He commenced this work in 1545, and carried it on with vigour so long as he lived. The cares and solicitude consequent upon this erection did not withdraw his attention from the business of the State. He attended a convention of peers, spiritual and temporal, which met at Stirling on the 10th of June 1545. Great efforts were made at this meeting to reconcile and unite the parties who opposed each other, and obstructed the establishment of peace, order, and security within the realm. Lord Fleming, although attached to the French party and the abettors of Popery, was strongly disposed to enter into healing measures; and therefore he approved of the proposal to select twenty peers, four of whom were to remain, alternately for a month;

with the Governor, the Earl of Arran, as his secret council. The first
four appointed to discharge the duties of this office, were, Lord Fleming; Patrick, Bishop of Orkney; Patrick, Earl of Bothwell; and
Gilbert, Earl of Cassillis.

In retaliation of the wrongs inflicted by the English on Scotland, an
army was sent into England on the 10th of August 1545, to burn,
plunder, and slay in return. Malcolm Lord Fleming, with his retainers, formed a portion of the rear division of this army. It burnt
and destroyed a number of villages, and returned laden with booty,
without meeting with any decided opposition, or incurring any great
loss.

Henry VIII. died in 1547, and as his son Edward was only in the
ninth year of his age, the Duke of Somerset was appointed Regent of
the kingdom. The Regent, unfortunately, resolved to prosecute the
same policy in regard to Scotland as his deceased master, and therefore levied an army ·of 18,000 men, and marched into Scotland,
determined still further to punish the Scots, and to carry off the
young Scottish Queen. The Scots, on their side, mustered a host
almost double in point of numbers; but, as was usual, it laboured
under the disadvantage of having no commander adequate to guide
and control the various sections of which it was composed. Malcolm
Lord Fleming mustered his vassals, and marched to the Scottish
camp near Musselburgh. Several of his near relatives had also taken
the field with their followers, particularly his two sons-in-law, the
Master of Livingstone and the Master of Montrose, both of them destined to meet with the same disastrous fate as himself. The position
of the Scots, on the left bank of the Esk, was well chosen; and on
Somerset reconnoitring it, he saw that he could not attack it with
advantage, and therefore gave orders to withdraw his troops to some
distance. This movement made the Scots imagine that the English
were retreating to their ships lying in the bay. In opposition to the
opinion and remonstrances of the most experienced leaders, the Scots
crossed the Esk, and thus gave their opponents the advantage of the
rising ground on which they stood. Lord Gray, with the English
cavalry, lost no time in rushing down on an advanced body of Scottish
infantry, who, drawn up in a firm and close phalanx, with their long
spears projecting in every direction, stood the dreadful charge quite
unshaken, while the southern horsemen were soon sent back reeling
in disorder. The want of cavalry on the part of the Scots prevented
them from following up their advantage. Lord Gray refused to renew
the conflict, declaring that he might as well charge a castle wall; and,
therefore, a body of musketeers and archers was advanced to assail
the Scots, whose compact array more fully exposed them to the effects
of the destructive shower of missiles that was hurled against them.
A change of position became necessary; and this was in the course of
being executed in good order, when the Highlanders, who had left

their ranks for the sake of plunder, supposing that their friends had commenced a retreat, immediately betook themselves to their heels. A panic was, consequently, infused into the whole Scottish army, and in an instant the country round was covered with fugitives. The English cavalry having now rallied, hastened after their foes, and cut them down without mercy. No fewer than 14,000 men were slain in the pursuit, so that dead bodies lay in the fields for five miles, as thick, according to Old Patten, as cattle in a well-stocked pasture. Lord Fleming, and many of his retainers from Biggar and his other estates, were among the slain. This battle was fought on the 10th of September 1547.

Lord Fleming, at his death, was in the fifty-third year of his age, and his body was, no doubt, conveyed to Biggar, and, according to his own directions, interred in the church which he had founded and partially built. He left two sons and five daughters by his wife Janet Stewart, and also several illegitimate children. On the 15th of February of the same year on which he was slain, he executed a testament, in which he left his family under the charge of several executors, and appointed his wife, so long as she remained unmarried, to be the principal 'intromittar' with all his goods, moveable and immoveable, with the advice of these executors. The inventory of his effects is of great length, and remarkably interesting, particularly as showing the sources from which he drew his income, and the amount and value of the grain, stock, and other produce which were paid to him in the shape of rent. We will quote such parts of it as are applicable to Biggar and its neighbourhood. 'The maills of the hale barony of Biggar, of the Whitsunday's term of xlvij zere, 106 merks, 4s., 4d., the said term's male of Kilboche, L.47, 5s., the said term's male of the Quarter 50s., the said term's male of Broghtown L.8, the said term's male of Burnatland 10 merks, the said term's male of Smalhoppis L.10, and the said term's male of Thankertoun L.9, 19s. 6d.' The sum-total of mails for that term, including those of Lenzie, Kers, Dreppis, Auchtermony, Lour, etc., amounted to L.399, 18s. 4d. The above seems to have been the money part of his rents, but from these places mentioned, and others, he drew besides a large revenue in name of multure meal, farm meal, and teind meal, and also in hens, capons, oxen, bulls, kye, stirks, horses, sheep, etc. The tenants on several parts of his lands, had, it would seem, fallen somewhat into arrears, and therefore we find such statements as follow : 'Item rests in Thankertoun of malt of the Martinmas term, the xlvj zeir, and Whitsunday term in the xlvij zeir the said xv day of Februar, iii score xij bolls malt, price of the boll xxx shill.,—sum, l^c iij lib, ij sh, ix d. Item rests of male in Thankertoun of the xlvj zeir crop, iiij chalders vj bolls,—price of the boll xx shill. Item rests within the barony of Biggar of malt and bear the said xv day of Februar, of the Martinmas term in the xlvj zeir, and Whitsunday term in

the xlvij zeir, xi chalders, x bolls, i ff, iii p, malt and bear, price of the
boll xxx shillings,—sum. xiij score xix lib, ii shil, ix d.   Item rests
of the former male on Biggar barony of the xlvj zeir crop, vij chalders, xv bolls, i ff, ii p,—price of the boll the forsaid sum,—vj score
vij lib, vij shil, vi d.   Item rests in Biggar barony, iiij score capons,
price of the peice ij shil,—sum viij lib.   Item in Louk Wilson's hands
in the Lyndsylands v chalders ats, at the price of the boll x shil,—
sum xi lib.   Item in Ick Kempis hands, xi kye price of the peice iiij
merks, sum is xliiij merks.   Item in his hand a bull, price xl shil.
Item in his hand iij stirks price of the peice xx shil,—sum iij lib.
Item in Jean Paterson elder's hand xi score vij yois, xiiij Kubbis, iij
score v yeld yois, iij tuppis, xi score vij hoges, and v score iiij gym-
mers, sum of sheep in Jean Paterson elder's hand xxxij score viij
sheep, price of the peice overheid, viij shils, sum xij score xix lib, iiij
shil.   In Jean Paterson younger's hand of schip xxxij score twa schip,
price of the peice overheid viij shil,—sum xij score xvj lib, xvj shil.
Item in the Boghall, that draws in plough and paddoch, xiij oxin—
price of the peice iiij lib, sum lij lib.   Item hele sawin in the Boghall
this instant zeir v chalders xiiij bolls ats, estimat to the third grain
price of the boll xx shil—sum xlviij lib.'   Among various other
tenants mentioned, may be noticed the miller of Killacke (Call-late),
whose mail was twenty bolls, and the miller of Glenholm, whose mail
was sixteen bolls oats and two bolls of sale bear.   The whole sum of
the inventory amounted to L.5006, 18s. 4d. Scots.

Among the legacies which he left, were 400 merks to his servants,
and L.20 to 'the poir householders within Lenzie and Biggar, that
pays me nocht, that are fallen folks, to pray for me.'   To his eldest
son James he left the 'insight,' that is, the furniture within the Place
of Cumbernauld; along with the silver 'wark, an bason, an cover,
twa gilt cups with covers, vi — of silver, vj silver spoons, an dozen
of silver trenchers, twa saltfats of silver,' etc.; and to his second son
John, L.1000; and to his daughters, Agnes and Mary, 1000 merks
each.   To his wife, in addition to the house of Boghall, with the 'insight within the same,' except the artillery, which was to be the property of James, his son and heir, he bequeathed all the oxen and kye,
corn and bear, on the Mains of Boghall.

CHAPTER XXV.

Historical Sketches of the Fleming Family—*Continued.*

MARY, one of the daughters of Lord Fleming who founded Biggar Kirk, and lost his life at Pinkie, was, when a child, selected to be a playmate of Mary, the young Scottish Queen, and to be trained up with her in all the branches of learning common at the period. She thus formed one of the Queen's four Marys; the others being, Mary, daughter of Lord Livingstone; Mary, daughter of Lord Seton; and Mary, daughter of Beton, Laird of Creich. The unsettled state of the country rendering it necessary that the Queen should live in places of security, she successively occupied several castles, and spent some time on the lone but pleasant isle of Inchmahon in the lake of Monteith. After the Battle of Pinkie, the Scottish people were more averse than ever to the marriage of the Queen with Edward of England, and becoming apprehensive that no place in their country might afford her adequate protection, they resolved to send her to France. Lady Fleming, the widow of Lord Malcolm, and the Queen's aunt, was appointed to accompany her in the capacity of governess. The Queen, attended by Lady Fleming and her four Marys, accordingly set sail for France in a French galley, commanded by Monsieur de Villegaignon, in the month of July 1548, when the Queen was in the sixth year of her age. When they had almost reached their destination, a violent storm arose, which lasted several days, and caused the youthful voyagers to suffer severely from sea-sickness. Lady Fleming repeatedly implored the captain to allow the Queen and her companions to land, and repose themselves a short time on shore; but his instructions being peremptory against any such step, he resisted all her solicitations, and at length, in a fit of ill humour, told her that she must either go to the place appointed for disembarkation, or be engulphed in the stormy ocean.

Lady Fleming was much respected and caressed at the French court. The attentions paid to her gave a handle to the English ambassador to make an attempt to injure her reputation, by alleging, in a letter which he sent to the English court, that an improper intimacy existed between her and the French king. The story appears to have been a mere fabrication, got up for the purpose of gratifying certain parties in England. It is certain, however, that Henry II.,

King of France, held Lady Fleming in very high estimation. As a
proof of this, we may a quote a letter which he wrote regarding her to
the Queen Dowager of Scotland :—

'Madame my Good Sister,
                'I believe that you think enough of the care, pains, and great
vigilance that my cousin, the Lady Fleming, constantly takes about the
person of our little daughter, the Queen of Scotland. The really good, virtuous, and honourable manner in which she performs her duties therein,
makes it only reasonable that you and I should have her, and the children
of her family, in perpetual remembrance on this account. She has been
lamenting to me that one of her sons is a prisoner in England, and I desire
to lend a helping hand, as far as possible, to obtain his deliverance; yet,
situated as I am, it is not quite easy to accomplish that wish. It appears
to me, Madame my good sister, that you ought to write and request, as you
have the means of doing so, to have him exchanged for some English prisoner. In doing this, you will perform a good work for a person who merits
it. Praying God, Madam,' etc.

Lady Fleming continued to superintend the education of the young
Queen for several years, when she was at length superseded by
Madame Parois, a bigoted devotee of the Romish Church, whom Cardinal Lorraine, the Queen's uncle, is said to have selected as a person
well qualified to instil into the mind of the Queen those extreme
popish opinions which, in Germany, in England, and in Scotland,
were now actively and successfully assailed, and which the ultra-
Romish party, therefore, felt all the more anxious to defend and
maintain. The services of Lady Fleming being no longer required
about the person of the Queen, she returned to her own country in
1555, and most likely took up her residence at Boghall Castle, as
assigned to her by her husband. Her daughter Mary, however,
remained with the Queen as one of her maids of honour, and no
doubt was present at all those amusements and festivities in which it
is said the Queen so largely participated, during her abode in France.
She would be one of her bridesmaids on the occasion of her marriage
to the Dauphin, and she would be called on to condole with her
when that young monarch was laid in a premature grave. She
accompanied her back to Scotland, and heard her take that affectionate
farewell of France which has been so pathetically described by many
historians, and which has furnished a theme of inspiration to not a few
gifted sons of song. She was afterwards a witness of some of those
scenes in the life of her royal mistress, which have invested her history
with a romantic interest beyond that of any monarch that ever lived,—
such as her warlike displays, her progresses through her dominions,
her interviews with Knox, her marriage to Darnley, the murder of
Rizzio, the birth of a son in Edinburgh Castle, the loss of her husband
by violence, etc. Mary Fleming was one of the ladies seated in an

outer chamber of the Palace of Holyrood, gorgeously apparelled, in 1563, whom Knox addressed after one of his stormy interviews with the Queen. 'O fair ladies,' said John, 'how plesing were this lyfe of yours, if it sould evir abyde, and then in the end that we mycht pas to heiven with all this gay gear. Bot fie upon that knave Death, that will come quhidder we will or not, and quhen he hes laid on his areist the foull wormes will be busie with this flesch, be it nevir so fair and so tender. And the silly saull sall be so feabill, that it can nyther cary with it gold, garnisching, targating, pearll, nor precious stones.'

In a court which Knox was fond of describing as utterly dissolute, and at which, as he maintained, fiddling, flinging, and dallying with dames formed the constant pastimes, it is not to be expected that the Queen's Marys would escape his reproach. Accordingly, in his 'History of the Reformation in Scotland,' after referring to several wicked practices which, he alleged, prevailed at Holyrood, he states, that 'Schame hastit mariage betwix Johne Sempill, called the Danser, and Marie Levingstoun, surnamed the Lustie;' and he then strikes a blow at the whole of the Marys and the dancers. 'What bruit,' says he, 'the Maries and the rest of the dawnsers of the court had the ballats of the age did witness, which we for modesties sake omitt.' We are disposed to take this sweeping denunciation with considerable limitation. Knox was incensed against Queen Mary because she gave her subjects toleration with regard to their religious opinions, and because she would not renounce the faith in which she had been brought up, and become an active promoter of the principles of the Reformation. He was evidently at bottom a hilarious sort of man; but in the discharge of his duties as a minister of the Gospel, he considered himself warranted to express a strong dislike of all harmless amusements, and to attempt the imposition of the most grave and depressing austerities, particularly on the young Queen and her courtiers. Freedom to practise popish rites, and the sound of music and dancing, were regarded by him as utter abominations; and hence, throughout his 'History,' he hurls against them his severest denunciations.

One of the amusements at that time practised at the Scottish court, was the cutting of a cake in which a bean had been concealed, and the distributing of it among the company present. The person who found the bean was denominated the Queen or King of the Bean, according as it might fall into the hands of a lady or a gentleman. The amusement of cutting the cake took place on the 5th of January, being the eve of Epiphany, and no doubt had its origin in connection with the ceremonies observed at the celebration of this Romish festival. On the day following, a banquet was served up in honour of the person to whose lot the bean had fallen; and, at this entertainment, the holder of the bean was saluted as King or Queen, and called on to act the part of a sovereign. On the 5th of January 1563 the bean fell into the hands of Mary Fleming; and Thomas Randolph, in a letter addressed a few days afterwards to Lord Robert Dudley, in the style of euphuism then in vogue, thus describes the success, the appearance, and effect of the mock Queen:—'The ladies and gentlewomen,' says he, ' are all in health and merrie, which your Lordship should have seen, if you had been here upon Tuesday, at the great solemnity and royall estate of the Queen of the Beene. Fortune was so favourable to faire Fleyming, that, if shee could have seen to have judged of her vertue and beauty, as blindly shee went to work and chose her at adventure, shee wold sooner have made her a Queen for ever, than for one only day to exalt her so high and the nixt to leave her in the state shee found her. Ther lacked only for so noble a hart a worthie realme to endue that which—That day yt was to be seen, by her princely pomp, how fite a match she wold be, wer she to contend ether with Venus in beauty, Minerva in witt, or Juno in worldly wealth, haveing the two former by nature, and of the third so much as is contained in this realme at her command and free disposition. The treasure of Solomon, I trowe, was not to be compared unto that which that day hanged upon her back. Happy was yt unto this realme that her raigne endured no longer. Two such sights in one state, in soe good accord, I beleeve was never seen, as to behold two worthie Queens possess, without envie, one kingdom both upon a day. I leave the rest unto your Lordship to be judged of. My pen staggereth, my hand faileth farther to wryt. Ther praises surmount whatsomever may be thought of them. The Queen of the Been was that ·day in a gowne of cloath of silver; her head, her neck, her shoulders, the rest of her whole body, so besett with stones, that more in our whole jewell house wer not to be found.' Mary Fleming was married at Stirling to Sir William Maitland, the celebrated Secretary of Queen Mary, on the 6th of January 1567, exactly four years after she had played with so much *eclat* the part of Queen of the Bean.

James Lord Fleming, who succeeded his father, who fell at Pinkie, was a nobleman of distinguished abilities, and took a prominent part in the public transactions of the period in which he lived. In September 1550, along with the Earls of Huntly, Sutherland, Marischal, Cassillis, and other noblemen, he accompanied Mary of Lorraine, the Queen Dowager, in a visit which she paid to her native country of France. They sailed from Leith, and landed at Dieppe, in Normandy, in the middle of October. They then proceeded to Rouen, where the French court was, and after spending some time there in mirth and jollity, they paid a visit to Paris, and participated in the gaiety and festivities that then characterized the French capital. The ostensible object of the Queen Dowager was to see her daughter, then receiving her education in France; but her principal design in reality was to prevail on the French king to exert his influence to secure for her the office of Regent of Scotland. The King promised that he would do

so, provided the Earl of Arran, at the time Regent, would voluntarily
resign his office. The Queen Dowager at length left France, and
landing at Portsmouth on the 2d of November 1551, repaired to
London, and had an interview with King Edward VI. at Whitehall.
After her return to Scotland, she set herself industriously to obtain
the great object of her ambition, the Regency of the kingdom. Her
efforts being crowned with success, she was, in 1554, exalted to the
office of chief ruler of the ancient realm of Scotland, and thus, as
Knox says, had 'a croun put upoun hir Heid, als seimlie a sicht, gif
men had eyes, as to put a Saidill upoun the Back of ane unrewlie Cow.'
As Lord Fleming stood high in the estimation of the Queen Dowager,
he was, by letters patent under the Great Seal, appointed to the office
of Lord Chamberlain of the kingdom, which had formerly been held
by his father. He was also, on the death of Patrick, Earl of Bothwell,
chosen Guardian and Lieutenant of the East and Middle Marches on
the Border, with the power of justiciary within the limits of his jurisdiction.

Lord Fleming was one of the Commissioners appointed by the
Scottish Parliament, on the 18th December 1557, to be present at the
marriage of Queen Mary with the Dauphin of France. His chief
colleagues in this embassy were, Beaton, Archbishop of Glasgow; Reid,
Bishop of Orkney; James Stewart, Prior of St Andrews, afterwards
Earl of Murray; the Earls of Cassillis and Rothes; Lord Seton; the
Provosts of Edinburgh and Montrose; and Mr Erskine of Dun. To
defray their expenses, a tax of L.15,000 Scots was imposed on the
burghs and the estates of the clergy and nobles. They set sail on the
8th February, and encountered extremely stormy weather; the consequence of which was, that one of the vessels that carried the rich
apparel, in which they intended to make an imposing appearance at
the French court, was lost off St Abb's head, and another foundered
in the roadstead off Boulogne, and all on board perished, except the
Earl of Rothes and the Bishop of Orkney, who were picked up by a
French fishing-boat, while the other ships were separated from each
other, and arrived at different French harbours. The Commissioners,
before leaving Scotland, had been carefully instructed to give no
sanction to the marriage unless they obtained the most ample guaran-
tees that the independence of the country would be maintained, and
its laws and liberty secured. Before their arrival, Henry, King of
France, had obtained the signature of Queen Mary to a document,
conferring on him and his heirs the crown of Scotland, and her right
to that of England in case of her decease without lineal succession;
and to another, transferring to him the revenues of her kingdom in
payment of one million of gold crowns, or any greater sum that might
be expended on her board and education in France or in defence of
her kingdom. The Commissioners readily agreed that the arms of
France and Scotland should be borne by the Queen and her husband,

on separate shields, surmounted by the French crown; that their eldest son should be sovereign of both realms; and that, in the event of their having only daughters, the eldest, who would be prevented by the Salic law from being sovereign of France, should, on her mother's death, succeed to the throne of Scotland; but, on being summoned before the French Council after the celebration of the marriage, and required to swear fealty to the Dauphin, and confer on him the emblems of royalty, they peremptorily refused, and asserted that they would not go a step beyond the instructions which they had received from their own Parliament. The French king, finding that they were inflexibly bent on adhering to their resolution, detained them several weeks amid the gaieties and festivities of the French capital; and on dismissing them, expressed a hope that they would at least support a proposal, which he intended to lay before the Estates of Scotland, to confer the crown-matrimonial of Scotland on the Dauphin. Their young Queen also preferred the same request; and after promising to give the subject a careful consideration, they took leave of the French court, and in a short time arrived at Dieppe. At this town the Bishop of Orkney died suddenly; and in a day or two afterwards, the Earls of Rothes and Cassillis, and several other members of the embassy, were also laid in the grave. Lord Fleming, alarmed at the sudden mortality among his colleagues, drew up his Last Will and Testament, which is still preserved in the archives of the family. To his brother John he left his 'chapel graith,' his silver plate, the furniture of Cumbernauld House, etc.; and, among all his bequests, it is interesting to note the following: 'Item to ye poore men of ye Westraw of Byggar one chalder of meill.' He also enjoined on his brother to 'set forthward ye proffet of ye Kirk of Byggar to beild ye prest's chalmers and ye provest's house, and desyn of ye kirk, and also ye said Ihone to set up my fadyr's toum.' Having executed this deed, and dreading infection, he hastened back to Paris; but, after all, he was seized with the same distemper, and died on the 18th December 1558, in the 24th year of his age. As no infectious disorder prevailed at the time, the general impression in Scotland was, that he and his colleagues died from the effects of poison, which had been administered to them in consequence of their refusal to comply with the ambitious designs of the French court.

Lord Fleming was married at an early age to Barbara, a daughter of the Duke of Chatelherault. On the 14th December 1553, he conferred on her a charter of part of the barony of Lenzie; and on the 21st December of the year following, he executed another charter in her favour, constituting her liferenter of the lands of Kildowan and Auchtermony. He left by this lady an only child—a daughter. Father Baillie, who wrote a work on the events of that period, says that John Knox, the Reformer, after the death of his first wife, in 1561, paid his addresses to Lady Fleming. Baillie's words are,—

'Having laid aside al feir of the panis of hel, and regarding na thing the honestie of the warld, as ane bund sklave of the Devil, being kendellit with ane unquenshible lust and ambition, he durst be sua bauld to enterpryse the sute of marriage with the maist honorabil ladie, my ladie Fleming, my Lord Duke's eldest dochter, to the end, that his seid being of the blude royal, and gydit be thair father's sperit, might have aspyrit to the crown. And becaus he receavit ane refusal, it is notoriouslie knawn how deidlie he hated the hail hous of the Hamiltons.' What truth there may be in that statement, it would not be very easy now to discover; but it is certain that Knox was anxious to ally himself in marriage with a family of the nobility. He accordingly made suit to Margaret Stewart, a daughter of Lord Ochiltree, who was connected with the royal family, and being accepted, he was married to that lady in March 1564.

John Fleming, the second son of Lord Malcolm, succeeded, on his brother's death, to the title and estates. On the 17th May 1564, he married Elizabeth, only daughter and heiress of Robert, Master of Ross, who was killed at Pinkie. The marriage, instead of being celebrated at the Castles of Biggar or Cumbernauld, took place in presence of Queen Mary and her court at Holyrood. From an account of the festivities which took place on this occasion, it would seem that they were celebrated in the Royal Park, at the lower end of the valley, between Arthur Seat and Salisbury Crags, a place at that time covered with water. Here the Queen, with her nobles, and foreign ambassadors, forgot for a time the cares and troubles of her unruly kingdom, and gave herself up to mirth and jollity. As Robert Chambers says, 'The incident is so pleasantly picturesque, and associates Mary so agreeably with one of her subjects, that it is gratifying to reflect on Lord Fleming proving a steady friend throughout her subsequent troubles.'

On the 1st of August 1565, the Queen and Parliament conferred on Lord Fleming the office of Lord Chamberlain, an office that had been held by three of his immediate predecessors. In 1567 he received a grant of a third of the profits and rents of the Priory of Whithorn, as a compensation, in part, for services which he had rendered to the Queen, and for the losses which he had sustained by depredations committed by marauders from the borders. About the same time he was appointed Governor of Dumbarton Castle, and 'Justiciar' within the bounds of the Upper Ward of Clydesdale.

Lord Fleming was one of the nobles who were in the Palace of Holyrood on the night of the 9th of March 1566, when a body of armed men, headed by Darnley, Morton, Ruthven, and others, rushed into the Palace, and in the Queen's presence assassinated David Rizzio, her foreign secretary and favourite musician. This outrage naturally caused a great uproar in the Palace. The attendants on the Queen were taken quite by surprise, and finding themselves utterly incom-

petent to contend against the assailing force, they escaped by the back
windows, and some of them did not stop till they reached the Castle
of Crichton. The persons connected with the Biggar district who
were implicated in this foul conspiracy, were William Tweedie of
Drummelzier, Adam Tweedie of Dreva, John Brown of Coultermains,
and Richard Muirhead of Crawford. These persons, along with the
other conspirators, were summoned on the 19th March following to
compear personally before the King and Queen, and the Lords of the
Secret Council, to answer such things as would be laid to their charge.
Their names, however, do not appear in the list of those who were put
to the horn for their participation in this outrage. It is not unlikely
that they submitted themselves to the Council, and were sentenced to
some slight punishment.

On the 19th of April 1567, Lord Fleming, along with other noblemen, subscribed a bond, acquitting the Earl of Bothwell of the murder
of Lord Darnley, recommending him as a fit and proper person to be
elevated to the honour of being the Queen's husband, and pledging
himself to stand up in defence of this unseemly and unnatural connection. The subscription of this bond was extorted by Bothwell
from Lord Fleming and the other nobles, whom he had invited to an
entertainment, and whom, it is said, he overawed, by surrounding
them with a strong body of his retainers. Armed with this document, Bothwell seized the Queen at Cramond, and carried her off to
the strong Castle of Dunbar. In a few days afterwards they appeared
publicly in the streets of Edinburgh; and Bothwell, having obtained
a divorce from his wife, was married to the Queen, on the 15th of
May, by the Bishop of Orkney. Lord Fleming was present at this
ill-starred solemnity, at which, as the author of the ' Diurnal of Remarkable Occurrents,' says, ' there was neither pleasure nor pastime
as was wont.'

It has long been a subject of disputation, whether Mary was accessory to the murder of her husband Darnley; but scarcely any doubt
was ever entertained, that the chief actor in this foul transaction was
Bothwell. He was, no doubt, acquitted of the charge by an ' assise;'
but this was effected by surrounding the court with armed men, and
preventing any person from giving evidence against him, by a dread
of personal violence. The Queen, therefore, by marrying Bothwell,
lost the sympathy and respect of a great portion of her subjects. A
report was spread, that Bothwell, having now obtained an entire control over the Queen, entertained the design of seizing the person of
her only son James, a child of two years of age, and most likely of
putting him to death also. Many of the nobles, therefore, flew to
arms, to protect the young Prince, to thwart the treacherous schemes
of Bothwell, and rescue the Queen from the fangs of her blood-
stained paramour. Mary summoned her subjects to rally to her
standard, and having assembled a considerable force, she left Dunbar

and advanced towards Edinburgh. The confederated lords with an equal number of retainers marched from the capital to Musselburgh, and learned, on reaching that town, that the Queen's army had taken possession of the neighbouring height of Carberry. They therefore made a detour by Wallyford, and ascended the hill until they came nearly in contact with the Queen's troops. The Queen, with her usual boldness and impetuosity, insisted on bringing the matters in dispute at once to the arbitration of the sword; but her friends by no means possessed the same ardour for the combat as herself. They counselled delay until the expected reinforcements from Clydesdale, under the command of the Hamiltons, should arrive. The Queen then proposed that she should go and meet them, promising that she would immediately return; but this design was opposed. It is likely that these reinforcements were at the very time on their way to join the Queen. The opposing forces came face to face on Carberry Hill on the 15th of June; and on the day preceding, the following letter was sent by Lord John Hamilton to Lord Fleming, at his Castle of Boghall :—

'MY LORD,—Efter maist hartie commendatioune ze sall understand that I resavit ane writtin fra the quenis Maistie, daitit at Dunbar, the xiij of this instant of Junij, that hir grace is reddy to cum fordwart this morning toward Haldingtoun, and therfore desiris me and my friendis to be in redines, quhen it sall pleise hir to charge us to merche fordwart. Heirfoir I haif thocht goid to send this berar, knawing that zour lordship sould be togidder this nicht, in to Beggar, to knaw zour dyet, and thinkis goid, safand better counsell, that we joyne us togidder or we cum to hir Maiestie, baith for zour surete and ouris. And we intend quhen we marche, to pass be Pentlandhills or neir therbie, and gif ze please to appoint ony place be that way, we being chargit to cum fordwart, we wald be glad to meit zou ther, as ye sall appoint; and the rest referris to zour advertisment with the berar; and sa committis zour lordship to the protectioune of God, this Saterday at vij houris afoirnoune the xiiij of Junij 1567.

Zour Lordship's loving friend at power,
JHONE HAMILTON.'

From a statement made in an old document, it would seem that Fleming and his Biggar retainers actually reached Carberry, but the whole of the Clydesdale forces did not arrive in time; and the Queen was thus induced to dismiss Bothwell, and surrender herself to the confederated lords. She was conducted with every mark of indignity and disrespect to Edinburgh, and next day, in violation of the conditions on which she had surrendered, she was placed in confinement in Lochleven Castle. Lords Fleming and Hamilton, after the Queen's surrender, withdrew their forces to Hamilton to watch the progress of events.

After the surrender of the Queen at Carberry, the Earl of Bothwell fled to the north of Scotland. It would seem from a letter of

Sir Nicholas Throkmorton to Queen Elizabeth, dated 18th July 1567,
that he had been joined there by Lords Fleming and Seton. The
likelihood is, that they had been despatched from Hamilton to hold a
conference with him, and learn his designs. It is evident from the
following extract from the letter, that their stay with him was short,
and that, to their credit, they left him to his fate :—' Bodwell doethe
still remaine in the northe partyes, bot the Lordis Seaton and
Flemynge, which have ben there, have utterlye abandoned hym, and
doe repayre hetherwardes.'

The party opposed to the Queen saw that it would be of importance
to gain the countenance and co-operation of the leaders of the Protestant Church, now in the ascendancy in Scotland, as thereby they
were likely to secure the favour of the great body of the people.
They, therefore, took an active part in the proceedings of the General
Assembly which met at Edinburgh in the month of June, and which
was presided over by the celebrated George Buchanan, Principal of
St Leonards College, St Andrews. Through their influence, letters
were addressed to Lord Fleming and a number of noblemen belonging
to the other faction, calling upon them to come to Edinburgh to engage in the important work of establishing the principles of true
religion in the Church, defining the just rules of ecclesiastical government, and providing a suitable maintenance for the clergy and the
poor. A commission, consisting of John Knox, John Douglas, John
Row, and John Craig, was appointed to wait upon these lords in
person ; but Lord Fleming was too zealous a Roman Catholic, and too
much devoted to the cause of the Queen, to comply with any such
proposal, even though he had entertained no apprehension of danger
in appearing in Edinburgh, which was then entirely in the hands of
his opponents.

Morton, Ruthven, Grange, and the other barons leagued against
the Queen, soon found that all their ostentatious zeal for the Protestant faith would not be sufficient to support their popularity. Their
treacherous and cruel treatment of the Queen was beginning to rouse
the indignation of the people, and the charge of rebellion both at
home and abroad was constantly rung in their ears. They considered that, in order to extenuate their conduct, it would be necessary
to make the Queen still more accessory to her own humiliation.
They therefore despatched Lord Lindsay, a man of stern and rough
manners, to Lochleven, to induce the Queen, by persuasion, or if
necessary by force, to abdicate the throne, to invest her infant son
James with the sovereign power, and to appoint her brother, the Earl
of Murray, Regent of the kingdom during the young King's minority.
The Queen was forced, from a dread of personal violence, to adhibit
her name to the degrading documents, which stript her of her crown.
Steps were immediately taken to have the young Prince crowned.
Sir James Melville was despatched to Hamilton, where Lords Hamilton,

Fleming, Boyd, and other friends of the Queen were still assembled, to invite them to be present at the coronation, which was to take place on the 29th of July.   They were, of course, astonished to hear of the Queen's abdication, and could scarcely believe that it had occurred ; but, after some consultation, John Hamilton, Archbishop of St Andrews, in reply to Sir James Melville, said, ' We ar beholden to the noble men wha has sent you with that frendly and discret commissioun, and following ther desyre ar redy to concure with them, gif they mak us sufficient securitie of that quhilk ye have said in ther name.   In sa doing they gif us occasion to supose the best of all ther proceadings past and to com ; sa that gif they had maid us foir-sean of ther first enterpryse to the punishment of the mourtheris we suld have tane plane pairt with them.   And wheras now we ar heir convenit, it is not till persew or offend any of them, bot to be vpon our awen gardis, vnderstanding of sa gret a concourse of noblemen, barrons, bourroues, and vthrs subiects.   Not being maid privy to ther enterpryse, we thocht meit to draw us togither till we mycht se whertu thingis wald turn.'

The confederated lords at Hamilton not having received satisfactory assurance of protection, and not approving of the business to be transacted, did not attend the coronation of the infant Prince at Stirling.   In the Castle of Dumbarton, held for the Queen by Lord Fleming, they entered into a bond for the purpose of restoring the Queen to liberty.   The document to which they appended their names commences by stating that they had no freedom of access to her Majesty for transacting their lawful business ; and therefore they bind themselves to use all diligence, and to adopt all reasonable means to set her at liberty, upon such conditions as may be consistent with her honour, the advantage of her kingdom, and the security of her subjects.   In the event of the refusal of the noblemen who had her in custody to open her prison-doors, they declared that they would employ themselves, their kin and friends, their servants and partakers, and their bodies and lives, to put her Highness at liberty, as well as to procure the punishment of the murderer of the King her husband, and the safe preservation of the Prince her son.   They also issued a proclamation from the same place, calling upon all good subjects to be ready on nine hours' warning to take arms for the delivery of the Queen.

Queen Mary, by the aid of William Douglas, a boy of fifteen or sixteen years of age, was at length enabled, on Sunday the 2d May 1568, to escape from Lochleven.   She was received, on landing from the boat that conveyed her ashore, by Lord Seton and a party of his retainers, and conveyed to Niddrie Castle, and next day to Hamilton. Intelligence of her escape soon spread far and wide, and brought large accessions to her ranks, so that in the course of a day or two her troops amounted to 6000 men. A bond was drawn up and signed by nine earls, nine bishops, eighteen lords, twelve abbots and priors, and about a hundred other barons, pledging themselves to protect the Queen and restore her to her rights. Lord Fleming, of course, was among the number of those who signed this bond. Mary's desire was to go with Lord Fleming to the strong Castle of Dumbarton, where she could remain in safety till she saw whether the nation in general would declare in favour of her restoration, or whether it would be necessary for her to abandon her kingdom, and retire once more to France. The Hamiltons being anxious to gain an ascendancy in the management of public affairs, thought that the presence of the Queen was necessary to the accomplishment of their designs, and therefore they detained her several days in the Castle of Draffen. The Earl of Murray had assembled a force of 4000 men at Glasgow, and a request was sent to him by the lords at Hamilton to agree to repone the Queen to her former status at the head of the government; but as he refused to do this, it was resolved to conduct the Queen in a sort of warlike procession to the Castle of Dumbarton on the 13th of May, under the direction of the Duke of Argyle, who had been appointed commander-in-chief of the Queen's forces. The Earl of Murray no sooner learned that the Queen's army was on its march towards Dumbarton, than he crossed the Clyde, and took possession of the little village of Langside, where he advantageously stationed his hagbutters among the cottages, hedges, and gardens that skirted the narrow road along which the Queen's forces were to pass. The Queen's vanguard, 2000 strong, commanded by Lord Claud Hamilton, soon advanced to dispute the passage, and were received by a murderous fire, which they were unable to return with any effect. Though thrown into a state of some confusion by the shower of balls to which they were exposed, yet being confident in the superiority of their numbers, they continued to press up the rising ground on which the village is situated. At this juncture they were charged by Murray's advanced division, consisting chiefly of border pikemen, and then the combat was carried on with the greatest obstinacy and fury. The shock of spears was tremendous; and these weapons from either side were so closely interlaced, that pistols and broken shafts flung on them were prevented from falling to the ground. 'Linked in the serried phalanx tight' the combat raged, till the right wing of the Regent's army, consisting of the barons of Renfrew, began to give way. Kirkcaldy of Grange, to retrieve this disaster, immediately brought up Lochleven, Lindsay, Balfour, and their retainers, and charged the victorious detachment of the Queen's troops with such fury, that they were driven back in their turn. The Regent seized this juncture to make an onset with his main body, and the effect of it was such, that the whole opposing force was chased in irretrievable rout and confusion from the field.

Lord Fleming himself took no part in the battle. Along with

Lords Herries and Livingstone and a small guard, he stood by the Queen's side at a thorn-tree, not far distant from Cathcart Castle, and watched the progress of the fight with breathless anxiety and suspense. When that small party saw that their hopes were blasted and their designs frustrated by the victory of the Regent, they lost no time in placing the Queen on horseback, and conveying her by a circuitous route through Ayrshire, Nithsdale, and Galloway, to the Abbey of Dundrennan. Mary, in a letter written to her uncle, the Cardinal Lorraine, during this journey, which lasted two days, states, 'I have suffered injuries, calumnies, hunger, cold, and heat; flying, without knowing whither, fourscore and twelve miles, without once pausing to alight; and then lay on the hard ground, having only sour milk to drink, and oatmeal to eat, without bread, passing three nights with the owls.' In the Abbey of Dundrennan she sat in council with her friends for the last time; and here she intimated her intention to proceed to England, and throw herself on the protection of Queen Elizabeth. Lord Fleming, Lord Herries, the Archbishop of St Andrews, and others who were present, implored her to abandon this design, and to put no faith in the specious promises and pretences of the English Queen. Finding her deaf to their remonstrances, they prevailed on her to sign an instrument exonerating them from all approval of, or complicity in, the step on which she had resolved. A boat was then procured, and the Queen, accompanied by Lords Fleming, Boyd, Livingstone, and others, amounting in all to sixteen persons, crossed the Solway Firth, and landed at Workington, a small town on the coast of Cumberland. She there surrendered herself to the English Deputy Warden, named Lowther, who assigned her a residence in the Castle of Carlisle, till such time as he should receive instructions from Elizabeth regarding her further disposal. Lords Fleming and Herries hastened up to the English court, with the view of entering into arrangements for the Queen's proper accommodation; but their mission was unsuccessful, and Mary was shortly afterwards removed to Bolton Castle in Yorkshire, where she was placed in the strictest confinement. Here, however, she found means to carry on a correspondence with her friends in Scotland, and, among others, with Lord Fleming. In a letter, dated 'Off Bowtoune, the 27th of September 1568,' and addressed to the Archbishop of St Andrews, she says, 'We haif vritten in ciphere to my Lord Flemyng, quha will mak zou participant therof.' We cannot find, however, that any of her letters to Lord Fleming have been preserved.

Lord John Fleming, after returning from London, was despatched by Queen Mary to the French court, to explain the late events in her history, to vindicate her character, and ask for advice and assistance. On the 24th of August 1568, most likely before his return from France, he and his relative, John Fleming of Boghall, were summoned to present themselves before Parliament and answer for their late conduct in supporting the Queen. Having failed to appear, their estates were liable to be forfeited; but at the request of the Regent, who in this case is said to have acted on the advice of Queen Elizabeth, it was agreed that the sentence of forfeiture should for a short time be suspended, in order that they might have a fair opportunity to acknowledge their faults, and be reconciled to Queen Mary's successor, her son James.

The Regent Murray, in order to justify his conduct in taking up arms against the Queen, publicly charged her with being accessory to the death of her husband Darnley. On this account, Queen Elizabeth refused to hold an interview with her until she could exonerate herself from this charge. Elizabeth's object was to obtain a plea to be constituted judge in a cause so important as a dispute between the Queen of Scotland and her subjects. She had no right to put the Scottish Queen on her trial for this or any other offence; but Mary, confident in her innocence, and acting under due protest, accepted the tribunal. Commissioners from both sides were thereupon appointed to meet at York in October 1568, and thither Mary sent Lords Fleming and Herries, the Bishop of Ross, and other able friends, to act in her defence. It was on this occasion that the Earl of Murray, in order to give a tangible proof of Queen Mary's guilt, produced the famous letters and sonnets which, it was alleged, had passed between the Queen and Bothwell, and had been taken from a servant of that nobleman's called Dalgleish. The investigation was carried on for five months; and Elizabeth, in the end, dismissed the Commissioners, declaring that the criminal charge against Queen Mary had not been proved.

Lord Fleming, after this period, took up his abode in Dumbarton Castle, of which he still continued to be Governor. The Master of Graham was several times sent to the Castle for the purpose of persuading him to surrender it to the Regent; but he obstinately persisted in rejecting all overtures on the subject. The Regent, therefore, invested it with a considerable force, and as any attempt to carry it by assault was considered hopeless, the siege was turned into a blockade; and on the 18th of November 1569, 'sentence of foirfaltour wes pronouncit aganis Lord John Fleming, and John Fleming of Boghall, for the keiping and halding the Castel of Dumbartane aganis the Kingis majestie.' This sentence was confirmed by the Scottish Parliament in 1571; and the Act then passed, among other things, states, 'And thairfoir decernis and ordanis all and sundrie ye landis, guidis, movable and vnmovable, alsweill landis as offices, and vther thingis quhatsomever pertening to thame and euerye ane of thame, to be confiscatt to our sourane lord, and to remane in propertie w^t his heynes for ewir. And thair persones to underlye ye panes of tressone extreme and just puncisment distinatt of ye lawes of yis Realme. Quhilk dome wes pronouncit be ye mowth of Andro Lindsay, dempstar of ye said Parliament.' The estate of Biggar, and the other estates of Lord Fleming, by this sentence were transferred to the Crown, and were held by it for eight years.

The garrison of Dumbarton began, ere long, to be straitened for want of provisions; but early on the morning of the 15th December, the Laird of Borg, taking advantage of the darkness that prevailed, and the want of vigilance on the part of the blockading force, succeeded in conveying into the Castle several 'ky' and 'laides of meill,' greatly to the satisfaction of the Governor and his men, but vastly to the displeasure of the Regent, who sharply rebuked his captains and men of war that they 'tholit the said furnischings to pas to ye Castel.' The Regent made various efforts to induce Lord Fleming to surrender the Castle during the month of January 1569–70; but intelligence having reached his Lordship that Thomas Fleming, a brother of the Laird of Boghall, had arrived in Lochryan from France, with two large ships laden with provisions and military stores for the use of the garrison, he refused to hold any further parley on the subject. The Regent, baffled in obtaining the object of his desire, left Dumbarton, and, in a few days afterwards, was shot at Linlithgow by Hamilton of Bothwellhaugh. The besiegers, so soon as they received intelligence of the Regent's death, broke up the blockade and retired to Stirling. In a few days afterwards, Thomas Fleming arrived at Dumbarton with his ships, and transferred the whole stores to the fortress without molestation. The Earl of Argyle, several of the Hamiltons, and other adherents of the Queen, repaired to the Castle, and held a conference with Lord Fleming on the posture of public affairs, consequent on the death of the Regent.

Queen Elizabeth, at the instigation of the King's faction, sent an army at this juncture into Scotland, under the command of Sir William Dury, which, during the spring of 1570, committed great havoc in Clydesdale on the estates of the adherents of the Queen. The devastation at Hamilton was such as had hardly ever been paralleled in Scotland before, and the ruthless soldiery 'herrit all the Monkland—my Lord Fleming's boundis, my Lord Livingstone's boundis, together with al their puir tennantis and freindis, in sic maner that nae heart can think theron bot the same must be dolorous.' Sir William, after perpetrating these enormities, had the audacity to repair to Dumbarton in the month of May, and request a parley with the Governor respecting the Archbishop of St Andrews, who had taken refuge in the fortress. Lord Fleming, justly enraged at the outrages which Sir William had committed, saluted him with a bullet discharged from one of the great guns on the ramparts. This was considered a grievous outrage by the King's party, and gave rise to a ballad, entitled 'The Tresson of Dumbartane,' which was printed in black letter, at Edinburgh, by Robert Lekpreuik, in 1570. The first verse of it is as follows:—

'In Mayis moneth, mening na dispute,
Quhen luffaris dois thair dailie obseruance
To Venus Quene, the goddes of delyte,
The fyftene day, befell the samen chance.'

After the death of the Earl of Murray, the Earl of Lennox was
chosen Regent. This nobleman manifested great anxiety to obtain
possession of the Castle of Dumbarton, as a rumour prevailed that
Lord Fleming intended to deliver it to the French. He craved assistance from England, in order that he might besiege it in due form;
and Queen Elizabeth sent an armament by sea, for the ostensible
purpose of furthering the designs of the Regent, but the real policy
of that monarch was to crush neither of the two factions into which
Scotland was divided, but allow them to weaken each other by continued quarrels and outrages. It does not therefore appear that the
English force ever invested the Castle. Indeed, Elizabeth became of
opinion that the Queen's party had been rather too much weakened
already; and therefore her lieutenant, the Earl of Sussex, caused the
Regent to give an assurance that he would, at least for a time, abstain
from inflicting any further outrages on his opponents. The Regent,
nevertheless, in violation of this compact, despatched a strong detachment of men to Biggar, and, according to the testimony of Richard
Bannatyne, the secretary of John Knox, who wrote a Journal of the
Transactions of Scotland from 1570 to 1573, they committed great
enormities; and as the estates of Lord Fleming had been forfeited,
they compelled the tenants in the Barony of Biggar, as well as in
Thankerton and Glenholm, to pay large contributions under the name
of the mails and rents of their lands. From Biggar they went to
Cumbernauld, and perpetrated similar outrages, besides destroying
the deer in the forest of that barony, 'and the quhit ky and bullis of
the said forrest, to the gryt distructione of polecie and hinder of the
commanweill.'

CHAPTER XXVI.

Historical Sketches of the Fleming Family—*Continued.*

THE Castle of Dumbarton, situated on a lofty and precipitous rock, and nearly surrounded by the Firth of Clyde, was in early times deemed impregnable. The use of battering artillery, at the time of which we are now speaking, 1571, was as yet but little known, and a blockade seemed unavailing, after the abundant supplies which the garrison had recently obtained from France. Captain Thomas Crawford of Jordanhill, a keen partisan of the Regent Lennox, was therefore entrusted with the apparently desperate enterprise of taking the Castle by escalade, during the darkness of night. He called to his aid the Laird of Drumwhassal, a skilful and intrepid soldier, and several other men of known courage, particularly a person of the name of Robertson, who at one time had been a member of the garrison, and was intimately acquainted with the fortifications and acclivities of the rock. The party assembled at Glasgow on the 2d of April 1571, and provided themselves with 'ledderis, coardis, crawes,' and other necessary implements, and despatched a few of their number to stop all travellers to the west, so that no intelligence of the intended enterprise might be conveyed to the Governor, Lord Fleming. Having appointed the Hill of Dumbeck, within a mile of Dumbarton, as the general rendezvous, they set out by different routes about an hour before sunset, and it was past midnight before they reached the foot of the rock. 'The geat with the gilteane horn,' as Richard Bannatyne styles Lord Fleming, and the other inmates of the Castle, with exception of a warder or two, had retired to rest, undisturbed by a single apprehension of an attack, and confident in the protection afforded by the crags and walls by which they were surrounded. A thick mist had by this time enveloped the top of the rock, and tended still more to conceal the operations of the party below. The 'crawes' were then thrown against the rock, and the soldiers began to ascend the ladders, when the whole gave way, and came to the ground with great noise and violence. Had the sentinels on the walls not been asleep, or utterly inattentive to their duty, the party must have been discovered, and their enterprise defeated. They eagerly listened for a time; but all being still, they made another attempt, and with greater success. Some of the soldiers landed on a shelving part of the rock, where an ash-tree sprung from

2 T

the crevices, and, by attaching ropes to it, they were able to render very effective aid to their companions below. They had now reached the middle of the ascent; but the most difficult part still remained, and the ruddy streaks of dawn began to appear in the east. They fixed the ladders once more; but an incident now occurred, which seemed likely to defeat the whole design. One of the soldiers, while climbing a ladder, overcome most likely by terror, was seized with a fit, and clung to the steps with such tenacity, that he could not be disengaged; but the self-possession and fertile mind of Crawford soon removed the obstruction by causing the man to be tied to the ladder, and turning it upside down. In a short time the whole assailants were at the foot of the walls, which were old and ruinous, and offered no great obstruction. They were now descried by the warders, who gave the alarm, and the inmates at once sprung out of bed, and rushed forth in bewilderment, without taking time to supply themselves either with clothes or arms. The assailants, having torn down a part of the wall, entered at the same time, and beating a drum, and shouting 'A Darnley, a Darnley!' fell upon the disordered and amazed garrison. Three or four of them were killed on the spot. Lord Fleming and several of his retainers hurried down a passage in the rock, and finding a boat, escaped to Argyleshire; while Lady Fleming, John Fleming of Boghall, John Hamilton, the Archbishop of St Andrews, Verac, the French ambassador, John Hall, an Englishman, and the rest, were made prisoners. Next day, at ten o'clock, the Regent Lennox arrived at the Castle, and showed Lady Fleming very great kindness and attention. He gave her liberty to depart, and take with her all her clothes, jewels, and silver plate. In the Castle were found a large quantity of war-like stores, twenty tuns of wine, twelve chalders of meal, ten bolls of wheat, eight bolls of malt, eight hogsheads of biscuit, and four puncheons of bacon. Lord Fleming found means to escape to France, the Archbishop of St Andrews was beheaded and quartered at Stirling, and John Fleming of Boghall was sent to the Castle of Blackness.

Lord Fleming returned from France on the 28th of May 1572, and brought with him a considerable sum of money, of which the adherents of the Queen stood very much in need. He landed in Galloway, and was met by Lord Herries, the Laird of Lochinvar, and others, who most likely escorted him to Biggar. On the 26th day of June, he arrived in Edinburgh at the head of a detachment of thirty horsemen, and took up his residence in the Castle, then held for the Queen by that stout warrior Sir William Kirkaldy of Grange. A few days afterwards, a party of twelve or fifteen French soldiers, who had been taken in a ship of war, and forced to serve in the King's army against their will, came up from Leith. Their design very likely was to desert the King's service, and to take refuge in the Castle. When they arrived at the Tolbooth, they were either opposed by another party, or were overjoyed to see Lord Fleming, whom they seem to have known, and

who is said to have been the cause of their leaving their quarters in
Leith. At all events, they fired a volley, and one of the balls re-
bounding from the causeway, struck his Lordship and wounded him
in a most serious manner. The author of the 'Diurnal of Remarkable
Occurrents' says that the gun by which his Lordship was wounded,
was only charged with powder and paper, and that the firing of it
caused 'the skalpis of the stanis' to fly up and hurt his Lordship in
the legs; but this statement is very improbable, as the mere concus-
sion of the shot was not very likely to split the stones on the street, and
make them fly up with such force as to inflict a deadly wound. His
Lordship was carried back to the Castle, where he remained till the
beginning of September. 'The sext of September,' to use the words
of Richard Bannatyne, 'the Lord Flemyng, wha wes hurt be the
Frenchemen which befoir staw out of Leyth, and that by his specialle
doingis and meanis, departit this lyfe in Biggar, where he wes careit
in ane litter furth of the Castell of Edinburgh; which litter not being
able to go furth at the Castell yeat, vntill the portcullious were raisit,
and liftit vp hier, which beand rasit vp, fele doun to the ground agane,
and pairt of a spelch therof fleing of, hurt Harie Balfour in the heid,
wha efter he had lyne a 10 or 11 dayis, deid the xi of September.
And so thair twa have gottin thare rewarde. God gif it be his pleasour
that that throw his judgments may be a warning to the rest to bring
tham to repentance; but *consuetudo mali est indelibilis.*'

Lord Fleming, by his wife Elizabeth, daughter and sole heiress of
Robert, Master of Ross, left a son, John, and three daughters, Mary,
Elizabeth, and Margaret.

Lady Fleming only survived her husband two or three years. At
her death she left a Will, still preserved, in which she appointed her
son John, her brother-in-law, John Earl of Athole, and her brother,
Thomas Scott of Abbotshall, her executors. It was in virtue of this
arrangement that John Fleming, styled 'Captain of Biggar,' on the
25th and 26th October 1578, delivered an inventory of the 'siluer
wark and garments, and vyer thingis' that pertained to the deceased
lady, to John Earl of Athole. As this inventory is remarkably curious,
and as the articles were most likely kept in Boghall Castle, we give
a copy in the original orthography :—

'In ye first xxvii dosoun viij pair and ane horne of gold Item sax
grit buttounis four ringis all of gold Tua crimter paciss of leid ane
for ane grit chinze and ane uyir for ane small qlk ar in michael gil-
bertis handis Item in ane buffet ane siluer lawar Tua siluer caupis
ane saltfalt ane luggit deiche Tua chandeleris ane dosane of truncheris
ane dosane of spunis sax caruig prikis Item mae of siluer wark Tua
coupis ane basin ane brokin saltfalt gilt elevin spunis Item ane ryding
clok ane skirt of blak begayrit wᵗ welnot Tua harnisingis The ane of
welnot pasmentit and wrocht wᵗ gold And ye uyir of blak welnot
plane Sevin pair of welnot schone This geir aboue writte is put in ane

coffer Item ane chapell ruif of reid skarlat cuttit out upoun quhit
satene & taffitie freinzeit w^t reid and quhit silk aucht tappis of beddis
of trie & gilt ane pein of purpour welnot freinzeit w^t blak and reid
silk ane round ruiff of blak satene bordourit w^t blak silk and freinzeit
w^t blak silk ane ruiff of gray dalmes pasmentit w^t gold ane blak silk
fur curtingis of gray dalmes for ye said ruif and thre bandis to y^e
beddis stuipis ane bairnis coit vnslevit of siluer & fugeirrit welnot ane
ruiff of ane bed of grene reid and zallow dalmes and thre curtingis to
ye samyne ane collat of gray must welnot pasmentit w^t siluer and
gold ane clok of blak dalmes w^t ane collat wärrit w^t welnot ane mat
of grene reid and zallow taffitie Tua collattis sewit of holene clay^t ane
w^t blak silk and ane uy reid Tua sarkis of holene clay^t ane sewit reid
and ane uyir blak Tua pokis w^t missiue writingis This geir forsaid put
in ane coffer Item ane harnising of blak welnot ane ruiff of ane bed of
purpour welnot borderit w^t siluer Thre curtingis of dalmes fussit w^t
siluer and silk ane pend of purpour welnot pasmentit w^t siluer four
stuipis of ye same pasmentit w^t siluer ane fute mantill of blak welnot
of my ladeis, ane goun of blak welnot w^t ye bodie w^{t}out slaues ane
cap clok of blak welnot pasmentit w^t silk ane almay clok of blak welnot freinzeit w^t blak silk and lynit w^t taffitie ane goun of quhit satein
w^t ane bodie but slaues pasmentit w^t clay^t of gold ane goun of cramosie welnot w^t ane bodie but slaues pasmentit w^t gold and siluer
ane skirt and slaues of clay^t of gold raisit ane skirt of clay^t of gold
and slaues raisit upoun cramosie satein ane ruiff of ane bed of quhit
dalmes freinzeit w^t quhit silk ane cap clok of purpour welnot pasmentit w^t gold and reid silk ane pair of breikis of purpour welnot but
schankis pasmentit w^t gold and reid silk ane coit of purpour welnot
pasmentit w^t gold and silk ane alman clok of blak satein barrit w^t
blak welnot and skirtit w^t matrikis ane uy alman clok of dalmes barrit
w^t welnot and skirtit w^t matrikis ane skirt of satein cuttit out in
doggrane sevin ourlaweris of sarkis w^t ye handis wro^t w^t gold silver
& silk This geir put in ye maist coffer ane burd clay^t of dornik of
dalmes champ w^t ane cupbur^t clay^t of ye same sax saruietis of ye
same champ uthir four burd clay^{ts} of dornik champit w^t ane copburd
clay^t of ye same seven towellis of dornik ane uyir burd clay^t of dornik
ane dosane saruietis of dornik Thre linnig burd clay^{ts} auchtene
saruietis of linnig spelnzeit w^t blew fyve wasching towellis speinzeit
w^t blew ane auld copburd of clay^t about ye rest ane auld furrin of
toddis This geir put up in ane uy coffer Item be ye cofferis ane kame
caiss and ane auld kimig clay^t about ye same ane blak buist w^t drawin
schottulis Twa cheiris ye ane. couerit w^t purpour welnot and ye uy
w^t gray fyve stuillis couerit w^t purpour welnot.

   'We Johnne erle of Athole chancellar of Scotland, &c. Be yir pntis
      grantis y^t Johnne flemig capitane of biggar hes deliuerit to us
      The haill guidis geir claithing and jewellis above specifat con-
      tenit in yis pnt Inventar qlk ye said Johnne had in keiping qlk

ptenit to Umq^{le} dame eli^t ross lady fiemig and we grant us to
have resauit ye same to be keipit be us to ye utilitie and proffeit
of ye said dame eli^{ts} bairnis [*Herefor we be yir pntis discharge
ye said Johnne flemig his airis excuturis and aasignais yairof
And we bind and obless us To warrand releiff and keip skaithles
him and his foirsaidis of ye same at ye handis of quhatsumever
persounis havand or pretentand to haif interes yairto for euer
and euer] Be yir pnts subscrivit w^t o^r hand in Edibrugh y^e
xxviii day of october the zeir of god (jav&^{o}.) thre scoir auchtene
zeiris.

'ERLL OF ATHOLL.'

John Fleming, at his father's death, was only four years of age.
In an account of the state of the Scottish nobility, published in 1583,
it is stated that he was, at that time, a youth in the fifteenth year of
his age, that his income was small, and that he was involved in debt
and trouble, in consequence of the efforts which his father had made
in upholding the cause of Queen Mary, and particularly in defending
and maintaining the Castle of Dumbarton. A great part of this
embarrassment was, no doubt, attributable to the forfeiture of the
family estates, by virtue of which their revenues were engrossed
either by the Crown, or by some of the partisans of the opposite faction. The Regent Lennox was graciously pleased to allow Lady
Fleming, after the capture of Dumbarton Castle, to occupy a portion
of her husband's lands; but this would likely be barely sufficient for
the maintenance of herself and her infant family. An Act was passed
by the Scottish Parliament in 1579, 'Restorand, rehabilitand, and
makand the said John (Fleming), lauchful to enter be brevis to the
landis and heretaige sumtyme pertaining to his said vmquhile father,
as gif he had deit at our soveran Lordis fayth and peace.' The following reservation made in this Act, was no doubt attributable to the
Earl of Morton, then Regent, and the most powerful man in the kingdom:—viz., that 'ye heritable dispositioun of ze landis of Edmestoun
to James Earle of Morton, Lord of Dalkeith, &c., nor the soume con-
signit be him for the redemptioun of the landis and barony of Kilbocho
and disponit to him by reason of escheat, &c., be not comprehendit
under this Act of present pacificatioun and restitution.' Immediately
on the execution of the Regent Morton in 1581, the Parliament decided that the clause regarding the lands of Edmonston should be
reversed. 'Sua that ye said Johne, now Lord Fleming, may bruik
and jois the saidis landis of Edmiston, conforme to his predicessouris
infeftmentis.' Archibald, Earl of Angus, as Morton's heir, laid claim
to the lands and barony of Kilbucho, that belonged to Lord Fleming.

* In the original, the words inserted within brackets are crossed with a pen, probably before signing. The place of signature, and day of the month, are in the
handwriting of the Earl of Athol.

Angus' claim was brought before Parliament in 1587, and it was decided that the matter in dispute should be settled by arbitration. The parties agreeing to this mode of adjustment, Lord John Fleming chose the Earl of Montrose and Sir John Maitland of Thirlestane on his side, and the Earl of Angus chose the Earl of Mar and the Master of Glamis on his. The decision seems to have been in favour of the Earl of Angus; for his descendants in 1641 disposed of the estate to John Dickson of Hartree, servitor to Alexander Gibson, younger of Durie.

At this same period, great feuds, as usual, prevailed among the nobility of Scotland, and kept the country in a state of constant turmoil and disorder. James VI., who was a rare compound of silliness and ability, of folly and sagacity, on the 14th of May 1587, assembled all the nobles at Holyrood, and exhorting them to give up their animosities, and to lead peaceable lives, caused them to join hands, and to walk two by two to the Cross of Edinburgh, where a grand collation of bread, wine, and sweetmeats had been provided. Amid salvoes of artillery, and the jubilant demonstrations of the inhabitants, he drank their healths, and wished that they might long enjoy happiness and peace. On the 13th of July following, an incident occurred at the opening of Parliament, which showed that the efforts of the King to establish concord had been of little avail. We give this incident in the words of the venerable historian, David Moysie:—'The Parliament,' says he, 'beguid the xiij day of the monethe of Julij, quhair his Majestie accompanied with his nobilitie red to the tolbuithe of Edinburgh. Bot befoir his vnlooping thaire arrose ane heiche contentioun betuix the erles of Crafurde and Bothuell, the lordis Fleming, Settoun, Home, and Innermeithe, anent thaire woites. The Counsell sat thairvpone, and fand that the erle of Crafurde sould have the prioritie of woite, and that the lord Flemyng sould have the woite afoir the rest of the lordis. Quhairvpone the Lord Home challendgit the lord Flemyng with the singular combat, quho wer not suffered to fecht, albeit they were baith weill willing.'

In the month of May 1590, the King brought home his bride, Ann of Denmark, to Leith, and lodged her in the house of Thomas Lindsay. Here the King took all the Danish nobles who had accompanied the Queen, one after another, by the hand, and gave them a gracious welcome to Scotland. Shortly afterwards the King and Queen repaired to church, to give thanks for their safe voyage; and there they were met by Lords Fleming and Hamilton, who escorted them into the place of worship, and sat beside them while Patrick Galloway preached a sermon. In six days afterwards, the Queen was conducted in state to the Palace of Holyrood, amid great manifestations of joy.

Lord Fleming was a great favourite of James VI., and received from him many tokens of his respect. In the beginning of the year 1595, as we have already stated, the King paid his Lordship a visit at his Castle of Boghall, where he remained several days, and enjoyed the sport of hawking.

After James ascended the English throne, Lord Fleming was one of the Scottish noblemen who were permitted to visit the court in London. He was appointed one of the members of the Scottish Council that sat in the English capital; and it was in virtue of this office that he was admitted to the presence chamber in 1607, when the King gave audience to the eight clergymen whom he had summoned from Scotland to confer with him on the state of the Scottish Church, at that time greatly disturbed by his controlling the freedom of the General Assembly, and appointing bishops as rulers in the Church. The prelates, who formed part of the delegation, of course readily came into the King's measures; but the inferior clergy, represented by the venerable Andrew Melville and his nephew James, would not renounce their opinions, or give up their opposition, and the consequence was, that in violation of everything like honour and justice, they were condemned to perpetual exile.

The King, to mark his appreciation of Lord Fleming's services and attachment to the throne, created him Earl of Wigton, Lord Fleming of Biggar and Cumbernauld, by letters patent, dated at Whitehall 19th March 1606. This dignity was 'to last and continue' to him, and his heirs male of lawful and lineal descent, in all time to come. Lord Fleming, in presence of a number of Scottish barons assembled at Perth on the 1st of July following, delivered the warrant for this honour, under the sign-manual, to the Earl of Montrose, his Majesty's Commissioner, and received investiture in due and ancient form. In the first place, his banner was displayed, and he himself was brought forward attired in his appropriate robes, and supported by two noblemen; and then, after the ceremony of 'belting,' or girding his person with a sword, the heralds, with a flare of trumpets, proclaimed his new style and titles.

The Roman Catholics in the north of Scotland, under the direction of the Earls of Huntly, Angus, and Errol, had, in the early part of 1608, shown considerable dissatisfaction, and a disposition to disturb the peace of the realm. A General Assembly was therefore convened at Linlithgow in the month of July of that year, by the King's command, at which several strong resolutions were passed against them, and a committee appointed to lay a petition before his Majesty, praying for the enforcement of the laws against Popery. The Earl of Wigton was chosen a member of this committee; and the King, in reply to the petition drawn up and presented by the Earl and his colleagues, said that he 'would give order for a Convention of Estates, which should ratifie the conclusions of the Assembly, assuring them that the Church, keeping that course, should never lack his patrociny and protection.' On the 24th of November, James wrote the following letter to the Earl in reference to these ecclesiastical proceedings:—

' James R.

            Right trusty and well-beloved Cosen, wee greete you well.
The reporte made to us by the Commissioners of the late generall assembly
of the procedingis therin, and of the greate zeale and affection kythed in
all sortes of people there, for the advancement of God's glory, and the suppressing of the common enemy, and also of the happie unity and concorde
amongst the clergy, did give us no small joy and contentment, that in this
last age of the worlde, wherein errour and superstition abroade had taken
so greate rooting, nevertheless, within these our dominions, God hath bene
pleased to reserve a handfull to him selfe, who have never bowed the knee
to Baal. And as wee acknowledge our selfe (in dewty to our God) bound
to be a nursing father to his churche, a protectour to all true professours,
and a prosequutour of all the enemyes of the treuth, so they may be eyther
reclamed, or then brought to that case as they may be no more feared (since
all those who are affected to this Romish superstition may justly be suspected
as daungerous subjectes in the estate), so for the better countenauncing of
the procedingis of the general assembly, wee have appoynted a convention
of the estates of that our kingdome to mete at Edinburgh, the **xxvj** of
Januarie nexte, to the entent that such thinges as may farder the advauncement of the gospell, and suppressing of the enemy, may be then treated of,
advised, and concluded, wherein there shall be no want eyther of our good
wille, power, or authority ; desiring you hereby to be present thereat, and
to utter your loving care and affection to the wele of that Churche. And
because wee have appoynted a preceding meeting of some selected oute of
every estate, to be at the same place the **xxiiij** of Januarie before, and
having made choice of you for one of that nomber, wee desire you also both
to keepe the time appoynted, and to kyth still as yee have done heretofore
affectioned, to the advauncement of the religion presentie profest, wherin
ye shall do us acceptable service ; and so bid you farewell. From our
Courte at Newmarket, the 24th November 1608.
    ' To our right trusty and well-beloved Cosen,
            The Earle of Wigtoun.'

      Several other letters, addressed by James VI. to the Earl of Wigton,
have been preserved by the family. They, among other things, declare, that the King had special confidence in the Earl's 'affection to
the advancement of religion and good estate of the cuntrie,' and therefore call on him to attend certain meetings of Parliament and of the
General Assembly, which had been summoned by the King, to adopt
measures, among other things, for 'hinderance of the encreas of Poperie.'
The King was not content with the meetings and deliberations of the
Scottish nobility regarding religious matters ; but, as is shown by a
document addressed to John Lord Fleming, he issued an edict in 1619,
calling upon the whole members of his Privy Council in Scotland to
repair to Edinburgh, 'and upon pashe day to convene at the heich
Kirk of Edinburgh, and thair to ressave the communioun, efter the
maner prescryvit by the ordoure and actis of the last generall assem-

blie, assureing thame that sal refuise to do the same, that they salbe deposit from thair placeis in counsall, as unworthie of the trust quhilk his Maiestie hes reposit in thame, by advanceing thame to sa heich a rowme.'

It appears that the Earl of Wigton, when frequenting the court at Whitehall, not only presented petitions to his Majesty from others, but that, like Richie Moniplies, he sometimes embraced an opportunity of slipping into the royal hand 'a sifflication' of his own. We have an instance of this in 1613. The Fleming family, at one time, were patrons of the Church of Stobo,* which had four pendicles or chapels, viz., Dawick, Drummelzier,† Broughton, and Glenholm. It is likely that they had also a right to appoint the vicars to these chapels, at least to Drummelzier and Glenholm, in which they had large possessions. At the Reformation, the rights of the Flemings in these respects had been disturbed, and the Earl of Wigton, of whom we now speak, had received a right to the patronage of the Church of Glenholm from his present Majesty, and had also given to the titular a large sum to secure his consent. The right of the Earl was, however, disputed by one John Gib, who attempted to establish his claim by an appeal to the legal tribunals of the country. The Earl presented a petition to the King regarding this matter, when he was at court; and he now addressed the following letter to his Majesty on the same subject :—

'Most Gratious and Dread Sourane,

At my laite being at your Heighnes Courte, the petitioun preferred by me for the Kirk of Glenquhome was gratiously acceptit by your Maistie, the samen Kirk being formerly giftit by your Heighnes to me, whiche nocht the less in purchessing the Titular's consent to the samen did stand me at no less rate than ten thousand poundis Scottis, as I did particularly signifie to your Maiestie, who then out of your Heighnes most gratious and bountifull dispositioun, pleased to promeis that efter a course sould be tane for securing wnto me the Patronage of that Kirk, acquyred by me at so deir a pryce, or then sufficient satisfactioun and recompence sould be gewen me for the samen. And now seing John Gib hathe of lait trovblit me with pursuite in the law, and heathe recovred decreit aganes me, I will most humblye intreat your Maistie to be pleased, according to your Heighnes promeis, that said Kirk, without farder trowble, be in my peaceble enjoying thairof, or dew recompance and satisfactioun be gewen to me for the samin. Thus humble crawing pardon for my bauldnes, and praying Almychtie God to encres your Maistie's happynes with long and happie regne ower ws and blissitnes elswheir, I taik my lief, and, as I am most bound, sall euir remane your Maistie's most humble serwand and subiect,

WIGTOUN.

Cummbernald, the 6ᵗʰ Oct. 1613.

To the King's his Most Excellent Maiestie.'

* Pennecuik's Description of Tweeddale.

† Drummelzier, in former times, included the present parish of Tweedsmuir. which was called Upper Drummelzier.

2 U

We are not aware how this dispute was settled. It is certain that the Flemings claimed, and perhaps exercised, the patronage of the other Tweeddale churches down to the close of the seventeenth century.

Lord Fleming married Lady Lillias Graham, a daughter of John, Earl of Montrose. Her Ladyship was distinguished for her piety and devotion, and her zealous efforts to promote the principles of the Reformation. Livingstone, in his 'Characteristics,' says of her, 'When I was a child, I have often seen her at my father's, at the preachings and communions. While dressing, she read the Bible, and every day, at that time, shed more tears (said one) than ever I did in my life.' The distinguished John Welch, son-in-law of John Knox, in 1605, addressed a lengthened epistle to her from the Castle of Blackness, in which he was imprisoned for attempting to hold meetings of the General Assembly, in opposition to the edicts of James VI. In this document, which has been printed, he expresses the consolations which he experienced in the midst of his sufferings; refers to the calamities which he anticipated would fall on his native country; vindicates the views which he held with regard to Church government, views which had led to his condemnation and imprisonment as a traitor; and declares his readiness 'to be offered up as a sacrifice' for the precious truths which he had maintained. The gist of his opinions on ecclesiastical polity, he says, was contained in the two propositions—that Christ is the Head of the Church; and that the Church is free in her government from all other jurisdiction except Christ's, yea, as free as any kingdom under heaven, not only to convocate, hold, and keep her meetings, conventions, and assemblies, but also to judge in all her affairs among her members and subjects. Such propositions as these, in the opinion of the King, were rank heresies. He maintained that no Assembly of the Kirk could be held without his authority, and under his special control; and, in the end, he came to be of opinion, that the deliberations of the Kirk should be altogether suppressed, as inconsistent with kingly power and prerogative. Lady Fleming, no doubt, held the views of Welch in regard to Church government; while her husband, although remaining an adherent of the Kirk of Scotland, appears to have countenanced the repressive measures of the King. The following entry in the Records of the Presbytery of Glasgow, under date 13th July 1596, shows that he was somewhat remiss in his attendance on religious ordinances in his Parish Church: —'The Presbyterie understanding that the absence of my Lord Fleming fra the Kirk of Lenzie upon the Sonday, his Lordship being then at Cumernald, within the bounds of Presbyterie, is the motive and great occasioune of moving his tennants, being parochiners of Lenzie, to byd away fra the Kirk to heir Godis word prechit on Sondaye, thairfore the Presbyterie ordenis Mr Niniane Drewe, person now present, ordinar minister of Lenzie, to summond the said Lord Fleming, how sone his Lordship cummis in Cumernald, to compeir befoir ye said Presbyterie to answer for his absence fra the said Kirk, and to sik wther thingis as the said Presbyterie sal happin to have to laye to his charge.'

The Earl died in April 1619, leaving three sons and five daughters, and was succeeded by his eldest son John, who warmly embraced his mother's ecclesiastical opinions, and was as zealous in the cause of Presbyterianism as his forefathers had been in the maintenance of Popery. He married Margaret, daughter of Alexander Livingston, first Earl of Linlithgow, a lady of amiable disposition and great piety, who entered cordially into the religious views and schemes of her husband. They not only attended the ministrations of the settled Protestant clergy, but for some time maintained a chaplain in their own family. The person who acted in this capacity was John Livingstone, a son of the Rev. William Livingstone, a distant relative of the Countess of Wigton, who was first settled at Monyabrock, and afterwards at Lanark. His father wished him to marry and settle on some lands which he had purchased in his former parish of Monyabrock, but young Livingstone's inclinations were altogether in favour of devoting himself to the work of the ministry. 'Now being in straits,' he says in his autobiography, 'I resolved I would spend one day before God my alone, and knowing of ane secret cave in the south side of Mouse Water, a little above the house of Jerviswood, over against Cleghorn Wood, I went thither, and after many too's and fro's, and much confusion and fear anent the state of my soul, I thought it was made out to me that I behoved to preach Jesus Christ, which if I did not, I should have no assurance of salvation.'

Mr Livingstone began to preach in January 1625, and for some time was employed in occasional ministrations in the pulpits of the neighbouring parishes, and in that of Biggar, no doubt, among the rest. His practice, he says, was to write out his sermons at length, and commit them to memory; but he was led to abandon this practice by an incident which took place at Quothquan. He had agreed to deliver a sermon at that place, on a Sunday after the communion; but he came with only one discourse in readiness, and he had preached it a short time before in the church of an adjoining parish. He observed in the early part of the day that a number of the worshippers at Quothquan had been his hearers in the church referred to, and, therefore, feeling reluctant to preach before them the same discourse, he, before ascending the pulpit in the afternoon, selected a new text, and merely noted some heads of the subject on which he proposed to enlarge. He says that he found more assistance in discoursing on these points, and more emotion in his heart than he had ever felt before, and so from that time he never wrote his sermons at full length.

In the autumn of 1626 he went, by desire of Lord Torphichen, to

Mid-Calder, and officiated as the assistant of the aged incumbent of
that charge. At the death of this official, which took place soon
afterwards, considerable exertions were made to get Mr Livingstone
appointed his successor; but this object was defeated by the bishops,
to whom he was obnoxious. He resolved to go back to his father's
house at Lanark, but before doing so, paid a visit to his uncle, William
Livingstone, at Falkirk; and here he received a letter from the Countess
of Wigton requesting him to come and see her mother, Eleanor,
Countess of Linlithgow, then on her death-bed. He complied with this
request, and the Earl and Countess of Wigton proposed, that as their
house of Cumbernauld was somewhat distant from the Parish Church,
he should reside with them, and in winter preach in the hall to their
household and such of their tenants as chose to attend. · He remained
in this situation two years and a half. The Fleming family treated
Livingstone with great respect. In 1635, when he was married by
his father in the West Kirk of Edinburgh to a daughter of Bartholo-
mew Fleming, a merchant of that city, the Earl and his son, John
Lord Fleming, honoured the nuptial ceremony with their presence.

In the month of July 1629, an event took place which reminds us
strongly of times still more remote, when the grandees very frequently
decided their quarrels by brute force. A difference regarding the
service to some land having arisen between the Earl of Wigton and
the Earl of Cassillis, it was discussed for some time with increasing
obstinacy and fury on both sides, and at last was submitted for decision to the Lords of Council and Session. The presence of the two
noblemen were, of course, required in Edinburgh; and as they either
considered themselves in danger of bodily harm, or wished to overawe
the judges by a display of force, they summoned all their retainers to
accompany them to the capital. The appearance of two large and
hostile bodies on the streets of Edinburgh, naturally caused great
disorder and alarm. The Privy Council met in haste, and appointed
a committee to wait on the belligerents, and remonstrate with them
on the impropriety of their conduct, and to prevent them, if possible,
from proceeding to actual blows and violence. The Council at the
same time decided, that so long as the two noblemen remained in
town, they would not be allowed to appear on the streets with more
than twelve followers each, or come to the bar with more than six,
that they should comport themselves in a peaceful manner, and dismiss from their attendance all persons who had no necessary cause to
be present. The Council also issued injunctions to all the other
noblemen who were in town, and were friends of the two litigants,
that they should 'forbear the backing of them at this time, on the
pain of censure as troublers of his Majesty's peace.'

CHAPTER XXVII.

Historical Sketches of the Fleming Family—*Continued.*

IN the chapter on the Covenanters in this volume, we have referred to various movements on the part of John, second Earl of Wigton, and his son John Lord Fleming. They attached themselves at first to the cause of the Covenant, but influenced by the solicitations of their relative Montrose, and by the blandishments of Charles II., they turned their backs on that movement, and lent their support to the measures of the King. After the Battle of Philiphaugh, they do not seem, however, to have taken a very active part in the public transactions of the time. The overthrow and the execution of Montrose, and the losses and injuries which they themselves sustained, most likely disposed them to withdraw from public life, and to spend the remainder of their days in retirement and peace. The Earl died at Cumbernauld on the 7th of May 1650, and was succeeded in his titles and estates by his son John. This Earl married Jane Drummond, a daughter of the Earl of Perth, by whom he had five sons and three daughters, and died in February 1665.

The Earl's second daughter, named Lillias, fell in love with one of her father's servants called Richard Storry, and having eloped with him, succeeded in forming with him a matrimonial union. She, with consent of her husband, in October 1673, resigned her portion, consisting of the five merk land of Smythson and others, lying in the barony of Lenzie, to her brother, Lieutenant-Colonel Fleming, and received from him a legal acknowledgment that the same would be redeemable in the manner there described. The family afterwards obtained for Storry a situation in the Custom-House. The marriage of this pair made a great noise at the time, and gave rise to a ballad, which has been preserved in some publications, and of which the following is a copy:—

> 'The Erle o' Wigtoun had three doughters,
>   O braw wallie they were bonnie;
> The youngest o' them, and the bonniest too,
>   Has fa'en in love wi' Richie Storrie.

> 'Here's a letter for ye, Madame,
>   Here's a letter for ye, Madame,
> The Erle o' Home wad fain presume,
>   To be a suitor to ye, Madame.

'I'll hae nane o' your letter, Richie,
    I'll hae nane o' your letter, Richie;
For I hae made a vow, and I'll keep it true,
    That I'll hae nane but you, Richie.

'O do not say so, Madame,
    O do not say so, Madame;
For I hae neither land nor rent,
    For to maintain you wi', Madame.

'Ribands ye maun wear, Madame,
    Ribands ye maun wear, Madame,
Wi' bands about your bonnie neck
    O' the goud that shines sae clear, Madame.

'I'll lie ayont a dyke, Richie,
    I'll lie ayont a dyke, Richie,
And I'll be aye at your command,
    And biding when ye like, Richie.

'Fair Powmoodie is a' my ain,
    And goud and pearlins too, Richie;
Gin ye'll consent to be my ain,
    I'll gie them a' to you, Richie,

'O he's gane on the braid braid road,
    And she's gane through the broom so bonnie,
Her sillar robes doun to her heels,
    And she's awa wi' Richie Storrie.

'The lady gaed up the Parliament Stairs,
    Wi' pendles in her lug sae bonnie;
Mony a lord lifted his hat,
    But little wist they she was Richie's lady.

'Up then spak the Erle of Home's lady,—
    Wasna ye richt sorrie, Lillie,
To leave the lands o' bonnie Cumbernald,
    And follow Richie Storrie, Lillie?

'O what need I be sorrie, Madame,
    O what need I be sorrie, Madame?
For I've got them that I like best,
    And war ordaned for me, Madame.

'Cumbernald is mine, Annie,
    Cumbernald is mine, Annie,
And a' that's mine it shall be thine,
    And we will sit at wine, Annie.'

The subject of this ballad formed the groundwork of a tale which appeared in the first and second numbers of 'Chambers' Edinburgh Journal' in 1832.

John Fleming, the eldest son of the last Earl, succeeded to the title and estates. Of his history very little is known. He married Anna, daughter of Henry Lord Ker, by whom he had a daughter, Jane, who became the wife of George Maule, Lord Panmure. He had only inherited the estates a period of three years, when he died, in 1668, and leaving no male issue, was succeeded by his brother William, who had entered the army the year previous, his commission as an ensign in General Thomas Dalziel's own company of foot being dated 26th July 1667. The following is a translation of the terms in which William, on the 5th of August of that year, was retoured heir of the Biggar estate to Chancery:—'William, Earl of Wigtoun, Lord Fleming of Cumbernauld, heir-male of John, Earl of Wigtoun, his brother-german, in the lands of Spittal, Easter Toft-Combes, Middle and Wester Toft-Combes, lands of Whinbush, Telfer's Oxengate,[*] and Gildie Oxengate,—the lands of Heavyside,—the lands of Stane and Chamberlane Oxengate, Mossyde Oxengate and Staneheid, four oxgates of land at Hillhead,—the town and burgh of Biggar, comprehending twenty-four burgh lands and two cotlands, with mill of Biggar,—lands of Westraw of Biggar, comprehending thirty oxgates,—two oxgates of lands of Westerraw of Biggar,—the three pound lands of the lordship of Boghall,—a part of the barony of Biggar,—the demesne lands of Lindsielands, the lands of Over and Nether Voltis, part of the barony of Biggar, two oxgates of the temple lands in the Westerraw of Biggar within the said barony and said burgh of Biggar, ancient extent L.36, new extent L.144,   acris of land of the said burgh of Biggar lying round in the lands and barony of Biggar, the six merk lands of ancient extent of Glentoers within the barony of Monkland, with the patronages of the Churches of Stobo, Drummelzier, Dawick, and Broughton ancient extent L.4, new extent L.8; the burghs of barony of Kirkintilloch and Biggar, all erected into the Earldom of Wigtoun.'

The Earl resigned his lands and honours to Charles II., and obtained a signature under the hand of the King, on the 18th of August 1669, authorizing a charter or regrant to pass the Great Seal of the dignities of Earl of Wigton, Lord Fleming and Cumbernauld, and also of his estates, in favour of himself and the heirs-male of his body, containing remainders also to Charles Fleming, his brother-german; Sir William Fleming, Chamberlain of the Household to the King, and son of John, second Earl of Wigton; to Lieutenant-Colonel Fleming, son of Malcolm Fleming, and grandson of John, first Earl; and to Jane Fleming, only daughter of John, fourth Earl, and afterwards wife of George, Earl of Panmure; to the heirs-male of their bodies *seriatim*, each and all of them, with an ultimate substitution, without

---

[*] An oxgate, oxgang, or bovate in Scotland, according to some writers, was 10 acres; Skene makes it 13 acres. In England, according to Spelman and Ducange, it contained 18 acres.

division, to the eldest heir-female of the body of the disponee. It is a very singular circumstance that this regrant was never completed; that, in the course of a few years, it became unknown to the family, and remained in oblivion until it was accidentally discovered some time after the middle of last century. By the above resignation of the Earldom, which was gratuitous and not onerous, and by the failure to carry into effect the new warrant obtained, the Earl may be legally held to have denuded himself of the honours conferred on the Fleming family by James VI., and perhaps also of his estates.

The Earl was appointed by Charles II. Sheriff of Dumbartonshire, and Governor of Dumbarton Castle, and also a member of the Privy Council. His name, however, does not appear in connection with any of the arbitrary and discreditable transactions with which the Privy Council during his time was so very largely engaged. He appears to have lived a good deal in retirement, for his name seldom occurs in any public document. From the numerous papers connected with the management of his estates still preserved, it is evident that he was a careful and methodical man of business. He seems to have exacted from his factors a full and satisfactory statement of all their transactions. Earl William died on the 8th of April 1681, and was succeeded by his son John.

This Earl, the sixth who bore the title since its revival by James VI., was a decided Royalist, and of course had no sympathy with the efforts made by the worthies of the Covenant to thwart the designs of the men of power, and overturn the Stewart dynasty. When William, Prince of Orange, landed in England, he took no part in the general rejoicing, but remained sulkily at his house of Cumbernauld. As might be expected, he lent no assistance to raise the Upper Ward Regiment, the 26th Cameronians, that was embodied at Douglas in 1687, for the purpose of supporting the principles of the Covenant, and the designs of King William. After James VII. had abandoned the throne, and settled in France, the Earl went over to the Continent, and remained for some time at the royal residence to console his fallen master. He returned to Scotland, and joined the party who were resolutely opposed to a union of the two kingdoms of Scotland and England. When the measure for effecting this union was brought before the Scottish Parliament, he voted against every one of the articles. This measure, as is well known, was highly obnoxious to all ranks in Scotland;—the noble, the divine, the merchant, the craftsman, and the peasant, could see nothing in it but ruin to their respective orders, and, of course, misery and degradation to their country. The inhabitants of the Biggar district were in a perfect flame during the whole time that the Union Parliament, as it was called, carried on its discussions. During the month of November 1706, addresses or petitions against the Union were presented to this Parliament from the parishioners of Covington, Symington, Libberton, Quothquan, Dun-

syre, Crawford, and Crawfordjohn. The address from the parish of
Biggar was presented on Friday, the 15th of that month, and was no
doubt gratifying to the Earl, who was present at this sederunt. A
design was entertained to bring some thousands of the men of Clydesdale to Edinburgh, to dissolve the Parliament by force. Cunningham
of Eckatt was entrusted with the task of carrying this design into
execution; but as he was in reality a Government spy, and as the
Duke of Hamilton, who possessed great influence in Clydesdale, and
pretended to be a resolute opponent of the scheme of Union, was, at
bottom, fainthearted, if not insincere, the whole affair, in the end,
came to nothing. The Government thus got a pretext to repeal the
Act of Security, the effect of which was, that any person afterwards
assuming arms without authority, was held to be guilty of rebellion.
The Articles of Union, after calling forth some creditable displays of
forensic eloquence and patriotic feeling in Parliament, and the grief
and resentment of nearly the entire nation, were, one after another,
passed into a law; and Scotland saw the majority of her senators, for
the most paltry bribes, barter away her independence, and sacrifice
their own dignity and power.

The first effects of the Union were disastrous to Scotland. The
abiding sense of humiliation and tarnished honour, the removal of
many of the nobles and gentry to London, the ignominious treatment
of the representatives of Scotland by the English senators, the improper
interference with Scottish commerce, the imposition of new and odious
taxes, and the dispersion over the country of a swarm of English revenue officers of dissolute habits and imperious dispositions, all contributed to keep the minds of the people in a state of intense irritation,
and to attach them more and more to the exiled House of Stewart.
Accordingly, when John, Earl of Mar, was repulsed from the presence
of George I. in 1715, then newly landed on the English shores, when
the address of loyalty and attachment from the chiefs of clans, which
he wished to present, was rejected, and the office of Secretary of State,
which he had held under Queen Anne, was taken from him, he set up
the standard of rebellion, and called on all true patriots to rally to the
rescue of their country.

No sooner was the note of rebellion sounded, than the Government,
in virtue of a statute, commonly called the Clan Act, summoned
upwards of fifty Scotsmen of note, and, among others, the Earl of
Wigton, to appear at Edinburgh in order to give bail for their orderly
and loyal behaviour. Only two persons, Sir Patrick Murray and Sir
Alexander Erskine, thought fit to comply. The consequence was, that
the others were declared rebels, and put to the horn. On a warrant
issued by Major-General Williams, the Earl of Wigton was accordingly
apprehended on the 20th August 1715, and placed in confinement in
Edinburgh Castle. The Earl, by an instrument dated 19th June 1716,
demanded that the Governor of Edinburgh Castle should set him at

2 x

liberty; but the Governor, in reply, said, that as he had been committed to prison in the time of war, he could not be released without a warrant from the King, or those acting under his authority. The Court of Justiciary, however, in the course of a few days, ordered the Governor to free him from his bonds; and accordingly he was immediately set at large, after he had been kept in ward for ten months.

Many of the gentlemen of the Upper Ward at that time belonged to the opposite side of politics from the Earl, and therefore made a stand in favour of the House of Hanover. Captain Daniel Weir of Stonebyres, the Laird of Corehouse, Sir James Carmichael of Bonniton, Sir James Lockhart of Lee, Baillie of Lamington, Alexander Menzies of Coulterallers, and others, assembled all their vassals, and had them regularly drilled and ready to take the field in support of the movements of the Duke of Argyle, Commander-in-Chief of the Royal Forces. The Duke of Douglas raised a regiment of 300 men, completely officered and trained. The first detachment, consisting of 100 men, commenced their march to the Royalist camp at Stirling on the 27th September 1715, and got the length of Carluke, when intelligence arrived that they were not to advance farther, in consequence of a scarcity of provisions in the camp. They consequently returned to Douglas; but the Duke himself, Baillie of Lamington, Sir James Carmichael, etc., proceeded onwards, and arrived at Stirling on the 29th. They were very likely present at the Battle of Sherriffmuir, which took place about a fortnight afterwards.

It was the Earl of whom we are now speaking, that in 1739 carried on a series of litigations with his vassals and feuars at Biggar regarding their respective rights to the Common. This was most likely done preparatory to his effecting the new entail of his estates in 1741. As already stated, he seems to have been altogether unaware of the regrant by Charles II. in 1669.

By the new deed of entail, he became bound to resign his estates and titles in favour of heirs-male lawfully procreated of his own body; but failing these, in favour of Charles Fleming, his brother-german, and his heirs-male lawfully begotten; and failing all these, in favour of heirs-female. One of the special objects of the Earl was, that as his brother was unmarried, and as his only daughter Clementina had in 1735 married Charles Elphinstone, son of Charles, ninth Lord Elphinstone, the peerage of Wigton should not be merged in or identified with any other title. It was therefore expressly stated, that the heir to succeed should be bound and obliged to assume and bear the title, name, arms, and designation of Lord or Baron Fleming, and no other. He therefore provided, that when any heir other than the heir-male of himself or his brother should succeed, or have a right to succeed, to the estates of Biggar and Cumbernauld, and should also succeed, or have a right to succeed, to the title and dignity of another peerage, then, in that case, and so soon as it should happen, he was bound to denude himself of the estates, and that they should go to the next heir, who should assume the name of Fleming.

The Earl died on the 10th of February 1742, in the 71st year of his age, and was interred in the Church of Biggar. He was three times married. His first wife was Margaret, a daughter of Colin Lindsay, third Earl of Balcarras; and by her he had a daughter, who appears to have died in early life. His second wife was Mary Keith, daughter of William, ninth Earl Marischall; and by her he had an only daughter, Clementina. His third wife was Miss Lockhart, daughter of the celebrated Sir George Lockhart of Carnwath; but by her he had no issue.

The Earl was succeeded by his brother Charles, of whom nothing of importance is known. He died unmarried in 1747, and the estates went to his niece Lady Clementina, and the title became extinct. Charles Ross Fleming, M.D., Dublin, claimed the title, and voted at some of the elections of Scottish Peers; but the House of Lords, in 1762, decided that his claim was without proper foundation. After the death of this gentleman in 1769, his son renewed the claim, but with no better success; so that the title of the Earl of Wigton has for more than a century been dropped from the roll of the Scottish nobility.

Lady Clementina Fleming, only child of John, sixth Earl of Wigton, in 1785 married Charles, second son of Charles, ninth Lord Elphinstone. On the death of her uncle Charles, seventh Earl of Wigton, as already stated, she became possessor of the estates of Biggar and Cumbernauld, and she was also, through her mother, heiress-of-line of William, ninth Earl Marischal. Her husband, on the death of his father in 1757, became Lord Elphinstone, his elder brother John having died some time previously. Her Ladyship by this union had four sons —John, Charles, William, and George Keith—and several daughters. Charles and George devoted themselves to the naval service, and rose to distinction. Charles perished at sea, on board the 'Prince George,' 90 gun ship, when she was destroyed by fire on the 18th of April 1758, during a voyage from England to Gibraltar. William, who was for many years an East India Company Director, married the eldest daughter of William Fullerton, Esq. of Carstairs; and from this couple, William, the present Lord Elphinstone, is directly descended. In the year 1773, Lady Clementina 'did for certain causes and considerations sell, alienate, and, in feu farm, dispone to and in favour of Sir Michael Bruce of Stenhouse, Bart., his heirs and assignees,' those parts of the lands of the barony of Biggar and Boghall which she inherited from her father and uncle. In the year following, Sir Michael Bruce, by disposition and deed of entail, sold, alienated, and disponed the same lands to and in favour of Lady Clementina, and the heirs whatsomever of her body, and failing them, to the heirs-female of her uncle Charles if any existed, to the heirs-male or female of Jean Fleming or Maule, relict of George Lord Ramsay, or to the heirs-male of the deceased William Fleming of Borochan, etc. This disposition and deed of entail was, however, not recorded in the Register of Tailzies.

John, Lady Clementina's eldest son, was born in 1739. He was an officer in the army, and served under the distinguished General Wolfe in Canada, where, at the Heights of Montmorenci, he was wounded in the neck by a musket-ball. He received the command of a company of invalids in 1760, and at a subsequent period was appointed Governor of Edinburgh Castle. He succeeded his father as eleventh Lord Elphinstone in 1781, and was several times chosen a representative peer for Scotland. He married Anne, daughter of Lord Ruthven; and by her he had four sons—John, Charles, James Ruthven, and Mountstuart. He died at Cumbernauld House on the 19th of August 1794. His mother, the venerable Clementina, outlived him upwards of four years, and died at Cavendish Square, London, on the 1st of January 1799, in the 80th year of her age, and, as formerly stated, was interred in Biggar Kirk. The last of the Flemings was thus appropriately laid in the tomb of her forefathers; and many ages, in all likelihood, will roll by before it is again opened.

With the death of Lady Clementina, the connection of the direct line of the Flemings with Biggar terminated. For four or five centuries at least this family reigned superior in the parish. Nay, we are strongly disposed to believe that they held uninterrupted possession of it from the time of the first David. The opinions opposed to this view rest merely on conjecture, while a probability at least exists in its favour. So soon as we obtain distinct and satisfactory evidence of the existence of the Fleming family, we find them in possession of Biggar parish; and, therefore, we are inclined to conclude that the family of de Bigris and the family of Fleming were the same. This evidently, at all events, was the opinion of some members of the Fleming family two centuries ago.

Biggar, no doubt, reaped very considerable advantages from its connection with this old and distinguished family. The presence of a chief who often resided at court, who fought in his country's battles, who went on important embassies to foreign kingdoms, and who took a prominent part in the great public movements of the age, must have inspired the inhabitants with pride and confidence, while his vigilant eye would rouse them up to industry and self-respect, causing them to cultivate their fields with care, maintain their dwellings in a state of comfort, and cultivate habits of decency and order. No evidence exists to show that they were ever harsh and tyrannical landlords or superiors, but much, on the contrary, to prove that they treated their tenants and vassals with leniency, and conferred on them many favours. It was through their influence that Biggar was erected into a free burgh of barony. They bestowed on the burgesses very ample possessions, and, with the exception of appointing a head bailie, they appear to have left them very much to manage their own affairs. The inhabitants of Biggar parish, no doubt, sustained occasional losses from their connection with the Flemings. In the days of feud and foray, revenge for the offences of a lord-superior was too often exercised on his unoffending vassals. The Flemings were at times obnoxious to men in power, or having at least the means of inflicting injuries; and hence their poor tenants were assailed, and their property destroyed or carried off. Murray, Lennox, and Cromwell made Biggar successively a scene of desolation.

The Flemings, as we have seen, were bountiful patrons of religious houses and the Romish faith. The altars in many a religious establishment received their benefactions, and many a mass must have been said for the salvation of their souls. The erection of the Collegiate Church of St Mary at Biggar, and its magnificent endowment, must ever keep their names fresh in the memory of the people of Biggar.

John, Lady Clementina's grandson, who became twelfth Lord Elphinstone, was an officer in the army, and served in different corps. He attained the rank of Major-General, and, on the 23d of April 1806, was appointed Colonel of the 26th or Cameronian Regiment. His brother Charles, who was born in 1774, entered the naval service, and attained the rank of Captain in 1794. He commanded the 'Tartar' frigate in April 1797, when she was lost by striking on a rock, while engaged in cutting out some valuable merchantmen from a French battery at St Domingo; but the crew were all saved. He afterwards commanded the 'Bulwark,' a 74 gun ship, and was stationed for some time in the Mediterranean. He rose to the rank of Admiral; and in the latter part of his life, held the important office of Governor of Greenwich Hospital. In virtue of the entail executed in 1741 by John, Earl of Wigton, to which we formerly referred, he laid claim to the estates of Biggar and Cumbernauld, the ancient inheritances of the Flemings; and as this was resisted by his elder brother, Lord Elphinstone, a litigation took place, in the early part of the present century, to settle the dispute. The Court of Session, on the 19th of January 1804, decerned in favour of Charles, the second brother; and this decision was afterwards confirmed by the House of Lords, and he consequently assumed the name of Fleming, and took possession of the estates. The Admiral for some time represented the county of Stirling in the Imperial Parliament. In 1816 he married Donna Catalina Paulina Alessandro, a Spanish lady, and by her he had one son and three daughters. Having fallen into pecuniary difficulties, his liabilities amounting to fully L.41,000, he obtained an Act of Parliament in 1826, empowering the Judges of the Court of Session to sell certain parts of the lands and barony of Biggar and lands and barony of Boghall, and to apply the price in payment of his debts. Three of the ten heirs next in succession being at the time of the passing of the Act in foreign countries, three years were allowed to obtain their con-

sent to the sale; and this having been procured, nearly the whole of
the ancient possessions of the Flemings in the parish of Biggar were,
about the year 1830, brought to the hammer, and, as formerly stated,
fell into the hands of five or six different proprietors.   The Admiral
died on the 30th of October 1840, and was succeeded by his only son
John, who was born on the 11th of December 1819.

John Elphinstone Fleming entered the army, and served for some
time in the 17th Lancers.   At the close of his active military career,
some five or six years ago, he was in command of the 2d Light Dragoons of the German Legion, and held the rank of Lieutenant-Colonel.
On the 19th of July 1860, he succeeded his cousin John as 14th Lord
Elphinstone; but dying at Bournemouth on the 13th of January following, he enjoyed his elevation to the peerage only a few months.
The estate of Cumbernauld, and such fragments of the estate of Biggar
as still remain in the hands of the family, are now the possession of
Viscountess Hawarden, eldest daughter of Admiral Fleming, and
sister of the late John Lord Elphinstone.

We close these brief and imperfect sketches of the Fleming family
with a cut, representing such fragments of their once spacious seat of
Boghall as still remain—a fitting emblem of the power and glory now
departed, that in former ages attached to their name in the district of
Biggar.

CHAPTER XXVIII.

Early Conterminous Proprietors.

HAVING given some details regarding the Fleming family, it may not be inappropriate to follow them up with a very brief notice of some of the early conterminous proprietors, to whom special reference has not yet been made. These men, though of inferior rank and influence to the Flemings, yet occupied a prominent place in the district. They were chiefs in their own localities, and had a number of retainers, who were bound to aid them in all their enterprises. Each of them occupied his grim baronial tower, in which he defended himself and his property from the attacks of marauding neighbours, and from which he occasionally led forth an armed band to revenge his wrongs, or obey the call of his lord-superior.

We will begin with the

BROWNS AND DICKSONS OF HARTREE.

Hartree is an estate which lies to the south of Biggar, and was long held by a family of the name of Brown. Richard Brown of Hartree is mentioned in a deed dated at Lanark, 20th December 1409, serving William Douglas heir of his father, by an inquest held at that town. Richard and his son John were, in 1431, appointed bailies to David Menzies, laird of one-half of the barony of Coulter. William Brown of Hartree appears in a suit before the Lord Auditors of Parliament in 1478-9, at the instance of John Martin of Medop. It appears that Richard Brown, son and apparent heir of Andrew Brown of Hartree, had married Janet, a daughter of Malcolm Lord Fleming; and his Lordship, on the 23d September 1536, granted a precept of sasine for infefting Richard and his wife, and the longest liver of the two, in the L.5 lands of Easter Hartry. Andrew Brown of Hartree was one of the witnesses of the charter of foundation of the Collegiate Church of Biggar in 1545. In 1587, John Lord Fleming granted a precept of *clare constat* for infefting Andrew Brown of Hartree, as heir to Andrew Brown, his grandfather, in the lands of Logan, lying in the barony of Glenholm, his Lordship being superior of these lands. On the 21st of June 1627, Andrew Brown of Hartree was served heir of his father, Gilbert, in the annual rent of 300 merks of the village, demesne lands, and mill of Kilbucho. In the muster roll of a Weapon-showing, held on the King's Muir, near Peebles, on the 15th June 1627, it is stated that the Laird of Hartree (Andrew Brown) was absent himself, but that ten of his men were present, 'horsed, with lances and swords.'

On the 13th of August 1630, John Dickson, 'servitor' to Sir Alexander Gibson of Durie, Clerk Register, received a charter from the Earl of Morton, of all and haill the town and lands of Kilbucho, the myln and mylnlands and multures thereof, the lands of 'Moitt or Maynis of Kilbucho,' of Raw, Blendewing, Cleugh, Goisland, with the patronage of the kirk, and the parsonage and vicarage teinds of the parish. The same John Dickson received, in 1635, two charters from the Earl of Traquair, conferring on him the lands of Burnfoot, Easter Place, Howslack, Blackbyres, Hartree Mill, and Threpland, 'with the toure, fortalice, and maner place of the same lands.' John Dickson, who thus became the founder of the family of Dickson of Hartree and Kilbucho, followed the law as a profession, and was raised to the Bench by the title of Lord Hartree. Some of Lord Hartree's successors have been distinguished men. We may refer to Lieutenant-Colonel William Dickson, who commanded the 42d Royal Highlanders at the commencement of the present century. He accompanied his regiment in the expedition to Egypt in 1801, and was wounded

> 'Whan Abercromby, gallant Scot,
> Made Britain's faes to tack again.'

On his return in 1802, he reviewed his Highlanders before George III., and an immense concourse of spectators, at Ashford; and then, at their head, commenced his march to Scotland, receiving great attention and applause from the inhabitants of all the towns through which he passed. At Peebles, he and his officers were entertained at a public dinner by the provost and inhabitants of that burgh; and, in course of the evening, the civic worthies, feeling proud of the Colonel as a native of their own county, offered to make exertions to return him as their representative to the next Parliament. They were as good as their word, and at next election succeeded in securing a majority of votes in his favour, and the Colonel sat one Parliament as the representative of the burghs of Lanark, Linlithgow, Peebles, and Selkirk, then united in returning a member to the Imperial Parliament. Shortly after this, Colonel Dickson was raised to the rank of Brigadier-General. He is understood to have been a free, hearty individual, and rather fond of a glass of good wine or whisky punch. In consequence of repeated applications to these inspiring beverages, his nose by and by assumed a somewhat rubicund appearance. On one of his visits to London, he happened to be in company with 'that daft buckie Geordie Wales,' when his Royal Highness said to him, 'Well, General, how much has it cost you to paint your nose?' 'I really canna say,' replied the General; 'I haena yet counted the cost, as I consider the wark still unfinished.' It is worthy of notice that the General's servant, Mr William Harlan, who attended him in his expedition to Egypt, and remained with him till his death, is still this year, 1862, alive at Biggar.

The Tower of Hartree, which was a conspicuous object from Biggar, stood on a knoll surrounded by marshes, near the site of the present mansion-house. It was demolished by the late Colonel Alexander Dickson, who erected the present building in its stead.

The Hartree estate is now the property of David Dickson, Esq., advocate. He generally resides a portion of the year at Hartree House, and takes a deep interest in all schemes for the benefit of the district.

THREPLAND.

Threpland, a farm lying at the foot of the Hartree Hills, a short distance to the west of Hartree House, was a separate holding in the time of Alexander III. At the commencement of the war of independence, in 1296, Robert, Laird of Threpelande, swore fealty to Edward I. The name of the proprietors of Threpland was Brown, at least it was so in 1526. At a short distance from the 'onstead' of Threpland, at one time stood a cottage or hamlet, called the Hole ayont Threpland, which very probably was built by the company of Germans to whom James V., in 1526, gave a grant of the precious mines of Scotland for forty-three years. These individuals made many excavations in our hills for the purpose of discovering ores of lead, silver, or gold. A hole in the hillside, supposed to be dug by them, can still be traced, and pieces of lead ore are occasionally picked up. This place is referred to in a rhyme, which, it is said, was composed by a vagrant, who had been disappointed in obtaining an 'awmous' at the different farm-houses mentioned :—

> 'Glenkirk and Glencotho,
> The Mains of Kilbucho,
> Blendewan and the Raw,
> Mitchelhill and the Shaw,
> The hole ayont the Threpland
> Wad had them a'.'

MENZIES OF COULTER.

One half of the lands of Coulter, at an early period, belonged to a family of the name of Bisset. It then passed in succession into the hands of the Newbiggings and Douglases. The other half was long the patrimony of a family named Menzies. In the year 1385, Robert Maynheis obtained a charter from Robert II. of half of the barony of Coulter, which his father John had resigned. It is interesting to note that David Menyheis, one of the members of this family, granted, in 1431, his part of the lands of Wolchclide 'in frankalmoigne' to the monks of Melrose.   At the Reformation, this and other possessions of the monks were conferred on Sir Thomas Hamilton of Byres, in Haddingtonshire, who, in 1619, was raised to the peerage by the title of Earl of Melrose, but who shortly afterwards was allowed to change this title for that of the Earl of Haddington.   In 1645, John, the fourth Earl of Haddington, was returned heir of the demesne lands of Melrose, comprehending, among others, those of Wolfclyde.   The farm of Wolfclyde appears to have been, at a subsequent period, the property of Sir William Menzies of Gladstanes.   It now forms part of the Hartree estate; and it is worthy of notice that it still pays annually a few shillings to the Duke of Buccleuch, as Lord of Erection of the Abbey of Melrose.   Alexander Menzies, yr. of Coulterallers, was appointed Commissioner of Supply and Lieutenant of the Upper Ward of Lanarkshire Militia, by an Act of the first Parliament of William and Mary, 14th March 1689.

The family of Menzies continued to hold a portion of the parish of Coulter, particularly Coulterallers, down to the death of Mr Robert Menzies, which happened in 1769; and the lands of Coulterallers and others were purchased two years afterwards by Mr James Baillie, writer, Edinburgh.   The family generally resided at Coulter, but their names do not appear very frequently in history.

BAILLIE OF COULTERALLERS.

The family of Baillie of Coulterallers, formerly of Bagbie, Hardington, and Hillhouse, is an offshoot from the Baillies of Lamington.   It is not accurately known at what time it branched off, but it has generally been stated that the founder of it was a younger son of William Baillie of Lamington, who flourished in the early part of the reign of Queen Mary.   This, however, appears not to be correct, as we find that the Baillies were in possession of Bagbie previous to 1555.   On the 22d of November of that year, William Baillie of Bagbie, Nicholas his brother, and Michael Short, his servant, and three others, were 'replegiated' by James, Earl of Morton, to his regality of Dalkeith, to underlie the law, on the 17th of January following, for the convocation of the lieges to the number of six score persons, armed in warlike manner, and attacking James, Lord Sommerville.

William Baillie of Bagbie, in 1574, purchased the farm of Unthank, in the parish of Coulter, of which his father Richard had been tenant. His son, Alexander, succeeded to the lands of Bagbie and Unthank, but does not seem to have made up any titles to Unthank.   He was appointed ruling elder for the parish of Roberton to the Presbytery of Lanark 18th July 1639.   His son, Major Alexander Baillie, made up titles to Unthank, as disponee of his father, in 1642. His brother, Major Claud Baillie, made up titles to Unthank, as heir to his brother, in 1644. The lands of Hardington seem to have belonged to a family named Baillie, probably cousins of Baillie of Bagbie; and on the 2d October 1645, the Moderator of the Presbytery of Lanark gave thanks to Lord Angus, the Laird of Lee, Sir William Carmichael, James Wondrone of Wiston, the Laird of Halcraig, Hardington, probably Alexander Baillie after-mentioned, Gilkerscleugh, and Gideon Jack, baillie of Lanark, all personally present, for their commendable adherence to the Covenant, and their resolute resistance to the enemy at this difficult time; and on 6th September 1666, Mr William Thomson reported to the Presbytery of Lanark, 'That as for the conventicle keept of late at young Hardington's house, he can prove by witnesses that Mr Nicol Blaick preached there. The Presbytery thinks fitt that it be recommended to Littilgill, Sainct John's Kirk, and William Somervil, the Justice of the Peace, to take notice thereof for the breach of the Act of Parliament.' Major Claud Baillie married Jane Baillie, daughter of William Baillie of Lamington. The Major was appointed one of the Commissioners for the county of Lanark, to gather in a supply, in 1666. He seems to have been of an extravagant disposition. He sold Unthank in 1666, and on 4th July 1661 he granted an heritable bond over all his lands and heritages to Alexander Baillie, son of the deceased William Baillie of Hardington, and Marjory Menzies, spouse of the said Alexander Baillie; and he granted another heritable bond to Alexander Baillie of Hillhouse, son to Richard Baillie, his brother-german, for 1300 merks, and to Joan Baillie, his sister, for 1000 merks, on 29th October 1661. Major Claud Baillie had a son named William, who succeeded him in the lands of Bagbie, against whom Mr Alexander Baillie of Hillhouse led an apprising, in which he obtained decree on 27th November 1672; and Mr William Baillie of Hardington (probably son of the above Alexander Baillie) also led apprisings and adjudications against Mr William Baillie of Bagbie, by which he acquired the lands of Bagbie, Shillowhead and Marchilands, Hillend and Bank, from him. Mr William Baillie of Hardington seems to have got into difficulties himself; for we find him denounced his Majesty's rebel, and put to the horn, for not making payment of some money he was owing. An action of ranking and sale of the lands of Bagbie and Shillowhead with the Kirklands thereof, Nether Hardington and Kirklands thereof, the Half West land of Hardington, Fallside, Smellgills, Hillend and Bank, was brought, in which decree was pronounced on 18th July 1721, declaring these lands to belong to Mr James Baillie, Writer to the Signet. This Mr James Baillie was son to Alexander Baillie of Hillhouse, who was son to Richard Baillie, brother of Major Claud Baillie of Bagbie, and son of Alexander Baillie of Bagbie and Unthank. He was born in the year 1660; married Miss Elizabeth

Johnston, daughter of David Johnston, merchant, burgess, and guild-brother, of Edinburgh; and passed Writer to the Signet in 1694. In right of his wife, he was made a burgess and guild-brother of Edinburgh 8th July 1696. He is designed of Wells in 1701, and seems to have sold this property previous to 1704, when he married Miss Anna Livington, daughter of George Livington of Saltcoats, in Haddingtonshire. He had three sons by his first marriage,—Robert, who was one of the magistrates of Edinburgh in 1745, and again in 1755; David, who married Miss Helen Bruce of Earlshall, and was killed at a horse-race at Cupar-Fife in 1725; and William, who was Governor of Guinea;—and by his second marriage he had an only son George.

Mr James Baillie purchased Hardington and Bagbie from the representatives of Mr William Baillie in 1721. Mr Baillie, who died in 1747, is represented as having been 'a very honest and bright gentleman,' and was private agent for the Earl of March, Baillie of Lamington, Menzies of Coulterallers, etc., and had a large and respectable practice. His son, Mr George Baillie, succeeded him in the lands of Hardington and Bagbie, and married Miss Euphemia Bertram, daughter of William Bertram of Nisbet, and had—with several other children—James, Robert, and Menzies. James, who was born in 1732, was a writer in Edinburgh. He purchased Coulterallers in 1771, and died unmarried in 1818. Robert, who was born in 1734, was apprentice to his uncle, the Edinburgh magistrate, and afterwards a settler in Georgia, in the United States of America. He distinguished himself very much in the American War, and was colonel of a regiment of Volunteers in the service of his Britannic Majesty. He married Miss M'Intosh, daughter of John Mohr M'Intosh, one of the earliest colonists of Georgia, and one of whose descendants again distinguished himself in the Mexican War. He died in 1782. Menzies was first an assistant surgeon in the army; then a partner of the firm of Bertram, Gardner, & Company, of Leith, and afterwards Barrack Master at Leith. He was born in 1741, and died in 1804. He married Miss Anne Hodgson. The present proprietor of Coulterallers, Robert Granbery Baillie, Esq., who is grandson to the above-mentioned Robert Baillie, succeeded to the estate of Coulterallers on the death of his granduncle, James Baillie, in 1818. He married Miss Anna Baillie, daughter of the above-named Menzies Baillie, and has two sons—James William Baillie, Esq., W.S., and John Menzies Baillie, Esq., C.A.

THE BROWNS OF COULTERMAINS.

The lands of Coultermains were held for a long period by a family of the name of Brown, a name that prevailed largely in the Biggar district. The Browns of Coultermains are supposed to be a branch

of the family of Brown of Hartree, to whom we have referred. The
period at which the Browns became proprietors of Coultermains
cannot now be exactly known. The earliest notice of them that
appears on record is in 1492, when John Brown of Cultre is mentioned
as attending an inquest of the gentlemen of the shire of Clydesdale.
Richard Brown of Coultermains, in 1512, along with John Tweedie of
Drummelzier, and James Lockhart of Lee, became surety for John
Symontoun of Symontoun, when he was arraigned on a charge of
treasonably forging false money; and as Symontoun did not appear
to underlie the law, Brown and his associates were 'amerceated' in
the sum of 1000 merks. Richard Brown of Coultermains, along with
Malcolm Lord Fleming, Andrew Brown of Hartree, and others, as
formerly mentioned, was in 1526 accused of treasonable communication with Englishmen in time of war, and received a respite for nineteen years. He also, along with Hugh Lord Sommerville, on the 24th
April 1536, became surety for William Chancellor of Quothquan, his
brother Robert, and James Chancellor, when they were accused of the
slaughter of Thomas Baillie of Cormiston.

In December 1562, James Tweedie of Fruid, most likely the son of
the individual who married Catherine Fraser, formerly referred to,
was attacked when seated before a fire in the house of William
Tweedie, burgess of Edinburgh, and mortally wounded, before he
could raise himself up, or parry the blows aimed at him. Patrick
Hunter, John Hunter, burgess of Edinburgh, John Burn of Over
Posso, George Paterson of Harestanes, and William Glen, the Laird
of Fruid's servant, were tried for this murder; and among the 'Pre-
locutouris' at the trial were the Laird of Coultermains, the Laird of
Carmichael, my Lord Semple, the Laird of Traquair, and the Laird of
Coilstone. The panels were on this occasion acquitted. John Brown
of Coultermains was arraigned for taking part in the murder of David
Rizzio, in March 1566; but it is not known whether he suffered any
punishment for this crime or not.

In the year 1571, during the regency of the Earl of Lennox, the
people of Scotland were divided into two inveterate factions, called
respectively Queensmen and Kingsmen; that is, those who favoured
Queen Mary, and those who favoured her son James. Both factions
held separate Parliaments, and pronounced condemnation and forfeiture on each other. The Queen's party held a Parliament at Edinburgh, in the autumn of the year referred to, under the protection of
William Kirkcaldy, the Governor of the Castle, and, of course, passed
the doom of forfeiture on their opponents, the Earl of Lennox, the
Earl of Morton, the Earl of Mar, and, among many others, James
Johnston of Westeraw, John Lindsay of Covington, and John Brown
of Coultermains, 'for certain crymes,' as the author of the 'Diurnal'
says, 'and poyntis of tressoune contenit in the summondis directit
thairupone; and decernit the saidis personis, and ilk ane of thame, to

have tint and foirfaltit thair lyvis, landis, and guidis, and ordaynit
thair airmes to be riffin, and thair namis and armis to be deleted out
of the buikis thairof for ever; and thairefter the saidis lieutennentis
and nobilitie, with sword, sceptour, and croun, past to the mercat
croce of Edinburgh, and thair causit proclame the said foirfaltour.'
From this it appears that the Laird of Coultermains was opposed to
the unfortunate Queen Mary, and took part with the Earl of Murray,
the Earl of Lennox, and others, who contended for the government
of her son James.

Robert Brown of Coulter, most likely a relative of the Browns of
Coultermains, was, in the June of 1596, cruelly slaughtered on the
Green of Coulter, and the goods and cattle of his brother carried off,
by Thomas Jardine of Birnock, and his two sons, Humphrey and
Alexander, individuals who, about that period, committed many barbarous outrages in the Upper Ward.   One of their most atrocious
deeds was their burning and destroying the place of Littlegill, in the
parish of Wandell, in 1589, 'with haill laiche housis, barnes, and
byres thairof, and haill insicht and plenessing being thairin, and their
crewall burning and slaying of umquhile Alexander Bailzie of Littlegill, Rachel Bailzie, dochter to Mathow Bailzie now of Littlegill, and
umquhile   Achiesone, servand to the said Mathow, the saidis
umquhile three persones being all within the said place the tyme of
the burning and destroying thairof.'

The estate of Coultermains consisted of two divisions.   The one
was called the dominical 50s. lands of old extent, and the other the
L.5 lands of old extent.   The 50s. lands lay on the west, and are
those which were first acquired by the family of Brown, and on which
the old mansion-house was built.   Till 1598, this mansion was a
tower, or, as it is called in the deeds, a fortalice, and the exact spot on
which it stood is the north-east corner of the present garden.   The
family abandoned the tower at that time, and erected a small but
commodious dwelling-house near it; and this building remained till
1838, when it was removed by the present proprietor, Mr Sim.   Two
stones of the old building were carefully preserved, and built into the
elegant new edifice then erected.   One of these stones has the inscription, J. B. 1598, K. L.; and the other, J. B., K. L., 1600.   The initials
refer to John Brown, and his spouse, Katherine Lockhart, a daughter
of the old Clydesdale House of Lee.

This Laird died in 1600, and was succeeded by his son Richard,
who, on the 12th of May of that year, was retoured heir of his father
of the 50s. lands called ' Coultermaneis,' within the barony of Coulter.
John Brown, and his son Richard, involved their affairs and estate in
pecuniary difficulties; but from what cause, does not appear; and
wadsets were granted over the lands to Sir James Lockhart of Lee,
Malcolm Fleming, younger, of Cardon, Menzies of Coulterallers and
Carlops, and Walter Carmichael.   It appears that in the end Sir

James Lockhart* exerted himself to set the affairs of his relatives the
Browns free from embarrassment, and that through his means a charter
of resignation in favour of John Brown, and his wife, Jean Sommerville, was granted by the various parties, restoring all their possessions
from wadsets, in 1637.

John Brown, the Laird of Coultermains of whom we are now speaking, was what was called a 'Malignant,' that is, he favoured the side
of Charles I.; and though he did not openly join Montrose, and take
part in his military movements, yet he secretly gave him his countenance and aid. The consequence of this was, that he came under the
lash of the Presbytery of Biggar. At a visitation of the Kirk of
Coulter, on the 16th of July 1645, one of the questions asked at
John Currie, the minister of the parish, was, 'if there was any in his
parish suspected of malignancie?' The answer was, that 'John
Brown, portioner of Cultermaines, was suspected, because it was reported that his reasoning in discourse with company did tend that
way. As also, when upon a time, ye minister in his sermon was
stirring up ye people to advance and hasten the levie, the said John
Brown was perceived to smyle.' Mr Brown denied that there was
any truth in these allegations, and, being removed, the elders of the
parish were called in; but though they admitted that 'he was bruited
and ill thought off,' yet they could not charge him with any special
act of malignancy. The case being referred to the minister and elders
of the parish for further examination, John Currie, on the 19th
November, reported that he and his session had been diligent in
trying the disaffection of John Brown, but had not found out anything against him of a serious character. This did not satisfy the
Presbytery, and therefore John Currie was ordered to cite the Laird
of Coultermains to appear before the Presbytery at their next meeting. The Laird accordingly appeared before the Presbytery on the
24th December, and admitted that he smiled in the Kirk when the
minister was insisting on constancy in the good cause; but he
asserted that the smile was extorted from him by the light behaviour
of a person that sat near him in the Kirk, and that he was very sorry
that such a thing had taken place. He declared 'that he thocht weill
of ye work of Reformation,' but denied that he received any protection
from Montrose, or was at the Battle of Philiphaugh. He confessed,
however, that he went in the cause of the King to Dumfries with the
Marquis of Douglas. These admissions not proving satisfactory to
the Presbytery, Robert Elliot of Kilbucho, George Bennet of Quoth-

---

* It may be mentioned that Sir James Lockhart was the father of the celebrated Sir
William Lockhart, who was the friend and minister of Oliver Cromwell, his ambas-
sador to France, and the commander of his army at the taking of Dunkirk. Sir
William married Robina Sewster, the niece of Cromwell, and thus the cousin of the
Coultermains family was intimately connected with the great head of the Common-
wealth.

quan, and the indefatigable John Currie of Coulter, were appointed a
committee to investigate still further into his conduct. These worthies
reported at the next meeting that they were unable to elicit any
further information, and therefore it was resolved to cite the Laird to
appear once more before the holy conclave. The result of the whole
was, that the Laird was forced to compear on the 21st of October
1646, when he humbled himself, confessed his malignancy, and craved
pardon. He was thereupon referred back to the Kirk of Coulter to
fulfil the rest of his censure. This, as laid down by the Presbytery
in cases of malignancy, was to appear before the congregation, and
' efter sermon, to stand before ye pulpitt, and mak open confessione
of yr offence, and falling down upone yr knies, craive pardon for ye
same.'

At the period to which we are now referring, when great commotions in Church and State prevailed, and property and even life were
insecure, John Brown of Coultermains removed the writs and evidents
of his lands to the house of his friend and brother-Malignant, William
Lindsay of Birthwood, situated in a solitary but beautiful glen at the
foot of Coulter Fell. Here an accident happened, by which the whole
papers and charters containing the history of the Browns, and the
rights and titles of their estate, were destroyed. The following extract from the Charter of Novodamus of both halves of Coultermains
in favour of John Brown of Coultermains, dated 4th February 1659,
tells the story :—' Richard, Lord Protector of the Commonwealth of
England, Scotland, and Ireland, and dominions thereto belonging, to
all men to whose knowledge this our present charter sall come, greeting,—Be it knowne that for-as-mekill as we understanding that our
loved Johne Broune of Coultermaynes stands heritablie infeft in all
and haill the fyve pund land of Coulter Maynes, alswell that halff
thereof called the auld or west halff, as in that other halff of the
samyne called the new or eister halff of the saidis lands, with houses,
biggings, yardis, pairts, pendicles, and pertinents thereof whatsomever,
lyand within the parochin of Coulter and our Shereffdome of Lanark,
holdin immediatelie of us and our predecessors, Kings of Scotland, be
service of warde and relieff, and siclyke, wee being certainlie informed
that in the time of the late *troubles* in the year ane thousand sex
hundreth and fiftie ane, the said Johne Broune, for securing his writes
and evidents of the saidis lands, haveing committed the samyne to the
custodie of William Lindsaye of Birthwode, to be keeped wtin his
hous, as a place remote and reteired frome all publice hieways, the
saide hous, and all within the samyne, and among the rest, the saidis
haill writs and evidents, were be ane sad and unexpected accident
totallie brunt, and destroyed with fyre, as hes beene sufficientlie instructed and made appear to our said Commissioner of Exchequere, be
twa severall certificates of the truith thereof produced before them,—
ane whereof subscribed be the Moderator and brethren of the Prisbitre

of Biggar, and the other, be the Justices of our Peace within that our countie,' etc., etc. The Brounes thought it necessary to get a similar charter from Charles II., July 1st, 1661, two years afterwards.

In July 1681, a deed was committed by the Laird of Coultermains, which strongly marks the disordered state of the country at the time, and the disposition of the local proprietors to disregard the laws and settle their disputes by brute force. Alexander Menzies, Laird of Coulterallers, about that period, for the accommodation of the house-wives of his neighbourhood, erected a waulk-mill on his own property, near the foot of Coulter Water, and a short time afterwards built a house contiguous to it, as a dwelling for the person in charge of the mill. Mr Brown offered no obstruction to the process of building this house; but after it was completed, he, on some ground or other, mani-fested his dissatisfaction. Mr Menzies, in consequence, took out a law-borrows against him; but Mr Brown paying no regard to this legal protection, assembled a considerable number of persons connected with Coulter, and among others, John Vallange, Luke Vallange his son, John Kemp, James Brown, William Brown, John Patoun, Mungo Inglis, and Alexander Inglis, ' all boddin in feir of weir, armed with swords, pistols, axes, and other instruments,' and leading them to the waulk-mill in question, there ' by force, bangistry, violence, and oppression, did demolish and throw down the said dwelling-house.' For this crime, the Laird and his accomplices, just named, were served with an indictment at the instance of Sir George Mackenzie of Rose-haugh, his Majesty's advocate, and Mr Alexander Menzies of Coulter-allers, on the 30th of the same month of July, to stand their trial; but, unfortunately, the result is not known.

In the chapter on the Covenanters, we have referred to the capture of a James Brown of Coulter by Claverhouse; but this person was not the Laird of Coultermains, though it is very possible he was a relation of the family. John Brown of Coultermains died in 1685, and was succeeded by his son Richard, of whom nothing of importance is known. His son William was the next Laird of Coultermains, who obtained a disposition of the estate from his father in 1704, upon which he expede a crown charter, and was infeft. The eldest son of William was John, who succeeded in 1736, and was at first minister of Symington, and afterwards of his native parish of Coulter.

The memory of this worthy clergyman is still held over the district in the very highest respect. As a minister of the Gospel, he was dis-tinguished for his piety and intelligence, as well as for his deeds of hospitality and benevolence; and as a proprietor, for the improvements he made on his ancestral property, by embankments, water-ducts, and planting, thus affording ample employment to his poorer parishioners. With the exception of the old trees which stood round the tower taken down in 1598, he was the planter of all the others, on this now well-timbered property. He built a considerable addition to the

2 z

mansion in 1753, which formed the principal part of the house that
was removed in 1838. An ornamental window, which was carefully
placed in the new house, has the above date, 1753, cut on it, and is
preserved as a sort of memorial of the worthy minister. His eldest
son, called William, was educated for the Church, but was carried off
by consumption in 1771, at a very early age. His worthy father received a severe blow from this bereavement; and when asked by the
family when the funeral should take place, he replied, 'Do not be in
a hurry, you may have two to bury.' He died the same night, and
the worthy minister and son were interred in the same grave. An
incident occurred at the funeral which we have heard related by an
eye-witness. The minister's man, an attached old servant, was so
overpowered by his feelings, that he fell, as if he had been dead, into
the grave. Water from the baptismal well soon restored him to consciousness; but the incident, of course, made a great noise at the time
at which it happened.

John Brown, before the Sheriff of Lanark, 3d July 1795, was
served heir to his father, John Brown, Laird of Coultermains, and
minister of the Gospel at Coulter, to whom we have just referred.
He married Miss Cecilia Grizel Bertram, a daughter of the old House
of Nisbet and Kersewell. Mr Brown was a Deputy-Lieutenant of the
county of Lanark, and a freemason, hailing from St Luke's Lodge,
Edinburgh. He was admitted an honorary member of the Lodge of
Biggar Free Operatives in April 1796, and on the occasion presented
the Lodge with a donation of two guineas. On the 19th of February
1817, Mr Brown sold Coultermains to the late David Sim, merchant,
Glasgow. The present representative of this old family is John
Brown, Esq., W.S., Edinburgh, a gentleman well known and univer-
sally respected.

We regret that the old documents connected with this family were
lost, and that we are thus left in ignorance of the time and manner
in which they acquired their estate, and other incidents in their early
history. In preparing even a brief notice of their proceedings and
their different successions, it is difficult to avoid confusion from the
continued repetition of the family names, Richard and John, which
evidently were favourites with the House of Coultermains. It was, in
fact, a common custom with great families, to adhere as closely as
possible to certain names, and hence, from this source, no small embarrassment is felt in writing family history. The Browns of Coultermains for three hundred years held their property in direct succession
from father to son, and, with one exception, were all called Richard
or John.

The present proprietor of Coultermains, Adam Sim, Esq., in 1838,
erected an elegant mansion on the estate. It is in the Elizabethan
style of architecture, from a design by Mr Spence, architect, Glasgow.
It stands on a lawn not far distant from the banks of the Clyde, and

is finely embowered amid luxuriant plantations. Internally it is fitted up in a style of great elegance and taste. The library is a fine apartment, stored with a rich collection of antiquarian lore; the drawing-room is magnificently adorned with costly furniture, and a perfect profusion of rare and choice works of art; and one of the rooms above stairs is fitted up in a very impressive manner, with carved oak pannelling in the mediæval style of art, with antique furniture and stained glass windows. The floor and walls of the lobby are covered with a variety of implements of the olden time; every apartment, in fact, has its store of curiosities; while scattered over the house is one of the largest collections of Lanarkshire antiquities that was ever made. The generous-hearted proprietor deserves the utmost gratitude for the immense labour, to say nothing of the cost, that he has expended in gathering these rare articles together, and also for the readiness, frankness, and evident delight that he, on all occasions, exhibits in showing them to his friends.

THE BAILLIES OF LAMINGTON.

To the south of Coulter are the lands of Lamington. The earliest proprietor of these lands of whom mention is made, is Hugh Braidfoot, who, according to Blind Harry, died previous to the year 1295, leaving a son and a daughter. Hesilrig, the English Sheriff of Lanark, put the young Laird to death; and his sister, whose name was Marion, purchased the protection of the English, and leaving the tower of Lamington, took up her abode at Lanark. Sir William Wallace, in the year 1296, occasionally sojourned at Gilbank, in the parish of Lesmahagow, the residence of his uncle, Nichol Auchinleck. It was his wont, when living here, to repair at times for recreation to the town of Lanark; and here he accidentally met with the heiress of Lamington. At the time at which Wallace first saw her, she was little more than eighteen years of age, possessed of great personal attractions, and distinguished no less for her modesty than for her amiable and generous disposition. Wallace fell deeply in love with her; and finding that his love was returned, he, after much hesitation, on account of his own unsettled mode of life and the disturbed state of the country, made her his wife, greatly to the mortification of the English Sheriff, who, it seems, had a design to wed her to his son. Some time after his marriage, Wallace received a visit from his attached companion-in-arms, Sir John Graham, accompanied by a small party of his followers. One morning the two chieftains and their retainers attended mass in the Parish Church of Lanark, which stood at a short distance from the town, and, on their return, the English soldiers, who at that time occupied the town and Castle of Lanark, intentionally fastened a quarrel on them in the streets. After some altercation, swords were drawn, and a sharp conflict ensuing, a strong party of the English were marched from the Castle to the aid of their friends. The Scots fought stoutly, and slew not a few of their opponents; but being overborne by numbers, they were forced to retreat, and naturally directed their steps with all speed to Wallace's mansion, where they were admitted by a female domestic, who had presence of mind to bolt the gate behind them. This retarded their pursuers; and by a back passage they succeeded in securing a safe retreat amid the woody fastnesses of Cartlane Craigs. The English, incensed at their escape, seized the wife of Wallace, and barbarously put her to death. The news of this sad event was conveyed to Wallace by an old female retainer of the House of Lamington, and naturally overwhelmed him with the deepest sorrow and distress. On recovering, he vowed from that time to devote himself entirely to the service of his country, and either to drive out the English, or perish in the attempt. It was instantly concerted that an attack should be made that night on the garrison of Lanark; and Auchinleck being apprised of this resolution, joined them with a small detachment of men. The Scots, divided into several little parties, came suddenly and unexpectedly to Lanark, and, by fire and sword, put the whole garrison, consisting of about 250 men, to death. Among the slain were Hesilrig the Sheriff, his son, Sir Robert Thorn, and other persons of distinction.

It is stated by the Minstrel, that Marion Braidfute had by Wallace a daughter, who was married to a person named Shaw, and that 'rycht gudly men came off yis lady zong.' It is supposed that either this lady herself afterwards, or that her daughter and heiress, was married to William, a member of the family of Baillie of Hoperig, in East Lothian. It was the opinion of the learned antiquary, Sir William Baillie of Castlecarry, that the name Baillie was the same as Baliol, and that the family of Hoperig was a branch of the illustrious House of Baliol, the head of which was Lord of Galloway, and, at one time, King of Scotland. William Baillie, who married the heiress of Lamington, was taken prisoner at the Battle of Durham in 1346. After his release, King David Bruce, in 1357, raised him to the rank of a knight; and on the 27th of January 1368, conferred on him and his heirs a new charter of the lands of 'Lambestown,' on condition of rendering the usual service.

William Baillie left two sons, William and Alexander. Alexander is supposed to be the founder of the family of Baillie of Carphin. William, the heir of Lamington, is designed in a charter, dated 4th Feb. 1395, also proprietor of Hoperig; and it thus seems that these two estates were for some time possessed by the same individual. He gave his son William as a hostage in exchange for David Lesly of that Ilk, in 1432; and this son is mentioned in a document, dated 1466, as still the possessor of the estates of Hoperig and Lamington. He was appointed by his country one of the conservators of peace; and in this capacity he took part in the negotiations at Nottingham that led to the conclusion of a treaty of peace with England in 1484. His daughter, Mary, was married to Lord Sommerville of Carnwath; and in 1485, he witnessed a charter of the lands of Cambusnethan, granted by that baron to his son.

Sir William Baillie left a son, William, who was his successor, and who married Marion, a daughter of Patrick Home of Polwarth, Comptroller of Scotland in the reign of James IV. He obtained a charter of his lands, under the Great Seal, in 1492; and left two sons, William, his heir, and John, the progenitor of the Baillies of St John's Kirk, Jerviswood, and Walston. William married Elizabeth, daughter of Lord John Lindsay of Byres, and had a son, also William, evidently a favourite name in the family, who, in 1542, was appointed to the office of Principal Keeper of the Wardrobe to Queen Mary. · This gentleman was a keen partisan of that Queen. He appeared on her side with his followers at the Battle of Langside; and on this account his lands were ravaged and afterwards forfeited by the Regent Murray. By his wife Janet, daughter of James, Earl of Arran, he had William, his successor, and another son, said to be the progenitor of the Baillies of Bagbie and Hardington, now represented by R. G. Baillie, Esq. of Coulterallers.

William, the next Laird of Lamington, married Margaret, a daughter of John Lord Maxwell, and relict of Archibald, Earl of Angus. By this lady he had one child, a daughter, who, by the negotiations of her mother, was induced to marry a relative of her own, Edward Maxwell, Commendator of Dundrenan, and third son of Lord Herries of Terregles. Baillie conferred the fee of his estate on his daughter and her heirs, on condition that they should assume the name of Baillie, and bear the arms of the House of Lamington, reserving only a life-interest in his estates to himself and his lady. While his wife was still living, he formed an improper intimacy with a Mrs Home, by whom he had a son. After his wife's death, he married this woman, with the view of legitimatizing his son; but in this object he failed. The son, thus prevented from inheriting his paternal estates, devoted himself to the profession of arms. Like many enterprising young Scotsmen, he went abroad, and fought with distinction under the banner of the renowned Gustavus Adolphus. When the contentions between Charles I. and the Parliament broke out, and both sides prepared to adjust their differences by the arbitration of the sword, Baillie returned to his native country, and threw in his lot with the opponents of royalty.

Under old Lesly, Earl of Leven, he was appointed Lieutenant of the Scots army that assembled at Berwick in 1644, and afterwards marched into England. He shared in the victory over the Royalists on Marston Moor, and took part in the siege of York and the capture of Newcastle. When the great Montrose was known to be carrying everything before him in Scotland in the cause of his royal master, Baillie was despatched from England to oppose his movements. He

encountered Montrose first at Alford, and afterwards at Kilsyth, and
in both cases sustained a defeat.   Historians have not failed to vindicate the generalship of Baillie, and to admit that his failures on these
occasions were attributable not to himself, but to the nobility and
Committee of Estates, by whom his counsels were thwarted and set
aside.   In the year 1648, he held a command in the army that was
raised in Scotland in favour of Charles I., and placed under the direction of the Duke of Hamilton.   This army was marched into England;
but was remarkably ill-conducted, as the Duke was no general.   The
consequence was, that his troops were defeated and dispersed by the
English Roundheads ; and Baillie, after being deserted by his commander, was forced to surrender at Uttoxeter to Lambert, one of
Cromwell's captains.   He is known to have made an effort to recover
his paternal estate of Lamington, but without success.

   William Maxwell, the son of the Commendator of Dundrenan, took
the name of Baillie, and married Elizabeth, daughter of Henry Stewart
of Craigiehall, Linlithgowshire.   He was the elder for Lamington
parish at the formation of the Presbytery of Biggar.   In 1648 he was
a member of the Scottish Parliament, and agreed to support the cause
of Charles I. after he was placed in confinement by Cromwell and his
party.   The engagement which a number of the other Scottish barons
entered into on this occasion, as is well known, gave great offence to
the Presbyterian clergy.   They denounced it from their pulpits, and
threatened to inflict spiritual censures on those who should obey the
edict of the Parliament, and take up arms in defence of the King.
Baillie of Lamington, in consequence of his connection with the 'sinful
engagement,' as it was called, was, along with others, pounced on by
the Presbytery of Biggar, and summoned to appear before them.   He
accordingly appeared on the 12th December 1649, and pled that by
taking part in the engagement he did not consider that he had done
anything wrong.   The members of Presbytery were of a different
opinion, and therefore they intimated to him, 'if he wold not be readie
to give satisfactione against ye next meiting, that they wold enter
into farther proces against him.'   He came up before the Presbytery
again on the 2d January 1650, and the reverend court laid down in
detail the charges which they brought against them.   They were as
follows :—' His being a member of that parliament consenting to yr
unjust proceedingis, and not dissenting with ye honest partie of that
parliament,—his being att ye committee of estaitts flowing from that
Parliament, and giveing his oath yr,—his keiping ye first rendezvous
at Lanerk moore wth his men verie willinglie,—his refusing to helpe
ye westerne forces, and not suffering his men to helpe theme or joyne
with theme,—his giveing furth his men to the enemie without
constraint,—his goeing a great way for joineing with Lanerkers,—
and his refuseing to cleare himself anent subscrybing the unlawfull
band.'

The Laird denied the greater number of these charges, but admitted that, in Parliament, he gave his consent to the engagement, and took no part with the 'honest partie,' and that he refused to render any help to the western forces. The Presbytery laboured hard to bring him to 'a sense of his guyltines;' but not succeeding, they appointed a committee of 'some breather and rewling elderis' to deal with him, and report at a future meeting. The clergy, in these days, when they entered on a case of this kind, pursued it with unwearied obstinacy; but in searching the records of Presbytery, we failed to discover any intimation that the Biggar divines had succeeded in extorting any further confession from the Laird, or inflicting on him any sort of punishment. The kirk-session of Lamington found him quite inexorable, and therefore deprived him of his office of elder, until he should give signs of penitence and make satisfaction.

Sir William Baillie was succeeded by his grandson William, who married Henrietta, a daughter of William, Earl of Crawford. By this lady he had only daughters, the eldest of whom married Sir James Carmichael of Bonninton. Sir James agreed that his estate should be sunk into the family of Lamington, and that his heirs-male should bear the title and surname of Baillie. During last century, the estate of Lamington was held by two other heiresses, the last of whom, Elizabeth, eldest daughter of Lord President Dundas, married Sir John Lockhart Ross of Balnagown. This lady's son, Sir Charles Ross, had a daughter named Matilda, who married Admiral Sir Thomas Cochrane, K.C.B. The eldest son of this lady, Alexander Dundas Ross Wishart Baillie Cochrane, Esq., as heir to his mother, is the present proprietor of the Lamington estate. He was born in 1816, and received his education at Eton, and Trinity College, Cambridge, where, in 1837, he took the degree of B.A. In 1844 he married Annabella, a daughter of A. R. Drummond, Esq. He represented Bridport for upwards of ten years in the Imperial Parliament, and the county of Lanark for three months in the spring of 1857. He was elected for Honiton in 1859, and this place he still continues to represent. Mr Cochrane has devoted a good portion of his time and attention to literary pursuits. On returning from his travels in Greece and the east of Europe in 1840, when he had only reached his 24th year, he published a poem entitled 'The Morea.' He has since published a work on Italy, and several novels, such as 'Lucille Belmont,' 'Ernest Vane,' 'Florence the Beautiful,' etc., and other productions. He has taken a warm interest in the affairs of the town of Biggar; and has especially been noted for his generous efforts to befriend the poor, and promote the cause of education. The old tower of Lamington, which it is supposed had stood from the days of Wallace, was greatly demolished eighty years ago, and thus rendered altogether uninhabitable. Mr Cochrane, some time ago, erected an elegant mansion on the estate, at which he usually resides a part of the year,

and, from his affability and active benevolence, is held in great and
deserved esteem, not only by his tenantry, but by the population of
the district at large.

LOCKHARTS OF SYMINGTON.

The first proprietor of Symington of whom we know anything was
Simon Lockhart, who flourished in the reigns of Malcolm IV. and
William the Lion.   Simon was one of the witnesses of a donation of
the Church of Weston, to the Abbey of Kelso, by Wicius of Weston, for
the safety of the soul of King Malcolm and his brother William, some
time previous to 1164.   The honour of knighthood was conferred
upon him by William, as appears from a gift, which he bestowed on
the Abbey of Kelso, of the Church of Wodechurch, with the whole of
its parish, as well of Thankerton as of the village of Sir Simon Lockhart.   This gift was confirmed by Jociline, Bishop of Glasgow, who
occupied that See from 1174 to 1199.   A controversy afterwards
arose between the Prior of Paisley and the Abbot of Kelso in regard
to the chapel of the village of Sir Symon Lockard; but a compromise
at last took place, by which it was agreed that the chaplain appointed
by Sir Simon should continue for life, and that the chapel should then
be resigned to the Abbot.   It is understood that it was from this
knight that the village and parish received the name of Symon's
Town, afterwards changed into Symington.

The Lockharts continued for a long period to be proprietors of
Symington; and their names occur repeatedly as witnesses in early
charters.   They became proprietors of the estate of Lee, in the parish
of Lanark, an estate still possessed by their descendants.   The lands
of Symington at length fell into the hands of a family who took the
name of Symington of that Ilk.   The Symingtons are often incident-
ally mentioned in our public muniments.   As already stated, John
Symontown of that Ilk, was, in 1512, charged with the crime of
forgery and making false money.   Robert Menzies of that Ilk, John
Tweedie of Drummelzier, James Lockhart of Lee, and Richard Brown
of Coultermains, conjointly and severally became caution that he
would appear and stand his trial, under a penalty of 1000 merks.
As he did not come forward, these parties forfeited this large sum.

THE BAILLIES OF ST JOHN'S KIRK.

The lands of St John's Kirk, in the suppressed parish of Thankerton, were long possessed by a family of the name of Baillie, a branch,
as we have already said, of the Baillies of Lamington.   Thomas Baillie
of St John's Kirk, like the rest of the Baillies, was a partisan of
Queen Mary.   On the 27th of February 1572-3, he was delatit for
the slaughter of the umquhile James Ballanye and others at the
Battle of Langside, 13th May 1568; but the case against him was in
the end deserted.   He had previously, however, sustained serious

losses by the ravages committed on his property by the Earl of
Murray, shortly after that battle. On the 4th of January 1642, John
Baillie was returned heir of the lands of Thankerton, lately St John's
Kirk, with the teinds and pasturage in the Common of Thankerton,
the lands of Lockharthill and a portion of Anneston commonly called
'Schawcruick,' in the barony of Symington, and the lands and meadow
called Annetscheill, with pasture in the Common of 'Wowstoun.' We
have already referred to the part which the Lady of St John's Kirk
played during the persecuting times of Charles II. and James VII.
She appears to have had a strong leaning in favour of the Covenanted
work of Reformation, but manifested some alarm and indecision at
a time when a terrible system of rapine and bloodshed, carried out
under the orders of Government, made the stoutest hearts tremble.
From this respected family sprung the Baillies of Walston and Jerviswood, that have given birth to men who have played a distinguished
part in the public transactions of their country. The estate of St
John's Kirk, which is pleasantly situated at the foot of Tinto, has been
out of the hands of the Baillies for a considerable period.

THE CHANCELLORS OF SHIELDHILL.

The Chancellors of Shieldhill are the oldest proprietors of land in
the neighbourhood of Biggar. They are supposed to have come to
this country from France at the time of the Norman Conquest, along
with the Sommervilles of Carnwath, whom they acknowledged as their
lords-superior. The alliance between them and the Sommervilles
appears, according to Nisbet, to have existed at least in 1317, in the
time of Robert Bruce. The oldest of their charters extant, is one
that is referred to in that curious gossiping work, 'The Memorie of
the Sommervilles,' and was granted by Thomas Lord Sommerville to
William, or, as Nisbet calls him, George Chancellor of Shieldhill, in
the year 1432. George was succeeded by his son Alexander, who
added some lands to the family estate, and obtained a charter from
Lord Sommerville in 1460. He was succeeded by his son George,
who resigned his lands into the hands of his superior, Lord Sommerville, in 1472, for new infeftment, and at that time received a new
charter. He is styed 'Nobilis vir Georgius Chanceler, dominus de
Quodquan.' By his wife, a daughter of Ramsay of Dalhousie, he left
a son, William, who was his successor, and in whose favour, and of his
wife Janet Geddes, a daughter of Geddes of Rachan and Kirkurd, a
sasine was registered in 1477. In the account of the famous incident
of 'Speates and Raxes,' which took place in July 1474, William
Chancellor of Quothquan is mentioned as one of the parties who
turned out to the assistance of his friend and superior, Lord Sommerville, when it was supposed that he was placed in a state of danger in
Edinburgh.

The next two Lairds of Shieldhill were John and Robert; but

nothing is known regarding them worthy of special notice. The successor of the last named was William, who was infeft in his lands in 1533, and was designated of Shieldhill, Quothquan, and Cormiston. In April 1535 he became surety for Hugh Lord Sommerville's underlying the law at the next Justice Aire at Lanark, for art and part of southrief and oppression done to John Tweedale, Carnwath, in reiving from him his cows, horses, crops, goods, and utensils. In the year following, his Lordship rendered a similar service to William Chancellor and his brother Robert, when they were charged with the crime of being art and part in the murder of Thomas Baillie, Laird of Cormiston. The Chancellors were fined in the sum of three hundred merks for not appearing to answer this charge; but Lord Sommerville and Richard Brown of Coultermains came forward as their cautioners, and a new trial having been appointed, they gave themselves up to justice, and were acquitted.

William Chancellor was succeeded by his son William, who had a charter from Lord Sommerville in 1546, and who married Agnes, a daughter of Sir John Hamilton of Crawfordjohn. Being allied with the Hamiltons, as might be expected, he was attached to the cause of Queen Mary. He accordingly, with his retainers, joined the Queen's party at Hamilton, and took part in the unhappy encounter at Langside in 1567. On this account his mansion-house at Quothquan was destroyed, and his lands were devastated by the Regent Murray. The successor of William was Robert, who married a daughter of Symington of that Ilk. His son John was the next Laird of Shieldhill, and the sasine of his lands is dated 1605. John was succeeded by his son Robert, who was distinguished for his loyalty to Charles I. and Charles II. In consequence of his attachment to the Stewarts, he was, no doubt, either opposed, or at all events indifferent, to the Presbyterian form of Church government then established. It was on this account perhaps that he and his family got into trouble with the Presbytery of Lanark. On the 24th of June 1630, he was summoned before that reverend court, when 'being convick of contempt of word, of raling against his pastor, wes ordainit to find cautione to obeye qlk thing he promisit to do, whairfor he wes injoined to make his publick repentance in his awin claithes only one day, if he maid a guid confessione, and so to be absolved.'

The minister of Quothquan was not content with the prosecution of Mr Chancellor himself. He laid an accusation before the Presbytery against Lady Chancellor, and her daughter Susanna, for having resorted to charming in order to restore a child to health. The *corpus delicti* was, that for the attainment of this end they had 'buried the claithes of a chyld betwixt laird's lands.' The worthy incumbent, on the 23d of September 1630, insisted before the Presbytery that the Lady of Shieldhill should appear before the brethren, and, in all humility, confess her fault, and give signs of unfeigned repentance. It is certain at least that Miss Chancellor, on the 14th October following, did appear before the Presbytery, 'and, in presence of the brethren, upon hir knees confessit her grit offence in having any medling with charmers, and promisit amendment in tyme coming.' The reverend gentleman had another contention with Mr Chancellor before the Presbytery of Lanark in 1639. The cause of offence on this occasion was, that Mr Chancellor had broken open the door of Quothquan Kirk, and interred the remains of his Lady in the interior of the said Kirk. As we have stated elsewhere, the Laird had to acknowledge his fault, and was ordered to be censured by the kirk-session of Quothquan.

Robert Chancellor died in 1664, and was succeeded by his son James. The opinions of James on the political and ecclesiastical topics of the day were somewhat 'different from those of his father. He appears to have attached himself to the cause of the Covenanters. After the Battle of Bothwell Bridge, he was for some time confined in prison on the charge of having given shelter to some of the poor countrymen who fled from that unhappy conflict. On another occasion, he got into trouble by taking violent possession of a piece of ground called the Parkholm, lying on the river Clyde. The river formed the boundary between the lands of Thankerton, belonging to Carmichael of Bonniton, and those belonging to James Chancellor, George Kello, and others. About the year 1638, a violent storm taking place, caused the Clyde to overflow its banks, and form a new channel, thus leaving a piece of ground belonging to Carmichael on the opposite side of the river. It got the name of the Parkholm, and remained for a number of years in a neglected state. Carmichael, considering it to be his property, at length put it under the plough, and year after year carried off the produce, much to the dissatisfaction of the neighbouring proprietors, who entertained an idea that the river should still form the boundary, as before. Carmichael dying about the year 1688, and his son and successor being a minor, James Chancellor and his friends thought the time favourable for establishing their claim to the piece of ground referred to. They mustered about eighty men, furnished with pitchforks, great staves, scythes, pistols, swords, and mastiff dogs, and in a rude and violent manner cut down 'the whole growth of fourteen bolls sowing of corn or thereby,' drove it home to their houses, and there made use of it in bedding their cattle, or converting it into dung. Thus 'corns which would have yielded at least ninety bolls, at eight pounds Scots the boll, were rendered useless for man or beast.' During the progress of the plunder, the tenants were confined to their houses under a guard; so it was altogether a riot and oppression, inferring severe punishment, which was accordingly called for by the curators of the young landlord. The Council having heard both parties, found the riot proven, and ordained Mr Chancellor of Shieldhill to pay 300 merks to the pur-

suer. The Lords of Session finally determined, in 1695, that the
Parkholm should remain the property of Sir James Carmichael.*

James Chancellor was returned an elder by the Presbytery of
Biggar to the first General Assembly that met after the Revolution in
1688.

The members of this family are not known to have taken a very
prominent part in the stormy and violent contentions of former ages,
which constitute the larger portion of written history. They appear
in general to have held on the noiseless tenor of their way, doing good
and receiving the esteem and approbation of their neighbours. They
have thus contrived to preserve their name and their property for
centuries, while the family of many a baron, once powerful and endowed with extensive domains, have disappeared. The present proprietor of Shieldhill estate is J. G. Chancellor, Esq.

THE LINDSAYS OF COVINGTON.

To the west of the possessions of the Chancellors lay the lands of
the Lindsays of Covington. For a considerable period they were
neighbouring proprietors of the Flemings of Biggar, while they held
the lands of Thankerton. The oldest writs of Thankerton in possession of the Fleming family do not indeed extend farther back
than the year 1465, but it is understood that these are not the
original titles. The lands and barony of Thankerton were sold on the
13th of February 1666 to Sir William Purves. The Lindsays of
Covington were not only neighbouring proprietors of the Flemings,
but several marriages took place between the two families that united
them in a greater bond of intimacy and friendship. The Lindsays of
Covington were descended from the Lindsays of Crawford. The first
of them was John Lindsay, who was the son of Sir Philip Lindsay, and
married the heiress of Covington some time previous to the year
1366. Lord Lindsay, in his 'Lives of the Lindsays,' gives a detail of
the successive Barons of Covington; but there is nothing very interesting in it, except to the genealogist. Margaret, a daughter of John
Lindsay of Covington, became the second wife of Robert Lord Fleming,
who died in 1494. John Lindsay of Covington was one of the persons who witnessed the Charter of Foundation of Biggar Kirk in 1545.
That baron, during the very year in which he signed that charter, was
arraigned, along with several of his relatives and eighteen other persons, for having assembled a party of two hundred men, armed with
lances, culverings, bows, and other invasive weapons, and on the 28th
September, marching to the barn of James Sommerville, Rector of
Libberton, and there wounding Robert Millar, the Rector's servant, in
the neck and other parts of his body, to the effusion of his blood and
the danger of his life. Lord Sommerville became surety for Lindsay
himself, and he was detained in Edinburgh 'until a royal license was

* Chambers's Domestic Annals, vol. iii.

granted for his departure.' The record does not say what was his ultimate punishment.

John Lindsay of Covington, about the commencement of the seventeenth century, married Agnes Fleming, only daughter and heir to John Fleming of Bord. Her tocher, amounting to 8000 merks, was paid on the 13th of November 1602 by John Lord Fleming. The oldest son of this pair was George Lindsay, who, on the 4th of November 1623, was retoured heir of his father in the barony of Covington, and also of two oxgates of temple lands called 'Stane,' in the barony of Biggar, the value of which, according to the ancient extent, was 16s. 8d., and according to the new extent, 3 merks. This Baron of Covington seems to have married Lady Rachel Fleming, a daughter of John, second Earl of Wigton; and a discharge for her tocher, dated 31st March 1630, is still preserved.

Sir William Lindsay, the last Baron of Covington, by profuse expenditure, squandered away the family inheritance, so that his lineal descendants became, ere long, merely labouring men. Lord Lindsay has given the following amusing anecdote regarding Sir William, the last Laird, who died previous to the year 1688:—'Sir William left four daughters, one of whom marrying John Baillie of St John's Kirk, was mother of a daughter married to William Somerville of Corehouse, representative of the Barons of Cambusnethan. Their daughter Isabella married Inglis of Eastshiel, whose only child, Violet, was the late Mrs Lockhart of Birkhill, who died in 1825. She used to relate to her grandchildren the following anecdote of her ancestor, Sir William, who, it appears, was a humorist, and noted, moreover, for preserving the picturesque appendage of a beard at a period when the fashion had long passed away. He had been extremely ill, and life was at last supposed to be extinct, though, as it afterwards turned out, he was only in a "dead faint," or trance. The female relatives were assembled for the "chesting" in a lighted chamber in the old tower of Covington, where the bearded knight lay stretched upon his bier. But when the servants were about to enter to assist at the ceremonies, Isabella Somerville, Sir William's great-granddaughter, and Mrs Lockhart's grandmother, then a child, creeping close to her mother, whispered in her ear, "The beard is wagging—the beard is wagging!" Mrs Somerville upon this looked to the bier, and, observing indications of life in the ancient knight, made the company retire, and Sir William soon came out of his faint. They explained that they believed him to be actually dead, and that arrangements had even been made for his funeral! In answer to his question, "Have the folks been warned?" (i.e., invited to the funeral), he was told that they had, that the funeral day had been fixed, an ox slain, and other preparations made for entertaining the company. Sir William then said, "All is as it should be; keep it a dead secret that I am in life, and let the folks come." His wishes were complied

with, and the company assembled for the burial at the appointed time.
After some delay, occasioned by the non-arrival of the clergyman, as
was supposed, and which afforded an opportunity for discussing the
merits of the deceased, the door suddenly opened, when, to their surprise and terror, in stepped the knight himself, pale in countenance,
and dressed in black, leaning on the arm of the minister of the parish
of Covington. Having quieted this alarm, and explained matters, he
called upon the clergyman to conduct an act of devotion, which included
thanksgiving for his recovery, and escape from being buried alive.
This done, the dinner succeeded. A jolly evening, after the manner
of the times, was passed, Sir William himself presiding over the
carousals.' This story will remind the reader of the resuscitation of
Athelstane, and his subsequent supper, in Ivanhoe.

THE COCKBURNS OF SKIRLING.

The barony of Skirling, or 'Scrawlin,' was possessed by a family of
the name of Cockburn for more than three hundred years. The
first Cockburn of Skirling appears to have been Alexander, who, some
time prior to the year 1362, married Margaret of Monfode, daughter
and heiress of Sir John of Monfode, to whom Robert I. granted the
whole lands of Skirling and the advowson of the church. The names
of many of the subsequent Barons of Skirling appear in our public
muniments. We may refer to one or two of them. In the year 1478,
the Auditors of Parliament decided that Walter Tweedie of Dreva
should restore to Adam Cockburn of Skirling a silver cup double gilt,
having a foot and a lid, which Cockburn had laid in pledge for twenty
merks. At a Justiciary Court held at Peebles on the 12th November
1498, Sir William Cockburn of Skirling, James, his brother, and
John Paterson, in 'Kingildurris,' produced a remission from the
charge of being art and part in the slaughter of Walter, son of John
Tweedie of Dreva; also of being art and part in the southrief of a
sword and shield from the said Walter,—and further, of forethought
of felony, in mutilating Andrew Tweedie within the town of Edinburgh during the sitting of Parliament.

William Cockburn of Skirling, who flourished in the early part of
the sixteenth century, appears to have had a feud with Alexander
Crichton of Newhall. He was, in addition to other acts of oppression,
charged with carrying off a box of documents belonging to that
gentleman, which he found in possession of Patrick Aitken, burgess,
Edinburgh,—with forcibly occupying his lands of Kirkrighill, pasturing on them seven score of cattle and sixty horses and mares,
overturning a 'fail dyke,' etc. This case was brought by the Councillors of State before James V. The King, who at the time was
sojourning at Crawfordjohn, wrote to his Councillors the following
reply :—

'Rex.

     . Traist Counsalouris, we grete you weil, and hes resavit zour writingis anent the Laird of Scraling, and thinkis zour avise and consel best anent the publishing of dome gevin aganis him. Quhair ze mentione of ane Minut send, we haue sene nane. Therefor we pray zou yat ye tak yat travil to pass to him and declair quhow it standis. Swa yat his lyf and guddis are in our handis. Gif he cummis in will we wilbe gracious to him. Fail-zeand yairof, we sall cause justice be keipit. And yairefter yat ze write to vs ane ansuir, as ze will do vs singular plesour.

    Gevin at Craufordjone, ye xxix day of March, and of our regne ye xxij zeir.'

James Cockburn thought it proper to come in the King's will, and this he did on the 31st of March 1536; but no statement has been left on record regarding the punishment assigned him by the King. Sir James Cockburn of Skirling, most likely a son of the preceding Laird, was a keen partisan of Queen Mary. The Queen, as a mark of her confidence and respect, appointed him Governor of Edinburgh Castle in the spring of 1567, in room of the Earl of Mar. Birrel, in noticing the event, says, 'The 21st of this month the Castell of Edin-burge was randred to Cockburne of Skirline at ye Queinis command. This same day ther rais ane vehement tempest of vunde, which blew a verey grate shipe out of the rode of Lieth, and sicklyk blew the taile from the cocke wich standis one the tope of ye steiple away frome it, so the old prophecy came trew,

> ' Quhen Skirline sall be Capitaine,
> Ye cock sall vant his taile.'

The author of the 'Diurnal' states that this change in the command of the Castle was made against the wishes of the inhabitants, who were in favour of the Earl of Mar, as he 'wes a guid man and na oppressour.' Sir James Cockburn, however, did not long enjoy the honour of holding this responsible office. James Balfour, Clerk Register, who had been instrumental in getting the banns proclaimed between the Queen and Bothwell, was appointed Governor on the 8th of May of the same year, most likely as a reward for his subserviency. Cockburn still remained faithful to the Queen; and the consequence was, that his lands were ravaged, and his house of Skirling was destroyed by the Regent Murray, while he himself had to seek security in exile.

James VI., as some compensation for the services which Sir James had performed, and the losses which he had sustained in defending the cause of his mother, Queen Mary, with the advice of his Parliament, erected Skirling in the year 1592 into a free burgh of barony, 'with all the easements, liberties, and commodities in as ample and large form as any burgh of barony within this realm, with power to keep and proclaim a fair to be observed within the said burgh on the fourth of September yearly, and a market day weekly upon Friday.' At that period, however, Sir James Cockburn had paid the debt of nature, and his son William possessed the estate of Skirling. This baron was succeeded by his son William, as we find from a 'Retour' that he was returned heir of his father, on the 20th Dec. 1603, of the lands and barony of Skirling, the L.20 lands of Roberton and Newholm, and the L.10 lands of 'Heidis,' all of old extent, annexed to the barony of Skirling. This was, most likely, the last proprietor of Skirling of the name of Cockburn, as, in the roll of the persons who attended the weaponshaw held on the Borrow Muir of Peebles on the 15th day of June 1627, it is stated that James Cockburn, bailie of Sir John Hamilton of Skirling, appeared for that knight, who was absent; and who thus seems by that time to have acquired the superiority of the barony of Skirling. Skirling is now the property of Sir William Gibson Carmichael, Bart. of Castlecraig.

We close this volume, which is principally of an antiquarian character, with a woodcut representing the Moat Knowe of Biggar, undoubtedly one of the oldest monuments of antiquity in the parish.

MURRAY AND GIBB, PRINTERS, EDINBURGH.

Lightning Source UK Ltd.
Milton Keynes UK
171300UK00001B/16/P